$$\text{Fixed Charge Coverage} = \frac{\text{Recurring Earnings, Excluding Interest Expense, Tax Expense, Equity Earnings, and Minority Earnings} + \text{Interest Portion of Rentals}}{\text{Interest Expense, Including Capitalized Interest} + \text{Interest Portion of Rentals}}$$

$$\text{Debt Ratio} = \frac{\text{Total Liabilities}}{\text{Total Assets}}$$

$$\text{Debt/Equity Ratio} = \frac{\text{Total Liabilities}}{\text{Stockholders' Equity}}$$

$$\text{Debt to Tangible Net Worth Ratio} = \frac{\text{Total Liabilities}}{\text{Stockholders' Equity} - \text{Intangible Assets}}$$

$$\text{Operating Cash Flow/Total Debt} = \frac{\text{Operating Cash Flow}}{\text{Total Debt}}$$

PROFITABILITY

$$\text{Net Profit Margin} = \frac{\text{Net Income Before Minority Share of Earnings, Equity Income and Nonrecurring Items}}{\text{Net Sales}}$$

$$\text{Total Asset Turnover} = \frac{\text{Net Sales}}{\text{Average Total Assets}}$$

$$\text{Return on Assets} = \frac{\text{Net Income Before Minority Share of Earnings and Nonrecurring Items}}{\text{Average Total Assets}}$$

$$\text{Operating Income Margin} = \frac{\text{Operating Income}}{\text{Net Sales}}$$

$$\text{Operating Asset Turnover} = \frac{\text{Net Sales}}{\text{Average Operating Assets}}$$

$$\text{Return on Operating Assets} = \frac{\text{Operating Income}}{\text{Average Operating Assets}}$$

$$\text{DuPont Return on Operating Assets} = \text{Operating Income Margin} \times \text{Operating Asset Turnover}$$

$$\text{Sales to Fixed Assets} = \frac{\text{Net Sales}}{\text{Average Net Fixed Assets (Exclude Construction in Progress)}}$$

$$\text{Return on Investment} = \frac{\text{Net Income Before Minority Share of Earnings and Nonrecurring Items} + [(\text{Interest Expense}) \times (1 - \text{Tax Rate})]}{\text{Average (Long-Term Liabilities} + \text{Equity)}}$$

FINANCIAL REPORTING & ANALYSIS

FINANCIAL REPORTING & ANALYSIS develops the basic principles of accounting on which financial reports are based. It includes many financial reporting topics that contribute to the understanding of financial reporting and builds skills in analyzing real financial reports through statements, exhibits, and cases of actual companies. Emphasis is placed on the analysis and interpretation of the end result of financial reporting — financial statements. Now with the integration of Thomson Analytics — *Business School Edition*™, readers of this text will be more prepared than ever for their business careers with practical, real-world analytical skills!

- ■ **RECENT CHANGES AND ISSUES:** This book has been completely updated to reflect recent changes in accounting standards and current financial reporting problems including: Enron, WorldCom, earnings management and FAS 148 among other topics.

- ■ **INTERNET EXERCISES:** In each chapter, "To the Net" exercises provide insight into the use of the World Wide Web for data. Numerous web sites of organizations and companies used in the book have been added.

- ■ **REAL-WORLD EXAMPLES:** Well-known companies (such as Nike, Reebok, Sears, Toys R Us and Wendy's) are used in illustrations, problems, cases, and analyses. These company examples connect theory to real application so the reader can easily see the relevance.

- ■ **EASY TO COMPREHEND:** Numerous pedagogical items, highlighted ratios, cases, illustrations, and an ongoing case study using a real company are designed to aid reader comprehension.

- ■ **NEW FinSAS FINANCIAL STATEMENT ANALYSIS SPREADSHEETS:** Allow students to perform analysis on any set of financial statements using the ratios in this text. These are available free at the companion web site.

SOUTH-WESTERN

THE CHOICE
IN ACCOUNTING & TAX

FINANCIAL

REPORTING

9E

& ANALYSIS

CHARLES H. GIBSON
THE UNIVERSITY OF TOLEDO

THOMSON
SOUTH-WESTERN

Australia · Canada · Mexico · Singapore · Spain · United Kingdom · United States

THOMSON

SOUTH-WESTERN

Financial Reporting & Analysis: Using Financial Accounting Information, 9e
Charles H. Gibson

VP/Editorial Director:
Jack W. Calhoun

VP/Editor-in-Chief:
George Werthman

Acquisitions Editor:
Julie Lindsay

Sr Developmental Editor:
Craig Avery

Marketing Manager:
Keith Chasse

Production Editor:
Amy McGuire

Media Developmental Editor:
Josh Fendley

Media Production Editor:
Kelly Reid

Manufacturing Coordinator:
Doug Wilke

Production House:
Cover to Cover Publishing, Inc.

Printer:
Quebecor World
Versailles, KY

Design Project Manager:
Rik Moore

Internal Designer:
Rik Moore

Cover Designer:
Rik Moore

Cover Images:
© PhotoDisc, Inc.

Material from the Certified Management Accountant Examination, Copyright ©1973, 1975, 1976, 1977, 1978, 1979,
1980, 1984, 1988, by the Institute of Certified Management
Accountants, is reprinted and/or adapted with permission.

Material identified as CFA Examination I, June 1987, is reproduced with permission from The Association of Investment Management and Research and The Institute of
Chartered Financial Analysts.

Material copyrighted by the Financial Accounting Standards
Board, 401 Merritt 7, P.O. Box 5116, Norwalk, Connecticut
06856-5116, U.S.A., is reprinted with permission. Copies of
the complete documents are available from the FASB.

Permission to reprint portions of the June 29, 1995 issue of
FASB status report was obtained from the Financial Accounting Standards Board.

Package ISBN 0-324-18643-6
Text ISBN 0-324-20158-3
Thomson Analytics access card ISBN 0-324-20156-7
International Student Edition ISBN 0-324-22227-0

PREFACE

Tell me, I'll forget.
Show me, I may remember.
Involve me, I'll understand.

This proverb describes the approach of the 9th edition—involving students in actual financial statements and their analysis and interpretation. Its premise is that students are better prepared to understand and analyze real financial reports when learning is not based on oversimplified financial statements.

From this basic premise come the many changes in the 9th edition. Those changes, discussed below, supported by our two new technology tools, focus on the goal of this text, which is to involve students in actively learning how to read, understand, and analyze the financial statements of actual companies.

CHANGES IN THIS EDITION

Significant changes have been made in this edition to improve its relevance to students and its flexibility for instructors. Among these changes are the following:

- Many **new exhibits and cases** have been based on actual companies such as Starbucks, Amazon.com, Intel, Walt Disney, and Eastman Kodak. The Toledo Mud Hens Baseball Club is also included.
- **Current topics** give students the latest edge in understanding the current business and regulatory climate affecting the reporting and analysis of financial statements.
  - **Options** (SFAS No. 148) (Chapter 9).
  - The SEC's **code of ethics** omission disclosure requirement for annual reports (Chapter 2).
  - The SEC's disclosure requirements for **pro forma financial information** (Chapter 8).
  - The **Sarbanes–Oxley Act** and the creation of the **Public Company Accounting Oversight Board** (PCAOB) (Chapter 1).
  - **Management of earnings**, including comments on Enron and WorldCom (Chapter 11).
  - The **North American Industry Classification System** (NAICS) (Chapter 5).
- **Access to Thomson Analytics—Business School Edition**™ is included with every new book. This access to a version of the professional research tool allows students to become familiar with the software they will likely need in professional practice. **Chapter cases** on the text Web site, for every chapter with the exception of Chapter 13, walk users step by step through these databases as they learn how to access financial information covered in the text. Thomson Analytics—Business School Edition provides information on 500 companies, combining a full range of fundamental financials, earnings estimates, market data, and source documents with powerful functionality.
- **FinSAS Financial Statement Analysis Spreadsheets** (by Donald V. Saftner, University of Toledo) allow students to perform analysis on any set of financial statements using the ratios covered in the text. Users enter income statement, balance sheet, and other data for 2 to 5 years. The result is a 2- to 5-year ratio comparison by liquidity, long-term debt-paying ability, profitability, and investor analysis. The result also includes common-size analysis of the income statement (horizontal and vertical) and common-size analysis of the balance sheet (horizontal and vertical). Downloadable in Excel from the product Web site, FinSAS can save users hours of number crunching, allowing them to concentrate on analysis and interpretation.

ACTUAL COMPANIES

The text explains financial reporting differences among industries, including manufacturing, retailing, and service firms, and regulated and non-regulated industries. This text also covers personal financial reports and financial reporting for governments and other not-for-profit institutions.

Statements of actual companies are used in illustrations and cases. The actual financial statements highlight current financial reporting problems, including comprehensive income, segment reporting, options, postretirement benefits, and the harmonization of international accounting standards.

EXTENSIVE USE OF ONE FIRM

An important feature of this text is that one firm, **Nike, Inc.**, is used extensively as an illustration. By using Nike's 2002 financial report and industry data, readers become familiar with a typical competitive market and a meaningful example for viewing financial statement analysis as a whole. (See Chapters 6 through 10 and Summary Analysis—Nike, Inc.). (Note also that FinSAS includes as example data the 2002 Nike financial numbers used in the Nike calculations for this text.)

FLEXIBLE ORGANIZATION

This text is used in a variety of courses with a variety of approaches to financial statement reporting and analysis. It provides the flexibility necessary to meet the needs of accounting and finance courses varying in content and length. Sufficient text, questions, "To the Net" exercises, problem materials, and cases are presented to allow the instructor latitude in the depth of coverage. Access to Thomson Analytics—Business School Edition™ is also included with every new book. Accounting principles are the basis for all discussion so that students may understand the methods used as well as the implications for analysis. Following is an outline of our chapter coverage:

Chapter 1 develops the basic principles of accounting on which financial reports are based. A review of the evolution of GAAP and the traditional assumptions of the accounting model helps the reader understand the statements and thus analyze them better.

Chapter 2 describes the forms of business entities and introduces financial reports. This chapter also reviews the sequence of accounting procedures completed during each accounting period. It includes other financial reporting topics that contribute to the understanding of financial reporting, such as the auditor's report, management's discussion, management's responsibility for financial statements, summary annual report, the efficient market hypothesis, ethics, harmonization of international accounting standards, consolidated statements, and accounting for business combinations.

Chapter 3 presents an in-depth review of the balance sheet, statement of stockholders' equity, and problems in balance sheet presentation. This chapter gives special emphasis to inventories and tangible assets.

Chapter 4 presents an in-depth review of the income statement, including special income statement items. Other topics included are earnings per share, retained earnings, dividends and stock splits, legality of distributions to stockholders, and comprehensive income.

Chapter 5 is an introduction to analysis and comparative statistics. Techniques include ratio analysis, common-size analysis, year-to-year change analysis, financial statement variations by type of industry, review of descriptive information, comparisons including Standard Industrial Classification (SIC) Manual and North American Industry Classification System (NAICS), relative size of firm, and many library sources of industry data.

Chapter 6 covers short-term liquidity. This chapter includes suggested procedures for analyzing short-term assets and the short-term debt-paying ability of an entity. This chapter includes a detailed discussion of four very important assets: cash, marketable securities, accounts receivable, and inventory. It is the first to extensively use Nike as an illustration.

Chapter 7 covers long-term debt-paying ability. This includes the income statement consideration and the balance sheet consideration. Topics include long-term leasing, pension plans, joint ventures, contingencies, financial instruments with off-balance-sheet risk, financial instruments with concentrations of credit risk and disclosures about fair value of financial instruments.

Chapter 8 covers the analysis of profitability, which is of vital concern to stockholders, creditors, and management. Besides profitability ratios, this chapter covers trends in profitability, segment reporting, gains and losses from prior period adjustments, comprehensive income, pro forma financial information, and interim reports.

Chapter 9, although not intended as a comprehensive guide to investment analysis, introduces analysis useful to the investor. Besides ratios, this chapter covers leverage and its effect on earnings, earnings per share, stock options, and stock appreciation rights.

Chapter 10 reviews the statement of cash flows, including ratios that relate to this statement. This chapter also covers procedures for developing the statement of cash flows.

A summary analysis of Nike is presented after Chapter 10, along with the Nike 2002 financial statements. The summary analysis includes Nike background information.

Chapter 11 covers an expanded utility of financial ratios. This includes the perception of financial ratios, the degree of conservatism and quality of earnings, forecasting financial failure, analytical review procedures, management's use of analysis, use of LIFO reserves, graphing financial information, and management of earnings.

Chapter 12 covers problems in analyzing six specialized industries: banks, electric utilities, oil and gas, transportation, insurance, and real estate. The chapter notes the differences in statements and suggests changes or additions to their analysis.

Chapter 13 covers personal financial statements and financial reporting for governments and other not-for-profit institutions.

A very extensive **Glossary** defines terms frequently found in annual reports. The text also includes a **Bibliography** of references that can be used in exploring further the topics in the text.

PRODUCT WEB SITE—HTTP://GIBSON.SWLEARNING.COM

Students and instructors have immediate access to financial statement analysis and classroom tools needed for the course at **http://gibson.swlearning.com**. Downloadable files for the solutions manual are password protected for adopting instructors, and FinSAS financial statement analysis spreadsheets (both blank and sample Nike versions) are available to students and instructors alike. For users of new books, the product Web site provides a link to **Thomson Analytics—Business School Edition**™ and its powerful suite of research tools for 500 companies, as well as **online cases** tied to the book's chapter content. Adopting instructors can download suggested solutions to the online Thomson Analytics—Business School Edition™ cases.

OTHER SUPPLEMENTARY MATERIALS

For the Student:

A well-regarded **Study Guide**, by the text author, includes objective problems that aid in reviewing chapter material. These self-quiz items include fill-ins, multiple choice, true/false, matching, classification, effect of selected transactions, and problems.

For the Instructor:

A combined Solutions Manual and Test Bank volume accompanies the text.
- The **Solutions Manual**, by the text author, includes a suggested solution for each "To the Net" exercise, question, problem, and case.
- The **Test Bank**, by the text author, includes problems, multiple choice, true/false, and other objective material for each chapter. The Test Bank is available in both printed and ExamView® versions. ExamView® is an easy-to-use test creation software compatible with Microsoft® Windows. Instructors can add or edit questions, instructions, and answers, and select questions (randomly or numerically) by previewing them on the screen. Instructors can also create and administer quizzes online, whether over the Internet, a local area network (LAN), or a wide area network (WAN).

ACKNOWLEDGMENTS

I am grateful to many people for their help and encouragement during the writing of this book. Comments received from colleagues and students who used the first eight editions resulted in many changes. I want to extend my appreciation to Nike, Inc. for permission to use its statements as illustrations. I am grateful to the numerous other firms and organizations that granted permission to reproduce their materials. Special thanks go to the American Institute of Certified Public Accountants, the Institute of Certified Management Accountants, and the Financial Accounting Standards Board. Permission has been received from the Institute of Certified Management Accountants of the Institute of Management Accountants to use questions and/or unofficial answers from past CMA examinations.

I am grateful to the following individuals for their useful and perceptive comments during the making of the 9th edition: Carol Dutton (South Florida Community College), Frank Flanegin (Robert Morris College), John Mahoney (New York University), Norman Meonske (Kent State University), and Howard G. Smith (Southwest Texas State University).

I am very grateful to Donald Saftner (University of Toledo) for his careful, timely, and effective revision of the FinSAS Spreadsheet tool for this edition.

Thanks also to the following at South-Western for their hard work on this edition: Julie Lindsay (acquisitions editor), Craig Avery (senior developmental editor), Keith Chasse (marketing manager), Amy McGuire (production editor), and Rik Moore (designer).

Charles H. Gibson

ACTUAL COMPANIES

Real world business examples are used extensively in the text, illustrations, and cases.

Albertson's, Inc.
Alexander and Baldwin
Amazon.com
Amedisys, Inc.
Amerada Hess Corporation
AMP
Andrew Corporation, The
Arch Chemicals
Arch Coal, Inc.
Arden Group, The
Argosy Gaming
Ashland Inc.
ASV Inc.
Barnes Group Inc.
Barr Laboratories, Inc.
Best Buy Co., Inc.
Blair
Boeing Company, The
Boston Celtics Ltd. Partnership II &
    Subsidiaries
Bridgford
Cabot Oil & Gas Corporation
Chubb Corporation, The
Chiquita Brands International, Inc.
City of Toledo
Clarcor
Coachmen Industries, Inc.
Conoco
Cooper Tire & Rubber Company
DaimlerChrysler
Dana Corporation
Dell Computer
Delta Airlines, Inc.
Denbury Resources Inc.
Dibrell Brothers Inc.
Digital Insight
Diodes Incorporated
Eastman Kodak Company
Ethan Allen Interiors Inc.
Exco Resources, Inc.
Florida Rock Industries, Inc.
Flowers Foods
Ford Motor Company
Frisch's Restraurants, Inc.
Gannett Company, Inc., The
Gap Inc.
General Electric
General Motors Corporation
Gentex Corporation
Good Year Tire
Harris Interactive Inc.
Hershey Foods Corporation

Hooper Holmes, Inc.
Independent Bank Corp.
Intel
Interpublic Group of Companies, The
International Business Machines
Institute of Mgmt. Accountants, Inc., The
JLG Industries, Inc.
Johnson & Johnson and Subsidiaries
Kroger Co.
Lands' End, Inc.
Lucas County, Ohio
Maine Public Service Company
McDonald's Corporation
Merck & Co., Inc.
Metro One Telecommunications, Inc.
Microsoft Corporation
Motorola, Inc.
MSC Software
Nacco Industries
National City
New England Electric System
Nike, Inc.
Nordson Corporation
Nord Resources Corp.
Northrop Grumman
Orphan Medical Inc.
Owens Corning Fiberglass Corporation
Owens-Illinois
Palatin Technologies Inc.
Procter & Gamble Company
Quantum Corporation
Reebok
Retek Inc.
Rowe Furniture
Royal Appliance Mfg. Co. and Subsidiaries
Safeway Inc.
Scientific Atlanta
Scientific Technologies
Scientific Technologies Inc.
Sears, Roebuck and Co.
Seaway Food Town
Shoe Carnival, Inc.
Smithfield Foods, Inc.
Snap On, Inc.
Southwest Gas Corporation
Starbucks
State Bancorp, Inc.
Sun Hydraulics®
Sun Micro Systems
Toledo Mud Hens Baseball Club, Inc.
Walgreen Co. and Subsidiaries
Wal-Mart

ABOUT THE AUTHOR

Charles Gibson is a certified public accountant who practiced with a Big Four accounting firm for four years and has had more than 30 years of teaching experience. His teaching experience encompasses a variety of accounting courses, including financial, managerial, tax, cost, and financial analysis.

Professor Gibson has taught seminars on financial analysis to financial executives, bank commercial loan officers, lawyers, and others. He has also taught financial reporting seminars for CPAs and review courses for both CPAs and CMAs. He has authored several problems used on the CMA exam.

Charles Gibson has written more than 60 articles in such journals as the *Journal of Accountancy, Accounting Horizons, Journal of Commercial Bank Lending, CPA Journal, Ohio CPA, Management Accounting, Risk Management, Taxation for Accountants, Advanced Management Journal, Taxation for Lawyers, California Management Review*, and *Journal of Small Business Management*. He is a co-author of the Financial Executives Research Foundation Study entitled, "Discounting in Financial Accounting and Reporting."

Dr. Gibson co-authored *Cases in Financial Reporting* (PWS-KENT Publishing Company). He has also co-authored two continuing education courses consisting of books and cassette tapes, published by the American Institute of Certified Public Accountants. These courses are entitled "Funds Flow Evaluation" and "Profitability and the Quality of Earnings."

Professor Gibson is a member of the American Accounting Association, American Institute of Certified Public Accountants, Ohio Society of Certified Public Accountants, and Financial Executives Institute. In the past, he has been particularly active in the American Accounting Association and the Ohio Society of Certified Public Accountants.

Dr. Gibson received the 1989 Outstanding Ohio Accounting Educator Award jointly presented by The Ohio Society of Certified Public Accountants and the Ohio Regional American Accounting Association. In 1993, he received the College of Business Research Award at The University of Toledo. In 1996, Dr. Gibson was honored as an "Accomplished Graduate" of the College of Business at Bowling Green State University. In 1999, he was honored by The Gamma Epsilon Chapter of Beta Alpha Psi of the University of Toledo.

DEDICATIONS

This book is dedicated to my wife Patricia and daughters Anne Elizabeth and Laura.

SPECIAL DEDICATION

To Dr. Gary John Previts, Professor of Accounting, Case Western Reserve University, recognized for his outstanding contribution to the accounting profession. This has included the teaching, research, and contributions to professional organizations such as the American Accounting Association, American Institute of Certified Public Accountants, and the Ohio Society of Certified Public Accountants.

CONTENTS

CHAPTER 4   INCOME STATEMENT   111

Basic Elements of the Income Statement   112
Net Sales (Revenues) • Cost of Goods Sold (Cost of Sales) • Other Operating Revenue • Operating Expenses • Other Income or Expense

Special Income Statement Items   114
(A) Unusual or Infrequent Item Disclosed Separately • (B) Equity in Earnings of Non-consolidated Subsidiaries • Income Taxes Related to Operations • (C) Discontinued Operations • (D) Extraordinary Items • (E) Cumulative Effect of Change in Accounting Principle • (F) Minority Share of Earnings

Earnings per Share   122

Retained Earnings   122

Dividends and Stock Splits   123

Legality of Distributions to Stockholders   124

Comprehensive Income   125

CHAPTER 7   LONG-TERM DEBT-PAYING ABILITY   209

CHAPTER 8   PROFITABILITY   251

CHAPTER 9   FOR THE INVESTOR   289

CHAPTER 13   PERSONAL FINANCIAL STATEMENTS AND ACCOUNTING FOR GOVERNMENTS AND NOT-FOR-PROFITS ORGANIZATIONS 523

INTRODUCTION TO FINANCIAL REPORTING

Users of financial statements include a company's managers, stockholders, bondholders, security analysts, suppliers, lending institutions, employees, labor unions, regulatory authorities, and the general public. They use the financial reports to make decisions. For example, potential investors use the financial reports as an aid in deciding whether to buy the stock. Suppliers use the financial reports to decide whether to sell merchandise to a company on credit. Labor unions use the financial reports to help determine their demands when they negotiate for employees. Management could use the financial reports to determine the company's profitability.

Demand for financial reports exists because users believe that the reports help them in decision making. In addition to the financial reports, users often consult competing information sources, such as new wage contracts and economy-oriented releases.

This book concentrates on using financial accounting information properly. Users must have a basic understanding of generally accepted accounting principles and traditional assumptions of the accounting model in order to recognize the limits of financial reports.

The ideas that underlie financial reports have developed over several hundred years. This development continues today to meet the needs of a changing society. A review of the evolution of generally accepted accounting principles and the traditional assumptions of the accounting model should help the reader understand the financial reports and thus analyze them better.

DEVELOPMENT OF GENERALLY ACCEPTED ACCOUNTING PRINCIPLES (GAAP)

Generally accepted accounting principles (GAAP) are accounting principles that have substantial authoritative support: The accountant must be familiar with acceptable reference sources in order to decide whether any particular accounting principle has substantial authoritative support.

The formal process of developing accounting principles that exist today in the United States began with the Securities Acts of 1933 and 1934. Prior to these securities acts, the New York Stock Exchange (NYSE), which was established in 1792, was the primary mechanism for establishing specific requirements for the disclosure of financial information. These requirements could be described as minimal and only applied to corporations whose shares were listed on the NYSE. The prevailing view of management was that financial information was for management's use.

The stock market crash of 1929 provoked widespread concern about external financial disclosure. Some alleged that the stock market crash was substantially influenced by the lack of adequate financial reporting requirements to investors and creditors. The Securities Act of 1933 was designed to protect investors from abuses in financial reporting that developed in the United States. This act was intended to regulate the initial offering and sale of securities in interstate commerce.

In general, the Securities Exchange Act of 1934 was intended to regulate securities trading on the national exchanges, and it was under this authority that the **Securities and Exchange Commission (SEC)** was created. In effect, the SEC has the authority to determine GAAP and to regulate the accounting profession. The SEC has elected to leave much of the determination of GAAP and the regulation of the accounting profession to the private sector. At times, the SEC will issue its own standards.

Currently the SEC issues Regulation S-X, which describes the primary formal financial disclosure requirements for companies. The SEC also issues Financial Reporting Releases (FRRs) that pertain to financial reporting requirements. Regulation S-X and FRRs are part of GAAP and are used to give the SEC's official position on matters relating to financial statements. The formal process that exists today is a blend of the private and public sectors.

A number of parties in the private sector have played a role in the development of GAAP. The American Institute of Certified Public Accountants (AICPA) and the Financial Accounting Standards Board (FASB) have had the most influence.

American Institute of Certified Public Accountants (AICPA)

The **AICPA** is a professional accounting organization whose members are certified public accountants (CPAs). During the 1930s, the AICPA had a special committee working with the New York Stock Exchange on matters of common interest. An outgrowth of this special committee was the establishment in 1939 of two standing committees, the **Committee on Accounting Procedures** and the **Committee on Accounting Terminology**. These committees were active from 1939 to 1959 and issued 51 Accounting Research Bulletins (ARBs). These committees took a problem-by-problem approach, because they tended to review an issue only when there was a problem related to that issue. This method became known as the brushfire approach. They were only partially successful in developing a well-structured body of accounting principles. ARBs are part of GAAP.

In 1959, the AICPA replaced the two committees with the **Accounting Principles Board (APB)** and the **Accounting Research Division**. The Accounting Research Division provided research to aid the APB in making decisions regarding accounting principles. Basic postulates would be developed that would aid in the development of accounting principles, and the entire process was intended to be based on research prior to an APB decision. However, the APB and the Accounting Research Division were not successful in formulating broad principles.

The combination of the APB and the Accounting Research Division lasted from 1959 to 1973. During this time, the Accounting Research Division issued 14 Accounting Research Studies. The APB issued 31 Opinions (APBOs) and 4 Statements (APBSs). The Opinions represented official positions of the Board, whereas the Statements represented the views of the Board but not the official opinions. APBOs are part of GAAP.

Various sources, including the public, generated pressure to find another way of developing GAAP. In 1972, a special study group of the AICPA recommended another approach—the establishment of the **Financial Accounting Standards Board (FASB)**. The AICPA adopted these recommendations in 1973.

Financial Accounting Standards Board (FASB)

The structure of the FASB is as follows: A panel of electors is selected from nine organizations. They are the AICPA, the Financial Executives Institute, the Institute of Management Accountants, the Financial Analysts Federation, the American Accounting Association, the Security Industry Association, and three not-for-profit organizations. The electors appoint the board of trustees that governs the **Financial Accounting Foundation (FAF).** There are 16 trustees.

The FAF appoints the **Financial Accounting Standards Advisory Council (FASAC)** and the FASB. The FAF also is responsible for funding the FASAC and the FASB.

There are approximately 30 members of the FASAC. This relatively large number is to obtain representation from a wide group of interested parties. The FASAC is responsible for advising the FASB. There are seven members of the FASB. Exhibit 1-1 illustrates the structure of the FASB.

The FASB issues four types of pronouncements:

1. **Statements of Financial Accounting Standards (SFASs).** These Statements establish GAAP for specific accounting issues.
2. **Interpretations.** These pronouncements provide clarifications to previously issued standards, including SFASs, APB Opinions, and Accounting Research Bulletins. The interpretations have the same authority and require the same majority votes for passage as standards (a supermajority of five or more of the seven members). Interpretations are part of GAAP.
3. **Technical bulletins.** These bulletins provide timely guidance on financial accounting and reporting problems. They may be used when the effect will not cause a major change in accounting practice for a number of companies and when they do not conflict with any broad fundamental accounting principle. Technical bulletins are part of GAAP.
4. **Statements of Financial Accounting Concepts (SFACs).** These Statements provide a theoretical foundation upon which to base GAAP. They are the output of the FASB's Conceptual Framework project, but they are not part of GAAP.

Operating Procedure for Statements of Financial Accounting Standards (SFASs)

The process of considering a SFAS begins when the Board elects to add a topic to its technical agenda. The Board receives suggestions and advice on topics from many sources, including the FASAC, the SEC, the AICPA, and industry organizations.

EXHIBIT 1-1   **STRUCTURE OF THE FASB**

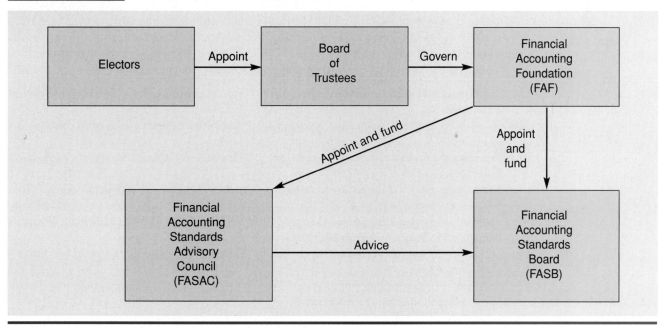

For its technical agenda, the Board considers only "broken" items. In other words, the Board must be convinced that a major issue needs to be addressed in a new area or an old issue needs to be reexamined.

The Board must rely on staff members for the day-to-day work on projects. A project is assigned a staff project manager, and informal discussions frequently take place among Board members, the staff project manager, and staff. In this way, Board members gain an understanding of the accounting issues and the economic relationships that underlie those issues.

On projects with a broad impact, a **Discussion Memorandum (DM)** or an **Invitation to Comment** is issued. A Discussion Memorandum presents all known facts and points of view on a topic. An Invitation to Comment sets forth the Board's tentative conclusions on some issues related to the topic or represents the views of others.

The Discussion Memorandum or Invitation to Comment is distributed as a basis for public comment. There is usually a 60-day period for written comments, followed by a public hearing. A transcript of the public hearing and the written comments become part of the public record. Then the Board begins deliberations on an **Exposure Draft (ED)** of a proposed Statement of Financial Accounting Standards. When completed, the Exposure Draft is issued for public comment. The Board may call for written comments only, or it may announce another public hearing. After considering the written comments and the public hearing comments, the Board resumes deliberations in one or more public Board meetings. The final Statement must receive affirmative votes from five of the seven members of the Board. The Rules of Procedure require dissenting Board members to set forth their reasons in the Statement. Developing a Statement on a major project generally takes at least two years, sometimes much longer. Some people believe that the time should be shortened to permit faster decision making.

The FASB standard-setting process includes aspects of accounting theory and political aspects. Many organizations, companies, and individuals have input into the process. Some input is directed toward achieving a standard less than desirable in terms of a strict accounting perspective. Often the end result is a standard that is not the best representation of economic reality.

FASB Conceptual Framework

The Conceptual Framework for Accounting and Reporting was on the agenda of the FASB from its inception in 1973. The Framework is intended to set forth a system of interrelated objectives and underlying concepts that will serve as the basis for evaluating existing standards of financial accounting and reporting.

Under this project, the FASB has established a series of pronouncements, **Statements of Financial Accounting Concepts (SFACs)**, intended to provide the Board with a common foundation and the basic reasons for considering the merits of various alternative accounting principles. SFACs do *not* establish GAAP; rather, the FASB eventually intends to evaluate current principles in terms of the concepts established.

To date, the Framework project has issued seven Concept Statements:

1. *Statement of Financial Accounting Concepts No. 1*, "Objectives of Financial Reporting by Business Enterprises."
2. *Statement of Financial Accounting Concepts No. 2*, "Qualitative Characteristics of Accounting Information."
3. *Statement of Financial Accounting Concepts No. 3*, "Elements of Financial Statements of Business Enterprises."
4. *Statement of Financial Accounting Concepts No. 4*, "Objectives of Financial Reporting by Nonbusiness Organizations."
5. *Statement of Financial Accounting Concepts No. 5*, "Recognition and Measurement in Financial Statements of Business Enterprises."
6. *Statement of Financial Accounting Concepts No. 6*, "Elements of Financial Statements" (a replacement of No. 3).
7. *Statement of Financial Accounting Concepts No. 7*, "Using Cash Flow Information and Present Value in Accounting Measurements."

Concepts Statement No. 1, issued in 1978, deals with identifying the objectives of financial reporting for business entities and establishes the focus for subsequent concept projects for business entities. Concepts Statement No. 1 pertains to general-purpose external financial reporting and is not restricted to financial statements. The following is a summary of the highlights of Concepts Statement No. 1.[1]

1. Financial reporting is intended to provide information useful in making business and economic decisions.
2. The information should be comprehensible to those having a reasonable understanding of business and economic activities. These individuals should be willing to study the information with reasonable diligence.
3. Financial reporting should be helpful to users in assessing the amounts, timing, and uncertainty of future cash flows.
4. The primary focus is information about earnings and its components.
5. Information should be provided about the economic resources of an enterprise and the claims against those resources.

Issued in May 1980, "Qualitative Characteristics of Accounting Information" (SFAC No. 2) examines the characteristics that make accounting information useful for investment, credit, and similar decisions. Those characteristics of information that make it a desirable commodity can be viewed as a hierarchy of qualities, with *understandability* and *usefulness for decision making* of most importance (see Exhibit 1-2).

Relevance and **reliability**, the two primary qualities, make accounting information useful for decision making. To be relevant, the information needs to have *predictive* and feedback value and must be *timely*. To be reliable, the information must be *verifiable*, subject to representational faithfulness, and *neutral*. **Comparability**, which includes consistency, interacts with relevance and reliability to contribute to the usefulness of information.

The hierarchy includes *two constraints*. To be useful and worth providing, the information should have *benefits that exceed its cost*. In addition, all of the qualities of information shown are *subject to a materiality threshold*.

SFAC No. 6, "Elements of Financial Statements," which replaced SFAC No. 3 in 1985, defines ten interrelated elements directly related to measuring performance and financial status of an enterprise. The ten elements are defined as follows:[2]

1. **Assets.** Assets are probable future economic benefits obtained or controlled by a particular entity as a result of past transactions or events.
2. **Liabilities.** Liabilities are probable future sacrifices of economic benefits arising from present obligations of a particular entity to transfer assets or provide services to other entities in the future as a result of past transactions or events.
3. **Equity.** Equity is the residual interest in the assets of an entity that remains after deducting its liabilities:

$$\text{Equity} = \text{Assets} - \text{Liabilities}$$

4. **Investments by owners.** Investments by owners are increases in equity of a particular business enterprise resulting from transfers to the enterprise from other entities of something of value to obtain or increase ownership interests (or equity) in it. Assets, most commonly received as investments by owners, may also include services or satisfaction or conversion of liabilities of the enterprise.
5. **Distribution to owners.** Distribution to owners is a decrease in equity of a particular business enterprise resulting from transferring assets, rendering services, or incurring liabilities by the enterprise to owners. Distributions to owners decrease ownership interest (or equity) in an enterprise.
6. **Comprehensive income.** Comprehensive income is the change in equity (net assets) of a business enterprise during a period from transactions and other events and circumstances from nonowner sources. It includes all changes in equity during a period except those resulting from investments by owners and distributions to owners.

EXHIBIT 1-2   **A HIERARCHY OF ACCOUNTING QUALITIES**

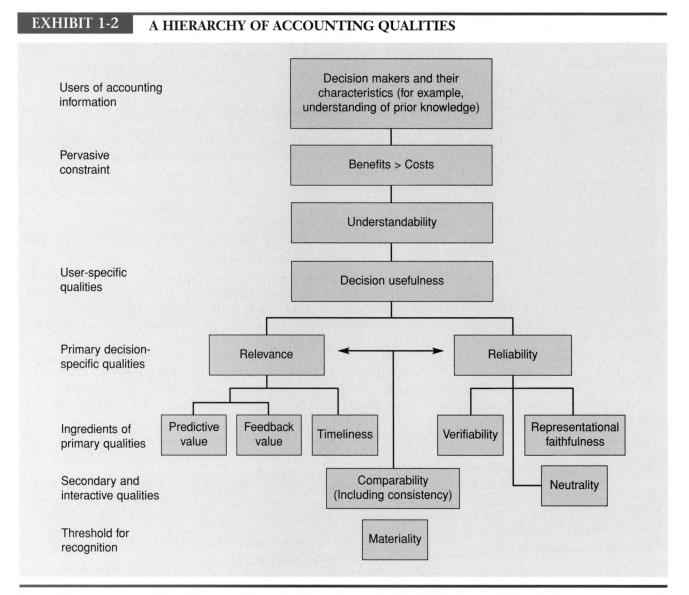

Source: "Qualitative Characteristics of Accounting Information." Adapted from Figure 1 in FASB Statement of Financial Accounting Concepts No. 2 (Stamford, CT: Financial Accounting Standards Board, 1980).

7. **Revenues.** Revenues are inflows or other enhancements of assets of an entity or settlements of its liabilities (or a combination of both) from delivering or producing goods, rendering services, or other activities that constitute the entity's ongoing major or central operations.

8. **Expenses.** Expenses are outflows or other consumption or using up of assets or incurrences of liabilities (or a combination of both) from delivering or producing goods, rendering services, or carrying out other activities that constitute the entity's ongoing major or central operations.

9. **Gains.** Gains are increases in equity (net assets) from peripheral or incidental transactions of an entity and from all other transactions and other events and circumstances affecting the entity during a period except those that result from revenues or investments by owners.

10. **Losses.** Losses are decreases in equity (net assets) from peripheral or incidental transactions of an entity and from all other transactions and other events and circumstances affecting the entity during a period except those that result from expenses or distributions to owners.

"Objectives of Financial Reporting by Nonbusiness Organizations" (SFAC No. 4) was completed in 1980. Organizations that fall within the focus of this statement include churches, foundations, and human-service organizations. Performance indicators for nonbusiness organizations include formal budgets and donor restrictions. These types of indicators are not ordinarily related to competition in markets.

Issued in 1984, "Recognition and Measurement in Financial Statements of Business Enterprises" (SFAC No. 5) indicates that an item, to be recognized, should meet four criteria, subject to the cost-benefit constraint and materiality threshold:[3]

1. **Definition.** The item fits one of the definitions of the elements.
2. **Measurability.** The item has a relevant attribute measurable with sufficient reliability.
3. **Relevance.** The information related to the item is relevant.
4. **Reliability.** The information related to the item is reliable.

This concept statement identifies *five* different *measurement attributes* currently used in practice and recommends the composition of a full set of financial statements for a period.

The following are five different measurement attributes currently used in practice:[4]

1. Historical cost (historical proceeds)
2. Current cost
3. Current market value
4. Net realizable (settlement) value
5. Present (or discounted) value of future cash flows

This concept statement probably accomplished little, relating to measurement attributes, because a firm, consistent position on recognition and measurement could not be agreed upon. It states: "Rather than attempt to select a single attribute and force changes in practice so that all classes of assets and liabilities use that attribute, this concept statement suggests that use of different attributes will continue."[5]

SFAC No. 5 recommended that a full set of financial statements for a period should show the following:[6]

1. Financial position at the end of the period
2. Earnings (net income)
3. Comprehensive income (total nonowner change in equity)
4. Cash flows during the period
5. Investments by and distributions to owners during the period

At the time of issuance of SFAC No. 5, financial position at the end of the period and earnings (net income) were financial statements being presented. Comprehensive income, cash flows during the period, and investments by and distributions to owners during the period are financial statements (disclosures) that have been subsequently developed. All of these financial statements (disclosures) will be extensively covered in this book.

SFAC No. 7, issued in February 2000, provides general principles for using present values for accounting measurements. It describes techniques for estimating cash flows and interest rates and applying present value in measuring liabilities.

The FASB Conceptual Framework for Accounting and Reporting project represents the most extensive effort undertaken to provide a conceptual framework for financial accounting. Potentially, the project can have a significant influence on financial accounting.

ADDITIONAL INPUT— AMERICAN INSTITUTE OF CERTIFIED PUBLIC ACCOUNTANTS (AICPA)

As indicated earlier, the AICPA played the primary role in the private sector in establishing GAAP prior to 1973. However, the AICPA continues to play a part, primarily through its Accounting Standards Division. The Accounting Standards Executive Committee (AcSEC) serves as the official voice of the AICPA in matters relating to financial accounting and reporting standards.

The Accounting Standards Division published numerous documents considered as sources of GAAP. These include Industry Audit Guides, Industry Accounting Guides, and Statements of Position (SOPs).

Industry Audit Guides and Industry Accounting Guides are designed to assist auditors in examining and reporting on financial statements of companies in specialized industries, such as insurance. SOPs were issued to influence the development of accounting standards. Some SOPs were revisions or clarifications to recommendations on accounting standards contained in Industry Audit Guides and Industry Accounting Guides.

Industry Audit Guides, Industry Accounting Guides, and SOPs were considered a lower level of authority than FASB Statements of Financial Accounting Standards (SFASs), FASB Interpretations, APB Opinions, and Accounting Research Bulletins. However, since the Industry Audit Guides, Industry Accounting Guides, and SOPs deal with material not covered in the primary sources, they, in effect, became the guide to standards for the areas they cover. They are part of GAAP.

EMERGING ISSUES TASK FORCE (EITF)

The FASB established the Emerging Issues Task Force (EITF) in July 1984 to help identify emerging issues affecting reporting and problems in implementing authoritative pronouncements. The Task Force had 15 members—senior technical partners of major national CPA firms and representatives of major associations of preparers of financial statements. The FASB's Director of Research and Technical Activities serves as Task Force chairperson. The SEC's Chief Accountant and the chairperson of the AICPA's Accounting Standards Executive Committee participated in Task Force meetings as observers.

The SEC's Chief Accountant has stated that any accounting that conflicts with the position of a consensus of the Task Force would be challenged. Agreement of the Task Force was recognized as a consensus if no more than two members disagreed with a position.

Task Force meetings were held about once every six weeks. Issues came to the Task Force from a variety of sources, including the EITF members, the SEC, and other federal agencies. The FASB also brought issues to the EITF in response to issues submitted by auditors and preparers of financial statements.

The EITF statements became a very important source of GAAP. The Task Force had the capability to review a number of issues within a relatively short period of time, in contrast to the lengthy deliberations that went into an SFAS.

EITF statements are considered to be less authoritative than the sources previously discussed in this chapter. However, since EITF addressed issues not covered by the other sources, its statements became important guidelines to standards for the areas they cover.

A NEW REALITY

In November 2001 Enron, one of the largest companies in the United States, recognized in a Federal filing that it overstated earnings by nearly $600 million since 1997. Within a month Enron declared bankruptcy. The Enron bankruptcy probably received more publicity than any prior bankruptcy in United States history. This was influenced by the size of Enron, the role of the auditors, the financial loss of investors, and the losses sustained by Enron employees. Many Enron employees lost their jobs and their pensions.

In June 2002 WorldCom announced it had inflated profits by $3.8 billion over the previous five quarters. This represented the largest financial fraud in corporate history. Soon after the WorldCom fraud announcement, WorldCom declared bankruptcy. (In November 2002 a special bankruptcy court examiner indicated that the restatement would likely exceed $7.2 billion.)

The WorldCom fraud compelled Congress and President George W. Bush to take action. Congress acted swiftly, with the support of President Bush, to pass legislation now known as the Sarbanes-Oxley Act of 2002.

The Sarbanes-Oxley Act has many provisions. While it is not practical to review the Act in detail, it is clear that it has far-reaching consequences for financial reporting and the CPA profession.

Sarbanes-Oxley creates a five-person oversight board, the Public Company Accounting Oversight Board (PCAOB). The PCAOB consists of five members appointed by the SEC. Two must be CPAs and the rest cannot be CPAs.

Among the many responsibilities of the PCAOB is to adopt auditing standards. This will materially decrease or eliminate the role of the AICPA in setting auditing standards.

The Chief Executive Officer (CEO), and the Chief Financial Officer (CFO), of each issuer must prepare a statement to accompany the audit report to certify disclosures fairly present, in all material respects, the operations and financial condition of the issuer.

In addition to appointing the five members of the PCAOB, the SEC is responsible for the oversight and enforcement authority over the Board. In effect the PCAOB is an arm of the SEC.

As described in this chapter, the setting of accounting standards has been divided among the SEC, FASB, EITF, and AcSEC. By law the setting of accounting standards is the responsibility of the SEC. The SEC elected to have most of the accounting standards be developed in the private sector with the oversight of the SEC. This substantially meant that the SEC allowed the FASB to determine accounting standards. The FASB allowed some of the standards to be determined by the EITF, and the AcSEC of the AICPA.

In November 2002 the FASB announced that it was streamlining the accounting rule-making process by taking back powers it had vested to EITF (an arm of the FASB), and AcSEC (an arm of the AICPA). The AcSEC will be allowed to continue with industry-specific accounting and audit guides (A&A guides). The AICPA is to stop issuing general purpose accounting Statements of Position (SOPs).

TRADITIONAL ASSUMPTIONS OF THE ACCOUNTING MODEL

The FASB's Conceptual Framework was influenced by several underlying assumptions. Some of these assumptions were addressed in the Conceptual Framework, and others are implicit in the Framework. These assumptions, along with the Conceptual Framework, are considered when a GAAP is established. Accountants, when confronted with a situation lacking an explicit standard, should resolve the situation by considering the Conceptual Framework and the traditional assumptions of the accounting model.

In all cases, the reports are to be a "fair representation." Even when there is an explicit GAAP, following the GAAP is not appropriate unless the end result is a "fair representation." Following GAAP is not an appropriate legal defense unless the statements represent a "fair representation."

Business Entity

The concept of separate **entity** means that the business or entity for which the financial statements are prepared is separate and distinct from the owners of the entity. In other words, the entity is viewed as an economic unit that stands on its own.

For example, an individual may own a grocery store, a farm, and numerous personal assets. To determine the economic success of the grocery store, we would view it separately from the other resources owned by the individual. The grocery store would be treated as a separate entity.

A corporation such as the Ford Motor Company has many owners (stockholders). The entity concept enables us to account for the Ford Motor Company entity separately from the transactions of the owners of the Ford Motor Company.

Going Concern or Continuity

The **going-concern assumption**, that the entity in question will remain in business for an indefinite period of time, provides perspective on the future of the entity. The going-concern assumption deliberately disregards the possibility that the entity will go bankrupt or be liquidated. If a particular entity is in fact threatened with bankruptcy or liquidation, then the going-concern assumption should be dropped. In such a case, the reader of the financial statements is interested in the liquidation values, not the values that can be used when making the assumption that the business will continue indefinitely. If the going-concern assumption has not been used for a particular set of financial statements, because of the threat of liquidation or bankruptcy, the financial statements must clearly disclose that the statements were prepared with the view that the entity will be liquidated or that it is a failing concern. In this case, conventional financial report analysis would not apply.

Many of our present financial statement figures would be misleading if it were not for the going-concern assumption. For instance, under the going-concern assumption, the value of prepaid insurance is computed by spreading the cost of the insurance over the period of the policy. If the entity were liquidated, then only the cancellation value of the policy would be meaningful. Inventories are basically carried at their accumulated cost. If the entity were liquidated, then the amount realized from the sale of the inventory, in a manner other than through the usual channels, usually would be substantially less than the cost. Therefore, to carry the inventory at cost would fail to recognize the loss that is represented by the difference between the liquidation value and the cost.

The going-concern assumption also influences liabilities. If the entity were liquidating, some liabilities would have to be stated at amounts in excess of those stated on the conventional statement. Also, the amounts provided for warranties and guarantees would not be realistic if the entity were liquidating.

The going-concern assumption also influences the classification of assets and liabilities. Without the going-concern assumption, all assets and liabilities would be current, with the expectation that the assets would be liquidated and the liabilities paid in the near future.

The audit opinion for a particular firm may indicate that the auditors have reservations as to the going-concern status of the firm. This puts the reader on guard that the statements are misleading if the firm does not continue as a going concern. For example, the annual report of Youthstream Media Networks, Inc. indicated a concern over the company's ability to continue as a going concern.

The Youthstream Media Networks, Inc. annual report included these comments in Note 1 and the auditor's report.

Youthstream Media Networks, Inc.

Note 1 Organization and Basis of Presentation (in Part)

FINANCIAL STATEMENT PRESENTATION—The Company has incurred recurring operating losses since its inception, as of June 30, 2002, had an accumulated deficit of $336,000,000, and expects to have insufficient capital to fund all of its obligations. In August and September 2002, the Company defaulted on approximately $18,000,000 of its long-term debt (see Note 6—Long-term Debt). In addition, the Company's retail sales have been on the decline. These conditions raise substantial doubt about the Company's ability to continue as a going concern. The financial statements do not include any adjustments to reflect the possible future effect of the recoverability and classification of assets or the amounts and classifications of liabilities that may result from the outcome of this uncertainty. The Company is also exploring strategic alternatives with respect to its business, which could include seeking to dispose of some or all of its remaining assets on terms favorable to the Company. The Company believes that consummation of disposition of all or substantially all of the assets associated with the retail business segment would require a vote of the Company's shareholders.

Report of Independent Auditors Board of Directors

Youthstream Media Networks, Inc. (in Part)

In our opinion, the consolidated financial statements referred to above present fairly, in all material respects, the consolidated financial position of Youthstream Media Networks, Inc. as of June 30, 2002 and 2001, and the consolidated results of its operations and its cash flows for each of the three years in the period ended June 30, 2002, in conformity with accounting principles generally accepted in the United States. Also, in our opinion, the related financial statement schedule, when considered in relation to the basic financial statements, takes as a whole, presents fairly, in all material respects, the information set forth therein.

The accompanying financial statements have been prepared assuming that Youthstream Media Networks, Inc. will continue as a going concern. As more fully described in Note 1, the Company has incurred recurring operating losses and has a working capital and stockholders' deficiency. In addition, the Company is in default with respect to its long-term debt. These conditions raise substantial doubt about the Company's ability to continue as a going concern. Management's plans in regard to these matters are also described in Note 1. The financial statements do not include any adjustments to reflect the possible future effect on the recoverability and classification of assets or the amounts and classification of liabilities that may result from the outcome of this uncertainty.

Ernst & Young LLP
New York, New York
September 27, 2002

Time Period

The only accurate way to account for the success or failure of an entity is to accumulate all transactions from the opening of business until the business eventually liquidates. Many years ago, this time period for reporting was acceptable, because it would be feasible to account for and divide up what remained at the completion of the venture. Today, the typical business has a relatively long duration, so it is not feasible to wait until the business liquidates before accounting for its success or failure.

This presents a problem: Accounting for the success or failure of the business in midstream involves inaccuracies. Many transactions and commitments are incomplete at any particular time between the opening and the closing of business. An attempt is made to eliminate the inaccuracies when statements are prepared for a period of time short of an entity's life span, but the inaccuracies cannot be eliminated completely. For example, the entity typically carries accounts receivable at the amount expected to be collected. Only when the receivables are collected can the entity account for them accurately. Until receivables are collected, there exists the possibility that collection cannot be made. The entity will have outstanding obligations at any time, and these obligations cannot be accurately accounted for until they are met. An example would be a warranty on products sold. An entity may also have a considerable investment in the production of inventories. Usually, until the inventory is sold in the normal course of business, the entity cannot accurately account for the investment in inventory.

With the time period assumption, we accept some inaccuracies of accounting for the entity short of its complete life span. We assume that the entity can be accounted for with reasonable accuracy for a particular period of time. In other words, the decision is made to accept some inaccuracy, because of incomplete information about the future, in exchange for more timely reporting.

Some businesses select an accounting period, known as a **natural business year**, that ends when operations are at a low ebb in order to facilitate a better measurement of income and financial position. Other businesses use the **calendar year** and thus end the accounting period on December 31. Some select a 12-month accounting period, known as a **fiscal year**, which closes at the end of a month other than December. The accounting period may be shorter than a year, such as a month. The shorter the period of time, the more inaccuracies we typically expect in the reporting.

Monetary Unit

Accountants need some standard of measure to bring financial transactions together in a meaningful way. Without some standard of measure, accountants would be forced to report in such terms as 5 cars, 1 factory, and 100 acres. This type of reporting would not be very meaningful.

There are a number of standards of measure, such as a yard, a gallon, and money. Of the possible standards of measure, accountants have concluded that money is the best for the purpose of measuring financial transactions.

Different countries call their monetary units by different names. For example, Japan uses the **yen**. Different countries also attach different values to their money—1 dollar is not equal to 1 yen. Thus, financial transactions may be measured in terms of money in each country, but the statements from various countries cannot be compared directly or added together until they are converted to a common monetary unit, such as the U.S. dollar.

In various countries, the stability of the monetary unit has been a problem. The loss in value of money is called **inflation**. In some countries, inflation has been more than 300% per year. In countries where inflation has been significant, financial statements are adjusted by an inflation factor that restores the significance of money as a measuring unit. However, a completely acceptable restoration of money as a measuring unit cannot be made in such cases because of the problems involved in determining an accurate index. To indicate one such problem, consider the price of a car in 1991 and in 2001. The price of the car in 2001 would be higher, but the explanation would not be simply that the general price level has increased. Part of the reason for the price increase would be that the type and quality of the equipment have changed between 1991 and 2001. Thus, an index that relates the 2001 price to the 1991 price is a mixture of inflation, technological advancement, and quality changes.

The rate of inflation in the United States prior to the 1970s was relatively low. Therefore, it was thought that an adjustment of money as a measuring unit was not appropriate, because the added expense and inaccuracies of adjusting for inflation were greater than the benefits. During the 1970s, however, the United States experienced double-digit inflation. This made it increasingly desirable to implement some formal recognition of inflation.

In September 1979, the FASB issued *Statement of Financial Accounting Standards No. 33*, "Financial Reporting and Changing Prices," which required that certain large, publicly held companies disclose certain supplementary information concerning the impact of changing prices in their annual reports for fiscal years ending on or after December 25, 1979. This disclosure later became optional in 1986. Currently no U.S. company provides this supplementary information.

Historical Cost

SFAC No. 5 identified five different measurement attributes currently used in practice: historical cost, current cost, current market value, net realizable value, and present value. Often, historical cost is used in practice because it is objective and determinable. A deviation from historical cost is accepted when it becomes apparent that the historical cost cannot be recovered. This deviation is justified by the conservatism concept. A deviation from historical cost is also found in practice where specific standards call for another measurement attribute such as current market value, net realizable value, or present value.

Conservatism

The accountant is often faced with a choice of different measurements of a situation, with each measurement having reasonable support. According to the concept of **conservatism**, the accountant must select the measurement with the least favorable effect on net income and financial position in the current period.

To apply the concept of conservatism to any given situation, there must be alternative measurements, each of which must have reasonable support. The accountant cannot use the conservatism concept to justify arbitrarily low figures. For example, writing inventory down to an arbitrarily low figure in order to recognize any possible loss from selling the inventory constitutes inaccurate accounting and cannot be justified under the concept of conservatism. An acceptable use of conservatism would be to value inventory at the lower of historical cost or market value.

The conservatism concept is used in many other situations, such as writing down or writing off obsolete inventory prior to sale, recognizing a loss on a long-term construction contract when it can be reasonably anticipated, and taking a conservative approach in determining the application of overhead to inventory. In estimating the lives of fixed assets, a conservative view is taken. Conservatism requires that the estimate of warranty expense reflects the least favorable effect on net income and the financial position of the current period.

Realization

Accountants face a problem of when to recognize revenue. All parts of an entity contribute to revenue, including the janitor, the receiving department, and the production employees. The problem becomes how to determine objectively the contribution of each of the segments toward revenue. Since this is not practical, accountants must determine *when* it is practical to recognize revenue.

In practice, revenue recognition has been the subject of much debate. This has resulted in fairly wide interpretations. The issue of revenue recognition has represented the basis of many SEC enforcement actions. In general, the point of recognition of revenue should be the point in time when revenue can be reasonably and objectively determined. It is essential that there be some uniformity regarding when revenue is recognized, so as to make financial statements meaningful and comparable.

Point of Sale
Revenue is usually recognized at the point of sale. At this time, the earning process is virtually complete, and the exchange value can be determined.

There are times when the use of the point-of-sale approach does not give a fair result. An example would be the sale of land on credit to a buyer who does not have a reasonable ability to pay. If revenue were recognized at the point of sale, there would be a reasonable chance that sales had been overstated because of the material risk of default. In such cases, there are other acceptable methods of recognizing revenue that should be considered, such as the following:

1. End of production
2. Receipt of cash
3. Revenue recognized during production
4. Cost recovery

End of Production
The recognition of revenue at the completion of the production process is acceptable when the price of the item is known and there is a ready market. The mining of gold or silver is an example, and the harvesting of some farm products would also fit these criteria. If corn is harvested in the fall and held over the winter in order to obtain a higher price in the spring, the realization of revenue from the growing of corn should be recognized in the fall, at the point of harvest. The gain or loss from the holding of the corn represents a separate consideration from the growing of the corn.

Receipt of Cash
The receipt of cash is another basis for revenue recognition. This method should be used when collection is not capable of reasonable estimation at the time of sale. The land sales business, where the purchaser makes only a nominal down payment, is one type of business where the collection of the full amount is especially doubtful. Experience has shown that many purchasers default on the contract.

During Production
Some long-term construction projects recognize revenue as the construction progresses. This exception tends to give a fairer picture of the results for a given period of time. For example, in the building of a utility plant, which may take several years, recognizing revenue as work progresses gives a fairer picture of the results than does having the entire revenue recognized in the period when the plant is completed.

Cost Recovery
The cost recovery approach is acceptable for highly speculative transactions. For example, an entity may invest in a venture search for gold, the outcome of which is completely unpredictable. In this case, the first revenue can be handled as a return of the investment. If more is received than has been invested, the excess would be considered revenue.

In addition to the methods of recognizing revenue described in this chapter, there are many other methods that are usually industry-specific. Being aware of the method(s) used by a specific firm can be important to your understanding of the financial reports.

Matching

The revenue realization concept involves when to recognize revenue. Accountants need a related concept that addresses when to recognize the costs associated with the recognized revenue: the **matching concept**. The basic intent is to determine the revenue first and then match the appropriate costs against this revenue.

Some costs, such as the cost of inventory, can be easily matched with revenue. When we sell the inventory and recognize the revenue, the cost of the inventory can be matched against the revenue. Other costs have no direct connection with revenue, so some systematic policy must be adopted in order to allocate these costs reasonably against revenues. Examples are research and development costs and public relations costs. Both research and development costs and public relations costs are charged off in the period incurred. This is inconsistent with the matching concept because the cost would benefit beyond the current period, but it is in accordance with the concept of conservatism.

Consistency

The **consistency concept** requires the entity to give the same treatment to comparable transactions from period to period. This adds to the usefulness of the reports, since the reports from one period are comparable to the reports from another period. It also facilitates the detection of trends.

Many accounting methods could be used for any single item, such as inventory. If inventory were determined in one period on one basis and in the next period on a different basis, the resulting inventory and profits would not be comparable from period to period.

Entities sometimes need to change particular accounting methods in order to adapt to changing environments. If the entity can justify the use of an alternative accounting method, the change can be made. The entity must be ready to defend the change—a responsibility that should not be taken lightly in view of the liability for misleading financial statements. Sometimes the change will be based on a new accounting pronouncement. When an entity makes a change in accounting methods, the justification for the change must be disclosed, along with an explanation of the effect on the statements.

Full Disclosure

The accounting reports must disclose all facts that may influence the judgment of an informed reader. If the entity uses an accounting method that represents a departure from the official position of the FASB, disclosure of the departure must be made, along with the justification for it.

Several methods of disclosure exist, such as parenthetical explanations, supporting schedules, cross-references, and footnotes. Often, the additional disclosures must be made by a footnote in order to explain the situation properly. For example, details of a pension plan, long-term leases, and provisions of a bond issue are often disclosed in footnotes.

The financial statements are expected to summarize significant financial information. If all the financial information is presented in detail, it could be misleading. Excessive disclosure could violate the concept of full disclosure. Therefore, a reasonable summarization of financial information is required.

Because of the complexity of many businesses and the increased expectations of the public, full disclosure has become one of the most difficult concepts for the accountant to apply. Lawsuits frequently charge accountants with failure to make proper disclosure. Since disclosure is often a judgment decision, it is not surprising that others (especially those who have suffered losses) would disagree with the adequacy of the disclosure.

Materiality

The accountant must consider many concepts and principles when determining how to handle a particular item. The proper use of the various concepts and principles may be costly and time-consuming. The **materiality concept** involves the relative size and importance of an item to a firm. A material item to one entity may not be material to another. For example, an item that costs $100 might be expensed by General Motors, but the same item might be carried as an asset by a small entity.

It is essential that material items be properly handled on the financial statements. Immaterial items are not subject to the concepts and principles that bind the accountant. They may be handled in the most economical and expedient manner possible. However, the accountant faces a judgment situation when determining materiality. It is better to err in favor of an item being material than the other way around.

A basic question when determining whether an item is material is: "Would this item influence an informed reader of the financial statements?" In answering this question, the accountant should consider the statements as a whole.

Industry Practices

Some industry practices lead to accounting reports that do not conform to the general theory that underlies accounting. Some of these practices are the result of government regulation. For example, some differences can be found in highly regulated industries, such as insurance, railroad, and utilities.

In the utility industry, an allowance for funds used during the construction period of a new plant is treated as part of the cost of the plant. The offsetting amount is reflected as other income. This amount is based on the utility's hypothetical cost of funds, including funds from debt and stock. This type of accounting is found only in the utility industry.

In some industries, it is very difficult to determine the cost of the inventory. Examples include the meat-packing industry, the flower industry, and farming. In these areas, it may be necessary to determine the inventory value by working backward from the anticipated selling price and subtracting the estimated cost to complete and dispose of the inventory. The inventory would thus be valued at a net realizable value, which would depart from the cost concept and the usual interpretation of the revenue realization concept. If inventory is valued at net realizable value, then the profit has already been recognized and is part of the inventory amount.

The accounting profession is making an effort to reduce or eliminate specific industry practices. However, industry practices that depart from typical accounting procedures will probably never be eliminated completely. Some industries have legitimate peculiarities that call for accounting procedures other than the customary ones.

Transaction Approach

The accountant records only events that affect the financial position of the entity and, at the same time, can be reasonably determined in monetary terms. For example, if the entity purchases merchandise on account (on credit), the financial position of the entity changes. This change can be determined in monetary terms as the inventory asset is obtained and the liability, accounts payable, is incurred.

Many important events that influence the prospects for the entity are not recorded and, therefore, are not reflected in the financial statements because they fall outside the transaction approach. The death of a top executive could have a material influence on future prospects, especially for a small company. One of the company's major suppliers could go bankrupt at a time when the entity does not have an alternative source. The entity may have experienced a long strike by its employees or have a history of labor problems. A major competitor may go out of business. All these events may be significant to the entity. They are not recorded because they are not transactions. When projecting the future prospects of an entity, it is necessary to go beyond current financial reports.

Some of the items not recorded will be disclosed. This is done under the full disclosure assumption.

Cash Basis

The **cash basis** recognizes revenue when cash is received and recognizes expenses when cash is paid. The cash basis usually does *not* provide reasonable information about the earning capability of the entity in the short run. Therefore, the cash basis is usually *not* acceptable.

Accrual Basis

The **accrual basis** of accounting recognizes revenue when realized (realization concept) and expenses when incurred (matching concept). If the difference between the accrual basis and the cash basis is not material, the entity may use the cash basis as an alternative to the accrual basis for income determination. Usually, the difference between the accrual basis and the cash basis is material.

A modified cash basis is sometimes used by professional practices and service organizations. The modified cash basis adjusts for such items as buildings and equipment.

The accrual basis requires numerous adjustments at the end of the accounting period. For example, if insurance has been paid for in advance, the accountant must determine the amounts that belong in prepaid insurance and insurance expense. If employees have not been paid all of their wages, the unpaid wages must be determined and recorded as an expense and as a liability. If revenue has been collected in advance, such as rent received in advance, this revenue relates to future periods and must, therefore, be deferred to those periods. At the end of the accounting period, the unearned rent would be considered a liability.

The use of the accrual basis complicates the accounting process, but the end result is more representative of an entity's financial condition than the cash basis. Without the accrual basis, accountants would not usually be able to make the time period assumption—that the entity can be accounted for with reasonable accuracy for a particular period of time.

The following illustration indicates why the accrual basis is generally regarded as a better measure of a firm's performance than the cash basis.

Assumptions:

1. Sold merchandise (inventory) for $25,000 on credit this year. The merchandise cost $12,500 when purchased in the prior year.
2. Purchased merchandise this year in the amount of $30,000 on credit.
3. Paid suppliers of merchandise $18,000 this year.
4. Collected $15,000 from sales.

Accrual Basis		**Cash Basis**	
Sales	$ 25,000	Receipts	$ 15,000
Cost of sales (expenses)	(12,500)	Expenditures	(18,000)
Income	$ 12,500	Loss	$ (3,000)

The accrual basis indicates a profitable business, whereas the cash basis indicates a loss. The cash basis does not reasonably indicate when the revenue was earned or when to recognize the cost that relates to the earned revenue. The cash basis does indicate when the receipts and payments (disbursements) occurred. The points in time when cash is received and paid do not usually constitute a good gauge of profitability. However, knowing the points in time is important; the flow of cash will be presented in a separate financial statement (statement of cash flows).

In practice, the accrual basis is modified. Immaterial items are frequently handled on a cash basis, and some specific standards have allowed the cash basis.

USING THE INTERNET

The **Internet** is a global collection of computer networks linked together and available for your use. Information passes easily among these networks because all connected networks use a common communication protocol. The Internet includes local, regional, national, and international backbone networks.

There are many reasons for using the Internet. Some of these reasons include: (1) retrieving information, (2) finding information, (3) sending and receiving electronic mail, (4) conducting research, and (5) accessing information databases.

Companies' Internet Web Sites

The majority of publicly held companies in the United States have established a web site on the Internet. The contents of these web sites vary. A few companies only provide advertisements and product information. In these cases, a phone number may be given to order more information. Other companies provide limited financial information, such as total revenues, net income, and earnings per share. These companies may also provide advertisements and a phone number for more information. The majority of companies provide comprehensive financial information and possibly advertisements. The comprehensive financial information may include the annual report and quarterly reports. It may also include the current stock price and the history of the stock price.

Helpful Web Sites

There are a number of web sites that can be very useful when performing analysis. Many of these web sites have highlighted text or graphics that can be clicked to go to another related site. Several excellent web sites follow:

1. SEC Edgar Database

   http://www.sec.gov

   The Securities and Exchange Commission provides a web site that includes its Edgar Database. This site allows users to download publicly available electronic filings submitted to the SEC from 1994 to the present. By citing the company name, you can select from a menu of recent filings. This will include the 10-K report and the 10-Q.

2. Rutgers Accounting Web

   http://www.rutgers.edu/accounting/

   This site provides links to many other accounting sites. RAW provides rapid access to many accounting sites without separately targeting each site. These include Edgar, the International Accounting Network, and many other accounting resources. Accounting organizations include the American Accounting Association, American Institute of Certified Public Accountants, and Institute of Management Accountants.

3. Report Gallery

   http://www.reportgallery.com

   This site lists web sites and annual reports of publicly traded companies.

4. Financial Accounting Standards Board (FASB)

   http://www.fasb.org

   Many useful items can be found here including publications, technical projects, and international activities.

5. General Services Administration

   http://www.info.gov

   This site serves as an entry point to find state, federal, and foreign government information.

6. IBM investor resources site

   http://www.ibm.com/investor

   This site attempts to give a good understanding of financials. There are many education-related items at this site. It includes a glossary and Internet links.

7. Yahoo Finance

   http://finance.yahoo.com/

   There are over 8,000 message board topics. This is an especially good financial site.

8. Virtual Finance Library

   http://www.cob.ohio-state.edu/dept/fin/

   Contains substantial financial information.

9. Financial markets/stock exchanges
   a. American Stock Exchange
      http://www.amex.com
   b. Chicago Mercantile Exchange
      http://www.cme.com
   c. NASDAQ Stock Market
      http://www.nasdaq.com
   d. New York Stock Exchange
      http://www.nyse.com

   The contents of the financial markets/stock exchange sites vary and are expanding.

SUMMARY

This chapter has reviewed the development of generally accepted accounting principles (GAAP) and the traditional assumptions of the accounting model. You need a broad understanding of GAAP and the traditional assumptions to reasonably understand financial reports. The financial reports can be no better than the accounting principles and the assumptions of the accounting model that are the basis for preparation.

To the Net

1. Go to the FASB web site (http://www.fasb.org).
   a. Click on "FASB Facts." Be prepared to discuss The Mission of the Financial Accounting Standards Board.
   b. Click on "FASAC—Financial Accounting Standards Advisory Council." Read "An Overview." Be prepared to discuss.

2. Go to the SEC site (http://www.sec.gov). Under Filings & Forms (Edgar), click on "Search for Company Filings." Click on "Search Companies and Filings." Enter the name of a company of your choice. Use this site to obtain the address of the company. Click on any form listed. The telephone number of the company can be found toward the top of the form. Contact the company, requesting a copy of their annual report, 10-K, and proxy.

Questions

Q 1-1.   Discuss the role of each of the following in the formulation of accounting principles:
   a.   American Institute of Certified Public Accountants
   b.   Financial Accounting Standards Board
   c.   Securities and Exchange Commission

Q 1-2.   How does the concept of consistency aid in the analysis of financial statements? What type of accounting disclosure is required if this concept is not applied?

Q 1-3.   The president of your firm, Lesky and Lesky, has little background in accounting. Today he walked into your office and said, "A year ago we bought a piece of land for $100,000. This year inflation has driven prices up by 6%, and an appraiser just told us we could easily resell the land for $115,000. Yet our balance sheet still shows it at $100,000. It should be valued at $115,000. That's what it's worth. Or, at a minimum, at $106,000." Respond to this statement with specific reference to accounting principles applicable in this situation.

Q 1-4.   Identify the accounting principle(s) applicable to each of the following situations:
   a.   Tim Roberts owns a bar and a rental apartment and operates a consulting service. He has separate financial statements for each.
   b.   An advance collection for magazine subscriptions is reported as a liability titled Unearned Subscriptions.
   c.   Purchases for office or store equipment for less than $25 are entered in Miscellaneous Expense.
   d.   A company uses the lower of cost or market for valuation of its inventory.
   e.   Partially completed television sets are carried at the sum of the cost incurred to date.
   f.   Land purchased 15 years ago for $40,500 is now worth $346,000. It is still carried on the books at $40,500.
   g.   Zero Corporation is being sued for $1,000,000 for breach of contract. Its lawyers believe that the damages will be minimal. Zero reports the possible loss in a footnote.

Q 1-5.   A corporation like General Motors has many owners (stockholders). Which concept enables the accountant to account for transactions of General Motors, separate and distinct from the personal transactions of the owners of General Motors?

Q 1-6.   Zebra Company has incurred substantial financial losses in recent years. Because of its financial condition, the ability of the company to keep operating is in question. Management prepares a set of financial statements that conform to generally accepted accounting principles. Comment on the use of GAAP under these conditions.

Q 1-7.   Because of assumptions and estimates that go into the preparation of financial statements, the statements are inaccurate and are, therefore, not a very meaningful tool to determine the profits or losses of an entity or the financial position of an entity. Comment.

Q 1-8.   The only accurate way to account for the success or failure of an entity is to accumulate all transactions from the opening of business until the business eventually liquidates. Comment on whether this is true. Discuss the necessity of having completely accurate statements.

Q 1-9.   Describe the following terms, which indicate the period of time included in the financial statements:
   a.   Natural business year
   b.   Calendar year
   c.   Fiscal year

Q 1-10.   Which standard of measure is the best for measuring financial transactions?

Q 1-11.   Countries have had problems with the stability of their money. Briefly describe the problem caused for financial statements when money does not hold a stable value.

Q 1-12.   In some countries where inflation has been material, an effort has been made to retain the significance of money as a measuring unit by adjusting the financial statements by an inflation factor. Can an accurate adjustment for inflation be made to the statements? Can a reasonable adjustment to the statements be made? Discuss.

Q 1-13.   An arbitrary write-off of inventory can be justified under the conservatism concept. Is this statement true or false? Discuss.

Q 1-14.   Inventory that has a market value below the historical cost should be written down in order to recognize a loss. Comment.

Q 1-15.   There are other acceptable methods of recognizing revenue when the point of sale is not acceptable. List and discuss the other methods reviewed in this chapter, and indicate when they can be used.

Q 1-16.   The matching concept involves the determination of when to recognize the costs associated with the revenue that is being recognized. For some costs, such as administrative costs, the matching concept is difficult to apply. Comment on when it is difficult to apply the matching concept. What do accountants often do under these circumstances?

Q 1-17.   The consistency concept requires the entity to give the same treatment to comparable transactions from period to period. Under what circumstances can an entity change its accounting methods, provided it makes full disclosure?

Q 1-18.   Discuss why the concept of full disclosure is difficult to apply.

Q 1-19.   No estimates or subjectivity is allowed in the preparation of financial statements. Discuss.

Q 1-20.   It is proper to handle immaterial items in the most economical, expedient manner possible. In other words, generally accepted accounting principles do not apply. Comment, including a concept that justifies your answer.

Q 1-21.   The same generally accepted accounting principles apply to all companies. Comment.

Q 1-22.   Many important events that influence the prospect for the entity are not recorded in the financial records. Comment and give an example.

Q 1-23.   Some industry practices lead to accounting reports that do not conform to the general theory that underlies accounting. Comment.

Q 1-24.   An entity may choose between the use of the accrual basis of accounting and the cash basis. Comment.

Q 1-25.   Generally accepted accounting principles have substantial authoritative support. Indicate the problem with determining substantial authoritative support.

Q 1-26.   Would an accountant record the personal assets and liabilities of the owners in the accounts of the business? Explain.

Q 1-27.   At which point is revenue from sales on account (credit sales) commonly recognized?

Q 1-28.   Elliott Company constructed a building at a cost of $50,000. A local contractor had submitted a bid to construct it for $60,000.
  a.   At what amount should the building be recorded?
  b.   Should revenue be recorded for the savings between the cost of $50,000 and the bid of $60,000?

Q 1-29.   Dexter Company charges to expense all equipment that costs $25 or less. What concept supports this policy?

Q 1-30.   Which U.S. government body has the legal power to determine generally accepted accounting principles?

Q 1-31.   What is the basic problem with the monetary assumption when there has been significant inflation?

Q 1-32.   Explain the matching principle. How is the matching principle related to the realization concept?

Q 1-33.   Briefly explain the term generally accepted accounting principles.

Q 1-34.   Briefly describe the operating procedure for Statements of Financial Accounting Standards.

Q 1-35.   What is the FASB Conceptual Framework for Accounting and Reporting intended to provide?

Q 1-36. Briefly describe the following:
  a. Committee on Accounting Procedures
  b. Committee on Accounting Terminology
  c. Accounting Principles Board
  d. Financial Accounting Standards Board

Q 1-37. The objectives of general-purpose external financial reporting are primarily to serve the needs of management. Comment.

Q 1-38. Financial accounting is designed to measure directly the value of a business enterprise. Comment.

Q 1-39. According to Concepts Statement No. 2, relevance and reliability are the two primary qualities that make accounting information useful for decision making. Comment on what is meant by relevance and reliability.

Q 1-40. SFAC No. 5 indicates that, to be recognized, an item should meet four criteria, subject to the cost-benefit constraint and materiality threshold. List these criteria.

Q 1-41. There are five different measurement attributes currently used in practice. List these measurement attributes.

Q 1-42. Briefly explain the difference between an accrual basis income statement and a cash basis income statement.

Q 1-43. The cash basis does not reasonably indicate when the revenue was earned and when the cost should be recognized. Comment.

Q 1-44. It is not important to know when cash is received and when payment is made. Comment.

Problems

P 1-1. FASB Statement of Concepts No. 2 indicates several qualitative characteristics of useful accounting information. Following is a list of some of these qualities, as well as a list of statements and phrases describing the qualities.
  a. Benefits > costs
  b. Decision usefulness
  c. Relevance
  d. Reliability
  e. Predictive value, feedback value, timeliness
  f. Verifiability, neutrality, representational faithfulness
  g. Comparability
  h. Materiality
  i. Relevance, reliability

  _____ 1. Without usefulness, there would be no benefits from information to set against its cost.
  _____ 2. Pervasive constraint imposed upon financial accounting information.
  _____ 3. Constraint that guides the threshold for recognition.
  _____ 4. A quality requiring that the information be timely and that it also have predictive value, or feedback value, or both.
  _____ 5. A quality requiring that the information have representational faithfulness and that it be verifiable and neutral.
  _____ 6. These are the two primary qualities that make accounting information useful for decision making.
  _____ 7. These are the ingredients needed to ensure that the information is relevant.
  _____ 8. These are the ingredients needed to ensure that the information is reliable.
  _____ 9. Includes consistency and interacts with relevance and reliability to contribute to the usefulness of information.

Required Place the appropriate letter identifying each quality on the line in front of the statement or phrase describing the quality.

P 1-2. Certain underlying considerations have had an important impact on the development of generally accepted accounting principles. Following is a list of these underlying considerations, as well as a list of statements describing them.
  a. Going concern or continuity
  b. Monetary unit
  c. Conservatism
  d. Matching
  e. Full disclosure
  f. Materiality
  g. Transaction approach
  h. Accrual basis
  i. Industry practices
  j. Verifiability

  k. Consistency
  l. Realization
  m. Historical cost

  n. Time period
  o. Business entity

____ 1. The business for which the financial statements are prepared is separate and distinct from the owners.

____ 2. The assumption is made that the entity will remain in business for an indefinite period of time.

____ 3. Accountants need some standard of measure to bring financial transactions together in a meaningful way.

____ 4. Revenue should be recognized when the earning process is virtually complete and the exchange value can be objectively determined.

____ 5. This concept deals with when to recognize the costs that are associated with the recognized revenue.

____ 6. Accounting reports must disclose all facts that may influence the judgment of an informed reader.

____ 7. This concept involves the relative size and importance of an item to a firm.

____ 8. The accountant is required to adhere as closely as possible to verifiable data.

____ 9. Some companies use accounting reports that do not conform to the general theory that underlies accounting.

____ 10. The accountant records only events that affect the financial position of the entity and, at the same time, can be reasonably determined in monetary terms.

____ 11. Revenue must be recognized when it is realized (realization concept), and expenses are recognized when incurred (matching concept).

____ 12. The entity must give the same treatment to comparable transactions from period to period.

____ 13. The measurement with the least favorable effect on net income and financial position in the current period must be selected.

____ 14. Of the various values that could be used, this value has been selected because it is objective and determinable.

____ 15. With this assumption, inaccuracies of accounting for the entity short of its complete life span are accepted.

Required Place the appropriate letter identifying each quality on the line in front of the statement describing the quality.

P 1-3.

Required Answer the following multiple-choice questions:

 a. Which of the following is a characteristic of information provided by external financial reports?
  1. The information is exact and not subject to change.
  2. The information is frequently the result of reasonable estimates.
  3. The information pertains to the economy as a whole.
  4. The information is provided at the least possible cost.
  5. None of the above.

 b. Which of the following is not an objective of financial reporting?
  1. Financial reporting should provide information that is useful to present and potential investors and creditors and other users in making rational investment, credit, and similar decisions.
  2. Financial reporting should provide information to help present and potential investors and creditors and other users in assessing the amounts, timing, and uncertainty of prospective cash receipts from dividends or interest and the proceeds from the sale, redemption, or maturity of securities or loans.
  3. Financial reporting should provide information about the economic resources of an enterprise, the claims against those resources, and the effects of transactions, events, and circumstances that change the resources and claims against those resources.
  4. Financial accounting is designed to measure directly the value of a business enterprise.
  5. None of the above.

 c. According to FASB Statement of Concepts No. 2, which of the following is an ingredient of the quality of relevance?
  1. Verifiability
  2. Representational faithfulness
  3. Neutrality
  4. Timeliness
  5. None of the above

d. The primary current source of generally accepted accounting principles for nongovernment operations is the
    1. New York Stock Exchange
    2. Financial Accounting Standards Board
    3. Securities and Exchange Commission
    4. American Institute of Certified Public Accountants
    5. None of the above

e. What is the underlying concept that supports the immediate recognition of a loss?
    1. Matching   4. Conservatism
    2. Consistency   5. Going concern
    3. Judgment

f. Which statement is not true?
    1. The Securities and Exchange Commission is a source of some generally accepted accounting principles.
    2. The American Institute of Certified Public Accountants is a source of some generally accepted accounting principles.
    3. The Internal Revenue Service is a source of some generally accepted accounting principles.
    4. The Financial Accounting Standards Board is a source of some generally accepted accounting principles.
    5. Numbers 1, 2, and 4 are sources of generally accepted accounting principles.

g. Which pronouncements are not issued by the Financial Accounting Standards Board?
    1. Statements of Financial Accounting Standards
    2. Statements of Financial Accounting Concepts
    3. Technical bulletins
    4. Interpretations
    5. Opinions

P 1-4.

Required   Answer the following multiple-choice questions:

a. Which of the following does the Financial Accounting Standards Board not issue?
    1. Statements of Position (SOPs)
    2. Statements of Financial Accounting Standards (SFASs)
    3. Interpretations
    4. Technical bulletins
    5. Statements of Financial Accounting Concepts (SFACs)

b. According to SFAC No. 6, assets can be defined by which of the following?
    1. Probable future sacrifices of economic benefits arising from present obligations of a particular entity to transfer assets or provide services to other entities in the future as a result of past transactions or events.
    2. Probable future economic benefits obtained or controlled by a particular entity as a result of past transactions or events.
    3. Residual interest on the assets of an entity that remains after deducting its liabilities.
    4. Increases in equity of a particular business enterprise resulting from transfers to the enterprise from other entities of something of value to obtain or increase ownership interests (or equity) in it.
    5. Decrease in equity of a particular business enterprise resulting from transferring assets, rendering services, or incurring liabilities by the enterprise.

c. According to SFAC No. 6, expenses can be defined by which of the following?
    1. Inflows or other enhancements of assets of an entity or settlements of its liabilities (or a combination of both) from delivering or producing goods, rendering services, or other activities that constitute the entity's ongoing major or central operations.
    2. Outflows or other consumption or using up of assets or incurrences of liabilities (or a combination of both) from delivering or producing goods, rendering services, or carrying out other activities that constitute the entity's ongoing major or central operations.
    3. Increases in equity (net assets) from peripheral or incidental transactions of an entity and from all other transactions and other events and circumstances affecting the entity during a period, except those that result from revenues or investments.
    4. Decreases in equity (net assets) from peripheral or incidental transactions of an entity and from all other transactions and other events and circumstances affecting the entity during a period, except those that result from expenses or distributions to owners.

5. Probable future economic benefits obtained or controlled by a particular entity as a result of past transactions or events.

d. SFAC No. 5 indicates that an item, to be recognized, should meet four criteria, subject to the cost-benefit constraint and the materiality threshold. Which of the following is not one of the four criteria?
   1. The item fits one of the definitions of the elements.
   2. The item has a relevant attribute measurable with sufficient reliability.
   3. The information related to the item is relevant.
   4. The information related to the item is reliable.
   5. The item has comparability, including consistency.

e. SFAC No. 5 identifies five different measurement attributes currently used in practice. Which of the following is not one of the measurement attributes currently used in practice?
   1. Historical cost
   2. Future cost
   3. Current market value
   4. Net realizable value
   5. Present, or discounted, value of future cash flows

f. Which of the following indicates how revenue is usually recognized?
   1. Point of sale
   2. End of production
   3. Receipt of cash
   4. During production
   5. Cost recovery

g. Statement of Financial Accounting Concepts No. 1, "Objectives of Financial Reporting by Business Enterprises," includes all of the following objectives, except one. Which objective does it not include?
   1. Financial accounting is designed to measure directly the value of a business enterprise.
   2. Investors, creditors, and others may use reported earnings and information about the elements of financial statements in various ways to assess the prospects for cash flows.
   3. The primary focus of financial reporting is information about earnings and its components.
   4. Financial reporting should provide information that is useful to present and potential investors and creditors and other users in making rational investment, credit, and similar decisions.
   5. The objectives are those of general-purpose external financial reporting by business enterprises.

P 1-5. The following data relate to Jones Company for the year ended December 31, 2002:

Sales on credit	$80,000
Cost of inventory sold on credit	65,000
Collections from customers	60,000
Purchase of inventory on credit	50,000
Payment for purchases	55,000
Cash collections for common stock	30,000
Dividends paid	10,000
Payment to salesclerk	10,000

Required
a. Determine income on an accrual basis.
b. Determine income on a cash basis.

Case 1-1

Standards Overload?*

Even though accounting records go back hundreds of years, there was little effort to develop accounting standards until the 1900s. The first major effort to develop accounting standards in the United States came in 1939 when the American Institute of Certified Public Accountants formed the Committee on Accounting Procedures.

As the number of standards increased, an issue called "standards overload" emerged. Essentially the charge of "standards overload" is that there are too many accounting standards and that the standards are too complicated. Many individuals charging that standards overload is a problem maintain that more professional judgment should be allowed in financial accounting. Some individuals take a position that selected standards should not apply to nonpublic companies. Others take a position that "little" companies should be exempt from selected standards. There has been some selective exclusion from standards in the past. Examples of selective exclusion are the following:

1. *Statement of Financial Accounting Standards No. 21*, "Suspension of the Reporting of Earnings per Share and Segment Information by Nonpublic Enterprises."
   "Although the presentation of earnings per share and segment information is not required in the financial statements of nonpublic enterprises, any such information that is presented in the financial statements of nonpublic enterprises shall be consistent with the requirements of APB Opinion No. 15 and FASB Statement No. 14."
2. *Statement of Financial Accounting Standards No. 33*, "Financial Reporting and Changing Prices."
   This statement required supplemental reporting on the effects of price changes. Only large public companies were required to present this information on a supplementary basis.

Required
a. Financial statements should aid the user of the statements in making decisions. In your opinion, would the user of the statements be aided if there were a distinction between financial reporting standards for public vs. nonpublic companies? Between little and big companies?
b. In your opinion, would CPAs favor a distinction between financial reporting standards for public vs. nonpublic companies? Discuss.
c. In your opinion, would small business owner-managers favor a distinction between financial reporting standards for small and large companies? Discuss.
d. In your opinion, would CPAs in a small CPA firm view standards overload as a bigger problem than CPAs in a large CPA firm? Discuss.
e. Comment on standards overload, considering *Statement of Financial Accounting Concepts No. 1*, "Objectives of Financial Reporting by Business Enterprises." Particularly consider the following objective:

   Financial reporting should provide information useful to present and potential investors and creditors and other users in making rational investment, credit, and similar decisions. The information should be comprehensible to those having a reasonable understanding of business and economic activities and willing to study the information with reasonable diligence.

---

*Note: The standards referenced in this case should not be considered current standards. The financial reporting issues referenced in this case are discussed in later chapters, using current requirements.

Case 1-2

Standard Setting: "A Political Aspect"

This case consists of a letter from Dennis R. Beresford, chairperson of the Financial Accounting Standards Board, to Senator Joseph I. Lieberman. The specific issue was proposed legislation relating to the accounting for employee stock options.

Permission to reprint the following letter was obtained from the Financial Accounting Standards Board.

August 3, 1993

Senator Joseph I. Lieberman
United States Senate
Hart Senate Office Building
Room 316
Washington, DC 20510

Dear Senator Lieberman:

Members of the Financial Accounting Standards Board (the FASB or the Board) and its staff routinely consult with members of Congress, their staffs, and other government officials on matters involving financial accounting. For example, FASB members and staff met with Senator Levin both before and after the introduction of his proposed legislation, Senate Bill 259, which also addresses accounting for employee stock options.

The attachment to this letter discusses the accounting issues (we have not addressed the tax issues) raised in your proposed legislation, Senate Bill 1175, and issues raised in remarks introduced in the *Congressional Record*. My comments in this letter address an issue that is more important than any particular legislation or any particular accounting issue: why we have a defined process for setting financial reporting standards and why it is harmful to the public interest to distort accounting reports in an attempt to attain other worthwhile goals.

Financial Reporting

Markets are enormously efficient information processors—when they have the information and that information faithfully portrays economic events. Financial statements are one of the basic tools for communicating that information. The U.S. capital market system is well-developed and efficient because of users' confidence that the financial information they receive is reliable. Common accounting standards for the preparation of financial reports contribute to their credibility. The mission of the FASB, an organization designed to be independent of all other business and professional organizations, is to establish and improve financial accounting and reporting standards in the United States.

Investors, creditors, regulators, and other users of financial reports make business and economic decisions based on information in financial statements. Credibility is critical whether the user is an individual contemplating a stock investment, a bank making lending decisions, or a regulatory agency reviewing solvency. Users count on financial reports that are evenhanded, neutral, and unbiased.

An efficiently functioning economy requires credible financial information as a basis for decisions about allocation of resources. If financial statements are to be useful, they must report economic activity without coloring the message to influence behavior in a particular direction. They must not intentionally favor one party over another. Financial statements must provide a neutral scorecard of the effects of transactions.

Economic Consequences of Accounting Standards

The Board often hears that we should take a broader view, that we must consider the economic consequences of a new accounting standard. The FASB should not act, critics maintain, if a new accounting standard would have undesirable economic consequences. We have been told that the effects of accounting standards could cause lasting damage to American companies and their employees. Some have suggested, for example, that recording the liability for retiree health care or the costs for stock-based compensation will place U.S. companies at a competitive disadvantage. These critics suggest that because of accounting standards, companies may reduce benefits or move operations overseas to areas where workers do not demand the same benefits. These assertions are usually combined with statements about desirable goals, like providing retiree health care or creating employee incentives.

There is a common element in those assertions. The goals are desirable, but the means require that the Board abandon neutrality and establish reporting standards that conceal the financial impact of certain transactions from those who use financial statements. Costs of transactions exist whether or not the FASB mandates their recognition in financial statements. For example, not requiring the recognition of the cost of stock options or ignoring the liabilities for retiree health benefits does not alter the economics of the transactions. It only withholds information from investors, creditors, policy makers, and others who need to make informed decisions and, eventually, impairs the credibility of financial reports.

One need only look to the collapse of the thrift industry to demonstrate the consequences of abandoning neutrality. During the 1970s and 1980s, regulatory accounting principles (RAP) were altered to obscure problems in troubled institutions. Preserving the industry was considered a "greater good." Many observers believe that the effect was to delay action and hide the true dimensions of the problem. The public interest is best served by neutral accounting standards that inform policy rather than promote it. Stated simply, truth in accounting is always good policy.

Neutrality does not mean that accounting should not influence human behavior. We expect that changes in financial reporting will have economic consequences, just as economic consequences are inherent in existing financial reporting practices. Changes in behavior naturally flow from more complete and representationally faithful financial statements. The fundamental question, however, is whether those who measure and report on economic events should somehow screen the information before reporting it to achieve some objective. In FASB Concepts Statement No. 2, "Qualitative Characteristics of Accounting Information" (paragraph 102), the Board observed:

> Indeed, most people are repelled by the notion that some "big brother," whether government or private, would tamper with scales or speedometers surreptitiously to induce people to lose weight or obey speed limits or would slant the scoring of athletic events or examinations to enhance or decrease someone's chances of winning or graduating. There is no more reason to abandon neutrality in accounting measurement.

The Board continues to hold that view. The Board does not set out to achieve particular economic results through accounting pronouncements. We could not if we tried. Beyond that, it is seldom clear which result we should seek because our constituents often have opposing viewpoints. Governments, and the policy goals they adopt, frequently change.

Standard Setting in the Private Sector

While the SEC and congressional committees maintain active oversight of the FASB to ensure that the public interest is served, throughout its history the SEC has relied on the Board and its predecessors in the private sector to establish and improve financial accounting and reporting standards. In fulfilling the Board's mission of improving financial reporting, accounting standards are established through a system of due process and open deliberation. On all of our major projects, this involves open Board meetings, proposals published for comment, "field testing" of proposals, public hearings, and redeliberation of the issues in light of comments.

Our due process has allowed us to deal with complex and highly controversial accounting issues, ranging from pensions and retiree health care to abandonment of nuclear power plants. This open, orderly process for standard setting precludes placing any particular special interest above the interests of the many who rely on financial information. The Board believes that the public interest is best served by developing neutral accounting standards that result in accounting for similar transactions similarly and different transactions differently. The resulting financial statements provide as complete and faithful a picture of an entity as possible.

Corporations, accounting firms, users of financial statements, and most other interested parties have long supported the process of establishing accounting standards in the private sector without intervention by Congress or other branches of government. Despite numerous individual issues on which the FASB and many of its constituents have disagreed, that support has continued. The resulting system of accounting standards and financial reporting, while not perfect, is the best in the world.

Conclusion

We understand that there are a number of people who believe that their particular short-term interests are more important than an effectively functioning financial reporting system. We sincerely hope, however, that you and others in the Congress will review the reasons that have led generations of lawmakers and regulators to conclude that neutral financial reporting is critical to the functioning of our economic system and that the best way to achieve that end is to allow the existing private sector process to proceed. We respectfully submit that the public interest will be best served by that course. As former SEC Chairman Richard Breeden said in testimony to the Senate Banking Committee in 1990:

> The purpose of accounting standards is to assure that financial information is presented in a way that enables decision-makers to make informed judgments. To the extent that accounting standards are subverted to achieve objectives unrelated to a fair and accurate presentation, they fail in their purpose.

The attachment to this letter discusses your proposed legislation. It also describes some aspects of our project on stock compensation and the steps in our due process procedures that remain before the project will be completed. In your remarks in the *Congressional Record*, you said that you will address future issues, including an examination of the current treatment of employee stock options, over the next weeks and months. We would be pleased to meet with you or your staff to discuss these topics and the details of our project. I will phone your appointments person in the next two weeks to see if it is convenient for you to meet with me.

Sincerely,

Dennis R. Beresford

Dennis R. Beresford

Enclosure
cc: The Honorable Connie Mack
       The Honorable Dianne Feinstein
       The Honorable Barbara Boxer
       The Honorable Carl S. Levin
       The Honorable Christopher J. Dodd
       The Honorable Arthur J. Levitt

Required   a.   "Financial statements must provide a neutral scorecard of the effects of transactions." Comment.
               b.   "Costs of transactions exist whether or not the FASB mandates their recognition in financial statements." Comment.
               c.   In the United States, standard setting is in the private sector. Comment.
               d.   Few, if any, accounting standards are without some economic impact. Comment.

Case 1-3   ## Standard Setting: "By the Way of the United States Congress"

In the summer of 1993, the Senate and the House introduced identical bills to amend the Internal Revenue Code of 1986. Section 4 of these bills addressed stock option compensation and financial reporting.

SEC. 4 STOCK OPTION COMPENSATION.

Section 14 of the Securities Exchange Act of 1934 (15 U.S.C. 78n) is amended by adding at the end the following new subsection:

"(h) STOCK OPTION COMPENSATION—The Commission shall not require or permit an issuer to recognize any expense or other charge in financial statements furnished to its security holders resulting from, or attributable to, either the grant, vesting, or exercise of any option or other right to acquire any equity security of such issuer (even if the right to exercise such option or right is subject to any conditions, contingencies or other criteria including, without limitation, the continued performance of services, achievement of performance objectives, or the occurrence of any event) which is granted to its directors, officers, employees, or other persons in connection with the performance of services, where the exercise price of such option or right is not less than the fair market value of the underlying security at the time such option or right is granted."

Required   a.   The United States Congress is well qualified to debate and set generally accepted accounting principles. Comment.
               b.   Speculate on why these bills were directed to amend the Securities Exchange Act of 1934.

Case 1-4   ## Recognizing Revenue and Related Costs—Part I

A.   The Boeing Company

Boeing is the leading aerospace company in the world.

1.   **Sales and Other Operating Revenues**—Commercial aircraft sales are recorded as deliveries made unless transfer of risk and rewards of ownership is not sufficient.
2.   **Contract and Program Accounting**—In the Military Aircraft and Missile Systems Segment and Space and Communications Segment, operations principally consist of performing work under contract, predominately for the U.S. Government and foreign governments. Cost of sales of such contracts is determined based on the estimated average total contract cost and revenue. Estimates of each contract's revenue and cost are revised and reassessed quarterly. Changes in estimates result in cumulate revisions to the contract profit recognized.

Required   a. **Sales and Other Operating Revenue**

Do you consider this revenue recognition to be reasonable?

b. **Contract and Program Accounting**

What would be the result if the estimate of sales would be revised downward?

B. General Motors Corporation

General Motors is the world's largest automotive corporation.

1. **Sales Allowances**—At the time of sale, GM records as a reduction of revenue the estimated impact of sales allowances in the form of dealer and customer incentives. There may be numerous types of incentives available at any particular time. This estimate is based upon the assumption that a certain number of vehicles in dealer stock will have a specific incentive applied against them. If the actual number of vehicles differs from the estimate, or if a different mix of incentives occurs, the sales allowances could be affected.

2. **Policy and Warranty**—Provisions for estimated expenses related to product warranties are made at the time products are sold. These estimates are established using historical information on the nature's frequency and average cost of warranty claims. Management actively studies trends of warranty claims and takes action to improve vehicle quality and minimize warranty claims. Management believes that the warranty reserve is appropriate; however, actual claims incurred could differ from the original estimates, requiring adjustments to the reserve.

Required   a. **Sales Allowances**

Assume that new car sales are less than expected from a sales allowances program. How will sales allowances be adjusted and how will this affect the recorded income at time of adjustment?

b. **Policy and Warranty**

Assume that warranty claims are substantially less than originally estimated. What adjustment will result?

C. Sun Hydraulics Corporation

Sun Hydraulics Corporation and its wholly owned subsidiaries (The "Company") design, manufacture, and sell screw-in cartridge valves and manifolds used in hydraulic systems.

Revenue Recognition—Sales are recognized when products are shipped. Sales incentives are granted to customers based upon the volume of purchases. These sales incentives are recorded at the time of sales as a reduction of gross sales.

Required   Is Sun Hydraulics Corporation using the cash basis of recognizing revenue? Explain.

D. Scientific Technologies

Scientific Technologies Incorporated (the "Company") develops, manufactures and markets safety light curtains, industrial sensors, optical profilers, microcomputers, and power monitoring devices for factory automation applications.

Revenue Recognition—Revenue from product sales to customers is recognized upon shipment if a signed purchase order exists, the price is fixed or determinable, collection of the resulting receivable is considered probable, and product returns can be reasonably estimated. Subsequent to the sale of the products, the Company has no obligation to provide any modification or customization, upgrades, enhancements, or post-contract customer support. Upon shipment, the Company provides for the estimated costs that may be incurred for product warranties.

Installation and engineering service revenue is recognized when services are rendered, or an identifiable portion of the contract is completed, no significant post-delivery obligations exist, and collection is probable.

Required   a. Describe the revenue recognition principle for product sales to customers.

b. Comment on the revenue recognition for installation and engineering service revenue.

| Case 1-5 | Recognizing Revenue and Related Costs—Part II |

A. Harris Interactive Inc.

Harris Interactive Inc. is a leading market research, polling, and consulting firm that uses Internet-based and traditional methodologies to provide our worldwide customers with critical market knowledge in many industries.

Revenue Recognition (in Part)—The Company recognizes revenue from services principally on the percentage of completion method in the ratio that costs incurred bear to estimated cost a completion.

Required Which revenue recognition method described in this book is being used?

B. Ethan Allen Interiors Inc.

Ethan Allen Interiors Inc. is a leading manufacturer and retailer of quality home furnishings, offering a full range of furniture products and home accessories.

Revenue Recognition—Sales are recorded to dealers when goods are shipped, at which point title has passed. Sales made through Ethan Allen-owned stores are recognized when delivery is made to the customer.

Required Comment on why sales are recorded to dealers when goods are shipped, while sales made through Ethan Allen-owned stores are not recognized until delivery is made.

C. Alexander and Baldwin, Inc.

The Company has three operating segments: Ocean Transportation, Property Development and Management, and Food Products.

Voyage Revenue Recognition—Voyage revenue and variable costs and expenses associated with Voyages are included in income at the time each voyage leg commences.

Real Estate Sales Revenue Recognition—Sales are recorded when the risks and benefits of ownership have passed to the buyers (generally on closing dates), adequate down payments have been received, and collection of remaining balances is reasonably assured.

Required Comment on the revenue recognition:
a. Voyage Revenue Recognition
b. Real Estate Sales Revenue Recognition

D. Orphan Medical, Inc.

Orphan Medical, Inc. (the "Company") acquires, develops, and markets products of high medical value intended to address inadequately treated or uncommon diseases within selected therapeutic areas segments.

Revenue Recognition—Sales are recognized at the time a product is shipped to the Company's customers and are recorded net of reserves for estimated returns of expired product and discounts. The Company is obligated to accept from all domestic customers the return of products that have reached their expiration date. The Company is not obligated to accept exchange of outdated product from its international distribution partners. The Company monitors the return of product and modifies its actual for outdated product returns as necessary. Management bases the reserve on historical experience and these estimates are subject to change.

Required Identify and discuss the estimates involved in the revenue recognition.

Case 1-6

Cash Basis—Accrual Basis?

1994 Annual Report—Dibrell Brothers Inc.

Note F—Employee Benefits (in Part)
Postretirement Health and Life Insurance Benefits

Effective July 1, 1992, the Company adopted Statement of Financial Accounting Standards, No. 106, "Employer's Accounting for Postretirement Benefits Other Than Pensions," for its U.S. operations. Employees retiring from the Company on or after attaining age 55 who have rendered at least ten years of service to the Company are eligible for postretirement health care coverage. The benefits are subject to deductibles, co-payment provisions, and other limitations. The Company reserves the right to change or terminate these benefits at any time.

SFAS 106 requires that the cost of postretirement benefits to the Company be recognized over the service lives of the employees, rather than on the cash basis. Employees of the Company are currently eligible to receive specified company-paid health care and life insurance benefits during retirement.

Required

a. Prior to July 1, 1992, what was the basis used to account for postretirement health care coverage?
b. Effective July 1, 1992, what was the basis used to account for postretirement health care coverage?
c. Why was the change made for reporting postretirement health care coverage?
d. Assume that this company used the accrual basis of accounting. Speculate on why such a company could report a potentially significant item on a cash basis.

Case 1-7

Going Concern?

Independent Auditors' Report

The Board of Directors and Stockholders
Palatin Technologies, Inc. (in Part)

In our opinion, based on our audit and the report of other auditors, the 2002 consolidated financial statements referred to above present fairly, in all material respects, the financial position of Palatin Technologies, Inc. (a development stage company) and subsidiaries as of June 30, 2002, and the results of their operations and their cash flows for the year then ended, and for the period from January 28, 2002, in conformity with accounting principles generally accepted in the United States of America.

The accompanying consolidated financial statements have been prepared assuming that the Company will continue as a going concern. As discussed on Note 1 to the consolidated financial statements, the Company has an accumulated deficit and has limited liquid resources that raise substantial doubt about its ability to continue as a going concern. Management's plans in regard to these matters are also described in Note 1. The consolidated financial statements do not include any adjustments that might result from the outcome of this uncertainty.

KPMG LLP

Philadelphia, Pennsylvania
September 20, 2002

Palatin Technologies, Inc.
(A Development Stage Enterprise)
Notes to Consolidated Financial Statements

Organization Activities (in Part)

BUSINESS RISK AND LIQUIDITY—As shown in the accompanying financial statements, the Company incurred a substantial loss of $16,138,577 for the year ended June 30, 2002, and has a deficit accumulated in the development stage of $70,243,616, cash and cash equivalents of $7,944,264, and investments of $1,178,717 as of June 30, 2002. The Company anticipates incurring additional losses in the future as it continues development of Leutech and expands clinical trials for other indications and PT-141, continues research and development of PT-141 and its MIDAS Technologies and proposed products, conducts pre-clinical studies and clinical trials, obtains required regulatory approvals, and successfully manufactures and markets such technologies and proposed products. The time required to reach profitability is highly uncertain, and there can be no assurance that the Company will be able to achieve profitability on a sustained basis, if at all.

The Company has incurred negative cash flows from operations since the inception; the Company has expended and expects to continue to expend in the future, substantial funds to complete its planned product development efforts. The Company expects that its existing capital resources, including the funds received pursuant to the July 2002 private placement, will be adequate to fund the Company's projected operations through December 2002, based on current expenditure levels. No assurance can be given that the Company will not consume a significant amount of its available resources before that time management plans to continue to refine its operations, control expenses, evaluate alternative methods to conduct its business, and seek available and attractive sources of financial and sharing of development costs through strategic collaboration agreements or other sources. Based on the Company's historical ability to raise capital, management believes that through one or a combination of such factors that it will obtain adequate financing to fund the Company's operations through fiscal year 2003, based on current expenditure levels. Should appropriate sources of financing not be available, management would delay certain clinical trials and research activities until such time as appropriate financing was available. There can be no assurance that the Company's financing efforts will be successful. If adequate funds are not available, our financial condition and results of operations will be materially and adversely affected.

These factors raise substantial doubt about the Company's ability to continue as a going concern. The consolidated financial statements do not include any adjustments that might result from the outcome of this uncertainty.

Required
a. What is the going-concern assumption?
b. Has Palatin Technologies prepared financial statements using the going-concern assumption? Comment.
c. What is the significance of the disclosure that this company may not be able to continue as a going concern?

Case 1-8

Economics and Accounting: The Uncongenial Twins*

"Economics and accountancy are two disciplines which draw their raw material from much the same mines. From these raw materials, however, they seem to fashion remarkably different products. They both study the operations of firms; they both are concerned with such concepts as income, expenditure, profits, capital, value, and prices. In spite of an apparently common subject-matter, however, they often seem to inhabit totally different worlds, between which there is remarkably little communication."

"It is not surprising that the economist regards much accounting procedure as in the nature of ritual. To call these procedures ritualistic is in no way to deny or decry their validity. Ritual is always the proper response when a man has to give an answer to a question, the answer to which he cannot really know. Ritual under these circumstances has two functions. It is comforting (and in the face of the great uncertainties of the future, comfort is not to be despised), and it is also an answer sufficient for action. It is the sufficient answer rather than the right answer which the accountant really seeks. Under these circumstances, however, it is important that we should know what the accountant's answer means, which means that we should know what procedure he has employed. The wise businessman will not believe his accountant although he takes what his accountant tells him as important evidence. The quality of that evidence, however, depends in considerable degree on the simplicity of the procedures and the awareness which we have of them. What the accountant tells us may not be true, but, if we know what he has done, we have a fair idea of what it means. For this reason, I am somewhat suspicious of many current efforts to reform accounting in the direction of making it more 'accurate'."

---

*Note: This case consists of quotes from the article "Economics and Accounting: The Uncongenial Twins," Kenneth E. Boulding. Professor Boulding was a professor of economics at the University of Michigan. Source: From *Studies in Accounting Theory*, edited by W.T. Baxter and Sidney Davidson (Homewood, IL: Richard D. Irwin, Inc., 1962), pp. 44–55.

"If accounts are bound to be untruths anyhow, as I have argued, there is much to be said for the simple untruth as against a complicated untruth, for if the untruth is simple, it seems to me that we have a fair chance of knowing what kind of an untruth it is. A known untruth is much better than a lie, and provided that the accounting rituals are well known and understood, accounting may be untrue but it is not lies; it does not deceive because we know that it does not tell the truth, and we are able to make our own adjustment in each individual case, using the results of the accountant as evidence rather than as definitive information."

Required   a. Assume that accounting procedures are in the form of ritual. Does this imply that the accountant's product does not serve a useful function? Discuss.
b. Does it appear that Kenneth Boulding would support complicated procedures and a complicated end product for the accountant? Discuss.
c. Accounting reports must be accurate in order to serve a useful function. Discuss.

Case 1-9

I Often Paint Fakes*

An art dealer bought a canvas signed "Picasso" and traveled all the way to Cannes to discover whether it was genuine. Picasso was working in his studio. He cast a single look at the canvas and said, "It's a fake."

A few months later the dealer bought another canvas signed "Picasso." Again he traveled to Cannes and again Picasso, after a single glance, grunted: "It's a fake."

"But cher maitre," expostulated the dealer, "it so happens that I saw you with my own eyes working on this very picture several years ago."

Picasso shrugged: "I often paint fakes."

Required   a. Assume that the accounting report was prepared using generally accepted accounting principles. Does this imply that the report is exactly accurate? Discuss.
b. In your opinion do accountants paint fakes? Discuss.

---

*Note: This case consists of a quote from *The Act of Creation*, Arthur Koestler (New York: Macmillan, 1964), p. 82.

Web Case

Thomson Analytics Business School Edition

Please complete the web case that covers material covered in this chapter at http://gibson.swlearning.com. You'll be using Thomson Analytics Business School Edition, a version of the powerful tool used by Wall Street professionals, that combines a full range of fundamental financial information, earnings estimates, market data, and source documents for 500 publicly traded companies.

Endnotes

1. *Statement of Financial Accounting Concepts No. 1*, "Objectives of Financial Reporting by Business Enterprises" (Stamford, CT: Financial Accounting Standards Board, 1978).
2. *Statement of Financial Accounting Concepts No. 6*, "Elements of Financial Statements" (Stamford, CT: Financial Accounting Standards Board, 1985).
3. *Statement of Financial Accounting Concepts No. 5*, "Recognition and Measurement of Financial Statements of Business Enterprises" (Stamford, CT: Financial Accounting Standards Board, 1984), paragraph 63.
4. *Statement of Financial Accounting Concepts No. 5*, paragraph 67.
5. *Statement of Financial Accounting Concepts No. 5*, paragraph 70.
6. *Statement of Financial Accounting Concepts No. 5*, paragraph 13.

INTRODUCTION TO FINANCIAL STATEMENTS AND OTHER FINANCIAL REPORTING TOPICS

This chapter introduces financial statements. Subsequent chapters present a detailed review of the principal financial statements. Chapter 3 covers the balance sheet, Chapter 4 covers the income statement, and Chapter 10 covers the statement of cash flows.

This chapter also reviews the forms of business entities and the sequence of accounting procedures (called the accounting cycle).

Other financial reporting topics included in this chapter that contribute to the understanding of financial reporting are: the auditor's report, management's responsibility for financial statements, the SEC's integrated disclosure system, the summary annual report, ethics, international accounting standards, consolidated statements, and accounting for business combinations.

FORMS OF BUSINESS ENTITIES

A business entity may be a **sole proprietorship**, a partnership, or a corporation. A sole proprietorship, a business owned by one person, is not a legal entity separate from its owner, but the accountant treats the business as a separate accounting entity. The profit or loss of the proprietorship goes on the income tax return of the owner. The owner is responsible for the debts of the sole proprietorship.

In the United States, a sole proprietorship may qualify to be treated as a limited liability company (LLC). As an LLC, the owner may limit the liability of the sole proprietor, but may increase the tax exposure of the proprietorship.

A **partnership** is a business owned by two or more individuals. Each owner, called a partner, is personally responsible for the debts of the partnership. The accountant treats the partners and the business as separate accounting entities. The profit or loss of the partnership goes on the individual income tax return of the partners. Like a proprietorship, a partnership may qualify to be treated as an LLC. As an LLC, the owners may limit the liability of the partners, but may increase the tax exposure of the partnership.

In the United States, a **business corporation** is a legal entity incorporated in a particular state. Ownership is evidenced by shares of stock. A corporation is considered to be separate and distinct from the stockholders. The stockholders risk only their investment; they are not responsible for the debts of the corporation.

Since a corporation is a legal entity, the profits or losses are treated as a separate entity on an income tax return. The owners are not taxed until profits are distributed to the owners (dividends). In the United States, some corporations qualify to be treated as a subchapter S Corporation. These corporations do not pay a corporate income tax. The profits or losses go directly on the income tax returns of the owners.

In the United States, most businesses operate as proprietorships, but corporations perform the bulk of business activity. Since the bulk of business activity is carried on in corporations and because much of financial accounting is concerned with reporting to the public, this book focuses on the corporate form of business.

Accounting for corporations, sole proprietorships, and partnerships is the same, except for the owners' equity section of the balance sheet. The owners' equity section for a sole proprietorship consists of the owner's capital account, while the owners' equity section for a partnership has a capital account for each partner. The more complicated owners' equity section for a corporation will be described in detail in this book.

THE FINANCIAL STATEMENTS

The principal financial statements of a corporation are the balance sheet, income statement, and statement of cash flows. Footnotes (notes) accompany these financial statements. To evaluate the financial condition, the profitability, and cash flows of an entity, the user needs to understand the statements and related notes.

Exhibit 2-1 illustrates the interrelationship of the balance sheet, income statement, and statement of cash flows. The most basic statement is the balance sheet. The other statements explain the changes between two balance sheet dates.

Balance Sheet (Statement of Financial Position)

A balance sheet shows the financial condition of an accounting entity as of a particular date. The balance sheet consists of three major sections: assets, the resources of the firm; liabilities, the debts of the firm; and stockholders' equity, the owners' interest in the firm.

At any point in time, the total assets amount must equal the total amount of the contributions of the creditors and owners. This is expressed in the accounting equation:

$$\text{Assets} = \text{Liabilities} + \text{Stockholders' Equity}$$

In simplistic form, the stockholders' equity of a corporation appears as follows:

Stockholders' Equity	
Common stock	$200,000
Retained earnings	50,000
	$250,000

EXHIBIT 2-1	**ABC COMPANY**
	The Interrelationship of Financial Statements

Balance Sheet December 31, 2003		Statement of Cash Flows for the Year Ended December 31, 2004		Balance Sheet December 31, 2004	
Assets		**Cash flows from operating activities:**		**Assets**	
Cash	$25,000	Net Income	$ 20,000	Cash	$ 40,000
Receivables	20,000	+ Decrease in inventory	10,000	Receivables	20,000
Inventory	30,000	– Decrease in accounts		Inventory	20,000
Land	10,000	payable	(5,000)	Land	20,000
Other assets	10,000	Net cash flow from		Other assets	10,000
Total assets	$95,000	operating activities	25,000	Total assets	$110,000
Liabilities		**Cash flow from investing activities:**		**Liabilities**	
Accounts payable	$25,000	– Increase in land	(10,000)	Accounts payable	$ 20,000
Wages payable	5,000	Net cash flow from		Wages payable	5,000
Total liabilities	$30,000	investing activities	(10,000)	Total liabilities	$ 25,000
Stockholders' equity		**Cash flow from financing activities:**		**Stockholders' equity**	
Capital stock	$40,000			Capital stock	$ 50,000
Retained earnings	25,000	+ Capital stock	10,000	Retained earnings	35,000
Total stockholders' equity	$65,000	– Dividends	(10,000)	Total stockholders' equity	$ 85,000
Total liabilities and stockholders' equity	$95,000	Net cash flow from financing activities	-0-	Total liabilities and stockholders' equity	$110,000
		Net increase in cash	$ 15,000		
		Cash at beginning of year	25,000		
		Cash at end of year	$ 40,000		

Income Statement for the Year Ended December 31, 2004

Revenues	$ 120,000
– Expenses	(100,000)
Net Income	$ 20,000

Statement of Retained Earnings for the Year Ended December 31, 2004

Beginning balance	$ 25,000
+ Net Income	20,000
– Dividends	(10,000)
Ending balance	$ 35,000

This indicates that stockholders contributed (invested) $200,000, and prior earnings less prior dividends have been retained in the entity in the net amount of $50,000 (retained earnings).

Statement of Stockholders' Equity (Reconciliation of Stockholders' Equity Accounts)

Firms are required to present reconciliations of the beginning and ending balances of their stockholders' equity accounts. This is accomplished by presenting a "statement of stockholders' equity." Retained earnings is one of the accounts in stockholders' equity.

Retained earnings links the balance sheet to the income statement. Retained earnings is increased by net income and decreased by net losses and dividends paid to stockholders. There are some other possible increases or decreases to retained earnings besides income (losses) and dividends. For the purposes of this chapter, retained earnings will be described as prior earnings less prior dividends.

Firms usually present the reconciliation of retained earnings within a "statement of stockholders' equity." Some firms present the reconciliation of retained earnings at the bottom of the income statement (combined income statement and retained earnings). In this case, the other stockholders' equity accounts may be reconciled in a statement that excludes retained earnings. An additional review of the statement of stockholders' equity is in Chapter 3.

Income Statement (Statement of Earnings)

The **income statement** summarizes revenues and expenses and gains and losses, ending with net income. It summarizes the results of operations for a particular period of time. Net income is included in retained earnings in the stockholders' equity section of the balance sheet. (This is necessary for the balance sheet to balance.)

Statement of Cash Flows (Statement of Inflows and Outflows of Cash)

The **statement of cash flows** details the inflows and outflows of cash during a specified period of time—the same period that is used for the income statement. The statement of cash flows consists of three sections: cash flows from operating activities, cash flows from investing activities, and cash flows from financing activities.

Footnotes (Notes)

The footnotes to the financial statements are used to present additional information about items included in the financial statements and to present additional financial information. Footnotes are an integral part of financial statements. A detailed review of footnotes is essential to understanding the financial statements.

Certain information must be presented in footnotes. Accounting policies are to be disclosed as the first note or be disclosed in a separate summary of significant accounting policies (preceding the first note). Accounting policies include such items as the method of inventory valuation and depreciation policies. Other information specifically requiring footnote disclosure is the existence of contingent liabilities and some subsequent events.

Contingent liabilities are dependent upon the occurrence or nonoccurrence of one or more future events to confirm the liability. The settlement of litigation or the ruling of a tax court would be examples of the confirmation of a contingent liability. Signing as guarantor on a loan creates another type of contingent liability.

An estimated loss from a contingent liability should be charged to income, and be established as a liability only if the loss is considered probable and the amount is reasonably determinable. A contingent liability that is recorded is also frequently described in a footnote. A loss contingency that is reasonably possible, but not probable, must be disclosed even if the loss is not reasonably estimable. (This loss contingency is not charged to income or established as a liability.) A loss contingency that is less than reasonably possible does not need to be disclosed, but disclosure may be desirable if there is an unusually large potential loss. Exhibit 2-2 illustrates a contingent liability footnote.

Subsequent events occur after the balance sheet date, but before the statements are issued. Two varieties of subsequent events occur. The first type consists of events related to conditions that existed at the balance sheet date, affect the estimates in the statements, and require adjustment of the statements before issuance. For example, if additional information is obtained indicating that a major customer's account receivable is not collectible, an adjustment would be made. The second type consists of events that provide evidence about conditions that did not exist at the balance sheet date and do not require adjustment of the statements. If failure to disclose these events would be misleading, disclosure should take the form of footnotes or supplementary schedules. Examples of the second type of such events include the sale of securities, the settlement of litigation, or casualty loss. Other

| EXHIBIT 2-2 | **INTERNATIONAL BUSINESS MACHINES**
Contingencies—2001 Annual Report |

Contingencies

The company is subject to a variety of claims and suits that arise from time to time in the ordinary course of its business, including actions with respect to contracts, intellectual property, product liability, employment and environmental matters. The company is a defendant and/or third-party defendant in a number of cases in which claims have been filed by current and former employees, independent contractors, estate representatives, offspring and relatives of employees seeking damages for wrongful death and personal injuries allegedly caused by exposure to chemicals in various of the company's facilities from 1964 to the present. The company believes that plaintiffs' claims are without merit and will defend itself vigorously.

While it is not possible to predict the ultimate outcome of the matters discussed above, the company believes that any losses associated with any of such matters will not have a material effect on the company's business, financial conditions or results of operations.

---

examples of subsequent events might be debt incurred, reduced, or refinanced; business combinations pending or effected; discontinued operations; employee benefit plans; and capital stock issued or purchased. Exhibit 2-3 describes a subsequent event for Microsoft, whose year-end was June 30, 2001.

THE ACCOUNTING CYCLE

The sequence of accounting procedures completed during each accounting period is called the accounting cycle. A broad summary of the steps of the accounting cycle include:

1. Recording transactions
2. Recording adjusting entries
3. Preparing the financial statements

Recording Transactions

A **transaction** is an event that causes a change in a company's assets, liabilities, or stockholders' equity, thus changing the company's financial position. Transactions may be external or internal to the company. External transactions involve outside parties, while internal transactions are confined within the company. For example, sales is an external transaction, while the use of equipment is internal.

Transactions must be recorded in a **journal** (book of original entry). All transactions could be recorded in the general journal. However, companies use a number of special journals to record most transactions. The special journals are designed to improve record keeping efficiency that could not be obtained by using only the general journal. The general journal is then used only to record transactions for which the company does not have a special journal. A transaction recorded in a journal is referred to as a **journal entry.**

| EXHIBIT 2-3 | **MICROSOFT**
Subsequent Events—2001 Annual Report |

Subsequent Event

On July 16, 2001, USA Networks, Inc. (USA) announced an agreement to acquire a controlling interest in Expedia, Inc. through the purchase of up to 37.5 million shares, approximately 75% of the current outstanding shares. If holders of more than 37.5 million Expedia shares elect to sell their shares to USA, there will be a pro rata reduction among all of those electing shareholders. Microsoft has agreed to transfer all of its 33.7 million shares and warrants, subject to pro-ration. It is expected that the transaction will close by December 31, 2001.

All transactions are recorded in a journal (journal entry) and are later posted from the journals to a **general ledger** (group of accounts for a company). After posting, the general ledger accounts contain the same information as the journals, but the information has been summarized by account.

Accounts store the monetary information from the recording of transactions. Examples of accounts include Cash, Land, and Buildings. An accounting system can be computerized or manual. A manual system using T-accounts is usually used for textbook explanations because a T-account is a logical format.

T-accounts have a left (debit) side and a right (credit) side. An example T-account follows:

Cash	
Debit	Credit

A double-entry system has been devised to handle the recording of transactions. In a double-entry system, each transaction is recorded with the total dollar amount of the debits equal to the total dollar amount of the credits. The scheme of the double-entry system revolves around the **accounting equation**:

$$\text{Assets} = \text{Liabilities} + \text{Stockholders' Equity}$$

With the double-entry system, *debit* merely means the left side of an account, while *credit* means the right side. Each transaction recorded must have an equal number of dollars on the left side as it does on the right side. Several accounts could be involved in a single transaction, but the debits and credits must still be equal.

The debit and credit approach is a technique that has gained acceptance over a long period of time. This book will not make you competent in the use of the double-entry (debit and credit) technique. This book will enhance your understanding of the end result of the accounting process and enable you to use the financial accounting information in a meaningful way.

Asset, liability, and stockholders' equity accounts are referred to as **permanent accounts** because the balances in these accounts carry forward to the next accounting period. Balances in revenue, expense, gain, loss, and dividend accounts, described as **temporary accounts**, are closed to retained earnings and not carried into the next period.

Exhibit 2-4 illustrates the double-entry system. Notice that the permanent accounts are represented by the accounting equation: assets = liabilities + stockholders' equity. The temporary accounts are represented by revenue, expense, and dividends. (Gains and losses would be treated like revenue and expense, respectively.) The balance sheet will not balance until the temporary accounts are closed to retained earnings.

Recording Adjusting Entries

Earlier a distinction was made between the accrual basis of accounting and the cash basis. It was indicated that the accrual basis requires that revenue be recognized when realized (realization concept) and expenses recognized when incurred (matching concept). The point of cash receipt for revenue and cash disbursement for expenses is not important under the accrual basis when determining income. Usually a company must use the accrual basis to achieve a reasonable result for the balance sheet and the income statement.

The accrual basis needs numerous adjustments to account balances at the end of the accounting period. For example, $1,000 paid for insurance on October 1 for a one-year period (October 1–September 30) could have been recorded as a debit to Insurance Expense ($1,000) and a credit to Cash ($1,000). If this company prepares financial statements on December 31, it would be necessary to adjust Insurance Expense because not all of the insurance expense should be recognized in the three-month period October 1–December 31. The adjustment would debit Prepaid Insurance, an asset account, for $750 and credit Insurance Expense for $750. Thus, insurance expense would be presented on the income statement for this period as $250, and an asset, prepaid insurance, would be presented on the balance sheet at $750.

Adjusting entries are recorded in the general journal and then posted to the general ledger. Once the accounts are adjusted to the accrual basis, the financial statements can be prepared.

EXHIBIT 2-4   DOUBLE-ENTRY SYSTEM
(Illustrating Relationship Between Permanent and Temporary Accounts)

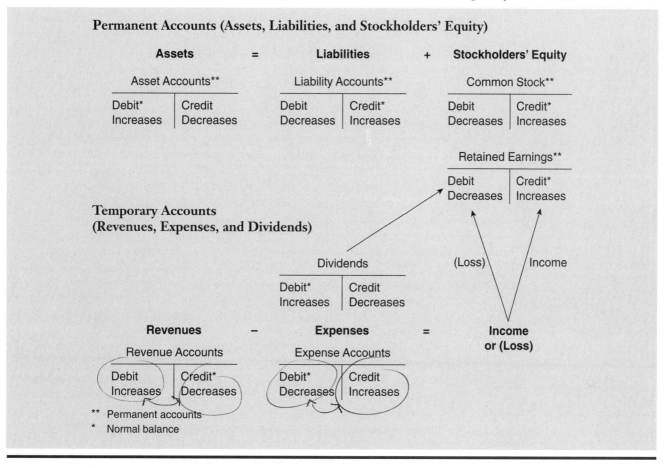

Permanent Accounts (Assets, Liabilities, and Stockholders' Equity)

** Permanent accounts
* Normal balance

Preparing the Financial Statements

The accountant uses the accounts after the adjustments have been made to prepare the financial statements. These statements represent the output of the accounting system. Two of the principal financial statements, the income statement and the balance sheet, can be prepared directly from the adjusted accounts. Preparation of the statement of cash flows requires further analysis of the accounts.

AUDITOR'S REPORT

An auditor (certified public accountant) conducts an independent examination of the accounting information presented by the business and issues a report thereon. An auditor's report is the formal statement of the auditor's opinion of the financial statements after conducting an audit. Audit opinions are classified as follows:

1. **Unqualified opinion.** This opinion states that the financial statements present fairly, in all material respects, the financial position, results of operations, and cash flows of the entity, in conformity with generally accepted accounting principles.
2. **Qualified opinion.** A qualified opinion states that, except for the effects of the matter(s) to which the qualification relates, the financial statements present fairly, in all material respects, the financial position, results of operations, and cash flows of the entity, in conformity with generally accepted accounting principles.

3. **Adverse opinion.** This opinion states that the financial statements do *not* present fairly the financial position, results of operations, and cash flows of the entity, in conformity with generally accepted accounting principles.

4. **Disclaimer of opinion.** A disclaimer of opinion states that the auditor does not express an opinion on the financial statements. A disclaimer of opinion is rendered when the auditor has not performed an audit sufficient in scope to form an opinion.

The typical unqualified (or clean) opinion has three paragraphs. The first paragraph indicates *the financial statements that have been audited* and states that these *statements are the responsibility of the company's management.* This paragraph indicates that the auditors have the responsibility to express an opinion on these statements based on the audit or to disclaim an opinion.

The second paragraph indicates that the audit has been conducted *in accordance with generally accepted auditing standards.* Auditing standards define the required level of audit quality. These standards are classified as to "general standards," "fieldwork standards," and "reporting standards." The paragraph goes on to state that these standards require the auditor to plan and perform the audit to obtain reasonable assurance that the financial statements are free of material misstatement. The second paragraph also includes a brief description of what is included in an audit.

The third paragraph gives an opinion on the statements—that they are in conformity with GAAP. In certain circumstances, an unqualified opinion on the financial statements may require that the auditor add an explanatory paragraph after the opinion paragraph. In this paragraph, the auditor may express agreement with a departure from a designated principle, describe a material uncertainty, describe a change in accounting principle, or express doubt as to the ability of the entity to continue as a going concern. An explanatory paragraph may also be added to emphasize a matter. Exhibit 2-5 illustrates a typical unqualified report.

When examining financial statements, review the independent auditor's report. It can be important to your analysis. From the point of view of analysis, financial statements accompanied by an unqualified opinion without an explanatory paragraph or explanatory language carry the highest degree of reliability. This type of report indicates that the financial statements do not contain a material departure from GAAP and that the audit was not limited as to scope.

When an unqualified opinion contains an explanatory paragraph or explanatory language, try to decide how seriously to regard the departure from a straight unqualified opinion. For example, an explanatory paragraph because of a change in accounting principle would not usually be regarded as

---

EXHIBIT 2-5	**TOYS "R" US** **Unqualified Opinion—2001 Annual Report**

Report of Independent Auditors

The Board of Directors and Stockholders
Toys "R" Us, Inc.

We have audited the accompanying consolidated balance sheets of Toys "R" Us, Inc. and subsidiaries as of February 2, 2002 and February 3, 2001, and the related consolidated statements of earnings, stockholders' equity and cash flows for each of the three years in the period ended February 2, 2002. These financial statements are the responsibility of the company's management. Our responsibility is to express an opinion on these financial statements based on our audits.

We conducted our audits in accordance with auditing standards generally accepted in the United States. Those standards require that we plan and perform the audit to obtain reasonable assurance about whether the financial statements are free of material misstatement. An audit includes examining, on a test basis, evidence supporting the amounts and disclosures in the financial

statements. An audit also includes assessing the accounting principles used and significant estimates made by management, as well as evaluating the overall financial statement presentation. We believe that our audits provide a reasonable basis for our opinion.

In our opinion, the financial statements referred to above present fairly, in all material respects, the consolidated financial position of Toys "R" Us, Inc. and subsidiaries at February 2, 2002 and February 3, 2001, and the consolidated results of their operations and their cash flows for each of the three years in the period ended February 2, 2002, in conformity with accounting principles generally accepted in the United States.

Ernst & Young LLP

New York, New York
March 14, 2002

serious, although it would be important to your analysis. An explanatory paragraph because of a material uncertainty would often be regarded as a serious matter.

You are likely to regard a qualified opinion or an adverse opinion as casting serious doubts on the reliability of the financial statements. In each case, you must read the auditor's report carefully to form your opinion.

A disclaimer of opinion indicates that you should not look to the auditor's report as an indication of the reliability of the statements. When rendering this type of report, the auditor has not performed an audit sufficient in scope to form an opinion, or the auditor is not independent.

In some cases, outside accountants are associated with financial statements when they have performed less than an audit. The accountant's report then indicates that the financial statements have been reviewed or compiled.

A **review** consists principally of inquiries made to company personnel and analytical procedures applied to financial data. It has substantially less scope than an examination in accordance with generally accepted auditing standards, the objective of which is the expression of an opinion regarding the financial statements taken as a whole. Accordingly, the accountant does not express an opinion. The accountant's report will indicate that the accountants are not aware of any material modifications that should be made to the financial statements in order for them to be in conformity with GAAP; or the report will indicate departures from GAAP. A departure from GAAP may result from using one or more accounting principles without reasonable justification, the omission of necessary footnote disclosures, or the omission of the statement of cash flows.

In general, the reliance that can be placed on financial statements accompanied by an accountant's review report is substantially less than those accompanied by an audit report. Remember that the accountant's report does not express an opinion on reviewed financial statements.

When the outside accountant presents only financial information as provided by management, he or she is said to have **compiled** the financial statements. The compilation report states that the accountant has not audited or reviewed the financial statements. Therefore, the accountant does not express an opinion or any other form of assurance about them. If an accountant performs a compilation and becomes aware of deficiencies in the statements, then the accountant's report characterizes the deficiencies as follows:

- Omission of substantially all disclosures
- Omission of statement of cash flows
- Accounting principles not generally accepted

Sometimes financial statements are presented without an accompanying accountant's report. This means that the statements have not been audited, reviewed, or compiled. Such statements are solely the representation of management.

Management's Responsibility for Financial Statements

The responsibility for the preparation and for the integrity of financial statements rests with management. The auditor is responsible for conducting an independent examination of the statements and expressing an opinion on the financial statements based on the audit. To make financial statement users aware of management's responsibility, companies have presented management statements to shareholders as part of the annual report. Exhibit 2-6 shows an example.

The SEC's Integrated Disclosure System

In general, in the United States, the SEC has the authority to prescribe external financial reporting requirements for companies with securities sold to the general public. Under this jurisdiction, the SEC requires that certain financial statement information be included in the annual report to shareholders. This annual report, along with certain supplementary information, must then be included, or incorporated by reference, in the annual filing to the SEC, known as the **10-K report** or **Form 10-K**. The Form 10-K is due three months following the end of the company's fiscal year. The annual report and the Form 10-K include audited financial statements.

EXHIBIT 2-6   **TOYS "R" US**
Management's Responsibility for Financial Reporting—2001 Annual Report

Report of Management

Responsibility for the integrity and objectivity of the financial information presented in this Annual Report rests with the management of Toys "R" Us. The accompanying financial statements have been prepared from accounting records which management believes fairly and accurately reflect the operations and financial position of the company. Management has established a system of internal controls to provide reasonable assurance that assets are maintained and accounted for in accordance with its policies and that transactions are recorded accurately on the company's books and records.

The company's comprehensive internal audit program provides for constant evaluation of the adequacy of the adherence to management's established policies and procedures. The company has distributed to key employees its policies for conducting business affairs in a lawful and ethical manner.

The Audit Committee of the Board of Directors, which is comprised solely of outside directors, provides oversight to the financial reporting process through periodic meetings with our independent auditors, internal auditors and management.

The financial statements of the company have been audited by Ernst & Young LLP, independent auditors, in accordance with auditing standards generally accepted in the United States, including a review of financial reporting matters and internal controls to the extent necessary to express an opinion on the consolidated financial statements.

[signed]   [signed]

John H. Eyler, Jr.   Louis Lipschitz
Chairman and   Executive Vice President
Chief Executive Officer   and Chief Financial Officer

The SEC promotes an integrated disclosure system between the annual report and the Form 10-K. The goals are to improve the quality of disclosure, lighten the disclosure load, standardize information requirements, and achieve uniformity of annual reports and Form 10-K filings.

In addition to the company's primary financial statements, the Form 10-K must include the following:

1. Information on the market for holders of common stock and related securities, including high and low sales price, frequency and amount of dividends, and number of shares.
2. Five-year summary of selected financial data, including net sales or operating revenues, income from continuing operations, total assets, long-term obligations, redeemable preferred stock, and cash dividends per share. (Some companies elect to present data for more than five years and/or expand the disclosure.) Trend analysis is emphasized.
3. Management's discussion and analysis (MDA) of financial condition and results of operations. Specifically required is discussion of liquidity, capital resources, and results of operations.
4. Two years of audited balance sheets and three years of audited income statements and statements of cash flow.
5. Disclosure of the domestic and foreign components of pretax income, unless foreign components are considered to be immaterial.

SEC requirements force management to focus on the financial statements as a whole, rather than on just the income statement and operations. Where trend information is relevant, discussion should center on the five-year summary. Emphasis should be on favorable or unfavorable trends and on identification of significant events or uncertainties. This discussion should provide the analyst with a reasonable summary of the position of the firm.

Exhibit 2-7 presents a summary of the major parts of the Form 10-K. In practice, much of the required information in the Form 10-K is incorporated by reference. Incorporated by reference means that the information is presented outside the Form 10-K, and a reference in the Form 10-K indicates where the information can be found. Usually the financial statements are incorporated into the Form 10-K by referencing the annual report.

A review of a company's Form 10-K can reveal information that is not available in the annual report. For example, Item 2 of the Form 10-K reveals a detailed listing of properties and indicates if the property is leased or owned.

The SEC requires that a quarterly report (Form 10-Q), containing financial statements and a management discussion and analysis, be submitted within 45 days following the end of the quarter.

EXHIBIT 2-7	**GENERAL SUMMARY OF FORM 10-K**

Part I

Item 1. Business.
Item 2. Properties.
Item 3. Legal Proceedings.
Item 4. Submission of Matters to a Vote of Security Holders.

Part II

Item 5. Market for Registrant's Common Equity and Related Stockholder Matters.
Item 6. Selected Financial Data.
Item 7. Management's Discussion and Analysis of Financial Condition and Results of Operations.
Item 8. Financial Statements and Supplementary Data.
Item 9. Changes in and Disagreements with Accountants on Accounting and Financial Disclosure.

Part III

Item 10. Directors and Executive Officers of Registrant.
Item 11. Executive Compensation.
Item 12. Security Ownership of Certain Beneficial Owners and Management.
Item 13. Certain Relationships and Related Transactions.
Item 14. Exhibits, Financial Statement Schedules, and Reports on Form 8-K.

(The Form 10-Q is not required for the fourth quarter of the fiscal year.) Most companies also issue a quarterly report to stockholders. The Form 10-Q and quarterly reports are unaudited.

In addition to the Form 10-K and Form 10-Q, a Form 8-K must be submitted to the SEC to report special events. Special events required to be reported are changes in principal stockholders, changes in auditors, acquisitions and divestitures, bankruptcy, and resignation of directors. The Form 8-K is due 15 days following the event.

The Forms 10-K, 10-Q, and 8-K filings are available to the public. Typically a company provides these reports to stockholders upon request only.

Proxy

The **proxy,** the solicitation sent to stockholders for the election of directors and for the approval of other corporation actions, represents the shareholder authorization regarding the casting of that shareholder's vote. The proxy contains notice of the annual meeting, beneficial ownership (name, address, and share ownership data of shareholders holding more than 5% of outstanding shares), board of directors, standing committees, compensation of directors, compensation of executive officers, employee benefit plans, certain transactions with officers and directors, relationship with independent accountants, and other business.

The proxy rules provided under the 1934 Securities Exchange Act are applicable to all securities registered under Section 12 of the Act. The SEC gains its influence over the annual report through provisions of the Act that cover proxy statements.

The SEC's proxy rules of particular interest to investors involve executive compensation disclosure, performance graph, and retirement plans for executive officers. These rules are designed to improve shareholders' understanding of the compensation paid to senior executives and directors, the criteria used in reaching compensation decisions, and the relationship between compensation and corporate performance.

Among other matters, the executive compensation rules call for four highly formatted disclosure tables and the disclosure of the compensation committee's basis for compensation decisions.

The four tables disclosing executive compensation are:

- A summary executive compensation table covering compensation for the company's chief executive officer and its four other most highly compensated executives for the last three years.

- Two tables detailing options and stock appreciation rights.
- A long-term incentive plan award table.

The performance graph is a line graph comparing the cumulative total shareholder return with performance indicators of the overall stock market and either the published industry index or the registrant-determined peer comparison. This performance graph must be presented for a five-year period.

The pension plan table for executive officers discloses the estimated annual benefits payable upon retirement for any defined benefit or actuarial plan under which benefits are determined primarily by final compensation (or average final compensation) and years of service. Immediately following the table, additional disclosure is required. This disclosure includes items such as the relationship of the covered compensation to the compensation reported in the summary compensation table and the estimated credited years of service for each of the named executive officers.

SUMMARY ANNUAL REPORT

A reporting option available to public companies is to issue a **summary annual report**. A summary annual report, a condensed report, omits much of the financial information typically included in an annual report. A typical full annual report has more financial pages than nonfinancial pages. A summary annual report generally has more nonfinancial pages.[1] When a company issues a summary annual report, the proxy materials it sends to shareholders must include a set of fully audited statements and other required financial disclosures.

A summary annual report is *not* adequate for reasonable analysis. For companies that issue a summary annual report, request a copy of their proxy and the Form 10-K. Even for companies that issue a full annual report, it is also good to obtain a copy of the proxy materials and the Form 10-K. Some companies issue a joint annual report and Form 10-K, while other companies issue a joint annual report and proxy.

THE EFFICIENT MARKET HYPOTHESIS

The **efficient market hypothesis (EMH)** relates to the ability of capital markets to generate prices for securities that reflect worth. The EMH implies that publicly available information is fully reflected in share prices. The market will not be efficient if the market does not have access to relevant information or if fraudulent information is provided.

There seems to be little doubt that the FASB and the SEC assess the impact of their actions on security prices. The SEC has been particularly sensitive to insider trading because abnormal returns could be achieved by the use of insider information.

If the market is efficient, investors may be harmed when firms do not follow a full disclosure policy. In an efficient market, the method of disclosure is not as important as whether the item is disclosed. It should not matter whether an item is disclosed in the body of the financial statements or in the footnotes. It is the disclosure rather than how to disclose that is the substantive issue.

Usually there is a cost to disclose. An attempt should be made to determine the value of additional disclosure in relation to the additional cost. Disclosure should be made when the perceived benefits exceed the additional cost to provide the disclosure.

It is generally recognized that the market is more efficient when dealing with large firms trading on large organized stock markets than it is for small firms that are not trading on large organized stock markets.

Although the research evidence regarding the EMH is conflicting, this hypothesis has taken on an important role in financial reporting in the United States.

ETHICS

"Ethics and morals are synonymous. While *ethics* is derived from Greek, *morals* is derived from Latin. They are interchangeable terms referring to ideals of character and conduct. These ideals, in the form of codes of conduct, furnish criteria for distinguishing between right and wrong."[2] Ethics has been a subject of investigation for hundreds of years. Individuals in financial positions must be able to recognize ethical issues and resolve them in an appropriate manner.

Ethics affect all individuals—from the financial clerk to the high-level financial executive. Individuals make daily decisions based on their individual values. Some companies and professional organizations have formulated a code of ethics as a statement of aspirations and a standard of integrity beyond that required by law (which can be viewed as the minimum standard of ethics).

Ten essential values can be considered central to relations between people.[3]

1. Caring
2. Honesty
3. Accountability
4. Promise keeping
5. Pursuit of excellence
6. Loyalty
7. Fairness
8. Integrity
9. Respect for others
10. Responsible citizenship

Ethics can be a particular problem with financial reports. Accepted accounting principles leave ample room for arriving at different results in the short run. Highly subjective estimates can substantially influence earnings. What provision should be made for warranty costs? What should be the loan loss reserve? What should be the allowance for doubtful accounts?

The American Accounting Association initiated a project in 1988 on professionalism and ethics. One of the goals of this project was to provide students with a framework for evaluating their courses of action when encountering ethical dilemmas. The American Accounting Association developed a decision model for focusing on ethical issues.[4]

1. Determine the facts—what, who, where, when, how.
2. Define the ethical issues (includes identifying the identifiable parties affected by the decision made or action taken).
3. Identify major principles, rules, and values.
4. Specify the alternatives.
5. Compare norms, principles, and values with alternatives to see if a clear decision can be reached.
6. Assess the consequences.
7. Make your decision.

Example 1: Questionable Ethics in Savings and Loans

In connection with the savings and loan (S & L) scandal, it was revealed that several auditors of thrift institutions borrowed substantial amounts from the S & L that their firm was auditing. It was charged that some of the loans involved special consideration.[5] In one case, dozens of partners of a major accounting firm borrowed money for commercial real estate loans, and some of the partners defaulted on their loans when the real estate market collapsed.[6] It was not clear whether these particular loans violated professional ethics standards. The AICPA subsequently changed its ethics standards to ban all such loans.

In another case, an accounting firm paid $1.5 million to settle charges by the California State Board of Accountancy that the accounting firm was grossly negligent in its 1987 audit of Lincoln Savings & Loan. The accounting board charged that the firm had agreed to the improper recognition of approximately $62 million in profits.[7]

Example 2: Questionable Ethics in the Motion Picture Industry

Hollywood's accounting practices have often been labeled "mysterious."[8] A case in point is Art Buchwald's lawsuit against Paramount Pictures for breach of contract regarding the film *Coming to America*. Paramount took an option on Buchwald's story "King for a Day" in 1983 and promised Buchwald 1.5% of the net profits of the film. Buchwald's attorney, Pierce O'Donnell, accused Paramount Studios of "fatal subtraction" in determining the amount of profit. Although the film grossed $350 million worldwide, Paramount claimed an $18 million net loss. As a result of the studio's accounting practices, Buchwald was to get 1.5% of nothing.[9] Buchwald was eventually awarded $150,000 in a 1992 court decision.[10]

Many Hollywood celebrities, in addition to Art Buchwald, have sued over Hollywood-style accounting. These include Winston Groom over the movie rights to *Forrest Gump*, Jane Fonda over a larger share of profits relating to *On Golden Pond*, and James Garner over his share of profits from *The Rockford Files* (a television program). Some of the best creative work in Hollywood is in accounting.

SEC Requirements—Code of Ethics

In January 2003 the SEC voted to require disclosure in a company's annual report whether it has a code of ethics that applies to the company's principal executive officer, principal financial officer, principal accounting officer or controller, or persons performing similar functions. The rules will define a code of ethics as written standards that are reasonably necessary to deter wrongdoing and to promote:

1. honest and ethical conduct, including the ethical handling of actual or apparent conflicts of interest between personal and professional relationships;
2. full, fair, accurate, timely, and understandable disclosure in reports and documents that a company files with, or submits to, the Commission and in other public communications made by the company;
3. compliance with applicable governmental laws, rules, and regulations;
4. the prompt internal reporting of code violations to an appropriate person or persons identified in the code; and
5. accountability for adherence to the code[11]

The SEC requires that a copy of the company's code of ethics be made available by filing an exhibit with its annual report, or by providing it on the company's Internet web site. These SEC requirements are effective for annual reports for fiscal years ending on or after July 15, 2003.

HARMONIZATION OF INTERNATIONAL ACCOUNTING STANDARDS

The impetus for changes in accounting practice has come from the needs of the business community and governments. With the expansion of international business and global capital markets, the business community and governments have shown an increased interest in the harmonization of international accounting standards.

Suggested problems caused by lack of harmonization of international accounting standards include:

1. A need for employment of key personnel in multinational companies to bridge the "gap" in accounting requirements between countries.
2. Difficulties in reconciling local standards for access to other capital markets.
3. Difficulties in accessing capital markets for companies from less developed countries.[12]
4. Negative effect on the international trade of accounting practice and services.[13]

International interest in harmonization of international accounting standards has been especially strong since the early 1970s. In 1973, nine countries, including the United States, formed the International Accounting Standards Committee (IASC). IASC included approximately 100 member nations and well over 100 professional accounting bodies. The IASC was the only private sector body involved in setting international accounting standards.

The IASC's objectives included:

1. Developing international accounting standards and disclosure to meet the needs of international capital markets and the international business community.
2. Developing accounting standards to meet the needs of developing and newly industrialized countries.

3.   Working toward increased comparability between national and international accounting standards.[14]

The International Accounting Standards Board (IASB) was established in January 2001 to replace the IASC. The IASB arose from a review of the structure of the IASC. The new structure has characteristics similar to that of the FASB. The IASB basically continues the objectives of the IASC.

The IASB does not have authority to enforce its standards, but these standards have been adopted in whole or in part by many countries. Some see the lack of enforcement authority as a positive factor because it enables the passing of standards that would not have had the necessary votes if they could be enforced. This allows standards to be more ideal than they would otherwise be if they were enforceable.

IASB follows a due-process procedure similar to that of the FASB. This includes exposure drafts and a comment period. All proposed standards and guidelines are exposed for comment for about six months.

The United Nations (UN) has shown a substantial interest in harmonization of international accounting standards. The UN appointed a group to study harmonization of international accounting standards in 1973. This has evolved into an ad hoc working group. Members of the working group represent governments and not the private sector. The working group does not issue standards but rather facilitates their development. The UN's concern is with how multinational corporations affect the developing countries.[15]

Many other organizations, in addition to the IASB and the UN, have played a role in the harmonization of international accounting standards. Some of these organizations include the Financial Accounting Standards Board (FASB), the European Economic Community (EEC), the Organization for Economic Cooperation and Development (OECD), and the International Federation of Accountants (IFAC).

Domestic accounting standards have developed to meet the needs of domestic environments. A few of the factors that influence accounting standards locally are:

1.   A litigious environment in the United States that has led to a demand for more detailed standards in many cases.
2.   High rates of inflation in some countries that have resulted in periodic revaluation of fixed assets and other price-level adjustments or disclosures.
3.   More emphasis on financial reporting/income tax conformity in certain countries (for example, Japan and Germany) that no doubt greatly influences domestic financial reporting.
4.   Reliance on open markets as the principal means of intermediating capital flows that has increased the demand for information to be included in financial reports in the United States and some other developed countries.[16]

The following have been observed to have an impact on a country's financial accounting operation:

1.   Who the investors and creditors—the information users—are (individuals, banks, the government).
2.   How many investors and creditors there are.
3.   How close the relationship is between businesses and the investor/creditor group.
4.   How developed the stock exchanges and bond markets are.
5.   The extent of use of international financial markets.[17]

With this backdrop of fragmentation, it will be difficult in the short run, if not impossible, to bring national standards into agreement with a meaningful body of international standards. But many see benefits to harmonization of international accounting standards and feel that accounting must move in that direction. In the short run, ways exist to cope with incomparable standards. One possible interim solution involves dual standards. International companies would prepare two sets of financial statements. One would be prepared under domestic GAAP, while the other would be prepared under international GAAP. This would likely put pressure on domestic GAAP to move toward international GAAP.

In the United States, a conflict exists between the SEC and the securities exchanges, such as the New York Stock Exchange (NYSE). In general, the SEC requires foreign registrants to conform to

U.S. GAAP, either directly or by reconciliation. This approach achieves a degree of comparability in the U.S. capital market, but it does not achieve comparability for investors who want to invest in several national capital markets. This approach poses a problem for U.S. securities exchanges, because the U.S. standards are perceived to be the most stringent. This puts exchanges such as the NYSE at a competitive disadvantage with foreign exchanges that have lower standards. The development of international standards would alleviate this problem.

In the United States, the FASB did not show a critical interest in harmonization of international accounting standards until the early 1990s. The FASB now actively participates in the harmonization of international accounting standards. This includes cooperating with the IASB and the UN.

CONSOLIDATED STATEMENTS

Financial statements of legally separate entities may be issued to show financial position, income, and cash flow as they would appear if the companies were a single entity (consolidated). Such statements reflect an economic, rather than a legal, concept of the entity. For consolidated statements, all transactions between the entities being consolidated—intercompany transactions—must be eliminated.

One corporation can own stock in another corporation in an amount sufficient to hold substantial voting rights in that corporation. The corporation owning the stock is the *parent corporation*. The corporation whose stock is owned is the *subsidiary corporation*. The financial statements of the parent and the subsidiary are consolidated for all majority-owned subsidiaries unless control is temporary or does not rest with the majority owner. These are termed **consolidated financial statements**. An *unconsolidated* subsidiary is accounted for as an investment on the parent's balance sheet.

When a subsidiary is less than 100% owned and its statements are consolidated, minority shareholders must be recognized in the consolidated financial statements by showing the minority interest in net assets on the balance sheet and the minority share of earnings on the income statement. Minority-related accounts are discussed in detail in Chapter 3.

The consolidation of financial statements has been a practice in the United States for years; however, this has not been the case for many other nations. In some countries like Japan, parent-only financial statements are the norm. In other countries like Germany, consolidation only includes domestic subsidiaries.

The IASC passed a standard that requires that all controlled subsidiaries be consolidated. Although IASC standards cannot be enforced, this standard will likely increase the acceptance of consolidation.

ACCOUNTING FOR BUSINESS COMBINATIONS

The combination of business entities by merger or acquisition is very frequent. There are many possible reasons for this external business expansion, including achieving economies of scale and savings of time in entering a new market. The combination must be accounted for using the **purchase method**.

The purchase method views the business combination as the acquisition of one entity by another. The firm doing the acquiring records the identifiable assets and liabilities at fair value at the date of acquisition. The difference between the fair value of the identifiable assets and liabilities and the amount paid is recorded as goodwill (an asset).

With a purchase, the acquiring firm picks up the income of the acquired firm from the date of acquisition. Retained earnings of the acquired firm do not continue.

SUMMARY

This chapter includes an introduction to the basic financial statements. Later chapters will cover these statements in detail.

An understanding of the sequence of accounting procedures completed during each accounting period, called the accounting cycle, will help in understanding the end result—financial statements.

This chapter describes the forms of business entities, which are sole proprietorship, partnership, and corporation.

Management is responsible for financial statements. These statements are examined by auditors who express an opinion regarding the statements' conformity to GAAP in the auditor's report. The auditor's report often points out key factors that can affect financial statement analysis. The SEC has begun a program to integrate the Form 10-K requirements with those of the annual report.

A reporting option available to public companies, a summary annual report (a condensed annual report), omits much of the financial information included in a typical annual report.

The EMH relates to the ability of capital markets to generate prices for securities that reflect worth. The market will not be efficient if the market does not have access to relevant information or if fraudulent information is provided.

Individuals in financial positions must be able to recognize ethical issues and resolve them appropriately.

With the expansion of international business and global capital markets, the business community and governments have shown an increased interest in the harmonization of international accounting standards.

The combination of business entities by merger or acquisition is very frequent. An understanding of how a business combination can impact the basic statements is important to the analyst.

To the Net

1. Go to the Carol and Lawrence Zicklin Center for Business Ethics Research site at http://www.zicklincenter.org. Click on "About." Copy the mission statement. Click on "Links." Click on "Academic Journal." Go to a library and review an article in the journal selected. Summarize the information provided by the article.

2. Go to the FASB web site (http://www.fasb.org) and click on International. Click on "International Accounting Standards Board." Be prepared to discuss the International Accounting Standards Board.

Questions

Q 2-1. Name the type of opinion indicated by each of the following situations:
   a. There is a material uncertainty.
   b. There was a change in accounting principle.
   c. There is no material scope limitation or material departure from GAAP.
   d. The financial statements do not present fairly the financial position, results of operations, or cash flows of the entity in conformity with GAAP.
   e. Except for the effects of the matter(s) to which the qualification relates, the financial statements present fairly, in all material respects, the financial position, results of operations, and cash flows of the entity, in conformity with GAAP.

Q 2-2. What are the roles of management and the auditor in the preparation and integrity of the financial statements?

Q 2-3. What is the purpose of the SEC's integrated disclosure system for financial reporting?

Q 2-4. Why do some unqualified opinions have explanatory paragraphs?

Q 2-5. Describe an auditor's review of financial statements.

Q 2-6. Will the accountant express an opinion on reviewed financial statements? Describe the accountant's report for reviewed financial statements.

Q 2-7. What type of opinion is expressed on a compilation?

Q 2-8. Are all financial statements presented with some kind of an accountant's report? Explain.

Q 2-9. What are the three principal financial statements of a corporation? Briefly describe the purpose of each statement.

Q 2-10. Why are footnotes to statements necessary?

Q 2-11. What are contingent liabilities? Are lawsuits against the firm contingent liabilities?

Q 2-12. Which of the following events, occurring subsequent to the balance sheet date, would require a footnote?
a. Major fire in one of the firm's plants
b. Increase in competitor's advertising
c. Purchase of another company
d. Introduction of new management techniques
e. Death of the corporate treasurer

Q 2-13. Describe a proxy statement.

Q 2-14. Briefly describe a summary annual report.

Q 2-15. If a company issues a summary annual report, where can the more extensive financial information be found?

Q 2-16. Comment on the typical number of financial pages in a summary annual report as compared to a full annual report.

Q 2-17. What are the major sections of a statement of cash flows?

Q 2-18. Which two principal financial statements explain the difference between two balance sheet dates? Describe how these financial statements explain the difference between two balance sheet dates.

Q 2-19. What are the three major categories on a balance sheet?

Q 2-20. Can cash dividends be paid from retained earnings? Comment.

Q 2-21. Why review footnotes to financial statements?

Q 2-22. Where do we find a description of a firm's accounting policies?

Q 2-23. Describe the relationship between the terms ethics and morals.

Q 2-24. What is the relationship between ethics and law?

Q 2-25. Identify the basic accounting equation.

Q 2-26. What is the relationship between the accounting equation and the double-entry system of recording transactions?

Q 2-27. Define the following:
a. Permanent accounts   b. Temporary accounts

Q 2-28. A typical accrual recognition for salaries is as follows:

Salaries Expense $1,000 (increase)
Salaries Payable   1,000 (increase)

Explain how the matching concept applies in this situation.

Q 2-29. Why are adjusting entries necessary?

Q 2-30. Why aren't all transactions recorded in the general journal?

Q 2-31. The NYSE has trouble competing with many foreign exchanges in the listing of foreign stocks. Discuss.

Q 2-32. Identify the usual forms of a business entity and describe the ownership characteristic of each.

Q 2-33. Why would the use of insider information be of concern if the market is efficient?

Q 2-34. Considering the EMH, it is best if financial disclosure is made in the body of the financial statements. Comment.

Q 2-35. Considering the EMH, how could abnormal returns be achieved?

Q 2-36. Describe the purchase method of accounting for a business combination.

Q 2-37. Consolidated statements may be issued to show financial position as it would appear if two or more companies were one entity. What is the objective of these statements?

Q 2-38. What is the basic guideline for consolidation?

Q 2-39. Where must a company's code of ethics be made available?

Problems

P 2-1. The Mike Szabo Company engaged in the following transactions during the month of December:

December 2 Made credit sales of $4,000 (accepted accounts receivable).
          6 Made cash sales of $2,500.
         10 Paid office salaries of $500.
         14 Sold land that originally cost $2,200 for $3,000 cash.
         17 Paid $6,000 for equipment.
         21 Billed clients $900 for services (accepted accounts receivable).
         24 Collected $1,200 on an account receivable.
         28 Paid an account payable of $700.

Required Record the transactions, using T-accounts.

P 2-2. The Darlene Cook Company engaged in the following transactions during the month of July:

July 1 Acquired land for $10,000. The company paid cash.
      8 Billed customers for $3,000. This represents an increase in revenue. The customer has been billed and will pay at a later date. An asset, accounts receivable, has been created.
     12 Incurred a repair expense for repairs of $600. Darlene Cook Company agreed to pay in 60 days. This transaction involves an increase in accounts payable and repair expense.
     15 Received a check for $500 from a customer who was previously billed. This is a reduction in accounts receivable.
     20 Paid $300 for supplies. This was previously established as a liability, account payable.
     24 Paid wages in the amount of $400. This was for work performed during July.

Required Record the transactions, using T-accounts.

P 2-3. The Gaffney Company had these adjusting entry situations at the end of December.

1. On July 1, Gaffney Company paid $1,200 for a one-year insurance policy. The policy was for the period July 1 through June 30. The transaction was recorded as prepaid insurance and a reduction in cash.
2. On September 10, Gaffney Company purchased $500 of supplies for cash. The purchase was recorded as supplies. On December 31, it was determined that various supplies had been consumed in operations and that supplies costing $200 remained on hand.
3. Gaffney Company received $1,000 on December 1 for services to be performed in the following year. This was recorded on December 1 as an increase in cash and as revenue. As of December 31, this needs to be recognized as unearned revenue, a liability account.
4. As of December 31, interest charges of $200 have been incurred because of borrowed funds. Payment will not be made until February. A liability for the interest needs to be recognized as does the interest expense.
5. As of December 31, a $500 liability for salaries needs to be recognized.
6. As of December 31, Gaffney Company had provided services in the amount of $400 for the Jones Company. An asset, account receivable, needs to be recognized along with the revenue.

Required Record the adjusting entries at December 31, using T-accounts.

P 2-4. The DeCort Company had these adjusting entry situations at the end of December:

1. On May 1, the DeCort Company paid $960 for a two-year insurance policy. The policy was for the period May 1 through April 30 (2 years). This is the first year of the policy. The transaction was recorded as insurance.
2. On December 1, the DeCort Company purchased $400 of supplies for cash. The purchase was recorded as an asset, supplies. On December 31, it was determined that various supplies had been consumed in operations and that supplies costing $300 remained on hand.
3. DeCort Company holds a note receivable for $4,000. This note is interest-bearing. The interest will be received when the note matures. The note is a one-year note receivable made on June 30, bearing 5% simple interest.
4. DeCort Company owes salaries in the amount of $800 at the end of December.
5. As of December 31, DeCort Company had received $600 for services to be performed. These services had not been performed as of December 31. A liability, unearned revenue needs to be recognized, and revenue needs to be reduced.

6. On December 20, DeCort Company received a $400 bill for advertising in December. The liability account, accounts payable, needs to be recognized along with the related expense.

Required   Record the adjusting entries at December 31, using T-accounts.

P 2-5.

Required   Answer the following multiple-choice questions:
  a. The balance sheet equation can be defined as which of the following?
      1. Assets + Stockholders' Equity = Liabilities
      2. Assets + Liabilities = Stockholders' Equity
      3. Assets = Liabilities – Stockholders' Equity
      4. Assets – Liabilities = Stockholders' Equity
      5. None of the above
  b. If assets are $40,000 and stockholders' equity is $10,000, how much are liabilities?
      1. $30,000
      2. $50,000
      3. $20,000
      4. $60,000
      5. $10,000
  c. If assets are $100,000 and liabilities are $40,000, how much is stockholders' equity?
      1. $40,000
      2. $50,000
      3. $60,000
      4. $30,000
      5. $140,000
  d. Which is a permanent account?
      1. Revenue
      2. Advertising Expense
      3. Accounts Receivable
      4. Dividends
      5. Insurance Expense
  e. Which is a temporary account?
      1. Cash
      2. Accounts Receivable
      3. Insurance Expense
      4. Accounts Payable
      5. Notes Payable
  f. In terms of debits and credits, which accounts have the same normal balances?
      1. Dividends, retained earnings, liabilities
      2. Capital stock, liabilities, expenses
      3. Revenues, capital stock, expenses
      4. Expenses, assets, dividends
      5. Dividends, assets, liabilities

P 2-6.

Required   Answer the following multiple-choice questions:
  a. Audit opinions cannot be classified as which of the following?
      1. All-purpose
      2. Disclaimer of opinion
      3. Adverse opinion
      4. Qualified opinion
      5. Unqualified opinion
  b. From the point of view of analysis, which classification of an audit opinion indicates that the financial statements carry the highest degree of reliability?
      1. Unqualified opinion
      2. All-purpose
      3. Disclaimer of opinion
      4. Qualified opinion
      5. Adverse opinion

c.   Which one of the following statements is false?
1.   The reliance that can be placed on financial statements that have been reviewed is substantially less than for those that have been audited.
2.   An accountant's report described as a compilation presents only financial information as provided by management.
3.   A disclaimer of opinion indicates that you should not look to the auditor's report as an indication of the reliability of the statements.
4.   A review has substantially less scope than an examination in accordance with generally accepted auditing standards.
5.   The typical unqualified opinion has one paragraph.

d.   If an accountant performs a compilation and becomes aware of deficiencies in the statements, the accountant's report characterizes the deficiencies by all but one of the following:
1.   Omission of substantially all disclosures
2.   Omission of statement of cash flows
3.   Accounting principles not generally accepted
4.   All of the above
5.   None of the above

e.   In addition to the company's principal financial statements, the Form 10-K and shareholder annual reports must include all but one of the following:
1.   Information on the market for holders of common stock and related securities, including high and low sales price, frequency and amount of dividends, and number of shares.
2.   Five-year summary of selected financial data.
3.   Management's discussion and analysis of financial condition and results of operations.
4.   Two years of audited balance sheets, three years of audited statements of income, and two years of statements of cash flows.
5.   Disclosure of the domestic and foreign components of pretax income.

f.   Which of these is not a suggested problem caused by lack of harmonization of international accounting standards?
1.   Positive effect on the international trade of accounting practice and services.
2.   A need for employment of key personnel in multinational companies to bridge the "gap" in accounting requirements between countries.
3.   Difficulties in reconciling local standards for access to other capital markets.
4.   Difficulties in accessing capital markets for companies from less developed countries.
5.   Negative effect on the international trade of accounting practice and services.

g.   Which of these organizations has not played a role in the harmonization of international accounting standards?
1.   United Nations (UN)
2.   Internal Revenue Service (IRS)
3.   International Accounting Standards Board (IASB)
4.   Financial Accounting Standards Board (FASB)
5.   European Economic Community (EEC)

h.   The Form 10-K is submitted to the
1.   American Institute of Certified Public Accountants
2.   Securities and Exchange Commission
3.   Internal Revenue Service
4.   American Accounting Association
5.   Emerging Issues Task Force

P 2-7.   The following are selected accounts of the Laura Gibson Company on December 31:

	Permanent (P) or Temporary (T)	Normal Balance (Dr.) or (Cr.)
Cash		
Accounts Receivable		
Equipment		
Accounts Payable		
Common Stock		
Sales		
Purchases		
Rent Expense		
Utility Expense		
Selling Expense		

Required   In the space provided:
1. Indicate if the account is a permanent (P) or temporary (T) account.
2. Indicate the normal balance in terms of debit (Dr.) or credit (Cr.).

P 2-8.   An auditor's report is the formal presentation of all the effort that goes into an audit. Below is a list of the classifications of audit opinions that can be found in an auditor's report as well as a list of phrases describing the opinions.

Classifications of Audit Opinions
a. Unqualified opinion
b. Qualified opinion
c. Adverse opinion
d. Disclaimer of opinion

Phrases
_____ 1. This opinion states that the financial statements do not present fairly the financial position, results of operations, or cash flows of the entity, in conformity with generally accepted accounting principles.

_____ 2. This type of report is rendered when the auditor has not performed an audit sufficient in scope to form an opinion.

_____ 3. This opinion states that, except for the effects of the matters to which the qualification relates, the financial statements present fairly, in all material respects, the financial position, results of operations, and cash flows of the entity, in conformity with generally accepted accounting principles.

_____ 4. This opinion states that the financial statements present fairly, in all material respects, the financial position, results of operations, and cash flows of the entity, in conformity with generally accepted accounting principles.

Required   Place the appropriate letter identifying each type of opinion on the line in front of the statement or phrase describing the type of opinion.

P 2-9.   A company prepares financial statements in order to summarize financial information. Below is a list of financial statements and a list of descriptions.

Financial Statements
a. Balance sheet
b. Income statement
c. Statement of cash flows
d. Statement of stockholders' equity

Descriptions
_____ 1. Details the sources and uses of cash during a specified period of time.
_____ 2. Summary of revenues and expenses and gains and losses for a specific period of time.
_____ 3. Shows the financial condition of an accounting entity as of a specific date.
_____ 4. Presents reconciliation of the beginning and ending balances of the stockholders' equity accounts.

Required   Match each financial statement with its description.

Case 2-1

The CEO Retires*

Dan Murphy awoke at 5:45 A.M., just like he did every workday morning. No matter that he went to sleep only four hours ago. The Orange Bowl game had gone late into the evening, and the New Year's Day party was so good, no one wanted to leave. At least Dan could awake easily this morning. Some of his guests had lost a little control celebrating the first day of the new year, and Dan was not a person who ever lost control.

The drive to the office was easier than most days. Perhaps there were a great many parties last night. All the better as it gave Dan time to think. The dawn of a new year; his last year. Dan would turn 65 next December, and the company had a mandatory retirement policy. A good idea he thought; to get new blood in the organization. At least that's what he thought on the climb up. From just another college graduate within the corporate staff, all the way to the Chief Executive Officer's suite. It certainly is a magnificent view from the top.

To be CEO of his own company. Well not really, as it was the stockholders' company, but he had been CEO for the past eight years. Now he too must turn the reins over. "Must," now that's the operative word. He knew it was the best thing for the company. Turnover kept middle management aggressive, but he also knew that he wouldn't leave if he had a choice. So Dan resolved to make his last year the company's best year ever.

It was that thought that kept his attention, yet the focus of consideration and related motivations supporting such a strategy changed as he continued to strategize. At first, Dan thought that it would be a fine way to give something back to a company that had given him so much. His 43 years with the company had given him challenges which filled his life with meaning and satisfaction, provided him with a good living, and made him a man respected and listened to in the business community. But the thought that the company was also forcing him to give all that up made his thoughts turn more inward.

Of course, the company had done many things for him, but what of all the sacrifices he had made? His whole heart and soul were tied to the company. In fact, one could hardly think of Dan Murphy without thinking of the company, in much the same way as prominent corporate leaders and their firms are intrinsically linked. But the company would still be here this time next year, and what of him? Yes, he would leave the company strong, because by leaving it strong, it would strengthen his reputation as a great leader. His legacy would carry and sustain him over the years. But would it? One must also live in a manner consistent with such esteem.

Being the CEO of a major company also has its creature comforts. Dan was accustomed to a certain style of living. How much will that suffer after the salary, bonuses, and stock options are no more?

Arriving at the office by 7:30 A.M., he left a note for his secretary that he was not to be disturbed until 9 A.M. He pulled out the compensation file and examined the incentive clauses in his own contract. The contract was created by the compensation committee of the Board of Directors. All of the committee members were outsiders; that is, not a part of the company's management. This lends the appearance of independence, but most were CEOs of their own companies, and Dan knew that, by and large, CEOs take care of their own. His suspicions were confirmed. If the company's financial results were the best ever this year, then so too would be his own personal compensation.

Yet what if there were uncontrollable problems? The general economy appeared fairly stable. However, another oil shock, some more bank failures, or a list of other disasters could turn things into a downward spiral quickly. Economies are easily influenced and consumer and corporate psychology can play a large part in determining outcomes. But even in apparently uncontrollable circumstances, Dan knew he could protect himself and the financial fortunes of his company during the short term, which after all, was the only thing that mattered.

Upon further review of his compensation contract, Dan saw that a large portion of his bonus and stock options was a function of operating income levels, earnings per share, and return on assets. So the trick was to maximize those items. If he did, the company would appear vibrant and posed for future growth at the time of his forced retirement, he reminded himself. Furthermore, his total compensation in the last year of his employment would reach record proportions. Additionally, since his pension is based on the average of his last three years' compensation, Dan will continue to reap the benefits of this year's results for hopefully a long time to come. And who says CEOs don't think long term?

Two remaining issues needed to be addressed. Those were (1) how to ensure a record-breaking year and (2) how to overcome any objections raised in attaining those results. Actually, the former was a

---

Prepared by Professor William H. Coyle, Babson College.
*Note: From "Ethics in the Accounting Curriculum: Cases & Readings," American Accounting Association, included with permission.

relatively simple goal to achieve. Since accounting allows so many alternatives in the way financial events are measured, Dan could just select a package of alternatives, which would maximize the company's earnings and return on assets. Some alternatives may result in changing an accounting method, but since the new auditing standards were issued, his company could still receive an unqualified opinion from his auditors, with only a passing reference to any accounting changes in the auditor's opinion and its effects disclosed in the footnotes. As long as the alternative was allowed by generally accepted accounting principles, and the justification for the change was reasonable, the auditors should not object. If there were objections, Dan could always threaten to change auditors. But still the best avenue to pursue would be a change in accounting estimates, since those changes did not even need to be explicitly disclosed.

So Dan began to mull over what changes in estimates or methods he could employ in order to maximize his firm's financial appearance. In the area of accounting estimates, Dan could lower the rate of estimated default on his accounts receivable, thus lowering bad debt expense. The estimated useful lives of his plant and equipment could be extended, thus lowering depreciation expense. In arguing that quality improvements have been implemented in the manufacturing process, the warranty expense on the products sold could also be lowered. In examining pension expense, he noted that the assumed rate of return on pension assets was at a modest 6.5%, so if that rate could be increased, the corresponding pension expense could be reduced.

Other possibilities occurred to Murphy. Perhaps items normally expensed, such as repairs, could be capitalized. Those repairs that could not be capitalized could simply be deferred. The company could also defer short-term expenses for the training of staff. Since research and development costs must now be fully expensed as incurred, a reduction in those expenditures would increase net income. Return on assets would be increased by not acquiring any new fixed assets. Production levels for inventory could be increased, thus spreading fixed costs over a greater number of units and reducing the total average cost per unit. Therefore, gross profit per unit will increase. Inventory levels would be a little bloated, but that should be easily handled by Dan's successor.

The prior examples are subtle changes that could be made. As a last resort, a change in accounting methods could be employed. This would require explicit footnote disclosure and a comment in the auditor's report, but if it came to that, it would still be tolerable. Examples of such changes would be to switch from accelerated to straight-line depreciation or to change from LIFO to FIFO.

How to make changes to the financial results of the company appeared easier than he first thought. Now back to the other potential problem of "getting away with it." At first thought, Dan considered the degree of resistance by the other members of top management. Mike Harrington, Dan's chief financial officer, would have to review any accounting changes that he suggested. Since Dan had brought Mike up the organization with him, Dan didn't foresee any strong resistance from Mike. As for the others, Dan believed he had two things going for him. One was their ambition. Dan knew that they all coveted his job, and a clear successor to Dan had yet to be chosen. Dan would only make a recommendation to the promotion committee of the Board of Directors, but everyone knew his recommendation carried a great deal of weight. Therefore, resistance to any accounting changes by any individual would surely end his or her hope to succeed him as CEO. Secondly, although not as lucrative as Dan's, their bonus package is tied to the exact same accounting numbers. So any actions taken by Dan to increase his compensation will also increase theirs.

Dan was actually beginning to enjoy this situation, even considering it one of his final challenges. Dan realized that any changes he implemented would have the tendency to reverse themselves over time. That would undoubtedly hurt the company's performance down the road, but all of his potential successors were in their mid-to-late 50s, so there would be plenty of time for them to turn things around in the years ahead. Besides, any near-term reversals would merely enhance his reputation as an excellent corporate leader, as problems would arise after his departure.

At that moment, his secretary called to inform him that Mike Harrington wanted to see him. Mike was just the man Dan wanted to see.

What are the ethical issues?

What should Mike do?

Required

a.   Determine the facts—what, who, where, when, how.

b.   Define the ethical issues.

c.   Identify major principles, rules, and values.

d.   Specify the alternatives.

e.   Compare norms, principles, and values with alternatives to see if a clear decision can be reached.

f.   Assess the consequences.

g.   Make your decision.

Case 2-2	The Dangerous Morality of Managing Earnings*

The Majority of Managers Surveyed Say It's Not Wrong to Manage Earnings

Occasionally, the morals and ethics executives use to manage their businesses are examined and discussed. Unfortunately, the morals that guide the timing of nonoperating events and choices of accounting policies largely have been ignored.

The ethical framework used by managers in reporting short-term earnings probably has received less attention than its operating counterpart because accountants prepare financial disclosures consistent with laws and generally accepted accounting principles (GAAP). Those disclosures are reviewed by objective auditors.

Managers determine the short-term reported earnings of their companies by:

- Managing, providing leadership, and directing the use of resources in operations.
- Selecting the timing of some nonoperating events, such as the sale of excess assets or the placement of gains or losses into a particular reporting period.
- Choosing the accounting methods that are used to measure short-term earnings.

Casual observers of the financial reporting process may assume that time, laws, regulation, and professional standards have restricted accounting practices to those that are moral, ethical, fair, and precise. But most managers and their accountants know otherwise—that managing short-term earnings can be part of a manager's job.

To understand the morals of short-term earnings management, we surveyed general managers and finance, control, and audit managers. The results are frightening.

We found striking disagreements among managers in all groups. Furthermore, the liberal definitions revealed in many responses of what is moral or ethical should raise profound questions about the quality of financial information that is used for decision-making purposes by parties both inside and outside a company. It seems many managers are convinced that if a practice is not explicitly prohibited or is only a slight deviation from rules, it is an ethical practice regardless of who might be affected either by the practice or the information that flows from it. This means that anyone who uses information on short-term earnings is vulnerable to misinterpretation, manipulation, or deliberate deception.

The Morals of Managing Earnings

To find a "revealed" consensus concerning the morality of engaging in earnings-management activities, we prepared a questionnaire describing 13 earnings-management situations we had observed either directly or indirectly. The actions described in the incidents were all legal (although some were in violation of GAAP), but each could be construed as involving short-term earnings management.

A total of 649 managers completed our questionnaire. Table 2-1 classifies respondents by job function. Table 2-2 summarizes the views on the acceptability of various earnings-management practices.

TABLE 2-1	SURVEY RESPONDENTS

Total Sample

General Managers	119
Finance, Control, & Audit Managers	262
Others or Position Not Known	268
	649

*Note: Prepared by William J. Bruns, Jr., Professor of Business Administration, Harvard University Graduate School of Business Administration, and Kenneth A. Merchant, Professor of Accounting, University of Southern California. Reprinted from *Management Accounting*, August 1990. Copyright by National Association of Accountants, Montvale, NJ.

TABLE 2-2	MANAGING SHORT-TERM EARNINGS

Proportion of Managers Who Judge the Practice

	Ethical	Questionable, or a Minor Infraction	Unethical, or a Serious Infraction
1. Managing short-term earnings by changing or manipulating operating decisions or procedures:			
When the result is to reduce earnings	79%	19%	2%
When the result is to increase earnings	57%	31%	12%
2. Managing short-term earnings by changing or manipulating accounting methods:			
When the change to earnings is small	5%	45%	50%
When the change to earnings is large	3%	21%	76%
3. Managing short-term earnings by deferring discretionary expenditures into the next accounting period:			
To meet an interim quarterly budget target	47%	41%	12%
To meet an annual budget target	41%	35%	24%
4. Increasing short-term earnings to meet a budget target:			
By selling excess assets and realizing a profit	80%	16%	4%
By ordering overtime work at year-end to ship as much as possible	74%	21%	5%
By offering customers special credit terms to accept delivery without obligation to pay until the following year	43%	44%	15%

Percentages are calculated from *Harvard Business Review* readers' sample.

A major finding of the survey was a striking lack of agreement. None of the respondent groups viewed any of the 13 practices unanimously as an ethical or unethical practice. The dispersion of judgments about many of the incidents was great. For example, here is one hypothetical earnings-management practice described in the questionnaire:

> In September, a general manager realized that his division would need a strong performance in the last quarter of the year in order to reach its budget targets. He decided to implement a sales program offering liberal payment terms to pull some sales that would normally occur next year into the current year. Customers accepting delivery in the fourth quarter would not have to pay the invoice for 120 days.

The survey respondents' judgments of the acceptability of this practice were distributed as follows:

Ethical	279
Questionable	288
Unethical	82
Total	649

Perhaps you are not surprised by these data. The ethical basis of an early shipment/liberal payment program may not be something you have considered, but, with the prevalence of such diverse views, how can any user of a short-term earnings report know the quality of the information?

Although the judgments about all earnings-management practices varied considerably, there are some other generalizations that can be made from the findings summarized in Table 2-2.

- On average, the respondents viewed management of short-term earnings by *accounting* methods as significantly less acceptable than accomplishing the same ends by changing or manipulating *operating decisions or procedures*.
- The direction of the effect on earnings matters. *Increasing* earnings is judged less acceptable than *reducing* earnings.
- Materiality matters. Short-term earnings management is judged less acceptable if the earnings effect is *large* rather than *small*.

- The time period of the effect may affect ethical judgments. Managing short-term earnings at the end of an interim *quarterly* reporting period is viewed as somewhat more acceptable than engaging in the same activity at the end of an *annual* reporting period.
- The method of managing earnings has an effect. Increasing profits by offering *extended credit terms* is seen as less acceptable than accomplishing the same end by *selling excess assets or using overtime* to increase shipments.

Managers Interviewed

Were the survey results simply hypothetical, or did managers recognize they can manage earnings and choose to do so? To find the answers, we talked to a large number of the respondents. What they told us was rarely reassuring.

On accounting manipulations, a profit center controller reported:

"Accounting is grey. Very little is absolute . . . You can save your company by doing things with sales and expenses, and, if it's legal, then you are justified in doing it."

A divisional general manager spoke to us about squeezing reserves to generate additional reported profit:

"If we get a call asking for additional profit, and that's not inconceivable, I would look at our reserves. Our reserves tend to be realistic, but we may have a product claim that could range from $50,000 to $500,000. Who knows what the right amount for something like that is? We would review our reserves, and if we felt some were on the high side, we would not be uncomfortable reducing them."

We also heard about operating manipulations. One corporate group controller noted:

"[To boost sales] we have paid overtime and shipped on Saturday, the last day of the fiscal quarter. If we totally left responsibility for the shipping function to the divisions, it could even slip over to 12:30 A.M. Sunday. There are people who would do that and not know it's wrong."

Managers often recognize that such actions "move" earnings from one period to another. For example, a division controller told us:

"Last year we called our customers and asked if they would take early delivery. We generated an extra $300,000 in sales at the last minute. We were scratching for everything. We made our plans, but we cleaned out our backlog and started in the hole this year. We missed our first quarter sales plan. We will catch up by the end of the second quarter."

And a group vice president said:

"I recently was involved in a situation where the manager wanted to delay the production costs for the advertising that would appear in the fall [so that he could meet his quarterly budget]."

Thus, in practice, it appears that a large majority of managers use at least some methods to manage short-term earnings. Although legal, these methods do not seem to be consistent with a strict ethical framework. While the managers' actions have the desired effect on reported earnings, the managers know there are no real positive economic benefits, and the actions might actually be quite costly in the long run. These actions are at best questionable because they involve deceptions that are not disclosed. Most managers who manage earnings, however, do not believe they are doing anything wrong.

We see two major problems. The most important is the generally high tolerance for operating manipulations. The other is the dispersion in managers' views about which practices are moral and ethical.

The Dangerous Allure

The essence of a moral or ethical approach to management is achieving a balance between individual interests and obligations to those who have a stake in what happens in the corporation (or what happens to a division or group within the corporation). These stakeholders include not only people who work in the firm, but customers, suppliers, creditors, shareholders, and investors as well.

Managers who take unproductive actions to boost short-term earnings may be acting totally within the laws and rules. Also they may be acting in the best interest of the corporation. But, if they fail to consider the adverse effects of their actions on other stakeholders, we may conclude that they are acting unethically.

The managers we interviewed explained that they rated accounting manipulations harshly because in such cases the "truth" has somehow been denied or misstated. The recipients of the earnings reports do not know what earnings would have been if no manipulation had taken place. Even if the accounting methods used are consistent with GAAP, they reason, the actions are not ethical because the interests of major stakeholder groups—including the recipients of the earnings reports—have been ignored.

The managers judge the operating manipulations more favorably because the earnings numbers are indicative of what actually took place. The operating manipulations have changed reality, and "truth" is fairly reported.

We see flaws in that reasoning. One is that the truth has not necessarily been disclosed completely. When sales and profits are borrowed from the future, for example, it is a rare company that discloses the borrowed nature of some of the profits reported.

A second flaw in the reasoning about the acceptability of operating manipulations is that it ignores a few or all of the effects of some types of operating manipulations on the full range of stakeholders. Many managers consider operating manipulations as a kind of "victimless crime."

But victims do exist. Consider, for example, the relatively common operating manipulation of early shipments. As one manager told us:

"Would I ship extra product if I was faced with a sales shortfall? You have to be careful there; you're playing with fire. I would let whatever happened fall to the bottom line. I've been in companies that did whatever they could to make the sales number, such as shipping lower quality product. That's way too short term. You have to draw the line there. You must maintain the level of quality and customer service. You'll end up paying for bad shipments eventually. You'll have returns, repairs, adjustments, ill will that will cause you to lose the account . . . [In addition] it's tough to go to your employees one day and say ship everything you can and then turn around the next day and say that the quality standards must be maintained."

Another reported:

"We've had to go to [one of our biggest customers] and say we need an order. That kills us in the negotiations. Our last sale was at a price just over our cost of materials."

These comments point out that customers—and sometimes even the corporation—may be victims.

Without a full analysis of the costs of operating manipulations, the dangers of such manipulations to the corporation are easily underestimated. Mistakes will be made because the quality of information is misjudged. The short term will be emphasized at the expense of the long term. If managers consistently manage short-term earnings, the messages sent to other employees create a corporate culture that lacks mutual trust, integrity, and loyalty.

A Lack of Moral Agreement

We also are troubled by the managers' inability to agree on the types of earnings-management activities that are acceptable. This lack of agreement exists even within corporations.

What this suggests is that many managers are doing their analyses in different ways. The danger is obfuscation of the reality behind the financial reports. Because managers are using different standards, individuals who try to use the information reported may be unable to assess accurately the quality of that information.

If differences in opinions exist, it is likely that financial reporting practices will sink to their lowest and most manipulative level. As a result, managers with strict definitions of what is moral and ethical will find it difficult to compete with managers who are not playing by the same rules. Ethical managers either will loosen their moral standards or fail to be promoted into positions of greater power.

Actions for Concerned Managers

We believe most corporations would benefit if they established clearer accounting and operating standards for all employees to follow. The standard-setting process should involve managers in discussions of the practices related to short-term earnings measurements.

Until these standards are in place, different managers will use widely varying criteria in assessing the acceptability of various earnings-management practices. These variations will have an adverse effect on the quality of the firm's financial information. Companies can use a questionnaire similar to the one in our study to encourage discussion and to communicate corporate standards and the reason for them.

Standards also enable internal and external auditors and management to judge whether the desired quality of earnings is being maintained. In most companies, auditors can depend on good standards to identify and judge the acceptability of the operating manipulations.

Ultimately, the line management chain-of-command, not auditors or financial staff, bears the primary responsibility for controlling operating manipulations. Often managers must rely on their prior experience and good judgment to distinguish between a decision that will have positive long-term benefits and one that has a positive short-term effect but a deleterious long-term effect.

Finally, it is important to manage the corporate culture. A culture that promotes openness and co-operative problem solving among managers is likely to result in less short-term earnings management than one that is more competitive and where annual, and even quarterly, performance shortfalls are punished. A corporate culture that is more concerned with managing for excellence rather than for reporting short-term profits will be less likely to support the widespread use of immoral earnings-management practices.

Required
a. Time, laws, regulation, and professional standards have restricted accounting practices to those that are moral, ethical, fair, and precise. Comment.

b. Most managers surveyed had a conservative, strict interpretation of what is moral or ethical in financial reporting. Comment.

c. The managers surveyed exhibited a surprising agreement as to what constitutes an ethical or unethical practice. Comment.

d. List the five generalizations from the findings in this study relating to managing earnings.

e. Comment on management's ability to manage earnings in the long run by influencing financial accounting.

Case 2-3

Frequent-Flier Awards—Tick-Tick, Tick-Tick, Tick-Tick

In the early 1980s, airlines introduced frequent-flier awards to develop passenger loyalty to a single airline. Free tickets and possibly other awards were made available to passengers when they accumulated a certain number of miles or flights on a particular air carrier. These programs were potentially good for the passenger and the airline as long as the awards were not too generous and the airlines could minimize revenue displacement from a paying passenger.

These programs were introduced by American Airlines in 1981. Originally there were no restrictions. Anyone with the necessary miles could take any flight that had an available seat. In the late 1980s, most airlines changed their no-restriction programs to programs with restrictions and blackout days. Airlines typically compensated passengers for these changes by cutting mileage requirements. The airlines also added partners in frequent-flier programs, such as car rental companies and hotels. These partners handed out frequent-flier miles compensating the airlines in some manner for the miles distributed. Airlines also added triple-mileage deals.

A consequence of these expanding frequent-flier programs was a surge in the number of passengers flying free and a surge in unused miles. To get a handle on the cost and the unused miles, airlines increased the frequent-flier miles needed for a flight and placed time limits on the award miles. Thus—tick-tick, tick-tick, tick-tick.

The increased frequent-flier miles needed for a flight and the time limits prompted lawsuits. Many of these lawsuits were filed in state courts. One of the suits filed in the District Court in Chicago in 1989 made its way to the United States Supreme Court. In 1995 the Supreme Court ruled that federal airline deregulation law would not bar the breach-of-contract claim in the state court. In June of 1995 a District Court in Dallas ruled in favor of the airline in a case involving an increase in miles needed to earn a trip. Airlines interpret this decision as upholding their right to make changes to their frequent-flier programs.

Required
a. In your opinion, are the outstanding (unused) miles a liability to the airline? (Substantiate your answer.)

b. Comment on the potential problems involved in estimating the dollar amount of any potential liability.

c. 1. What is a contingent liability?
   2. In your opinion, are unused miles a contingent liability to the air carrier?
   3. Recommend the recognition (if any) for unused miles.

Case 2-4

International Accounting—Harmonization in Practice

Dennis R. Beresford, Chairman, Financial Accounting Standards Board, included these comments in the June 1995 Financial Accounting Series of the Financial Accounting Foundation. This case represents a quote from page 2, Notes from the Chairman. (Permission to reprint obtained from the Financial Accounting Standards Board.)

Notes from the Chairman (in Part)

Last month Jim Leisenring and I attended what is now becoming more or less an annual meeting of accounting standards setters from more than a dozen countries. The first of those meetings, initiated by the FASB, was held in 1991 in Brussels, and similar get-togethers have followed in our offices, London, and now Amsterdam. This year's meeting was held in conjunction with a regular meeting of the International Accounting Standards Committee and the centenary celebrations of NIVRA, the professional accounting body in the Netherlands.

Earlier, this group had devoted its attention mainly to conceptual issues and general communications about what the various countries were working on at the time. For example, the first gathering concentrated on the objectives of external financial reporting and whether individual countries had explicit or implicit conceptual frameworks. In London, most of the time was spent on how future events are considered in accounting recognition and measurement decisions. That discussion was facilitated by a paper prepared by the FASB and our counterparts from Australia, Canada, the United Kingdom, and the IASC. The paper later was jointly published as the Special Report, "Future Events—A Conceptual Study of Their Significance for Recognition and Measurement."

In Amsterdam, we spent most of the time on two specific technical issues that are hot topics here as well as in the rest of the world: accounting for environmental liabilities and derivative financial instruments. Papers were presented by Canada, Denmark, England, and the European Commission, which covered the current state-of-the-art regarding disclosure of and accounting for environmental costs. As in the U.S., the key issues are deciding when an obligation has been incurred, under what circumstances can any resulting debit be considered an asset (e.g., costs incurred to "improve" a productive facility), and when an amount is measurable with sufficient reliability.

Required

a. Comment on the trend in harmonization of international accounting as represented by the comments included in this case.

b. Can we expect harmonization of international accounting to be accomplished in the foreseeable future? Comment.

Case 2-5

Materiality: In Practice

Professional standards require auditors to make a preliminary judgment about materiality levels during the planning of an audit. Statement of Auditing Standards (SAS) No. 47 states that "the auditor plans the audit to obtain reasonable assurance of detecting misstatements that he/she believes could be large enough, individually or in the aggregate, to be quantitatively material to the financial statements."*

SAS No. 47 indicates that materiality judgments involve both quantitative and qualitative considerations. This statement recognizes that it ordinarily is not practical to design procedures to detect misstatements that could be qualitatively material.

A number of rule-of-thumb materiality calculations have emerged, such as percentages of income, total assets, revenues, and equity. These rule-of-thumb calculations result in differing amounts for audit planning purposes. In fact, sizeable differences can result, depending on the rule of thumb and the industry.

Required

a. It would seem prudent for auditors to give careful consideration to planning materiality decisions. Comment.

b. It is difficult to design procedures to detect misstatements that could be qualitatively material. Comment.

c. It is difficult to design procedures to detect misstatements that could be quantitatively material. Comment.

d. In your opinion, would the application of materiality be a frequent issue in court cases involving financial statements? Comment.

*Note: This case is based on SAS No. 47 as updated and presented in AV312 of the *Codification of Statements on Auditing Standards* (American Institute of Certified Public Accountants), January 1989.

Case 2-6   Who is Responsible?

Report of Management

The accompanying consolidated financial statements, including the notes thereto, and other financial information presented in the annual report were prepared by management, which is responsible for their integrity and objectivity. The financial statements have been prepared in accordance with generally accepted accounting principles and include amounts that are based upon our best estimates and judgments.

We maintain an effective system of internal accounting control. We believe this system provides reasonable assurance that transactions are executed in accordance with management authorization and are appropriately recorded in order to permit preparation of financial statements in conformity with generally accepted accounting principles and to adequately safeguard, verify, and maintain accountability of assets. The concept of reasonable assurance is based on the recognition that the cost of a system of internal control should not exceed the benefits derived.

PricewaterhouseCoopers LLP, independent certified public accountants, is retained to audit our financial statements. Their accompanying report is based on audits conducted in accordance with generally accepted auditing standards. The audits include a review of the internal accounting control structure to gain a basic understanding of the accounting system in order to design an effective and efficient audit approach and not for the purpose of providing assurance on the system of internal control.

The Audit Committee of the Board of Directors is composed of three outside directors and is responsible for recommending the independent accounting firm to be retained for the coming year, subject to shareholder approval. The audit Committee meets periodically and privately with the independent accountants, as well as with management, to review accounting, auditing, internal accounting controls, and financial reporting matters.

[signed]

Gregory A. Effertz

Vice President, Finance and Administration,
Chief Financial Officer, Treasurer and Secretary

[signed]

Steven D. Ladwig
President and Chief Executive Officer

Report of Independent Accountants

To the Board of Directors and Stockholders of Retek Inc.

In our opinion, the consolidated financial statements present fairly, in all material respects, the financial position of Retek Inc. (the Company) and its subsidiaries at December 31, 2001 in conformity with accounting principles generally accepted in the United States of America. These financial statements are the responsibility of the Company's management; our responsibility is to express an opinion on these financial statements based on our audits. We conducted our audits of these statements in accordance with auditing standards generally accepted in the United States of America, which require that we plan and perform the audit to obtain reasonable assurance about whether the financial statements are free of material misstatement. An audit includes examining, on a test basis, evidence supporting the amounts and disclosures in the financial statements, assessing the accounting principles used and significant estimates made by management, and evaluating the overall financial statement presentation. We believe that our audits provide a reasonable basis for our opinion.

[signed]

PricewaterhouseCoopers LLP
Minneapolis, Minnesota
January 21, 2002

Required   a.   Who has the responsibility for the financial statements?

b.   What is the role of the accountant (auditor) as to the financial statements?

c.   Accountants (auditors) are often included as defendants in lawsuits that relate to the financial statements. Speculate as to why this is the case.

d.   What type of auditor's opinion is represented in this case?

e.   Would we expect these audited financial statements to be free of misstatement? Comment.

Case 2-7   Safe Harbor

In 1995, Congress passed the Private Securities Litigation Reform Act (the Act). The principal provisions of the Act are intended to curb abusive litigation and improve the quality of information available to investors through the creation of a safe harbor for forward-looking statements.

Forward-looking statements were defined to include statements relating to projections of revenues and other financial items, plans and objectives, future economic performance, assumptions, reports issued by outside reviewers, or other projections or estimates specified by rule of the SEC. The safe harbor applies to both oral and written statements.

Management frequently uses signals as "we estimate," "we project," and the like, where forward-looking statements are not otherwise identified as such. The forward-looking statements must be accompanied by meaningful cautionary statements. The cautionary statement may be contained in a separate risk section elsewhere in the disclosure document.

Flowers Foods included this statement in their 2001 Annual Report.

FORWARD-LOOKING STATEMENTS

Certain statements made in this discussion are "forward-looking statements" within the meaning of the Private Securities Litigation Reform Act of 1995 (the "Reform Act"). These statements are subject to the safe harbor provisions of the Reform Act. Such forward-looking statements include, without limitation, statements about: the competitiveness of the baking industry; the future availability and prices of raw and packaging materials; potential regulatory obligations; our strategies; and other statements that are not historical facts.

When used in this discussion, the words "anticipate," "believe," "estimate" and similar expressions are generally intended to identify forward-looking statements. Because such forward-looking statements involve risks and uncertainties, there are important factors that could cause actual results to differ materially from those expressed or implied by such forward-looking statements, including but not limited to: changes in general economic or business conditions (including in the baking industry); actions of competitors; our ability to retain or procure capital on terms acceptable to us; our ability to recover material costs in the pricing of our products; the extent to which we are able to develop new products and markets for our products; the time required for such development; the level of demand for such products; and changes in our business strategies.

Required   a.   Demand for financial reports exists because users believe that the reports help them in decision making. In your opinion, will forward-looking statements as provided by the Private Securities Litigation Reform Act aid users of financial reports in decision making?

b.   To some extent, investors' rights are limited by the curb of abusive litigation. In your opinion, is there a net benefit to investors from a safe harbor for forward-looking statements?

Web Case   Thomson Analytics *Business School Edition*

Please complete the web case that covers material covered in this chapter at http://gibson.swlearning.com. You'll be using Thomson Analytics Business School Edition, a version of the powerful tool used by Wall Street professionals, that combines a full range of fundamental financial information, earnings estimates, market data, and source documents for 500 publicly traded companies.

Endnotes

1.   Charles H. Gibson and Nicholas Schroeder, "How 21 Companies Handled Their Summary Annual Reports," *Financial Executive* (November/December 1989), pp. 45–46.

2. Mary E. Guy, *Ethical Decision Making in Everyday Work Situations* (New York: Quarum Books, 1990), p. 5.
3. *Ibid.*, p. 14.
4. William W. May, ed., *Ethics in the Accounting Curriculum: Cases & Readings* (Sarasota, FL: American Accounting Association, 1990), pp. 1–2.
5. "Regulators Investigate Peat on Its Auditing of S & L," *The New York Times* (May 23, 1991), p. D-1.
6. "S.E.C. Inquiry Is Reported on Loans to Accountants," *The New York Times* (February 7, 1991), p. D-1.
7. "Ernst & Young Settles Negligence Charge," *Business Insurance* (May 6, 1991), p. 2.
8. Ronald Grover, "Curtains for Tinseltown Accounting?" *Business Week* (January 14, 1991), p. 35.
9. Shahram Victory, "Pierce O'Donnell Pans 'Fatal Subtraction,'" *American Lawyer* (March 1991), p. 43.
10. "Buchwald Wins Just $150,000 in Film Lawsuit," *The Wall Street Journal* (March 17, 1992), p. B-1.
11. SEC Adopts Rules on Provisions of Sarbanes-Oxley Act, SEC Internet web site, http://www.sec.gov/news/press/1-16-03.
12. Dennis E. Peavey and Stuart K. Webster, "Is GAAP the Gap to International Markets?" *Management Accounting* (August 1990), pp. 31–32.
13. John Hagarty, "Why We Can't Let GATT Die," *Journal of Accountancy* (April 1991), p. 74.
14. Peavey and Webster, "Is GAAP the Gap to International Markets?" p. 34.
15. Gerhard G. Mueller, Helen Gernan, and Gary Meek, *Accounting: An International Perspective*, 2d ed. (Homewood, IL: Richard D. Irwin, Inc., 1991), pp. 45–46.
16. Dennis Beresford, "Internationalization of Accounting Standards," *Accounting Horizons* (March 1990), p. 10.
17. Mueller, Gernan, and Meek, *Accounting*, pp. 11–12.

BALANCE SHEET

The Principal Financial Statements are the balance sheet, income statement, and statement of cash flows. This chapter will review the balance sheet in detail. Another statement, called the statement of stockholders' equity, reconciles the changes in stockholders' equity, a section of the balance sheet. This statement will also be reviewed in this chapter.

**BASIC
ELEMENTS
OF THE
BALANCE
SHEET**

A **balance sheet** shows the financial condition of an accounting entity as of a particular date. The balance sheet consists of assets, the resources of the firm; liabilities, the debts of the firm; and stockholders' equity, the owners' interest in the firm.

The assets are derived from two sources, creditors and owners. At any point in time, the assets must equal the contribution of the creditors and owners. The accounting equation expresses this relationship:

$$\text{Assets} = \text{Liabilities} + \text{Stockholders' Equity}$$

On the balance sheet, the assets equal the liabilities plus the stockholders' equity. This may be presented side by side (account form) or with the assets at the top and the liabilities and stockholders' equity at the bottom (report form). Exhibit 3-1 presents a typical report form format, and Exhibit 3-2 presents a typical account form format.

EXHIBIT 3-1

BRIDGFORD—2001 ANNUAL REPORT
Consolidated Balance Sheets (Statement of Financial Position) Report Form

CONSOLIDATED BALANCE SHEETS (in thousands)

	November 2, 2001	November 3, 2000
ASSETS		
Current assets:		
Cash and cash equivalents	$12,974	$18,301
Accounts receivable, less allowance for doubtful accounts of $779 and $694, respectively	14,282	13,642
Inventories	19,165	18,191
Prepaid expenses	864	528
Refundable income taxes	2,041	
Deferred income taxes	2,451	2,438
Total current assets	51,777	53,100
Property, plant and equipment, net of accumulated depreciation of $35,378 and $31,599, respectively	19,471	18,964
Other non-current assets	7,649	6,836
Deferred income taxes	3,441	3,781
	$82,338	$82,681
LIABILITIES AND SHAREHOLDERS' EQUITY		
Current liabilities:		
Accounts payable	$6,958	$7,723
Accrued payroll and other expenses	6,464	6,788
Income taxes payable	330	120
Total current liabilities	13,752	14,631
Non-current liabilities	11,251	11,854
Contingencies and commitments (Note 6)		
Shareholders' equity:		
Preferred stock, without par value		
Authorized—1,000 shares		
Issued and outstanding—none		
Common stock, $1.00 par value		
Authorized—20,000 shares		
Issued and outstanding—10,448 and 10,615, respectively	10,505	10,672
Capital in excess of par value	17,475	19,459
Retained earnings	29,355	26,065
Total shareholders' equity	57,335	56,196
	$82,338	$82,681

EXHIBIT 3-2	**SMITHFIELD FOODS, INC.—2001 ANNUAL REPORT**

Consolidated Balance Sheets Account Form

FISCAL YEARS ENDED (in thousands, except share data)	April 29, 2001	April 30, 2000
Assets		
Current assets:		
Cash and cash equivalents	$ 56,532	$ 49,882
Accounts receivable less allowances of $6,392 and $4,899	387,841	390,037
Inventories	729,167	665,143
Prepaid expenses and other current assets	90,155	127,664
Total current assets	1,263,695	1,232,726
Property, plant and equipment:		
Land	76,100	73,753
Buildings and improvements	711,124	666,428
Machinery and equipment	855,838	732,217
Breeding stock	94,286	100,576
Construction in progress	59,307	39,069
	1,796,655	1,612,043
Less accumulated depreciation	(522,178)	(398,469)
Net property, plant and equipment	1,274,477	1,213,574
Other assets:		
Goodwill, net of accumulated amortization of $18,925 and $8,695	347,342	320,148
Investments in partnerships	88,092	102,551
Other	277,282	260,614
Total other assets	712,716	683,313
	$3,250,888	$3,129,613

(continued)

Balance sheet formats differ across nations. For example, nations influenced by British financial reporting report the least liquid assets first and cash last. Nations influenced by the United States report a balance sheet emphasizing liquidity, as illustrated in this chapter.

Assets

Assets are probable future economic benefits obtained or controlled by an entity as a result of past transactions or events.[1] Assets may be *physical*, such as land, buildings, inventory of supplies, material, or finished products. Assets may also be *intangible*, such as patents and trademarks.

Assets are normally divided into two major categories: current and noncurrent (long-term). **Current assets** are assets (1) in the form of cash, (2) that will normally be realized in cash, or (3) that conserve the use of cash during the operating cycle of a firm or for one year, whichever is longer. The *operating cycle* covers the time between the acquisition of inventory and the realization of cash from selling the inventory. Noncurrent or **long-term** assets take longer than a year or an operating cycle to be converted to cash or to conserve cash. Some industries, such as banking (financial institutions), insurance, and real estate, do not divide assets (or liabilities) into current and noncurrent. Chapter 12 reviews specialized industries.

When a significant subsidiary is consolidated from an industry that does not use the concept of current and noncurrent, then the consolidated statements will not use the concept of current and noncurrent. These companies often present supplementary statements, handling the subsidiary as an investment (nonconsolidated).

For example, General Electric does not use the concept of current and noncurrent. General Electric Company's consolidated financial statements represent the combination of manufacturing

| EXHIBIT 3-2 | SMITHFIELD FOODS, INC.—2001 ANNUAL REPORT |

Consolidated Balance Sheets Account Form (*continued*)

FISCAL YEARS ENDED (in thousands, except share data)	April 29, 2001	April 30, 2000
Liabilities and Shareholder's Equity		
Current liabilities:		
Notes payable	$ 35,504	$ 64,924
Current portion of long-term debt and		
capital lease obligations	79,590	48,505
Accounts payable	278,093	270,004
Accrued expenses and other current liabilities	235,095	239,436
Total current liabilities	628,282	622,869
Long-term debt and capital lease obligations	1,146,223	1,187,770
Other noncurrent liabilities:		
Deferred income taxes	271,516	274,329
Pension and postretirement benefits	77,520	78,656
Other	25,820	30,311
Total other noncurrent liabilities	374,856	383,296
Minority interests	48,395	32,769
Commitments and contingencies		
Shareholders' equity:		
Preferred stock, $1.00 par value, 1,000,000		
authorized shares	—	—
Common stock, $.50 par value, 100,000,000		
authorized shares; 52,502,951 and		
54,705,386 issued and outstanding	26,251	27,353
Additional paid-in capital	405,665	473,974
Retained earnings	638,779	415,266
Accumulated other comprehensive loss	(17,563)	(13,684)
Total shareholders' equity	1,053,132	902,909
	$3,250,888	$3,129,613

and nonfinancial services businesses of General Electric Company (GE) and the accounts of General Electric Capital Services, Inc. (GECS).

Current Assets

Current assets are listed on the balance sheet in order of **liquidity** (the ability to be converted to cash). Current assets typically include cash, marketable securities, short-term receivables, inventories, and prepaids. In some cases, assets other than these may be classified as current. If so, management is indicating that it expects the asset to be converted into cash during the operating cycle or within a year, whichever is longer. An example is land held for immediate disposal. Exhibit 3-3 includes the items that the 2001 edition of *Accounting Trends & Techniques* reported as being disclosed as other current assets. The definition of current assets excludes restricted cash, investments for purposes of control, long-term receivables, the cash surrender value of life insurance, land and other natural resources, depreciable assets, and long-term prepayments.

Cash **Cash**, the most liquid asset, includes negotiable checks and unrestricted balances in checking accounts, as well as cash on hand. Savings accounts are classified as cash even though the bank may not release the money for a specific period of time. Exhibit 3-4 illustrates the presentation of cash.

Marketable Securities **Marketable securities** (also labeled short-term investments) are characterized by their marketability at a readily determinable market price. A firm holds marketable secu-

EXHIBIT 3-3	**OTHER CURRENT ASSET ITEMS**

| | **Number of Companies** | | | |
Nature of Asset	**2000**	**1999**	**1998**	**1997**
Deferred income taxes	359	364	400	375
Property held for sale	38	31	28	33
Unbilled costs	8	13	20	14
Advances or deposits	4	9	6	4
Derivatives	3	N/C*	N/C*	N/C*
Other—identified	59	42	46	29

*N/C = Not compiled. Line item was not included in table for year shown.

Source: *Accounting Trends & Techniques*, copyright © 2001 by American Institute of Certified Public Accountants, Inc., p. 159. Reprinted with permission.

rities to earn a return on near-cash resources. Management must intend to convert these assets to cash during the current period for them to be classified as marketable securities.

The carrying basis of debt and equity marketable securities is fair value. Refer to Exhibit 3-4 for a presentation of marketable securities.

Accounts Receivable **Accounts receivable** are monies due on accounts that arise from sales or services rendered to customers. Accounts receivable are shown net of allowances to reflect their realizable value. This amount is expected to be collected. The most typical allowances are for bad debts (uncollectible accounts). Other allowances may account for expected sales discounts, which are given for prompt payment or for sales returns. These types of allowances recognize expenses in the period of sale, at which time the allowance is established. In future periods, when the losses occur, they are

EXHIBIT 3-4	**VERIZON COMMUNICATIONS INC.—2001 ANNUAL REPORT** **Consolidated Balance Sheets (in Part)** **Illustration of Cash, Marketable Securities, and Accounts Receivable**

(dollars in millions, except per share amounts)	**December 31,**	
	2001	**2000**
ASSETS		
Current assets:		
Cash and cash equivalents	$ 979	$ 757
Short-term investments	1,991	1,613
Accounts receivable, net of allowance of		
$2,153 and $1,562	14,254	14,010
Inventories	1,968	1,910
Net assets held for sale	1,199	518
Prepaid expenses and other	2,796	3,313
Total current assets	23,187	22,121
Plant, property and equipment	169,586	158,957
Less accumulated depreciation	95,167	89,453
	74,419	69,504
Investments in unconsolidated businesses	10,202	13,115
Intangible assets, net	44,262	41,990
Other assets	18,725	18,005
Total assets	$170,795	$164,735

charged to the allowance. Exhibit 3-4 presents the accounts receivable of Verizon Communications Inc. (less allowances). At year-end 2001, the firm expects to realize $14,254,000,000. The gross receivables can be reconciled as follows:

Receivables, net	$14,254,000,000
Plus: Allowances	2,153,000,000
Receivables, gross	$16,407,000,000

Other receivables may also be included in current assets. These receivables may result from contracts, tax refund claims, sales of assets, retained interest in sold receivables, employees, and installment notes or accounts.[2]

Inventories **Inventories** are the balance of goods on hand. In a manufacturing firm, they include raw materials, work in process, and finished goods. Inventories will be carried at cost, expressed in terms of lower-of-cost-or-market. (Cost methods and lower-of-cost-or-market are covered in Chapter 7.) Refer to Exhibit 3-5 for a presentation of inventory.

EXHIBIT 3-5	**BARR LABORATORIES, INC.—2001 ANNUAL REPORT**

Illustration of Inventory

Consolidated Balance Sheets (in Part)

	June 30,	
(in thousands of dollars, except share amounts)	2001	2000
Assets		
Current Assets		
Cash and cash equivalents	$222,339	$155,922
Marketable securities	—	96
Accounts receivable (including receivables from related parties of $3,603 in 2001 and $865 in 2000) less allowances of $8,230 and $4,140 in 2001 and 2000, respectively	73,050	54,669
Other receivables	20,272	23,811
Inventories	115,615	79,482
Deferred income taxes	2,716	—
Prepaid expenses	2,782	1,428
Total current assets	436,774	315,408
Property, plant and equipment, net	102,583	95,296
Other assets	4,037	13,149
Total assets	$543,394	$423,853

Notes (in Part)

1. Summary of Significant Accounting Policies (in Part):

(d) Inventories

Inventories are stated at the lower of cost, determined on a first-in, first-out (FIFO) basis, or market

Inventories

A summary of inventories is as follows:

	June 30,	
	2001	2000
Raw materials and supplies	$ 22,656	$16,884
Work-in-process	5,825	5,102
Finished goods	87,134	57,496
	$115,615	$79,482

Tamoxifen Cirate, purchased as a finished product, accounted for $66,890 and $42,730 of finished goods inventory at June 30, 2001 and 2000, respectively.

Raw Materials These are goods purchased for direct use in manufacturing a product, and they become part of the product. For example, in the manufacture of shirts, the fabric and buttons would be raw materials.

Work in Process Work in process represents goods started but not ready for sale. Work in process includes the cost of materials, labor costs for workers directly involved in the manufacture, and factory overhead. Factory overhead includes such cost items as rent, indirect wages, and maintenance.

Finished Goods Finished goods are inventory ready for sale. These inventory costs also include the cost of materials, labor costs for workers directly involved in the manufacture, and a portion of factory overhead.

Since retailing and wholesaling firms do not engage in the manufacture of a product but only in the sale, their only inventory item is merchandise. These firms do not have raw materials, work in process inventory, or finished goods.

Supplies In addition to goods on hand, the firm may have supplies. Supplies could include register tapes, pencils, or sewing machine needles for the shirt factory. Details relating to inventory are usually disclosed in a footnote.

Prepaids A **prepaid** is an expenditure made in advance of the use of the service or goods. It represents future benefits that have resulted from past transactions. For example, if insurance is paid in advance for three years, at the end of the first year, two years' worth of the outlay will be prepaid. The entity retains the right to be covered by insurance for two more years.

Typical prepaids include advertising, taxes, insurance, promotion costs, and early payments on long-term contracts. Prepaids are often not disclosed separately. In Exhibit 3-1, the prepaid account is disclosed separately. In Exhibit 3-2, prepaids are part of prepaid expenses and other current assets.

Long-Term Assets

Long-term assets are usually divided into four categories: tangible assets, investments, intangible assets, and other.

Tangible Assets These are the physical facilities used in the operations of the business. The tangible assets of land, buildings, machinery, and construction in progress will now be reviewed. Accumulated depreciation related to buildings and machinery will also be reviewed.

Land Land is shown at acquisition cost and is not depreciated because land does not get used up. Land containing resources that will be used up, however, such as mineral deposits and timberlands, is subject to depletion. Depletion expense attempts to measure the wearing away of these resources. It is similar to depreciation except that depreciation deals with a tangible fixed asset and depletion deals with a natural resource.

Buildings Structures are presented at cost plus the cost of permanent improvements. Buildings are depreciated (expensed) over their estimated useful life.

Machinery Machinery is listed at historical cost, including delivery and installation, plus any material improvements that extend its life or increase the quantity or quality of service. Machinery is depreciated over its estimated useful life.

Construction in Progress Construction in progress represents cost incurred for projects under construction. These costs will be transferred to the proper tangible asset account upon completion of construction. The firm cannot use these assets while they are under construction. Some analysis is directed at how efficiently the company is using operating assets. This analysis can be distorted by construction in progress, since construction in progress is classified as part of tangible assets. To avoid this distortion, classify construction in progress under long-term assets, other.

Accumulated Depreciation   Depreciation is the process of allocating the cost of buildings and machinery over the periods benefited. The depreciation expense taken each period is accumulated in a separate account (Accumulated Depreciation). Accumulated depreciation is subtracted from the cost of plant and equipment. The net amount is the **book value** of the asset. It does not represent the current market value of the asset.

There are a number of depreciation methods that a firm can use. Often a firm depreciates an asset under one method for financial statements and another for income tax returns. A firm often wants to depreciate slowly for the financial statements because this results in the highest immediate income and highest asset balance. The same firm would want to depreciate faster for income tax returns because this results in the lowest immediate income and thus lower income taxes. Over the life of an asset, the total depreciation will be the same regardless of the depreciation method selected.

Three factors are usually considered when computing depreciation: (1) the asset cost, (2) length of the life of the asset, and (3) its salvage value when retired from service. The length of the asset's life and the salvage value must be estimated at the time that the asset is placed in service. These estimates may be later changed if warranted.

Exhibit 3-6 indicates the depreciation methods used for financial reporting purposes by the firms surveyed for the 2001 edition of *Accounting Trends & Techniques*. The most popular methods were straight-line, accelerated methods, and units-of-production. Many firms use more than one depreciation method.

The following assumptions will be made to illustrate depreciation methods:

1. Cost of asset—$10,000
2. Estimated life of asset—5 years
3. Estimated salvage (or residual) value—$2,000
4. Estimated total hours of use—16,000

Straight-Line Method The **straight-line method** recognizes depreciation in equal amounts over the estimated life of the asset. Compute depreciation using the straight-line method as follows:

$$\frac{\text{Cost} - \text{Salvage Value}}{\text{Estimated Life}} = \text{Annual Depreciation}$$

For the asset used for illustration, the annual depreciation would be computed as follows:

$$\frac{\$10,000 - \$2,000}{5 \text{ years}} = \$1,600$$

The $1,600 depreciation amount would be recognized each year of the five-year life of the asset. Do not depreciate the salvage value.

Declining-Balance Method The **declining-balance method**, an accelerated method, applies a multiple times the straight-line rate to the declining book value (cost minus accumulated depreciation) to achieve a declining depreciation charge over the estimated life of the asset. This book will use

| EXHIBIT 3-6 | DEPRECIATION METHODS |

	Number of Companies			
	2000	**1999**	**1998**	**1997**
Straight-line	576	577	577	578
Declining balance	22	27	25	26
Sum-of-the-years'-digits	7	7	9	10
Accelerated method—not specified	53	53	43	50
Units-of-production	34	31	36	39
Other	10	6	9	10

Source: *Accounting Trends & Techniques*, copyright © 2001 by American Institute of Certified Public Accountants, Inc., p. 359. Reprinted with permission.

double the straight-line rate, which is the maximum rate that can be used. Compute depreciation using the declining balance method as follows:

$$\frac{1}{\text{Estimated life of asset}} \times 2 \times \text{Book amount at beginning of the year} = \text{Annual depreciation}$$

For the asset used for illustration, the first year's depreciation would be computed as follows:

$$\frac{1}{5} \times 2 \times (\$10,000 - 0) = \$4,000$$

The declining-balance method results in the following depreciation amounts for each of the five years of the asset's life:

Year	Cost	Accumulated Depreciation at Beginning of Year	Book Amount at Beginning of Year	Depreciation for Year	Book Amount at End of Year
1	$10,000	—	$10,000	$4,000	$6,000
2	10,000	$4,000	6,000	2,400	3,600
3	10,000	6,400	3,600	1,440	2,160
4	10,000	7,840	2,160	160	2,000
5	10,000	8,000	2,000	—	2,000

Estimated salvage value is not considered in the formula, but the asset should not be depreciated below the estimated salvage value. For the sample asset, the formula produced a depreciation amount of $864 in the fourth year. Only $160 depreciation can be used in the fourth year because the $160 amount brings the book amount of the asset down to the salvage value. Once the book amount is equal to the salvage value, no additional depreciation may be taken.

Sum-of-the-Years'-Digits Method   The **sum-of-the-years'-digits method** is an accelerated depreciation method. Thus, the depreciation expense declines steadily over the estimated life of the asset. This method takes a fraction each year times the cost less salvage value. The numerator of the fraction changes each year. It is the remaining number of years of the asset's life. The denominator of the fraction remains constant; it is the sum of the digits representing the years of the asset's life. Compute depreciation using the sum-of-the-years'-digits method as follows:

$$\frac{\text{Remaining Number of Years of Life}}{\text{Sum of the Digits Representing the Years of Life}} \times (\text{Cost} - \text{Salvage}) = \text{Annual Depreciation}$$

For the asset used for illustration, the first year's depreciation would be computed as follows:

$$\frac{5}{(5 + 4 + 3 + 2 + 1) \text{ or } 15} \times (\$10,000 - \$2,000) = \$2,666.67$$

The sum-of-the-years'-digits method results in the following depreciation amounts for each year of the five years of the asset's life:

Year	Cost Less Salvage Value	Fraction	Depreciation for Year	Accumulated Depreciation at End of Year	Book Amount at End of Year
1	$8,000	5/15	$2,666.67	$2,666.67	$7,333.33
2	8,000	4/15	2,133.33	4,800.00	5,200.00
3	8,000	3/15	1,600.00	6,400.00	3,600.00
4	8,000	2/15	1,066.67	7,466.67	2,533.33
5	8,000	1/15	533.33	8,000.00	2,000.00

Unit-of-Production Method   The **unit-of-production method** relates depreciation to the output capacity of the asset, estimated for the life of the asset. The capacity is stated in terms most appropriate for the asset, such as units of production, hours of use, or miles. Hours of use will be used for the asset in our example. For the life of the asset, it is estimated that there will be 16,000 hours of use. The estimated output capacity is divided into the cost of the asset less the salvage value to determine the depreciation per unit of output. For the example asset, the depreciation per hour of use would be $.50 [(cost of asset, $10,000 – salvage, $2,000) divided by 16,000 hours].

The depreciation for each year is then determined by multiplying the depreciation per unit of output by the output for that year. Assuming that the output was 2,000 hours during the first year, the depreciation for that year would be $1,000 ($.50 × 2,000). Further depreciation cannot be taken when the accumulated depreciation equals the cost of the asset less the salvage value. For the example asset, this will be when accumulated depreciation equals $8,000.

In Exhibit 3-7, Weatherford International Inc. presents these assets as property, plant, and equipment at cost. Added detail information is disclosed in the notes.

EXHIBIT 3-7	**WEATHERFORD INTERNATIONAL, INC.—2001 ANNUAL REPORT**

Consolidated Balance Sheets (in Part)
Properties and Depreciation

(in thousands, except shares and par values)	December 31,	
	2001	**2000**
ASSETS		
Current Assets:		
Cash and Cash Equivalents	$ 88,832	$ 153,808
Accounts Receivable, Net of Allowance for Uncollectible		
Accounts of $18,021 in 2001 and $23,281 in 2000	462,145	498,663
Inventories	504,986	443,588
Current Deferred Tax Assets	69,985	72,054
Other Current Assets	105,385	73,474
	1,231,333	1,241,587
Property, Plant and Equipment, at Cost:		
Land, Buildings and Other Property	226,288	193,290
Rental and Service Equipment	1,274,017	1,255,907
Machinery and Other	484,257	405,765
	1,984,562	1,854,962
Less: Accumulated Depreciation	944,946	881,937
	1,039,616	973,025
Goodwill, Net	1,383,272	1,051,562
Equity Investments in Unconsolidated Affiliates	483,038	9,229
Other Assets	159,103	186,176
	$4,296,362	$3,461,579

Notes to Consolidated Financial Statements (in Part)

1. Summary of Significant Accounting Policies (in Part)

Property, Plant and Equipment

Property, plant and equipment, both owned and under capital lease, is carried at cost. Maintenance and repairs are expensed as incurred. The cost of renewals, replacements and betterments is capitalized. Depreciation on fixed assets, including those under capital leases, is computed using the straight-line method over the estimated useful lives for the respective categories. The estimated useful lives of the major classes of property, plant and equipment are as follows:

	Estimated Useful Lives
Buildings and other property	5–45 years
Rental and service equipment	3–15 years
Machinery and other	3–20 years

Leases   Leases are classified as *operating* leases or *capital* leases. If the lease is in substance an ownership arrangement, it is a capital lease; otherwise, the lease is an operating lease. Assets leased under a capital lease are classified as long-term assets. They are shown net of amortization (depreciation) and listed with plant, property, and equipment. (The discounted value of the obligation, a liability, will be part current and part long term.) Chapter 7 covers the topic of leases in more length.

Investments   Long-term investments, usually stocks and bonds of other companies, are often held to maintain a business relationship or to exercise control. Long-term investments are different from marketable securities, where the intent is to hold for short-term profits and to achieve liquidity. (Financial reports often refer to marketable securities as investments.)

Debt securities under investments are to be classified as held-to-maturity securities or available-for-sale securities. *Held-to-maturity securities* are securities that the firm has the intent and ability to hold to maturity. Debt securities classified as held-to-maturity securities are carried at amortized cost. Debt securities classified as available-for-sale securities are carried at fair value.

Equity securities under investments are to be carried at fair value. An exception for fair value is used for common stock where there is significant influence. For these common stock investments, the investment is carried under the equity method. Under the equity method, the cost is adjusted for the proportionate share of the rise (fall) in retained profits of the subsidiary (investee). For example, a parent company owns 40% of a subsidiary company, purchased at a cost of $400,000. When the subsidiary company earns $100,000, the parent company increases the investment account by 40% of $100,000, or $40,000. When the subsidiary company declares dividends of $20,000, the parent company decreases the investment account by 40% of $20,000, or $8,000. This decrease occurs because the investment account changes in direct proportion to the retained earnings of the subsidiary.

Investments can also include tangible assets not currently used in operations, such as an idle plant, as well as monies set aside in special funds, such as pensions. The investments of Gentex Corporation are illustrated in Exhibit 3-8.

EXHIBIT 3-8	**GENTEX CORPORATION** **Consolidated Balance Sheets as of December 31, 2001 and 2000 (in Part)** **Investments**

	2001	2000
ASSETS		
Current Assets:		
Cash and cash equivalents	$139,784,721	$110,195,583
Short-term investments	65,859,016	28,246,967
Accounts receivable, less allowances of		
$375,000 and $350,000 in 2001 and 2000	31,994,939	35,614,669
Inventories	14,405,350	12,087,513
Prepaid expenses and other	7,814,468	4,411,118
Total current assets	259,858,494	190,555,850
Plant and Equipment:		
Land, buildings and improvements	45,923,054	40,400,929
Machinery and equipment	118,809,575	84,480,366
Construction-in-process	6,446,221	4,816,097
	171,178,850	129,697,392
Less: Accumulated depreciation and amortization	(60,316,540)	(47,777,724)
	110,862,310	81,919,668
Other Assets:		
Long-term investments	132,771,234	153,016,195
Parents and other assets, net	3,330,760	2,636,980
	136,101,994	155,653,175
	$506,822,798	$428,128,693

(continued)

EXHIBIT 3-8   **GENTEX CORPORATION** (*continued*)

Notes to Consolidated Financial Statements (in Part)

(1) Summary of Significant Accounting and Reporting Policies (in Part)

Investments. Equity securities and U.S. Treasuries are available for sale and are stated at fair value based on quoted market prices. Adjustments to the fair value of available for sale investments are recorded as increases or decreases, net of income taxes, within accumulated other comprehensive income in shareholders' investment. Fixed income securities, excluding U.S. Treasuries, are considered held to maturity and, accordingly, are carried at amortized cost.

The amortized cost, unrealized gains and losses, and market value of securities held to maturity and available for sale are shown as of December 31, 2001 and 2000:

2001	**Cost**	**Gains**	**Losses**	**Market Value**
U.S. Treasuries	$ 69,991,935	$2,172,456	$ —	$ 72,164,391
Municipal	27,008,487	227,952	(42,554)	27,193,885
Other fixed income	34,427,986	506,260	(7,375)	34,926,871
Equity	61,306,343	5,345,938	(1,622,895)	65,029,386
	$192,734,751	$8,252,606	$(1,672,824)	$199,314,533
2000				
U.S. Treasuries	$ 80,010,620	$ 1,109,708	$ (5,062)	$ 81,115,266
Municipal	21,070,646	51,298	(29,381)	21,092,563
Other fixed income	27,095,719	175,666	(39,377)	27,232,088
Equity	45,586,289	7,130,465	(735,222)	51,981,532
	$ 173,763,274	$ 8,467,137	$ (809,042)	$ 181,421,369

Fixed income securities as of December 31, 2001, have contractual maturities as follows:

	Held to Maturity	**U.S. Treasuries**
Due within one year	$16,546,500	$48,239,263
Due between one and five years	44,598,954	21,752,672
Due over five years	291,019	—
	$61,436,473	$69,991,935

During 2000, the Company sold approximately $947,000 of securities classified as held to maturity for $952,000. The decision to sell these securities was based on deterioration in the credit worthiness of the issuer.

Intangibles   Intangibles are nonphysical assets, such as patents and copyrights. Intangibles are recorded at historical cost and amortized over their useful lives or their legal lives, whichever is shorter. Purchased goodwill resulting from an acquisition represents an exception to amortization. Research and development costs must be expensed as incurred. Thus, research and development costs in the United States represent an immediate expense, not an intangible. This requirement is not common in many other countries. The following are examples of intangibles that are recorded in the United States.

Goodwill   **Goodwill** arises from the acquisition of a business for a sum greater than the physical asset value, usually because the business has unusual earning power. It may result from good customer relations, a well-respected owner, and so on. Purchased goodwill is not amortized but is subject to annual impairment reviews.[3]

The global treatment of goodwill varies significantly. In some countries, goodwill is not recorded because it is charged to stockholders' equity. In this case, there is no influence to reported income. In some countries, goodwill is expensed in the year acquired. In many countries goodwill is recorded and amortized.

Patents **Patents**, exclusive legal rights granted to an inventor for a period of 20 years, are valued at their acquisition cost. The cost of a patent should be amortized over its legal life or its useful life, whichever is shorter.

Trademarks **Trademarks** are distinctive names or symbols. Rights are granted indefinitely as long as the owner uses it in connection with the product or service and files the paperwork.

Organizational Costs **Organizational costs** are legal costs incurred when a business is organized. These costs are carried as an asset and are usually written off over a period of five years or longer.

Franchises **Franchises** are the legal right to operate under a particular corporate name, providing trade-name products or services. The cost of a franchise with a limited life should be amortized over the life of the franchise.

Copyrights **Copyrights** are rights that authors, painters, musicians, sculptors, and other artists have in their creations and expressions. A copyright is granted for the life of the creator, plus 70 years. The costs of the copyright should be amortized over the period of expected benefit.

Exhibit 3-9 displays the Microsoft Corporation presentation of intangibles. It consists of goodwill, and other intangibles.

Other Assets Firms will occasionally have assets that do not fit into one of the previously discussed classifications. These assets, termed "other," might include noncurrent receivables and noncurrent prepaids. Exhibit 3-10 summarizes types of other assets from a financial statement compilation in *Accounting Trends & Techniques*.

Liabilities

Liabilities are probable future sacrifices of economic benefits arising from present obligations of a particular entity to transfer assets or provide services to other entities in the future as a result of past transactions or events.[4] Liabilities are usually classified as either current or long-term liabilities.

Current Liabilities

Current liabilities are obligations whose liquidation is reasonably expected to require the use of existing current assets or the creation of other current liabilities within a year or an operating cycle, whichever is longer. They include the following items. Exhibit 3-11 shows the current liabilities of Royal Appliance Mfg. Co. and Subsidiaries.

Payables These include short-term obligations created by the acquisition of goods and services, such as accounts payable (for materials or goods bought for use or resale), wages payable, and taxes payable. Payables may also be in the form of a written promissory note, notes payable.

Unearned Income Payments collected in advance of the performance of service are termed unearned. They include rent income and subscription income. Rather than cash, a future service or good is due the customer.

Other Current Liabilities There are many other current obligations requiring payment during the year. Exhibit 3-12 on page 82 displays other current liabilities reported by *Accounting Trends & Techniques* in 2001.

Long-Term Liabilities

Long-term liabilities are those due in a period exceeding one year or one operating cycle, whichever is longer. Long-term liabilities are generally of two types: financing arrangements of assets and operational obligations.

Liabilities Relating to Financing Agreements The long-term liabilities that are financing arrangements of assets usually require systematic payment of principal and interest. They include notes payable, bonds payable, and credit agreements.

| **EXHIBIT 3-9** | **MICROSOFT CORPORATION—2001 ANNUAL REPORT**
Intangibles |

Balance Sheets (in Part)

In millions	June 30	
	2001	2002
Assets		
Current assets		
Cash and cash equivalents	$ 3,922	$ 3,016
Short-term investments	27,678	35,636
Total cash and short-term investments	31,600	38,652
Accounts receivable, net	3,671	5,129
Inventories	83	673
Deferred income taxes	1,522	2,112
Other	2,334	2,010
Total current assets	39,210	48,576
Property and equipment, net	2,309	2,268
Equity and other investments	14,361	14,191
Goodwill	1,511	1,426
Intangible assets, net	401	243
Other long-term assets	1,038	942
Total assets	$58,830	$67,646

Notes to Financial Statements (in Part)

NOTE 8   GOODWILL

During fiscal 2002, goodwill was reduced by $85 million, principally in connection with Microsoft's exchange of all of its 33.7 million shares and warrants of Expedia, Inc. to USA Networks, Inc. No goodwill was acquired or impaired during fiscal 2002. As of June 30, 2002, Desktop and Enterprise Software and Services goodwill was $1.1 billion, Consumer Software, Services, and Devices goodwill was $258 million, and Consumer Commerce Investments goodwill was $72 million.

NOTE 9   INTANGIBLE ASSETS

During fiscal 2002, changes in intangible assets primarily relates to the Company's acquisition of $25 million in patents and licenses and $27 million in existing technology, which will be amortized over approximately 3 years. No significant residual value is estimated for these intangible assets. Intangible assets amortization expense was $202 million for fiscal 2001 and $194 million for fiscal 2002. The components of intangible assets were as follows:

In millions	June 30			
	2001		2002	
	Gross Carrying Amount	Accumulated Amortization	Gross Carrying Amount	Accumulated Amortization
Patents and licenses	$407	$(177)	$421	$(290)
Existing technology	157	(27)	172	(71)
Trademarks, tradenames and other	83	(42)	15	(4)
Intangible assets	$647	$(246)	$608	$(365)

Amortization expense for the net carrying amount of intangible assets at June 30, 2002 is estimated to be $115 million in fiscal 2003, $90 million in fiscal 2004, $36 million in fiscal 2005, and $2 million in fiscal 2006.

Notes Payable   Promissory notes due in periods greater than one year or one operating cycle, whichever is longer, are classified as long term. If secured by a claim against real property, they are called mortgage notes.

Bonds Payable   A **bond** is a debt security normally issued with $1,000 par per bond and requiring semiannual interest payments based on the coupon rate. Bonds payable is similar to notes payable. Bonds payable are usually for a longer duration than notes payable.

EXHIBIT 3-10 OTHER NONCURRENT ASSETS

| | Number of Companies | | | |
	2000	1999	1998	1997
Deferred income taxes	129	165	177	177
Prepaid pension costs	94	100	88	101
Software	84	85	65	53
Debt issue costs	49	48	55	48
Segregated cash or securities	34	32	38	34
Property held for sale	29	37	41	43
Cash surrender value of life insurance	18	30	24	29
Assets leased to others	9	8	11	20
Contracts	8	N/C*	N/C*	N/C*
Assets of nonhomogeneous operations	7	5	10	9
Derivatives	4	N/C*	N/C*	N/C*
Estimated insurance recoveries	2	4	10	13
Other identified noncurrent assets	44	45	43	40

*N/C = Not compiled. Line item was not included in the table for the year shown.

Source: *Accounting Trends & Techniques,* copyright © 2001 by American Institute of Certified Public Accountants, Inc., p. 200. Reprinted with permission.

Bonds are not necessarily sold at par. They are sold at a premium if the stated rate of interest exceeds the market rate and at a discount if the stated rate of interest is less than the market rate. If sold for more than par, a premium on bonds payable arises and increases bonds payable to obtain the current carrying value. Similarly, if sold at less than par, a discount on bonds payable arises and decreases bonds payable on the balance sheet. Each of these accounts, discount or premium, will be gradually written off (amortized) to interest expense over the life of the bond. At the maturity date, the carrying value of bonds payable will be equal to the par value. Amortization of bond discount increases interest expense; amortization of bond premium reduces it. Exhibit 3-13 illustrates bonds sold at par, premium, or discount.

Bonds that are convertible into common stock at the option of the bondholder (creditor) are exchanged for a specified number of common shares, and the bondholder becomes a common stockholder. Often, convertible bonds are issued when the common stock price is low, in management's opinion, and the firm eventually wants to increase its common equity. By issuing a convertible bond, the firm may get more for the specified number of common shares than could be obtained by issuing the common shares. The conversion feature allows the firm to issue the bond at a more favorable

EXHIBIT 3-11 ROYAL APPLIANCE MFG. CO. AND SUBSIDIARIES—2001 ANNUAL REPORT
Current Liabilities

| | December 31 | |
(Dollars in thousands)	2001	2000
Current Liabilities:		
Trade accounts payable	$27,433	$22,209
Accrued liabilities:		
Advertising and promotion	11,196	13,103
Salaries, benefits, and payroll taxes	7,258	3,355
Warranty and customer returns	9,950	9,800
Income taxes	1,370	—
Other	6,479	6,091
Current portions of capital lease obligations and notes payable	147	136
Total current liabilities	$63,833	$54,694

EXHIBIT 3-12	OTHER CURRENT LIABILITIES

	Number of Companies			
	2000	**1999**	**1998**	**1997**
Interest	110	107	112	110
Taxes other than federal income taxes	106	111	107	116
Deferred revenue	79	86	74	69
Estimated costs related to discontinued operations	76	100	93	87
Warranties	60	67	64	66
Customer advances, deposits	58	54	52	50
Dividends payable	58	62	69	69
Insurance	56	64	64	63
Advertising	48	60	57	56
Deferred taxes	47	45	47	39
Environmental costs	40	48	55	49
Due to affiliated companies	16	19	19	21
Royalties	15	17	18	15
Billings on uncompleted contracts	14	18	21	16
Rebates	12	N/C*	N/C*	N/C*
Litigation	11	14	17	16
Derivatives	6	N/C*	N/C*	N/C*
Other—described	158	125	92	91

*N/C = Not compiled. Line item was not included in the table for the year shown.

Source: *Accounting Trends & Techniques*, copyright © 2001 by American Institute of Certified Public Accountants, Inc., p. 219. Reprinted with permission.

EXHIBIT 3-13	BONDS AT PAR, PREMIUM, OR DISCOUNT

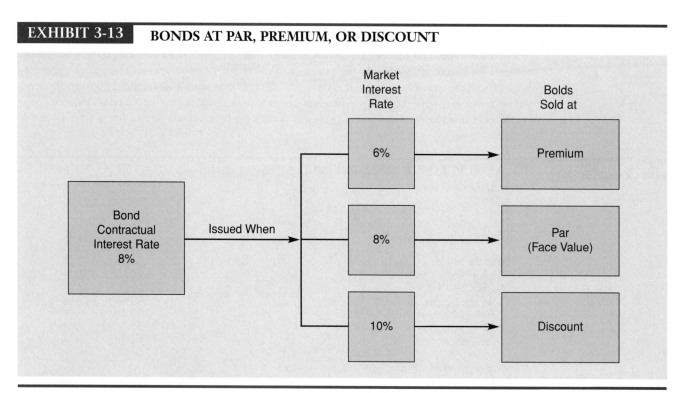

Note: The market interest rate becomes the effective rate of interest.

interest rate than would be the case with a bond lacking the conversion feature. Also, the tax deductible interest paid on the convertible bond reduces the firm's cost for these funds. If common stock had been issued, the dividend on the common stock would not be tax deductible. Thus, a firm may find that issuing a convertible bond can be an attractive means of raising common equity funds in the long run. However, if the firm's stock price stays depressed after issuing a convertible bond, then the firm will have the convertible bond liability until the bond comes due. Convertible bonds of Quantum Corporation are displayed in Exhibit 3-14.

Credit Agreements   Many firms arrange loan commitments from banks or insurance companies for future loans. Often, the firm does not intend to obtain these loans but has arranged the credit agreement just in case a need exists for additional funds. Such credit agreements do not represent a liability unless the firm actually requests the funds. From the point of view of analysis, the existence of a substantial credit agreement is a positive condition in that it could relieve pressure on the firm if there is a problem in meeting existing liabilities.

In return for giving a credit agreement, the bank or insurance company obtains a fee. This commitment fee is usually a percentage of the unused portion of the commitment. Also, banks often require the firm to keep a specified sum in its bank account, referred to as a compensating balance. Exhibit 3-15 shows credit agreements.

Liabilities Relating to Operational Obligations   Long-term liabilities relating to operational obligations include obligations arising from the operation of a business, mostly of a service nature, such as pension obligations, postretirement benefit obligations other than pension plans, deferred taxes, and service warranties. Chapter 7 covers at length pensions and postretirement benefit obligations other than pension plans.

Deferred Taxes   Deferred taxes are caused by using different accounting methods for tax and reporting purposes. For example, a firm may use accelerated depreciation for tax purposes and straight-line depreciation for reporting purposes. This causes tax expense for reporting purposes to be higher than taxes payable according to the tax return. The difference is deferred tax. Any situation where revenue or expense is recognized in the financial statements in a different time period

EXHIBIT 3-14	QUANTUM CORPORATION—2001 ANNUAL REPORT

Consolidated Balance Sheet (in Part)
Convertible Bonds

(dollars in thousands)	March 31	
	2002	**2001**
Current liabilities:		
Accounts payable	$ 65,503	$ 86,510
Accrued warranty	43,210	54,771
Short-term debt	41,363	—
Accrued compensation	28,581	36,326
Income taxes payable	29,638	22,424
Accrued special charges	24,227	8,081
Deferred revenue	15,539	12,373
Due to the Hard Disk Drive group	—	34,000
Other accrued liabilities	49,074	25,572
Total current liabilities	297,135	280,057
Long-term liabilities:		
Deferred income taxes	48,636	35,807
Convertible subordinated debt	287,500	287,500
Total long-term liabilities	336,136	323,307

EXHIBIT 3-15   **CHIQUITA BRANDS INTERNATIONAL, INC.—2001 ANNUAL REPORT**
Credit Agreements

Notes to Consolidated Financial Statements (in Part)

Note 9—Debt (in Part)
In January 2001, the Company announced its intention to re-structure $861 million principal amount of outstanding senior notes and subordinated debentures ("Old Notes") of CBII, which is a parent holding company without business operations of its own. As part of this initiative, CBII discontinued all interest and principal payments on this parent company public debt. CBII filed its Plan of Reorganization on November 28, 2001 under Chapter 11 of the U.S. Bankruptcy Code, and the Plan became effective on March 19, 2002. In accordance with the Plan of Re-organization (see Note 2), the Old Notes and the accrued and un-paid interest thereon are being converted into $250 million of 10.56% senior notes ("New Notes") and 95.5% of the common stock of the reorganized entity. The consolidated balance sheet at December 31, 2001 reflects $861 million principal amount of Old Notes and $102 million of accrued and unpaid interest on such debt as "Liabilities subject to compromise."

The indenture for the New Notes contains restrictions on the payment of dividends. At March 19, 2002, these restrictions limited the aggregate amount that could be paid by CBII as dividends to $25 million.

than for the tax return will create a deferred tax situation (asset or liability). For example, in the later years of the life of a fixed asset, straight-line depreciation will give higher depreciation and, there-fore, lower net income than an accelerated method. Then tax expense for reporting purposes will be lower than taxes payable, and the deferred tax will be reduced (paid). Since firms often buy more and higher-priced assets, however, the increase in deferred taxes may exceed the decrease. In this case, a partial or a total reversal will not occur. The taxes may be deferred for a very long time, perhaps per-manently. Chapter 7 covers deferred taxes in more detail.

Warranty Obligations   Warranty obligations are estimated obligations arising out of product war-ranties. Product warranties require the seller to correct any deficiencies in quantity, quality, or per-formance of the product or service for a specific period of time after the sale. Warranty obligations are estimated in order to recognize the obligation at the balance sheet date and to charge the expense to the period of the sale.

Exhibit 3-16 shows warranty obligations of General Motors.

EXHIBIT 3-16   **GENERAL MOTORS CORPORATION AND SUBSIDIARIES—**
2001 ANNUAL REPORT
Warranty Obligations

Note 12—Accrued Expenses, Other Liabilities, and Deferred Income Taxes (in Part)

Automotive, Communications Services, and Other Operations

Accrued expenses, other liabilities, and deferred income taxes included the following (dollars in millions):

	December 31	
	2001	2000
Warranties, dealer and customer allowances, claims, and discounts	$16,421	$15,993
Deferred revenue[1]	8,331	9,974
Payrolls and employee benefits (excludes postemployment)	6,069	4,609
Unpaid losses under self-insurance programs	2,016	2,031
Taxes, other than income taxes	1,082	1,009
Interest	904	1,401
Deferred income taxes	2,420	2,430
Postemployment benefits (including extended disability benefits)	2,218	2,380
Other	8,423	9,193
Total accrued expenses, other liabilities and deferred income taxes	$47,884	$49,020

[1] Principally relates to sales of vehicles to rental companies.

Minority Interest   Minority interest reflects the ownership of minority shareholders in the equity of consolidated subsidiaries less than wholly owned. Minority interest does not represent a liability or stockholders' equity in the firm being analyzed. Consider the following simple example. Parent P owns 90% of the common stock of Subsidiary S.

	Parent P **Balance Sheet** **December 31, 2003**	**Subsidiary S** **Balance Sheet** **December 31, 2003**
	(In millions)	
Current assets	$100	$10
Investment in Subsidiary S	18	–
Other long-term assets	382	40
	$500	$50
Current liabilities	$100	$10
Long-term liabilities	200	20
Stockholders' equity	200	20
	$500	$50

In consolidation, the assets and liabilities of the subsidiary are added to those of the parent, with the elimination of the investment in Subsidiary S. Parent P owns 90% of the subsidiary's net assets of $20 ($50 – $30), and the minority shareholders own 10%.

This will be shown on the consolidated balance sheet:

PARENT P AND SUBSIDIARY
Consolidated Balance Sheet
December 31, 2003

	(In millions)
Current assets	$110
Long-term assets	422
	$532
Current liabilities	$110
Long-term liabilities	220
Minority interest	2
Stockholders' equity	200
	$532

Because of the nature of minority interest, it is usually presented after liabilities and before stockholders' equity. Some firms include minority interest in liabilities; others present it in stockholders' equity. Since minority interest is seldom material, consider it a liability to simplify the analysis. In a firm where the minority interest is material, the analysis can be performed twice—once with minority interest as a liability and then as a stockholders' equity item.

Including minority interest as a long-term liability is also conservative when analyzing a firm. The primary analysis should be conservative. Refer to Exhibit 3-17 for an illustration of minority interest.

Other Noncurrent Liabilities   Many other noncurrent liabilities may be disclosed. It would not be practical to discuss all of the possibilities. An example would be deferred profit on sales.

Redeemable Preferred Stock   Redeemable preferred stock is subject to mandatory redemption requirements or has a redemption feature outside the control of the issuer. If this feature is coupled with such characteristics as no vote or fixed return, often preferred stock and bond characteristics, then this type of preferred stock is more like debt than equity. For this reason, the SEC directs that the three categories of stock—redeemable preferred stock, non-redeemable preferred stock, and

EXHIBIT 3-17   **DIODES INCORPORATED—2001 ANNUAL REPORT**
Minority Interest

(in thousands, except share data)	December 31 2000	2001
LIABILITIES AND STOCKHOLDERS' EQUITY		
CURRENT LIABILITIES		
Line of credit	$ 7,750	$ 6,503
Accounts payable		
Trade	10,710	6,098
Related parties	1,008	3,149
Accrued liabilities	8,401	5,062
Income taxes payable	1,370	—
Current portion of long-term debt		
Related party	11,049	2,500
Other	3,811	5,833
Total current liabilities	44,099	29,145
LONG-TERM DEBT, net of current portion		
Related party	2,500	7,500
Other	13,497	13,664
MINORITY INTEREST IN JOINT VENTURE	1,601	1,825
STOCKHOLDERS' EQUITY		
Class A convertible preferred stock—par value $1 per share; 1,000,000 shares authorized; no shares issued and outstanding	—	—
Common stock—par value $.66 2/3 per share; 30,000,000 shares authorized; 9,201,663 shares in 2000 and 9,227,664 shares in 2001 issued and outstanding	6,134	6,151
Additional paid-in capital	7,143	7,310
Retained earnings	39,758	39,882
	53,035	53,343
Less: Treasury stock—1,075,672 shares of common stock, at cost	1,782	1,782
Accumulated other comprehensive loss	—	437
	1,782	2,219
Total stockholders' equity	51,253	51,124
Total liabilities and stockholders' equity	$112,950	$103,258

common stock—not be totaled in the balance sheet. Further, the stockholders' equity section should not include redeemable preferred stock. Redeemable preferred stock is illustrated in Exhibit 3-18. Because redeemable preferred stock is more like debt than equity, consider it as part of total liabilities for purposes of financial statement analysis.

Stockholders' Equity

Stockholders' equity is the residual ownership interest in the assets of an entity that remains after deducting its liabilities.[5] Usually divided into two basic categories, paid-in capital and retained earnings, other accounts may appear in stockholders' equity that are usually presented separately from paid-in capital and retained earnings. Other accounts include accumulated other comprehensive income, equity-oriented deferred compensation, and employee stock ownership plans (ESOPs).

Corporations do not use a standard title for owners' equity. Exhibit 3-19 shows the titles for owners' equity used by the companies surveyed by *Accounting Trends & Techniques*.

Paid-in Capital

The first type of paid-in capital account is capital stock. Two basic types of capital stock are preferred and common.

**WENDY'S INTERNATIONAL, INC. AND SUBSIDIARIES—
2001 ANNUAL REPORT
Redeemable Preferred Stock**

(Dollars in thousands)	December 30, 2001	December 30, 2000
Long-term obligations		
Term debt	$ 401,511	$ 204,027
Capital leases	49,735	44,357
	451,246	248,384
Deferred income taxes	82,287	72,750
Other long-term liabilities	16,044	14,023
Commitments and contingencies		
Company-obligated mandatorily redeemable preferred securities of subsidiary Wendy's Financing I, holding solely Wendy's Convertible Debentures	200,000	200,000
Shareholders' equity		
Preferred stock, Authorized: 250,000 shares		
Common stock, $.10 stated value per share, Authorized: 200,000,000 shares, Issued and Exchangeable: 138,452,000 and 136,188,000 shares, respectively	13,271	12,074
Capital in excess of stated value	467,687	423,144
Retained earnings	1,377,840	1,211,015
Accumulated other comprehensive expense	(48,754)	(27,133)
	1,810,044	1,619,100
Treasury stock, at cost: 33,277,000 and 21,978,000 shares, respectively	(780,265)	(492,957)
	1,029,779	1,126,143
	$2,076,043*	$1,957,716*

*Represents total liabilities and shareholders' equity

Both preferred stock and common stock may be issued as par-value stock. (Some states call this *stated value stock*.) The articles of incorporation establish the par value, a designated dollar amount per share. Many states stipulate that the par value of issued stock times the number of shares outstanding constitutes the **legal capital**. Many states also designate that, if original-issue stock is sold

TITLE OF OWNER'S EQUITY

	Number of Companies			
	2000	1999	1998	1997
Stockholders' Equity	286	284	271	271
Shareholders' Equity	229	238	244	246
Shareowners' Equity	25	25	26	25
Shareholders' Investment	12	12	12	12
Common Stockholders' Equity	6	8	9	11
Common Shareholders' Equity	7	7	12	10
Other or no title	35	26	26	25
Total Companies	**600**	**600**	**600**	**600**

Source: *Accounting Trends & Techniques*, copyright © 2001 by American Institute of Certified Public Accountants, Inc., p. 271. Reprinted with permission.

below par value, the buyer is contingently liable for the difference between the par value and the lower amount paid. This does not usually pose a problem because the par value has no direct relationship to market value, the selling price of the stock. To avoid selling a stock below par, the par value is usually set very low in relation to the intended selling price. For example, the intended selling price may be $25.00, and the par value may be $1.00.

Some states allow the issuance of no-par stock (either common or preferred). Some of these states require that the entire proceeds received from the sale of the no-par stock be designated as legal capital.

Additional paid-in capital arises from the excess of amounts paid for stock over the par or stated value of the common and preferred stock. Also included here are amounts over cost from the sale of treasury stock (discussed later in this chapter), capital arising from the donation of assets to the firm, and transfer from retained earnings through stock dividends when the market price of the stock exceeds par.

Common Stock

Common stock shares in all the stockholders' rights and represents ownership that has voting and liquidation rights. Common stockholders elect the board of directors and vote on major corporate decisions. In the event of liquidation, the liquidation rights of common stockholders give them claims to company assets after all creditors' and preferred stockholders' rights have been fulfilled.

Preferred Stock

Preferred stock seldom has voting rights. When preferred stock has voting rights, it is usually because of missed dividends. For example, the preferred stockholders may possibly receive voting rights if their dividends have been missed two consecutive times. Some other preferred stock characteristics include the following:

* Preference as to dividends
* Accumulation of dividends
* Participation in excess of stated dividend rate
* Convertibility into common stock
* Callability by the corporation
* Redemption at future maturity date (see the previous discussion of redeemable preferred stock)
* Preference in liquidation

Preference as to Dividends   When preferred stock has a preference as to dividends, the current year's preferred dividend must be paid before a dividend can be paid to common stockholders. For par-value (or stated value) stock, the dividend rate is usually stated as a percentage of par. For example, if the dividend rate were 6% and the par were $100 per share, then the dividend per share would be $6. For no-par stock, if the dividend rate is stated as $5, then each share should receive $5 if a dividend is paid. A preference as to dividends does not guarantee that a preferred dividend will be paid in a given year. The Board of Directors must declare a dividend before a dividend is paid. The lack of a fixed commitment to pay dividends and the lack of a due date on the principal are the primary reasons that many firms elect to issue preferred stock instead of bonds. Preferred stock usually represents an expensive source of funds, compared to bonds. The preferred stock dividends are not tax deductible, while interest on bonds is deductible.

Accumulation of Dividends   If the Board of Directors does not declare dividends in a particular year, a holder of noncumulative preferred stock will never be paid that dividend. To make the preferred stock more attractive to investors, a corporation typically issues cumulative preferred stock. If a corporation fails to declare the usual dividend on the cumulative preferred stock, the amount of passed dividends becomes **dividends in arrears**. Common stockholders cannot be paid any dividends until the preferred dividends in arrears and the current preferred dividends are paid.

To illustrate dividends in arrears, assume a corporation has outstanding 10,000 shares of 8%, $100 par cumulative preferred stock. If dividends are not declared in 2001 and 2002, but are declared in 2003, the preferred stockholders would be entitled to dividends in arrears of $160,000 and current dividends in 2003 of $80,000 before any dividends could be paid to common stockholders.

Participation in Excess of Stated Dividend Rate   When preferred stock is participating, preferred stockholders may receive an extra dividend beyond the stated dividend rate. The terms of the participation depend on the terms included with the stock certificate. For example, the terms may state that any dividend to common stockholders over $10 per share will also be given to preferred stockholders.

To illustrate participating preferred stock, assume that a corporation has 8%, $100 par preferred stock. The terms of the participation are that any dividend paid on common shares over $10 per share will also be paid to preferred stockholders. For the current year, a dividend of $12 per share is declared on the common stock. Therefore, a dividend of $10 must be paid per share of preferred stock for the current year: (8% × $100) + $2.00 = $10.00.

Convertibility into Common Stock   Convertible preferred stock contains a provision that allows the preferred stockholders, at their option, to convert the share of preferred stock at a specific exchange ratio into another security of the corporation. The other security is almost always common stock. The conversion feature is very attractive to investors. For example, the terms may be that each share of preferred stock can be converted to four shares of common stock.

Convertible preferred stock is similar to a convertible bond, except that there are no fixed payout commitments with the convertible preferred stock. The preferred dividend need not be declared, and the preferred stock does not have a due date. The major reason for issuing convertible preferred stock is similar to that for issuing convertible bonds: If the current common stock price is low, in the opinion of management, and the firm eventually wants to increase its common equity, then the firm can raise more money for a given number of common shares by first issuing convertible preferred stock.

A firm usually prefers to issue convertible bonds rather than convertible preferred stock if its capital structure can carry more debt without taking on too much risk. The interest on the convertible bond is tax deductible while the dividend on the preferred stock is not.

Callability by the Corporation   Callable preferred stock may be retired (recalled) by the corporation at its option. The call price is part of the original stock contract. When the preferred stock is also cumulative, the call terms normally require payment of dividends in arrears before the call is executed.

The call provision favors the company because the company decides when to call. Investors do not like call provisions. Therefore, to make a security that has a call provision marketable, the call provision can normally not be exercised for a given number of years. For example, callable preferred stock issued in 2001 may have a provision that the call option cannot be exercised prior to 2011.

Preference in Liquidation   Should the corporation liquidate, the preferred stockholders normally have priority over common stockholders for settlement of claims. However, the claims of preferred stockholders are secondary to the claims of creditors, including bondholders.

Preference in liquidation for preferred stock over common stock is not usually considered to be an important provision. This is because often, in liquidation, funds are not sufficient to pay claims of preferred stock. Even creditors may receive only a few cents on the dollar in satisfaction of their claims.

Disclosures   Preferred stock may carry various combinations of provisions. The provisions of each preferred stock issue should be disclosed either parenthetically in the stockholders' equity section of the balance sheet or in a footnote. A company may have various preferred stock issues, each with different provisions. Preferred stock is illustrated in Exhibit 3-20.

Donated Capital

Donated capital may be included in the paid-in capital. Capital is donated to the company by stockholders, creditors, or other parties (such as a city). For example, a city may offer land to a company as an inducement to locate a factory there to increase the level of employment. The firm records the donated land at the appraised amount and records an equal amount as donated capital in stockholders' equity.

| EXHIBIT 3-20 | **CHIQUITA BRANDS INTERNATIONAL—2001 ANNUAL REPORT**
Preferred Stock |

Consolidated Balance Sheet (in Part)

	December 31, 2001	2000
(In thousands, except share amounts)	**2001**	**2000**
Shareholders' equity		
Preferred and preference stock	$ 139,729	$ 253,475
Common stock, $.01 par value		
(78,273,183 and 66,705,622 shares outstanding, respectively)	783	667
Capital surplus	881,192	766,217
Accumulated deficit	(530,068)	(411,300)
Accumulated other comprehensive loss	(43,042)	(26,516)
Total shareholders' equity	$ 448,594	$ 582,543

Notes to Consolidated Financial Statements (in Part)

Note 12—Shareholders' Equity (in Part)

At December 31, 2001, three series of Old Preferred Stock were outstanding, each series having the number of shares outstanding as set forth in the table below. Each share of the outstanding series of Old Preferred Stock had a liquidation preference of $50.00, and had an annual dividend rate and was convertible at the holder's option into a number of shares of Old Common Stock as follows:

	Shares outstanding	Annual dividend rate	Holders' conversion rate
$2.875 Non-Voting Cumulative Preferred Stock, Series A	1,653,930	$2.875	2.6316
$3.75 Convertible Preferred Stock, Series B	1,168,700	3.750	3.3333
$2.50 Convertible Preference Stock, Series C	75,650	2.500	2.9220

The Series A and Series B shares were non-voting. The Series C shares had one vote per share, voting with the common stock. If the Company failed to pay quarterly dividends on Series A, B and C shares for six quarters, the holders of such shares, voting as a class, had the right to elect two directors in addition to the regular directors. In the fourth quarter of 2000, the Company discontinued payment of dividends on its Old Preferred Stock, and accordingly, the Company has five quarters of accumulated and unpaid dividends at December 31, 2001. The following table sets forth the accumulated dividend arrearage on Old Preferred Stock at December 31, 2001:

	Total arrearage
$2.875 Non-Voting Cumulative Preferred Stock, Series A	$5.9 million
$3.75 Convertible Preferred Stock, Series B	5.5 million
$2.50 Convertible Preference Stock, Series C	0.2 million

Pursuant to the Plan of Reorganization, all rights with respect to such dividend arrearages have been cancelled.

At December 31, 2001, each Series A share was convertible at the Company's option into a number of shares of common stock (not exceeding 10 shares) having a total market value of $50.00.

At December 31, 2001, each Series C share was convertible at the Company's option into a number of shares of common stock (not exceeding 10 shares) having a total market value of $50.75.

Another example would be a company that needs to increase its available cash. A plan is devised, calling for existing common stockholders to donate a percentage of their stock to the company. When the stock is sold, the proceeds are added to the cash account, and the donated capital in stockholders' equity is increased. Exhibit 3-21 illustrates the presentation of donated capital by Lands' End.

EXHIBIT 3-21 **LANDS' END, INC. AND SUBSIDIARIES—2002 ANNUAL REPORT**
Donated Capital

Consolidated Balance Sheets (in Part)		
(In thousands)	February 1, 2002	January 26, 2001
Shareholders' investment		
Common stock, 40,221 shares issued	$ 402	$ 402
Donated capital	8,400	8,400
Additional paid-in capital	39,568	31,908
Deferred compensation	(56)	(121)
Accumulated other comprehensive income	3,343	5,974
Retained earnings	556,003	489,087
Treasury stock, 10,236 and 10,945 shares at cost, respectively	(206,942)	(221,462)
Total shareholders' investment	$ 400,718	$ 314,188

Retained Earnings

Retained earnings are the undistributed earnings of the corporation—that is, the net income for all past periods minus the dividends (both cash and stock) that have been declared. Retained earnings, cash dividends, and stock dividends are reviewed in more detail in Chapter 4. Exhibit 3-21 illustrates the presentation of retained earnings.

Quasi-Reorganization

A **quasi-reorganization** is an accounting procedure equivalent to an accounting fresh start. A company with a deficit balance in retained earnings "starts over" with a zero balance rather than a deficit. A quasi-reorganization involves the reclassification of a deficit in retained earnings. It removes the deficit and an equal amount from paid-in capital. A quasi-reorganization may also include a restatement of the carrying values of assets and liabilities to reflect current values.

When a quasi-reorganization is performed, the retained earnings should be dated as of the readjustment date and disclosed in the financial statements for a period of five to ten years. Exhibit 3-22 illustrates a quasi-reorganization of Exco Resources.

Accumulated Other Comprehensive Income

Conceptually, **accumulated other comprehensive income** represents retained earnings from other comprehensive income. In addition to the aggregate amount, companies are required to disclose the separate categories that make up accumulated other comprehensive income. The disclosure of the separate components can be made on the face of the balance sheet, in the statement of stockholders' equity, or in the footnotes. Chapter 4 covers comprehensive income. Exhibit 3-21 illustrates the presentation of accumulated other comprehensive income.

Equity-Oriented Deferred Compensation

Equity-oriented deferred compensation arrangements encompass a wide variety of plans. The deferred compensation element of an equity-based deferred compensation arrangement is the amount of compensation cost deferred and amortized (expensed) to future periods as the services are provided.

If stock is issued in a plan before some or all of the services are performed, the unearned compensation should be shown as a reduction to stockholders' equity. This unearned compensation amount should be accounted for as an expense of future period(s) as services are performed. Thus,

EXHIBIT 3-22

EXCO RESOURCES, INC.—1998 ANNUAL REPORT
Quasi-Reorganization

Balance Sheet (in Part)

(In thousands)	December 31, 1997	1998
Stockholders' equity		
Preferred stock, $.01 par value		
Authorized shares—10,000,000		
Outstanding shares—none	—	—
Common stock, $.02 par value		
Authorized shares—25,000,000		
Issued and outstanding shares—502,650 and		
6,687,696 at December 31, 1997 and 1998, respectively	10	134
Additional paid-in capital	9,716	46,241
Notes receivable—officers		(825)
Deficit eliminated	(8,799)	(8,799)
Retained earnings (deficit), as adjusted for		
quasi-reorganization at December 31, 1997	—	(511)
Total stockholders' equity	$ 927	$36,240

Notes (in Part)

Quasi-Reorganization

Effective December 31, 1997, we effected a quasi-reorganization by applying approximately $8.8 million of our additional paid-in capital account to eliminate our accumulated deficit. Our board of directors decided to effect a quasi-reorganization given the change in management, the infusion of new equity capital and increase in activities. Our accumulated deficit was primarily related to past operations and properties that have been disposed of. We did not adjust the historical carrying values of our assets and liabilities in connection with the quasi-reorganization.

the unearned compensation amount is removed from stockholders' equity (amortized) and is recognized as an expense in future periods.

When a plan involves the potential issuance of only stock, then the unearned compensation is shown as a reduction in stockholders' equity, and the offsetting amount is also in the stockholders' equity section. If the plan involves cash or a subsequent election of either cash or stock, the unearned compensation appears as a reduction in stockholders' equity, and the offsetting amount appears as a liability.

Exhibit 3-23 illustrates an equity-oriented deferred compensation plan for AMP. It is apparently a stock-only plan. The deferred compensation will be amortized to expense over subsequent periods.

Employee Stock Ownership Plans (ESOPs)

An **ESOP** is a qualified stock-bonus, or combination stock-bonus and money-purchase pension plan, designed to invest primarily in the employer's securities. A qualified plan must satisfy certain requirements of the Internal Revenue Code. An ESOP must be a permanent trusteed plan for the exclusive benefit of the employees.

The trust that is part of the plan is exempt from tax on its income, and the employer/sponsor gets a current deduction for contributions to the plan. The plan participants become eligible for favorable taxation of distributions from the plan.

An ESOP may borrow the funds necessary to purchase the employer stock. These funds may be borrowed from the company, its stockholders, or a third party such as a bank. The company can guarantee the loan to the ESOP. Financial leverage—the ability of the ESOP to borrow in order to buy employer securities—is an important aspect.

EXHIBIT 3-23	**AMP—1998 ANNUAL REPORT**

Equity-Oriented Deferred Compensation

(Dollars in thousands)	December 31, 1998	December 31, 1997
Shareholders' Equity:		
Common stock, without par value—Authorized 700,000,000 shares, issued 232,496,129 shares	$ 81,912	$ 81,670
Other capital	91,872	91,575
Deferred compensation	(19,752)	(11,169)
Cumulative other comprehensive income	17,204	18,606
Retained earnings	2,706,614	2,940,488
Treasury stock, at cost	(213,512)	(177,735)
Total shareholders' equity	$2,664,338	$2,943,435

The Internal Revenue Code favors borrowing for an ESOP. Commercial lending institutions, insurance companies, and mutual funds are permitted an exclusion from income for 50% of the interest received on loans used to finance an ESOP's acquisition of company stock. Thus, these institutions are willing to charge a reduced rate of interest for the loan.

From a company's perspective, there are advantages and disadvantages to an ESOP. One advantage is that an ESOP serves as a source of funds for expansion at a reasonable rate. Other possible advantages follow:

1. A means to buy the stock from a major shareholder or possibly an unwanted shareholder.
2. Help financing a leveraged buyout.
3. Reduction of potential of an unfriendly takeover.
4. Help in creating a market for the company's stock.

Some firms do not find an ESOP attractive, because it can result in a significant amount of voting stock in the hands of their employees. Existing stockholders may not find an ESOP desirable because it will probably dilute their proportional ownership.

The employer contribution to an ESOP reduces cash, and an unearned compensation item decreases stockholders' equity. The unearned compensation is amortized on the income statement in subsequent periods. When an ESOP borrows funds and the firm (in either an informal or formal guarantee) commits to future contributions to the ESOP to meet the debt-service requirements, then the firm records this commitment as a liability and as a deferred compensation deduction within stockholders' equity. As the debt is liquidated, the liability and deferred compensation are reduced.

Exhibit 3-24 shows the reporting of the ESOP of Hershey Foods.

Treasury Stock

A firm creates treasury stock when it repurchases its own stock and does not retire it. Since treasury stock lowers the stock outstanding, it is subtracted from stockholders' equity. Treasury stock is, in essence, a reduction in paid-in capital.

A firm may record treasury stock in two ways. One method records the treasury stock at par or stated value, referred to as the par value method of recording treasury stock. This method removes the paid-in capital in excess of par (or stated value) from the original issue. The treasury stock appears as a reduction of paid-in capital.

The other method, referred to as the *cost method*, records treasury stock at the cost of the stock (presented as a reduction of stockholders' equity). Most firms record treasury stock at cost.

Exhibit 3-25 illustrates the presentation of treasury stock for Hooper Holmes, Inc. Note that a firm cannot record gains or losses from dealing in its own stock. Any apparent gains or losses related to treasury stock must impact stockholders' equity, such as a reduction in retained earnings.

EXHIBIT 3-24   **HERSHEY FOODS CORPORATION—2001 ANNUAL REPORT**
Employee Stock Ownership Plan (ESOP)

	December 31	
(In thousands of dollars)	2001	2000
Stockholders' equity:		
Preferred stock, shares issued: none in 2001 and 2000	—	—
Common stock, shares issued: 149,517,064 in 2001 and 149,509,014 in 2000	$ 149,516	$ 149,508
Class B common stock, shares issued: 30,433,808 in 2001 and 30,441,858 in 2000	30,434	30,442
Additional paid-in capital	3,263	13,124
Unearned ESOP compensation	(15,967)	(19,161)
Retained earnings	2,755,333	2,702,927
Treasury—common stock shares, at cost: 44,311,870 in 2001 and 43,669,284 in 2000	(1,689,243)	(1,645,088)
Accumulated other comprehensive loss	(86,132)	(56,716)
Total stockholders' equity	1,147,204	1,175,036
Total liabilities and stockholders' equity	$ 3,247,430	$ 3,447,764

Notes to Consolidated Financial Statements (in Part)
13. EMPLOYEE STOCK OWNERSHIP TRUST

The Corporation's employee stock ownership trust ("ESOP") serves as the primary vehicle for contributions to its existing Employee Savings Stock Investment and Ownership Plan for participating domestic salaried and hourly employees. The ESOP was funded by a 15-year 7.75% loan of $47.9 million from the Corporation. During 2001 and 2000, the ESOP received a combination of dividends on unallocated shares and contributions from the Corporation equal to the amount required to meet its principal and interest payments under the loan. Simultaneously, the ESOP allocated to participants 159,176 shares of Common Stock each year. As of December 31, 2001, the ESOP held 1,139,966 allocated shares and 795,872 unallocated shares. All ESOP shares are considered outstanding for income per share computations.

The Corporation recognized net compensation expense equal to the shares allocated multiplied by the original cost of $20.06 per share less dividends received by the ESOP on unallocated shares. Compensation expense related to the ESOP for 2001, 2000 and 1999 was $1.6 million, $3.2 million and $1.6 million, respectively. Dividends paid on unallocated ESOP shares for 2001, 2000 and 1999 were $1.0 million, $1.1 million and $1.2 million, respectively. Dividends paid on all ESOP shares are recorded as a reduction to retained earnings. The unearned ESOP compensation balance in stockholders' equity represented deferred compensation expense to be recognized by the Corporation in future years as additional shares are allocated to participants.

Stockholders' Equity in Unincorporated Firms

These firms do not have stockholders. Stockholders' equity in an unincorporated firm is termed capital. The amount invested by the owner plus the retained earnings may be shown as one sum. A sole proprietorship form of business has only one owner (one capital account). A partnership form of business has more than one owner (capital account for each owner). Chapter 2 reviewed these forms of business.

STATEMENT OF STOCKHOLDERS' EQUITY   Firms are required to present reconciliations of the beginning and ending balances of their stockholder accounts. This is accomplished by presenting a "statement of stockholders' equity."

This statement will include all of the stockholders' equity accounts. It is important when performing analysis to be aware of changes in these accounts. For example, common stock will indicate changes in common stock, retained earnings will indicate changes in retained earnings, and treasury stock will indicate changes in treasury stock. This statement is illustrated in Chapter 4.

For many firms, changes to the account accumulated other comprehensive income (loss) will be important to observe. This account is related to comprehensive income, which is covered in Chapter 4.

EXHIBIT 3-25 **HOOPER HOLMES, INC.—2001 ANNUAL REPORT**
Treasury Stock

| | December 31, | |
	2001	2000
Stockholders' equity:		
Common stock, par value $.04 per share; authorized 240,000,000 shares, issued 67,499,074 in 2001 and 67,454,174 in 2000	$ 2,699,963	$ 2,698,167
Additional paid-in capital	134,482,010	135,419,195
Unrealized gains on marketable securities	201,589	—
Retained earnings	84,308,815	71,009,995
	221,692,377	209,127,357
Less: Treasury stock at cost (2,949,459 shares in 2001 and 1,993,564 shares in 2000)	25,285,503	18,050,736
Total stockholders' equity	$196,406,874	$191,076,621

PROBLEMS IN BALANCE SHEET PRESENTATION

Numerous problems inherent in balance sheet presentation may cause difficulty in analysis. First, many assets are valued at cost, so one cannot determine the market value or replacement cost of many assets and should not assume that their balance sheet amount approximates current valuation.

Second, varying methods are used for asset valuation. For example, inventories may be valued differently from firm to firm and, within a firm, from product to product. Similar problems exist with long-term asset valuation and the related depreciation alternatives.

A different type of problem exists in that not all items of value to the firm are included as assets. For example, such characteristics as good employees, outstanding management, and a well-chosen location do not appear on the balance sheet. In the same vein, liabilities related to contingencies also may not appear on the balance sheet. Chapters 6 and 7 present many of the problems of the balance sheet.

These problems do not make statement analysis impossible. They merely require that qualitative judgment be applied to quantitative data in order to assess the impact of these problem areas.

SUMMARY

The balance sheet shows the financial condition of an accounting entity as of a particular date. It is the most basic financial statement, and it is read by various users as part of their decision-making process.

To the Net

1. Go to the SEC site (http://www.sec.gov). Under Filings & Forms (Edgar), click on "Search for Company Filings." Click on Search Companies and Filings." Under Company name enter "Cooper Tire." Select the 10-K405 filed March 3, 2002.
   a. What is the total stockholders' equity at December 31, 2001?
   b. What is the cost of treasury shares at December 31, 2001?
   c. Why is treasury stock subtracted from stockholders' equity?

2. Go to the SEC site (http://www.sec.gov). Under Filings & Forms (Edgar), click on "Search for Company Filings." Click on "Search Companies and Filings." Under Company name enter "Reebok." Select the 10-K405 filed March 27, 2002.
   a. What is the total current assets at December 31, 2001?
   b. What is the net intangibles at December 31, 2001?
   c. Why are intangibles amortized?

3.   Go to the SEC site (http://www.sec.gov). Under Filings & Forms (Edgar), click on "Search for Company Filings." Click on "Search Companies and Filings." Under Company name enter "Gap Inc." Select the 10-K filed April 2, 2002.
    a.   What is the balance in retained earnings at February 2, 2002?
    b.   In what balance sheet accounts is retained earnings?

Questions

Q 3-1.   Name and describe the three major categories of balance sheet accounts.

Q 3-2.   Are the following balance sheet items (A) assets, (L) liabilities, or (E) stockholders' equity?

a. Cash dividends payable	k. Retained earnings
b. Mortgage notes payable	l. Donated capital
c. Investments in stock	m. Accounts receivable
d. Cash	n. Taxes payable
e. Land	o. Accounts payable
f. Inventory	p. Organizational costs
g. Unearned rent	q. Prepaid expenses
h. Marketable securities	r. Goodwill
i. Patents	s. Tools
j. Capital stock	t. Buildings

Q 3-3.   Classify the following as (CA) current asset, (IV) investments, (IA) intangible asset, or (TA) tangible asset:

a. Land	g. Tools
b. Cash	h. Prepaids
c. Copyrights	i. Buildings
d. Marketable securities	j. Accounts receivable
e. Goodwill	k. Long-term investment in stock
f. Inventories	l. Machinery

Q 3-4.   Usually current assets are listed in a specific order, starting with cash. What is the objective of this order of listing?

Q 3-5.   Differentiate between marketable securities and long-term investments. What is the purpose of owning each?

Q 3-6.   Differentiate between accounts receivable and accounts payable.

Q 3-7.   What types of inventory will a retailing firm have? A manufacturing firm?

Q 3-8.   What is depreciation? Which tangible assets are depreciated and which are not? Why?

Q 3-9.   For reporting purposes, management prefers higher profits; for tax purposes, lower taxable income is desired. To meet these goals, firms often use different methods of depreciation for tax and reporting purposes. Which depreciation method is best for reporting and which for tax purposes? Why?

Q 3-10.   A rental agency collects rent in advance. Why is the rent collected treated as a liability?

Q 3-11.   A bond carries a stated rate of interest of 6% and par of $1,000. It matures in 20 years. It is sold at 83 (83% of $1,000, or $830).
    a.   Under normal conditions, why would the bond sell at less than par?
    b.   How would the discount be disclosed on the statements?

Q 3-12.   To be conservative, how should minority interest on the balance sheet be handled for primary analysis?

Q 3-13.   Many assets are presented at historical cost. Why does this accounting principle cause difficulties in financial statement analysis?

Q 3-14.   Explain how the issuance of a convertible bond can be a very attractive means of raising common equity funds.

Q 3-15.   Classify each of the following as a (CA) current asset, (NA) noncurrent asset, (CL) current liability, (NL) noncurrent liability, or (E) equity account. Choose the best or most frequently used classification.

a.	Supplies	k.	Wages payable
b.	Notes receivable	l.	Mortgage bonds payable
c.	Unearned subscription revenue	m.	Unearned interest
d.	Accounts payable	n.	Marketable securities
e.	Retained earnings	o.	Paid-in capital from sale of treasury stock
f.	Accounts receivable	p.	Land
g.	Preferred stock	q.	Inventories
h.	Plant	r.	Taxes accrued
i.	Prepaid rent	s.	Cash
j.	Capital		

Q 3-16.   Explain these preferred stock characteristics:
a.   Accumulation of dividends
b.   Participation in excess of stated dividend rate
c.   Convertibility into common stock
d.   Callability by the corporation
e.   Preference in liquidation

Q 3-17.   Describe the account "unrealized exchange gains or losses."

Q 3-18.   What is treasury stock? Why is it deducted from stockholders' equity?

Q 3-19.   A firm, with no opening inventory, buys 10 units at $6 each during the period. In which accounts might the $60 appear on the financial statements?

Q 3-20.   How is an unconsolidated subsidiary presented on a balance sheet?

Q 3-21.   When would minority interest be presented on a balance sheet?

Q 3-22.   DeLand Company owns 100% of Little Florida, Inc. Will DeLand Company show a minority interest on its balance sheet? Would the answer change if it owned only 60%? Will there ever be a case in which the subsidiary, Little Florida, is not consolidated?

Q 3-23.   Describe the item "unrealized decline in market value of noncurrent equity investments."

Q 3-24.   What is redeemable preferred stock? Why should it be included with debt for purposes of financial statement analysis?

Q 3-25.   Describe donated capital.

Q 3-26.   Assume that a city donated land to a company. What accounts would be affected by this donation, and what would be the value?

Q 3-27.   Describe quasi-reorganization.

Q 3-28.   Assume that an equity-oriented deferred compensation plan involves cash or a subsequent election of either cash or stock. Describe the presentation of this plan on the balance sheet.

Q 3-29.   Describe employee stock ownership plans (ESOPs).

Q 3-30.   Why are commercial lending institutions, insurance companies, and mutual funds willing to grant loans to an employee stock ownership plan at favorable rates?

Q 3-31.   What are some possible disadvantages of an employee stock ownership plan?

Q 3-32.   How does a company recognize, in an informal or formal way, that it has guaranteed commitments to future contributions to an ESOP to meet debt-service requirements?

Q 3-33.   Describe depreciation, amortization, and depletion. How do they differ?

Q 3-34.   What are the three factors usually considered when computing depreciation?

Q 3-35.   An accelerated system of depreciation is often used for income tax purposes but not for financial reporting. Why?

Q 3-36.   Which depreciation method will result in the most depreciation over the life of an asset?

Q 3-37.   Should depreciation be recognized on a building in a year in which the cost of replacing the building rises? Explain.

Q 3-38.   Describe the account "accumulated other comprehensive income."

Problems

P 3-1.   The following information was obtained from the accounts of Airlines International dated December 31, 2003. It is presented in alphabetical order.

Accounts payable	$ 77,916
Accounts receivable	67,551
Accrued expenses	23,952
Accumulated depreciation	220,541
Allowance for doubtful accounts	248
Capital in excess of par	72,913
Cash	28,837
Common stock (par $0.50, authorized 20,000 shares, issued 14,304 shares)	7,152
Current installments of long-term debt	36,875
Deferred income tax liability (long term)	42,070
Inventory	16,643
Investments and special funds	11,901
Long-term debt, less current portion	393,808
Marketable securities	10,042
Other assets	727
Prepaid expenses	3,963
Property, plant, and equipment at cost	809,980
Retained earnings	67,361
Unearned transportation revenue (airline tickets expiring within one year)	6,808

Required   Prepare a classified balance sheet in report form.

P 3-2.   The following information was obtained from the accounts of Lukes, Inc. as of December 31, 2003. It is presented in scrambled order.

Common stock, no par value, 10,000 shares authorized, 5,724 shares issued	$ 3,180
Retained earnings	129,950
Deferred income tax liability (long term)	24,000
Long-term debt	99,870
Accounts payable	35,000
Buildings	75,000
Machinery and equipment	300,000
Land	11,000
Accumulated depreciation	200,000
Cash	3,000
Receivables, less allowance of $3,000	58,000
Accrued income taxes	3,000
Inventory	54,000
Other accrued expenses	8,000
Current portion of long-term debt	7,000
Prepaid expenses	2,000
Other assets (long term)	7,000

Required   Prepare a classified balance sheet in report form. For assets, use the classifications of current assets, plant and equipment, and other assets. For liabilities, use the classifications of current liabilities and long-term liabilities.

P 3-3.   The following information was obtained from the accounts of Alleg, Inc. as of December 31, 2003. It is presented in scrambled order.

Common stock, authorized 21,000 shares at $1 par value, issued 10,000 shares	$ 10,000
Additional paid-in capital	38,000
Cash	13,000
Marketable securities	17,000
Accounts receivable	26,000
Accounts payable	15,000
Current maturities of long-term debt	11,000
Mortgages payable	80,000
Bonds payable	70,000
Inventory	30,000
Land and buildings	57,000
Machinery and equipment	125,000
Goodwill	8,000
Patents	10,000
Other assets	50,000
Deferred income taxes (long-term liability)	18,000
Retained earnings	33,000
Accumulated depreciation	61,000

Required Prepare a classified balance sheet in report form. For assets, use the classifications of current assets, plant and equipment, intangibles, and other assets. For liabilities, use the classifications of current liabilities and long-term liabilities.

P 3-4. The following is the balance sheet of Ingram Industries.

INGRAM INDUSTRIES
Balance Sheet
June 30, 2003

Assets

Current assets:		
Cash (including $13,000 in sinking fund for bonds payable)	$ 70,000	
Marketable securities	23,400	
Investment in subsidiary company	23,000	
Accounts receivable	21,000	
Inventories (lower-of-cost-or-market)	117,000	$254,400
Plant assets:		
Land and buildings	$160,000	
Less: Accumulated depreciation	100,000	60,000
Investments:		
Treasury stock		4,000
Deferred charges:		
Discount on bonds payable	$ 6,000	
Prepaid expenses	2,000	8,000
		$326,400

Liabilities and Stockholders' Equity

Liabilities:			
Notes payable to bank		$ 60,000	
Accounts payable		18,000	
Bonds payable		61,000	
Total liabilities			$139,000
Stockholders' equity:			
Preferred and common (each $10 par, 5,000 shares preferred and 6,000 shares common)		$110,000	
Capital in excess of par		61,000	
Retained earnings, beginning of year	$11,400		
Net income	15,000		
Less: Dividends	10,000	16,400	187,400
Total liabilities and stockholders' equity			$326,400

Required | Indicate your criticisms of the balance sheet and briefly explain the proper treatment of any item criticized.

P 3-5. | The following is the balance sheet of Rubber Industries.

RUBBER INDUSTRIES
Balance Sheet
For the Year Ended December 31, 2003

Assets

Current assets:

Cash	$ 50,000
Marketable equity securities	19,000
Accounts receivable, net	60,000
Inventory	30,000
Treasury stock	20,000
Total current assets	$179,000

Plant assets:

Land and buildings, net	160,000

Investments:

Short-term U.S. notes	20,000

Other assets:

Supplies	4,000
Total assets	$363,000

Liabilities and Stockholders' Equity

Liabilities:

Bonds payable	$120,000
Accounts payable	40,000
Wages payable	10,000
Premium on bonds payable	3,000
Total liabilities	$173,000

Stockholders' equity:

Common stock ($20 par, 20,000 shares authorized, 6,000 shares outstanding)	120,000
Retained earnings	30,000
Minority interest	20,000
Redeemable preferred stock	20,000
Total liabilities and stockholders' equity	$363,000

Required | Indicate your criticisms of the balance sheet and briefly explain the proper treatment of any item criticized.

P 3-6. | The following is the balance sheet of McDonald Company.

McDONALD COMPANY
December 31, 2003

Assets

Current assets:

Cash (including $10,000 restricted for payment of note)	$ 40,000	
Marketable equity securities	20,000	
Accounts receivable, less allowance for doubtful accounts of $12,000	70,000	
Inventory	60,000	
Total current assets		$190,000

Plant assets:

Land	$ 40,000	
Buildings, net	100,000	
Equipment	$80,000	
Less: Accumulated depreciation	20,000	60,000
Patent		20,000
Organizational costs		15,000
		235,000

Other assets:

Prepaid insurance		5,000
Total assets		$430,000

Liabilities and Stockholders' Equity

Current liabilities:		
Accounts payable	$ 60,000	
Wages payable	10,000	
Notes payable, due July 1, 2006	20,000	
Bonds payable, due December 2013	100,000	
Total current liabilities		$190,000
Dividends payable		4,000
Deferred tax liability, long term		30,000
Stockholders' equity:		
Common stock ($10 par, 10,000 shares authorized, 5,000 shares outstanding)	$ 50,000	
Retained earnings	156,000	
Total stockholders' equity		206,000
Total liabilities and stockholders' equity		$430,000

Required   Indicate your criticisms of the balance sheet and briefly explain the proper treatment of any item criticized.

P 3-7.   You have just started as a staff auditor for a small CPA firm. During the course of the audit, you discover the following items related to a single client firm:
a.   During the year, the firm declared and paid $10,000 in dividends.
b.   Your client has been named defendant in a legal suit involving a material amount. You have received from the client's counsel a statement indicating little likelihood of loss.
c.   Because of cost control actions and general employee dissatisfaction, it is likely that the client will suffer a costly strike in the near future.
d.   Twenty days after closing, the client suffered a major fire in one of its plants.
e.   The cash account includes a substantial amount set aside for payment of pension obligations.
f.   Marketable securities include a large quantity of shares of stock purchased for control purposes.
g.   Land is listed on the balance sheet at its market value of $1,000,000. It cost $670,000 to purchase 12 years ago.
h.   During the year, the government of Uganda expropriated a plant located in that country. There was substantial loss.

Required   How would each of these items be reflected in the year-end balance sheet, including footnotes?

P 3-8.   Corvallis Corporation owns 80% of the stock of Little Harrisburg, Inc. At December 31, 2003, Little Harrisburg had the following summarized balance sheet:

LITTLE HARRISBURG, INC.
Balance Sheet
December 31, 2003

Current assets	$100,000	Current liabilities	$ 50,000
Property, plant, and		Long-term debt	150,000
equipment (net)	400,000	Capital stock	50,000
		Retained earnings	250,000
	$500,000		$500,000

The earnings of Little Harrisburg, Inc. for 2003 were $50,000 after tax.

Required   a.   What would be the amount of minority interest on the balance sheet of Corvallis Corporation? How should minority interest be classified for financial statement analysis purposes?
b.   What would be the minority share of earnings on the income statement of Corvallis Corporation?

P 3-9.   The Aggarwal Company has had 10,000 shares of 10%, $100 par-value preferred stock and 80,000 shares of $5 stated-value common stock outstanding for the last three years. During that period, dividends paid totaled $0, $200,000, and $220,000 for each year, respectively.

Required   Compute the amount of dividends that must have been paid to preferred stockholders and common stockholders in each of the three years, given the following four independent assumptions:
a.   Preferred stock is nonparticipating and cumulative.
b.   Preferred stock participates up to 12% of its par value and is cumulative.

    c.   Preferred stock is fully participating and cumulative.

    d.   Preferred stock is nonparticipating and noncumulative.

P 3-10. The Rosewell Company has had 5,000 shares of 9%, $100 par-value preferred stock and 10,000 shares of $10 par-value common stock outstanding for the last two years. During the most recent year, dividends paid totaled $65,000; in the prior year, dividends paid totaled $40,000.

Required Compute the amount of dividends that must have been paid to preferred stockholders and common stockholders in each year, given the following independent assumptions:

    a.   Preferred stock is fully participating and cumulative.

    b.   Preferred stock is nonparticipating and noncumulative.

    c.   Preferred stock participates up to 10% of its par value and is cumulative.

    d.   Preferred stock is nonparticipating and cumulative.

P 3-11. An item of equipment acquired on January 1 at a cost of $100,000 has an estimated life of 10 years.

Required Assuming that the equipment will have a salvage value of $10,000, determine the depreciation for each of the first three years by the:

    a.   Straight-line method

    b.   Declining-balance method

    c.   Sum-of-the-years'-digits method

P 3-12. An item of equipment acquired on January 1 at a cost of $60,000 has an estimated use of 25,000 hours. During the first three years, the equipment was used 5,000 hours, 6,000 hours, and 4,000 hours, respectively. The estimated salvage value of the equipment is $10,000.

Required Determine the depreciation for each of the three years, using the unit-of-production method.

P 3-13. An item of equipment acquired on January 1 at a cost of $50,000 has an estimated life of five years and an estimated salvage of $10,000.

Required
    a.   From a management perspective, from among the straight-line method, declining-balance method, and the sum-of-the-years'-digits method of depreciation, which method should be chosen for the financial statements if income is to be at a maximum the first year? Which method should be chosen for the income tax returns, assuming that the tax rate stays the same each year? Explain and show computations.

    b.   Is it permissible to use different depreciation methods in financial statements than those used in tax returns?

Case 3-1

Balance Sheet Review

The December 31, 1998 and 1997 consolidated balance sheets of Merck & Co., Inc. follow.

CONSOLIDATED BALANCE SHEET
Merck & Co., Inc. and Subsidiaries

December 31 ($ in millions)	1998	1997
Assets		
Current Assets		
Cash and cash equivalents	$ 2,606.2	$ 1,125.1
Short-term investments	749.5	1,184.2
Accounts receivable	3,374.1	2,876.7
Inventories	2,623.9	2,145.1
Prepaid expenses and taxes	874.8	881.9
Total current assets	10,228.5	8,213.0
Investments	3,607.7	2,533.4
Property, Plant and Equipment (at cost)		
Land	228.8	216.4
Buildings	3,664.0	3,257.8
Machinery, equipment and office furnishings	6,211.7	5,388.6
Construction in progress	1,782.1	1,169.8
	11,886.6	10,032.6
Less allowance for depreciation	4,042.8	3,423.2
	7,843.8	6,609.4
Goodwill and Other Intangibles (net of accumulated amortization of $1,123.9 million in 1998 and $815.8 million in 1997)	8,287.2	6,780.5
Other Assets	1,886.2	1,599.6
	$31,853.4	$25,735.9
Liabilities and Stockholders' Equity		
Current Liabilities		
Accounts payable and accrued liabilities	$ 3,682.1	$ 3,268.9
Loans payable and current portion of long-term debt	624.2	902.5
Income taxes payable	1,125.1	859.6
Dividends payable	637.4	537.6
Total current liabilities	6,068.8	5,568.6
Long-Term Debt	3,220.8	1,346.5
Deferred Income Taxes and Noncurrent Liabilities	6,057.0	5,060.1
Minority Interests	3,705.0	1,166.1
Stockholders' Equity		
Common stock, one cent par value		
Authorized—5,400,000,000 shares		
Issued— 2,967,851,980 shares	29.7	29.7
Other paid-in capital	5,614.5	5,224.3
Retained earnings	20,186.7	17,291.5
Accumulated other comprehensive (loss) income	(21.3)	9.0
	25,809.6	22,554.5
Less treasury stock, at cost		
607,399,428 shares—1998		
580,555,052 shares—1997	13,007.8	9,959.9
Total stockholders' equity	12,801.8	12,594.6
	$31,853.4	$25,735.9

NOTES TO CONSOLIDATED FINANCIAL STATEMENTS (in Part)

Merck & Co., Inc. and Subsidiaries
($ in millions except per share amounts)

1. **Nature of Operations**

   Merck is a global research-driven pharmaceutical company that discovers, develops, manufactures and markets a broad range of human and animal health products, directly and through its joint ventures, and provides pharmaceutical benefit services through Merck-Medco Managed Care (Merck-Medco). Human health products include therapeutic and preventive agents, generally sold by prescription, for the treatment of human disorders. Pharmaceutical benefit services primarily include managed prescription drug programs and programs to manage health and drug utilization.

   Merck sells its human health products and provides pharmaceutical benefit services to drug wholesalers and retailers, hospitals, clinics, government agencies, corporations, labor unions, retirement systems, insurance carriers, managed health care providers such as health maintenance organizations and other institutions.

2. **Summary of Accounting Policies (In Part)**

   Principles of Consolidation—The consolidated financial statements include the accounts of the Company and all of its subsidiaries in which a controlling interest is maintained. For those consolidated subsidiaries where Company ownership is less than 100%, the outside stockholders' interests are shown as Minority interests. Investments in affiliates over which the Company has significant influence but not a controlling interest are carried on the equity basis.

   Inventories—The majority of domestic inventories are valued at the lower of last-in, first-out (LIFO) cost or market. Remaining inventories are valued at the lower of first-in, first-out (FIFO) cost or market.

   Depreciation—Depreciation is provided over the estimated useful lives of the assets, principally using the straight-line method. For tax purposes, accelerated methods are used.

   Goodwill and Other Intangibles—Goodwill of $4.3 billion in 1998 and $3.6 billion in 1997 (net of accumulated amortization) represents the excess of acquisition costs over the fair value of net assets of businesses purchased and is amortized on a straight-line basis over periods up to 40 years. Other acquired intangibles principally include customer relationships of $2.7 billion in 1998 and $2.8 billion in 1997 (net of accumulated amortization) that arose in connection with the acquisition of Medco Containment Services, Inc. (renamed Merck-Medco Managed Care) and patent rights approximating $9 billion in 1998 (net of accumulated amortization) acquired as part of the restructuring of Astra Merck Inc. (AMI). (See Note 4.) These acquired intangibles are recorded at cost and are amortized on a straight-line basis over their estimated useful lives of up to 40 years. The Company reviews goodwill and other intangibles to assess recoverability from future operations using undiscounted cash flows. Impairments are recognized in operating results to the extent that carrying value exceeds fair value.

5. **Affiliates Accounted for Using the Equity Method**

   Investments in affiliates accounted for using the equity method are included in Other assets and were $1.1 billion at December 31, 1998 and $693.7 million at December 31, 1997. This increase primarily reflects the restructuring of the Company's investment in AMI into APLP, partially offset by the sale of the Company's one-half interest in DMPC. (See Notes 3 and 4.) Dividends and distributions received from these affiliates were $919.3 million in 1998, $791.0 million in 1997 and $476.2 million in 1996. Summarized information for these affiliates is as follows:

Years Ended December 31	**1998**	**1997**	**1996**
Sales	$7,095.6	$5,655.8	$4,441.4
Materials and production costs	2,191.1	1,349.3	959.4
Other expense, net	2,757.8	1,852.9	1,725.2
Income before taxes	2,146.7	2,453.6	1,756.8
December 31	**1998**	**1997**	
Current assets	$2,693.0	$2,475.9	
Noncurrent assets	2,036.6	2,824.0	
Current liabilities	2,280.2	1,920.1	
Noncurrent liabilities	281.4	699.8	

7. **Inventories**

Inventories at December 31 consisted of:

	1998	1997
Finished goods	$1,701.2	$1,230.6
Raw materials and work in process	851.6	849.7
Supplies	71.1	64.8
Total (approximates current cost)	2,623.9	2,145.1
Reduction to LIFO cost	—	—
	$2,623.9	$2,145.1

Inventories valued under the LIFO method comprised approximately 37% and 42% of inventories at December 31, 1998 and 1997, respectively.

Required
a. 1. The statement is entitled "Consolidated Balance Sheet." What does it mean to have a consolidated balance sheet?
   2. For subsidiaries (affiliates) where control is present, does Merck have 100% ownership? Explain.
   3. For subsidiaries (affiliates) where control is not present, have these investments been consolidated? Explain.
   4. For subsidiaries (affiliates) where control is not present, have assets of these affiliates been included on Merck's consolidated balance sheet? Explain.
b. 1. What are the gross receivables at December 31, 1998?
   2. What is the estimated amount that will be collected on receivables outstanding at December 31, 1998?
c. 1. What is the total amount of inventory at December 31, 1998?
   2. How much of the inventory was costed at LIFO at December 31, 1998?
   3. What proportion of the inventory was in finished goods at December 31, 1997 and 1998, respectively. Give your opinion as to this trend.
d. 1. What is the net property, plant, and equipment at December 31, 1998?
   2. What is the gross property, plant, and equipment at December 31, 1998?
   3. What depreciation method is used for financial reporting purposes?
   4. What depreciation method is used for tax purposes?
   5. Does it appear that property, plant, and equipment is relatively old? Explain.
e. What is the total amount of current assets at December 31, 1998?
f. 1. What is the gross amount for goodwill and other intangibles at December 31, 1998?
   2. What is the net amount for goodwill and other intangibles at December 31, 1998?
g. 1. Describe treasury stock.
   2. How many shares of treasury stock are held at December 31, 1998?
h. 1. How many common stock shares have been issued at December 31, 1998?
   2. How many common stock shares are outstanding at December 31, 1998?
i. 1. What is the total amount of assets at December 31, 1998?
   2. What is the total amount of liabilities at December 31, 1998?
   3. What is the amount of stockholders' equity at December 31, 1998?
   4. Demonstrate that the balance sheet balances at December 31, 1998.

Case 3-2	**Insight on Liabilities**

The September 30, 2001 and 2000 liabilities section of the Consolidated Balance Sheet for Florida Rock Industries, Inc. follow.

(Dollars in thousands)	2001	2000
Liabilities and Shareholders' Equity		
Current liabilities:		
Short-term notes payable to banks	$ —	$ 2,500
Accounts payable	42,583	40,624
Dividends payable	2,406	2,319
Federal and state income taxes	—	3,239
Accrued payroll and benefits	17,213	19,029
Accrued insurance reserves, current portion	2,678	3,191
Accrued liabilities, other	12,245	9,072
Long-term debt due within one year	9,145	743
Total current liabilities	86,270	80,717
Long-term debt	138,456	163,620
Deferred income taxes	55,298	34,074
Accrued employee benefits	16,788	14,765
Long-term accrued insurance reserves	7,258	8,591
Other accrued liabilities	4,852	8,329

Commitments and contingent liabilities (Notes 11, 15 and 16)

Required a. 1. The statement is entitled "Consolidated Balance Sheet." What does it mean to have a consolidated balance sheet?
2. Does it appear that the subsidiaries are wholly owned? Explain.
b. Describe deferred income taxes.
c. 1. Describe long-term debt.
2. Why is the current part of long-term debt disclosed under current liabilities?
d. Describe the following:
1. Accrued insurance reserves, current portion.
2. Long-term accrued insurance reserves.

Case 3-3	**Insight on Shareholders' Equity**

The 2001 annual report of Sears, Roebuck and Co. included shareholders' equity as follows:

CONSOLIDATED BALANCE SHEETS (in Part)

(millions, except per share data)	December 29, 2001	December 30, 2000
SHAREHOLDERS' EQUITY		
Common shares ($.75 per value per share, 1,000 shares authorized, 320.4 and 333.2 shares outstanding, respectively)	$ 323	$ 323
Capital in excess of par value	3,500	3,538
Retained earnings	7,413	6,979
Treasury stock—at cost	(4,223)	(3,726)
Deferred ESOP expense	(63)	(96)
Accumulated other comprehensive loss	(831)	(249)
Total Shareholders' equity	$ 6,119	$ 6,769

Required a. Describe the following accounts:
1. Shareholders' equity.
2. Capital in excess of par value.

3. Retained earnings.
4. Treasury stock—at cost.
5. Deferred ESOP expense.
b. Determine the number of shares of:
1. Common stock issued at December 29, 2001.
2. Common stock authorized at December 29, 2001.
c. 1. What is the dollar amount of shareholders' equity at December 29, 2001?
2. Would the dollar amount of shareholders' equity at December 29, 2001, equal the market value of the shareholders' equity at December 29, 2001? Explain.

Case 3-4

Insight on Assets

The December 31, 2001 and 2000 consolidated balance sheets of Barnes Group Inc. included the following assets.

(Dollars in thousands) December 31,	**2001**	**2000**
ASSETS		
Current assets:		
Cash and cash equivalents	$ 48,868	$ 23,303
Accounts receivable, less allowances (2001—$3,114; 2000—$2,720)	94,124	107,434
Inventories	85,721	88,514
Deferred income taxes	16,702	12,647
Prepaid expenses	11,120	9,450
Total current assets	256,535	241,348
Deferred income taxes	5,783	15,010
Property, plant and equipment	152,943	163,766
Goodwill	159,836	155,667
Other assets	61,408	61,150
Total assets	$636,505	$636,941

Notes to Consolidated Financial Statements (in Part)

(All dollar amounts included in the notes are stated in thousands except per share data and the tables in note 13.)

1. **Summary of Significant Accounting Policies (in Part)**
   General: The preparation of financial statements requires management to make estimates and assumptions that affect the reported amounts of assets and liabilities at the date of the financial statements and the reported amounts of revenues and expenses during the reporting period. Actual results could differ from those estimates.

   Certain reclassifications have been made to prior year amounts to conform to the current year presentation.

   Inventories: Inventories are valued at the lower of cost or market. The last-in, first-out (LIFO) method was used to accumulate the cost of the majority of U.S. inventories, which represent 77% of total inventories. The cost of all other inventories was determined using the first-in, first-out (FIFO) method.

   Property, plant and equipment: Property, plant and equipment is stated at cost. Depreciation is recorded over estimated useful lives, ranging from 20 to 50 years for buildings and three to 17 years for machinery and equipment. The straight-line method of depreciation was adopted for all property, plant and equipment placed in service after March 31, 1999. For property, plant and equipment placed into service prior to April 1, 1999, depreciation is calculated using accelerated methods. The change in accounting principle was made to reflect improvements in the design and durability of machinery and equipment. Management believes that the straight-line method results in a better matching of revenues and costs, and the new method is prevalent in the industries in which the Company operates.

3. **Inventories**

Inventories at December 31 consisted of:

	2001	2000
Finished goods	**$51,840**	$59,665
Work-in-process	**15,506**	13,605
Raw materials and supplies	**18,375**	15,244
	$85,721	$88,514

Inventories valued by the LIFO method aggregated $66,092 and $64,422 at December 31, 2001, and 2000, respectively. If LIFO inventories had been valued using the FIFO method, they would have been $13,135 and $13,283 higher at those dates.

4. **Property, Plant and Equipment**

Property, plant and equipment at December 31 consisted of:

	2001	2000
Land	**$ 4,046**	$ 4,181
Buildings	**74,191**	73,400
Machinery and equipment	**328,402**	322,738
	406,639	400,319
Less accumulated depreciation	**253,696**	236,553
	$152,943	$163,766

Depreciation expense was $30,008, $30,314 and $27,606 for 2001, 2000 and 1999, respectively.

Required   a.   The statement is entitled "Consolidated Balance Sheets." What does it mean to have a consolidated balance sheet?

b.   What is the estimated amount that will be collected from receivables at December 31, 2001?

c.   1.   What is the gross amount of property, plant, and equipment at December 31, 2001?
    2.   What is the net amount of property, plant, and equipment at December 31, 2001?
    3.   Describe the account Accumulated Depreciation.
    4.   What would be the accumulated depreciation to land at December 31, 2001?
    5.   Does it appear that property, plant, and equipment is relatively old at December 31, 2001?

d.   1.   What is the amount of total assets at December 31, 2001?
    2.   What is the amount of current assets at December 31, 2001?

e.   Assets are stated at their exact amounts as of December 31, 2001. Comment.

Case 3-5   Our Principal Asset Is Our People

Dana Corporation included the following in its 2001 financial report.

Foundation Business: Focused Excellence

Dana's foundation businesses are: axles, drive shafts, structures, brake and chassis products, fluid systems, filtration products, and bearing and sealing products.

These products hold strong market positions—number one or two in the markets they serve. They provide value-added manufacturing, are technically advanced, and each has features that are unique and patented.

Management Statement (in Part)

We believe people are Dana's most important asset. The proper selection, training and development of our people as a means of ensuring that effective internal controls are fair, uniform reporting are maintained as standard practice throughout the Company.

Required   a.   Dana states that "We believe people are Dana's most important asset." Currently, generally accepted accounting principles do not recognize people as an asset. Speculate on why people are not considered to be an asset.

b.   Speculate on what concept of an asset Dana is considering when they state "We believe people are Dana's most important asset."

Case 3-6	**Brands Are Dead?**

The September 1, 1993 issue of *Financial World* estimated that the brand value of Intel was $178 billion. *Financial World* arrived at this estimate using a valuation method developed by London-based Interbrand Group.

Required   a.   Define an asset.
b.   In your opinion, do brands represent a valuable asset? Comment.
c.   Under generally accepted accounting principles, should an internally generated brand value be recognized as an asset? Comment.
d.   If the brand was purchased, should it be recognized as an asset? Comment.

Case 3-7	**Advertising—Asset?**

The Big Car Company did substantial advertising in late December. The company's year-end date was December 31. The president of the firm was concerned that this advertising campaign would reduce profits.

Required   a.   Define an asset.
b.   Would the advertising represent an asset? Comment.

Web Case	# Thomson Analytics *Business School Edition*

Please complete the web case that covers material covered in this chapter at http://gibson.swlearning.com. You'll be using Thomson Analytics Business School Edition, a version of the powerful tool used by Wall Street professionals, that combines a full range of fundamental financial information, earnings estimates, market data, and source documents for 500 publicly traded companies.

Endnotes

1.   *Statement of Financial Accounting Concepts No. 6*, "Elements of Financial Statements" (Stamford, CT: Financial Accounting Standards Board, 1985), paragraph 25.
2.   *Accounting Trends & Techniques* (Jersey City, NJ: American Institute of Certified Public Accountants, 1998), p. 167.
3.   *Statement of Financial Accounting Standards No. 142*, Goodwill and Other Intangible Assets, issued June 1, 2001, represents the current standard relating to goodwill. Prior to this standard goodwill was amortized over a period of 40 years or less. SFAS No. 142 was required to be applied starting with fiscal years beginning after December 15, 2001.
4.   *Statement of Financial Accounting Concepts No. 6*, paragraph 35.
5.   *Statement of Financial Accounting Concepts No. 6*, paragraph 212.

INCOME STATEMENT

The income statement is often considered to be the most important financial statement. Frequently used titles for this statement include Statement of Income, Statement of Earnings, and Statement of Operations. This chapter covers the income statement in detail.

<table>
<tr><td>BASIC
ELEMENTS OF
THE INCOME
STATEMENT</td><td></td></tr>
</table>

An income statement summarizes revenues and expenses and gains and losses, and ends with the net income for a specific period. A multiple-step income statement usually presents separately the gross profit, operating income, income before income taxes, and net income.

A simplified multiple-step income statement might look as follows:

	Net Sales (Revenues)	$XXX
−	*Cost of Goods Sold (cost of sales)*	XXX
	Gross Profit	XXX
−	*Operating Expenses (selling and administrative)*	XXX
	Operating Income	XXX
+(−)	*Other Income or Expense*	XXX
	Income Before Income Taxes	XXX
−	*Income Taxes*	XXX
	Net Income	$XXX
	Earnings per Share	$XXX

Many firms use a single-step income statement, which totals revenues and gains (sales, other income, etc.) and then deducts total expenses and losses (cost of goods sold, operating expenses, other expenses, etc.). A simplified single-step income statement might look as follows:

Revenue:	
Net Sales	$XXX
Other Income	XXX
Total Revenue	XXX
Expenses:	
Cost of Goods Sold (cost of sales)	XXX
Operating Expenses (selling and administrative)	XXX
Other Expense	XXX
Income Tax Expense	XXX
Total Expenses	XXX
Net Income	$XXX
Earnings per Share	$XXX

A single-step income statement lists all revenues and gains (usually in order of amount), then lists all expenses and losses (usually in order of amount). Total expense and loss items deducted from total revenue and gain items determine the net income. Most firms that present a single-step income statement modify it in some way, such as presenting federal income tax expense as a separate item.

Exhibits 4-1 and 4-2 (pages 113 and 114) illustrate the different types of income statements. In Exhibit 4-1, Blair uses a single-step income statement, while in Exhibit 4-2, Sun Hydraulics® uses a multiple-step format.

For firms that have cost of goods sold, cost of goods manufactured, or cost of services, a multiple-step income statement should be used for analysis. The multiple-step provides intermediate profit figures useful in analysis. You may need to construct the multiple-step format from the single-step.

Exhibit 4-3 (page 115) contains a comprehensive multiple-step income statement illustration. This illustration resembles the vast majority of income statements as presented in the United States.

Net Sales (Revenues)

Sales (revenues) represent revenue from goods or services sold to customers. The firm earns revenue from the sale of its principal products. Sales are usually shown net of any discounts, returns, and allowances.

EXHIBIT 4-1	**BLAIR**

Consolidated Statements of Income

Single-Step Income Statement

	Year Ended December 31,		
	2001	**2000**	**1999**
Net sales	**$580,700,163**	$574,595,907	$522,197,334
Other income—Note 7	**47,766,066**	44,792,832	40,686,195
	628,466,229	619,388,739	562,883,529
Costs and expenses:			
Cost of goods sold	**285,923,186**	282,011,613	269,460,019
Advertising	**169,102,381**	140,860,571	134,892,301
General and administrative	**127,260,554**	125,458,465	109,340,500
Provision for doubtful accounts	**31,333,326**	35,932,526	22,468,075
Interest	**2,142,636**	1,835,120	2,557,945
	615,762,083	586,098,295	538,718,840
Income Before Income Taxes	**12,704,146**	33,290,444	24,164,689
Income taxes—Note 6	**3,412,000**	12,186,000	8,852,000
Net Income	**$ 9,292,146**	$ 21,104,444	$ 15,312,689
Basic and diluted earnings per share based on weighted average shares outstanding	**$1.17**	$2.63	$1.84

Notes to Consolidated Financial Statements (in Part)

7. OTHER INCOME			
Other income consists of:	**2001**	**2000**	**1999**
Finance charges on time payment accounts	**$ 37,791,524**	$ 37,270,749	$ 33,906,734
Commissions earned	**3,658,633**	3,246,282	2,936,178
Interest from tax settlement	**4,061,253**	-0-	-0-
Other items	**2,254,656**	4,275,801	3,843,283
	$ 47,766,066	$ 44,792,832	$ 40,686,195

Cost of Goods Sold (Cost of Sales)

This category shows the cost of goods sold to produce revenue. For a retailing firm, the cost of goods sold equals beginning inventory plus purchases minus ending inventory. In a manufacturing firm, the cost of goods manufactured replaces purchases since the goods are produced rather than purchased. A service firm will not have cost of goods sold or cost of sales, but it will often have cost of services.

Other Operating Revenue

Depending on the operations of the business, there may be other operating revenue, such as lease revenue and royalties.

Operating Expenses

Operating expenses consist of two types: selling and administrative. **Selling expenses,** resulting from the company's effort to create sales, include advertising, sales commissions, sales supplies used, and so on. **Administrative expenses** relate to the general administration of the company's

EXHIBIT 4-2

SUN HYDRAULICS® CORPORATION
Consolidated Statements of Operations

Multi-Step Income Statement

(in thousands except per share data)

For the Year Ended	December 29, 2001	December 30, 2000	January 1, 2000
Net sales	$64,983	$79,967	$70,449
Cost of sales	50,358	58,502	54,033
Gross profit	14,625	21,465	16,416
Selling, engineering, and administrative expenses	12,565	14,109	12,378
Operating income	2,060	7,356	4,038
Interest expense	878	1,114	954
Miscellaneous expense (income)	(130)	323	420
Income before income taxes	1,312	5,919	2,664
Income tax provision	362	1,998	833
Net income	$ 950	$ 3,921	$ 1,831
Basic net income per common share	$0.15	$0.61	$0.29
Weighted average basic shares outstanding	6,392	6,385	6,380
Diluted net income per common share	$0.14	$0.60	$0.28
Weighted average diluted shares outstanding	6,554	6,574	6,569

operation. They include office salaries, insurance, telephone, bad debt expense, and other costs difficult to allocate.

Other Income or Expense

In this category are secondary activities of the firm, not directly related to the operations. For example, if a manufacturing firm has a warehouse rented, this lease income would be other income. Dividend and interest income and gains and losses from the sale of assets are also included here. Interest expense is categorized as other expense.

SPECIAL INCOME STATEMENT ITEMS

To comprehend and analyze profits, you need to understand income statement items that require special disclosure. Exhibit 4-3 contains items that require special disclosure. These items are lettered to identify them for discussion. Note that some of these items are presented before tax and some are presented net of tax.

(A) Unusual or Infrequent Item Disclosed Separately

Certain income statement items are either unusual or occur infrequently. They might include such items as a gain on sale of securities, write-downs of receivables, or write-downs of inventory. These items are shown with normal, recurring revenues and expenses, and gains and losses. If material, they will be disclosed separately, before tax. Unusual or infrequent items are typically left in primary analysis because they relate to operations.

In supplementary analysis, unusual or infrequent items should be removed net after tax. Usually an estimate of the tax effect will be necessary. A reasonable estimate of the tax effect can be made by using the effective income tax rate, usually disclosed in a footnote, or by dividing income taxes by income before taxes.

Refer to Exhibit 4-4 (page 116), which illustrates an unusual or infrequent item disclosed separately for Arch Coal, Inc. The unusual or infrequent item was a write-down of impaired assets in 1999.

EXHIBIT 4-3   **ILLUSTRATION OF SPECIAL ITEMS**

G AND F COMPANY
Income Statement (Multiple-Step Format)
For the Year Ended December 31, 2002

Net sales			$ XXX
Cost of products sold			XXX
Gross profit			XXX
Other operating revenue			XXX
Operating expenses:			
Selling expenses		$ XXX	
General expenses		XXX	(XXX)
Operating income			XXX
Other income (includes interest income)			XXX
Other expenses (includes interest expense)			(XXX)
[A] Unusual or infrequent item disclosed separately [loss]			(XXX)
[B] Equity in earnings of nonconsolidated subsidiaries [loss]			XXX
Income before taxes			XXX
Income taxes related to operations			XXX
Net income from operations			XXX
[C] Discontinued operations:			
Income [loss] from operations of discontinued segment			
(less applicable income taxes of $XXX)		$(XXX)	
Income [loss] on disposal of division X (less applicable			
income taxes of $XXX)		(XXX)	(XXX)
[D] Extraordinary gain [loss] (less applicable income taxes of $XXX)			(XXX)
[E] Cumulative effect of change in accounting principle [loss]			
(less applicable income taxes of $XXX)			XXX
Net income before minority interest			$ XXX
[F] Minority share of earnings (income) loss			(XXX)
Net income			$ XXX
Earnings per share			$X.XX

The unusual or infrequent items in 1999 would be removed as follows:

Write-down of impaired assets	$364,579,000
Less estimated tax effect (15.80% × $364,579,000)	57,603,482
Write-down of impaired assets, net of tax	$306,975,518

Arch Coal, Inc. reported a loss before cumulative effect of accounting change of $350,093,000 in 1999. Removal of the write-down of impaired assets would reduce the loss to $43,117,482 ($350,093,000 – $306,975,518).

(B) Equity in Earnings of Nonconsolidated Subsidiaries

When a firm accounts for its investments in stocks using the equity method (the investment is not consolidated), the investor reports equity earnings (losses). **Equity earnings** (losses) are the investor's proportionate share of the investee's earnings (losses). If the investor owns 20% of the stock of the investee, for example, and the investee reports income of $100,000, then the investor reports $20,000 on its income statement. In this book, the term equity earnings will be used unless equity losses are specifically intended.

To the extent that equity earnings are not accompanied by cash dividends, the investor reports earnings greater than the cash flow from the investment. If an investor company reports material

EXHIBIT 4-4	**ARCH COAL, INC.**
	Consolidated Statements of Operations

Unusual or Infrequent Item

	Year Ended December 31,		
(in thousands of dollars except per share data)	**2001**	**2000**	**1999**
Revenues			
Coal sales	**$1,403,370**	$1,342,171	$1,509,596
Income from equity investment	**26,250**	12,837	11,129
Other revenues	**59,108**	49,613	46,657
	1,488,728	1,404,621	1,567,382
Costs and Expenses			
Cost of coal sales	**1,336,788**	1,237,378	1,426,105
Selling, general and administrative expenses	**43,834**	38,887	46,357
Amortization of coal supply agreements	**27,460**	39,803	36,532
Write-down of impaired assets	**—**	—	364,579
Other expenses	**18,190**	14,569	20,835
	1,426,272	1,330,637	1,894,408
Income (loss) from operations	**62,456**	73,984	(327,026)
Interest expense, net:			
Interest expense	**(64,211)**	(92,132)	(90,058)
Interest income	**4,264**	1,412	1,291
	(59,947)	(90,720)	(88,767)
Income (loss) before income taxes and cumulative effect of accounting change	**2,509**	(16,736)	(415,793)
Benefit from income taxes	**(4,700)**	(4,000)	(65,700)
Income (loss) before cumulative effect of accounting change	**7,209**	(12,736)	(350,093)
Cumulative effect of accounting change, net of taxes	**—**	—	3,813
Net Income (Loss)	**$ 7,209**	$ (12,736)	$ (346,280)
Basic and diluted earnings (loss) per common share:			
Income (loss) before cumulative effect of accounting change	**$.15**	$(.33)	$(9.12)
Cumulative effect of accounting change, net of taxes	**—**	—	.10
Basic and diluted earnings (loss) per common share	**$.15**	$(.33)	$(9.02)

equity earnings, its net income could be much greater than its ability to pay dividends or cover maturing liabilities.

For purposes of analysis, the equity in the net income of nonconsolidated subsidiaries raises practical problems. For example, the equity earnings represent earnings of other companies, not earnings from the operations of the business. Thus, equity earnings can distort the reported results of a business' operations. For each ratio influenced by equity earnings, this book suggests a recommended approach described when the ratio is introduced.

Refer to Exhibit 4-5, which illustrates equity in earnings of nonconsolidated subsidiaries for Dana. Leaving these accounts in the statements presents a problem for profitability analysis because most of the profitability measures relate income figures to other figures (usually balance sheet figures). Because these earnings are from nonconsolidated subsidiaries, an inconsistency can result between the numerator and the denominator when computing a ratio.

Some ratios are distorted more than others by equity earnings. (Chapter 5 presents a detailed discussion of ratios.) For example, the ratio that relates income to sales can be distorted because of equity earnings. The numerator of the ratio includes the earnings of the operating company and the equity earnings of nonconsolidated subsidiaries. The denominator (sales) includes only the sales of

EXHIBIT 4-5	**DANA CORPORATION**

Statement of Income

	Equity Income		
In millions except per share amounts	**Year Ended December 31,**		
	1999	**2000**	**2001**
Net sales	$13,159	$12,317	**$10,271**
Revenue from lease financing	111	143	**115**
Other income, net	83	231	**83**
	13,353	12,691	**10,469**
Costs and expenses			
Cost of sales	10,964	10,599	**9,268**
Selling, general and administrative expenses	1,192	1,132	**985**
Restructuring and integration changes	181	173	**390**
Interest expense	279	323	**309**
	12,616	12,227	**10,952**
Income (loss) before income taxes	737	464	**(483)**
Estimated taxes on income	251	171	**(161)**
Income (loss) before minority interest and equity in earnings of affiliates	486	293	**(322)**
Minority interest	(13)	(13)	**(8)**
Equity in earnings of affiliates	40	54	**32**
Net income (loss)	$ 513	$ 334	**$ (298)**
Net income (loss) per common share			
Basic income (loss) per share	$3.10	$2.20	**$(2.01)**
Diluted income (loss) per share	$3.08	$2.18	**$(2.01)**
Cash dividends declared and paid per common share	$1.24	$1.24	**$0.94**
Average shares outstanding—Basic	165	152	**148**
Average shares outstanding—Diluted	166	153	**148**

the operating company. The sales of the unconsolidated subsidiaries will not appear on the investor's income statement because the subsidiary was not consolidated. This causes the ratio to be distorted.

Equity in earnings of nonconsolidated subsidiaries (equity earnings) will be presented before tax. Any tax will be related to the dividend received, and it will typically be immaterial. When removing equity earnings for analysis, do not attempt a tax computation.

Income Taxes Related to Operations

Federal, state, and local income taxes, based on reported accounting profit, are shown here. Income tax expense includes taxes paid and taxes deferred. Income taxes reported here will not include taxes on items presented net of tax.

(C) Discontinued Operations

A common type of unusual item is the disposal of a business or product line. If the disposal meets the criteria of a discontinued operation, then a separate income statement category for the gain or loss from disposal of a segment of the business must be provided. In addition, the results of operations of the segment that has been or will be disposed of are reported in conjunction with the gain or loss on disposal. These effects appear as a separate category after continuing operations.

Discontinued operations pose a problem for profitability analysis. Ideally, income from continuing operations would be the better figure to use to project future income. Several practical problems associated with the removal of a gain or loss from the discontinued operations occur in the primary profitability analysis. These problems revolve around two points: (1) an inadequate disclosure of data related to the discontinued operations, in order to remove the balance sheet amounts associated with the discontinued operations; and (2) the lack of past profit and loss data associated with the discontinued operations.

Exhibit 4-6 illustrates the presentation of discontinued operations in net income. The best analysis would remove the income statement items that relate to the discontinued operations.

The income statement items that relate to a discontinued operation are always presented net of applicable income taxes. Therefore, the items as presented on the income statement can be removed for primary analysis without further adjustment for income taxes. Supplementary analysis considers discontinued operations in order to avoid disregarding these items.

Ideally, the balance sheet accounts that relate to the discontinued operations should be removed for primary analysis. Consider these items on a supplemental basis because they will not contribute to future operating revenue. However, inadequate disclosure often makes it impossible to remove these items from your analysis.

The balance sheet items related to discontinued operations are frequently disposed of when the business or product line has been disposed of prior to the year-end balance sheet date. In this case, the balance sheet accounts related to discontinued operations do not present a problem for the current year.

(D) Extraordinary Items

Extraordinary items are material events and transactions distinguished by their unusual nature and by the infrequency of their occurrence. Examples include a major casualty (such as a fire), prohibition under a newly enacted law, or an expropriation. These items, net of their tax effects, must be shown separately. Some pronouncements have specified items that must be considered extraordinary, including material tax loss carryovers and gains and losses from extinguishment of debt. The effect of an extraordinary item on earnings per share must also be shown separately. Exhibit 4-7 (page 120) presents an extraordinary loss on extinguishment of debt.

In analysis of income for purposes of determining a trend, extraordinary items should be eliminated since the extraordinary item is not expected to recur. In supplementary analysis, these extraordinary items should be considered, as this approach avoids disregarding these items.

Extraordinary items are always presented net of applicable income taxes. Therefore, the items as presented on the income statement are removed without further adjustment for income taxes.

(E) Cumulative Effect of Change in Accounting Principle

Some changes in accounting principles do not require retroactive adjustments to reflect the adoption of a new accounting principle. The new principle is used for the current year, while the prior years continue to be presented based on the prior accounting principle. This makes comparability a problem. The comparability problem is compounded by the additional reporting guideline that directs that the income effect of the change on prior years be reported net of tax as a cumulative effect of a change in accounting principle on the income statement in the year of change. The cumulative effect is shown separately on the income statement in the year of change. It is usually shown just above net income.

When there is a cumulative effect of a change in accounting principle, the reporting standards require that income before extraordinary items and net income, computed on a pro forma basis (as if the new principle had been in effect), should be shown on the face of the income statements for all periods as if the newly adopted accounting principle had been applied during all periods affected. The pro forma presentation is an additional presentation at the bottom of the income statement. In practice, this pro forma material is often not presented or only partially presented.

The accounting standard of not changing the statements retroactively is the general case when an accounting principle changes. APB Opinion No. 20, the basis of this reporting standard, provides for only a few exceptions. For most exceptions, the prior statements are retroactively changed using the new accounting principle. In the case when the cumulative effect cannot be determined, the firm should include a footnote explaining the change in accounting principle and the fact that the cumulative effect is not determinable.

EXHIBIT 4-6

AMEDISYS, INC. AND SUBSIDIARIES
Consolidated Statements of Operations

Discontinued Operations

For the Years Ended December 31, 2001, 2000 and 1999
(in 000s except share data)

	2001	2000	1999
Income:			
Net service revenues	$110,174	$88,155	$97,411
Cost of service revenues	49,046	41,468	46,890
Gross margin	61,128	46,687	50,521
General and Administrative Expenses:			
Salaries and benefits	30,495	29,038	30,089
Other	23,170	20,213	23,057
Total general and administrative expenses	53,665	49,251	53,146
Operating income (loss)	7,463	(2,564)	(2,625)
Other Income (Expense):			
Interest expense	(2,785)	(2,159)	(3,625)
Interest income	328	249	66
Miscellaneous	290	141	(1,160)
Total other expense	(2,167)	(1,769)	(4,719)
Income (Loss) Before Income Taxes, Discontinued Operations, and Extraordinary Item	5,296	(4,333)	(7,344)
Income Tax (Expense) Benefit (Note 8)	(220)	1,647	3,263
Income (loss) before discontinued operations and extraordinary item	5,076	(2,686)	(4,081)
Discontinued Operations:			
Loss from discontinued operations, net of income tax	(566)	(3,281)	(784)
Gain on dispositions, net of income tax	876	4,684	6,165
Extraordinary Item, Net of Income Tax	—	5,053	—
Net income	$ 5,386	$ 3,770	$ 1,300
Weighted Average Common Shares Outstanding—Basic (Note 1)	5,941,000	4,336,000	3,093,000
Basic Earnings per Common Share (Note 1):			
Income (loss) before discontinued operations and extraordinary item	$ 0.85	$(0.62)	$(1.32)
Loss from discontinued operations, net of income tax	(0.10)	(0.76)	(0.25)
Gain on dispositions of discontinued operations, net of income tax	0.15	1.08	1.99
Extraordinary item, net of income tax	—	1.17	—
Net income	$ 0.90	$ 0.87	$ 0.42
Weighted Average Common Shares Outstanding—Diluted (Note 1)	7,980,000	4,336,000	3,093,000
Diluted Earnings per Common Share (Note 1):			
Income (loss) before discontinued operations and extraordinary item	$ 0.64	$(0.62)	$(1.32)
Loss from discontinued operations, net of income tax	(0.07)	(0.76)	(0.25)
Gain on dispositions of discontinued operations, net of income tax	0.11	1.08	1.99
Extraordinary item, net of income tax	—	1.17	—
Net income	$ 0.68	$ 0.87	$ 0.42

| EXHIBIT 4-7 | **ARGOSY GAMING COMPANY**
Consolidated Statements of Income |

Extraordinary Gain (Loss)

(in thousands, except share and per share data)	Years Ended December 31,		
	2001	**2000**	**1999**
Revenues:			
Casino	$783,405	$658,883	$559,147
Admissions	18,465	18,998	18,893
Food, beverage and other	82,060	66,146	57,998
	883,930	744,027	636,038
Less promotional allowances	(99,180)	(93,394)	(76,387)
Net revenues	784,750	650,633	559,651
Costs and Expenses:			
Casino	337,538	272,138	237,809
Selling, general and administrative	118,698	107,240	95,365
Food, beverage and other	61,682	46,575	41,528
Other operating expenses	36,343	30,230	27,866
Depreciation and amortization	47,316	36,094	34,058
Write-down of assets held for sale	—	6,800	—
	601,577	499,077	436,626
Income from operations	183,173	151,556	123,025
Other Income (Expense):			
Interest income	752	1,368	2,870
Interest expense	(67,569)	(34,768)	(48,594)
	(66,817)	(33,400)	(45,724)
Income before minority interests, income taxes and extraordinary items	116,356	118,156	77,301
Minority interests	(4,086)	(40,466)	(34,975)
Income tax expense	(46,185)	(31,161)	(5,900)
Income before extraordinary items	66,085	46,529	36,426
Extraordinary loss on extinguishments of debt (net of income tax benefit of $—, $770 and $13,500, respectively)	—	(1,154)	(24,920)
Net income	66,085	45,375	11,506
Preferred stock dividends and accretion	—	—	(27)
Net income attributable to common stockholders	$ 66,085	$ 45,375	$ 11,479
Basic net income per share	$2.31	$1.60	$0.41
Diluted net income per share	$2.25	$1.56	$0.40

The accounting standard of not changing the statements retroactively when there has been a change in accounting principle is not always followed in practice. APB opinions subsequent to No. 20 and later SFASs frequently directed that the new principles included in the respective pronouncement be handled retroactively by changing prior years' statements.

The accounting standard of not changing the statements retroactively when there has been a change in accounting principle presents major problems for analysis. It is not good theory because it places on the income statement, in the year of change, a potentially material income or loss amount that has nothing to do with operations of that year. Comparability with prior years (consistency) is also a problem.

Statement of Financial Accounting Concepts No. 5 (December 1985) recommends that the cumulative effects of changes in accounting principles not be included in earnings in the year of change in principle. To date, this recommendation has not been the subject of a FASB statement.

No ideal way exists to handle the analysis problem when a change in accounting principle is not handled retroactively. The cumulative effect of a change in accounting principle should be removed from the income statement for primary analysis. This still leaves the comparability problem that the income in the year of change, and subsequent years, is based on the new principle; while the years prior to the change are based on the prior principle. If, in your opinion, the income effect is so extreme that comparability is materially distorted, then do not use years prior to the change in comparability analysis. Also note the pro forma presentation, if provided, at the bottom of the income statement. The pro forma numbers will be comparable, but limited. Exhibit 4-8 illustrates a cumulative effect of a change in accounting principle.

EXHIBIT 4-8

SUN MICROSYSTEMS, INC.
Consolidated Statements of Income

Cumulative Effect of Change in Accounting Principle

(in millions, except per share amounts)	2001	2000	1999
	Years Ended June 30,		
Net revenues:			
Products	$15,015	$13,421	$10,171
Services	3,235	2,300	1,635
Total net revenues	18,250	15,721	11,806
Cost of sales:			
Cost of sales—products	7,961	6,096	4,696
Cost of sales—services	2,080	1,453	974
Total cost of sales	10,041	7,549	5,670
Gross margin	8,209	8,172	6,136
Operating expenses:			
Research and development	2,016	1,630	1,280
Selling, general and administrative	4,544	4,072	3,196
Goodwill amortization	261	65	19
Purchased in-process research and development	77	12	121
Total operating expenses	6,898	5,779	4,616
Operating income	1,311	2,393	1,520
Gain (loss) on strategic investments	(90)	208	—
Interest income, net	363	170	85
Income before income taxes and cumulative effect of change in accounting principle	1,584	2,771	1,605
Provision for income taxes	603	917	575
Income before cumulative effect of change in accounting principle	981	1,854	1,030
Cumulative effect of change in accounting principle, net	(54)	—	—
Net income	$ 927	$ 1,854	$ 1,030
Net income per common share—basic:			
Income before cumulative effect of change in accounting principle	$ 0.30	$0.59	$0.33
Cumulative effect of change in accounting principle	(0.02)	—	—
Net income per common share—basic	$ 0.28	$0.59	$0.33
Net income per common share—diluted:			
Income before cumulative effect of change in accounting principle	$ 0.29	$0.55	$0.31
Cumulative effect of change in accounting principle	(0.02)	—	—
Net income per common share—diluted	$ 0.27	$0.55	$0.31
Shares used in the calculation of net income per common share—basic	3,234	3,151	3,087
Shares used in the calculation of net income per common share—diluted	3,417	3,379	3,282

(F) Minority Share of Earnings

If a firm consolidates subsidiaries not wholly owned, the total revenues and expenses of the subsidiaries are included with those of the parent. However, to determine the income that would accrue to the parent, it is necessary to deduct the portion of income that would belong to the minority owners. This is labeled "minority share of earnings" or "minority interest." Note that this item sometimes appears before and sometimes after the tax provision on the income statement. When presented before the tax provision, it is usually presented gross of tax. When presented after the tax provision, it is presented net of tax. In this book, assume net-of-tax treatment. Exhibit 4-9 illustrates minority share of earnings.

Some ratios can be materially distorted because of a minority share of earnings. For each ratio influenced by a minority share of earnings, this book suggests a recommended approach.

EARNINGS PER SHARE

In general, **earnings per share** is earnings divided by the number of shares of outstanding common stock. Chapter 9 presents earnings per share in detail, and explains its computation. Meanwhile, use the formula of net income divided by outstanding shares of common stock.

RETAINED EARNINGS

Retained earnings, an account on the balance sheet, represents the undistributed earnings of the corporation. A reconciliation of retained earnings summarizes the changes in retained earnings.

EXHIBIT 4-9

CLARCOR
Consolidated Statements of Earnings

	Minority Share of Earnings		
For the Years Ended November 30, 2001, 2000, and 1999			
(Dollars in thousands except per share data)	**2001**	**2000**	**1999**
Net sales	**$666,964**	$652,148	$477,869
Cost of sales	**471,477**	453,803	329,282
Gross profit	**195,487**	198,345	148,587
Selling and administrative expenses	**119,677**	122,358	92,510
Operating profit	**75,810**	75,987	56,077
Other income (expense):			
Interest expense	**(10,270)**	(11,534)	(3,733)
Interest income	**654**	698	1,451
Other, net	**(460)**	(1,664)	1,820
	(10,076)	(12,500)	(462)
Earnings before income taxes and minority interests	**65,734**	63,487	55,615
Provision for income taxes	**23,804**	23,201	20,137
Earnings before minority interests	**41,930**	40,286	35,478
Minority interests in earnings of subsidiaries	**(37)**	(49)	(66)
Net earnings	**$ 41,893**	$ 40,237	$ 35,412
Net earnings per common share:			
Basic	**$1.71**	$1.66	$1.48
Diluted	**$1.68**	$1.64	$1.46
Average number of common shares outstanding:			
Basic	**24,535,199**	24,269,675	23,970,011
Diluted	**24,892,062**	24,506,171	24,313,607

It shows the retained earnings at the beginning of the year, the net income for the year as an addition, the dividends as a subtraction, and concludes with end-of-year retained earnings. It also includes, if appropriate, prior period adjustments (net of tax) and some adjustments for changes in accounting principles (net of tax). These restate beginning retained earnings. Other possible changes to retained earnings are beyond the scope of this book.

Sometimes a portion of retained earnings may be unavailable for dividends because it has been appropriated (restricted). Appropriated retained earnings remain part of retained earnings. The appropriation of retained earnings may or may not have significance.

Appropriations that result from legal requirements (usually state law) and appropriations that result from contractual agreements are potentially significant. They may leave unappropriated retained earnings inadequate to pay dividends. (Note: A corporation will not be able to pay a cash dividend even with an adequate unrestricted balance in retained earnings unless it has adequate cash or ability to raise cash and has complied with the state law where it is incorporated.)

Most appropriations result from management decisions. These are usually not significant because management can choose to remove the appropriation.

Caution should be exercised not to confuse retained earnings or appropriated retained earnings with cash or any other asset. There is no cash or any other asset in retained earnings. The reason for an appropriation will be disclosed either in the reconciliation of retained earnings or in a footnote. From this disclosure, try to arrive at an opinion as to the significance, if any. For example, Cooper Tire & Rubber Company had retained earnings of $1,103,080,000 at December 31, 2001. A debt footnote discloses that retained earnings of $206,593,000 at December 31, 2001, are available for the payment of cash dividends and purchases of the Company's common shares. This is likely not significant because the dividends paid were only $30,475,000 in 2001. Although Cooper appears to have adequate cash and adequate unrestricted retained earnings, it must also be in compliance with the applicable state law where it is incorporated in order to pay a dividend.

The reconciliation of retained earnings usually appears as part of a statement of stockholders' equity. Sometimes it is combined with the income statement. Exhibit 4-10 gives an example of a reconciliation of retained earnings being presented with a stockholders' equity statement.

DIVIDENDS AND STOCK SPLITS

Dividends return profits to the owners of a corporation. A cash dividend declared by the board of directors reduces retained earnings by the amount of the dividends declared and creates the current liability, dividends payable. The date of payment occurs after the date of declaration. The dividend payment eliminates the liability, dividends payable, and reduces cash. Note that the date of the declaration of dividends, not the date of the dividend payment, affects retained earnings and creates the liability.

The Board of Directors may elect to declare and issue another type of dividend, termed a *stock dividend*. The firm issues a percentage of outstanding stock as new shares to existing shareholders. If the Board declares a 10% stock dividend, for example, an owner holding 1,000 shares would receive an additional 100 shares of new stock. The accounting for a stock dividend, assuming a relatively small distribution (less than 25% of the existing stock), requires removing the fair market value of the stock at the date of declaration from retained earnings and transferring it to paid-in capital. With a material stock dividend, the amount removed from retained earnings and transferred to paid-in capital is determined by multiplying the par value of the stock by the number of additional shares. Note that the overall effect of a stock dividend leaves total stockholders' equity and each owner's share of stockholders' equity unchanged. However, the total number of outstanding shares increases.

A stock dividend should reduce the market value of individual shares by the percentage of the stock dividend. Total market value considering all outstanding shares should not change in theory. In practice, the market value change may not be the same percentage as the stock dividend.

A more drastic device to change the market value of individual shares is by declaring a stock split. A 2-for-1 split should reduce the market value per share to one half the amount prior to the split. The market value per share in practice may not change exactly in proportion to the split. The market value will result from the supply and demand for the stock.

Lowering the market value is sometimes desirable for stocks selling at high prices (as perceived by management). Stocks with high prices are less readily traded. A stock dividend or stock split can influence the demand for the stock.

EXHIBIT 4-10   **METRO ONE TELECOMMUNICATIONS, INC.**
Statement of Shareholders' Equity

Shareholders' Equity (in thousands)

	Common Stock		Retained Earnings (Accumulated Deficit)	Shareholders' Equity
	Shares	Amount		
Balances at December 31, 1998	16,782	$ 38,477	$(10,235)	$ 28,242
Employee stock options exercised, net	339	1,831	—	1,831
Net income	—	—	1,906	1,906
Balances at December 31, 1999	17,121	40,308	(8,329)	31,979
Employee stock options exercised, net	587	3,426	—	3,426
Employee stock purchase plan	39	257	—	257
Net income	—	—	9,742	9,742
Balances at December 31, 2000	17,747	43,991	1,413	45,404
Issuance of common stock, net	6,000	64,607	—	64,607
Shares issued in business combination	155	3,200	—	3,200
Employee stock options exercised	510	3,300	—	3,300
Tax benefit from stock plans	—	1,730	—	1,730
Employee stock purchase plan	51	706	—	706
Net income	—	—	28,422	28,422
Balances at December 31, 2001	24,463	$117,534	$ 29,835	$147,369

A stock split merely increases the number of shares of stock. It does not usually change retained earnings or paid-in capital. For example, if a firm had 1,000 shares of common stock, a 2-for-1 stock split would result in 2,000 shares.

For a stock split, the par or stated value of the stock is changed in proportion to the stock split, and no change is made to retained earnings, additional paid-in capital, or capital stock. For example, a firm with $10 par common stock that declares a 2-for-1 stock split would reduce the par value to $5.

Since the number of shares changes under both a stock dividend and stock split, any ratio based on the number of shares must be restated for a meaningful comparison. For example, if a firm had earnings per share of $4 in 2002, a 2-for-1 stock split in 2003 would require restatement of the earnings per share to $2 in 2002 because of the increase in the shares. Restatement will be made for all prior financial statements presented with the current financial statements, including a 5- or 10-year summary.

LEGALITY OF DISTRIBUTIONS TO STOCKHOLDERS

The legality of distributions to stockholders is governed by applicable state law. Currently, the 50 states may be classified into one of three groups for purposes of distributions to stockholders. These groups are the following:[1]

1. Distributions to stockholders are acceptable as long as the firm has the ability to pay debts as they come due in the normal course of business.
2. Distributions to stockholders are acceptable as long as the firm is solvent and the distributions do not exceed the fair value of net assets.
3. Distributions consist of solvency and balance sheet tests of liquidity and risk.

Thus, the appropriateness of a distribution to stockholders is a legal interpretation. Accountants have not accepted the role of disclosing the firm's capacity to make distributions to stockholders. Accountants have accepted the role of disclosing appropriations (restrictions) of retained earnings. Appropriations can temporarily limit the firm's ability to make distributions. These appropriations are typically directed toward limiting or prohibiting the payment of cash dividends.

During the 1980s and 1990s, there were many distributions to stockholders that exceeded the net book value of the firms' assets. These were often accompanied by debt-financed restructurings. Often the result was a deficit balance in retained earnings and sometimes a deficit balance in total stockholders' equity.

During 1988, Holiday Corporation (owner of Holiday Inns of America) distributed a $65 per share dividend to prevent a hostile takeover. The result was a substantial deficit to retained earnings and approximately a $770 million deficit to total stockholders' equity.[2]

A similar situation took place at Owens Corning during the 1980s as it made a substantial distribution to stockholders by way of a debt-financed restructuring. Owens Corning also had substantial expenses related to asbestos-related illnesses. At the end of 1995, Owens Corning had a deficit in retained earnings of $781,000,000, and a deficit in total stockholders' equity of $212,000,000.

An Owens Corning news release of June 20, 1996, stated (in part):

> The Board of Directors has approved an annual dividend policy of 25 cents per share and declared a quarterly dividend of 6-1/4 cents per share payable on October 15, 1996 to shareholders of record as of September 30, 1996.
>
> In reference to the dividend, we were able to initiate this action because debt has been reduced to target levels and cash flow from operations will be in excess of internal funding requirements.
>
> We are delighted to be able to reward our shareholders with a dividend. Reinstating the dividend has been a priority of mine since joining the company and I am pleased that we now are in a position to set the date.

COMPREHENSIVE INCOME

Chapter 1 described the Concept Statements that serve as the basis for evaluating existing standards of financial accounting and reports. Concept Statements Nos. 5 & 6 included the concept of comprehensive income. Comprehensive income was described in SFAC No. 6 as the change in equity of a business enterprise during a period from transactions and other events and circumstances from nonowner sources.

Subsequently, SFAS No. 130 was issued that required the reporting of comprehensive income, but using a narrower definition than in SFAC No. 6. Under SFAS No. 130, comprehensive income is net income plus the period's change in accumulated other comprehensive income. Accumulated other comprehensive income is a category within stockholders' equity, described in Chapter 3.

Categories within accumulated other comprehensive income are:

1. *Foreign currency translation adjustments.* The expansion of international business and extensive currency realignment have created special accounting problems. The biggest difficulty has been related to translating foreign financial statements into the financial statements of a U.S. enterprise.

   U.S. financial reporting calls for postponing the recognition of unrealized exchange gains and losses until the foreign operation is substantially liquidated. This postponement is accomplished by creating a separate category within stockholders' equity to carry unrealized exchange gains and losses. This method eliminates the wide fluctuations in earnings from translation adjustments for most firms. For subsidiaries operating in highly inflationary economies, translation adjustments are charged to net earnings. Also, actual foreign currency exchange gains (losses) are included in net earnings.

2. *Unrealized holding gains and losses on available-for-sale marketable securities.* Debt and equity securities classified as available-for-sale securities are carried at fair value. Unrealized holding gains and losses are included in a separate category within stockholders' equity until realized. Thus, the unrealized holding gains and losses are not included in net earnings. Note that this accounting only applies to securities available for sale. Trading securities are reported at their fair values on the balance sheet date, and unrealized holding gains and losses are included in income of the current period. Debt securities held to maturity are reported at their amortized cost on the balance sheet date.

3. *Changes to stockholders' equity resulting from additional minimum pension liability adjustments.* Accounting standards require a reduction in stockholders' equity for a minimum pension liability under a defined benefit plan. Accounting for a defined benefit plan is reviewed in Chapter 7.

4. *Unrealized gains and losses from derivative instruments.* Derivative instruments are financial instruments or other contracts where rights or obligations meet the definitions of assets or liabilities. The gain or loss for some derivative instruments are reported in current earnings. For other derivative instruments, the gain or loss is reported as a component of other comprehensive income. The gain or loss for these instruments is recognized in subsequent periods in income as the hedged forecasted transactions affect earnings.

The reporting of this component of accumulated other comprehensive income was effective for fiscal quarters of fiscal years beginning after June 15, 2000. For the other items, the effective date was for fiscal years beginning after December 15, 1997.

Required disclosures are the following:

- Comprehensive income
- Each category of other comprehensive income
- Reclassification adjustments for categories of other comprehensive income
- Tax effects for each category of other comprehensive income
- Balances for each category of accumulated other comprehensive income

The accounting standard provides considerable flexibility in reporting comprehensive income. One format uses a single income statement to report net income and comprehensive income. The second format reports comprehensive income in a separate statement of financial activity. The third format reports comprehensive income within the statement of changes in stockholders' equity. Exhibit 4-11 illustrates the three format options provided for in the accounting standard.

The first two options are not popular because comprehensive income would be closely tied to the income statement. Comprehensive income will typically be more volatile than net income. This is because the items within accumulated other comprehensive income have the potential to be volatile. A good case could be made that comprehensive income is a better indication of long-run profitability than is net income. Some firms have elected to disclose comprehensive income as a note to the financial statements. The coverage of comprehensive income in analysis is in Chapter 12.

SUMMARY

The income statement summarizes the profit for a specific period of time. To understand and analyze profitability, the reader must be familiar with the components of income, as well as income statement items that require special disclosure. This chapter presented special income statement items, such as unusual or infrequent items disclosed separately, equity in earnings of nonconsolidated subsidiaries, discontinued operations, extraordinary items, changes in accounting principle, and minority shares of earnings. This chapter also covered the reconciliation of retained earnings, dividends and stock splits, and comprehensive income.

To the Net

1. Go to the SEC site (http://www.sec.gov). Under Filings & Forms (Edgar), click on "Search for Company Filings." Click on "Search Companies and Filings." Under company name enter "Owens-Illinois." Select the 10-K405 filed April 1, 2002.
   a. What is the amount of equity earnings for 2001? Describe equity earnings.
   b. What is the amount of minority share of earnings for 2001? Describe minority share of earnings.

2. Go to the SEC site (http://www.sec.gov). Under Filings & Forms (Edgar), click on "Search for Company Filings." Click on "Search Companies and Filings." Under company name enter "Amazon." Select the 10-K405 filed January 24, 2002.
   a. What were the net sales for 2001, 2000, and 1999?
   b. What were loss from operations for 2001, 2000, and 1999?
   c. What was the interest expense for 2001, 2000, and 1999?
   d. Comment considering the data in a, b, and c.

EXHIBIT 4-11	REPORTING COMPREHENSIVE INCOME

Format A Single Income Statement
to Report Net Income and Comprehensive Income

XYZ Corporation
Statement of Income and Comprehensive Income
For the Year Ended December 31, 2003

(Dollars in thousands, except per share)

Sales	$230,000
Cost of goods sold	140,000
Gross profit	90,000
Operating expenses	40,000
Operating income	50,000
Other income	4,000
Income before income taxes	54,000
Income taxes	20,000
Net income	34,000

Other comprehensive income

Available-for-sale securities adjustment, net of $2,500 income tax	5,500
Minimum pension liability adjustment, net of $1,000 income tax	3,500
Foreign currency translation adjustment, net of $1,500 income tax benefit	(5,000)
Other comprehensive income	4,000
Comprehensive income	$ 38,000

Earnings per share

(Earnings per share continue to be calculated based on net income.)	$2.80

Format B Separate Comprehensive
Income Statement

XYZ Corporation
Statement of Comprehensive Income
For the Year Ended December 31, 2003

(Dollars in thousands)

Net income		$34,000
Other comprehensive income		
Available-for-sale securities adjustment, net of $2,500 income tax	5,500	
Minimum pension liability adjustment, net of $1,000 income tax	3,500	
Foreign currency translation adjustments, net of $1,500 income tax benefit	(5,000)	
Total Other comprehensive income		4,000
Comprehensive income		$38,000

Format C Comprehensive Income Presented with
Statement of Changes in Stockholders' Equity

XYZ Corporation
Statement of Stockholders' Equity For the Year Ended December 31, 2003

(Dollars in thousands)

	Total	Retained Earnings	Accumulated Other Comprehensive Income	Common Stock Amount	Common Stock Shares
Beginning balance	$180,000	$60,000	$10,000	$110,000	55,000
Net income	34,000	34,000			
Other comprehensive income:					
Available-for-sale securities adjustment, net of $2,500 income tax	5,500		5,500		
Minimum pension liability adjustment, net of $1,000 income tax	3,500		3,500		
Foreign currency translation adjustment, net of $1,500 income tax benefit	(5,000)		(5,000)		
Comprehensive income	38,000				
Ending balance	$218,000	$94,000	$14,000	$110,000	55,000

Questions

Q 4-1.   What are extraordinary items? How are they shown on the income statement? Why are they shown in that manner?

Q 4-2.   Which of the following would be classified as extraordinary?
a. Selling expense
b. Interest expense
c. Gain on the sale of marketable securities
d. Loss from flood
e. Income tax expense
f. Loss from prohibition of red dye
g. Loss from the write-down of inventory

Q 4-3.   Give three examples of unusual or infrequent items that are disclosed separately. Why are they shown separately? Are they presented before or after tax? Why or why not?

Q 4-4.   Why is the equity in earnings of nonconsolidated subsidiaries sometimes a problem in profitability analysis? Discuss with respect to income versus cash flow.

Q 4-5.   A health food distributor selling wholesale dairy products and vitamins decides to discontinue the division that sells vitamins. How should this discontinuance be classified on the income statement?

Q 4-6.   Why are unusual or infrequent items disclosed before tax?

Q 4-7.   In 2003, Jensen Company decided to change its depreciation method from units-of-production to straight-line. The cumulative effect of the change to the new method, prior to 2003, was to increase depreciation by $30,000 before tax. How would the change be presented in the financial statements?

Q 4-8.   How does the declaration of a cash dividend affect the financial statements? How does the payment of a cash dividend affect the financial statements?

Q 4-9.   What is the difference in the impact on financial statements of a stock dividend versus a stock split?

Q 4-10.   Why is minority share of earnings deducted before arriving at net income?

Q 4-11.   Explain the relationship between the income statement and the reconciliation of retained earnings.

Q 4-12.   List the three types of appropriated retained earnings accounts. Which of these types is most likely not a detriment to the payment of a dividend? Explain.

Q 4-13.   A balance sheet represents a specific date, such as "December 31," while an income statement covers a period of time, such as "For the Year Ended December 31, 2003." Why does this difference exist?

Q 4-14.   Describe the following items:
a. Minority share of earnings
b. Equity in earnings of nonconsolidated subsidiaries

Q 4-15.   An income statement is a summary of revenues and expenses and gains and losses, ending with net income for a specific period of time. Indicate the two traditional formats for presenting the income statement. Which of these formats is preferable for analysis? Why?

Q 4-16.   Melcher Company reported earnings per share in 2003 and 2002 of $2.00 and $1.60, respectively. In 2004 there was a 2-for-1 stock split, and the earnings per share for 2004 were reported to be $1.40. Give a three-year presentation of earnings per share (2002–2004).

Q 4-17.   Comment on your ability to determine a firm's capacity to make distributions to stockholders, using published financial statements.

Q 4-18.   Management does not usually like to tie comprehensive income closely with the income statement. Comment.

Problems

P 4-1.   The following information for Decher Automotives covers the year ended 2003:

Administrative expense	$ 62,000
Dividend income	10,000
Income taxes	100,000

Interest expense	20,000
Merchandise inventory, 1/1	650,000
Merchandise inventory, 12/31	440,000
Flood loss (net of tax)	30,000
Purchases	460,000
Sales	1,000,000
Selling expenses	43,000

Required   a. Prepare a multiple-step income statement.
b. Assuming that 100,000 shares of common stock are outstanding, calculate the earnings per share before extraordinary items and the net earnings per share.
c. Prepare a single-step income statement.

P 4-2.   The following information for Lesky Corporation covers the year ended December 31, 2003:

LESKY CORPORATION
Income Statement
For the Year Ended December 31, 2003

Revenue:		
Revenues from sales		$362,000
Rental income		1,000
Interest		2,400
Total revenue		365,400
Expenses:		
Cost of products sold	$242,000	
Selling expenses	47,000	
Administrative and general expenses	11,400	
Interest expense	2,200	
Federal and state income taxes	20,300	
Total expenses		322,900
Net income		$ 42,500

Required   Change this statement to a multiple-step format, as illustrated in this chapter.

P 4-3.   The accounts of Consolidated Can contain the following amounts at December 31, 2003:

Cost of products sold	$410,000
Dividends	3,000
Extraordinary gain (net of tax)	1,000
Income taxes	9,300
Interest expense	8,700
Other income	1,600
Retained earnings, 1/1	270,000
Sales	480,000
Selling and administrative expense	42,000

Required   Prepare a multiple-step income statement combined with a reconciliation of retained earnings for the year ended December 31, 2003.

P 4-4.   The following items are from Taperline Corporation on December 31, 2003. Assume a flat 40% corporate tax rate on all items, including the casualty loss.

Sales	$670,000
Rental income	3,600
Gain on the sale of fixed assets	3,000
General and administrative expenses	110,000
Selling expenses	97,000
Interest expense	1,900
Depreciation for the period	10,000
Extraordinary item (casualty loss—pretax)	30,000
Cost of sales	300,000
Common stock (30,000 shares outstanding)	150,000

Required   a.   Prepare a single-step income statement for the year ended December 31, 2003. Include earnings per share for earnings before extraordinary items and net income.

b.   Prepare a multiple-step income statement. Include earnings per share for earnings before extraordinary items and net income.

P 4-5.   The income statement of Rawl Company for the year ended December 31, 2003 shows:

Net sales	$360,000
Cost of sales	190,000
Gross profit	170,000
Selling, general, and administrative expense	80,000
Income before unusual write-offs	90,000
Provision for unusual write-offs	50,000
Earnings from operations before income taxes	40,000
Income taxes	20,000
Net earnings from operations before extraordinary charge	20,000
Extraordinary charge, net of tax of $10,000	(50,000)
Net earnings (loss)	$ (30,000)

Shows tax rate = 50%.

Required   Compute the net earnings remaining after removing unusual write-offs and the extraordinary charge. Remove these items net of tax. Estimate the tax rate for unusual write-offs based on the taxes on operating income.

P 4-6.   At the end of 2003, vandals destroyed your financial records. Fortunately, the controller had kept certain statistical data related to the income statement, as follows:

a.   Cost of goods sold was $2,000,000.
b.   Administrative expenses were 20% of the cost of sales but only 10% of sales.
c.   Selling expenses were 150% of administrative expenses.
d.   Bonds payable were $1,000,000, with an average interest rate of 11%.
e.   The tax rate was 48%.
f.   50,000 shares of common stock were outstanding for the entire year.

Required   From the information given, reconstruct a multiple-step income statement for the year. Include earnings per share.

P 4-7.   The following information applies to Bowling Green Metals Corporation for the year ended December 31, 2003.

Total revenues from regular operations	$832,000
Total expenses from regular operations	776,000
Extraordinary gain, net of applicable income taxes	30,000
Dividends paid	20,000
Number of shares of common stock outstanding during the year	10,000

Required   Compute earnings per share before extraordinary items and net earnings. Show how this might be presented in the financial statements.

P 4-8.   You were recently hired as the assistant treasurer for Victor, Inc. Yesterday the treasurer was injured in a bicycle accident and is now hospitalized, unconscious. Your boss, Mr. Fernandes, just informed you that the financial statements are due today. Searching through the treasurer's desk, you find the following notes:

a.   Income from continuing operations, based on computations done so far, is $400,000. No taxes are accounted for yet. The tax rate is 30%.
b.   Dividends declared and paid were $20,000. During the year, 100,000 shares of stock were outstanding.
c.   The corporation experienced an uninsured $20,000 pretax loss from a freak hailstorm. Such a storm is considered to be unusual and infrequent.
d.   The company decided to change its inventory pricing method from average cost to the FIFO method. The effect of this change is to increase prior years' income by $30,000 pretax. The FIFO method has been used for 2000. (Hint: This adjustment should be placed just prior to net income.)

e.   In 2003, the company settled a lawsuit against it for $10,000 pretax. The settlement was not previously accrued and is due for payment in February 2004.

f.   In 2003, the firm sold a portion of its long-term securities at a gain of $30,000 pretax.

g.   The corporation disposed of its consumer products division in August 2003, at a loss of $90,000 pretax. The loss from operations through August was $60,000 pretax.

Required   Prepare an income statement for 2003, in good form, starting with income from continuing operations. Compute earnings per share for income from continuing operations, discontinued operations, extraordinary loss, cumulative effect of a change in accounting principle, and net income.

P 4-9.   List the statement on which each of the following items may appear. Choose from (A) income statement, (B) balance sheet, or (C) neither.

a.   Net income
b.   Cost of goods sold
c.   Gross profit
d.   Retained earnings
e.   Paid-in capital in excess of par
f.   Sales
g.   Supplies expense
h.   Investment in G. Company
i.   Dividends
j.   Inventory
k.   Common stock

l.   Interest payable
m.   Loss from flood
n.   Land
o.   Taxes payable
p.   Interest income
q.   Gain on sale of property
r.   Dividend income
s.   Depreciation expense
t.   Accounts receivable
u.   Accumulated depreciation
v.   Sales commissions

P 4-10.   List where each of the following items may appear. Choose from (A) income statement, (B) balance sheet, or (C) reconciliation of retained earnings.

a.   Dividends paid
b.   Notes payable
c.   Minority share of earnings
d.   Accrued payrolls
e.   Loss on disposal of equipment
f.   Minority interest in consolidated subsidiary
g.   Adjustments of prior periods
h.   Redeemable preferred stock
i.   Treasury stock
j.   Extraordinary loss

k.   Unrealized exchange gains and losses
l.   Equity in net income of affiliates
m.   Goodwill
n.   Unrealized decline in market value of equity investment
o.   Cumulative effect of change in accounting principle
p.   Common stock
q.   Costs of good sold
r.   Supplies
s.   Land

P 4-11.   The income statement of Tawls Company for the year ended December 31, 2003 shows:

Revenue from sales		$ 980,000
Cost of products sold		510,000
Gross profit		470,000
Operating expenses:		
Selling expenses	$110,000	
General expenses	140,000	250,000
Operating income		220,000
Equity on earnings of nonconsolidated subsidiary		60,000
Operating income before income taxes		280,000
Taxes related to operations		100,000
Net income from operations		180,000
Extraordinary loss from flood		
(less applicable taxes of $50,000)		(120,000)
Minority share of earnings		(40,000)
Net income		$ 20,000

Required   a.   Compute the net earnings remaining after removing nonrecurring items.

b.   Determine the earnings from the nonconsolidated subsidiary.

c.   For the subsidiary that was not consolidated, what amount of income would have been included if this subsidiary had been consolidated?

d. What earnings relate to minority shareholders of a subsidiary that was consolidated?
e. Determine the total tax amount.

P 4-12.   The income statement of Jones Company for the year ended December 31, 2003 follows.

Revenue from sales		$790,000
Cost of products sold		410,000
Gross profit		380,000
Operating expenses:		
Selling expenses	$ 40,000	
General expenses	80,000	120,000
Operating income		260,000
Equity in earnings of non-consolidated subsidiaries (loss)		(20,000)
Operating income before income taxes		240,000
Taxes related to operations		(94,000)
Net income from operations		146,000
Discontinued operations:		
Loss from operations of discontinued segment		
(less applicable income tax credit of $30,000)	$ (70,000)	
Loss on disposal of segment (less applicable		
income tax credit of $50,000)	(100,000)	(170,000)
Income before cumulative effect of change		
in accounting principle		(24,000)
Cumulative effect of change in accounting principle		
(less applicable income taxes of $25,000)		50,000
Net income		$ 26,000

Required   a. Compute the net earnings remaining after removing nonrecurring items.
              b. Determine the earnings (loss) from the nonconsolidated subsidiary.
              c. Determine the total tax amount.

P 4-13.   Uranium Mining Company, founded in 1970 to mine and market uranium, purchased a mine in 1971 for $900 million. It estimated that the uranium had a market value of $150 per ounce. By 2003, the market value had increased to $300 per ounce. Records for 2003 indicate the following:

Production	200,000 ounces
Sales	230,000 ounces
Deliveries	190,000 ounces
Cash collection	210,000 ounces
Costs of production including depletion*	$50,000,000
Selling expense	$2,000,000
Administrative expenses	$1,250,000
Tax rate	50%

*Production cost per ounce has remained constant over the last few years, and the company has maintained the same production level.

Required   a. Compute the income for 2003, using each of the following bases:
                  1. Receipt of cash
                  2. Point of sale
                  3. End of production
                  4. Based on delivery
              b. Comment on when each of the methods should be used. Which method should be used by Uranium Mining Company?

P 4-14.   Each of the following statements represents a decision made by the accountant of Growth Industries:
              a. A tornado destroyed $200,000 in uninsured inventory. This loss is included in the cost of goods sold.
              b. Land was purchased 10 years ago for $50,000. The accountant adjusts the land account to $100,000, which is the estimated current value.
              c. The cost of machinery and equipment is charged to a fixed asset account. The machinery and equipment will be expensed over the period of use.

d. The value of equipment increased this year, so no depreciation of equipment was recorded this year.

e. During the year, inventory that cost $5,000 was stolen by employees. This loss has been included in the cost of goods sold for the financial statements. The total amount of the cost of goods sold was $1,000,000.

f. The president of the company, who owns the business, used company funds to buy a car for personal use. The car was recorded on the company's books.

Required State whether you agree or disagree with each decision.

P 4-15. The following information for Gaffney Corporation covers the year ended December 31, 2003:

GAFFNEY CORPORATION
Income Statement
For the Year Ended December 31, 2003

Revenue:		
Revenues from sales		$450,000
Other		5,000
Total revenue		455,000
Expenses:		
Cost of products sold	$280,000	
Selling expenses	50,000	
Administrative and general expenses	20,000	
Federal and state income taxes	30,000	
Total expenses		380,000
Net income		75,000
Other comprehensive income		
Available-for-sale securities adjustment, net of $5,000 income tax	$ 7,000	
Foreign currency translation adjustment, net of $3,000 income tax	8,000	
Other comprehensive income		15,000
Comprehensive income		$ 90,000

Required

a. Will net income or comprehensive income tend to be more volatile? Comment.

b. Which income figure will be used to compute earnings per share?

c. What is the total tax expense reported?

d. Will the items within other comprehensive income always net out as an addition to net income? Comment.

Case 4-1

Under the Arch

McDonald's Corporation presented these consolidated statements of income for 2001, 2000, and 1999.

Consolidated statements of income

In millions, except per share data

Years ended December 31,	2001	2000	1999
Revenues			
Sales by Company-operated restaurants	**$11,040.7**	$10,467.0	$ 9,512.5
Revenues from franchised and affiliated restaurants	**3,829.3**	3,776.0	3,746.8
Total revenues	**14,870.0**	14,243.0	13,259.3
Operating costs and expenses			
Food and packaging	**3,802.1**	3,557.1	3,204.6
Payroll and employee benefits	**2,901.2**	2,690.2	2,418.3
Occupancy and other operating expenses	**2,750.4**	2,502.8	2,206.7
Total Company-operated restaurant expenses	**9,453.7**	8,750.1	7,829.6
Franchised restaurants—occupancy expenses	**800.2**	772.3	737.7
Selling, general & administrative expenses	**1,661.7**	1,587.3	1,477.6
Special charge—global change initiatives	**200.0**		
Other operating (income) expense, net	**57.4**	(196.4)	(105.2)
Total operating costs and expenses	**12,173.0**	10,913.3	9,939.7
Operating income	**2,697.0**	3,329.7	3,319.6
Interest expense—net of capitalized interest of $15.2, $16.3 and $14.3	**452.4**	429.9	396.3
McDonald's Japan IPO gain	**(137.1)**		
Nonoperating expense, net	**52.0**	17.5	39.2
Income before provision for income taxes	**2,329.7**	2,882.3	2,884.1
Provision for income taxes	**693.1**	905.0	936.2
Net income	**$ 1,636.6**	$ 1,977.3	$ 1,947.9
Net income per common share	**$1.27**	$1.49	$1.44
Net income per common share—diluted	**$1.25**	$1.46	$1.39
Dividends per common share	**$ .23**	$ .22	$ .20
Weighted-average shares	**1,289.7**	1,323.2	1,355.3
Weighted-average shares—diluted	**1,309.3**	1,356.5	1,404.2

Required

a. Does it appear that there is 100% ownership in all consolidated subsidiaries? Discuss.

b. If a subsidiary were not consolidated but rather accounted for using the equity method, would this change net income? Explain.

c. Determine the net income for each year with the special charge–global change initiatives removed.

Case 4-2

Hidden Treasure

Denbury Resources Inc. presented these consolidated statements of operations for the year ended December 31, 2001, 2000, and 1999.

| | Year Ended December 31, | | |
Amounts in Thousands Except Per Share Amounts	**2001**	**2000**	**1999**
Revenues			
Oil, natural gas and related product sales	**$260,398**	$204,636	$90,991
CO_2 sales	**5,210**	—	—
Gain (loss) on settlements of derivative contracts	**18,654**	(25,264)	(9,416)
Interest income and other	**849**	2,279	1,415
Total revenues	**285,111**	181,651	82,990
Expenses			
Lease operating costs	**55,049**	38,676	26,029
Production taxes and marketing expenses	**10,963**	8,051	3,662
CO2 operating costs	**891**	—	—
General and administrative	**9,297**	8,055	7,029
Interest	**22,335**	15,255	15,795
Depletion and depreciation	**71,345**	36,214	25,515
Franchise taxes	**877**	467	346
Loss on Enron related assets	**25,164**	—	—
Amortization of derivative contracts and other non-cash hedging adjustments	**7,816**	—	—
Total expenses	**203,737**	106,718	78,376
Income before income taxes	**81,374**	74,933	4,614
Income tax provision (benefit)			
Current income taxes	**640**	558	—
Deferred income taxes	**24,184**	(67,852)	—
Net income	**$ 56,550**	$142,227	$ 4,614
Net income per common share			
Basic	**$1.15**	$3.10	$0.12
Diluted	**1.12**	3.07	0.12
Weighted average common shares outstanding			
Basic	**49,325**	45,823	39,928
Diluted	**50,361**	46,352	39,987

Required

a. What does it mean that the statements are "Consolidated Statements of Operations"?

b. Does it appear that Denbury Resources Inc. has consolidated subsidiaries in which it has less than 100% ownership? Explain.

c. Assume that "Loss on Enron related assets" is nonrecurring. What would be the net income if this item were removed?

Case 4-3

Take My Picture

Eastman Kodak Company presented these consolidated statements of earnings for the year ended December 31, 2001, 2000, and 1999.

Eastman Kodak Company and Subsidiary Companies
CONSOLIDATED STATEMENT OF EARNINGS

(in millions, except per share data)	2001	2000	1999
	For the Year Ended December 31,		
Net sales	$13,234	$13,994	$14,089
Cost of goods sold	8,670	8,375	8,086
Gross profit	4,564	5,619	6,003
Selling, general and administrative expenses	2,627	2,514	2,701
Research and development costs	779	784	817
Goodwill amortization	154	151	145
Restructuring costs (credits) and other	659	(44)	350
Earnings from operations	345	2,214	1,990
Interest expense	219	178	142
Other income (charges)	(18)	96	261
Earnings before income taxes	108	2,132	2,109
Provision for income taxes	32	725	717
NET EARNINGS	$ 76	$ 1,407	$ 1,392
Basic earnings per share	$ .26	$ 4.62	$ 4.38
Diluted earnings per share	$ .26	$ 4.59	$ 4.33
Earnings used in basic and diluted earnings per share	$ 76	$ 1,407	$ 1,392
Number of common shares used in basic earnings per share	290.6	304.9	318.0
Incremental shares from assumed conversion of options	0.4	1.7	3.5
Number of common shares used in diluted earnings per share	291.0	306.6	321.5
Cash dividends per share	$ 2.21	$ 1.76	$ 1.76

Required
a. What does it mean that the statements are "Consolidated Statements of Earnings"?
b. Does it appear that Eastman Kodak has 100% ownership of the subsidiaries consolidated?
c. Determine net earnings with restructuring costs (credits) and other removed.

Case 4-4

The Big Order

On October 15, 1990, United Airlines (UAL Corporation) placed the largest wide-body aircraft order in commercial aviation history—60 Boeing 747-400s and 68 Boeing 777s—with an estimated value of $22 billion. With this order, United became the launch customer for the B777. This order was equally split between firm orders and options.

Required
a. Comment on when United Airlines should record the purchase of these planes.
b. Comment on when Boeing should record the revenue from selling these planes.
c. Speculate on how firm the commitment was on the part of United Airlines to accept delivery of these planes.
d. 1. Speculate on the disclosure for this order in the 1990 financial statements and footnotes of United Airlines.
  2. Speculate on the disclosure for this order in the 1990 annual report of United Airlines. (Exclude the financial statements and footnotes.)
e. 1. Speculate on the disclosure for this order in the 1990 financial statements and footnotes of Boeing.
  2. Speculate on the disclosure for this order in the 1990 annual report of Boeing (exclude the financial statements and footnotes).

Case 4-5   Celtics

Boston Celtics Limited Partnership II and subsidiaries presented these consolidated statements of income for 1998, 1997, and 1996.

CONSOLIDATED STATEMENTS OF INCOME
BOSTON CELTICS LIMITED PARTNERSHIP II AND SUBSIDIARIES

	For The Year Ended		
	June 30, 1998	June 30, 1997	June 30, 1996
Revenues:			
Basketball regular season	$39,107,960	$31,813,019	$35,249,625
Ticket sales	28,002,469	23,269,159	22,071,992
Television and radio broadcast rights fees	8,569,485	7,915,626	7,458,651
Other, principally promotional advertising	75,679,914	62,997,804	64,780,268
Costs and expenses:			
Basketball regular season			
Team	40,401,643	40,941,156	27,891,264
Game	2,820,107	2,386,042	2,606,218
General and administrative	13,464,566	13,913,893	15,053,333
Selling and promotional	4,819,478	4,680,168	2,973,488
Depreciation	208,162	189,324	140,894
Amortization of NBA franchise and other intangible assets	165,035	164,702	164,703
	61,878,991	62,275,285	48,829,900
	13,800,923	722,519	15,950,368
Interest expense	(6,017,737)	(5,872,805)	(6,387,598)
Interest income	6,402,366	6,609,541	8,175,184
Net realized gains (losses) on disposition of marketable securities and other short-term investments	(18,235)	361,051	(101,138)
Income from continuing operations before income taxes	14,167,317	1,820,306	17,636,816
Provision for income taxes	1,900,000	1,400,000	1,850,000
Income from continuing operations	12,267,317	420,306	15,786,816
Discontinued operations:			
Income from discontinued operations (less applicable income taxes of $30,000)			82,806
Gain from disposal of discontinued operations (less applicable income taxes of $17,770,000)			38,330,907
NET INCOME	12,267,317	420,306	54,200,529
Net income applicable to interests of General Partners	306,216	62,246	1,291,014
Net income applicable to interests of Limited Partners	$11,961,101	$ 358,060	$52,909,515
Per unit:			
Income from continuing operations—basic	$2.45	$0.07	$2.68
Income from continuing operations—diluted	$2.17	$0.06	$2.59
Net income—basic	$2.45	$0.07	$9.18
Net income—diluted	$2.17	$0.06	$8.89
Distributions declared	$2.00	$1.00	$1.50

Required

a. Comment on the amortization of NBA franchise and other intangible assets.

b. Would the discontinued operations be included in projecting the future? Comment.

c. The costs and expenses include team costs and expenses. Speculate on the major reason for the increase in this expense between 1996 and 1997.

d. What were the major reasons for the increase in income from continuing operations between 1997 and 1998?

e. Speculate on why distributions declared were higher in 1998 than 1996. (Notice that net income was substantially higher in 1996.)

Case 4-6	**Always Low Prices**

Wal-Mart presented these consolidated statements of income for 2002, 2001, and 2000.

Consolidated Statements of Income

(Amounts in millions except per share data)

Fiscal years ended January 31,	2002	2001	2000
Revenues			
Net sales	**$217,799**	$191,329	$165,013
Other income—net	**2,013**	1,966	1,796
	219,812	193,295	166,809
Costs and Expenses			
Cost of sales	**171,562**	150,255	129,664
Operating, selling and general and administrative expenses	**36,173**	31,550	27,040
Interest Costs			
Debt	**1,052**	1,095	756
Capital leases	**274**	279	266
	209,061	183,179	157,726
Income Before Income Taxes, Minority Interest and			
Cumulative Effect of Accounting Change	**10,751**	10,116	9,083
Provision for Income Taxes			
Current	**3,712**	3,350	3,476
Deferred	**185**	342	(138)
	3,897	3,692	3,338
Income Before Minority Interest and			
Cumulative Effect of Accounting Change	**6,854**	6,424	5,745
Minority Interest	**(183)**	(129)	(170)
Income Before Cumulative Effect of Accounting Change	**6,671**	6,295	5,575
Cumulative Effect of Accounting Change,			
net of tax benefit of $119	**—**	—	(198)
Net Income	**$ 6,671**	$ 6,295	$ 5,377
Net Income Per Common Share:			
Basic Net Income Per Common Share:			
Income before cumulative effect of accounting change	**$ 1.49**	$ 1.41	$ 1.25
Cumulative effect of accounting change, net of tax	**—**	—	(0.04)
Net Income Per Common Share	**$ 1.49**	$ 1.41	$ 1.21
Average Number of Common Shares	**4,465**	4,465	4,451
Diluted Net Income Per Common Share:			
Income before cumulative effect of accounting change	**$ 1.49**	$ 1.40	$ 1.25
Cumulative effect of accounting change, net of tax	**—**	—	(0.04)
Net Income Per Common Share	**$ 1.49**	$ 1.40	$ 1.21
Average Number of Common Shares	**4,481**	4,484	4,474

Required

a. Describe minority interest.

b. Describe cumulative effect of accounting change.

c. Determine net income using generally accepted accounting principles on a consistent basis for the years 2002, 2001, and 2000.

Web Case	**Thomson Analytics** *Business School Edition*

Please complete the web case that covers material covered in this chapter at http://gibson.swlearning.com. You'll be using Thomson Analytics Business School Edition, a version of the powerful tool used by Wall Street professionals, that combines a full range of fundamental financial information, earnings estimates, market data, and source documents for 500 publicly traded companies.

Endnotes

1. Michael L. Roberts, William D. Samson, and Michael T. Dugan, "The Stockholders' Equity Section: Form Without Substance," *Accounting Horizon* (December 1990), pp. 35–46.
2. Ibid., p. 36.

5

BASICS OF ANALYSIS

The analysis of financial data employs various techniques to emphasize the comparative and relative importance of the data presented and to evaluate the position of the firm. These techniques include ratio analysis, common-size analysis, study of differences in components of financial statements among industries, review of descriptive material, and comparisons of results with other types of data. The information derived from these types of analysis should be blended to determine the overall financial position. No one type of analysis supports overall findings or serves all types of users. This chapter provides an introduction to different analyses and uses of financial information.

Financial statement analysis is a judgmental process. One of the primary objectives is identification of major changes (turning points) in trends, amounts, and relationships and investigation of the reasons underlying those changes. Often, a turning point may signal an early warning of a significant shift in the future success or failure of the business. The judgment process can be improved by experience and by the use of analytical tools.

RATIO ANALYSIS	Financial ratios are usually expressed as a percent or as times per period. The following ratios will be discussed fully in future chapters.

1. Liquidity ratios measure a firm's ability to meet its current obligations. They may include ratios that measure the efficiency of the use of current assets and current liabilities (Chapter 6).
2. Borrowing capacity (leverage) ratios measure the degree of protection of suppliers of long-term funds (Chapter 7).
3. Profitability ratios measure the earning ability of a firm. Discussion will include measures of the use of assets in general (Chapter 8).
4. Investors are interested in a special group of ratios, in addition to liquidity, debt, and profitability ratios (Chapter 9).
5. Cash flow ratios can indicate liquidity, borrowing capacity, or profitability (Chapter 10).

A ratio can be computed from any pair of numbers. Given the large quantity of variables included in financial statements, a very long list of meaningful ratios can be derived. A standard list of ratios or standard computation of them does not exist. Each author and source on financial analysis uses a different list. This book presents frequently utilized and discussed ratios.

Ratios are interpretable in comparison with (1) prior ratios, (2) ratios of competitors, (3) industry ratios, and (4) predetermined standards. The trend of a ratio and the variability of a ratio are important considerations.

Comparison of income statement and balance sheet numbers, in the form of ratios, can create difficulties due to the timing of the financial statements. Specifically, the income statement covers the entire fiscal period; whereas, the balance sheet applies to a single point in time, the end of the period. Ideally, then, to compare an income statement figure such as sales to a balance sheet figure such as receivables, we need to know the average receivables for the year that the sales figure covers. However, these data are not available to the external analyst. In some cases, the analyst uses an average of the beginning and ending balance sheet figures. This approach smooths out changes from beginning to end, but it does not eliminate problems due to seasonal and cyclical changes. It also does not reflect changes that occur unevenly throughout the year.

Be aware that computing averages from two similar balance sheet dates can be misleading. It is possible that a representative average cannot be computed from externally published statements.

A ratio will usually represent a fairly accurate trend, even when the ratio is distorted. If the ratio is distorted, then it does not represent a good absolute number.

Applying the U.S. techniques of ratio analysis to statements prepared in other countries can be misleading. The ratio analysis must be understood in terms of the accounting principles used and the business practices and culture of the country.

COMMON-SIZE ANALYSIS (VERTICAL AND HORIZONTAL)	Common-size analysis expresses comparisons in percentages. For example, if cash is $40,000 and total assets is $1,000,000, then cash represents 4% of total assets. The use of percentages is usually preferable to the use of absolute amounts. An illustration will make this clear. If Firm A earns $10,000 and Firm B earns $1,000, which is more profitable? Firm A is probably your response. However, the total owners' equity of A is $1,000,000, and B's is $10,000. The return on owners' equity is as follows:

	Firm A	**Firm B**
$\dfrac{\text{Earnings}}{\text{Owners' Equity}}$	$\dfrac{\$10,000}{\$1,000,000} = 1\%$	$\dfrac{\$1,000}{\$10,000} = 10\%$

The use of common-size analysis makes comparisons of firms of different sizes much more meaningful. Care must be exercised in the use of common-size analysis with small absolute amounts because a small change in amount can result in a very substantial percentage change. For example, if profits last year amounted to $100 and increased this year to $500, this would be an increase of only $400 in profits, but it would represent a substantial percentage increase.

Vertical analysis compares each amount with a base amount selected from the same year. For example, if advertising expenses were $1,000 in 2003 and sales were $100,000, the advertising would have been 1% of sales.

Horizontal analysis compares each amount with a base amount for a selected base year. For example, if sales were $400,000 in 2002 and $600,000 in 2003, then sales increased to 150% of the 2002 level in 2003, an increase of 50%.

Exhibit 5-1 illustrates common-size analysis (vertical and horizontal).

YEAR-TO-YEAR CHANGE ANALYSIS

Comparing financial statements over two time periods using absolute amounts and percentages can be meaningful. This approach aids in keeping absolute and percentage changes in perspective.

EXHIBIT 5-1

MELCHER COMPANY
Income Statement

Illustration of Common Size Analysis (Vertical and Horizontal)

(Absolute dollars)	For the Years Ended December 31, 2001	2000	1999
Revenue from sales	$100,000	$95,000	$ 91,000
Cost of products sold	65,000	60,800	56,420
Gross profit	35,000	34,200	34,580
Operating expenses			
Selling expenses	14,000	11,400	10,000
General expenses	16,000	15,200	13,650
Total operating expenses	30,000	26,600	23,650
Operating income before income taxes	5,000	7,600	10,930
Taxes related to operations	1,500	2,280	3,279
Net income	$ 3,500	$ 5,320	$ 7,651
Vertical Common Size			
Revenue from sales	100.0%	100.0%	100.0%
Cost of goods sold	65.0	64.0	62.0
Gross profit	35.0	36.0	38.0
Operating expenses			
Selling expenses	14.0	12.0	11.0
General expenses	16.0	16.0	15.0
Total operating expenses	30.0	28.0	26.0
Operating income before income taxes	5.0	8.0	12.0
Taxes related to operations	1.5	2.4	3.6
Net income	3.5%	5.6%	8.4%
Horizontal Common Size			
Revenue from sales	109.9%	104.4%	100.0%
Cost of goods sold	115.2	107.8	100.0
Gross profit	101.2	98.9	100.0
Operating expenses			
Selling expenses	140.0	114.0	100.0
General expenses	117.2	111.4	100.0
Total operating expenses	126.8	112.5	100.0
Operating income before income taxes	45.7	69.5	100.0
Taxes related to operations	45.7	69.5	100.0
Net income	45.7	69.5	100.0

For example, a substantial percentage change may not be relevant because of an immaterial absolute change. When performing year-to-year change analysis, follow these rules:

1. When an item has value in the base year and none in the next period, the decrease is 100%.
2. A meaningful percent change cannot be computed when one number is positive and the other number is negative.
3. No percent change is computable when there is no figure for the base year.

These rules are illustrated in Exhibit 5-2.

FINANCIAL STATEMENT VARIATION BY TYPE OF INDUSTRY

The components of financial statements, especially the balance sheet and the income statement, will vary by type of industry. Exhibits 5-3, 5-4, and 5-5 (pages 145–151) illustrate, respectively, a merchandising firm (Walgreen Co.), a service firm (The Interpublic Group of Companies), and a manufacturing firm (Cooper Tire & Rubber Company).

Merchandising (retail-wholesale) firms sell products purchased from other firms. A principal asset is inventory, which consists of finished goods. For some merchandising firms, a large amount of sales may be for cash. In such cases, the receivables balance will be relatively low. Other merchandising firms have a large amount of sales charged but also accept credit cards such as VISA, so they also have a relatively low balance in receivables. Other firms extend credit and carry the accounts receivable and thus have a relatively large receivables balance. Because of the competitive nature of the industry, profit ratios on the income statement are often quite low, with the cost of sales and operating expenses constituting a large portion of expenses. Refer to Exhibit 5-3, Walgreen Co.

A service firm generates its revenue from the service provided. Because service cannot typically be stored, inventory is low or nonexistent. In people-intensive services, such as advertising, investment in property and equipment is also low compared with that of manufacturing firms. Refer to Exhibit 5-4, The Interpublic Group of Companies.

A manufacturing firm will usually have large inventories composed of raw materials, work in process, and finished goods, as well as a material investment in property, plant, and equipment. Notes and accounts receivable may also be material, depending on the terms of sale. The cost of sales often represents the major expense. Refer to Exhibit 5-5, Cooper Tire & Rubber Company.

REVIEW OF DESCRIPTIVE INFORMATION

The descriptive information found in an annual report, in trade periodicals, and in industry reviews helps us understand the financial position of a firm. Descriptive material might discuss the role of research and development in producing future sales, present data on capital expansion and the goals related thereto, discuss aspects of employee relations such as minority hiring or union negotiations, or help explain the dividend policy of the firm.

EXHIBIT 5-2   **YEAR-TO-YEAR CHANGE ANALYSIS**
(Illustrating Rules)

Item	Year 1	Year 2	Change Analysis Amount	Percent
Advertising expense	$20,000	—	$(20,000)	(100%)
Operating income	6,000	(3,000)	(9,000)	—
Net income	(7,000)	8,000	15,000	—
Other	—	4,000	4,000	—

EXHIBIT 5-3	**WALGREEN CO. AND SUBSIDIARIES** **Merchandising Firm**

Consolidated Balance Sheets

Walgreen Co. and Subsidiaries at August 31, 2001 and 2000 (Dollars in Millions)

Assets	2001	2000
Current Assets		
Cash and cash equivalents	$ 16.9	$ 12.8
Accounts receivable, net	798.3	614.5
Inventories	3,482.4	2,830.8
Other current assets	96.3	92.0
Total Current Assets	4,393.9	3,550.1
Non-Current Assets		
Property and equipment, at cost, less accumulated depreciation and amortization	4,345.3	3,428.2
Other non-current assets	94.6	125.4
Total Assets	$8,833.8	$7,103.7
Liabilities and Shareholders' Equity		
Current Liabilities		
Short-term borrowings	$ 440.7	$ —
Trade accounts payable	1,546.8	1,364.0
Accrued expenses and other liabilities	937.5	847.7
Income taxes	86.6	92.0
Total Current Liabilities	3,011.6	2,303.7
Non-Current Liabilities		
Deferred income taxes	137.0	101.6
Other non-current liabilities	478.0	464.4
Total Non-Current Liabilities	615.0	566.0
Shareholders' Equity		
Preferred stock, $.0625 par value; authorized 32 million shares; none issued	—	—
Common stock, $.078125 par value; authorized 3.2 billion shares; issued and outstanding 1,019,425,052 in 2001 and 1,010,818,890 in 2000	79.6	79.0
Paid-in capital	596.7	367.2
Retained earnings	4,530.9	3,787.8
Total Shareholders' Equity	5,207.2	4,234.0
Total Liabilities and Shareholders' Equity	$8,833.8	$7,103.7

(continued)

COMPARISONS   Absolute figures or ratios appear meaningless unless compared to other figures or ratios. If a person were asked if ten dollars is a lot of money, the frame of reference would determine the answer. To a small child, still in awe of a quarter, ten dollars is a lot. To a millionaire, a ten-dollar bill is nothing. Similarly, having 60% of total assets composed of buildings and equipment would be normal for some firms but disastrous for others. One must have a guide to determine the meaning of the ratios and other measures. Several types of comparisons offer insight.

Trend Analysis

Trend analysis studies the financial history of a firm for comparison. By looking at the trend of a particular ratio, one sees whether that ratio is falling, rising, or remaining relatively constant. This helps detect problems or observe good management.

EXHIBIT 5-3   **WALGREEN CO. AND SUBSIDIARIES**
Merchandising Firm (*continued*)

Consolidated Statement of Earnings and Shareholders' Equity

Walgreen Co. and Subsidiaries for the Years Ended August 31, 2001, 2000, and 1999
(Dollars in Millions, except per share data)

Earnings	2001	2000	1999
Net Sales	$24,623.0	$21,206.9	$17,838.8
Costs and Deductions			
Cost of sales	18,048.9	15,465.9	12,978.6
Selling, occupancy and administration	5,175.8	4,516.9	3,844.8
	23,224.7	19,982.8	16,823.4
Other (Income) Expense			
Interest income	(5.4)	(6.1)	(12.3)
Interest expense	3.1	.4	.4
Other income	(22.1)	(33.5)	
	(24.4)	(39.2)	(11.9)
Earnings			
Earnings before income tax provision	1,422.7	1,263.3	1,027.3
Income tax provision	537.1	486.4	403.2
Net Earnings	$ 885.6	$ 776.9	$ 624.1
Net Earnings per Common Share			
Basic	$.87	$.77	$.62
Diluted	$.86	$.76	$.62
Average shares outstanding	1,016,197,785	1,007,393,572	1,000,363,234
Dilutive effect of stock options	12,748,828	12,495,236	13,918,481
Average shares outstanding assuming dilution	1,028,946,613	1,019,888,808	1,014,281,715

	Common Stock		Paid-in	Retained
Shareholder's Equity	**Shares**	**Amount**	**Capital**	**Earnings**
Balance, August 31, 1998	996,487,044	$77.8	$118.1	$2,653.0
Net earnings	—	—	—	624.1
Cash dividends declared ($.13 per share)	—	—	—	(130.1)
Employee stock purchase and option plans	7,535,214	.6	140.8	
Balance, August 31, 1999	1,004,022,258	78.4	258.9	3,147.0
Net earnings	—	—	—	776.9
Cash dividends declared ($.135 per share)	—	—	—	(136.1)
Employee stock purchase and option plans	6,796,632	.6	108.3	
Balance, August 31, 2000	1,010,818,890	79.0	367.2	3,787.8
Net earnings	—	—	—	885.6
Cash dividends declared ($.14 per share)	—	—	—	(142.5)
Employee stock purchase and option plans	8,606,162	.6	229.5	
Balance, August 31, 2001	1,019,425,052	$79.6	$596.7	$4,530.9

Standard Industrial Classification (SIC) Manual

The Standard Industrial Classification is a statistical classification of business by industry. The National Technical Information Service publishes the classification manual. The manual is the responsibility of the Office of Management and Budget, which is under the executive office of the President.

Use of the SIC promotes comparability of various facets of the U.S. economy and defines industries in accordance with the composition and structure of the economy. An organization's SIC

| EXHIBIT 5-4 | **THE INTERPUBLIC GROUP OF COMPANIES**
Financial Statements—Service Firm |

CONSOLIDATED BALANCE SHEET

The Interpublic Group of Companies, Inc. and its Subsidiaries

(Amounts in Millions, Except Per Share Amounts)

December 31	2001	2000
ASSETS		
CURRENT ASSETS:		
Cash and cash equivalents (includes certificates of deposit: 2001—$93.8; 2000—$110.9)	$ 935.2	$ 844.6
Accounts receivable (net of allowance for doubtful accounts: 2001—$90.7; 2000—$85.7)	4,780.5	5,735.7
Expenditures billable to clients	333.0	437.9
Deferred taxes on income	80.0	—
Prepaid expenses and other current assets	338.5	277.8
Total current assets	6,467.2	7,296.0
FIXED ASSETS, AT COST:		
Land and buildings	161.1	174.1
Furniture and equipment	1,085.8	1,103.7
Leasehold improvements	461.4	427.8
	1,708.3	1,705.6
Less: accumulated depreciation	(858.0)	(879.2)
Total fixed assets	850.3	826.4
OTHER ASSETS:		
Investment in unconsolidated affiliates	165.0	178.9
Deferred taxes on income	492.8	380.3
Other assets and miscellaneous investments	432.5	525.4
Intangible assets (net of accumulated amortization: 2001—$1,024.8; 2000—$861.5)	3,106.9	3,155.0
Total other assets	4,197.2	4,239.6
TOTAL ASSETS	$11,514.7	$12,362.0

(continued)

consists of a two-digit major group number, a three-digit industry group number, and a four-digit industry number. These numbers describe the business's identifiable level of industrial detail.

Determining a company's SIC is a good starting point in researching a company, an industry, or a product. Many library sources use the SIC number as a method of classification.

North American Industry Classification System (NAICS)

The North American Industry Classification System (NAICS) was created jointly by the United States, Canada, and Mexico. It is to replace the existing classification of each country: the Standard Industrial Classification of Canada (1980), the Mexican Classification of Activities and Products (1994), and the Standard Industrial Classification of the United States (1987).

For the NAICS economic units with similar production processes are classified in the same industry, and the lines drawn between industries demarcate differences in production processes. This supply based economic concept was adopted because an industry classification system is a framework for collecting information on both inputs and outputs. This will aid in the collection of statistics on such things as productivity, unit labor costs, and capital intensity.

NAICS provides enhanced industry comparability among the three NAFTA trading partners. It also increases compatibility with the two-digit level of the International Standard Industrial Classification (ISIC Rev. 3) of the United Nations.

EXHIBIT 5-4

THE INTERPUBLIC GROUP OF COMPANIES
Financial Statements—Service Firm (*continued*)

CONSOLIDATED BALANCE SHEET

The Interpublic Group of Companies, Inc. and its Subsidiaries

(Amounts in Millions, Except Per Share Amounts)

December 31	2001	2000
LIABILITIES AND STOCKHOLDERS' EQUITY		
CURRENT LIABILITIES:		
Accounts payable	$ 4,525.2	$ 5,751.3
Accrued expenses	1,316.5	1,081.7
Accrued income taxes	103.1	210.3
Dividends payable	36.0	29.4
Short-term bank borrowings	418.5	483.8
Current portion of long-term debt	34.6	65.5
Total current liabilities	6,433.9	7,622.0
NON-CURRENT LIABILITIES:		
Long-term debt	1,356.8	998.7
Convertible subordinated notes	548.5	533.1
Zero-coupon convertible senior notes	575.3	—
Deferred compensation	376.7	464.3
Accrued postretirement benefits	54.4	55.2
Other non-current liabilities	100.5	105.7
Minority interests in consolidated subsidiaries	89.3	100.6
Total non-current liabilities	3,101.5	2,257.6
Commitments and contingencies (Note 16)		
STOCKHOLDERS' EQUITY:		
Preferred stock, no par value,		
shares authorized: 20.0, shares issued: none		
Common stock, $0.10 par value,		
shares authorized: 550.0,		
shares issued: 2001—385.8; 2000—377.3	38.6	37.7
Additional paid-in capital	1,785.2	1,514.7
Retained earnings	1,011.2	1,667.5
Accumulated other comprehensive loss, net of tax	(451.5)	(411.6)
	2,383.5	2,808.3
Less:		
Treasury stock, at cost: 2001—7.3 shares; 2000—5.5 shares	(290.2)	(194.8)
Unamortized deferred compensation	(114.0)	(131.1)
Total stockholders' equity	1,979.3	2,482.4
TOTAL LIABILITIES AND STOCKHOLDERS' EQUITY	$11,514.7	$12,362.0

(continued)

NAICS divides the economy into 20 sectors. Industries within these sectors are grouped according to the production criterion. Four sectors are largely goods-producing and 16 are entirely services-producing industries.

In most sectors, NAICS provides for compatibility at the industry (five-digit) level. For some sectors the compatibility level is less at four-digit, three-digit, or two-digit levels. Each country can add additional detailed industries, provided the additional detail aggregates to the NAICS level.

The United States adopted the NAICS in 1997. Most of the United States government agencies now use the NAICS in place of the Standard Industrial Classification (SIC). A major exception is the Securities and Exchange Commission (SEC). Companies reporting to the SEC include their SIC on their reports to the SEC. For private companies that publish industry data, some now only use the NAICS, some use the SIC, and some include both the NAICS and the SIC.

| EXHIBIT 5-4 | **THE INTERPUBLIC GROUP OF COMPANIES** **Financial Statements—Service Firm (*continued*)** |

CONSOLIDATED STATEMENT OF OPERATIONS

The Interpublic Group of Companies, Inc. and its Subsidiaries

(Amounts in Millions, Except Per Share Amounts)

Year Ended December 31	2001	2000	1999
REVENUE	$6,726.8	$7,182.7	$6,417.2
OPERATING EXPENSES:			
Salaries and related expenses	3,787.1	4,035.2	3,617.4
Office and general expenses	2,026.1	1,976.4	1,862.5
Amortization of intangible assets	173.0	144.3	128.4
Restructuring and other merger related costs	645.6	177.7	159.5
Goodwill impairment and other charges	303.1	—	—
Total operating expenses	6,934.9	6,333.6	5,767.8
OPERATING INCOME (LOSS)	(208.1)	849.1	649.4
OTHER INCOME (EXPENSE):			
Interest expense	(164.6)	(126.3)	(99.5)
Interest income	43.0	57.5	56.2
Other income	13.7	46.2	65.8
Investment impairment	(208.3)	—	—
Total other income (expense)	(316.2)	(22.6)	22.5
Income (loss) before provision for (benefit of) income taxes	(524.3)	826.5	671.9
Provision for (benefit of) income taxes	(43.9)	348.8	285.3
Income (loss) of consolidated companies	(480.4)	477.7	386.6
Income applicable to minority interests	(30.3)	(42.8)	(38.2)
Equity in net income (loss) of unconsolidated affiliates	5.4	(14.6)	11.0
NET INCOME (LOSS)	$ (505.3)	$ 420.3	$ 359.4
Earnings (loss) per share:			
Basic EPS	$ (1.37)	$ 1.17	$ 1.02
Diluted EPS	$ (1.37)	$ 1.14	$ 0.99
Weighted average shares:			
Basic	369.0	359.6	352.0
Diluted	369.0	370.6	364.6
Cash dividends per share	$ 0.38	$ 0.37	$ 0.33

Industry Averages and Comparison with Competitors

The analysis of an entity's financial statements is more meaningful if the results are compared with industry averages and with results of competitors. Several financial services provide composite data on various industries.

The analyst faces a problem when the industries reported do not clearly include the company being examined because the company is diversified into many industrial areas. Since many companies do not clearly fit into any one industry, it is often necessary to use an industry that best fits the firm. The financial services have a similar problem in selecting an industry in which to place a company. Thus, a financial service uses its best judgment as to which industry the firm best fits.

This section briefly describes some financial services. For a more extensive explanation, consult the service's literature. Each service explains how it computes its ratios and the data it provides.

The Department of Commerce Financial Report is a publication of the federal government for manufacturing, mining, and trade corporations. Published by the Economic Surveys Division of the Bureau of the Census, it includes income statement data and balance sheet data in total industry dollars. It also includes an industry-wide common-size vertical income statement (Income Statement in Ratio Format) and an industry-wide common-size vertical balance sheet (Selected Balance Sheet

EXHIBIT 5-5

COOPER TIRE & RUBBER COMPANY
Manufacturing Firm

Consolidated Balance Sheets

(Dollar amounts in thousands except per share amounts)

Assets	December 31 2000	2001
Current assets:		
Cash and cash equivalents	$ 45,795	$ 71,835
Accounts receivable, less allowance or $11,000 in 2000 and $13,159 in 2001	581,142	497,180
Inventories:		
Finished goods	192,357	207,484
Work in process	32,882	32,838
Raw materials and supplies	71,221	66,156
	296,460	306,478
Prepaid expenses, deferred income taxes and assets held for sale	74,793	76,604
Total current assets	998,190	952,097
Property, plant and equipment:		
Land and land improvements	47,737	47,713
Buildings	408,332	393,065
Machinery and equipment	1,568,760	1,636,773
Molds, cores and rings	138,588	156,209
	2,163,417	2,233,760
Less accumulated depreciation and amortization	878,020	1,027,686
Net property, plant and equipment	1,285,397	1,206,074
Goodwill, net of accumulated amortization of $17,237 in 2000 and $33,199 in 2001	439,443	427,895
Intangibles, net of accumulated amortization of $10,492 in 2000 and $14,698 in 2001, and other assets	173,643	178,184
	$ 2,896,673	$2,764,250

Liabilities and Stockholders' Equity

	2000	2001
Current liabilities:		
Notes payable	$ 154,997	$ 15,875
Accounts payable	186,284	191,802
Accrued liabilities	218,021	222,503
Income taxes	4,249	564
Current portion of long-term debt	15,193	217,161
Total current liabilities	578,744	647,905
Long-term debt	1,036,960	882,134
Postretirement benefits other than pensions	190,175	197,757
Other long-term liabilities	75,791	106,202
Deferred income tax	62,447	20,012
Stockholders' equity:		
Preferred stock, $1 per share par value; 5,000,000 shares authorized: none issued	—	—
Common stock, $1 per share par value; 300,000,000 shares authorized; (83,848,027 in 2000) 83,903,845 shares issued in 2001	83,848	83,904
Capital in excess of par value	3,982	4,658
Retained earnings	1,115,389	1,103,080
Cumulative other comprehensive loss	(53,642)	(84,390)
	1,149,577	1,107,252
Less: (11,304,400 in 2000) 11,303,900 shares in treasury at cost	(197,021)	(197,012)
Total stockholders' equity	952,556	910,240
	$ 2,896,673	$2,764,250

(continued)

EXHIBIT 5-5

COOPER TIRE & RUBBER COMPANY
Manufacturing Firm (*continued*)

Consolidated Statements of Income

(Dollar amounts in thousands except per share amounts)

| | Years ended December 31 | | |
	1999	2000	2001
Net sales	$2,196,343	$3,472,372	**$3,154,702**
Cost of products sold	1,810,524	2,939,815	**2,724,692**
Gross profit	385,819	532,557	**430,010**
Selling, general and administrative	144,189	225,824	**227,229**
Class action costs	—	—	**72,194**
Amortization of goodwill	2,550	15,553	**15,705**
Restructuring	—	38,699	**8,648**
Operating profit	239,080	252,481	**106,234**
Interest expense	24,445	97,461	**90,695**
Other income—net	(862)	(5,136)	**(13,619)**
Income before income taxes	215,497	160,156	**29,158**
Provision for income taxes	80,023	63,422	**10,992**
Net income	$ 135,474	$ 96,734	**$ 18,166**
Basic and diluted earnings per share	$1.79	$1.31	**$0.25**

Ratios). This source also includes selected operating and balance sheet ratios. This government publication uses NAICS for classification.

This report, updated quarterly, probably offers the most current source. It typically becomes available within six or seven months after the end of the quarter. It is a unique source of industry data in total dollars and would enable a company to compare its dollars (such as sales) with the industry dollars (sales). This service is free and is now on the Internet.

Robert Morris Associates Annual Statement Studies is published by Robert Morris Associates, the association of lending and credit risk professionals. Submitted by institutional members of Robert Morris Associates, the data cover several hundred different industries in manufacturing, wholesaling, retailing, service, agriculture, and construction.

Annual Statement Studies groups the data by industry, using the SIC number, and the NAICS number. It provides common-size balance sheets, income statements, and 16 selected ratios.

The data are sorted by assets and sales and are particularly useful because the financial position and operations of small firms are often quite different from those of larger firms. The Robert Morris presentation also includes a five-year comparison of historical data that presents all firms under a particular SIC code number.

In each category, the ratios are computed for the median and the upper and lower quartiles. For example:

Number of firms (9)
Ratio—Return on total assets
Results for the nine firms (in order, from highest to lowest):
   12%, 11%, 10.5%, 10%, 9.8%, 9.7%, 9.6%, 7.0%, 6.5%
The middle result is the median: 9.8%
The result halfway between the top result and the median is the upper quartile: 10.5%
The result halfway between the bottom result and the median is the lower quartile: 9.6%

For ratios in which a low value is desirable, the results are presented from low values to high:
For example, 2% (upper quartile), 5% (median), and 8% (lower quartile).

Because of the combination of common-size statements, selected ratios, and comparative historical data, *Robert Morris Associates Annual Statement Studies* is one of the most extensively used sources of industry data. Commercial loan officers in banks frequently use this source.

Notice the section called "Interpretation of Statement Studies Figures," Exhibit 5-6, which indicates that statement studies should be "regarded only as general guidelines and not as absolute industry norms." It then proceeds to list reasons why the data may not be fully representative of a given industry. This word of caution is useful in keeping the user from concluding that the data represent an absolute norm for a given industry.

Standard & Poor's Industry Surveys contains a five-year summary on several firms within an industry group. Some of the data include:

1. Operating revenues
2. Net income
3. Return on revenues (%)
4. Return on assets (%)
5. Return on equity (%)
6. Current ratio
7. Debt/capital ratio (%)
8. Debt as a percent of net working capital
9. Price-earnings ratio (high-low)
10. Dividend payout ratio (%)
11. Yield (high %-low %)
12. Earnings per share
13. Book value per share
14. Share price (high-low)

Industry Surveys also includes composite industry data. Industry surveys are of particular interest to investors.

Almanac of Business and Industrial Financial Ratios, published by Prentice Hall, is a compilation of corporate tax return data. It includes a broad range of industries and presents 50 statistics for 11 size categories of firms. Some of the industries include manufacturing, construction, transportation, retail trade, banking, and wholesale trade. Each *Almanac* industry is cross-referenced to a NAICS number.

Industry Norms and Key Business Ratios, desktop edition published by Dun & Bradstreet, includes over 800 different lines of business as defined by the SIC code numbers. It includes one-year data consisting of a condensed balance sheet and income statement in dollars and common size. It also includes working capital and ratios.

EXHIBIT 5-6	**ROBERT MORRIS ASSOCIATES** **Annual Statement Studies**

Interpretation of Statement Studies Figures

RMA recommends that *Statement Studies* data be regarded only as general guidelines and not as absolute industry norms. There are several reasons why the data may not be fully representative of a given industry.

(1) The financial statements used in the *Statement Studies* are not selected by any random or statistically reliable method. RMA member banks voluntarily submit the raw data they have available each year with no limitation on company size.

(2) Many companies have varied product lines; however, the *Statement Studies* categorize them by their primary product Standard Industrial Classification (SIC) number only.*

(3) Some of our industry samples are rather small in relation to the total number of firms in a given industry. A relatively small sample can increase the chances that some of our composites do not fully represent an industry.

(4) There is the chance that an extreme statement can be present in a sample, causing a disproportionate influence on the industry composite. This is particularly true in a relatively small sample.

(5) Companies within the same industry may differ in their method of operations which in turn can directly influence their financial statements. Since they are included in our sample, too, these statements can significantly affect our composite calculations.

(6) Other considerations that can result in variations among different companies engaged in the same general line of business are different labor markets, geographical location, different account methods, quality of products handled, sources and methods of financing, and terms of sale.

For these reasons, RMA does not recommend the Statement Studies *figures be considered as absolute norms for a given industry. Rather the figures should be used only as general guidelines and in addition to the other methods of financial analysis. RMA makes no claim as to the representativeness of the figures printed in this book.*

---

* As noted on page 151, Annual Statement Studies now uses the SIC number and the NAICS number.

There are 14 ratios presented for the upper quartile, median, and lower quartile. The 14 ratios are:

Solvency
  Quick Ratio (Times)
  Current Ratio (Times)
  Current Liabilities to Net Worth (%)
  Current Liabilities to Inventory (%)
  Total Liabilities to Net Worth (%)
  Fixed Assets to Net Worth (%)
Efficiency
  Collection Period (days)
  Sales to Inventory (Times)
  Assets to Sales (%)
  Sales to Net Working Capital (Times)
  Accounts Payable to Sales (%)
Profitability
  Return on Sales (%)
  Return on Assets (%)
  Return on Net Working Capital (%)

Dun & Bradstreet advises that the industry norms and key business ratios are to be used as yardsticks and not as absolutes. *Industry Norms and Key Business Ratios* is also published in an expanded set in the following five segments:

1. Agriculture/Mining/Construction/Transportation/Communication/Utilities
2. Manufacturing
3. Wholesaling
4. Retailing
5. Finance/Real Estate/Services

All five segments are available in three different formats, for a total of 15 books. The three formats follow:

1. Industry Norms for last three years
2. Industry Norms one-year edition
3. Key Business Ratios one-year edition

Value Line Investment Service contains profitability and investment data for 1,700 individual firms and for industries in general. *Value Line* places companies in 1 of 96 industries. This service rates each stock's timeliness and safety. It is very popular with investors.

The data included in *Value Line* for a company are largely for a relatively long period of time (5 to 10 years). Some of the data provided for each company are as follows:

1. Revenues per share
2. Cash flow per share
3. Earnings per share
4. Dividends declared per share
5. Capital spending per share
6. Book value per share
7. Common shares outstanding
8. Average annual P/E ratio
9. Relative P/E ratio
10. Average annual dividend yield
11. Revenues
12. Net profit
13. Income tax rate
14. AFUDC % to net profit
15. Long-term debt ratio

16. Common equity ratio
17. Total capital
18. Net plant
19. Percent earned total capital
20. Percent earned net worth
21. Percent earned common equity
22. Percent retained to common equity
23. Percent all dividends to net profit

Tax Financial Statement Benchmarks, published by John Wiley & Sons, provides industry benchmarks from IRS tax return data representing approximately 4 million corporations in the United States. The data are aggregated into 235 industries and industry groups, identified by both SIC and IRS Principal Business Activity (PBA) codes. The corporations in each industry are categorized by asset size into 13 size-classes. Income statement, balance sheet, and operating data are presented in percentage form. There are also profitability, liquidity, leverage, and other financial ratios.

As indicated previously, comparison has become more difficult in recent years as more firms become conglomerates and diversify into many product lines. To counteract this problem, the SEC has implemented line-of-business reporting requirements for companies that must submit their reports to the SEC. These reports are made available to the public. SFAS No. 14 also addresses line-of-business reporting requirements. Such reporting requirements ease the analysis problem created by conglomerates but cannot eliminate it because the entity must decide how to allocate administrative and joint costs.

If industry figures are unavailable or if comparison with a competitor is desired, another firm's statements may be analyzed. Remember, however, that the other firm is not necessarily good or bad, nor does it represent a norm or standard for its industry.

Alternative accounting methods are acceptable in many situations. Since identical companies may use different valuation or expense methods, read statements and footnotes carefully to determine if the statements are reasonably comparable.

Ideally, the use of all types of comparison would be best. Using trend analysis, industry averages, and comparisons with a major competitor will give support to findings and will provide a concrete basis for analysis.

In analyzing ratios, the analyst will sometimes encounter negative profit figures. **Analysis of ratios that have negative numerators or denominators is meaningless, and the negative sign of the ratio should simply be noted.**

Caution in Using Industry Averages

Financial analysis requires judgment decisions on the part of the analyst. Users of financial statements must be careful not to place complete confidence in ratios or comparisons.

Remember that ratios are simply fractions with a numerator (top) and a denominator (bottom). There are as many for financial analysis as there are pairs of figures. There is no set group, nor is a particular ratio always computed using the same figures. Even the industry ratio formulas vary from source to source. Adequate detailed disclosure of how the industry ratios are computed is often lacking. Major problems can result from analyzing a firm according to the recommendations of a book and then making comparisons to industry ratios that may have been computed differently.

The use of different accounting methods causes a problem. Since identical firms may use different valuation or revenue recognition methods, read statements and footnotes carefully to determine the degree of comparability between statements. Trend analysis for each firm, however, will usually be meaningful. Industry averages group firms that use different accounting principles.

Different year-ends can also produce different results. Consider the difference in the inventory of two toy stores if one ends November 30 and the other ends December 31. The ratios of firms with differing year-ends are all grouped together in industry averages.

Firms with differing financial policies might be included in the same industry average. Possibly capital-intensive firms are grouped with labor-intensive companies. Firms with large amounts of debt may be included in the same average as firms that prefer to avoid the risk of debt.

Some industry averages come from small samples that may not be representative of the industry. An extreme statement, such as one containing a large loss, can also distort industry data.

Ratios may have alternative forms of computation. In comparing one year to the next, one firm to another, or a company to its industry, meaningful analysis requires that the ratios be computed using the same formula. For example, Robert Morris computes income ratios before tax; Dun & Bradstreet profit figures are after tax. The analyst should compute the enterprise ratios on the same basis as is used for industry comparisons, but this is often not possible.

Finally, ratios are not absolute norms. They are general guidelines to be combined with other methods in formulating an evaluation of the financial condition of a firm. Despite the problems with using ratios, they can be very informative if reasonably used.

RELATIVE SIZE OF FIRM

Comparisons of firms of different sizes may be more difficult than comparisons of firms of equal size. For example, larger firms often have access to wider and more sophisticated capital markets, can buy in large quantities, and service wider markets. Ratios and common-size analysis help to eliminate some of the problems related to the use of absolute numbers.

Be aware of the different sizes of firms under comparison. These differences can be seen by looking at relative sales, assets, or profit sizes. Investment services such as *Value Line* often make available another meaningful figure—percent of market.

OTHER LIBRARY SOURCES

The typical business library has many sources of information relating to a particular company, industry, and product. Some of these sources are described here to aid you in your search for information about a company, its industry, and its products.

Ward's Business Directory

Ward's Business Directory covers domestic private and public companies. Up to 20 items of information are provided for each company listed. The data may include names, addresses, telephone numbers, e-mails and URLs, sales, employee figures, and up to five names and titles of executive officers.

The directory is published in eight volumes. Volumes 1, 2, and 3 contain profiles of private and public companies arranged alphabetically. Volume 4 provides profiles of all the companies listed in Volumes 1, 2, and 3 organized by state and lists each company in ascending ZIP Code order. Volume 5 organizes the companies by the 4-digit SIC code that most closely resembles their principal industry and ranks them according to revenue. Volume 6 and 7 organizes the companies by state, then by the 4-digit SIC code. Volume 8 organizes the companies by the 5- or 6-digit NAICS code and ranks them according to revenue. A number of the volumes include special features that are too extensive to describe here.

Ward's Business Directory is good for obtaining the SIC and NAICS code for a company. It also includes a conversion guide from SIC to NAICS codes, and from NAICS to SIC codes.

Standard & Poor's Reports

Standard & Poor's Reports covers companies on the New York Stock Exchange, American Stock Exchange, over-the-counter companies, and regional exchanges. Arranged alphabetically by stock exchange, they contain a brief narrative analysis of companies regularly traded and provide key financial data. Company information is updated four times per year on a rotating basis.

Standard & Poor's Register of Corporations, Directors, and Executives

This annual source is arranged in three volumes. Volume 1 contains an alphabetical list of approximately 55,000 corporations, including such data as ZIP Codes, telephone numbers, and functions of officers, directors, and other principals. The NAICS code is included at the end of each listing.

Volume 2 contains an alphabetical list of individuals serving as officers, directors, trustees, partners, and so on. It provides such data as principal business affiliations, business address, and residence address.

Volume 3 contains seven sections:

- *Section 1*—Explains the construction and use of the NAICS code numbers and lists these numbers by major groups and by alphabetical and numerical division of major groups.
- *Section 2*—Lists corporations under the six-digit NAICS codes, which are arranged in numerical order.
- *Section 3*—Lists companies geographically by states and by major cities.
- *Section 4*—Lists and cross-references subsidiaries, divisions, and affiliates in alphabetical sequence and links them to their ultimate parent company listed in Volume 1.
- *Section 5*—Lists the deaths of which publishers have been notified in the past year.
- *Section 6*—Lists individuals whose names appear in the Register for the first time.
- *Section 7*—Lists the companies appearing in the Register for the first time.

Standard & Poor's Analyst's Handbook

This source contains selected income account and balance sheet items and related ratios as applied to the Standard & Poor's industry group stock price indexes. The progress of a given company may possibly be compared with a composite of its industry groups. Brief monthly updates for selected industries supplement the annual editions of the handbook.

Standard & Poor's Corporation Records

This source provides background information and detailed financial statistics on U.S. corporations, with extensive coverage for some corporations. Historical information is arranged in a multivalue section separate from the "Daily News" section. The contents and the index are updated throughout the year.

America's Corporate Families:® The Billion Dollar Directory®

The directory listings include 12,700 parent companies. Corporate family listings are alphabetical, geographical, and by SIC classification. This annual directory provides a cross-reference index of divisions, subsidiaries, and ultimate parent companies, as well as such data as lines of business and telephone numbers of parent and subsidiary companies.

D&B® Million Dollar Directory®

This directory provides information on more than 160,000 U.S. companies. Company listings are shown alphabetically, geographically, and by SIC classification. Data include lines of business, accounting firm, stock ticker symbol, and names of officers.

Directory of Corporate Affiliations

This directory gives an in-depth view of companies and their divisions, subsidiaries, and affiliates. It contains an alphabetical index, geographical index, and SIC classifications. The parent company listing consists of address, telephone number, stock ticker symbol, stock exchange(s), approximate sales, number of employees, type of business, and top corporate officers.

Thomas Register of American Manufacturers

This is a comprehensive "yellow pages" of products and services, as follows:

- *Red section*—Products and services listed alphabetically.
- *Yellow section*—Company profiles with addresses, ZIP Codes, telephone numbers, branch officials, asset ratings, and company officials.
- *Blue section*—Catalogs of companies; cross-referenced to the red volumes.

Moody's Investors' Services

Moody's Industrial Manual examines corporations with detailed summary coverage of the history, principal products and services, and detailed financial tables. They are color-coded and arranged in major industry/service groups: Bank and finance, Industrial, OTC industrial, OTC unlisted, International, Municipal government, Public utility, and Transportation.

Also available from Moody's are the following:

- *Moody's Bond Record*
- *Moody's Bond Survey*
- *Moody's Dividend Record*
- *Moody's Handbook of Common Stock*

Securities Owner's Stock Guide

This monthly guide, published by Standard & Poor's, covers over 5,300 common and preferred stocks. It contains trading activity, price range, dividends, and so on for companies traded on the New York Stock Exchange, American Stock Exchange, over the counter, and regional exchanges. The information is displayed with numerous abbreviations and footnotes, in order to fit concisely into one single line, for each publicly traded security.

The Wall Street Transcript

The Wall Street Transcript newspaper provides access to corporate management presentations to financial analysts and brokerage house assessment reports of corporations and industries. Each issue contains a cumulative index for the current quarter. Each issue also has a reference to the cumulative index for a relatively long period of time, such as for the prior year.

The Wall Street Journal Index

This index provides abstracts and comprehensive indexing of all articles in the 3-Star Eastern Edition of *The Wall Street Journal*. Some of the items included are feature articles, editorials, news items, and earnings reports.

The Official Index to The Financial Times

This index is compiled from the final London editions of *The Financial Times* and *The Weekend Financial Times*. It can be used to locate reports and articles in these publications.

Predicasts F & S Index

This family of indexes, previously known as the Funk & Scott Index of Corporations and Industries, includes:

- *Predicasts F & S Index—United States*
- *Predicasts F & S Index—Europe*
- *Predicasts F & S Index—International*

This comprehensive family of indexes to articles on corporations and industries issued monthly covers 1965 to the present. Each listing includes business periodicals, newspapers, government documents, and investment services reports. The material is arranged by company and industry by SIC code number.

Reference Book of Corporate Managements

The four volumes contain profile information on over 200,000 principal corporate officers in over 12,000 companies. The information includes the year of birth, education, military service, present business position, and previous positions. Names and titles of other officers, as well as names of directors who are not officers, are also provided.

Compact Disclosure

This database of textual and financial information on approximately 14,000 public companies can be accessed by a menu-driven screen. The information is taken from annual and periodic reports filed by each company with the Securities and Exchange Commission. A full printout for a company is approximately 14 pages. It includes the major financial statements (annual and quarterly), many financial ratios for the prior three years, institutional holdings, ownership by insiders, president's letter, and financial footnotes.

A company can be accessed by keying its name or ticker symbol. In addition, the system can be searched by type of business (SIC), by geographic area (state, city, ZIP Code, or telephone area code), stock price financial ratios, and much more.

THE USERS OF FINANCIAL STATEMENTS	The financial statements are prepared for a group of diversified users. Users of financial data have their own objectives in analysis.

Management, an obvious user of financial data, must analyze the data from the viewpoints of both investors and creditors. Management must be concerned about the current position of the entity to meet its obligations, as well as the future earning prospects of the firm.

Management is interested in the financial structure of the entity in order to determine a proper mix of short-term debt, long-term debt, and equity from owners. Also of interest is the asset structure of the entity: the combination of cash, inventory, receivables, investments, and fixed assets.

Management must guide the entity toward sound short-term and long-term financial policies and also earn a profit. For example, liquidity and profitability are competitive since the most highly liquid assets (cash and marketable securities) are usually the least profitable. It does the entity little good to be guided toward a maximum profitability goal if resources are not available to meet current obligations. The entity would soon find itself in bankruptcy as creditors cut off lines of credit and demand payment. Similarly, management must utilize resources properly to obtain a reasonable return.

The investing public, another category of users, is interested in specific types of analysis. Investors are concerned with the financial position of the entity and its ability to earn future profits. The investor uses an analysis of past trends and the current position of the entity to project the future prospects of the entity.

Credit grantors are interested in the financial statements of the entity. Pure credit grantors obtain a limited return from extending credit: a fixed rate of interest (as in the case of banks) or the profit on the merchandise or services provided (as in the case of suppliers). Since these rewards are limited and the possibility exists that the principal will not be repaid, credit grantors tend to be conservative in extending credit.

The same principle applies to suppliers that extend credit. If merchandise with a 20% markup is sold on credit, it takes five successful sales of the same amount to make up for one sale not collected. In addition, the creditor considers the cost of the funds when extending credit. Extending credit really amounts to financing the entity.

A difference exists between the objectives of short-term grantors of credit and those of long-term grantors. The short-term creditor can look primarily to current resources that appear on the financial statements in order to determine if credit should be extended. Long-term creditors must usually look to the future prospects of earnings in order to be repaid. For example, if bonds are issued that are to be repaid in 30 years, the current resources of the entity will not be an indication of its ability to meet this obligation. The repayment for this obligation will come from future earnings. Thus, the objectives of financial analysis by credit grantors will vary, based on such factors as the term of the credit and the purpose. Profitability of the entity may not be a major consideration, as long as the resources for repayment can be projected. |

The financial structure of the entity is of interest to creditors because the amount of equity capital in relation to debt indicates the risk that the owners bear in relation to the creditors. The equity capital provides creditors with a cushion against loss. When this equity cushion is small, creditors are bearing the risk of the entity.

Many other parties are interested in analyzing financial statements. Unions that represent employees are interested in the ability of the entity to grant wage increases and fringe benefits, such as pension plans. The government also has an interest in analyzing financial statements for tax purposes and to ensure compliance with antitrust laws.

SUMMARY

Financial analysis consists of the quantitative and qualitative aspects of measuring the relative financial position among firms and among industries. Analysis can be done in different ways, depending on the type of firm or industry and the specific needs of the user. Financial statements will vary by size of firm and among industries.

To the Net

1. Go to the SEC site (http://www.sec.gov). Under Filings & Forms (Edgar), click on "Search for Company Filings." Click on "Search Companies and Filings." Under company name enter "Novell." Select the 10-K filed January 28, 2002. For the following partial consolidated statements of operations compute horizontal and vertical common-size analysis. Use October 31, 1999, for the base in the horizontal common-size analysis. Use net sales for the vertical common-size analysis. Comment on the results.

| | **Fiscal Year Ended** | | |
	October 31 2001	October 31 2000	October 31 1999
Net sales			
Cost of sales			
Gross profit			
Operating expenses			
Sales and marketing			
Product development			
General and administrative			
Restructuring changes			
Total operating expenses			

2. Go to the SEC site (http://www.sec.gov). Under Filings & Forms (Edgar), click on "Search for Company Filings." Click on "Search Companies and Filings." Under company name enter "Amazon." Select the 10-K405 filed January 24, 2002. Copy the following from the consolidated statements of operations. Comment on the results.

| | **Years Ended December 31,** | | |
	2001	*2000*	*1999*
Net sales			
Loss from operations			
Interest expense			

3. Go to the SEC site (http://www.sec.gov). Under Filings & Forms (Edgar), click on "Search for Company Filings." Click on "Search Companies and Filings." Under company name enter "Kroger." Select the 10-K filed May 1, 2002. For the following partial consolidated statement of income prepare a horizontal common-size analysis with change in dollars. Use the year ended February 3, 2001 as the base. Comment on the results.

Consolidated Statement of Income
Years Ended February 2, 2002 and February 3, 2001
(in millions)

	2001 52 Weeks	2000 53 Weeks	Increase (Decrease) Dollars	Percent
Sales				
Merchandise costs, including advertising, warehousing and transportation				
Gross profit				
Operating, general and administrative				
Rent				
Depreciation and amortization				
Goodwill amortization				
Asset impairment charges				
Restructuring charges				
Merger related costs				
Operating profit				

Questions

Q 5-1. What is a ratio? How do ratios help to alleviate the problems of size differences among firms?

Q 5-2. What does each of the following categories of ratios attempt to measure? (a) liquidity; (b) long-term borrowing capacity; (c) profitability. Name a group of users who might be interested in each category.

Q 5-3. Brown Company earned 5.5% on sales in 2003. What further information would be needed to evaluate this result?

Q 5-4. Differentiate between absolute and percentage changes. Which is generally a better measure of change? Why?

Q 5-5. Differentiate between horizontal and vertical analysis. Using sales as a component for each type, give an example that explains the difference.

Q 5-6. What is trend analysis? Can it be used for ratios? For absolute figures?

Q 5-7. Suppose you are comparing two firms within an industry. One is large and the other is small. Will relative or absolute numbers be of more value in each case? What kinds of statistics can help evaluate relative size?

Q 5-8. Are managers the only users of financial reports? Discuss.

Q 5-9. Briefly describe how each of these groups might use financial reports: managers, investors, and creditors.

Q 5-10. Refer to Exhibits 5-3, 5-4, and 5-5 to answer the following questions:
a. For each of the firms illustrated, what is the single largest asset category? Does this seem typical of this type of firm?
b. Which of the three firms has the largest amount in current assets in relation to the amount in current liabilities? Does this seem logical? Explain.

Q 5-11. Differentiate between the types of inventory typically held by a retailing firm and a manufacturing firm.

Q 5-12. Sometimes manufacturing firms have only raw materials and finished goods listed on their balance sheets. This is true of Avon Products, a manufacturer of cosmetics, and it might be true of food canners also. Explain the absence of work in process.

Q 5-13. Using these results for a given ratio, compute the median, upper quartile, and lower quartile. 14%, 13.5% 13%, 11.8%, 10.5% 9.5% 9.3% 9%, 7%.

Q 5-14. You want profile information on the president of a company. Which reference book should be consulted?

Q 5-15. Answer the following concerning the *Almanac of Business and Industrial Financial Ratios*:
a. This service presents statistics for how many size categories of firms?
b. Indicate the industries covered by this service.

Q 5-16. Using the *Department of Commerce Quarterly Financial Report* discussion in the text, answer the following:
   a. Could we determine the percentage of total sales income after income taxes that a particular firm had in relation to the total industry sales? Explain.
   b. Could we determine the percentage of total assets that a particular firm had in relation to the total industry? Explain.

Q 5-17. a. What is the SIC number? How can it aid in the search of a company, industry, or product?
   b. What is the NAICS number? How can it aid in the search of a company, industry, or product?

Q 5-18. You want to know if there have been any reported deaths of officers of a company you are researching. What library source will aid you in your search?

Q 5-19. You want to compare the progress of a given company with a composite of that company's industry group for selected income statement and balance sheet items. Which library source will aid you?

Q 5-20. You are considering buying the stock of a large publicly traded company. You need an opinion of timeliness of the industry and the company. Which publication could you use?

Q 5-21. You want to know the trading activity (volume of its stock sold) for a company. Which service provides this information?

Q 5-22. You need to research articles on a company that you are analyzing. Which source will aid you?

Q 5-23. You read in your local newspaper that an executive of a company that you are interested in is giving a presentation to financial analysts in New York. How could you learn the content of the presentation without getting in touch with the company?

Q 5-24. You would like to determine the principal business affiliations of the president of a company you are analyzing. Which reference service may have this information?

Q 5-25. Indicate some sources that contain an appraisal of the outlook for particular industries.

Q 5-26. You want to determine if there is a fairly recent brokerage house assessment report on a company that you are analyzing. Which reference may aid you?

Problems

P 5-1. The Walgreen Co. and subsidiaries balance sheets from its 2001 annual report are presented in Exhibit 5-3.

Required a. Using the balance sheets, prepare a vertical common-size analysis for 2001 and 2000. Use total assets as a base.
   b. Using the balance sheets, prepare a horizontal common-size analysis for 2001 and 2000. Use 2000 as the base.
   c. Comment on significant trends that appear in (a) and (b).

P 5-2. The Walgreen Co. and subsidiaries statements of earnings from its 2001 annual report is presented in Exhibit 5-3.

Required a. Using the income statement, prepare a vertical common-size analysis for 2001, 2000, and 1999. Use net sales as a base.
   b. Using the income statement, prepare a horizontal common-size analysis for 2001, 2000, and 1999. Use 1999 as the base.
   c. Comment on significant trends that appear in (a) and (b).

P 5-3. The Interpublic Group of Companies balance sheet from its 2001 annual report is presented in Exhibit 5-4.

Required a. Using the balance sheet, prepare a vertical common-size analysis for 2001 and 2000. Use total assets as a base.
   b. Using the balance sheet, prepare a horizontal common-size analysis for 2001 and 2000. Use 2000 as the base.
   c. Comment on significant trends that appear in (a) and (b).

P 5-4. The Interpublic Group of Companies income statement from its 2001 annual report is presented in Exhibit 5-4.

Required   a. Using the income statement, prepare a vertical common-size analysis for 2001, 2000, and 1999. Use gross income as the base.

b. Using the income statement, prepare a horizontal common-size analysis for 2001, 2000, and 1999. Use 1999 as the base.

c. Comment on significant trends that appear in (a) and (b).

P 5-5.

Item	Year 1	Year 2	Change Analysis	
			Amount	Percent
1	—	3,000		
2	6,000	(4,000)		
3	(7,000)	4,000		
4	4,000	—		
5	8,000	10,000		

Required   Determine the absolute change and the percentage for these items.

P 5-6.

Item	Year 1	Year 2	Change Analysis	
			Amount	Percent
1	4,000	—		
2	5,000	(3,000)		
3	(9,000)	2,000		
4	7,000	—		
5	—	15,000		

Required   Determine the absolute change and the percentage for these items.

P 5-7.

Rapid Retail
Comparative Statements of Income
(in thousands of dollars)

	December 31		Increase (Decrease)	
	2003	2002	Dollars	Percent
Net sales	$30,000	$28,000		
Cost of goods sold	20,000	19,500		
Gross profit	10,000	8,500		
Selling, general and administrative expense	3,000	2,900		
Operating income	7,000	5,600		
Interest expense	100	80		
Income before taxes	6,900	5,520		
Income tax expense	2,000	1,600		
Net income	$ 4,900	$ 3,920		

Required   a. Complete the increase (decrease) in dollars and percent.

b. Comment on trends.

Web Case   # Thomson Analytics Business School Edition

Please complete the web case that covers material covered in this chapter at http://gibson.swlearning.com. You'll be using Thomson Analytics Business School Edition, a version of the powerful tool used by Wall Street professionals, that combines a full range of fundamental financial information, earnings estimates, market data, and source documents for 500 publicly traded companies.

LIQUIDITY OF SHORT-TERM ASSETS; RELATED DEBT-PAYING ABILITY

An entity's ability to maintain its short-term debt-paying ability is important to all users of financial statements. If the entity cannot maintain a short-term debt-paying ability, it will not be able to maintain a long-term debt-paying ability, nor will it be able to satisfy its stockholders. Even a very profitable entity will find itself bankrupt if it fails to meet its obligations to short-term creditors. The ability to pay current obligations when due is also related to the cash-generating ability of the firm. This will be discussed in Chapter 10.

When analyzing the short-term debt-paying ability of the firm, we find a close relationship between the current assets and the current liabilities. Generally, the current liabilities will be paid with cash generated from the current assets. As previously indicated, the profitability of the firm does not determine the short-term debt-paying ability. In other words, using accrual accounting, the entity may report very high profits but may not have the ability to pay its current bills because it lacks available funds. If the entity reports a loss, it may still be able to pay short-term obligations.

This chapter suggests procedures for analyzing short-term assets and the short-term debt-paying ability of an entity. The procedures require an understanding of current assets, current liabilities, and the notes to financial statements.

This chapter also includes a detailed discussion of four very important assets—cash, marketable securities, accounts receivable, and inventory. Accounts receivable and inventory, two critical assets, often substantially influence the liquidity and profitability of a firm.

Chapters 6 through 10 will extensively use the 2002 financial statements of Nike, Inc. (Nike) to illustrate the technique of financial analysis. This will aid readers in viewing financial analysis as a whole. The Nike, Inc. 2002 financial statements are presented following Chapter 10. With the Nike statements is an analysis that summarizes and expands on the Nike analysis in Chapters 6 through 10.

CURRENT ASSETS, CURRENT LIABILITIES, AND THE OPERATING CYCLE

Current assets (1) are in the form of cash, (2) will be realized in cash, or (3) conserve the use of cash *within the operating cycle of a business or one year, whichever is longer.*[1]

The five categories of assets usually found in current assets, listed in their order of liquidity, include cash, marketable securities, receivables, inventories, and prepayments. Other assets may also be classified in current assets, such as assets held for sale. This chapter will examine in detail each type of current asset.

The **operating cycle** for a company is the time period between the acquisition of goods and the final cash realization resulting from sales and subsequent collections. For example, a food store purchases inventory and then sells the inventory for cash. The relatively short time that the inventory remains an asset of the food store represents a very short operating cycle. In another example, a car manufacturer purchases materials and then uses labor and overhead to convert these materials into a finished car. A dealer buys the car on credit and then pays the manufacturer. Compared to the food store, the car manufacturer has a much longer operating cycle, but it is still less than a year. Only a few businesses have an operating cycle longer than a year. For example, if a business is involved in selling resort property, the average time period that the property is held before sale, plus the average collection period, is typically longer than a year.

Cash

Cash is a medium of exchange that a bank will accept for deposit and a creditor will accept for payment. To be classified as a current asset, cash must be free from any restrictions that would prevent its deposit or use to pay creditors classified as current. If restricted for specific short-term creditors, many firms still classify this cash under current assets, but they disclose the restrictions. Cash restricted for short-term creditors should be eliminated along with the related amount of short-term debt when determining the short-term debt-paying ability. Cash should be available to pay general short-term creditors to be considered as part of the firm's short-term debt-paying ability.

It has become common for banks to require a portion of any loan to remain on deposit in the bank for the duration of the loan period. These deposits, termed **compensating balances**, reduce the amount of cash available to the borrower to meet obligations, and they increase the borrower's effective interest rate.

Compensating balances against short-term borrowings are separately stated in the current asset section or footnoted. Compensating balances for long-term borrowings are separately stated as noncurrent assets under either investments or other assets.

The cash account on the balance sheet is usually entitled *cash, cash and equivalents,* or *cash and certificates of deposit.* The cash classification typically includes currency and unrestricted funds on deposit with a bank.

There are two major problems encountered when analyzing a current asset: determining a fair valuation for the asset and determining the liquidity of the asset. These problems apply to the cash asset only when it has been restricted. Thus, it is usually a simple matter to decide on the amount of cash to use when determining the short-term debt-paying ability of an entity.

Marketable Securities

The business entity has varying cash needs throughout the year. Because an inferred cost arises from keeping money available, management does not want to keep all of the entity's cash needs in the form of cash throughout the year. The available alternative turns some of the cash into productive use through short-term investments (marketable securities), which can be converted into cash as the need arises.

To qualify as a **marketable security**, the investment must be readily marketable, and it must be the intent of management to convert the investment to cash within the current operating cycle or one year, whichever is longer. The key element of this test is **managerial intent**.

It is to management's advantage to show investments under marketable securities, instead of long-term investments, because this classification improves the liquidity appearance of the firm. When the same securities are carried as marketable securities year after year, they are likely held for a business purpose. For example, the other company may be a major supplier or customer of the firm being analyzed. The firm would not want to sell these securities to pay short-term creditors. Therefore, to be conservative, it is better to reclassify them as investments for analysis purposes.

Investments classified as marketable securities should be temporary. Examples of marketable securities include treasury bills, short-term notes of corporations, government bonds, corporate bonds, preferred stock, and common stock. Investments in preferred stock and common stock are referred to as *marketable equity securities*.

Debt and equity securities are to be carried at fair value. An exception is that debt securities can be carried at amortized cost if classified as held-to-maturity securities, but these debt securities would be classified under investments (not classified under current assets).[2]

A security's liquidity must be determined in order for it to be classified as a marketable security. The analyst must assume that securities classified as marketable securities are readily marketable.

Exhibit 6-1 presents the marketable securities on the 2001 annual report of ASV Inc. It discloses the detail of the marketable securities account. Many companies do not disclose this detail.

Receivables

An entity usually has a number of claims to future inflows of cash. These claims are usually classified as **accounts receivable** and **notes receivable** on the financial statements. The primary claim that most entities have comes from the selling of merchandise or services on account to customers, referred to as *trade receivables*, with the customer promising to pay within a limited period of time, such as 30 days. Other claims may be from sources such as loans to employees or a federal tax refund.

Claims from customers, usually in the form of accounts receivable, neither bear interest nor involve claims against specific resources of the customer. In some cases, however, the customer signs a note instead of being granted the privilege of having an open account. Usually, the interest-bearing note will be for a longer period of time than an account receivable. In some cases, a customer who does not pay an account receivable when due signs a *note receivable* in place of the account receivable.

The common characteristic of receivables is that the company expects to receive cash some time in the future. This causes two valuation problems. First, a period of time must pass before the

---

EXHIBIT 6-1	**ASV INC.**

Marketable Securities (Short-Term Investments)

Consolidated Balance Sheets (in Part)

	December 31,	
Assets (in Part)	**2001**	**2000**
Current Assets		
Cash and cash equivalents	$ 5,221,591	$ 9,483,861
Short-term investments	725,249	1,278,282
Accounts receivable (net of allowance for doubtful accounts of $75,000)	16,828,489	10,557,907
Inventories	28,614,053	28,064,998
Prepaid expenses and other	1,756,844	965,026
Total current assets	$53,146,226	$50,350,074

Note B—Short-Term Investments

Short-term investments consist primarily of a diversified portfolio of taxable governmental agency bonds, which mature between 2002 and 2004. The Company considers the investments as "available-for-sale." At December 31, 2001 and 2000, cost was equal to fair value and no amount was included as a separate component of shareholders' equity.

receivable can be collected, so the entity incurs costs for the use of these funds. Second, collection might not be made.

The valuation problem from waiting to collect is *ignored in the valuation of receivables and of notes classified as current assets* because of the short waiting period and the immaterial difference in value. The waiting period problem is not ignored if the receivable or note is long-term and classified as an investment. The stipulated rate of interest is presumed to be fair, except when:

1. No interest is stated.
2. The stated rate of interest is clearly unreasonable.
3. The face value of the note is materially different from the cash sales price of the property, goods, or services, or the market value of the note at the date of the transaction.[3]

Under the condition that the face amount of the note does not represent the fair value of the consideration exchanged, *the note is recorded as a present value amount on the date of the original transaction*. The note is recorded at less than (or more than) the face amount, taking into consideration the time value of money. The difference between the recorded amount and the face amount is subsequently amortized as interest income (note receivable) or as interest expense (note payable).

The second problem in valuing receivables or notes is that collection may not be made. Usually, an allowance provides for estimated uncollectible accounts. Estimated losses must be accrued against income, and the impairment of the asset must be recognized (or liability recorded) under the following conditions:

1. Information available prior to the issuance of the financial statements indicates that it is probable that an asset has been impaired, or a liability has been incurred at the date of the financial statements.
2. The amount of the loss can be reasonably estimated.[4]

Both of these conditions are normally met with respect to the uncollectibility of receivables, and the amount subject to being uncollectible is usually material. Thus, in most cases, the company must estimate bad debt expense and indicate the impairment of the receivable. The expense is placed on the income statement, and the impairment of the receivable is disclosed by the use of an account, **allowance for doubtful accounts**, which is subtracted from the gross receivable account. Later, a specific customer's account, identified as being uncollectible, is charged against allowance for doubtful accounts and the gross receivable account on the balance sheet. (This does not mean that the firm will stop efforts to collect.)

It is difficult for the firm to estimate the collectibility of any individual receivable, but when it considers all of the receivables in setting up the allowance, the total estimate should be reasonably accurate. The problem of collection applies to each type of receivable, including notes. The company normally provides for only one allowance account as a matter of convenience, but it considers possible collection problems with all types of receivables and notes when determining the allowance account.

The impairment of receivables may come from causes other than uncollectibility, such as cash discounts allowed, sales returns, and allowances given. Usually, the company considers all of the causes that impair receivables in allowance for doubtful accounts, rather than setting up a separate allowance account for each cause.

Nike presented its receivable account for May 31, 2002, and 2001 as follows:

	2002	2001
Accounts receivable, less allowance of $77,400,000 in 2002 and $72,100,000 in 2001	$1,807,100,000	$1,621,400,000

This indicates that net receivables were $1,807,100,000 at May 31, 2002, and $1,621,400,000 at May 31, 2001, after subtracting allowances for doubtful accounts.

The use of the allowance for doubtful accounts approach results in the bad debt expense being charged to the period of sale, thus matching this expense with its related revenue. It also results in the recognition of the impairment of the asset. The later charge-off of a specified account receivable does not influence the income statement or net receivables on the balance sheet. The charge-off reduces accounts receivable and allowance for doubtful accounts.

When both conditions specified are not met, or the receivables are immaterial, the entity recognizes bad debt expense using the direct write-off method. With this method, bad debt expense is recognized when a specific customer's account is identified as being uncollectible. At this time, the bad debt expense is recognized on the income statement, and gross accounts receivable is decreased on the balance sheet. This method recognizes the bad debt expense in the same period for both the income statement and the tax return.

The direct write-off method frequently results in the bad debt expense being recognized in the year subsequent to the sale, and thus does not result in a proper matching of expense with revenue. This method reports gross receivables, which does not recognize the impairment of the asset from uncollectibility.

When a company has receivables that are due beyond one year (or accounting cycle) from the balance sheet date, and when it is the industry practice to include these receivables in current assets, they are included in current assets even though they do not technically meet the guidelines to qualify as a current asset. The company should disclose the fact that these receivables do not meet the technical guidelines for current assets. Exhibit 6-2 indicates the disclosure made by Snap On, Inc. in its 1998 annual report.

When a company has receivables classified as current, but due later than one year from the balance sheet date, the analyst should make special note of this when making comparisons with competitors. If competitors do not have the same type of receivables, the receivables may not be comparable. For example, a retail company that has substantial installment receivables, with many of them over a year from their due date, is not comparable to a retail company that does not have installment receivables. Installment receivables are considered to be of lower quality than other receivables because of the length of time needed to collect the installment receivables. More importantly, the company with installment receivables should have high standards when granting credit and should closely monitor its receivables.

Customer concentration can be an important consideration in the quality of receivables. When a large portion of receivables is from a few customers, the firm can be highly dependent on those customers. This information is usually not available in the Form 10-K. Nike's Form 10-K disclosed

---

EXHIBIT 6-2	**SNAP ON, INC.** **Receivables Due Beyond One Year**

Consolidated Balance Sheets (in Part)		
(Amounts in thousands except per share data)	**January 2,** **1999**	**January 3,** **1998**
Asset (in Part)		
Current assets		
Cash and cash equivalents	$ 15,041	$ 25,679

Accounts receivable, less allowance for doubtful
    accounts of $29.2 million in 1998 and
    $20.6 million in 1997
	554,703	539,589

Inventories	375,436	373,155
Prepaid expenses and other assets	134,652	83,286
Total current assets	$1,079,832	$1,021,709

Note 4 Receivables (in Part)

Accounts receivable include installment receivable amounts that are due beyond one year from balance sheet dates. These amounts were approximately $16.5 million and $15.6 million at the end of 1998 and 1997. Gross installment receivables amounted to $176.9 million and $174.0 million at the end of 1998 and 1997. Of these amounts, $16.8 million and $14.6 million represented unearned finance charges at the end of 1998 and 1997.

that Foot Locker, Inc., which operates a chain of retail stores specializing in athletic footwear and apparel, accounted for approximately 11% of global net sales of Nike brand products during fiscal 2002. No other customer accounted for 10% or more of net sales during fiscal 2002.

The liquidity of the trade receivables for a company can be examined by making *two computations*. *The first computation* determines the number of days' sales in receivables at the end of the accounting period, and *the second computation* determines the accounts receivable turnover. The turnover figure can be computed to show the number of times per year receivables turn over or to show how many days on the average it takes to collect the receivables.

Days' Sales in Receivables

The number of days' sales in receivables relates the amount of the accounts receivable to the average daily sales on account. For this computation, the accounts receivable amount should include trade notes receivable. Other receivables not related to sales on account should not be included in this computation. Compute the days' sales in receivables as follows:

$$\text{Days' Sales in Receivables} = \frac{\text{Gross Receivables}}{\text{Net Sales}/365}$$

This formula divides the number of days in a year into net sales on account, and then divides the resulting figure into gross receivables. Exhibit 6-3 presents the computation for Nike at the end of 2002 and 2001. The increase in days' sales in receivables from 65.13 days at the end of 2001 to 69.54 days at the end of 2002 appears to indicate a slight deterioration in the control of receivables. It could also indicate an increase in sales on account late in 2002.

An internal analyst compares days' sales in receivables with the company's credit terms as an indication of how efficiently the company manages its receivables. For example, if the credit term is 30 days, days' sales in receivables should not be materially over 30 days. If days' sales in receivables are materially more than the credit terms, the company has a collection problem. An effort should be made to keep the days' sales in receivables close to the credit terms.

Consider the effect on the quality of receivables from a change in the *credit terms*. Shortening the credit terms indicates that there will be less risk in the collection of future receivables, and a lengthening of the credit terms indicates a greater risk. Credit term information is readily available for internal analysis and may be available in footnotes.

Right of return privileges can also be important to the quality of receivables. Liberal right of return privileges can be a negative factor in the quality of receivables and on sales that have already been recorded. Pay particular attention to any change in the right of return privileges. Right of return privileges can readily be determined for internal analysis, and this information should be available in a footnote if considered to be material.

The net sales figure includes collectible and uncollectible accounts. The uncollectible accounts *would not exist* if there were an accurate way, prior to sale, of determining which credit customers would not pay. Firms make an effort to determine credit standing when they approve a customer for credit, but this process does not eliminate uncollectible accounts. Since the net sales figure includes

---

EXHIBIT 6-3   **NIKE, INC.**

Days' Sales in Receivables

Years Ended May 31, 2002 and 2001

	2002	2001
	(in millions)	
Accounts receivable, less allowance for doubtful accounts of $77.4 and $72.1	$1,807.1	$1,621.4
Gross receivables (net plus allowance) [A]	1,884.5	1,693.5
Net sales	9,893.0	9,488.8
Average daily sales on account (net sales on account divided by 365) [B]	27.10	26.00
Days' sales in receivables [A ÷ B]	69.54 days	65.13 days

both collectible and uncollectible accounts (gross sales), the comparable receivables figure should include gross receivables, rather than the net receivables figure that remains after the allowance for doubtful accounts is deducted.

The days' sales in receivables gives an indication of the length of time that the receivables have been outstanding at the end of the year. *The indication can be misleading if sales are seasonal and/or the company uses a natural business year.* If the company uses a natural business year for its accounting period, the days' sales in receivables will tend to be understated because the actual sales per day at the end of the year will be low when compared to the average sales per day for the year. The understatement of days' sales in receivables can also be explained by the fact that gross receivables will tend to be below average at that time of year.

The following is an example of how days' sales in receivables will tend to be understated when a company uses a natural business year:

Average sales per day for the entire year	$ 2,000
Sales per day at the end of the natural business year	1,000
Gross receivables at the end of the year	100,000

Days' sales in receivables based on the formula:

$$\frac{\$100,000}{\$2,000} = 50 \text{ Days}$$

Days' sales in receivables based on sales per day at the end of the natural business year:

$$\frac{\$100,000}{\$1,000} = 100 \text{ Days}$$

The liquidity of a company that uses a natural business year tends to be overstated. However, the only positive way to know if a company uses a natural business year is through research. The information may not be readily available.

It is unlikely that a company that has a seasonal business will close the accounting year during peak activity. At the peak of the business cycle, company personnel are busy and receivables are likely to be at their highest levels. If a company closed during peak activity, the days' sales in receivables would tend to be overstated and the liquidity understated.

The length of time that the receivables have been outstanding gives an indication of their collectibility. The days' sales in receivables should be compared for several years. A comparison should also be made between the days' sales in receivables for a particular company and comparable figures for other firms in the industry and industry averages. This type of comparison can be made when doing either internal or external analysis.

Assuming that the days' sales in receivables computation is *not* distorted because of a seasonal business and/or the company's use of a natural business year, consider the following reasons to explain why the days' sales in receivables appears to be abnormally high:

1. Sales volume expands materially late in the year.
2. Receivables are uncollectible and should have been written off.
3. The company seasonally dates invoices. (An example would be a toy manufacturer that ships in August with the receivable due at the end of December.)
4. A large portion of receivables are on the installment basis.

Assuming that the distortion is *not* from a seasonal situation or the company's use of a natural business year, the following should be considered as possible reasons why the days' sales in receivables appears to be abnormally low:

1. Sales volume decreases materially late in the year.
2. A material amount of sales are on a cash basis.
3. The company has a factoring arrangement in which a material amount of the receivables is sold. (With a factoring arrangement, the receivables are sold to an outside party.)

When doing external analysis, many of the reasons why the days' sales in receivables is abnormally high or low cannot be determined without access to internal information.

Accounts Receivable Turnover

Another computation, accounts receivable turnover, indicates the liquidity of the receivables. Compute the accounts receivable turnover measured in times per year as follows:

$$\text{Accounts Receivable Turnover} = \frac{\text{Net Sales}}{\text{Average Gross Receivables}}$$

Exhibit 6-4 presents the computation for Nike at the end of 2002 and 2001. The turnover of receivables slightly decreased between 2001 and 2002 from 5.70 times per year to 5.53 times per year. For Nike, this would be a negative trend.

Computing the average gross receivables based on beginning-of-year and end-of-year receivables can be misleading if the business has seasonal fluctuations or if the company uses a natural business year. To avoid problems of seasonal fluctuations or of comparing a company that uses a natural business year with one that uses a calendar year, the monthly balances (or even weekly balances) of accounts receivable should be used in the computation. This is feasible when performing internal analysis, but not when performing external analysis. In the latter case, quarterly figures can be used to help eliminate these problems. If these problems cannot be eliminated, companies not on the same basis should not be compared. The company with the natural business year tends to overstate its accounts receivable turnover, thus overstating its liquidity.

Accounts Receivable Turnover in Days

The accounts receivable turnover can be expressed in terms of days instead of times per year. Turnover in number of days also gives a comparison with the number of days' sales in the ending receivables. The accounts receivable turnover in days also results in an answer directly related to the firm's credit terms. Compute the accounts receivable turnover in days as follows:

$$\text{Accounts Receivable Turnover in Days} = \frac{\text{Average Gross Receivables}}{\text{Net Sales}/365}$$

This formula is the same as that for determining number of days' sales in receivables, except that the accounts receivable turnover in days is computed using the average gross receivables. Exhibit 6-5 presents the computation for Nike at the end of 2002 and 2001. Accounts receivable turnover in days increased from 64.01 days in 2001 to 66.01 days in 2002. This would represent a modest negative trend.

EXHIBIT 6-4	**NIKE, INC.**

Accounts Receivable Turnover

Years Ended May 31, 2002 and 2001

	2002	2001
	(in millions)	
Net sales [A]	$9,893.0	$9,488.8
End-of-year receivables, less allowance for doubtful accounts	1,807.1	1,621.4
Beginning-of-year receivables, less allowance for doubtful accounts	1,621.4	1,569.4
Allowance for doubtful accounts		
End of 2002 $77.4		
End of 2001 $72.1		
End of 2000 $65.4		
Ending gross receivables (net plus allowance)	1,884.5	1,693.5
Beginning gross receivables (net plus allowance)	1,693.5	1,634.8
Average gross receivables [B]	1,789.00	1,664.25
Accounts receivable turnover [A ÷ B]	5.53 times	5.70 times

The accounts receivable turnover in times per year and days can both be computed by alternative formulas, using Nike's 2002 figures, as follows:

1.   Accounts Receivable Turnover in Times per Year

$$\frac{365}{\text{Accounts Receivable Turnover in Days}} = \frac{365}{66.01} = \frac{5.53 \text{ Times}}{\text{per Year}}$$

2.   Accounts Receivable Turnover in Days

$$\frac{365}{\text{Accounts Receivable Turnover in Times per Year}} = \frac{365}{5.53 \text{ Times per Year}} = 66.00 \text{ Days}$$

The answers obtained for both accounts receivable turnover in number of times per year and accounts receivable turnover in days, using the alternative formulas, may differ slightly from the answers obtained with the previous formulas. The difference is due to rounding.

Credit Sales Versus Cash Sales

A difficulty in computing receivables' liquidity is the problem of credit sales versus cash sales. Net sales includes both credit sales and cash sales. To have a realistic indication of the liquidity of receivables, only the credit sales should be included in the computations. If cash sales are included, the liquidity will be overstated.

The internal analyst determines the credit sales figure and eliminates the problem of credit sales versus cash sales. The external analyst should be aware of this problem, and not be misled by the liquidity figures. The distinction between cash sales and credit sales is not usually a major problem for the external analyst because certain types of businesses tend to sell only on cash terms, and others sell only on credit terms. For example, a manufacturer usually sells only on credit terms. Some businesses, such as a retail department store, have a mixture of credit sales and cash sales.

In cases of mixed sales, the proportion of credit and cash sales tends to stay rather constant. Therefore, the liquidity figures are comparable (but overstated), enabling the reader to compare figures from period to period as well as figures of similar companies.

Inventories

Inventory is often the most significant asset in determining the short-term debt-paying ability of an entity. Often the inventory account is more than half of the total current assets. Because of the significance of inventories, a special effort should be made to analyze properly this important area.

To be classified as **inventory**, the asset should be for sale in the ordinary course of business, or used or consumed in the production of goods. A trading concern purchases merchandise in a form to sell to customers. Inventories of a trading concern, whether wholesale or retail, usually appear in one inventory account (merchandise inventory). A manufacturing concern produces goods to be sold. Inventories of a manufacturing concern are normally classified in three distinct inventory

EXHIBIT 6-5	NIKE, INC.

Accounts Receivable Turnover in Days

Years Ended May 31, 2002 and 2001

	2002	2001
	(in millions)	
Net sales	$9,893.0	$9,488.8
Average gross receivables [A]	1,789.0	1,664.3
Sales per day (net sales divided by 365) [B]	27.10	26.00
Accounts receivable turnover in days [A ÷ B]	66.01 days	64.01 days

accounts: inventory available to use in production (raw materials inventory), inventory in production (work in process inventory), and inventory completed (finished goods inventory).

Usually, the determination of the inventory figures is much more difficult in a manufacturing concern than in a trading concern. The manufacturing concern deals with materials, labor, and overhead when determining the inventory figures, while the trading concern only deals with purchased merchandise. The overhead portion of the work in process inventory and the finished goods inventory is often a problem when determining a manufacturer's inventory. The overhead consists of all the costs of the factory other than direct materials and direct labor. From an analysis viewpoint, however, many of the problems of determining the proper inventory value are solved before the entity publishes financial statements.

Inventory is particularly sensitive to changes in business activity, so management must keep inventory in balance with business activity. Failure to do so leads to excessive costs (such as storage cost), production disruptions, and employee layoffs. For example, it is difficult for automobile manufacturers to balance inventories with business activities. When sales decline rapidly, the industry has difficulty adjusting production and the resulting inventory to match the decline. Manufacturers have to use customer incentives, such as price rebates, to get the large inventory buildup back to a manageable level. When business activity increases, inventory shortages can lead to overtime costs. The increase in activity can also lead to cash shortages because of the length of time necessary to acquire inventory, sell the merchandise, and collect receivables.

Inventory quantities and costs may be accounted for using either the **perpetual** or **periodic** system. Using the perpetual system, the company maintains a continuous record of physical quantities in its inventory. When the perpetual system includes costs (versus quantities only), then the company updates its inventory and cost of goods sold continually as purchases and sales take place. (The inventory needs to be verified by a physical count at least once a year.)

Using the periodic system, physical counts are taken periodically, which should be at least once a year. The cost of the ending inventory is determined by attaching costs to the physical quantities on hand based on the cost flow assumption used. The cost of goods sold is calculated by subtracting the ending inventory from the cost of goods available for sale.

Inventory Cost

The most critical problem that most entities face is determining which cost to use, since the cost prices have usually varied over time. If it were practical to determine the specific cost of an item, this would be a good cost figure to use. It would also substantially reduce inventory valuation problems. In practice, because of the different types of inventory items and the constant flow of these items, it is not practical to determine the specific costs. Exceptions to this are large items and/or expensive items. For example, it would be practical to determine the specific cost of a new car in the dealer's showroom or the specific cost of an expensive diamond in a jewelry store. When specific costs are used, this is referred to as the **specific identification** method.

Because the cost of specific items is not usually practical to determine and because other things are considered (such as the income result), companies typically use a cost flow assumption. The most common cost flow assumptions are first-in, first-out (FIFO), last-in, first-out (LIFO), or some average computation. These assumptions can produce substantially different results because of changing prices.

The **FIFO method** assumes that the first inventory acquired is the first sold. This means that the cost of goods sold account consists of beginning inventory and the earliest items purchased. The latest items purchased remain in inventory. These latest costs are fairly representative of the current costs to replace the inventory. If the inventory flows slowly (low turnover), or if there has been substantial inflation, even FIFO may not produce an inventory figure for the balance sheet representative of the replacement cost. Part of the inventory cost of a manufacturing concern consists of overhead, some of which may represent costs from several years prior, such as depreciation on the plant and equipment. Often the costs transferred to cost of goods sold under FIFO are low in relation to current costs, so current costs are not matched against current revenue. During a time of inflation, the resulting profit is overstated. To the extent that inventory does not represent replacement cost, an understatement of the inventory cost occurs.

The **LIFO method** assumes that the costs of the latest items bought or produced are matched against current sales. This assumption usually materially improves the matching of current costs against current revenue, so the resulting profit figure is usually fairly realistic. The first items (and oldest costs) in inventory can materially distort the reported inventory figure in comparison with its replacement cost. A firm that has been on LIFO for many years may have some inventory costs that go back 20 years or more. Because of inflation, the resulting inventory figure will not reflect current replacement costs. LIFO accounting was started in the United States. It is now accepted in a few other countries.

Averaging methods lump the costs to determine a midpoint. An average cost computation for inventories results in an inventory amount and a cost of goods sold amount somewhere between FIFO and LIFO. During times of inflation, the resulting inventory is more than LIFO and less than FIFO. The resulting cost of goods sold is less than LIFO and more than FIFO.

Exhibit 6-6 summarizes the inventory methods used by the 600 companies surveyed for *Accounting Trends & Techniques*. The table covers the years 2000, 1999, 1998, and 1997. (Notice that the number of companies in the table does not add up to 600 because many companies use more than one method.) Exhibit 6-6 indicates that the most popular inventory methods are FIFO and LIFO. It is perceived that LIFO requires more cost to administer than FIFO. LIFO is not as popular during times of relatively low inflation. During times of relatively high inflation, LIFO becomes more popular because LIFO matches the latest costs against revenue. LIFO results in tax benefits because of the matching of recent higher costs against revenue.

Exhibit 6-6 includes a summary of companies that use LIFO for all inventories, 50% or more of inventories, less than 50% of inventories, and not determinable. This summary indicates that only a small percentage of companies that use LIFO use it for all of their inventories.

For the following illustration, the periodic system is used with the inventory count at the end of the year. The same answer would result for FIFO and specific identification under either the perpetual or periodic system. A different answer would result for LIFO or average cost, depending on whether a perpetual or periodic system is used.

To illustrate the major costing methods for determining which costs apply to the units remaining in inventory at the end of the year and which costs are allocated to cost of goods sold, consider the following:

Date	Description	Number of Units	Cost per Unit	Total Cost
January 1	Beginning inventory	200	$ 6	$ 1,200
March 1	Purchase	1,200	7	8,400
July 1	Purchase	300	9	2,700
October 1	Purchase	400	11	4,400
		2,100		$16,700

EXHIBIT 6-6   **INVENTORY COST DETERMINATION**

	Number of Companies			
	2000	**1999**	**1998**	**1997**
Methods				
First-in, first-out (FIFO)	386	404	409	415
Last-in, first-out (LIFO)	283	301	319	326
Average cost	180	176	176	188
Other	38	34	40	32
Use of LIFO:				
All inventories	23	24	30	17
50% or more of inventories	148	159	152	170
Less than 50% of inventories	82	83	95	99
Not determinable	30	35	42	40
Companies using LIFO	283	301	319	326

A physical inventory count on December 31 indicates 800 units on hand. There were 2,100 units available during the year, and 800 remained at the end of the year; therefore, 1,300 units were sold.

Four cost assumptions will be used to illustrate the determination of the ending inventory costs and the related cost of goods sold: *first-in, first-out (FIFO), last-in, first-out (LIFO), average cost,* and *specific identification.*

First-In, First-Out Method (FIFO)   The cost of ending inventory is found by attaching cost to the physical quantities on hand, based on the FIFO cost flow assumption. The costs of goods sold is calculated by subtracting the ending inventory cost from the cost of goods available for sale.

		Number of Units	Cost per Unit	Inventory Cost	Cost of Goods Sold
October 1	Purchase	400 @	$11	$4,400	
July 1	Purchase	300 @	9	2,700	
March 1	Purchase	100 @	7	700	
Ending inventory		800		$7,800	
Cost of goods sold ($16,700 − $7,800)					$8,900

Last-In, First-Out Method (LIFO)   The cost of the ending inventory is found by attaching costs to the physical quantities on hand, based on the LIFO cost flow assumption. The cost of goods sold is calculated by subtracting the ending inventory cost from the cost of goods available for sale.

		Number of Units	Cost per Unit	Inventory Cost	Cost of Goods Sold
January 1	Beginning inventory	200 @	$6	$1,200	
March 1	Purchase	600 @	7	4,200	
Ending inventory		800		$5,400	
Cost of goods sold ($16,700 − $5,400)					$11,300

Average Cost   There are several ways to compute the average cost. The weighted average divides the total cost by the total units to determine the average cost per unit. The average cost per unit is multiplied by the inventory quantity to determine inventory cost. The cost of goods sold is calculated by subtracting the ending inventory cost from the cost of goods available for sale.

	Inventory Cost	Cost of Goods Sold
$\dfrac{\text{Total cost} \quad \$16,700}{\text{Total units} \quad 2,100} = \$7.95$		
Ending inventory (800 × $7.95)	$6,360	
Cost of goods sold ($16,700 − $6,360)		$10,340

Specific Identification   With the specific identification method, the items in inventory are identified as coming from specific purchases. For this example, assume that the 800 items in inventory can be identified with the March 1 purchase. The cost of goods sold is calculated by subtracting the ending inventory cost from the cost of goods available for sale.

	Inventory Cost	Cost of Goods Sold
Ending inventory (800 × $7.00)	$5,600	
Cost of goods sold ($16,700 − $5,600)		$11,100

The difference in results for inventory cost and cost of goods sold from using different inventory methods may be material or immaterial. The major impact on the results usually comes from the rate of inflation. In general, the higher the inflation rate, the greater the differences between the inventory methods.

Because the inventory amounts can be substantially different under the various cost flow assumptions, the analyst should be cautious when comparing the liquidity of firms that have different inventory cost flow assumptions. Caution is particularly necessary when one of the firms is using the LIFO method because LIFO may prove meaningless with regard to the firm's short-term debt-paying ability. If two firms that have different cost flow assumptions need to be compared, this problem should be kept in mind to avoid being misled by the indicated short-term debt-paying ability.

Since the resulting inventory amount will not be equal to the cost of replacing the inventory, regardless of the cost method, another problem needs to be considered when determining the short-term debt-paying ability of the firm: the inventory must be sold for more than cost in order to realize a profit. To the extent that the inventory is sold for more than cost, the short-term debt-paying ability has been understated. However, the extent of the understatement is materially reduced by several factors. One, the firm will incur substantial selling and administrative costs in addition to the inventory cost, thereby reducing the understatement of liquidity to the resulting net profit. Two, the replacement cost of the inventory usually exceeds the reported inventory cost, even if FIFO is used. Therefore, more funds will be required to replace the inventory sold. This will reduce the future short-term debt-paying ability of the firm. Also, since accountants support the conservatism concept, they would rather have a slight understatement of the short-term debt-paying ability of the firm than an overstatement.

The impact on the entity of the different inventory methods must be understood. Since the extremes in inventory costing are LIFO and FIFO, the following summarizes these methods. This summary assumes that the entity faces a period of inflation. The conclusions arrived at in this summary would be reversed if the entity faces a deflationary period.

1. LIFO generally results in a lower profit than does FIFO, as a result of a higher cost of goods sold. This difference can be substantial.
2. Generally, reported profit under LIFO is closer to reality than profit reported under FIFO because the cost of goods sold is closer to replacement cost under LIFO. This is the case under both inflationary and deflationary conditions.
3. FIFO reports a higher inventory ending balance (closer to replacement cost). However, this figure falls short of true replacement cost.
4. The cash flow under LIFO is greater than the cash flow under FIFO because of the difference in tax liability between the two methods, an important reason why a company selects LIFO.
5. Some companies use a periodic inventory system, which updates the inventory in the general ledger once a year. Purchases made late in the year become part of the cost of goods sold under LIFO. If prices have increased during the period, the cost of goods sold will increase and profits will decrease. It is important that accountants inform management that profits will be lower if substantial purchases of inventory are made near the end of the year, and a periodic inventory system is used.
6. A company using LIFO could face a severe tax problem and a severe cash problem if sales reduce or eliminate the amount of inventory normally carried. The reduction in inventory would result in older costs being matched against current sales. This distorts profits on the high side. Because of the high reported profit, income taxes would increase. When the firm needs to replenish the inventory, it has to use additional cash. These problems can be reduced by planning and close supervision of production and purchases. A method called dollar-value LIFO is now frequently used by companies that use LIFO. The dollar-value LIFO method uses price indexes related to the inventory instead of units and unit costs. With dollar-value LIFO, inventory each period is determined for pools of inventory dollars. (See an intermediate accounting book for a detailed explanation of dollar-value LIFO.)
7. LIFO would probably not be used for inventory that has a high turnover rate because there would be an immaterial difference in the results between LIFO and FIFO.
8. LIFO results in a lower profit figure than does FIFO, the result of a higher cost of goods sold.

A firm using LIFO must disclose a LIFO reserve account, usually in a footnote to the financial statement. Usually, the amount disclosed must be added to inventory to approximate the inventory at FIFO. An inventory at FIFO is usually a reasonable approximation of the current replacement cost of the inventory.

Nike uses the FIFO inventory method. Walgreens 2001 annual report will be used to illustrate LIFO.

Walgreens annual report for 2001 indicates inventories are valued on a lower of last-in, first-out (LIFO) cost or market basis. At August 31, 2001, and 2000, inventories would have been greater by $637.6 million and $574.8 million, respectively, if they had been valued on a lower of first-in, first-out (FIFO) cost or market basis. Cost of sales is primarily derived from an estimate based upon point-of-sale scanning information and adjusted based on periodic inventories. The approximate current cost of the Walgreen's inventory for August 31, 2001 and 2000 follow:

	2001	2000
Balance sheet inventories	$3,482,400,000	$2,830,800,000
Additional amount in footnote		
(LIFO reserve)	637,600,000	574,800,000
Approximate current costs	$4,120,000,000	$3,405,600,000

Lower-of-Cost-or-Market Rule   We have reviewed the inventory cost-based measurements of FIFO, LIFO, average, and specific identification. These cost-based measurements are all considered to be historical cost approaches. The accounting profession decided that a "departure from the cost basis of inventory pricing is required when the utility of the goods is no longer as great as its cost." Utility of the goods has been measured through market values. When the market value of inventory falls below cost, it is necessary to write the inventory down to the lower market value. This is known as the **lower-of-cost-or-market (LCM) rule**. Market is defined in terms of current replacement cost, either by purchase or manufacture.

Following the LCM rule, inventories can be written down below cost but never up above cost. The LCM rule provides for the recognition of the loss in utility during the period in which the loss occurs. The LCM rule is consistent with both the matching and the conservatism assumptions.

The LCM rule is used by many countries other than the United States. As indicated, market is defined in the United States in terms of current replacement cost. Market in other countries may be defined differently, such as "net realizable value."

Liquidity of Inventory   The analysis of the liquidity of the inventories can be approached in a manner similar to that taken to analyze the liquidity of accounts receivable. One computation determines the *number of days' sales in inventory* at the end of the accounting period, another computation determines the *inventory turnover in times per year*, and a third determines the *inventory turnover in days*.

Days' Sales in Inventory   The number of days' sales in inventory ratio relates the amount of the ending inventory to the average daily cost of goods sold. All of the inventory accounts should be included in the computation. The computation gives an indication of the length of time that it will take to use up the inventory through sales. This can be misleading if sales are seasonal or if the company uses a natural business year.

If the company uses a natural business year for its accounting period, the number of days' sales in inventory will tend to be understated because the average daily cost of goods sold will be at a low point at this time of year. If the days' sales in inventory is understated, the liquidity of the inventory is overstated. The same caution should be observed here as was suggested for determining the liquidity of receivables, when one company uses a natural business year and the other uses a calendar year.

If the company closes its year during peak activity, the number of days' sales in inventory would tend to be overstated and the liquidity would be understated. As indicated with receivables, no good business reason exists for closing the year when activities are at a peak, so this situation should rarely occur.

Compute the number of days' sales in inventory as follows:

$$\text{Days' Sales in Inventory} = \frac{\text{Ending Inventory}}{\text{Cost of Goods Sold}/365}$$

The formula divides the number of days in a year into the cost of goods sold, and then divides the resulting figure into the ending inventory. Exhibit 6-7 presents the number of days' sales in inventory for Nike for May 31, 2002, and May 31, 2001. The number of days' sales in inventory has decreased from 89.85 days at the end of 2001 to 83.51 days at the end of 2002. This represents a positive trend.

If sales are approximately constant, then the lower the number of days' sales in inventory, the better the inventory control. An inventory buildup can be burdensome if business volume decreases. However, it can be good if business volume expands, since the increased inventory would be available for customers.

The days' sales in inventory estimates the number of days that it will take to sell the current inventory. For several reasons, this estimate may not be very accurate. The cost of goods sold figure is based on last year's sales, divided by the number of days in a year. Sales next year may not be at the same pace as last year. Also, the ending inventory figure may not be representative of the quantity of inventory actually on hand, especially if using LIFO.

A seasonal situation, with inventory unusually low or high at the end of the year, would also result in an unrealistic days' sales in inventory computation. Also, a natural business year with low inventory at the end of the year would result in an unrealistic days' sales in inventory. Therefore, the resulting answer should be taken as a rough estimate, but it helps when comparing periods or similar companies.

The number of days' sales in inventory could become too low, resulting in lost sales. A good knowledge of the industry and the company is required to determine if the number of days' sales in inventory is too low.

In some cases, not only will the cost of goods sold not be reported separately, but the figure reported will not be a close approximation of the cost of goods sold. This, of course, presents a problem for the external analyst. In such cases, use net sales in place of the cost of goods sold. The result will not be a realistic number of days' sales in inventory, but it can be useful in comparing periods within one firm and in comparing one firm with another. Using net sales produces a much lower number of days' sales in inventory, which materially overstates the liquidity of the ending inventory. Therefore, only the trend determined from comparing one period with another and one firm with other firms should be taken seriously (not actual absolute figures). When you suspect that the days' sales in inventory computation does not result in a reasonable answer, consider using this ratio only to indicate a trend.

If the dollar figures for inventory and/or the cost of goods sold are not reasonable, the ratios calculated with these figures may be distorted. These distortions can be eliminated to some extent by using quantities rather than dollars in the computation. The use of quantities in the computation may work very well for single products or groups of similar products. It does not work very well for a large diversified inventory because of possible changes in the mix of the inventory. Also, using quantities rather than dollars will not be feasible when using externally published statements.

EXHIBIT 6-7	**NIKE, INC.**

Days' Sales in Inventory

Years Ended May 31, 2002 and 2001

	2002	2001
	(in millions)	
Inventories, end of year [A]	$1,373.8	$1,424.1
Cost of goods sold	6,004.7	5,784.9
Average daily cost of goods sold (cost of goods sold divided by 365) [B]	16.45	15.85
Number of days' sales in inventory [A ÷ B]	83.51 days	89.85 days

An example of the use of quantities, instead of dollars, follows:

Ending inventory	50 units
Cost of goods sold	500 units

$$\text{Days' sales in inventory} = \frac{50}{500 / 365} = 36.50 \text{ Days}$$

Inventory Turnover   Inventory turnover indicates the liquidity of the inventory. This computation is similar to the accounts receivable turnover computation.

The inventory turnover formula follows:

$$\text{Inventory Turnover} = \frac{\text{Cost of Goods Sold}}{\text{Average Inventory}}$$

Exhibit 6-8 presents the inventory turnover using the 2002 and 2001 figures for Nike. For Nike, the inventory turnover was up in 2002. This represents a positive trend.

Computing the average inventory based on the beginning-of-year and end-of-year inventories can be misleading if the company has seasonal fluctuations or if the company uses a natural business year. The solution to the problem is similar to that used when computing the receivables turnover—that is, use the monthly (or even weekly) balances of inventory. Monthly estimates of inventory are available for internal analysis, but not for external analysis. Quarterly figures may be available for external analysis. If adequate information is not available, avoid comparing a company on a natural business year with a company on a calendar year. The company with the natural business year tends to overstate inventory turnover and therefore the liquidity of its inventory.

Over time, the difference between the inventory turnover for a firm that uses LIFO and one that uses a method that results in a higher inventory figure can become very material. The LIFO firm will have a much lower inventory and therefore a much higher turnover. Also, it may not be reasonable to compare firms in different industries.

When you suspect that the inventory turnover computation does not result in a reasonable answer because of unrealistic inventory and/or cost of goods sold dollar figures, perform the computation using quantities rather than dollars. As with the days' sales in inventory, this alternative is feasible only when performing internal analysis. (It may not be feasible even for internal analysis because of product line changes.)

Inventory Turnover in Days   The inventory turnover figure can be expressed in number of days instead of times per year. This is comparable to the computation that expressed accounts receivable turnover in days. Compute the inventory turnover in days as follows:

$$\text{Inventory Turnover in Days} = \frac{\text{Average Inventory}}{\text{Cost of Goods Sold} / 365}$$

EXHIBIT 6-8	**NIKE, INC.**

Merchandise Inventory Turnover

Years Ended May 31, 2002 and 2001

	2002	2001
	(in millions)	
Cost of goods sold [A]	$6,004.7	$5,784.9
Inventories:		
Beginning of year	1,424.1	1,446.0
End of year	1,373.8	1,424.1
Total	2,797.9	2,870.1
Average inventory [B]	1,398.95	1,435.05
Merchandise inventory turnover [A ÷ B]	4.29 times per year	4.03 times per year

This is the same formula for determining the days' sales in inventory, except that it uses the average inventory. Exhibit 6-9 uses the 2002 and 2001 Nike data to compute the inventory turnover in days. There was a decrease in inventory turnover in days for Nike in 2002. This represents a negative trend.

The inventory turnover in days can be used to compute the inventory turnover per year, as follows:

$$\frac{365}{\text{Inventory Turnover in Days}} = \text{Inventory Turnover per Year}$$

Using the 2002 Nike data, the inventory turnover is as follows:

$$\frac{365}{\text{Inventory Turnover in Days}} = \frac{365}{85.04} = 4.29 \text{ Times per Year}$$

Operating Cycle   The operating cycle represents the period of time elapsing between the acquisition of goods and the final cash realization resulting from sales and subsequent collections. An approximation of the operating cycle can be determined from the receivables liquidity figures and the inventory liquidity figures. Compute the operating cycle as follows:

$$\text{Operating Cycle} = \frac{\text{Accounts Receivable}}{\text{Turnover in Days}} + \frac{\text{Inventory Turnover}}{\text{in Days}}$$

Exhibit 6-10 uses the 2002 and 2001 Nike data to compute the operating cycle. For Nike, the operating cycle decreased, which is a positive trend.

The estimate of the operating cycle is not realistic if the accounts receivable turnover in days and the inventory turnover in days are not realistic. Remember that the accounts receivable turnover in days and the inventory turnover in days are understated, and thus the liquidity overstated, if the company uses a natural business year and computed the averages based on beginning-of-year and end-of-year data. It should also be remembered that the inventory turnover in days is understated, and the liquidity of the inventory overstated, if the company uses LIFO inventory. Also note that

---

EXHIBIT 6-9   **NIKE, INC.**

Inventory Turnover in Days

Years Ended May 31, 2002 and 2001

	2002	2001
	(in millions)	
Cost of goods sold	$6,004.7	$5,784.9
Average inventory [A]	1,398.95	1,435.05
Sales of inventory per day (cost of goods sold divided by 365) [B]	16.45	15.85
Inventory turnover in days [A ÷ B]	85.04 days	90.54 days

EXHIBIT 6-10   **NIKE, INC.**

Operating Cycle

Years Ended May 31, 2002 and 2001

	2002	2001
Accounts receivable turnover in days [A]	66.01	64.01
Inventory turnover in days [B]	85.04	90.54
Operating cycle [A + B]	151.05	154.55

accounts receivable turnover in days is understated, and liquidity of receivables overstated, if the sales figures used included cash and credit sales.

The operating cycle should be helpful when comparing a firm from period to period and when comparing a firm with similar companies. This would be the case, even if understated or overstated, as long as the figures in the computation are comparable.

Related to the operating cycle figure is a computation that indicates how long it will take to realize cash from the ending inventory. This computation consists of combining the number of days' sales in ending receivables and the number of days' sales in ending inventory. The 2002 Nike data produced a days' sales in ending receivables of 69.54 days and a days' sales in ending inventory of 83.51 days, for a total of 153.05 days. In this case, there is an increase, considering the year-end numbers. Therefore, the receivables and inventory at the end of the year are higher than the receivables and inventory carried during the year. This indicates less liquidity at the end of the year than during the year.

Prepayments

Prepayments consist of unexpired costs for which payment has been made. These current assets are expected to be consumed within the operating cycle or one year, whichever is longer. Prepayments normally represent an immaterial portion of the current assets. Therefore, they have little influence on the short-term debt-paying ability of the firm.

Since prepayments have been paid for and will not generate cash in the future, they differ from other current assets. Prepayments relate to the short-term debt-paying ability of the entity because they conserve the use of cash.

Because of the nature of prepayments, the problems of valuation and liquidity are handled in a simple manner. Valuation is taken as the cost that has been paid. Since a prepayment is a current asset that has been paid for in a relatively short period before the balance sheet date, the cost paid fairly represents the cash used for the prepayment. Except in rare circumstances, a prepayment will not result in a receipt of cash; therefore, no liquidity computation is needed. An example of a circumstance where cash is received would be an insurance policy canceled early. No liquidity computation is possible, even in this case.

Other Current Assets

Current assets other than cash, marketable securities, receivables, inventories, and prepayments may be listed under current assets. These other current assets may be very material in any one year and, unless they are recurring, may distort the firm's liquidity.

These assets will, in management's opinion, be realized in cash or conserve the use of cash within the operating cycle of the business or one year, whichever is longer. Examples of other current assets include property held for sale and advances or deposits, often explained in a footnote.

Current Liabilities

Current liabilities are "obligations whose liquidation is reasonably expected to require the use of existing resources properly classifiable as current assets or the creation of other current liabilities."[5] Thus, the definition of current liabilities correlates with the definition of current assets.

Typical items found in current liabilities include accounts payable, notes payable, accrued wages, accrued taxes, collections received in advance, and current portions of long-term liabilities. The 2002 Nike annual report listed current liabilities as follows:

	(In millions)
Current liabilities:	
Current portion of long-term debt	$ 55.3
Notes payable	425.2
Accounts payable	504.4
Accrued liabilities	768.3
Income taxes payable	83.0
Total current liabilities	$1,836.2

For a current liability, liquidity is not a problem, and the valuation problem is immaterial and is disregarded. Theoretically, the valuation of a current liability should be the present value of the required future outlay of money. Since the difference between the present value and the amount that will be paid in the future is immaterial, the current liability is carried at its face value.

CURRENT ASSETS COMPARED WITH CURRENT LIABILITIES

A comparison of current assets with current liabilities gives an indication of the short-term debt-paying ability of the entity. Several comparisons can be made to determine this ability:

1. Working capital
2. Current ratio
3. Acid-test ratio
4. Cash ratio

Working Capital

The working capital of a business is an indication of the short-run solvency of the business. Compute working capital as follows:

$$\text{Working Capital} = \text{Current Assets} - \text{Current Liabilities}$$

Exhibit 6-11 presents the working capital for Nike at the end of 2002 and 2001. Nike had $2,321,500,000 in working capital in 2002 and $1,838,600,000 in working capital in 2001. These figures tend to be understated because some of the current assets, such as inventory, may be understated, based on the book figures.

The inventory as reported may be much less than its replacement cost. The difference between the reported inventory amount and the replacement amount is normally material when the firm is using LIFO inventory. The difference may also be material when using one of the other cost methods.

The current working capital amount should be compared with past amounts to determine if working capital is reasonable. Because the relative size of a firm may be expanding or contracting, comparing working capital of one firm with that of another firm is usually meaningless because of their size differences. If the working capital appears to be out of line, find the reasons by analyzing the individual current asset and current liability accounts.

Current Ratio

Another indicator, the current ratio, determines short-term debt-paying ability and is computed as follows:

$$\text{Current Ratio} = \frac{\text{Current Assets}}{\text{Current Liabilities}}$$

EXHIBIT 6-11   **NIKE, INC.**

Working Capital

Years Ended May 31, 2002 and 2001

	2002	2001
	(in millions)	
Current assets [A]	$4,157.7	$3,625.3
Current liabilities [B]	1,836.2	1,786.7
Working capital [A – B]	$2,321.5	$1,838.6

Exhibit 6-12 presents the current ratio for Nike at the end of 2002 and 2001. For Nike, the current ratio was 2.26 at the end of 2002 and 2.03 at the end of 2001. This indicates a positive trend considering liquidity.

For many years, the guideline for the minimum current ratio has been 2.00. Until the mid-1960s, the typical firm successfully maintained a current ratio of 2.00 or better. Since that time, the current ratio of many firms has declined to a point below the 2.00 guideline. Currently, many firms are not successful in staying above a current ratio of 2.00. This indicates a decline in the liquidity of many firms. It also could indicate better control of receivables and/or inventory.

A comparison with industry averages should be made to determine the typical current ratio for similar firms. In some industries, a current ratio substantially below 2.00 is adequate, while other industries require a much larger ratio. In general, the shorter the operating cycle, the lower the current ratio. The longer the operating cycle, the higher the current ratio.

A comparison of the firm's current ratio with prior periods, and a comparison with industry averages, will help to determine if the ratio is high or low. These comparisons do not indicate why it is high or low. Possible reasons can be found from an analysis of the individual current asset and current liability accounts. Often, the major reasons for the current ratio being out of line will be found in a detailed analysis of accounts receivable and inventory.

The current ratio is considered to be more indicative of the short-term debt-paying ability than the working capital. Working capital only determines the absolute difference between the current assets and current liabilities. The current ratio shows the relationship between the size of the current assets and the size of the current liabilities, making it feasible to compare the current ratio, for example, between IBM and Intel. A comparison of the working capital of these two firms would be meaningless because IBM is a larger firm than Intel.

LIFO inventory can cause major problems with the current ratio because of the understatement of inventory. The result is an understated current ratio. Extreme caution should be exercised when comparing a firm that uses LIFO and a firm that uses some other costing method.

Before computing the current ratio, the analyst should compute the accounts receivable turnover and the merchandise inventory turnover. These computations enable the analyst to formulate an opinion as to whether liquidity problems exist with receivables and/or inventory. An opinion as to the quality of receivables and inventory should influence the analyst's opinion of the current ratio. If liquidity problems exist with receivables and/or inventory, the current ratio needs to be much higher.

Acid-Test Ratio (Quick Ratio)

The current ratio evaluates an enterprise's overall liquidity position, considering current assets and current liabilities. At times, it is desirable to access a more immediate position than that indicated by the current ratio. The acid-test (or quick) ratio relates the most liquid assets to current liabilities.

Inventory is removed from current assets when computing the acid-test ratio. Some of the reasons for removing inventory are that inventory may be slow-moving or possibly obsolete, and parts of the inventory may have been pledged to specific creditors. For example, a winery's inventory re-

---

EXHIBIT 6-12   **NIKE, INC.**

Current Ratio

Years Ended May 31, 2002 and 2001

	2002	2001
	(in millions)	
Current assets [A]	$4,157.7	$3,625.3
Current liabilities [B]	1,836.2	1,786.7
Current ratio [A ÷ B]	2.26	2.03

quires considerable time for aging and, therefore, a considerable time before sale. To include the wine inventory in the acid-test computation would overstate the liquidity. A valuation problem with inventory also exists because it is stated at a cost figure that may be materially different from a fair current valuation.

Compute the acid-test ratio as follows:

$$\text{Acid-Test Ratio} = \frac{\text{Current Assets} - \text{Inventory}}{\text{Current Liabilities}}$$

Exhibit 6-13 presents the acid-test ratio for Nike at the end of 2002 and 2001. For Nike, the acid-test ratio was 1.52 at the end of 2002 and 1.23 at the end of 2001. This represents a positive trend.

It may also be desirable to exclude some other items from current assets that may not represent current cash flow, such as prepaid and miscellaneous items. Compute the more conservative acid-test ratio as follows:

$$\text{Acid-Test Ratio} = \frac{\text{Cash Equivalents} + \text{Marketable Securities} + \text{Net Receivables}}{\text{Current Liabilities}}$$

Usually, a very immaterial difference occurs between the acid-test ratios computed under the first method and this second method. Frequently, the only difference is the inclusion of prepayments in the first computation.

Exhibit 6-14 presents the conservative acid-test ratio for Nike at the end of 2002 and 2001. This approach resulted in an acid-test ratio of 1.30 at the end of 2002 and 1.08 at the end of 2001.

EXHIBIT 6-13   **NIKE, INC.**

Acid-Test Ratio

Years Ended May 31, 2002 and 2001

	2002	2001
	(in millions)	
Current assets	$4,157.7	$3,625.3
Less: ending inventory	1,373.8	1,424.1
Remaining current assets [A]	$2,783.9	$2,201.2
Current liabilities [B]	$1,836.2	$1,786.7
Acid-test Ratio [A ÷ B]	1.52	1.23

EXHIBIT 6-14   **NIKE, INC.**

Acid-Test Ratio (Conservative Approach)

Years Ended May 31, 2002 and 2001

	2002	2001
	(in millions)	
Cash, including short-term investments	$ 575.5	$ 304.0
Net receivables	1,807.1	1,621.4
Total quick assets [A]	$2,382.6	$1,925.4
Current liabilities [B]	$1,836.2	$1,786.7
Acid-test Ratio [A ÷ B]	1.30	1.08

From this point on in this book, the more conservative computations will be used for the acid-test ratio. When a company needs to view liquidity with only inventory removed, the alternative computation should be used.

For many years, the guideline for the minimum acid-test ratio was 1.00. A comparison should be made with the firm's past acid-test ratios and with major competitors and the industry averages. Some industries find that a ratio less than 1.00 is adequate, while others need a ratio greater than 1.00. For example, a grocery store may sell only for cash and not have receivables. This type of business can have an acid-test ratio substantially below the 1.00 guideline and still have adequate liquidity.

Before computing the acid-test ratio, compute the accounts receivable turnover. An opinion as to the quality of receivables should help the analyst form an opinion of the acid-test ratio.

There has been a major decline in the liquidity of companies in the United States, as measured by the current ratio and the acid-test ratio. Exhibit 6-15 shows the dramatically reduced liquidity of U.S. companies. Reduced liquidity leads to more bankruptcies and greater risk for creditors and investors.

Cash Ratio

Sometimes an analyst needs to view the liquidity of a firm from an extremely conservative point of view. For example, the company may have pledged its receivables and its inventory, or the analyst

| EXHIBIT 6-15 | **TRENDS IN CURRENT RATIO AND ACID-TEST RATIO**
All U.S. Manufacturing Companies, 1947–2001* |

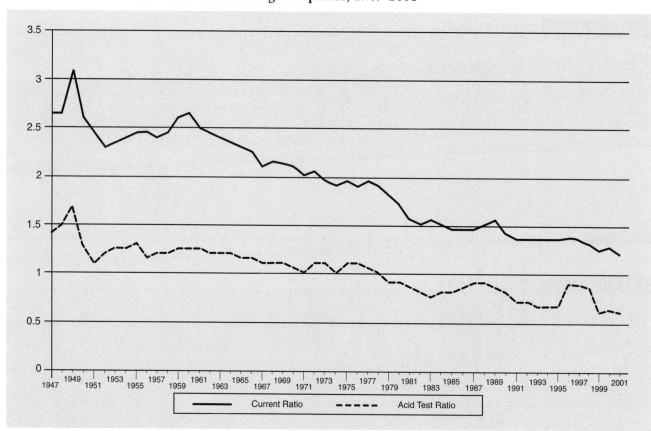

*1980–2001 extended by author.

Source: Adapted from Financial Accounting Standards Board, "FASB Discussion Memorandum—Reporting Funds Flow, Liquidity, and Financial Flexibility," 1980, p. 7.

suspects severe liquidity problems with inventory and receivables. The best indicator of the company's short-run liquidity may be the cash ratio. Compute the cash ratio as follows:

$$\text{Cash Ratio} = \frac{\text{Cash Equivalents} + \text{Marketable Securities}}{\text{Current Liabilities}}$$

The analyst seldom gives the cash ratio much weight when evaluating the liquidity of a firm because it is not realistic to expect a firm to have enough cash equivalents and marketable securities to cover current liabilities. If the firm must depend on cash equivalents and marketable securities for its liquidity, its solvency may be impaired.

Analysts should consider the cash ratio of companies that have naturally slow-moving inventories and receivables and companies that are highly speculative. For example, a land development company in Florida may sell lots paid for over a number of years on the installment basis, or the success of a new company may be in doubt.

The cash ratio indicates the immediate liquidity of the firm. A high cash ratio indicates that the firm is not using its cash to its best advantage; cash should be put to work in the operations of the company. Detailed knowledge of the firm is required, however, before drawing a definite conclusion. Management may have plans for the cash, such as a building expansion program. A cash ratio that is too low could indicate an immediate problem with paying bills.

Exhibit 6-16 presents this ratio for Nike at the end of 2002 and 2001. For Nike, the cash ratio was .31 at the end of 2002 and .17 at the end of 2001. Nike's cash ratio increased materially at the end of 2002 in relation to the end of 2001.

| **OTHER LIQUIDITY CONSIDERATIONS** | Another ratio that may be useful to the analyst is the sales to working capital ratio. In addition, there may be liquidity considerations that are not on the face of the statements. This ratio and other liquidity considerations are discussed in this section. |

Sales to Working Capital (Working Capital Turnover)

Relating sales to working capital gives an indication of the turnover in working capital per year. The analyst needs to compare this ratio with the past, with competitors, and with industry averages in order to form an opinion as to the adequacy of the working capital turnover. Like many ratios, no rules of thumb exist as to what it should be. Since this ratio relates a balance sheet number (working capital) to an income statement number (sales), a problem exists if the balance sheet number is not representative of the year. To avoid this problem, use the average monthly working capital figure when available. Compute the working capital turnover as follows:

$$\text{Sales to Working Capital} = \frac{\text{Sales}}{\text{Average Working Capital}}$$

A low working capital turnover ratio tentatively indicates an unprofitable use of working capital. In other words, sales are not adequate in relation to the available working capital. A high ratio tenta-

---

EXHIBIT 6-16   **NIKE, INC.**

Cash Ratio

Years Ended May 31, 2002 and 2001

	2002	2001
	(in millions)	
Cash, including short-term investments [A]	$575.5	$304.0
Current liabilities [B]	$1,836.2	$1,786.7
Cash ratio [A ÷ B]	0.31	0.17

tively indicates that the firm is undercapitalized (overtrading). An undercapitalized firm is particularly susceptible to liquidity problems when a major adverse change in business conditions occurs.

Exhibit 6-17 presents this ratio for Nike at the end of 2002 and 2001. The sales to working capital ratio decreased substantially from 2001 to 2002. (Working capital in 2002 was higher in relation to sales than it was in 2001.) This tentatively indicates a slightly less profitable use of working capital in 2002 in relation to 2001.

Liquidity Considerations Not on the Face of the Statements

A firm may have a better liquidity position than indicated by the face of the financial statements. The following paragraphs present several examples:

1. Unused bank credit lines would be a positive addition to liquidity. They are frequently disclosed in footnotes.
2. A firm may have some long-term assets that could be converted to cash quickly. This would add to the firm's liquidity. Extreme caution is advised if there is any reliance on long-term assets for liquidity. For one thing, the long-term assets are usually needed in operations. Second, even excess long-term assets may not be easily converted into cash in a short period of time. An exception might be investments, depending on the nature of the investments.
3. A firm may be in a very good long-term debt position and therefore have the capability to issue debt or stock. Thus, the firm could relieve a severe liquidity problem in a reasonable amount of time.

A firm may not be in as good a position of liquidity as indicated by the ratios, as the following examples show:

1. A firm may have notes discounted on which the other party has full recourse against the firm. Discounted notes should be disclosed in a footnote. (A company that discounts a customer note receivable is in essence selling the note to the bank with recourse.)
2. A firm may have major contingent liabilities that have not been recorded, such as a disputed tax claim. Unrecorded contingencies that are material are disclosed in a footnote.
3. A firm may have guaranteed a bank note for another company. This would be disclosed in a footnote.

EXHIBIT 6-17	**NIKE, INC.**

Sales to Working Capital

Years Ended May 31, 2002 and 2001

	2002	2001
	(in millions)	
Net sales [A]	$9,893.0	$9,488.8
Working capital at beginning of year	1,838.6	1,456.4
Working capital at end of year	2,321.5	1,838.6
Average working capital [B]	2,080.05	1,647.50
Sales to working capital [A ÷ B]	4.76 times per year	5.76 times per year

---

SUMMARY   The ratios related to the liquidity of short-term assets and the short-term debt-paying ability follow:

$$\text{Days' Sales in Receivables} = \frac{\text{Gross Receivables}}{\text{Net Sales}/365}$$

$$\text{Accounts Receivable Turnover} = \frac{\text{Net Sales}}{\text{Average Gross Receivables}}$$

$$\text{Accounts Receivable Turnover in Days} = \frac{\text{Average Gross Receivables}}{\text{Net Sales}/365}$$

$$\text{Days' Sales in Inventory} = \frac{\text{Ending Inventory}}{\text{Cost of Goods Sold}/365}$$

$$\text{Inventory Turnover} = \frac{\text{Cost of Goods Sold}}{\text{Average Inventory}}$$

$$\text{Inventory Turnover in Days} = \frac{\text{Average Inventory}}{\text{Cost of Goods Sold}/365}$$

$$\text{Operating Cycle} = \frac{\text{Accounts Receivable}}{\text{Turnover in Days}} + \frac{\text{Inventory Turnover}}{\text{in Days}}$$

$$\text{Working Capital} = \text{Current Assets} - \text{Current Liabilities}$$

$$\text{Current Ratio} = \frac{\text{Current Assets}}{\text{Current Liabilities}}$$

$$\text{Acid-Test Ratio} = \frac{\text{Cash Equivalents} + \text{Marketable Securities} + \text{Net Receivables}}{\text{Current Liabilities}}$$

$$\text{Cash Ratio} = \frac{\text{Cash Equivalents} + \text{Marketable Securities}}{\text{Current Liabilities}}$$

$$\text{Sales to Working Capital} = \frac{\text{Sales}}{\text{Average Working Capital}}$$

To the Net

1. Go to the SEC site (http://www.sec.gov). Under Filings & Forms (Edgar), click on "Search for Company Filings." Click on "Search Companies and Filings." Under company names enter "Cooper Tire" and then "Kroger Co." For Cooper Tire use the 10-K405 submitted March 18, 2002. For the Kroger Co. use the 10-K submitted May 1, 2002.
    a. For both companies determine the SIC.
    b. Considering the nature of the business of these companies, speculate on which firm has the higher current ratio. Comment.
    c. Compute the current ratio for both firms. Did the results agree with your speculation in part (b)?

2. Go to the SEC site (http://www.sec.gov). Under Filings & Forms (Edgar), click on "Search for Company Filings." Click on "Search Companies and Filings." Under company name enter "Eastman Kodak." Use the 10-K submitted March 20, 2002.
    a. What is the net receivables at December 31, 2001?
    b. What is the gross receivables at December 31, 2001?
    c. What is the inventory method?

3. Go to the Sears, Roebuck & Co. site at http://www.sears.com. Using the 2001 financial statements determine the following:
    a. What was the inventory balance at December 29, 2001, and December 30, 2000?
    b. Describe the inventory costing method used by Sears.
    c. If the inventory costing method had been FIFO, how much higher would the inventory cost have been for December 29, 2001 and December 30, 2000?

Questions

Q 6-1.   It is proposed at a stockholders' meeting that the firm slow its rate of payments on accounts payable in order to make more funds available for operations. It is contended that this procedure will enable the firm to expand inventory, which will in turn enable the firm to generate more sales. Comment on this proposal.

Q 6-2.   Jones Wholesale Company has been one of the fastest growing wholesale firms in the United States for the last five years in terms of sales and profits. The firm has maintained a current ratio above the average for the wholesale industry. Mr. Jones has asked you to explain possible reasons why the firm is having difficulty meeting its payroll and its accounts payable. What would you tell Mr. Jones?

Q 6-3.   What is the reason for separating current assets from the rest of the assets found on the balance sheet?

Q 6-4.   Define the operating cycle.

Q 6-5.   Define current assets.

Q 6-6.   List the major categories of items usually found in current assets.

Q 6-7.   Rachit Company has cash that has been frozen in a bank in Cuba. Should this cash be classified as a current asset? Discuss.

Q 6-8.   A. B. Smith Company has guaranteed a $1,000,000 bank note for Alender Company. How would this influence the liquidity ratios of A. B. Smith Company? How should this situation be considered?

Q 6-9.   Arrow Company has invested funds in a supplier to help ensure a steady supply of needed materials. Would this investment be classified as a marketable security (current asset)?

Q 6-10.   List the two computations that are used to determine the liquidity of receivables.

Q 6-11.   List the two computations that are used to determine the liquidity of inventory.

Q 6-12.   Would a company that uses a natural business year tend to overstate or understate the liquidity of its receivables? Explain.

Q 6-13.   T. Melcher Company uses the calendar year. Sales are at a peak during the holiday season, and T. Melcher Company extends 30-day credit terms to customers. Comment on the expected liquidity of its receivables, based on the days' sales in receivables and the accounts receivable turnover.

Q 6-14.   A company that uses a natural business year, or ends its year when business is at a peak, will tend to distort the liquidity of its receivables when end-of-year and beginning-of-year receivables are used in the computation. Explain how a company that uses a natural business year or ends its year when business is at a peak can eliminate the distortion in its liquidity computations.

Q 6-15.   If a company has substantial cash sales and credit sales, is there any meaning to the receivable liquidity computations that are based on gross sales?

Q 6-16.   Describe the difference in inventories between a firm that is a trading concern and a firm that is a manufacturing concern.

Q 6-17.   During times of inflation, which of the inventory costing methods listed below would give the most realistic valuation of inventory? Which method would give the least realistic valuation of inventory? Explain.
a.   LIFO
b.   Average
c.   FIFO

Q 6-18.   The number of days' sales in inventory relates the amount of the ending inventory to the average daily cost of goods sold. Explain why this computation may be misleading under the following conditions:
a.   The company uses a natural business year for its accounting period.
b.   The company closes the year when activities are at a peak.
c.   The company uses LIFO inventory, and inflation has been a problem for a number of years.

Q 6-19.   The days' sales in inventory is an estimate of the number of days that it will take to sell the current inventory.
a.   What is the ideal number of days' sales in inventory?
b.   In general, does a company want many days' sales in inventory?
c.   Can days' sales in inventory be too low?

Q 6-20.   Some firms do not report the cost of goods sold separately on their income statements. In such a case, how should you proceed to compute days' sales in inventory? Will this procedure produce a realistic days' sales in inventory?

Q 6-21.   One of the computations used to determine the liquidity of inventory determines the inventory turnover. In this computation, usually the average inventory is determined by using the beginning-of-the-year and the end-of-the-year inventory figures, but this computation can be misleading if the company has seasonal fluctuations or uses a natural business year. Suggest how to eliminate these distortions.

Q 6-22.   Explain the influence of the use of LIFO inventory on the inventory turnover.

Q 6-23.   Define working capital.

Q 6-24.   Define current liabilities.

Q 6-25.   Several comparisons can be made to determine the short-term debt-paying ability of an entity. Some of these are:
  a.   Working capital
  b.   Current ratio
  c.   Acid-test ratio
  d.   Cash ratio
     1.   Define each of these terms.
     2.   If the book figures are based on cost, will the results of the preceding computations tend to be understated or overstated? Explain.
     3.   What figures should be used in order to avoid the problem referred to in (2)?

Q 6-26.   Discuss how to use working capital in analysis.

Q 6-27.   Both current assets and current liabilities are used in the computation of working capital and the current ratio, yet the current ratio is considered to be more indicative of the short-term debt-paying ability. Explain.

Q 6-28.   In determining the short-term liquidity of a firm, the current ratio is usually considered to be a better guide than the acid-test ratio, and the acid-test ratio is considered to be a better guide than the cash ratio. Discuss when the acid-test ratio would be preferred over the current ratio and when the cash ratio would be preferred over the acid-test ratio.

Q 6-29.   Discuss some benefits that may accrue to a firm from reducing its operating cycle. Suggest some ways that may be used to reduce a company's operating cycle.

Q 6-30.   Discuss why some firms have longer natural operating cycles than other firms.

Q 6-31.   Would a firm with a relatively long operating cycle tend to charge a higher markup on its inventory cost than a firm with a short operating cycle? Discuss.

Q 6-32.   Is the profitability of the entity considered to be of major importance in determining the short-term debt-paying ability? Discuss.

Q 6-33.   Does the allowance method for bad debts or the direct write-off method result in the fairest presentation of receivables on the balance sheet and the fairest matching of expenses against revenue?

Q 6-34.   When a firm faces an inflationary condition and the LIFO inventory method is based on a periodic basis, purchases late in the year can have a substantial influence on profits. Comment.

Q 6-35.   Why could a current asset such as "net assets of business held for sale" distort a firm's liquidity, in terms of working capital or the current ratio?

Q 6-36.   Before computing the current ratio, the accounts receivable turnover and the inventory turnover should be computed. Why?

Q 6-37.   Before computing the acid-test ratio, compute the accounts receivable turnover. Comment.

Q 6-38.   Which inventory costing method results in the highest balance sheet amount for inventory? (Assume inflationary conditions.)

Q 6-39.   Indicate the single most important factor that motivates a company to select LIFO.

Q 6-40.   A relatively low sales to working capital ratio is a tentative indication of an efficient use of working capital. Comment. A relatively high sales to working capital ratio is a tentative indication that the firm is undercapitalized. Comment.

Q 6-41.   List three situations in which the liquidity position of the firm may be better than that indicated by the liquidity ratios.

Q 6-42.   List three situations in which the liquidity position of the firm may not be as good as that indicated by the liquidity ratios.

Q 6-43.   Indicate the objective of the sales to working capital ratio.

Q 6-44.   Why does LIFO result in a very unrealistic ending inventory figure in a period of rising prices?

Q 6-45.   The cost of inventory at the close of the calendar year of the first year of operation is $40,000, using LIFO inventory, resulting in a profit before tax of $100,000. If the FIFO inventory would have been $50,000, what would the reported profit before tax have been? If the average cost method would have resulted in an inventory of $45,000, what would the reported profit before tax have been? Should the inventory costing method be disclosed? Why?

Problems

P 6-1.   In this problem, compute the acid-test ratio as follows:

$$\frac{\text{Current Assets} - \text{Inventory}}{\text{Current Liabilities}}$$

Required   Determine the cost of sales of a firm with the financial data given below:

Current ratio	2.5
Quick ratio or acid-test	2.0
Current liabilities	$400,000
Inventory turnover	3 times

P 6-2.   The Hawk Company wants to determine the liquidity of its receivables. It has supplied you with the following data regarding selected accounts for December 31, 2003, and 2002:

	2003	**2002**
Net sales	$1,180,178	$2,200,000
Receivables, less allowance for losses and discounts		
Beginning of year (allowance for losses and discounts, 2003—$12,300; 2002—$7,180)	240,360	230,180
End of year (allowance for losses and discounts, 2003—$11,180; 2002—$12,300)	220,385	240,360

Required   a.   Compute the number of days' sales in receivables at December 31, 2003, and 2002.
b.   Compute the accounts receivable turnover for 2003 and 2002. (Use year-end gross receivables.)
c.   Comment on the liquidity of the Hawk Company receivables.

P 6-3.   Mr. Williams, the owner of Williams Produce, wants to maintain control over accounts receivable. He understands that days' sales in receivables and accounts receivable turnover will give a good indication of how well receivables are being managed. Williams Produce does 60% of its business during June, July, and August. Mr. Williams provided the pertinent data:

	For Year Ended December 31, 2003	**For Year Ended July 31, 2003**
Net sales	$800,000	$790,000
Receivables, less allowance for doubtful accounts		
Beginning of period (allowance January 1, $3,000; August 1, $4,000)	50,000	89,000
End of period (allowance December 31, $3,500; July 31, $4,100)	55,400	90,150

Required   a.   Compute the days' sales in receivables for July 31, 2003, and December 31, 2003, based on the accompanying data.
b.   Compute the accounts receivable turnover for the period ended July 31, 2003, and December 31, 2003. (Use year-end gross receivables.)
c.   Comment on the results from (a) and (b).

P 6-4.   The L. Solomon Company would like to compare its days' sales in receivables with that of a competitor, L. Konrath Company. Both companies have had similar sales results in the past, but the L. Konrath Company has had better profit results. The L. Solomon Company suspects that one reason for the better profit results is that the L. Konrath Company did a better job of managing receivables. The L. Solomon Company uses a calendar year that ends on December 31, while the L. Konrath Company uses a fiscal year that ends on July 31. Information related to sales and receivables of the two companies follows:

	For Year Ended December 31, 20XX
L. Solomon Company	
Net sales	$1,800,000
Receivables, less allowance for doubtful accounts of $8,000	110,000

	For Year Ended July 31, 20XX
L. Konrath Company	
Net sales	$1,850,000
Receivables, less allowance for doubtful accounts of $4,000	60,000

Required
a. Compute the days' sales in receivables for both companies. (Use year-end gross receivables.)
b. Comment on the results.

P 6-5a. The P. Gibson Company has computed its accounts receivable turnover in days to be 36.

Required Compute the accounts receivable turnover per year.

P 6-5b. The P. Gibson Company has computed its accounts receivable turnover per year to be 12.

Required Compute the accounts receivable turnover in days.

P 6-5c. The P. Gibson Company has gross receivables at the end of the year of $280,000 and net sales for the year of $2,158,000.

Required Compute the days' sales in receivables at the end of the year.

P 6-5d. The P. Gibson Company has net sales of $3,500,000 and average gross receivables of $324,000.

Required Compute the accounts receivable turnover.

P 6-6. The J. Shaffer Company has an ending inventory of $360,500 and a cost of goods sold for the year of $2,100,000. It has used LIFO inventory for a number of years because of persistent inflation.

Required
a. Compute the days' sales in inventory.
b. Is the J. Shaffer Company days' sales in inventory as computed realistic in comparison with the actual days' sales in inventory?
c. Would the days' sales in inventory computed for the J. Shaffer Company be a helpful guide?

P 6-7. The J. Szabo Company had an average inventory of $280,000 and a cost of goods sold of $1,250,000.

Required Compute the following:
a. The inventory turnover in days
b. The inventory turnover

P 6-8. The following inventory and sales data for this year for the G. Rabbit Company are:

	End of Year	Beginning of Year
Net sales	$3,150,000	
Gross receivables	180,000	$160,000
Inventory	480,000	390,000
Cost of goods sold	2,250,000	

Required Using the above data from the G. Rabbit Company, compute:
a. The accounts receivable turnover in days
b. The inventory turnover in days
c. The operating cycle

P 6-9. The Anna Banana Company would like to estimate how long it will take to realize cash from its ending inventory. For this purpose, the following data are submitted:

Accounts receivable, less allowance for doubtful accounts of $30,000	$ 560,000
Ending inventory	680,000
Net sales	4,350,000
Cost of goods sold	3,600,000

Required   Estimate how long it will take to realize cash from the ending inventory.

P 6-10.   The Laura Badora Company has been using LIFO inventory. The Company is required to disclose the replacement cost of its inventory and the replacement cost of its cost of goods sold on its annual statements. Selected data for the year ended 2004 are as follows:

Ending accounts receivable, less allowance for doubtful accounts of $25,000	$ 480,000
Ending inventory, LIFO (estimated replacement $900,000)	570,000
Net sales	3,650,000
Cost of goods sold (estimated replacement cost $3,150,000)	2,850,000

Required   a.   Compute the days' sales in receivables.
      b.   Compute the days' sales in inventory, using the cost figure.
      c.   Compute the days' sales in inventory, using the replacement cost for the inventory and the cost of goods sold.
      d.   Should replacement cost of inventory and cost of goods sold be used, when possible, when computing days' sales in inventory? Discuss.

P 6-11.   A partial balance sheet and income statement for the King Corporation follow.

KING CORPORATION
Partial Balance Sheet
December 31, 2004

Assets
  Current assets:

Cash	$ 33,493
Marketable securities	215,147
Trade receivables, less allowance of $6,000	255,000
Inventories, LIFO	523,000
Prepaid expenses	26,180
Total current assets	$1,052,820

Liabilities
  Current liabilities:

Trade accounts payable	$ 103,689
Notes payable (primarily to banks) and commercial paper	210,381
Accrued expenses and other liabilities	120,602
Income taxes payable	3,120
Current maturities of long-term debt	22,050
Total current liabilities	$ 459,842

KING CORPORATION
Partial Income Statement
For Year Ended December 31, 2004

Net sales	$3,050,600
Miscellaneous income	45,060
	$3,095,660
Costs and expenses:	
Cost of sales	2,185,100
Selling, general, and administrative expenses	350,265
Interest expense	45,600
Income taxes	300,000
	2,880,965
Net income	$ 214,695

Note: The trade receivables at December 31, 2003, were $280,000, net of an allowance of $8,000, for a gross receivables figure of $288,000. The inventory at December 31, 2003, was $565,000.

Required   Compute the following:
   a.   Working capital   f.   Accounts receivable turnover in days
   b.   Current ratio   g.   Days' sales in inventory
   c.   Acid-test ratio   h.   Inventory turnover in days
   d.   Cash ratio   i.   Operating cycle
   e.   Days' sales in receivables

P 6-12.   Individual transactions often have a significant impact on ratios. This problem will consider the direction of such an impact.

	Total Current Assets	Total Current Liabilities	Net Working Capital	Current Ratio
a. Cash is acquired through issuance of additional common stock.	____	____	____	____
b. Merchandise is sold for cash. (Assume a profit.)	____	____	____	____
c. A fixed asset is sold for more than book value.	____	____	____	____
d. Payment is made to trade creditors for previous purchases.	____	____	____	____
e. A cash dividend is declared and paid.	____	____	____	____
f. A stock dividend is declared and paid.	____	____	____	____
g. Cash is obtained through long-term bank loans.	____	____	____	____
h. A profitable firm increases its fixed assets depreciation allowance account.	____	____	____	____
i. Current operating expenses are paid.	____	____	____	____
j. Ten-year notes are issued to pay off accounts payable.	____	____	____	____
k. Accounts receivable are collected.	____	____	____	____
l. Equipment is purchased with short-term notes.	____	____	____	____
m. Merchandise is purchased on credit.	____	____	____	____
n. The estimated taxes payable are increased.	____	____	____	____
o. Marketable securities are sold below cost.	____	____	____	____

Required   Indicate the effects of the previous transactions on each of the following: total current assets, total current liabilities, net working capital, and current ratio. Use + to indicate an increase, – to indicate a decrease, and 0 to indicate no effect. Assume an initial current ratio of more than 1 to 1.

P 6-13.   Current assets and current liabilities for companies D and E are summarized as follows:

	Company D	Company E
Current assets	$400,000	$900,000
Current liabilities	200,000	700,000
Working capital	$200,000	$200,000

Required   Evaluate the relative solvency of companies D and E.

P 6-14.   Current assets and current liabilities for companies R and T are summarized below:

	Company R	Company T
Current assets	$400,000	$800,000
Current liabilities	200,000	400,000
Working capital	$200,000	$400,000

Required   Evaluate the relative solvency of companies R and T.

P 6-15.   The following financial data were taken from the annual financial statements of the Smith Corporation:

	2002	2003	2004
Current assets	$ 450,000	$ 400,000	$ 500,000
Current liabilities	390,000	300,000	340,000
Sales	1,450,000	1,500,000	1,400,000
Cost of goods sold	1,180,000	1,020,000	1,120,000
Inventory	280,000	200,000	250,000
Accounts receivable	120,000	110,000	105,000

Required   a.   Based on these data, calculate the following for 2003 and 2004:
   1.   Working capital
   2.   Current ratio
   3.   Acid-test ratio
   4.   Accounts receivable turnover
   5.   Merchandise inventory turnover
   6.   Inventory turnover in days

   b.   Evaluate the results of your computations in regard to the short-term liquidity of the firm.

P 6-16.   The Anne Elizabeth Corporation is engaged in the business of making toys. A high percentage of its products are sold to consumers during November and December. Therefore, retailers need to have the toys in stock prior to November. The corporation produces on a relatively stable basis during the year in order to retain its skilled employees and to minimize its investment in plant and equipment. The seasonal nature of its business requires a substantial capacity to store inventory.

   The gross receivables balance at April 30, 2003, was $75,000, and the inventory balance was $350,000 on this date. Sales for the year ended April 30, 2004, totaled $4,000,000, and the cost of goods sold totaled $1,800,000.

   The Anne Elizabeth Corporation uses a natural business year that ends on April 30. Inventory and accounts receivable data are given in the following table for the year ended April 30, 2004.

| | Month-End Balance | |
Month	Gross Receivables	Inventory
May, 2003	$ 60,000	$525,000
June, 2003	40,000	650,000
July, 2003	50,000	775,000
August, 2003	60,000	900,000
September, 2003	200,000	975,000
October, 2003	800,000	700,000
November, 2003	1,500,000	400,000
December, 2003	1,800,000	25,000
January, 2004	1,000,000	100,000
February, 2004	600,000	150,000
March, 2004	200,000	275,000
April, 2004	50,000	400,000

Required   a.   Using averages based on the year-end figures, compute the following:
   1.   Accounts receivable turnover in days
   2.   Accounts receivable turnover per year
   3.   Inventory turnover in days
   4.   Inventory turnover per year

   b.   Using averages based on monthly figures, compute the following:
   1.   Accounts receivable turnover in days
   2.   Accounts receivable turnover per year
   3.   Inventory turnover in days
   4.   Inventory turnover per year

   c.   Comment on the difference between the ratios computed in (a) and (b).
   d.   Compute the days' sales in receivables.
   e.   Compute the days' sales in inventory.
   f.   How realistic are the days' sales in receivables and the days' sales in inventory that were computed in (d) and (e)?

P 6-17.   The following data relate to inventory for the year ended December 31, 2003:

Date	Description	Number of Units	Cost per Unit	Total Cost
January 1	Beginning inventory	400	$5.00	$ 2,000
March 1	Purchase	1,000	6.00	6,000
August 1	Purchase	200	7.00	1,400
November 1	Purchase	200	7.50	1,500
		1,800		$10,900

A physical inventory on December 31, 2003, indicates that 400 units are on hand and that they came from the March 1 purchase.

Required   Compute the cost of goods sold for the year ended December 31, 2003, and the ending inventory under the following cost assumptions:
a.   First-in, first-out (FIFO)
b.   Last-in, first-out (LIFO)
c.   Average cost (weighted average)
d.   Specific identification

P 6-18.   The following data relate to inventory for the year ended December 31, 2004. A physical inventory on December 31, 2004, indicates that 600 units are on hand and that they came from the July 1 purchase.

Date	Description	Number of Units	Cost per Unit	Total Cost
January 1	Beginning inventory	1,000	$4.00	$ 4,000
February 20	Purchase	800	4.50	3,600
April 1	Purchase	900	4.75	4,275
July 1	Purchase	700	5.00	3,500
October 22	Purchase	500	4.90	2,450
December 10	Purchase	500	5.00	2,500
		4,400		$20,325

Required   Compute the cost of goods sold for the year ended December 31, 2004, and the ending inventory under the following cost assumptions:
a.   First-in, first-out (FIFO)
b.   Last-in, first-out (LIFO)
c.   Average cost (weighted average)
d.   Specific identification

P 6-19.   The J.A. Appliance Company has supplied you with the following data regarding working capital and sales for the years 2004, 2003, and 2002.

	2004	2003	2002
Working capital	$270,000	$260,000	$240,000
Sales	$650,000	$600,000	$500,000
Industry average for the ratio sales to working capital	4.10 times	4.05 times	4.00 times

Required   a.   Compute the sales to working capital ratio for each year.
b.   Comment on the sales to working capital ratio for J.A. Appliance in relation to the industry average and what this may indicate.

P 6-20.   The Depoole Company manufactures industrial products and employs a calendar year for financial reporting purposes. Items (a) through (e) present several of Depoole's transactions during 2004. The total of cash equivalents, marketable securities, and net receivables exceeded total current liabilities both before and after each transaction described. Depoole has positive profits in 2004 and a credit balance throughout 2004 in its retained earnings account.

Required   Answer the following multiple-choice questions.
a.   Payment of a trade account payable of $64,500 would:
1.   Increase the current ratio, but the acid-test ratio would not be affected.
2.   Increase the acid-test ratio, but the current ratio would not be affected.
3.   Increase both the current and acid-test ratios.
4.   Decrease both the current and acid-test ratios.
5.   Have no effect on the current and acid-test ratios.
b.   The purchase of raw materials for $85,000 on open account would:
1.   Increase the current ratio.
2.   Decrease the current ratio.
3.   Increase net working capital.
4.   Decrease net working capital.
5.   Increase both the current ratio and net working capital.

c. The collection of a current accounts receivable of $29,000 would:
    1. Increase the current ratio.
    2. Decrease the current ratio.
    3. Increase the acid-test ratio.
    4. Decrease the acid-test ratio.
    5. Not affect the current or acid-test ratios.
d. Obsolete inventory of $125,000 was written off during 2004. This would:
    1. Decrease the acid-test ratio.
    2. Increase the acid-test ratio.
    3. Increase net working capital.
    4. Decrease the current ratio.
    5. Decrease both the current and acid-test ratios.
e. The early liquidation of a long-term note with cash would:
    1. Affect the current ratio to a greater degree than the acid-test ratio.
    2. Affect the acid-test ratio to a greater degree than the current ratio.
    3. Affect the current and acid-test ratios to the same degree.
    4. Affect the current ratio, but not the acid-test ratio.
    5. Affect the acid-test ratio, but not the current ratio.

CMA Adapted

P 6-21.   Information from the Greg Company's balance sheet follows:

Current assets:

Cash	$ 2,100,000
Marketable securities	7,200,000
Accounts receivable	50,500,000
Inventories	65,000,000
Prepaid expenses	1,000,000
Total current assets	$125,800,000

Current liabilities:

Notes payable	$ 1,400,000
Accounts payable	18,000,000
Accrued expenses	11,000,000
Income taxes payable	600,000
Payments due within one year on long-term debt	3,000,000
Total current liabilities	$ 34,000,000

Required   Answer the following multiple-choice questions:
a. What is the acid-test ratio for the Greg Company?
    1. 1.60
    2. 1.76
    3. 1.90
    4. 2.20
b. What is the effect of the collection of accounts receivable on the current ratio and net working capital, respectively?

	Current Ratio	Net Working Capital
1.	No effect	No effect
2.	Increase	Increase
3.	Increase	No effect
4.	No effect	Increase

P 6-22.   The following data apply to items (a) and (b). Mr. Sparks, the owner of School Supplies, Inc., wants to maintain control over accounts receivable. He understands that accounts receivable turnover will give a good indication of how well receivables are being managed. School Supplies, Inc. does 70% of its business during June, July, and August. The terms of sale are 2/10, net/60.

Net sales for the year ended December 31, 2004, and receivables balances follow.

Net sales	$1,500,000
Receivables, less allowance for doubtful accounts of $8,000 at January 1, 2004	72,000
Receivables, less allowance for doubtful accounts of $10,000 at December 31, 2004	60,000

Required   Answer the following multiple-choice questions:

a.   The average accounts receivable turnover calculated from the previous data is:
  1.   20.0 times.
  2.   25.0 times.
  3.   22.7 times.
  4.   18.75 times.
  5.   20.8 times.

b.   The average accounts receivable turnover computed for School Supplies, Inc., in item (a) is:
  1.   Representative for the entire year.
  2.   Overstated.
  3.   Understated.

CMA Adapted

P 6-23.   Items (a) through (d) are based on the following information:

SHARKEY CORPORATION
Selected Financial Data

| | As of December 31 | |
	2004	2003
Cash	$ 8,000	$ 60,000
Marketable securities	32,000	8,000
Accounts receivable	40,000	110,000
Inventory	80,000	140,000
Net property, plant, and equipment	240,000	280,000
Accounts payable	60,000	100,000
Short-term notes payable	30,000	50,000
Cash sales	1,500,000	1,400,000
Credit sales	600,000	900,000
Cost of goods sold	1,260,000	1,403,000

Required   Answer the following multiple-choice questions:

a.   Sharkey's acid test ratio as of December 31, 2004 is
  1.   0.63.
  2.   0.70.
  3.   0.89.
  4.   0.99.

b.   Sharkey's receivables turnover for 2004 is
  1.   8 times.
  2.   6 times.
  3.   12 times.
  4.   14 times.

c.   Sharkey's inventory turnover for 2004 is
  1.   11.45 times.
  2.   10.50 times.
  3.   9.85 times.
  4.   8.45 times.

d.   Sharkey's current ratio at December 31, 2004, is
  1.   1.40.
  2.   2.60.
  3.   1.90.
  4.   1.78.

e.   If current assets exceed current liabilities, payments to creditors made on the last day of the year will
  1.   Decrease current ratio.
  2.   Increase current ratio.
  3.   Decrease working capital.
  4.   Increase working capital.

P 6-24.

Required   Answer the following multiple-choice questions:

a.   A company's current ratio is 2.2 to 1 and quick (acid-test) ratio is 1.0 to 1 at the beginning of the year. At the end of the year, the company has a current ratio of 2.5 to 1 and a quick ratio of .8 to 1. Which of the following could help explain the divergence in the ratios from the beginning to the end of the year?

1. An increase in inventory levels during the current year.
2. An increase in credit sales in relationship to cash sales.
3. An increase in the use of trade payables during the current year.
4. An increase in the collection rate of accounts receivable.
5. The sale of marketable securities at a price below cost.

b. If, just prior to a period of rising prices, a company changed its inventory measurement method from FIFO to LIFO, the effect in the next period would be to

1. Increase both the current ratio and inventory turnover.
2. Decrease both the current ratio and inventory turnover.
3. Increase the current ratio and decrease inventory turnover.
4. Decrease the current ratio and increase inventory turnover.
5. Leave the current ratio and inventory turnover unchanged.

c. Selected year-end data for the Bayer Company are as follows:

Current liabilities	$600,000
Acid-test ratio	2.5
Current ratio	3.0
Cost of sales	500,000

The Bayer Company's inventory turnover based on this year-end data is

1. 1.20.
2. 2.40.
3. 1.67.
4. Some amount other than those given.
5. Not determinable from the data given.

d. If a firm has a high current ratio but a low acid-test ratio, one can conclude that

1. The firm has a large outstanding accounts receivable balance.
2. The firm has a large investment in inventory.
3. The firm has a large amount of current liabilities.
4. The cash ratio is extremely high.
5. The two ratios must be recalculated because both conditions cannot occur simultaneously.

e. Investment instruments used to invest temporarily idle cash balances should have which of the following characteristics?

1. High expected return, low marketability, and a short term to maturity
2. High expected return, readily marketable, and no maturity date
3. Low default risk, low marketability, and a short term to maturity
4. Low default risk, readily marketable, and a long term to maturity
5. Low default risk, readily marketable, and a short term to maturity

f. The primary objective in the management of accounts receivable is

1. To achieve a combination of sales volume, bad-debt experience, and receivables turnover that maximizes the profits of the corporation.
2. To realize no bad debts because of the opportunity cost involved.
3. To provide the treasurer of the corporation with sufficient cash to pay the company's bills on time.
4. To coordinate the activities of manufacturing, marketing, and financing so that the corporation can maximize its profits.
5. To allow the most liberal credit acceptance policy because increased sales mean increased profits.

g. A firm requires short-term funds to cover payroll expenses. These funds can come from

1. Trade credit.
2. Collections of receivables.
3. Bank loans.
4. Delayed payments of accounts payable.
5. All of the above.

CMA Adapted

P 6-25.   Text-of-the-Quarter, Inc. (TQI) is a new retailer of accounting texts. Sales are made via contracts that provide for TQI to send the customer an accounting text each quarter for twelve quarters. The selling price of each text is $15, with payment due within 30 days of delivery. Sales can be accurately estimated because of the contracts.

The number of contracts TQI sold in its first four quarters of existence, along with the number of texts purchased by TQI, were as follows:

Quarter	Contracts Sold	Text Purchased	Texts Remaining from Each Quarter's Purchase at End of First Year
First	10,000	50,000	0
Second	20,000	40,000	0
Third	30,000	50,000	10,000
Fourth	40,000	120,000	50,000

All deliveries start in the quarter of contract sale, and all deliveries are up-to-date. Texts were purchased from the publisher at an average cost of $9 for the first quarter, $10 for the second and third quarters, and $11 for the fourth quarter. Selling and administrative costs for the year were $270,000. TQI's tax rate is 40%.

Required Using generally accepted accounting principles for revenue and expense recognition and inventory accounting, prepare an income statement in such a way as to minimize the company's taxes.

CFA Adapted

P 6-26. Consecutive five-year balance sheets and income statements of the Anne Gibson Corporation follow.

Anne Gibson Corporation
Balance Sheet
December 31, 2001 through December 31, 2005

Dollars in thousands	2005	2004	2003	2002	2001
Assets:					
Current assets					
Cash	$ 47,200	$ 46,000	$ 45,000	$ 44,000	$ 43,000
Marketable securities	2,000	2,500	3,000	3,000	3,000
Accounts receivable, less allowance of $1,000, December 31, 2005; $ 900, December 31, 2004; $ 900, December 31, 2003; $ 800, December 31, 2002; $1,200, December 31, 2001	131,000	128,000	127,000	126,000	125,000
Inventories	122,000	124,000	126,000	127,000	125,000
Prepaid expenses	3,000	2,500	2,000	1,000	1,000
Total current assets	305,200	303,000	303,000	301,000	297,000
Property, plant and equipment, net	240,000	239,000	238,000	237,500	234,000
Other assets	10,000	8,000	7,000	6,500	7,000
Total assets	$555,200	$550,000	$548,000	$545,000	$538,000
Liabilities and stockholders' equity:					
Current liabilities					
Accounts payable	$ 72,000	$ 73,000	$ 75,000	$ 76,000	$ 78,500
Accrued compensation	26,000	25,000	25,500	26,000	26,000
Income taxes	11,500	12,000	13,000	12,500	11,000
Total current liabilities	109,500	110,000	113,500	114,500	115,500
Long-term debt	68,000	60,000	58,000	60,000	62,000
Deferred income taxes	25,000	24,000	23,000	22,000	21,000
Stockholders' equity	352,700	356,000	353,500	348,500	339,500
Total liabilities and stockholders' equity	$555,200	$550,000	$548,000	$545,000	$538,000

Anne Gibson Corporation
Statement of Earnings
For Years Ended December 31, 2001–2005

In thousands, except per share	**2005**	**2004**	**2003**	**2002**	**2001**
Net sales	$880,000	$910,000	$840,000	$825,000	$820,000
Cost of goods sold	740,000	760,000	704,000	695,000	692,000
Gross profit	140,000	150,000	136,000	130,000	128,000
Selling and administrative expense	53,000	52,000	50,000	49,800	49,000
Interest expense	6,700	5,900	5,800	5,900	6,000
Earnings from continuing operations before income taxes	80,300	92,100	80,200	74,300	73,000
Income taxes	26,000	27,500	28,000	23,000	22,500
Net earnings	$ 54,300	$ 64,600	$ 52,200	$ 51,300	$ 50,500
Earnings per share	$1.40	$1.65	$1.38	$1.36	$1.33

Required

a. Using year-end balance sheet figures, compute the following for the maximum number of years, based on the available data:
   1. Days' sales in receivables
   2. Accounts receivable turnover
   3. Accounts receivable turnover in days
   4. Days' sales in inventory
   5. Inventory turnover
   6. Inventory turnover in days
   7. Operating cycle
   8. Working capital
   9. Current ratio
   10. Acid-test ratio
   11. Cash ratio
   12. Sales to working capital

b. Using average balance sheet figures, as suggested in the chapter, compute the following for the maximum number of years, based on the available data:
   1. Days' sales in receivables
   2. Accounts receivable turnover
   3. Accounts receivable turnover in days
   4. Days' sales in inventory
   5. Inventory turnover
   6. Inventory turnover in days
   7. Operating cycle
   8. Working capital
   9. Current ratio
   10. Acid-test ratio
   11. Cash ratio
   12. Sales to working capital

c. Comment on trends indicated in short-term liquidity.

Case 6-1	**LIFO-FIFO**

The current assets and current liabilities section of the NACCO Industries balance sheet for 1998 and 1997, along with selected footnotes, follows.

	December 31	
	1998	**1997**
	(in millions)	
Assets		
Current assets:		
Cash and cash equivalents	$ 34.7	$ 24.1
Accounts receivable, net of allowance of $15.6 and $14.1	275.1	240.8
Inventories	356.2	302.9
Prepaid expenses and other	37.2	31.8
Total current assets	$703.2	$599.6
Liabilities		
Current liabilities:		
Accounts payable	$252.9	$244.7
Revolving credit agreements	31.2	23.5
Current maturities of long-term debt	28.4	18.9
Income taxes	10.9	12.8
Accrued payroll	44.7	36.4
Accrued warranty obligations	36.3	27.9
Other current liabilities	144.2	142.3
Total current liabilities	$548.6	$506.5

Note 2 Accounting Policies (in part)

Inventories: Inventories are stated at the lower of cost or market. Cost is determined under the last-in, first-out (LIFO) method for manufacturing inventories in the United States and for certain retail inventories. The first-in, first-out (FIFO) method is used with respect to all other inventory.

Note 6 Inventories

	December 31	
	1998	**1997**
	(in millions)	
Manufacturing inventories:		
Finished goods and service parts		
NMHG	$125.3	$ 86.9
Housewares	41.5	31.8
	166.8	118.7
Raw materials and work in process		
NMHG	136.6	135.6
Housewares	17.5	15.1
	154.1	150.7
Lifo reserve		
NMHG	(12.6)	(13.4)
Housewares	1.8	1.1
	(10.8)	(12.3)
Total manufacturing inventories	310.1	257.1
Coal—NA Coal	9.5	10.7
Mining supplies—NA Coal	19.4	19.2
Housewares	17.2	15.9
	$356.2	$302.9

The cost of manufacturing inventories has been determined by the LIFO method for 72% and 66% of such inventories at December 31, 1998, and 1997, respectively.

Required

a. What is the working capital at the end of 1998?

b. What is the balance in the LIFO reserve account at the end of 1998? Describe this account.

c. If the LIFO reserve account was added to the inventory at LIFO, what would be the resulting inventory number at the end of 1998? Which inventory amount do you consider to be more realistic?

d. Does the use of LIFO or FIFO produce higher, lower, or the same income during (1) price increases, (2) price decreases, and (3) constant prices? (Assume no decrease or increase in inventory quantity.)

e. Does the use of LIFO or FIFO produce higher, lower, or the same amount of cash flow during (1) price increases, (2) price decreases, and (3) constant costs? Answer the question for both pretax cash flows and after-tax cash flows. (Assume no decrease or increase in inventory quantity.)

f. Assume that the company purchased inventory on the last day of the year, beginning inventory equaled ending inventory, and inventory records for the item purchased were maintained periodically on the LIFO basis. Would that purchase be included on the income statement or the balance sheet at year-end?

| **Case 6-2** | **Rising Prices, a Time to Switch Off LIFO?** |

The following information was taken directly from an annual report of a firm that wishes to remain anonymous. (The dates have been changed.)

Financial Summary
Effects of LIFO Accounting

For a number of years, the corporation has used the last-in, first-out (LIFO) method of accounting for its steel inventories. In periods of extended inflation, coupled with uncertain supplies of raw materials from foreign sources, and rapid increases and fluctuations in prices of raw materials such as nickel and chrome nickel scrap, earnings can be affected unrealistically for any given year.

Because of these factors, the corporation will apply to the Internal Revenue Service for permission to discontinue using the LIFO method of accounting for valuing those inventories for which this method has been used. If such application is granted, the LIFO reserve at December 31, 2002, of $12,300,000 would be eliminated, which would require a provision for income taxes of approximately $6,150,000. The corporation will also seek permission to pay the increased taxes over a ten-year period. If the corporation had not used the LIFO method of accounting during 2001, net earnings for the year would have been increased by approximately $1,500,000.

The 2002 annual report also disclosed the following:

		2002	**2001**
1.	Sales and revenues	$536,467,782	$487,886,449
2.	Earnings per common share	$3.44	$3.58

Required

a. The corporation indicates that earnings can be affected unrealistically by rapid increases and fluctuations in prices when using LIFO. Comment.

b. How much taxes will need to be paid on past earnings from the switch from LIFO? How will the switch from LIFO influence taxes in the future?

c. How will a switch from LIFO affect 2002 profits?

d. How will a switch from LIFO affect future profits?

e. How will a switch from LIFO affect 2002 cash flow?

f. How will a switch from LIFO affect future cash flow?

g. Speculate on the real reason that the corporation wishes to switch from LIFO.

Case 6-3

Moments to Remember

The information on this case came from the Eastman Kodak 2001 financial report.

Eastman Kodak Company and Subsidiary Companies
Consolidated Statement of Financial Position

(in millions, except share and per share data)	At December 31, 2001	At December 31, 2000
Assets		
Current Assets		
Cash and cash equivalents	$ 448	$ 246
Receivables, net	2,337	2,653
Inventories, net	1,137	1,718
Deferred income taxes	521	575
Other current assets	240	299
Total current assets	4,683	5,491
Property, plant and equipment, net	5,659	5,919
Goodwill, net	948	947
Other long-term assets	2,072	1,855
Total Assets	$13,362	$14,212
Liabilities and Shareholders' Equity		
Current Liabilities		
Accounts payable and other current liabilities	$ 3,276	$ 3,403
Short-term borrowings	1,378	2,058
Current portion of long-term debt	156	148
Accrued income taxes	544	606
Total current liabilities	5,354	6,215
Long-term debt, net of current portion	1,666	1,166
Postemployment liabilities	2,728	2,722
Other long-term liabilities	720	681
Total Liabilities	10,468	10,784
Commitments and Contingencies (Note 10)		
Shareholders' Equity		
Common stock, $2.50 par value		
950,000,000 shares authorized; issued 391,292,760 shares in 2001 and 2000; 290,929,701 and 290,484,266 shares outstanding in 2001 and 2000	978	978
Additional paid in capital	849	871
Retained earnings	7,431	7,869
Accumulated other comprehensive loss	(597)	(482)
	8,661	9,236
Treasury stock, at cost		
100,363,059 shares in 2001 and 100,808,494 shares in 2000	5,767	5,808
Total Shareholders' Equity	2,894	3,428
Total Liabilities and Shareholders' Equity	$13,362	$14,212

Eastman Kodak Company and Subsidiary Companies
Consolidated Statement of Earnings

(in millions, except per share data)	For the Year Ended December 31,		
	2001	2000	1999
Net sales	$13,234	$13,994	$14,089
Cost of goods sold	8,670	8,375	8,086
Gross profit	4,564	5,619	6,003
Selling, general and administrative expenses	2,627	2,514	2,701
Research and development costs	779	784	817
Goodwill amortization	154	151	145
Restructuring costs (credits) and other	659	(44)	350
Earnings from operations	345	2,214	1,990
Interest expense	219	178	142
Other income (charges)	(18)	96	261
Earnings before income taxes	108	2,132	2,109
Provision for income taxes	32	725	717
Net Earnings	$ 76	$ 1,407	$ 1,392
Basic earnings per share	$ .26	$ 4.62	$ 4.38
Diluted earnings per share	$ .26	$ 4.59	$ 4.33
Earnings used in basic and diluted earnings per share	$ 76	$ 1,407	$ 1,392
Number of common shares used in basic earnings per share	290.6	304.9	318.0
Incremental shares from assumed conversion of options	0.4	1.7	3.5
Number of common shares used in diluted earnings per share	291.0	306.6	321.5
Cash dividends per share	$ 2.21	$ 1.76	$ 1.76

Notes to Financial Statements (in Part)

Note 2: Receivables, net

(in millions)	2001	2000
Trade receivables	$1,966	$2,245
Miscellaneous receivables	371	408
Total (net of allowances of $109 and $89)	$2,337	$2,653

In the fourth quarter of 2001, the Company recorded a charge of $20 million to provide for the potential uncollectible amounts due from Kmart, who filed a petition for reorganization under Chapter 11 of the United States Bankruptcy Code in January 2002. The amount of $20 million is included in selling, general and administrative expenses and in the total allowance of $109 million at December 31, 2001.

Note 7: Accounts Payable and Other Current Liabilities

(in millions)	2001	2000
Accounts payable, trade	$ 674	$ 817
Accrued advertising and promotional expenses	568	578
Accrued employment-related liabilities	749	780
Accrued restructuring liabilities	318	—
Dividends payable	—	128
Other	967	1,100
Total payables	$3,276	$3,403

The Other component above consists of other miscellaneous current liabilities which, individually, are less than 5% of the Total current liabilities component within the Consolidated Statement of Financial Position, and therefore, have been aggregated in accordance with Regulation S-X.

Required   a.   Based on these data, calculate the following for 2001 and 2000.
1. Days' sales in receivables (Use trade receivables.)
2. Accounts receivable turnover (Use gross trade receivables at year-end.)

3. Days' sales in inventory
4. Inventory turnover (use year-end inventory)
5. Working capital
6. Current ratio
7. Acid-test ratio

b. Comment on each ratio individually.
c. Prepare a vertical common-size analysis for the balance sheets using 2001 and 2000. (Use total assets as the base.)
d. Comment on the vertical common-size analysis.
e. Comment on the apparent total liquidity.

Case 6-4 The Other Side of LIFO

What happens when a company using LIFO sells a greater quantity of goods than it purchases? In the following article,* Allen I. Schiff, Ph.D., Associate Professor of Accounting at Fordham University, New York City, discusses the implications of this phenomenon, which is known as LIFO liquidation.

Discussion of the LIFO cost basis for inventory valuation usually focuses on the superiority of this method and its widespread adoption. The conventional rationale for LIFO is its consistency with the matching principle during a period of rising prices. Historically, the most significant adoption of LIFO by U.S. corporations occurred during the period from 1973 to 1974, which was characterized by rapidly rising prices and sharp increases in interest rates. However, the motivation for the widespread use of LIFO didn't derive from the desire to achieve better matching of cost and revenue but, rather, from the reduced reported income that led to tax savings and increased cash flow.

Recently, another facet of LIFO has appeared in the annual reports of some companies. Known as LIFO liquidation, this process occurs during a reporting period when a company sells (withdraws) goods in a greater quantity than the quantity purchased (entered). As a result, inventories are reduced to a point at which cost layers of prior years are related to current inflated sales prices.

Relatively little attention has been given to the implications of LIFO inventory liquidations. Accounting texts discuss LIFO liquidations in a superficial fashion—and for good reason, it wasn't a phenomenon frequently encountered in the past. Indeed, until recently the only significant attempted LIFO liquidation related to the steel industry during the Korean War period. During this period, the demand for steel was strong, prices were high, and a steelworker's strike contributed to decreasing inventory levels. Congress was petitioned to modify the tax result from a matching of "old" costs against their then-current high-selling prices. Congress refused and steel inventories weren't liquidated despite market demand.

The Incentives for LIFO Liquidation

The economic environment at this writing is quite different. Possible factors causing LIFO liquidations at present are:

- Decreased expected demand associated with a recessionary economy.
- High interest rates resulting in high inventory carrying costs. These high rates also present alternative economic opportunities for funds invested in inventories if there is a belief that the inflation rate will decrease in relation to interest rates.
- A sluggish economy that could lead management to minimize losses or improve reported profit.

To get a notion about the extent, if any, to which companies that recorded a LIFO liquidation increased net income, the financial reports of 17 LIFO companies for the years 1980 and 1981 were randomly selected. Nine of these companies reported an increase in pretax income (or a reduction of loss) of at least 10 percent for either 1980, 1981 or both as a direct result of LIFO liquidation. What these preliminary results suggest is that there are other aspects of LIFO which require more extensive study. The original justification for LIFO was its superiority in reflecting results consistent with the matching

---

* Copyright © 1983 by the AICPA, Inc. Opinions expressed in the *Journal of Accountancy* are those of the editors and contributors. Publication in the *Journal of Accountancy* does not constitute endorsement by the AICPA or its committees.

principle. The liquidation of LIFO layers in recent years has had the opposite effect; it mismatches current revenues and historical costs, which results in the inclusion of inventory holding gains in reported income.

Conclusion

Thus, we have come full circle. FIFO valuation methods, originally criticized for poor matching when compared to LIFO, may actually be superior in the sense that, compared to companies experiencing LIFO liquidations, FIFO companies match costs and revenues relatively well. Furthermore, it may be argued that the sole motivation attributed to companies for switching to LIFO—to improve cash flows—may need broadening. Since the timing of the decision to liquidate LIFO inventories is entirely up to management, it would appear that such liquidations may give rise to income smoothing; it must be stressed that the smoothing may enhance the image conveyed by financial statements, but it has a negative impact on cash flow to the extent that taxes are paid (or loss carryforwards reduced) on the incremental profit associated with the sale of the liquidated inventories.

More extensive research is, of course, needed to fully document the incidence of LIFO inventory liquidation during the last two years. Even my limited examination of reports suggests the need to emphasize the "other side of LIFO."

Required   a.   Briefly describe why an inventory method that uses historical costs (such as LIFO) can distort profits.

b.   Indicate probable reasons why the steel industry did not sell its available inventory during the steel strike.

c.   For the firms that were using LIFO, explain the anticipated effect on the following variables because of reducing inventories during 1980 and 1981:
   1.   Profits
   2.   Taxes paid
   3.   Cash flow

d.   In your opinion, what effect did the reduction in inventories during 1980 and 1981, for the LIFO firms, have on the quality of earnings?

e.   Explain why many firms voluntarily reduced their inventories during 1980 and 1981.

Case 6-5   Network Supreme

The following information is from the 1998 financial statements of Novell. Novell is a large network software company.

Novell
Consolidated Balance Sheet (in Part)

(Dollars in thousands)	October 31 1998	October 31 1997
Assets		
Current assets:		
Cash and short-term investments	$1,007,167	$1,033,473
Receivables, less allowances ($47,921—1998, $33,053—1997)	246,577	211,531
Inventories	3,562	10,656
Prepaid expenses	63,165	57,685
Deferred and refundable income taxes	95,343	134,210
Other current assets	19,886	22,827
Total current assets	1,435,700	1,470,382
Property, plant, and equipment, net	346,196	373,865
Long-term investments	114,815	19,107
Other assets	27,401	47,295
Total assets	$1,924,112	$1,910,649

Liabilities and shareholders' equity

Current liabilities

Accounts payable	$ 77,987	$ 82,759
Accrued compensation	52,348	51,397
Accrued marketing liabilities	16,383	27,728
Other accrued liabilities	62,206	85,157
Income taxes payable	64,057	—
Deferred revenue	141,714	74,915
Total current liabilities	414,695	321,956
Minority interests	15,919	23,276
Shareholders' equity (detail omitted)	1,493,498	1,565,417
Total liabilities and shareholders' equity	$1,924,112	$1,910,649

Novell
Consolidated Statements of Operations (in Part)
Fiscal Year Ended

(Amounts in millions except per share data)	October 31, 1998	October 31, 1997	October 31, 1996
Net sales	$1,083,887	$1,007,311	$1,374,856
Cost of sales	238,649	277,446	306,761
Gross profit	845,238	729,865	1,068,095
Operating expenses (detail omitted)	746,792	929,869	959,151
Income (loss) from operations	98,446	(200,004)	108,944
Other income (expense)			
Investment income	44,727	61,315	58,195
Gain on sale of assets	—	—	19,815
Other, net	(1,539)	(11,881)	(6,966)
Other income, net	43,188	49,434	71,044
Income (loss) before taxes	141,634	(150,570)	179,988
Income tax expense (benefit)	39,658	(72,274)	53,997
Net income (loss)	$ 101,976	$ (78,296)	$ 125,991
Weighted average shares outstanding			
Basic	350,525	348,149	355,478
Diluted	356,437	349,429	357,919
Net income (loss) per share			
Basic	$.29	$(.22)	$.35
Diluted	$.29	$(.22)	$.35

Note: Repurchases of common stock

1998	$244,964,000
1997	—
1996	$455,701,000

Decrease in inventories

1998	$7,094,000
1997	$6,181,000
1996	$6,188,000

Required   a. Based on these data, calculate the following for 1998 and 1997:

1. Days' sales in receivables
2. Accounts receivable turnover (gross receivables at year-end)
3. Days' sales in inventory
4. Inventory turnover (Use inventory at year-end.)
5. Working capital
6. Current ratio
7. Acid-test ratio

b. Prepare a vertical common-size analysis for the balance sheets, using 1998 and 1997. (Use total assets as the base.)
c. Comment on each ratio individually.
d. Comment on the vertical common-size analysis.
e. Comment on the apparent total liquidity.

Case 6-6

Booming Retail

The Grand retail firm reported the following financial data for the past several years:

	Year				
	5	**4**	**3**	**2**	**1**
	(amounts in 000s)				
Sales	$1,254,131	$1,210,918	$1,096,152	$979,458	$920,797
Net accounts receivable	419,731	368,267	312,776	72,450	230,427

The Grand retail firm had a decentralized credit operation allowing each store to administer its credit operation. Many stores provided installment plans allowing the customer up to 36 months to pay. Gross profits on installment sales were reflected in the financial statements in the period when the sales were made.

Required

a. Using Year 1 as the base, prepare horizontal common-size analysis for sales and net accounts receivable.
b. Compute the accounts receivable turnover for Years 2–5. (Use net accounts receivable.)
c. Would financial control of accounts receivable be more important with installment sales than with sales on 30-day credit? Comment.
d. Comment on what is apparently happening at The Grand retail firm.
Note: Data from an actual retail company.

Web Case

Thomson Analytics *Business School Edition*

Please complete the web case that covers material covered in this chapter at http://gibson.swlearning.com. You'll be using Thomson Analytics Business School Edition, a version of the powerful tool used by Wall Street professionals, that combines a full range of fundamental financial information, earnings estimates, market data, and source documents for 500 publicly traded companies.

Endnotes

1. *Accounting Research Bulletins No. 43*, "Restatement and Revision of Accounting Research Bulletins," 1953, Chapter 3, Section A, paragraph 4.
2. *Statement of Financial Accounting Standards No. 115*, "Accounting for Certain Investments in Debt and Equity Securities" (Norwalk, CT: Financial Accounting Standards Board, 1993).
3. *Opinions of the Accounting Principles Board No. 21*, "Interest on Receivables and Payables" (New York: American Institute of Certified Public Accountants, 1971), paragraph 11.
4. *Statement of Financial Accounting Standards No. 5*, "Accounting for Contingencies" (Stamford, CT: Financial Accounting Standards Board, 1975), paragraph 8.
5. Committee on Accounting Procedure, American Institute of Certified Public Accountants, "Accounting Research and Terminology Bulletins" (New York: American Institute of Certified Public Accountants, 1961), p. 21.

CHAPTER

7

LONG-TERM
DEBT-PAYING ABILITY

This chapter covers two approaches to viewing a firm's long-term debt-paying ability. One approach views the firm's ability to carry the debt as indicated by the income statement, and the other considers the firm's ability to carry debt as indicated by the balance sheet.

In the long run, a relationship exists between the reported income resulting from the use of accrual accounting and the ability of the firm to meet its long-term obligations. Although the reported income does not agree with the cash available in the short run, the revenue and expense items eventually do result in cash movements. Because of the close relationship between the reported income and the ability of the firm to meet its long-run obligations, the entity's profitability is an important factor when determining long-term debt-paying ability.

In addition to the profitability of the firm, the amount of debt in relation to the size of the firm should be analyzed. This analysis indicates the amount of funds provided by outsiders in relation to those provided by owners of the firm. If a high proportion of the resources has been provided by outsiders, the risks of the business have been substantially shifted to the outsiders. A large proportion of debt in the capital structure increases the risk of not meeting the principal or interest obligation because the company may not generate adequate funds to meet these obligations.

INCOME STATEMENT CONSIDERATION WHEN DETERMINING LONG-TERM DEBT-PAYING ABILITY

The firm's ability to carry debt, as indicated by the income statement, can be viewed by considering the times interest earned and the fixed charge coverage. These ratios are now reviewed.

Times Interest Earned

The **times interest earned ratio** indicates a firm's long-term debt-paying ability from the income statement view. If the times interest earned is adequate, little danger exists that the firm will not be able to meet its interest obligation. If the firm has good coverage of the interest obligation, it should also be able to refinance the principal when it comes due. In effect, the funds will probably never be required to pay off the principal if the company has a good record of covering the interest expense. A relatively high, stable coverage of interest over the years indicates a good record. A low, fluctuating coverage from year to year indicates a poor record.

Companies that maintain a good record can finance a relatively high proportion of debt in relation to stockholders' equity and, at the same time, obtain funds at favorable rates. Utility companies have traditionally been examples of companies that have a high debt structure, in relation to stockholders' equity. They accomplished this because of their relatively high, stable coverage of interest over the years. This stability evolved in an industry with a regulated profit and a relatively stable demand. During the 1970s, 1980s, and 1990s, utilities experienced a severe strain on their profits, as rate increases did not keep pace with inflation. In addition, the demand was not as predictable as in prior years. The strain on profits and the uncertainty of demand influenced investors to demand higher interest rates from utilities than had been previously required in relation to other companies.

A company issues debt obligations to obtain funds at an interest rate less than the earnings from these funds. This is called **trading on the equity** or **leverage**. With a high interest rate, the added risk exists that the company will not be able to earn more on the funds than the interest cost on them.

Compute times interest earned as follows:

$$\text{Times Interest Earned} = \frac{\begin{array}{c}\text{Recurring Earnings, Excluding Interest}\\\text{Expense, Tax Expense, Equity Earnings,}\\\text{and Minority Earnings}\end{array}}{\text{Interest Expense, Including Capitalized Interest}}$$

The income statement contains several figures that might be used in this analysis. In general, the primary analysis of the firm's ability to carry the debt as indicated by the income statement should include only income expected to occur in subsequent periods. Thus, the following nonrecurring items should be excluded:

1. Discontinued operations
2. Extraordinary items
3. Cumulative effect of a change in accounting principle

In addition to these nonrecurring items, additional items that should be excluded for the times interest earned computation include:

1. **Interest expense.** This is added back to net income because the interest coverage would be understated by one if interest expense were deducted before computing times interest earned.
2. **Income tax expense.** Income taxes are computed after deducting interest expense, so they do not affect the safety of the interest payments.
3. **Equity earnings (losses) of nonconsolidated subsidiaries.** These are excluded because they are not available to cover interest payments, except to the extent that they are accompanied by cash dividends.
4. **Minority income (loss).** This adjustment at the bottom of the income statement should be excluded; use income before minority interest. Minority income (loss) results from consolidating a firm in which a company has control but less than 100% ownership. All of the interest expense of the firm consolidated is included in the consolidated income statement. Therefore, all of the income of the firm consolidated should be considered in the coverage.

Capitalization of interest results in interest being added to a fixed asset instead of expensed. The interest capitalized should be included with the total interest expense in the denominator of the times interest earned ratio because it is part of the interest payment. The capitalized interest must be added to the interest expense disclosed on the income statement or in footnotes.

An example of capitalized interest would be interest during the current year on a bond issued to build a factory. As long as the factory is under construction, this interest would be added to the asset account, construction in process, on the balance sheet. This interest does not appear on the income statement, but it is as much of a commitment as the interest expense deducted on the income statement.

When the factory is completed, the annual interest on the bond issued to build the factory will be expensed. When expensed, interest appears on the income statement.

Capitalized interest is usually disclosed in a footnote. Some firms describe the capitalized interest on the face of the income statement.

Exhibit 7-1 shows times interest earned for Nike for the years 2002 and 2001. Many would consider this ratio to be high. To evaluate the adequacy of coverage, the times interest earned ratio should be computed for a period of three to five years and compared to competitors and the industry average. Computing interest earned for three to five years provides insight on the stability of the interest coverage. Because the firm needs to cover interest in the bad years as well as the good years, the lowest times interest earned in the period is used as the primary indication of the interest coverage. A cyclical firm may have a very high times interest earned ratio in highly profitable years, but interest may not be covered in low profit years.

Interest coverage on long-term debt is sometimes computed separately from the normal times interest earned. For this purpose only, use the interest on long-term debt, thus focusing on the long-term interest coverage. Since times interest earned indicates long-term debt-paying ability, this revised computation helps focus on the long-term position. For external analysis, it is usually not practical to compute times interest coverage on long-term debt because of the lack of data. However, this computation can be made for internal analysis.

In the long run, a firm must have the funds to meet all of its expenses. In the short run, a firm can often meet its interest obligations even when the times interest earned is less than 1.00. Some of the expenses, such as depreciation expense, amortization expense, and depletion expense, do not require funds in the short run. The airline industry has had several bad periods when the times interest earned was less than 1.00, but it was able to maintain the interest payments.

To get a better indication of a firm's ability to cover interest payments in the short run, the noncash expenses such as depreciation, depletion, and amortization can be added back to the numerator of the times interest earned ratio. The resulting ratio, which is less conservative, gives a type of cash basis times interest earned useful for evaluating the firm in the short run.

Exhibit 7-2 shows that Nike's short-run times interest earned ratio is substantially higher than its long-run ratio.

EXHIBIT 7-1	NIKE, INC.

Times Interest Earned

Year Ended May 31, 2002 and 2001

	2002	2001
	(in millions)	
Income before income taxes and cumulative effect accounting change	$1,017.3	$921.4
Plus: Interest expense	47.6	58.7
Income before income taxes, cumulative effect accounting change and interest expense [A]	$1,064.9	$980.1
Interest expense	$ 47.6	$ 58.7
Capitalized interest	1.7	8.4
Total interest paid [B]	$ 49.3	$ 67.1
Times interest earned [A ÷ B]	21.60 times per year	14.61 times per year

EXHIBIT 7-2   NIKE, INC.

Times Interest Earned (Short-Run Perspective)

Year Ended May 31, 2002 and 2001

	2002	2001
	(in millions)	
Income before income taxes and cumulative effect accounting change	$1,017.3	$ 921.4
Plus: Interest expense	47.6	58.7
Depreciation	223.5	197.4
Amortization and other*	53.1	16.7
Earnings adjusted [A]	$1,341.5	$1,194.2
Interest expense	$ 47.6	$ 58.7
Capitalized interest	1.7	8.4
Total interest paid [B]	$ 49.3	$ 67.1
Times interest earned (short-run perspective) [A ÷ B]	27.21 times per year	17.80 times per year

*In the financial report, amortization and other were combined. The total amount was used because there was no way to determine the amount for amortization and the amount for other.

Fixed Charge Coverage

The **fixed charge coverage ratio**, an extension of the times interest earned ratio, also indicates a firm's long-term debt-paying ability from the income statement view. The fixed charge coverage ratio indicates a firm's ability to cover fixed charges. It is computed as follows:

$$\text{Fixed Charge Coverage} = \frac{\begin{array}{c}\text{Recurring Earnings, Excluding Interest Expense, Tax Expense, Equity}\\\text{Earnings, and Minority Earnings + Interest Portion of Rentals}\end{array}}{\begin{array}{c}\text{Interest Expense, Including Capitalized Interest}\\\text{+ Interest Portion of Rentals}\end{array}}$$

A difference of opinion occurs in practice as to what should be included in the fixed charges. When assets are leased, the lessee classifies leases as either capital leases or operating leases. The lessee treats a capital lease as an acquisition and includes the leased asset in fixed assets and the related obligation in liabilities. Part of the lease payment is considered to be interest expense. Therefore, the interest expense on the income statement includes interest related to capital leases.

A portion of operating lease payments is an item frequently included in addition to interest expense. Operating leases are not on the balance sheet, but they are reflected on the income statement in the rent expense. An operating lease for a relatively long term is a type of long-term financing, so part of the lease payment is really interest. When a portion of operating lease payments is included in fixed charges, it is an effort to recognize the true total interest that the firm pays.

SEC reporting may require a more conservative computation than the times interest earned ratio in order to determine the firm's long-term debt-paying ability. The SEC refers to its ratio as the **ratio of earnings to fixed charges.** The major difference between the times interest earned computation and the ratio of earnings to fixed charges is that the latter computation includes a portion of the operating leases.

Usually, one-third of the operating leases' rental charges is included in the fixed charges because this is an approximation of the proportion of lease payment that is interest. The SEC does not accept the one-third approximation automatically, but requires a more specific estimate of the interest portion based on the terms of the lease. Individuals interested in a company's ratio of earnings to fixed charges can find this ratio on the face of the income statement included with the SEC registration statement (Form S-7) when debt securities are registered.

The same adjusted earnings figure is used in the fixed charge coverage ratio as is used for the times interest earned ratio, except that the interest portion of operating leases (rentals) is added to the adjusted earnings for the fixed charge coverage ratio. The interest portion of operating leases is added to the adjusted earnings because it was previously deducted on the income statement as rental charges.

Nike's 2002 annual report disclosed "the Company leases space for its offices, warehouses and retail stores under leases expiring from one to fifteen years after May 31, 2002. Rent expense was $159.9 million, $152.0 million and $145.5 million for the years ended May 31, 2002, 2001 and 2000, respectively."

Exhibit 7-3 shows the fixed charge coverage for Nike for 2002 and 2001, with the interest portion of rentals considered. This figure, more conservative than the times interest earned, is still very good for Nike.

Among the other items sometimes considered as fixed charges are depreciation, depletion and amortization, debt principal payments, and pension payments. Substantial preferred dividends may also be included, or a separate ratio may be computed to consider preferred dividends. The more items considered as fixed charges, the more conservative the ratio. The trend is usually similar to that found for the times interest earned ratio.

BALANCE SHEET CONSIDERATION WHEN DETERMINING LONG-TERM DEBT-PAYING ABILITY

The firm's ability to carry debt, as indicated by the balance sheet, can be viewed by considering the debt ratio and the debt/equity ratio. These ratios are now reviewed.

Debt Ratio

The debt ratio indicates the firm's long-term debt-paying ability. It is computed as follows:

$$\text{Debt Ratio} = \frac{\text{Total Liabilities}}{\text{Total Assets}}$$

Total liabilities includes short-term liabilities, reserves, deferred tax liabilities, minority shareholders' interests, redeemable preferred stock, and any other noncurrent liability. It does not include stockholders' equity.

The debt ratio indicates the percentage of assets financed by creditors, and it helps to determine how well creditors are protected in case of insolvency. If creditors are not well protected, the company is not in a position to issue additional long-term debt. From the perspective of long-term debt-paying ability, the lower this ratio, the better the company's position.

Exhibit 7-4 shows the debt ratio for Nike for May 31, 2002, and May 31, 2001. The exhibit indicates that substantially less than one-half of the Nike assets were financed by outsiders in both

EXHIBIT 7-3	NIKE, INC.

Fixed Charge Coverage

Years Ended May 31, 2002 and 2001

	2002	2001
	(in millions)	
Income before income taxes and cumulative effect accounting change	$1,017.3	$ 921.4
Plus: Interest expense	47.6	58.7
Interest portion of rentals	53.30	50.67
Earnings adjusted [A]	$1,118.20	$1,030.77
Interest expense	$ 47.6	$ 58.7
Capitalized interest	1.7	8.4
Interest portion of rentals	53.30	50.67
Adjusted interest [B]	$ 102.60	$ 117.77
Fixed charge coverage [A ÷ B]	10.90 times per year	8.75 times per year

EXHIBIT 7-4   **NIKE, INC.**

Debt Ratio

Years Ended May 31, 2002 and 2001

	2002	2001
	(in millions)	
Total liabilities compiled:		
Current Liabilities	$1,836.2	$1,786.7
Long-term debt	625.9	435.9
Deferred income taxes and other liabilities	141.6	102.2
Redeemable Preferred Stock	0.3	0.3
Total liabilities [A]	$2,604.0	$2,325.1
Total assets [B]	$6,443.0	$5,819.6
Debt ratio [A ÷ B]	40.42%	39.95%

2002 and 2001. This debt ratio is a conservative computation because all of the liabilities and near liabilities have been included. At the same time, the assets are understated because no adjustments have been made for assets that have a fair market value greater than book value.

The debt ratio should be compared with competitors and industry averages. Industries that have stable earnings can handle more debt than industries that have cyclical earnings. This comparison can be misleading if one firm has substantial hidden assets, or liabilities that other firms do not (such as substantial land carried at historical cost).

In practice, substantial disagreement occurs on the details of the formula to compute the debt ratio. Some of the disagreement revolves around whether short-term liabilities should be included. Some firms exclude short-term liabilities because they are not long-term sources of funds and are, therefore, not a valid indication of the firm's long-term debt position. Other firms include short-term liabilities because these liabilities become part of the total source of outside funds in the long run. For example, individual accounts payable are relatively short term, but accounts payable in total becomes a rather permanent part of the entire sources of funds. This book takes a conservative position that includes the short-term liabilities in the debt ratio.

Another issue involves whether certain other items should be included in liabilities. Under current GAAP, some liabilities clearly represent a commitment to pay out funds in the future, whereas other items may never result in a future payment. Items that present particular problems as to a future payment of funds include reserves, deferred taxes, minority shareholders' interests, and redeemable preferred stock. Each of these items will be reviewed in the sections that follow.

Reserves

The reserve accounts classified under liabilities (some short-term and some long-term) result from an expense charge to the income statement and an equal increase in the reserve account on the balance sheet. These reserve accounts do not represent definite commitments to pay out funds in the future, but they are estimates of funds that will be paid out.

Reserve accounts are used infrequently in U.S. financial reporting. It is thought that they provide too much discretion in determining the amount of the reserve and the related impact on reported income. When the reserve account is increased, income is reduced. When the reserve account is decreased, income is increased. Reserve accounts are popular in some other countries like Germany. This book takes a conservative position that includes the reserves in liabilities in the debt ratio.

Deferred Taxes (Interperiod Tax Allocation)

In the United States, a firm may recognize certain income and expense items in one period for the financial statements and in another period for the federal tax return. This can result in financial statement income in any one period that is substantially different from tax return income. For many other countries, this is not the case. For example, there are few timing differences in Germany, and there are no timing differences in Japan. For these countries, deferred taxes are not a substantial issue or are not an issue at all. In the United States, taxes payable based on the tax return can be substantially different from income tax expense based on financial statement income. Current GAAP directs that the tax expense for the financial statements be based on the tax-related items on the financial statements. Taxes payable are based on the actual current taxes payable, determined by the tax return. (The Internal Revenue Code specifies the procedures for determining taxable income.) The tax expense for the financial statements often does not agree with the taxes payable. The difference between tax expense and taxes payable is recorded as deferred income taxes. The concept that results in deferred income taxes is called **interperiod tax allocation.**

As an illustration of deferred taxes, consider the following facts related to machinery purchase for $100,000:

Three-year write-off for tax purposes:

1st year	$ 25,000
2nd year	38,000
3rd year	37,000
	$100,000

Five-year write-off for financial statements:

1st year	$ 20,000
2nd year	20,000
3rd year	20,000
4th year	20,000
5th year	20,000
	$100,000

For both tax and financial statement purposes, $100,000 was written off for the equipment. The write-off on the tax return was three years, while the write-off on the financial statements was five years. The faster write-off on the tax return resulted in lower taxable income than the income reported on the income statement during the first three years. During the last two years, the income statement income was lower than the tax return income.

In addition to temporary differences, the tax liability can be influenced by an **operating loss carryback** and/or **operating loss carryforward**. The tax code allows a corporation reporting an operating loss for income tax purposes in the current year to carry this loss back and forward to offset reported taxable income. The company may first carry an operating loss back two years in sequential order, starting with the earliest of the two years. If the taxable income for the past two years is not enough to offset the operating loss, then the remaining loss is sequentially carried forward 20 years and offset against future taxable income.

A company can elect to forgo a carryback and, instead, only carry forward an operating loss. A company would not normally forgo a carryback because an operating loss carryback results in a definite and immediate income tax refund. A carryforward will reduce income taxes payable in future years to the extent of earned taxable income. A company could possibly benefit from forgoing a carryback if prospects in future years are good and an increase in the tax rate is anticipated.

Interperiod tax allocation should be used for all temporary differences. A temporary difference between the tax basis of an asset or liability and its reported amount in the financial statements will result in taxable or deductible amounts in future years when the reported amount of the asset or liability is recovered or settled, respectively.

A corporation reports deferred taxes in two classifications: a net current amount and a net noncurrent amount. The net current amount could result in a current asset or a current liability being reported. The net noncurrent amount could result in a noncurrent asset or a noncurrent liability being reported.

Classification as current or noncurrent is usually based on the classification of the asset or liability responsible for the temporary difference. For example, a deferred tax liability resulting from the excess of tax depreciation over financial reporting depreciation would be reported as a noncurrent liability. This is because the temporary difference is related to noncurrent assets (fixed assets).

When a deferred tax asset or liability is not related to an asset or liability, the deferred tax asset or liability is classified according to the expected reversal date of the temporary difference. For example, a deferred tax amount resulting from an operating loss carryforward would be classified based on the expected reversal date of the temporary difference.

There should be a valuation allowance against a deferred tax asset if sufficient uncertainty exists about a corporation's future taxable income. A valuation allowance reduces the deferred tax asset to its expected realizable amount. At the time that the valuation allowance is recognized, tax expense is increased.

A more likely than not criterion is used to measure uncertainty. If more likely than not a deferred asset will not be realized, a valuation allowance would be required.

Nike discloses deferred taxes in long-term assets and long-term liabilities. For many firms, the long-term liability, deferred taxes, has grown to a substantial amount, which often increases each year. This occurs because of the growth in the temporary differences that cause the timing difference. The Nike amount increased substantially in 2002 for the long-term liability.

Deferred taxes must be accounted for, using the liability method, which focuses on the balance sheet. Deferred taxes are recorded at amounts at which they will be settled when underlying temporary differences reverse. Deferred taxes are adjusted for tax rate changes. A change in tax rates can result in a material adjustment to the deferred account and can substantially influence income in the year of the tax rate change.

Some individuals disagree with the concept of deferred taxes (interperiod tax allocation). It is uncertain that the deferred tax will be paid. If it will be paid (received), it is uncertain when it will be paid (or received). The deferred tax accounts are, therefore, often referred to as **soft accounts**.

Because of the uncertainty over whether (and when) a deferred tax liability (asset) will be paid (received), some individuals elect to exclude deferred tax liabilities and assets when performing analysis. This is inconsistent with GAAP, which recognize deferred taxes.

Some revenue and expense items, referred to as **permanent differences**, never go on the tax return, but do go on the income statement. Examples would be premiums on life insurance and life insurance proceeds. Federal tax law does not allow these items to be included in expense and revenue, respectively. These items never influence either the tax expense or the tax liability, so they never influence the deferred tax accounts.

Minority Shareholders' Interest

The account, minority shareholders' interest, results when the firm has consolidated another company of which it owns less than 100%. The proportion of the consolidated company that is not owned appears on the balance sheet just above stockholders' equity.

Some firms exclude the minority shareholders' interest when computing debt ratios because this amount does not represent a commitment to pay funds to outsiders. Other firms include the minority shareholders' interest when computing debt ratios because these funds came from outsiders and are part of the total funds that the firm uses. This book takes the conservative position of including minority shareholders' interest in the primary computation of debt ratios. To review minority shareholders' interest, refer to the section of Chapter 3 on minority interest.

Redeemable Preferred Stock

Redeemable preferred stock is subject to mandatory redemption requirements or has a redemption feature outside the control of the issuer. Some redeemable preferred stock agreements require the firm to purchase certain amounts of the preferred stock on the open market. The Securities and Exchange Commission dictates that redeemable preferred stock not be disclosed under stockholders' equity.

The nature of redeemable preferred stock leaves open to judgment how it should be handled when computing debt ratios. One view excludes it from debt and includes it in stockholders' equity, on the grounds that it does not represent a normal debt relationship. A conservative position includes it as debt when computing the debt ratios. This book uses the conservative approach and includes redeemable preferred stock in debt for the primary computation of debt ratios. For a more detailed review, refer to the section of Chapter 3 that describes redeemable preferred stock.

Debt/Equity Ratio

The **debt/equity ratio** is another computation that determines the entity's long-term debt-paying ability. This computation compares the total debt with the total shareholders' equity. The debt/equity ratio also helps determine how well creditors are protected in case of insolvency. From the perspective of long-term debt-paying ability, the lower this ratio is, the better the company's debt position.

In this book, the computation of the debt/equity ratio is conservative because all of the liabilities and near liabilities are included, and the stockholders' equity is understated to the extent that assets have a value greater than book value. This ratio should also be compared with industry averages and competitors. Compute the debt/equity ratio as follows:

$$\text{Debt /Equity Ratio} = \frac{\text{Total Liabilities}}{\text{Shareholders' Equity}}$$

Exhibit 7-5 shows the debt/equity ratio for Nike for May 31, 2002, and May 31, 2001. Using a conservative approach to computing debt/equity, Exhibit 7-5 indicates the debt/equity ratio was 67.83% at the end of 2002, up from 66.54% at the end of 2001.

The debt ratio and the debt/equity ratio have the same objectives. Therefore, these ratios are alternatives to each other if computed in the manner recommended here. Because some financial services may be reporting the debt ratio and others may be reporting the debt/equity ratio, the reader should be familiar with both.

As indicated previously, a problem exists with the lack of uniformity in the way some ratios are computed. This especially occurs with the debt ratio and the debt/equity ratio. When comparing the debt ratio and the debt/equity ratio with industry ratios, try to determine how the industry ratios were computed. A reasonable comparison may not be possible because the financial sources sometimes do not indicate what elements of debt the computations include.

Debt to Tangible Net Worth Ratio

The debt to tangible net worth ratio also determines the entity's long-term debt-paying ability. This ratio also indicates how well creditors are protected in case of the firm's insolvency. As with the debt ratio and the debt/equity ratio, from the perspective of long-term debt-paying ability, it is better to have a lower ratio.

The debt to tangible net worth ratio is a more conservative ratio than either the debt ratio or the debt/equity ratio. It eliminates intangible assets, such as goodwill, trademarks, patents, and copyrights, because they do not provide resources to pay creditors—a very conservative position. Compute the debt to tangible net worth ratio as follows:

$$\text{Debt to Tangible Net Worth Ratio} = \frac{\text{Total Liabilities}}{\text{Shareholders' Equity} - \text{Intangible Assets}}$$

EXHIBIT 7-5	**NIKE, INC.**		
Debt/Equity Ratio			
Years Ended May 31, 2002 and 2001		**2002**	**2001**
		(in millions)	
Total liabilities [Exhibit 7-4] [A]		$2,604.0	$2,325.1
Shareholders' equity [B]		$3,839.0	$3,494.5
Debt/equity ratio [A ÷ B]		67.83%	66.54%

In this book, the computation of the debt to tangible net worth ratio is conservative. All of the liabilities and near liabilities are included, and the stockholders' equity is understated to the extent that assets have a value greater than book value.

Exhibit 7-6 shows the debt to tangible net worth ratios for Nike for May 31, 2002, and May 31, 2001. This is a conservative view of the debt-paying ability.

Other Long-Term Debt-Paying Ability Ratios

A number of additional ratios indicate perspective on the long-term debt-paying ability of a firm. This section describes some of these ratios.

The **current debt/net worth ratio** indicates a relationship between current liabilities and funds contributed by shareholders. The higher the proportion of funds provided by current liabilities, the greater the risk.

Another ratio, the **total capitalization ratio**, compares long-term debt to total capitalization. Total capitalization consists of long-term debt, preferred stock, and common stockholders' equity. The lower the ratio, the lower the risk.

Another ratio, the **fixed asset/equity ratio**, indicates the extent to which shareholders have provided funds in relation to fixed assets. Some firms subtract intangibles from shareholders' equity to obtain tangible net worth. This results in a more conservative ratio. The higher the fixed assets in relation to equity, the greater the risk.

Exhibit 7-7 indicates the trend in current liabilities, total liabilities, and owner's equity of firms in the United States between 1964 and 2001. It shows that there has been a major shift in the capital structure of firms, toward a higher proportion of debt in relation to total assets. This indicates a substantial increase in risk as management more frequently faces debt coming due. It also indicates that short-term debt is a permanent part of the financial structure of firms. This supports the decision to include short-term liabilities in the ratios determining long-term debt-paying ability (debt ratio, debt/equity ratio, and debt to tangible net worth ratio).

SPECIAL ITEMS THAT INFLUENCE A FIRM'S LONG-TERM DEBT-PAYING ABILITY

There are a number of special items that influence a firm's long-term debt-paying ability. These items are now reviewed.

Long-Term Assets Versus Long-Term Debt

The specific assets of the firm are important if the firm becomes unprofitable and the assets are sold. Therefore, consider the assets of the firm when determining the long-term debt-paying ability. The assets are insurance should the firm become unprofitable. The ability to analyze the assets, in relation to the long-term debt-paying ability, is limited, based on the information reported in the

---

EXHIBIT 7-6	**NIKE, INC.**

Debt to Tangible Net Worth Ratio

Years Ended May 31, 2002 and 2001

	2002	2001
	(in millions)	
Total liabilities [Exhibit 7-4] [A]	$2,604.0	$2,325.1
Shareholders' equity	$3,839.0	$3,494.5
Less: Intangible assets	437.8	397.3
Adjusted shareholders' equity [B]	$3,401.20	$3,097.20
Debt to tangible net worth ratio [A ÷ B]	76.56%	75.07%

| EXHIBIT 7-7 | TRENDS IN CURRENT LIABILITIES, LONG-TERM LIABILITIES, AND OWNER'S EQUITY 1964–2001 |

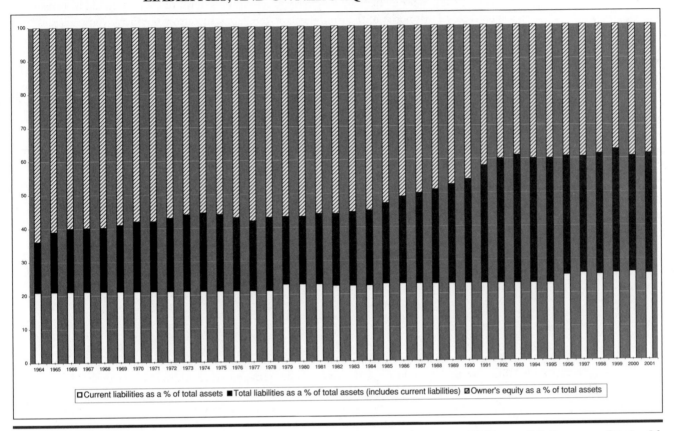

□ Current liabilities as a % of total assets ■ Total liabilities as a % of total assets (includes current liabilities) ▨ Owner's equity as a % of total assets

Source: Quarterly Financial Reports of Manufacturing, Mining & Trading, Department of Commerce. Washington, DC: Government Printing Office.

published financial statements. The statements do not extensively disclose market or liquidation values; they disclose only unrecovered cost for many items. The market value figure reported for some investments has been an exception.

A review of the financial statements is often of value if the firm liquidates or decides to reduce the scope of its operations. Examples of assets that may have substantial value would be land, timberlands, and investments.

When the Penn Central Company went bankrupt, it had substantial debt and operating losses. Yet because of assets that had substantial market values, creditors were repaid. In other cases, creditors receive nothing or only nominal amounts when a firm goes bankrupt.

Substantial assets that have a potential value higher than the book figures may also indicate an earnings potential that will be realized later. For example, knowing that a railroad owns land that contains millions or billions of tons of coal could indicate substantial profit potential, even if the coal is not economical to mine at the present time. In future years, as the price of competitive products such as oil and gas increase, the coal may become economical to mine. This happened in the United States in the late 1970s. Several railroads that owned millions or billions of tons of unmined coal found that the coal became very valuable as the price of oil and gas increased.

Long-Term Leasing

Earlier, this chapter explained the influence of long-term leasing in relation to the income statement. Now we will consider the influence of long-term leasing from the balance sheet perspective.

First, review some points made previously. The lessee classifies leases as either capital leases or operating leases. A capital lease is handled as if the lessee acquired the asset. The leased asset is classified as a fixed asset, and the related obligation is included in liabilities. Operating leases are not reflected on the balance sheet but in a footnote and on the income statement as rent expense.

Operating leases for a relatively long term (a type of long-term financing) should be considered in a supplemental manner as to their influence on the debt structure of the firms. Capital leases have already been considered in the debt ratios computed because the capital leases were part of the total assets and also part of the total liabilities on the balance sheet.

The capitalized asset amount will not agree with the capitalized liability amount because the liability is reduced by payments and the asset is reduced by depreciation taken. Usually, a company depreciates capital leases faster than payments are made. This would result in the capitalized asset amount being lower than the related capitalized liability amount. On the original date of the capital lease, the capitalized asset amount and the capitalized liability amount are the same.

The Nike footnote relating to long-term leases indicates the minimum future rentals under operating leases for years subsequent to May 31, 2002. These figures, as the following shows, do not include an amount for any possible contingent rentals because they are not practicable to estimate.

	Operating Leases
2003	$158.2 million
2004	143.4
2005	119.1
2006	95.3
2007	98.2
2008 and later	288.0
	$902.2

If these leases had been capitalized, the amount added to fixed assets and the amount added to liabilities would be the same at the time of the initial entry. As indicated previously, the amounts would not be the same, subsequently, because the asset is depreciated at some selected rate, while the liability is reduced as payments are made. When incorporating the operating leases into the debt ratios, use the liability amount and assume that the asset and the liability amount would be the same since no realistic way exists to compute the difference.

It would not be realistic to include the total future rentals that relate to operating leases in the lease commitments footnote ($902.2 million) because part of the commitment would be an interest consideration. Earlier, this chapter indicated that some firms estimate that one-third of the operating lease commitment is for interest. With a one-third estimate for interest, two-thirds is estimated for principal. For Nike, this amount is $601.5 million ($902.2 × 2/3). This amount can be added to fixed assets and long-term liabilities in order to obtain a supplemental view of the debt ratios that relate to the balance sheet. Exhibit 7-8 shows the adjusted debt ratio and debt/equity ratio for Nike at May 31, 2002; this increases the debt position by a substantial amount.

Pension Plans

The Employee Retirement Income Security Act (ERISA) became law in 1974 and substantially influenced the administration of pension plans, while elevating their liability status for the firm. This act includes provisions requiring minimum funding of plans, minimum rights to employees upon termination of their employment, and the creation of a special federal agency, the Pension Benefit Guaranty Corporation (PBGC), to help fund employee benefits when pension plans are terminated. The PBGC receives a fee for every employee covered by a pension plan subject to the PBGC. The PBGC has the right to impose a lien against a covered firm of 30% of the firm's net worth. This lien has the status of a tax lien and, therefore, ranks high among creditor claims. In practice, the PBGC has been reluctant to impose this lien except when a firm is in bankruptcy proceedings. This has resulted in the PBGC receiving a relatively small amount of assets when it has imposed the lien.

An important provision in a pension plan is the vesting provision. An employee vested in the pension plan is eligible to receive some pension benefits at retirement, regardless of whether the employee continues working for the employer. ERISA has had a major impact on reducing the vesting time. The original ERISA has been amended several times to increase the responsibility of firms regarding their pension plans.

EXHIBIT 7-8	**NIKE, INC.**

Adjusted Debt Ratio and Debt/Equity Ratio Considering Operating Leases	
	May 31, 2002 (in millions)
Adjusted debt ratio:	
Unadjusted total liabilities [Exhibit 7-4]	$2,604.0
Plus: Estimated for operating leases ($902.20 × 2/3)	601.50
Adjusted liabilities [A]	$3,205.50
Unadjusted total assets	$6,443.0
Plus: Estimated for operating leases	601.50
Adjusted assets [B]	$7,044.50
Adjusted debt ratio [A ÷ B]	45.50%
Unadjusted debt ratio [Exhibit 7-4]	40.42%
Adjusted debt/equity:	
Adjusted liabilities (above) [A]	$3,205.50
Shareholders' equity [B]	$3,839.0
Adjusted debt/equity [A ÷ B]	83.50
Unadjusted debt/equity [Exhibit 7-5]	67.83%

In 1980, Congress passed the Multiemployer Pension Plan Amendment Act. Multiemployer pension plans are plans maintained jointly by two or more unrelated employers. This act provides for significant increased employer obligations for multiemployer pension plans and makes the PBGC coverage mandatory for multiemployer plans.

When a firm has a multiemployer pension plan, it normally covers union employees. Such a firm usually has other pension plans that cover nonunion employees. When disclosing a multiemployer pension plan, the firm normally includes the cost of the plan with the cost of the other pension plans. It is usually not practical to isolate the cost of these plans because of commingling. These plans operate usually on a pay-as-you-go basis, so no liability arises unless a payment has not been made. A potential significant liability arises if the company withdraws from the multiemployer plan. Unfortunately, the amount of this liability often cannot be ascertained from the pension footnote.

Albertson's, Inc. included the following comment in a footnote with its 2001 annual report:

> The Company also contributes to various plans under industry collective bargaining agreements, primarily for defined benefit plans. Total contributions to these plans were $49,000,000 for 2001, $58,000,000 for 2000, and $98,000,000 for 1999.

Defined Contribution Plan

A company-sponsored pension plan is either a defined contribution plan or a defined benefit plan. A **defined contribution plan** defines the contributions of the company to the pension plan. Once this defined contribution is paid, the company has no further obligation to the pension plan. This type of plan shifts the risk to the employee as to whether the pension funds will grow to provide for a reasonable pension payment upon retirement. With this type of plan, which gained popularity during the 1980s, there is no problem of estimating the company's pension liability or pension expense. Thus, defined contribution plans do not present major financial reporting problems.

A **401K** is a type of defined contribution plan. These plans may or may not require a company's contribution. They may provide for an employee's contribution. When a company makes a required contribution, this ends any pension liability.

For firms with defined contribution plans, try to grasp the significance by doing the following:

1. For a three-year period, compare pension expense with operating revenue. This will indicate the materiality of pension expense in relation to operating revenue and the trend.

2. For a three-year period, compare pension expense with income before income taxes. This will indicate the materiality of pension expense in relation to income and the trend.
3. Note any balance sheet items. (There will usually not be a balance sheet item because the firm is paying on a pay-as-you-go basis.)

Nike does not have a defined contribution plan, but they do have a voluntary 401(k) employee savings plan. We can approach analysis of this plan in a manner similar to the analysis of a defined contribution pension plan. Note 10 (benefit plans) explains the following:

> The Company has a voluntary 401(k) employee savings plan. The Company matches a portion of employee contributions with common stock. Plan changes during the year ended May 31, 2001 included a larger Company match percentage and a change to immediate vesting of the Company match, compared to a previous vesting schedule over 5 years. Company contributions to the savings plan were $13.7 million, $12.7 million and $6.7 million for the years ended May 31, 2002, 2001, and 2000, respectively, and are included in selling and administrative expenses.

Thus the savings plan expenses as a percentage of revenues 0.14%, 0.13%, and 0.07% in 2002, 2001, and 2000, respectively. Savings plan expenses as a percentage of income before income taxes were 1.35%, 1.38%, and 0.73% in 2002, 2001, and 2000, respectively. Savings plans appear to be immaterial. No balance sheet items are disclosed.

Defined Benefit Plan

A defined benefit plan defines the benefits to be received by the participants in the plan. For example, the plan may call for the participant to receive 40% of his or her average pay for the three years before retirement. This type of plan leaves the company with the risk of having insufficient funds in the pension fund to meet the defined benefit. This type of plan was the predominant type of plan prior to the 1980s. Most companies still have a defined benefit plan, partly because of the difficulties involved in switching to a defined contribution plan. Some companies have terminated their defined benefit plan by funding the obligations of the plan and starting a defined contribution plan. In some cases, this has resulted in millions of dollars being transferred to the company from the pension plan after the defined benefit plan obligations have been met. The U.S. Congress added an excise tax on "reversions" in 1990. This excise tax can be as high as 50%. This has substantially slowed down the "reversions."

A number of assumptions about future events must be made regarding a defined benefit plan. Some of these assumptions that relate to the future are interest rates, employee turnover, mortality rates, compensation, and pension benefits set by law. Assumptions about future events contribute materially to the financial reporting problems in the pension area. Two firms with the same plan may make significantly different assumptions, resulting in major differences in pension expense and liability.

There are many technical terms associated with defined benefit plans. A description of all of these terms is beyond the scope of this book.

For firms with defined benefit plans, try to grasp the significance by doing the following:

1. For a three-year period, compare pension expense with operating revenue. This will indicate the materiality of pension expense in relation to operating revenue and the trend.
2. For a three-year period, compare pension expense with income before income taxes. This will indicate the materiality of pension expense in relation to income and the trend.
3. Compare the benefit obligations with the value of plan assets. This can indicate significant underfunding or overfunding. Underfunding represents a potential liability. Overfunding represents an opportunity to reduce future pension expense. Overfunding can also be used to reduce related costs, such as disability benefits, retiree health costs, staff downsizings. Overfunding can also be used to take credits to the income statement.
4. Note the net balance sheet liability (asset) recognized.
5. Note assumptions as to the following:
    a. Discount rate
        The interest (discount) rate used to discount benefit obligations will have a significant impact on the benefit obligations. The higher the interest rate used, the lower the present

value of the liability and the lower the immediate pension cost. Changes in this interest rate could significantly increase (decrease) the present value of the liability and increase (decrease) the pension cost.

b. Rate of compensation increase

The more compensation increase assumed, the greater is the future pay that increases the benefit obligations. Changes in the rate of compensation could significantly increase (decrease) the projected benefit obligations. An increase in the rate of compensation projected would increase the projected benefit obligations. A decrease in the rate of compensation projected would decrease the projected benefit obligations.

c. Expected return on plan assets

The higher the expected return on plan assets, the lower is the projected benefit obligation. The lower the expected return on plan assets, the higher is the projected benefit obligation.

Exhibit 7-9 shows the Ashland Inc. pension footnote. We note that Ashland's pension plans are mostly defined benefit plans. Observe the following relating to Ashland's defined benefit plans:

1. Pension expense (cost) in relation to operating revenue:

	2001	2000	1999
Pension expense [A]	$46,000,000	$50,000,000	$46,000,000
Operating revenue [B]	$7,719,000,000	$7,961,000,000	$6,801,000,000
Pension expense/operating revenue [A ÷ B]	0.60%	0.63%	0.68%

Pension expense in relation to operating revenue appears to be under control.

2. Pension expense (cost) in relation to income before taxes:

	2001	2000	1999
Pension expense [A]	$46,000,000	$50,000,000	$46,000,000
Income before income taxes [B]	$681,000,000	$483,000,000	$485,000,000
Pension expense/income before income taxes [A ÷ B]	6.75%	10.35%	9.48%

Ashland's pension expense has declined in relation to income before income taxes, but it would likely be considered to be material.

3. Comparison of benefit obligations with the value of the plan assets:

	2001		2000	
	Qualified Plans	**Nonqualified Plans**	**Qualified Plans**	**Nonqualified Plans**
Benefit obligations	$715,000,000	$103,000,000	$595,000,000	$87,000,000
Plan assets	518,000,000		506,000,000	—
Excess of obligations over plan assets	$197,000,000	$103,000,000	$ 89,000,000	$87,000,000

There appears to be a significant underfunding of pension plans. This could result in future pension expense increases.

4. Net balance sheet liability (asset) recognized:

	2001		2000	
	Qualified Plans	**Nonqualified Plans**	**Qualified Plans**	**Nonqualified Plans**
Net liability recognized	$8,000,000	$59,000,000	$50,000,000	$60,000,000

A significant balance sheet liability has been recognized. The liability recognized is materially less than the excess of obligations over plan assets.

EXHIBIT 7-9	ASHLAND INC.
	Pension and Other Postretirement Plans

Partial Income Statement

NOTE 0—EMPLOYEE BENEFIT PLANS

PENSION AND OTHER POSTRETIREMENT PLANS

Ashland and its subsidiaries sponsor noncontributory, defined benefit pension plans that cover substantially all employees. Benefits under these plans are generally based on employees' years of service and compensation during the years immediately preceding their retirement. For certain plans, 50% of employees' leveraged employee stock ownership plan (LESOP) accounts are coordinated with and used to fund their pension benefits. Ashland determines the level of contributions to its pension plans annually and contributes amounts within the limitations imposed by Internal Revenue Service regulations.

Ashland and its subsidiaries also sponsor unfunded postretirement benefit plans, which provide health care and life insurance benefits for eligible employees who retire or are disabled. Retiree contributions to Ashland's health care plans are adjusted periodically, and the plans contain other cost-sharing features, such as deductibles and coinsurance. Life insurance plans are generally noncontributory for base level coverage, and fully contributory for any additional coverage elected by employees. Ashland funds the costs of benefits as they are paid.

Summaries of the changes in the benefit obligations and plan assets (primarily listed stocks and debt securities) and of the funded status of the plans follow.

	Pension benefits				Other postretirement benefits	
	2001		2000			
(in millions)	Qualified plans	Nonqualified plans	Qualified plans	Nonqualified plans	2001	2000
Change in benefit obligations						
Benefit obligations at October 1	$ 595	$ 87	$529	$ 88	$269	$262
Service cost	35	2	35	2	11	9
Interest cost	46	7	40	7	22	19
Retiree contributions	—	—	—	—	7	5
Benefits paid	(28)	(5)	(24)	(7)	(28)	(25)
Other—primarily actuarial loss (gain)	67	12	15	(3)	52	(1)
Benefit obligations at September 30	$ 715	$103	$595	$ 87	$333	$269
Change in plan assets						
Value of plan assets at October 1	$ 506	$ —	$429	$ —	$ —	$ —
Actual return on plan assets	(40)	—	50	—	—	—
Employer contributions	76	5	46	7	21	20
Retiree contributions	—	—	—	—	7	5
Benefits paid	(28)	(5)	(24)	(7)	(28)	(25)
Other	4	—	5	—	—	—
Value of plan assets at September 30	$ 518	$ —	$506	$ —	$ —	$ —
Funded status of the plans						
Under- (over-) funded accumulated obligation	$ 53	$ 91	$ (29)	$73	$333	$269
Provision for future salary increases	144	12	118	14	—	—
Excess of obligations over plan assets	197	103	89	87	333	269
Unrecognized actuarial loss	(186)	(44)	(35)	(27)	(56)	(6)
Unrecognized prior service credit (cost)	(3)	—	(4)	—	24	31
Net liability recognized	$ 8	$ 59	$ 50	$60	$301	$294
Balance sheet liabilities (assets)						
Prepaid benefit costs	$ (4)		$ (3)		$ —	$ —
Accrued benefit liabilities	144		127		301	294
Intangible assets	(2)		—		—	—
Accumulated other comprehensive loss	(71)		(14)		—	—
Net liability recognized	$ 67		$110		$301	$294
Assumptions as of September 30						
Discount rate	7.25%		7.75%		7.25%	7.75%
Rate of compensation increase	5.00		5.00		5.00	5.00
Expected return on plan assets	9.00		9.00		—	—

EXHIBIT 7-9	**ASHLAND INC.**

Pension and Other Postretirement Plans (*continued*)

The following table details the components of pension and other postretirement benefit costs.

(in millions)	Pension benefits			Other postretirement benefits		
	2001	2000	1999	**2001**	2000	1999
Service cost	$ 37	$ 37	$ 34	$11	$ 9	$ 8
Interest cost	53	47	41	22	19	18
Expected return on plan assets	(48)	(39)	(34)	—	—	—
Other amortization and deferral	4	5	5	(6)	(9)	(7)
	$ 46	$ 50	$ 46	$27	$19	$19

Ashland amended nearly all of its retiree health care plans in 1992 to place a cap on its contributions and to adopt a cost-sharing method based upon years of service. The cap limits Ashland's contributions to base year per capita costs, plus annual increases of up to 4.5% per year. These amendments reduced Ashland's obligations under its retiree health care plans, with the reduction amortized to income over approximately 12 years. The remaining credit at September 30, 2001, amounted to $22 million, and will be amortized over approximately three years in declining amounts from $8 million in 2002 to $6 million in 2004.

OTHER PLANS

Ashland sponsors a qualified savings plan to assist eligible employees in providing for retirement or other future needs. Under that plan, Ashland contributes up to 4.2% of a participating employee's earnings. Company contributions amounted to $16 million in 2001 and $15 million in both 2000 and 1999.

Ashland Inc. and Consolidated Subsidiaries
STATEMENTS OF CONSOLIDATED INCOME (in Part)
Years Ended September 30

(In millions except per share data)	2001	2000	1999
Revenues			
Sales and operating revenues	$7,719	$7,961	$6,801
Equity income—Note F	754	394	351
Other income	74	81	101
	8,547	8,436	7,253
Costs and expenses			
Cost of sales and operating expenses	6,319	6,434	5,346
Selling, general and administrative expenses	1,127	1,094	1,054
Depreciation, depletion and amortization	250	237	228
	7,696	7,765	6,628
Operating income	851	671	625
Net interest and other financial costs—Note G	(170)	(188)	(140)
Income from continuing operations before income taxes	681	483	485
Income taxes—Note E	(275)	(191)	(194)
Income from continuing operations	406	292	291
Results form discontinued operations (net of income taxes)—Note B	19	(218)	(1)
Income before extraordinary loss and cumulative effect of accounting change	425	74	290
Extraordinary loss on early retirement of debt (net of income taxes)—Note G	(3)	(4)	—
Cumulative effect of accounting change (net of income taxes)—Note A	(5)	—	—
Net income	$ 417	$ 70	$ 290

5. Assumptions as to discount rate, rate of compensation increase, and expected return on plan assets:

	2001	**2000**
Discount rate	7.25%	7.75%

The discount rate was reduced to 7.25% from 7.75%. This increased the benefit obligations and the pension expense. According to the 2001 *Accounting Trends & Techniques*, the weighted average assumptions were 7.50% (2000); 7.75% (1999); and 7.00% (1998).[1]

	2001	**2000**
Rate of compensation increase	5.00%	5.00%

According to the 2001 *Accounting Trends & Techniques*, the weighted average assumptions were 4.00% (2000); 4.50% (1999); and 4.00% (1998).[2] Note that there was no change in the rate for Ashland.

	2001	**2000**
Expected return on plan assets	9.00%	9.00%

According to the 2001 *Accounting Trends & Techniques*, the weighted average assumptions were 9.50% in 2001 and 2000.[3] Note that there was no change in the rate for Ashland.

In Exhibit 7-9 are "Other Plans." These appear to be multiemployee plans. These plans should also be considered.

Postretirement Benefits Other than Pensions

Some benefits other than pensions, such as medical insurance and life insurance contracts, accrue to employees upon retirement. These benefits can be substantial. Many firms have obligations in the millions of dollars. Prior to 1993, most firms did not have these obligations funded; therefore, for these firms, a potential for a significant liability existed.

Beginning in 1993, firms were required to accrue, or set up a reserve for, future postretirement benefits other than pensions (rather than deduct these costs when paid). Firms can usually spread the catch-up accrual costs over 20 years or take the charge in one lump sum. The amount involved is frequently material, so this choice can represent a major problem when comparing financial results of two or more firms. For some firms, the catch-up charge for medical insurance was so material that it resulted in a deficit in retained earnings or even a deficit to the entire stockholders' equity section.

Many firms reduce costs by changing their plans to limit health care benefits to retirees to a maximum fixed amount. This type of plan, in contrast to open-ended medical benefits, could materially reduce the firm's health care costs for retirees. Review the footnotes closely to determine how the firm records health care costs for retirees.

For firms with postretirement benefits other than pensions, you should try to grasp the significance using the same basic approach as was used for defined benefit plans for pensions. The exception is that there will be no rate of compensation increase.

Exhibit 7-9 shows the postretirement benefits other than pensions for Ashland Inc.

1. Expense (cost) in relation to operating revenue:

	2001	**2000**	**1999**
Expense [A]	$27,000,000	$19,000,000	$19,000,000
Operating revenue [B]	$7,719,000,000	$7,961,000,000	$6,801,000,000
Expense/operating revenue [A ÷ B]	0.35%	0.24%	0.28%

Expense in relation to operating revenue fluctuated substantially. This expense would likely be considered to be immaterial.

2. Expense (cost) in relation to income before taxes:

	2001	2000	1999
Expense [A]	$27,000,000	$19,000,000	$19,000,000
Income before income taxes [B]	$681,000,000	$483,000,000	$485,000,000
Expense/income before income taxes [A ÷ B]	3.96%	3.93%	3.92%

Postretirement expense was very steady in relation to income before income taxes. This expense could be considered substantial.

3. Comparison of benefit obligations with the value of the plan assets:

	2001	2000
Benefit obligation	$333,000,000	$269,000,000
Plan assets	—	—
Excess of obligations over plan assets	$333,000,000	$269,000,000

This appears to be a significant underfunding of postretirement benefit obligation.

4. Net balance sheet liability (asset) recognized:

	2001	2000
Net liability recognized	$301,000,000	$294,000,000

A significant balance sheet liability has been recognized.

5. Assumptions as to discount rate, rate of compensation increase, and expected return on plan assets:

	2001	2000
Discount rate	7.25%	7.75%

The same rate as used for pension plans. The discount rate was reduced from 7.75% to 7.25%. This increased the benefit obligations and the expense.

	2001	2000
Rate of compensation increase	5.00%	5.00%

The same rate as used for pension plans.

	2001	2000
Expected return on plan assets	—	—

A rate was not used for plan assets because there were no plan assets.

Joint Ventures

A **joint venture** is an association of two or more businesses established for a special purpose. Some joint ventures are in the form of partnerships or other unincorporated forms of business. Others are in the form of corporations jointly owned by two or more other firms.

The accounting principles for joint ventures are flexible because of their many forms. The typical problem concerns whether a joint venture should be carried as an investment or consolidated. Some joint ventures are very significant in relation to the parent firm. There is typically a question as to whether the parent firm has control or only significant influence. When the parent firm has control, it usually consolidates joint ventures by using a pro rata share. Other joint ventures are usually carried in an investment account by using the equity method. In either case, disclosure of significant information often appears in a footnote.

When a firm enters into a joint venture, it frequently makes commitments such as guaranteeing a bank loan for the joint venture or a long-term contract to purchase materials with the joint venture. This type of action can give the company significant potential liabilities or commitments that do not appear on the face of the balance sheet. This potential problem exists with all joint ventures, including those that have been consolidated. To be aware of these significant potential liabilities or commitments, read the footnote that relates to the joint venture. Then consider this information in relation to the additional liabilities or commitments to which the joint venture may commit the firm.

Arch Chemicals disclosed a joint venture in a footnote to its 2001 annual report (in millions):

> Joint Venture—In April 2000, the Company formed a joint venture with Wacker Silicones Corporation, to produce and market chemical mechanical planarization slurry products used in the advanced computer chip manufacturing process. The joint venture, called Planar, is expected to provide opportunities in this high growth area of the semiconductor industry. The Company contributed cash of approximately $3.4 and intellectual property to the venture, and has guaranteed up to $5.0 of its debt.

Contingencies

A **contingency** is an existing condition, situation, or set of circumstances involving uncertainty as to possible gain or loss to an enterprise that will ultimately be resolved when one or more future events occur or fail to occur.[4]

A contingency is characterized by an existing condition, uncertainty as to the ultimate effect, and its resolution depending on one or more future events. A loss contingency should be accrued if two conditions are met:[5]

1. Information prior to issuance of the financial statements indicates that it is *probable* that an asset has been impaired or a liability has been incurred at the date of the financial statements.
2. The amount of the loss can be *reasonably estimated*.

If a contingency loss meets one, but not both, of the criteria for recording and is, therefore, not accrued, disclosure by footnote is made when it is at *least reasonably possible* that there has been an impairment of assets or that a liability has been incurred. Examples of contingencies include warranty obligations and collectibility of receivables. If the firm guarantees the indebtedness of others, the contingency is usually disclosed in a footnote.

When examining financial statements, a footnote that describes contingencies should be closely reviewed for possible significant liabilities not disclosed on the face of the balance sheet.

The following covers gain contingencies:

1. Contingencies that might result in gains usually are not reflected in the accounts, since to do so might be to recognize revenue prior to its realization.
2. Adequate disclosure shall be made of contingencies that might result in gains, but care shall be exercised to avoid misleading implications as to the likelihood of realization.[6]

The footnotes of the firm should be reviewed for gain contingencies.

Scientific Technologies Inc. disclosed the following in the notes to its 2001 annual report:

> From time to time, the Company is involved in litigation in the normal course of business. Management believes that the outcome of matters to date will not have a material adverse effect on the Company's consolidated financial position, results of operations or cash flows.

Financial Instruments with Off-Balance-Sheet Risk and Financial Instruments with Concentrations of Credit Risk

Credit and market risk for all financial instruments with off-balance-sheet risk require the following disclosure:

1. The face or contract amount.
2. The nature and terms including, at a minimum, a discussion of credit and market risk, cash requirements, and accounting policies.[7]

Disclosure is also required of the following regarding financial instruments with off-balance-sheet credit risk:

1. The amount of accounting loss the entity would incur if any party failed completely to perform according to the terms of the contract and the collateral or other security, if any, proved worthless.

2. The entity's policy of requiring collateral and a brief description of the collateral it currently holds.[8]

Accounting loss represents the worst-case loss if everything related to a contract went wrong. This includes the possibility that a loss may occur from the failure of another party to perform according to the terms of a contract, as well as the possibility that changes in market prices may make a financial instrument less valuable or more troublesome.

In addition to requiring disclosure of matters relating to off-balance-sheet financial instruments, disclosure is required of credit risk concentration. This disclosure includes information on the extent of risk from exposures to individuals or groups of counterparties in the same industry or region. The activity, region, or economic characteristic that identifies a concentration requires a narrative description. The provision of requiring disclosure of credit risk concentration can be particularly significant to small companies. Examples are a retail store whose receivables are substantially with local residents and a local bank with a loan portfolio concentrated with debtors dependent on the local tourist business.

Exhibit 7-10 presents financial instruments with off-balance-sheet risk and financial instruments with concentrations of credit risk for Nordson Corporation as disclosed in its 2001 annual report.

Disclosures About Fair Value of Financial Instruments

Disclosure is required about the fair value of financial instruments. This includes financial instruments recognized and not recognized in the balance sheet (both assets and liabilities). When estimating fair value is not practicable, then descriptive information pertinent to estimating fair value should be disclosed.

The disclosure about fair value of financial instruments can be either in the body of the financial statements or in the footnotes.[9] This disclosure could possibly indicate significant opportunity or additional risk to the company. For example, long-term debt disclosed at a fair value above the carrying amount increases the potential for a loss.

Exhibit 7-11 (page 231) presents the fair value of financial instruments for Intel, as disclosed in its 2001 annual report.

SUMMARY

This chapter covered two approaches to a firm's long-term debt-paying ability. One approach considers the firm's ability to carry debt as indicated by the income statement, and the other approach views it as indicated by the balance sheet. The ratios related to debt include the following:

$$\text{Times Interest Earned} = \frac{\substack{\text{Recurring Earnings, Excluding Interest}\\ \text{Expense, Tax Expense, Equity Earnings,}\\ \text{and Minority Earnings}}}{\text{Interest Expense, Including Capitalized Interest}}$$

$$\text{Fixed Charge Coverage} = \frac{\substack{\text{Recurring Earnings, Excluding Interest Expense, Tax Expense, Equity}\\ \text{Earnings, and Minority Earnings} + \text{Interest Portion of Rentals}}}{\substack{\text{Interest Expense, Including Capitalized Interest}\\ + \text{Interest Portion of Rentals}}}$$

$$\text{Debt Ratio} = \frac{\text{Total Liabilities}}{\text{Total Assets}}$$

$$\text{Debt/Equity Ratio} = \frac{\text{Total Liabilities}}{\text{Shareholders' Equity}}$$

$$\text{Debt to Tangible Net Worth Ratio} = \frac{\text{Total Liabilities}}{\text{Shareholders' Equity} - \text{Intangible Assets}}$$

EXHIBIT 7-10

NORDSON CORPORATION
Off-Balance-Sheet Risk and Concentrations of Credit Risk

Note 10—Financial instruments

The Company enters into foreign currency forward contracts, which are derivative financial instruments, to reduce the risk of foreign currency exposures resulting from the collection of intercompany receivables, payables and loans denominated in foreign currencies. The maturities of these contracts are usually less than 90 days. Forward contracts are marked to market each accounting period, and resulting gains or losses are included in other income (expense) on the Consolidated Statement of Income. Gains of $146,000, $248,000 and $562,000 were recognized from changes in the fair value of these contracts for the years ended October 28, 2001, October 29, 2000 and October 31,1999, respectively.

At October 28, 2001 the Company had outstanding forward exchange contracts that mature at various dates through December 2001. The following table summarizes, by currency, the Company's forward exchange contacts at October 28, 2001 and October 29, 2000:

	Sell		Buy	
	Notional Amounts	Fair Market Value	Notional Amounts	Fair Market Value
	(In thousands)			
October 28, 2001 contract amounts:				
Euro	$ 9,302	$ 9,339	$14,620	$14,726
British pound	14,603	14,723	4,549	4,572
Japanese yen	7,733	8,372	10,199	10,639
Others	1,495	1,491	8,534	8,428
Total	$33,133	$33,925	$37,902	$38,365

	Sell		Buy	
	Notional Amounts	Fair Market Value	Notional Amounts	Fair Market Value
	(In thousands)			
October 29, 2000 contract amounts:				
Euro	$15,386	$15,271	$ 2,577	$ 2,540
British pound	8,340	8,636	558	574
Japanese yen	9,729	9,380	467	462
Others	6,917	6,899	7,196	7,146
Total	$40,372	$40,186	$10,798	$10,722

The Company also uses foreign denominated fixed-rate debt and intercompany foreign currency transactions of a long-term investment nature to protect the value of its investment in its wholly owned subsidiaries. For hedges of the net investment in foreign operations, realized and unrealized gains and losses are shown in the cumulative translation adjustment account included in total comprehensive income. For the years ended October 28, 2001 and October 29, 2000, net gains of $1,914,000 and $6,322,000, respectively, were included in the cumulative translation adjustment account related to foreign denominated fixed-rate debt designated as a hedge of net investment in foreign operations.

The Company has an interest-rate swap that it has designated as a fair-value hedge. This derivative qualified for the short-cut method. The swap is recorded with a fair market value of $204,000 in other assets in the Consolidated Balance Sheet. The Company is exposed to credit-related losses in the event of non-performance by counterparties to financial instruments. The Company uses major banks throughout the world for cash deposits, forward exchange contracts and interest rate swaps. The Company's customers represent a wide variety of industries and geographic regions. As of October 28, 2001, there were no significant concentrations of credit risk. The Company does not use financial instruments for trading or speculative purposes.

The carrying amounts and fair values of the Company's financial instruments, other than receivables and accounts payable, are as follows:

2001

	Carrying Amount	Fair Value
	(In thousands)	
Cash and cash equivalents	$ 7,881	$ 7,881
Marketable securities	62	62
Notes payable	(194,964)	(194,964)
Long-term debt	(202,658)	(211,144)
Forward exchange contracts	254	278

2000

	Carrying Amount	Fair Value
	(In thousands)	
Cash and cash equivalents	$ 785	$ 785
Marketable securities	30	30
Notes payable	(91,697)	(91,697)
Long-term debt	(61,728)	(58,936)
Forward exchange contracts	108	210
Interest rate swaps	—	448

To the Net

1. Go to the SEC site (http://sec.gov). Under Filings & Forms (Edgar), click on "Search for Company Filings." Click on "Search Companies and Filings." Under company name, enter "Walt Disney." Select the 10-K submitted December 10, 2001.
    a. Determine the standard industrial classification.
    b. Determine contractual commitments.

EXHIBIT 7-11
INTEL—2001 ANNUAL REPORT
Fair Value of Financial Instruments

Fair values of financial instruments

The estimated fair values of financial instruments outstanding at fiscal year-ends were as follows:

(In millions—assets (liabilities))	2001		2000	
	Carrying amount	Estimated fair value	Carrying amount	Estimated fair value
Cash and cash equivalents	$7,970	$7,970	$2,976	$2,976
Short-term investments	$2,356	$2,356	$10,498	$10,498
Trading assets	$1,224	$1,224	$355	$355
Marketable strategic equity securities	$155	$155	$1,915	$1,915
Other long-term investments	$1,319	$1,319	$1,801	$1,801
Non-marketable equity securities	$1,276	$1,719	$1,726	$2,912
Other non-marketable instruments	$161	$161	$148	$148
Warrants and other equities marked-to-market as derivatives in 2001	$172	$172	$12	$36
Options hedging or offsetting equities	$51	$51	$—	$—
Swaps related to investments in debt securities	$12	$12	$12	$12
Options related to deferred compensation liabilities	$(6)	$(6)	$(5)	$(5)
Short-term debt	$(409)	$(409)	$(378)	$(378)
Long-term debt	$(1,050)	$(1,045)	$(707)	$(702)
Swaps hedging debt	$4	$4	$—	$(1)
Currency forward contracts	$1	$1	$2	$6

Due to restrictions on sales extending beyond one year, publicly traded securities with a carrying value of $85 million and an estimated fair value of $210 million were classified as non-marketable equity securities at December 29, 2001. At December 30, 2000, similarly restricted securities had a carrying amount of $109 million and an estimated fair value of $631 million.

2. Go to the SEC site (http://www.sec.gov). Under Filings & Forms (Edgar), click on "Search for Company Filings." Click on "Search Companies and Filings." Under company name enter "Goodyear Tire." Select the 10-K submitted March 11, 2002.
   For pensions determine the following:
   a. Net periodic pension cost for the year ended December 31, 2001? How material is the expense in relation to net sales? How material is this expense in relation to net income (loss) for the year ended December 31, 2001?
   b. Projected benefit obligation in excess of plan assets?
   c. For plans that are not fully funded what is the accumulated benefit obligation at December 31, 2001? For plans that are not fully funded what are the plan assets at December 31, 2001?

3. Go to the SEC site (http://www.sec.gov). Under Filings & Forms (Edgar), click on "Search for Company Filings." Click on "Search Companies and Filings." Under company name enter "Flowers Foods." Select the 10-K submitted March 29, 2002.
   Compute the following ratios for the 52 weeks ended December 29, 2001:
   1. Times interest earned
   2. Debt ratio
   3. Operating cash flow/total debt
   4. Comment on the above ratios.

Questions

Q 7-1.   Is profitability important to a firm's long-term debt-paying ability? Discuss.

Q 7-2.   List the two approaches to examining a firm's long-term debt-paying ability. Discuss why each of these approaches gives an important view of a firm's ability to carry debt.

Q 7-3.   What type of times interest earned ratio would be desirable? What type would not be desirable?

Q 7-4.   Would you expect an auto manufacturer to finance a relatively high proportion of its long-term funds from debt? Discuss.

Q 7-5.   Would you expect a telephone company to have a high debt ratio? Discuss.

Q 7-6.   Why should capitalized interest be added to interest expense when computing times interest earned?

Q 7-7.   Discuss how noncash charges for depreciation, depletion, and amortization can be used to obtain a short-run view of times interest earned.

Q 7-8.   Why is it difficult to determine the value of assets?

Q 7-9.   Is it feasible to get a precise measurement of the funds that could be available from long-term assets to pay long-term debts? Discuss.

Q 7-10.   One of the ratios used to indicate long-term debt-paying ability compares total liabilities to total assets. What is the intent of this ratio? How precise is this ratio in achieving its intent?

Q 7-11.   For a given firm, would you expect the debt ratio to be as high as the debt/equity ratio? Explain.

Q 7-12.   Explain how the debt/equity ratio indicates the same relative long-term debt-paying ability as does the debt ratio, only in a different form.

Q 7-13.   Why is it important to compare long-term debt ratios of a given firm with industry averages?

Q 7-14.   How should lessees account for operating leases? Capital leases? Include both income statement and balance sheet accounts.

Q 7-15.   A firm with substantial leased assets that have not been capitalized may be overstating its long-term debt-paying ability. Explain.

Q 7-16.   Capital leases that have not been capitalized will decrease the times interest earned ratio. Comment.

Q 7-17.   Indicate the status of pension liabilities under the Employee Retirement Income Security Act.

Q 7-18.   Why is the vesting provision an important provision of a pension plan? How has the Employee Retirement Income Security Act influenced vesting periods?

Q 7-19.   Indicate the risk to a company if it withdraws from a multiemployer pension plan or if the multiemployer pension plan is terminated.

Q 7-20.   Operating leases are not reflected on the balance sheet, but they are reflected on the income statement in the rent expense. Comment on why an interest expense figure that relates to long-term operating leases should be considered when determining a fixed charge coverage.

Q 7-21.   What portion of net worth can the federal government require a company to use to pay for pension obligations?

Q 7-22.   Consider the debt ratio. Explain a position for including short-term liabilities in the debt ratio. Explain a position for excluding short-term liabilities from the debt ratio. Which of these approaches would be more conservative?

Q 7-23.   Consider the accounts of bonds payable and reserve for rebuilding furnaces. Explain how one of these accounts could be considered a firm liability and the other could be considered a soft liability.

Q 7-24.   Explain why deferred taxes that are disclosed as long-term liabilities may not result in actual cash outlays in the future.

Q 7-25.   A firm has a high current debt/net worth ratio in relation to prior years, competitors, and the industry. Comment on what this tentatively indicates.

Q 7-26.   Comment on the implications of relying on a greater proportion of short-term debt in relation to long-term debt.

Q 7-27. When a firm guarantees a bank loan for a joint venture that it participates in and the joint venture is handled as an investment, then the overall potential debt position will not be obvious from the face of the balance sheet. Comment.

Q 7-28. When examining financial statements, a footnote that describes contingencies should be reviewed closely for possible significant liabilities that are not disclosed on the face of the balance sheet. Comment.

Q 7-29. There is a chance that a company may be in a position to have large sums transferred from the pension fund to the company. Comment.

Q 7-30. Indicate why comparing firms for postretirement benefits other than pensions can be difficult.

Q 7-31. Speculate on why the disclosure of the concentrations of credit risk is potentially important to the users of financial reports.

Q 7-32. Comment on the significance of disclosing off-balance-sheet risk of accounting loss.

Q 7-33. Comment on the significance of disclosing the fair value of financial instruments.

Problems

P 7-1. Consider the following operating figures:

Net sales	$1,079,143
Cost and deductions:	
Cost of sales	792,755
Selling and administration	264,566
Interest expense, net	4,311
Income taxes	5,059
	1,066,691
	$ 12,452

Note: Depreciation expense totals $40,000.

Required   a. Compute the times interest earned.
              b. Compute the cash basis times interest earned.

P 7-2. The Jones Petro Company reports the following consolidated statement of income:

Operating revenues	$2,989
Costs and expenses:	
Cost of rentals and royalties	543
Cost of sales	314
Selling, service, administrative, and general expense	1,424
Total costs and expenses	2,281
Operating income	708
Other income	27
Other deductions (interest)	60
Income before income taxes	675
Income taxes	309
Income before outside shareholders' interests	366
Outside shareholders' interests	66
Net income	$ 300

Note: Depreciation expense totals $200; operating lease payments total $150; and preferred dividends total $50. Assume that 1/3 of operating lease payments is for interest.

Required   a. Compute the times interest earned.
              b. Compute the fixed charge coverage.

P 7-3. The Sherwill statement of consolidated income is as follows:

Net sales	$658
Other income	8
	666
Costs and expenses:	
Cost of products sold	418
Selling, general, and administrative expenses	196
Interest	16
	630
Income before income taxes and extraordinary charges	36
Income taxes	18
Income before extraordinary charge	18
Extraordinary charge—losses on tornado damage (net)	4
Net income	$ 14

Note: Depreciation expense totals $200; operating lease payments total $150; and preferred dividends total $50. Assume that 1/3 of operating lease payments is for interest.

Required   a.   Compute the times interest earned.
 b.   Compute the fixed charge coverage.

P 7-4.   The Kaufman Company balance sheet follows.

Assets

Current assets		
Cash		$ 13,445
Short-term investments—at cost (approximate market)		5,239
Trade accounts receivable, less allowance of $1,590		88,337
Inventories—at lower of cost (average method) or market:		
Finished merchandise	$113,879	
Work in process, raw materials and supplies	47,036	
		160,915
Prepaid expenses		8,221
Total current assets		276,157
Other assets:		
Receivables, advances, and other assets		4,473
Intangibles		2,324
Total other assets		6,797
Property, plant, and equipment:		
Land		5,981
Buildings		78,908
Machinery and equipment		162,425
		247,314
Less allowances for depreciation		106,067
Net property, plant, and equipment		141,247
Total assets		$424,201

Liabilities and Shareholders' Equity

Current liabilities:		
Notes payable		$ 2,817
Trade accounts payable		23,720
Pension, interest, and other accruals		33,219
Taxes, other than income taxes		4,736
Income taxes		3,409
Total current liabilities		67,901
Long-term debt, 12% debentures		86,235
Deferred income taxes		8,768
Minority interest in subsidiaries		12,075
Total liabilities		174,979

(continued)

Stockholders' equity:	
Serial preferred	9,154
Common $5.25 par value	33,540
Additional paid-in capital	3,506
Retained earnings	203,712
	249,912
Less cost of common shares in treasury	690
Total shareholders' equity	249,222
Total liabilities and shareholders' equity	$424,201

Required
a. Compute the debt ratio.
b. Compute the debt/equity ratio.
c. Compute the ratio of total debt to tangible net worth.
d. Comment on the amount of debt that the Kaufman Company has.

P 7-5. Individual transactions often have a significant impact on ratios. This problem will consider the direction of such an impact.

Ratio Transaction	Times Interest Earned	Debt Ratio	Debt/ Equity Ratio	Debt to Tangible Net Worth	
a. Purchase of buildings financed by mortgage.	−	+	+	+	
b. Purchase of inventory on short-term loan at 1% over prime rate.	−	+	+	+	
c. Declaration and payment of cash dividend.	0	⌐	⊥	+	cash goes ↓
d. Declaration and payment of stock dividend.	0	0	0	0	
e. Firm increases profits by cutting cost of sales.	+	−	−	−	
f. Appropriation of retained earnings.	0	0	0	0	
g. Sale of common stock.	0	←	←	−	cash come in
h. Repayment of long-term bank loan.	+	−	−	−	intrest reduced
i. Conversion of bonds to common stock outstanding.	+	⌣	~	−	
j. Sale of inventory at greater than cost.	+	~	~	−	

Required Indicate the effect of each of the transactions on the ratios listed. Use + to indicate an increase, − to indicate a decrease, and 0 to indicate no effect. Assume an initial times interest earned of more than 1, and a debt ratio, debt/equity ratio, and a total debt to tangible net worth of less than 1.

P 7-6. Mr. Parks has asked you to advise him on the long-term debt-paying ability of the Arodex Company. He provides you with the following ratios:

	2004	2003	2002
Times interest earned	8.2	6.0	5.5
Debt ratio	40%	39%	40%
Debt to tangible net worth	80%	81%	81%

Required
a. Give the implications and the limitations of each item separately and then the collective influence that could be drawn from them about the Arodex Company's long-term debt position.
b. What warnings should you offer Mr. Parks about the limitations of ratio analysis for the purpose stated here?

P 7-7. For the year ended June 30, 2004, A.E.G. Enterprises presented the financial statements shown on the following page.

Early in the new fiscal year, the officers of the firm formalized a substantial expansion plan. The plan will increase fixed assets by $190,000,000. In addition, extra inventory will be needed to support expanded production. The increase in inventory is purported to be $10,000,000.

The firm's investment bankers have suggested the following three alternative financing plans:

Plan A: Sell preferred stock at par.
Plan B: Sell common stock at $10 per share.
Plan C: Sell long-term bonds, due in 20 years, at par ($1,000), with a stated interest rate of 16%.

A.E.G. ENTERPRISES
Balance Sheet for June 30, 2004 (in thousands)

Assets
  Current assets:
    Cash $ 50,000
    Accounts receivable   60,000
    Inventory   106,000
      Total current assets $216,000
    Property, plant, and equipment $504,000
    Less: accumulated depreciation   140,000   364,000
    Patents and other intangible assets   20,000
      Total assets $600,000

Liabilities and Stockholders' Equity
  Current liabilities:
    Accounts payable $ 46,000
    Taxes payable   15,000
    Other current liabilities   32,000
      Total current liabilities $ 93,000
  Long-term debt   100,000
  Stockholders' equity:
    Preferred stock ($100 par, 10% cumulative, 500,000 shares
      authorized and issued)   50,000
    Common stock ($1 par, 200,000,000 shares authorized,
      100,000,000 issued)   100,000
    Premium on common stock   120,000
    Retained earnings   137,000
      Total liabilities and stockholders' equity $600,000

A.E.G. ENTERPRISES
Income Statement
For the Year Ended June 30, 2004
(in thousands except earnings per share)

Sales $936,000
Cost of sales   671,000

Gross profit $265,000
Operating expenses
  Selling $ 62,000
  General   41,000   103,000

Operating income $162,000
Other items:
  Interest expense   20,000

Earnings before provision for income tax $142,000
Provision for income tax   56,800

  Net income $ 85,200

Earnings per share $ 0.83

Required   a.   For the year ended June 30, 2004, compute:
                    1.   Times interest earned
                    2.   Debt ratio
                    3.   Debt/equity ratio
                    4.   Debt to tangible net worth ratio
               b.   Assuming the same financial results and statement balances, except for the increased assets and fi-
                    nancing, compute the same ratios as in (a) under each financing alternative. Do not attempt to adjust
                    retained earnings for the next year's profits.

c. Changes in earnings and number of shares will give the following earnings per share: Plan A—0.73 Plan B—0.69 Plan C—0.73. Based on the information given, discuss the advantages and disadvantages of each alternative.

d. Why does the 10% preferred stock cost the company more than the 16% bonds?

P 7-8. The consolidated statement of earnings of Anonymous Corporation for the year ended December 31, 2004 is as follows:

Net sales	$1,550,010,000
Other income, net	10,898,000
	1,560,908,000
Costs and expenses:	
Cost of goods sold	1,237,403,000
Depreciation and amortization	32,229,000
Selling, general and administrative	178,850,000
Interest	37,646,000
	1,486,128,000
Earnings from continuing operations before income taxes and equity earnings	74,780,000
Income taxes	37,394,000
Earnings from continuing operations before equity earnings	37,386,000
Equity in net earnings of unconsolidated subsidiaries and affiliated companies	27,749,000
Earnings from continuing operations	65,135,000
Earnings (losses) from discontinued operations, net of applicable income taxes	6,392,000
Net earnings	$ 71,527,000

Required

a. Compute the times interest earned for 2004.

b. Compute the times interest earned for 2004, including the equity income in the coverage.

c. What is the impact of including equity earnings from the coverage? Why should equity income be excluded from the times interest earned coverage?

P 7-9. The Allen Company and the Barker Company are competitors in the same industry. Selected financial data from their 2004 statements follow.

Balance Sheet
December 31, 2004

	Allen Company	Barker Company
Cash	$ 10,000	$ 35,000
Accounts receivable	45,000	120,000
Inventory	70,000	190,000
Investments	40,000	100,000
Intangibles	11,000	20,000
Property, plant, and equipment	180,000	520,000
Total assets	$356,000	$985,000
Accounts payable	$ 60,000	$165,000
Bonds payable	100,000	410,000
Preferred stock, $1 par	50,000	30,000
Common Stock, $10 par	100,000	280,000
Retained earnings	46,000	100,000
Total liabilities and capital	$356,000	$985,000

Income Statement
For the Year Ended December 31, 2004

	Allen Company	Barker Company
Sales	$1,050,000	$2,800,000
Cost of goods sold	725,000	2,050,000
Selling and administrative expenses	230,000	580,000
Interest expense	10,000	32,000
Income taxes	42,000	65,000
Net income	$ 43,000	$ 73,000

Industry Averages:

Times interest earned		7.2 times
Debt ratio		40.3%
Debt/equity		66.6%
Debt to tangible net worth		72.7%

Required

a. Compute the following ratios for each company:
1. Times interest earned
2. Debt ratio
3. Debt/equity ratio
4. Debt to tangible net worth

b. Is Barker Company in a position to take on additional long-term debt? Explain.

c. Which company has the better long-term debt position? Explain.

P 7-10. Consecutive five-year balance sheets and income statements of the Laura Gibson Corporation are shown below and on the following page.

Required

a. Compute the following for the years ended December 31, 2000–2004:
1. Times interest earned
2. Fixed charge coverage
3. Debt ratio
4. Debt/equity ratio
5. Debt to tangible net worth

b. Comment on the debt position and the trends indicated in the long-term debt-paying ability.

Laura Gibson Corporation
Balance Sheets
December 31, 2000 through December 31, 2004

(Dollars in thousands)	2004	2003	2002	2001	2000
Assets					
Current Assets					
Cash	$ 27,000	$ 26,000	$ 25,800	$ 25,500	$ 25,000
Accounts receivable, net	135,000	132,000	130,000	129,000	128,000
Inventories	128,000	130,000	134,000	132,000	126,000
Total current assets	290,000	288,000	289,800	286,500	279,000
Property, plant and equipment, net	250,000	248,000	247,000	246,000	243,000
Intangibles	20,000	18,000	17,000	16,000	15,000
Total assets	$560,000	$554,000	$553,800	$548,500	$537,000
Liabilities and stockholders' equity					
Current liabilities					
Accounts payable	$ 75,000	$ 76,000	$ 76,500	$ 77,000	$ 78,000
Income taxes	13,000	13,500	14,000	13,000	13,500
Total current liabilities	88,000	89,500	90,500	90,000	91,500
Long-term debt	170,000	168,000	165,000	164,000	262,000
Stockholders' equity	302,000	296,500	298,300	294,500	183,500
Total liabilities and stockholders' equity	$560,000	$554,000	$553,800	$548,500	$537,000

Laura Gibson Corporation
Statement of Earnings
Years Ended December 31, 2000–2004

(In thousands, except per share)	2004	2003	2002	2001	2000
Net sales	$920,000	$950,000	$910,000	$850,000	$800,000
Cost of goods sold	640,000	648,000	624,000	580,000	552,000
Gross margin	280,000	302,000	286,000	270,000	248,000
Selling and administrative expense	156,000	157,000	154,000	150,000	147,000
Interest expense	17,000	16,000	15,000	14,500	23,000
Earnings from continuing operations before income taxes	107,000	129,000	117,000	105,500	78,000
Income taxes	36,300	43,200	39,800	35,800	26,500
Earnings from continuing operations	70,700	85,800	77,200	69,700	51,500
Discontinued operating earnings (loss), net of taxes:					
From operations	(1,400)	1,300	1,400	1,450	1,600
On disposal	(900)	—	—	—	—
Earnings (loss) from discontinued operation	(2,300)	1,300	1,400	1,450	1,600
Net earnings	$ 68,400	$ 87,100	$ 78,600	$ 71,150	$ 53,100
Earnings (loss) per share:					
Continuing operations	$ 1.53	$ 1.69	$ 1.46	$ 1.37	$ 1.25
Discontinued operations	(.03)	.01	.01	.01	.01
Net earnings per share	$ 1.50	$ 1.70	$ 1.47	$ 1.38	$ 1.26

Note: Operating lease payments were as follows: 2004, $30,000; 2003, $27,000; 2002, $28,500; 2001, $30,000; 2000, $27,000. (Dollars in thousands)

Case 7-1

Expensing Interest Now and Later

Johnson & Johnson and Subsidiaries
Consolidated Statement of Earnings

(Dollars in Millions Except Per Share Figures) (Note 1)	2001	2000	1999
Sales to customers	$33,004	$29,846	$28,007
Cost of products sold	9,536	8,908	8,498
Gross profit	23,468	20,938	19,509
Selling, marketing and administrative expenses	11,992	11,218	10,756
Research expense	3,591	3,105	2,768
Purchased in-process research and development (Note 17)	105	66	—
Interest income	(456)	(429)	(266)
Interest expense, net of portion capitalized (Note 3)	153	204	255
Other (income) expense, net	185	(94)	119
	15,570	14,070	13,632
Earnings before provision for taxes on income	7,898	6,868	5,877
Provision for taxes on income (Note 8)	2,230	1,915	1,604
Net earnings	$ 5,668	$ 4,953	$ 4,273
Basic net earnings per share (Notes 1 and 19)	$1.87	$1.65	$1.43
Diluted net earnings per share (Notes 1 and 19)	$1.84	$1.61	$1.39

Selected Note

3 Property, Plant and Equipment

At the end of 2001 and 2000, property, plant and equipment at cost and accumulated depreciation were:

(Dollars in Millions)	2001	2000
Land and land improvements	$ 459	$ 427
Buildings and building equipment	3,911	3,659
Machinery and equipment	6,805	6,312
Construction in progress	1,283	1,468
	12,458	11,866
Less accumulated depreciation	4,739	4,457
	$ 7,719	$ 7,409

The Company capitalizes interest expense as part of the cost of construction of facilities and equipment. Interest expense capitalized in 2001, 2000 and 1999 was $95 million, $97 million and $84 million, respectively.

Upon retirement or other disposal of fixed assets, the cost and related amount of accumulated depreciation or amortization are eliminated from the asset and accumulated depreciation accounts, respectively. The difference, if any, between the net asset value and the proceeds is adjusted to earnings.

Required
a. What is the amount of gross interest expense for 2001, 2000, and 1999?
b. What is the interest reported on the income statement for 2001, 2000, and 1999?
c. What was the interest added to the cost of property, plant, and equipment during 2001, 2000, and 1999?
d. When is capitalized interest recognized as an expense? Describe.
e. What was the effect on income from capitalizing interest? Describe.

Case 7-2

Consideration of Leases

Wal-Mart included the following statements in its 1998 annual report:

Consolidated Statements of Income
(Amounts in millions except per share data)

Fiscal years ended January 31,	1998	1997	1996
Revenues:			
Net sales	$117,958	$104,859	$93,627
Other income—net	1,341	1,319	1,146
	119,299	106,178	94,773
Costs and Expenses:			
Cost of sales	93,438	83,510	74,505
Operating, selling and general and administrative expenses	19,358	16,946	15,021
Interest Costs:			
Debt	555	629	692
Capital leases	229	216	196
	113,580	101,301	90,414
Income Before Income Taxes, Minority Interest and Equity in Unconsolidated Subsidiaries	5,719	4,877	4,359
Provision for Income Taxes			
Current	2,095	1,974	1,530
Deferred	20	(180)	76
	2,115	1,794	1,606
Income Before Minority Interest and Equity in Unconsolidated Subsidiaries	3,604	3,083	2,753
Minority Interest and Equity in Unconsolidated Subsidiaries	(78)	(27)	(13)
Net Income	$ 3,526	$ 3,056	$ 2,740
Net Income Per Share—Basic and Dilutive	$1.56	$1.33	$1.19

Consolidated Balance Sheets
(Amounts in millions)

January 31,	1998	1997
Assets		
Current Assets:		
Cash and cash equivalents	$ 1,447	$ 883
Receivables	976	845
Inventories at replacement cost	16,845	16,193
Less LIFO reserve	348	296
Inventories at LIFO cost	16,497	15,897
Prepaid expenses and other	432	368
Total Current Assets	19,352	17,993
Property, Plant and Equipment, at Cost:		
Land	4,691	3,689
Building and improvements	14,646	12,724
Fixtures and equipment	7,636	6,390
Transportation equipment	403	379
	27,376	23,182
Less accumulated depreciation	5,907	4,849
Net property, plant and equipment	21,469	18,333
Property Under Capital Lease:		
Property under capital lease	3,040	2,782
Less accumulated amortization	903	791
Net property under capital leases	2,137	1,991
Other Assets and Deferred Charges	2,426	1,287
Total Assets	$ 45,384	$ 39,604

Liabilities and Shareholders' Equity
Current Liabilities:

Accounts payable	**$ 9,126**	$ 7,628
Accrued liabilities	**3,628**	2,413
Accrued income taxes	**565**	298
Long-term debt due within one year	**1,039**	523
Obligations under capital leases due within one year	**102**	95
Total Current Liabilities	**14,460**	10,957
Long-Term Debt	**7,191**	7,709
Long-Term Obligations Under Capital Leases	**2,483**	2,307
Deferred Income Taxes and Other	**809**	463
Minority Interest	**1,938**	1,025
Shareholders' Equity		
Preferred stock ($.10 par value; 100 shares authorized, none issued)		
Common stock ($.10 par value; 5,500 shares authorized, 2,241and 2,285 issued and outstanding in 1998 and 1997, respectively)	**224**	228
Capital in excess of par value	**585**	547
Retained earnings	**18,167**	16,768
Foreign currency translation adjustment	**(473)**	(400)
Total Shareholders' Equity	**18,503**	17,143
Total Liabilities and Shareholders' Equity	**$ 45,384**	$ 39,604

Selected Note

8 Long-term Lease Obligations

The Company and certain of its subsidiaries have long-term leases for stores and equipment. Rentals (including, for certain leases, amounts applicable to taxes, insurance, maintenance, other operating expenses and contingent rentals) under all operating leases were $596 million, $561 million and $531 million in 1998, 1997 and 1996, respectively. Aggregate minimum annual rentals at January 31, 1998, under non-cancelable leases are as follows (in millions):

Fiscal year	Operating leases	Capital leases
1999	$ 404	$ 347
2000	384	345
2001	347	344
2002	332	343
2002	315	340
Thereafter	2,642	3,404
Total minimum rentals	$ 4,424	5,123
Less estimated executory costs		73
Net minimum lease payments		5,050
Less imputed interest at rates ranging from 6.1% to 14.0%		2,465
Present value of minimum lease payments		$ 2,585

Certain of the leases provide for contingent additional rentals based on percentage of sales. Such additional rentals amounted to $46 million, $51 million and $41 million in 1998, 1997 and 1996, respectively. Substantially all of the store leases have renewal options for additional terms from 5 to 25 years at comparable rentals.

The Company has entered into lease commitments for land and buildings for 38 future locals. These lease commitments with real estate developers provide for minimum rentals for 20 to 25 years, excluding renewal options, which if consummated based on current cost estimates, will approximate $38 million annually over the lease terms.

Required   a.   Compute the following for 1998:
1. Times interest earned
2. Fixed charge coverage

3. Debt ratio
4. Debt/equity ratio
b. Compute the debt ratio, considering operating leases.
c. Give your opinion of the significance of considering operating leases in the debt ratio.
d. Net property under capital leases totaled $2,137,000,000 at January 31, 1998. Obligations under capital leases totaled $2,585,000,000 at January 31, 1998. Why do the assets under capital leases not equal the liabilities under capital leases?

Case 7-3   **Lockout**

The Celtics Basketball Holdings, L.P. and Subsidiary included the following footnote in its 1998 annual report:

Note G—Commitments and Contingencies (In Part)

National Basketball Association ("NBA") players, including those that play for the Boston Celtics, are covered by a collective bargaining agreement between the NBA and the NBA Players Association (the "NBPA") that was to be in effect through June 30, 2001 (the "Collective Bargaining Agreement"). Under the terms of the Collective Bargaining Agreement, the NBA had the right to terminate the Collective Bargaining Agreement after the 1997–98 season if it was determined that the aggregate salaries and benefits paid by all NBA teams for the 1997–98 season exceeded 51.8% of projected Basketball Related Income, as defined in the Collective Bargaining Agreement ("BRI"). Effective June 30, 1998, the Board of Governors of the NBA voted to exercise that right and reopen the Collective Bargaining Agreement, as it had been determined that the aggregate salaries and benefits paid by the NBA teams for the 1997–98 season would exceed 51.8% of projected BRI. Effective July 1, 1998, the NBA commenced a lockout of NBA players in support of its attempt to reach a new collective bargaining agreement. The NBA and the NBPA have been engaged in negotiations regarding a new collective bargaining agreement, but as of September 18, 1998, no agreement has been reached. In the event that the lockout extends into the 1998–99 season, NBA teams, including the Boston Celtics, will refund amounts paid by season ticket holders (plus interest) for any games that are canceled as a result of the lockout. In addition, as a result of the lockout, NBA teams have not made any payments due to players with respect to the 1998–99 season. The NBPA has disputed the NBA's position on this matter, and both the NBA and the NBPA have presented their cases to an independent arbitrator, who will make his ruling no later than the middle of October 1998. As of September 18, 1998, the arbitrator has not ruled on this matter.

Although the ultimate outcome of this matter cannot be determined at this time, any loss of games as a result of the absence of a collective bargaining agreement or the continuation of the lockout will have a material adverse effect on the Partnership's financial condition and its results of operations. Further, if NBA teams, including the Boston Celtics, are required to honor the player contracts for the 1998–99 season and beyond without agreeing to a new collective bargaining agreement or without ending the lockout, which would result in the loss of games, the Partnership's financial condition and results of operations will be materially and adversely affected.

The Partnership has employment agreements with officers, coaches and players of the basketball team (Celtics Basketball). Certain of the contracts provide for guaranteed payments which must be paid even if the employee is injured or terminated. Amounts required to be paid under such contracts in effect as of September 18, 1998, including option years and $8,100,000 included in accrued expenses at June 30, 1998, but excluding deferred compensation commitments disclosed in Note E—Deferred Compensation, are as follows:

Years ending June 30,	1999	$32,715,000
	2000	33,828,000
	2001	27,284,000
	2002	20,860,000
	2003	19,585,000
	2004 and thereafter	10,800,000

Commitments for the year ended June 30, 1999, include payments due to players under contracts for the 1998–99 season in the amount of $18,801,000, which are currently not being paid as a result of the lockout described above.

Celtics Basketball maintains disability and life insurance policies on most of its key players. The level of insurance coverage maintained is based on management's determination of the insurance proceeds which would be required to meet its guaranteed obligations in the event of permanent or total disability of its key players.

Required   Discuss how to incorporate the contingency footnote into an analysis of Celtics Basketball Holdings, L.P. and Subsidiary.

Case 7-4   Many Employers

Safeway Inc. presented the following as part of a footnote in its 2001 annual report.

Multi-Employer Pension Plans Safeway participates in various multi-employer pension plans, covering virtually all Company employees not covered under the Company's non-contributory pension plans, pursuant to agreements between the Company and employee bargaining units that are members of such plans. These plans are generally defined benefit plans; however, in many cases, specific benefit levels are not negotiated with or known by the employer-contributors. Contributions of $158 million in 2001, $154 million in 2000 and $144 million in 1999 were made and charged to expense.

Under U.S. legislation regarding such pension plans, a company is required to continue funding its proportionate share of a plan's unfunded vested benefits in the event of withdrawal (as defined by the legislation) from a plan or plan termination. Safeway participates in a number of these pension plans, and the potential obligation as a participant in these plans may be significant. The information required to determine the total amount of this contingent obligation, as well as the total amount of accumulated benefits and net assets of such plans, is not readily available. During 1988 and 1987, the Company sold certain operations. In most cases the party acquiring the operation agreed to continue making contributions to the plans. Safeway is relieved of the obligations related to these sold operations to the extent that the acquiring parties continue to make contributions. Whether such sales could result in withdrawal under ERISA and, if so, whether such withdrawals could result in liability to the Company, is not determinable at this time.

Note: Sales were $34,301,000,000, $31,976,900,000, and $28,859,900,000 in 2001, 2000, and 1999 respectively.

Required   a.   What were the contributions to multi-employer pension plans for 2001, 2000, and 1999? Comment.
b.   Determine the total liability for multi-employer pension plans at the end of 2001.

Case 7-5   Play It Safe

Safeway Inc. presented the following consolidated statements of income and partial pension footnote with its 2001 Annual Report.

SAFEWAY INC. AND SUBSIDIARIES
Consolidated Statements of Income

(In millions, except per-share amounts)	52 weeks 2001	52 Weeks 2000	52 Weeks 1999
Sales	$ 34,301.0	$ 31,976.9	$ 28,859.9
Cost of goods sold	(23,696.7)	(22,482.4)	(20,349.2)
Gross profit	10,604.3	9,494.5	8,510.7
Operating and administrative expense	(7,875.1)	(7,086.6)	(6,411.4)
Goodwill amortization	(140.4)	(126.2)	(101.4)
Operating profit	2,588.8	2,281.7	1,997.9
Interest expense	(446.9)	(457.2)	(362.2)
Other (loss) income, net	(46.9)	42.0	38.3
Income before income taxes	2,095.0	1,866.5	1,674.0
Income taxes	(841.1)	(774.6)	(703.1)
Net income	$ 1,253.9	$ 1,091.9	$ 970.9
Basic earnings per share	$2.49	$2.19	$1.95
Diluted earnings per share	$2.44	$2.13	$1.88
Weighted average shares outstanding—basic	503.3	497.9	498.6
Weighted average shares outstanding—diluted	513.2	511.6	515.4

Note I: Employee Benefit Plans and Collective Bargaining Agreements

RETIREMENT PLANS The Company maintains defined benefit, non-contributory retirement plans for substantially all of its employees not participating in multi-employer pension plans.

In connection with the Genuardi's and Randall's Acquisitions, and the Vons merger in 1997, the Company assumed the obligations of Genuardi's, Randall's and Vons retirement plans. The actuarial assumptions for the existing Genuardi's, Randall's and Vons retirement plans are comparable to those existing plans of the Company. Genuardi's, Randall's and Vons retirement plans have been combined with Safeway's for financial statement presentation.

The following tables provide a reconciliation of the changes in the retirement plans' benefit obligation and fair value of assets over the two-year period ended December 29, 2001 and a statement of the funded status as of year-end 2001 and 2000 (in millions):

	2001	2000
Change in benefit obligation:		
Beginning balance	**$ 1,181.9**	$ 1,119.7
Service cost	**58.2**	47.2
Interest cost	**76.4**	84.1
Plan amendments	**19.0**	17.8
Actuarial loss	**51.3**	28.3
Acquisition of Genuardi's	**22.7**	—
Benefit payments	**(85.3)**	(85.1)
Transfer of plan liabilities	**(21.5)**	(20.0)
Curtailment	**—**	(2.3)
Currency translation adjustment	**(15.8)**	(7.8)
Ending balance	**$ 1,286.9**	$ 1,181.9

	2001	2000
Change in fair value of plan assets:		
Beginning balance	**$ 1,956.7**	$ 2,153.4
Actual loss on plan assets	**(56.1)**	(60.4)
Acquisition of Genuardi's	**24.4**	—
Employer contributions	**5.9**	0.6
Benefit payments	**(85.3)**	(85.1)
Transfer of plan assets	**(46.9)**	(43.0)
Currency translation adjustment	**(15.9)**	(8.8)
Ending balance	**$ 1,782.8**	$ 1,956.7

	2001	2000
Funded status:		
Fair value of plan assets	**$ 1,782.8**	$ 1,956.7
Projected benefit obligation	**(1,286.9)**	(1,181.9)
Funded status	**495.9**	774.8
Adjustment for difference in book and tax basis of assets	**(165.1)**	(165.1)
Unamortized prior service cost	**99.0**	94.3
Unrecognized loss (gain)	**101.5**	(212.5)
Prepaid pension cost	**$ 531.3**	$ 491.5

The following table provides the components of 2001, 2000 and 1999 net pension income for the retirement plans (in millions):

	2001	2000	1999
Estimated return on assets	**$ 158.9**	$182.3	$162.7
Service cost	**(58.2)**	(47.7)	(54.4)
Interest cost	**(76.4)**	(84.7)	(81.6)
Amortization of prior service cost	**(14.0)**	(14.8)	(15.4)
Amortization of unrecognized gains	**17.0**	42.2	23.8
Net pension income	**$ 27.3**	$ 77.3	$ 35.1

Prior service costs are amortized on a straight-line basis over the average remaining service period of active participants. Actuarial gains and losses are amortized over the average remaining service life of active participants when the accumulation of such gains and losses exceeds 10% of the greater of the projected benefit obligation and the fair value of plan assets.

In May 2000, Safeway entered into an agreement to have a third party operate the Company's Maryland distribution center. Pursuant to the agreement, Safeway and the third party jointly established a new multiple employer defined benefit pension plan to provide benefits for the employees who were to be transferred as a result of this agreement. The Company recorded settlement gains of $9.3 million in 2001 and $15.0 million in 2000 as a result of transfers of employees and their related accrued benefits and assets from the Safeway Plan to the Multiple Employer Plan.

The actuarial assumptions used to determine year-end plan status were as follows:

	2001	2000	1999
Discount rate used to determine the projected benefit obligation:			
United States Plans	**7.5%**	7.8%	7.8%
Canadian Plans	**7.0**	7.0	7.5
Combined weighted average rate	**7.4**	7.6	7.7
Expected return on plan assets:			
United States Plans	**9.0%**	9.0%	9.0%
Canadian Plans	**8.0**	8.0	8.0
Rate of compensation increase:			
United States Plans	**5.0%**	5.0%	5.0%
Canadian Plans	**5.0**	5.0	5.0

RETIREMENT RESTORATION PLAN The Retirement Restoration Plan provides death benefits and supplemental income payments for senior executives after retirement. The Company recognized expense of $5.5 million in 2001, $4.7 million in 2000 and $5.4 million in 1999. The aggregate projected benefit obligation of the Retirement Restoration Plan was approximately $55.8 million at year-end 2001 and $53.1 million at year-end 2000.

Required

a. For 2001, 2000, and 1999, compare pension expense (income) with operating revenue. Comment.

b. For 2001, 2000, and 1999, compare pension expense (income) with income before income taxes. Comment.

c. Compare the benefit obligations with the value of plan assets. Comment.

d. Note the assumptions for the discount rate used to determine the projected benefit obligation, expected return on plan assets, and the rate of compensation increase. Comment.

Case 7-6

Retirement Plans Revisited

Lands' End, Inc. & Subsidiaries
Consolidated Statements of Operations

(In thousands, except per share data)	For the Period Ended		
	February 2, 1996	January 27, 1995	January 28, 1994
Net sales	$1,031,548	$ 992,106	$ 869,975
Cost of sales	588,017	571,265	514,052
Gross profit	443,531	420,841	355,923
Selling, general, and administrative expenses	(392,484)	(357,516)	(285,513)
Charges from sale of subsidiary	(1,882)	(3,500)	—
Income from operations	49,165	59,825	70,410
Other income (expense):			
Interest expense	(2,771)	(1,769)	(359)
Interest income	253	307	346
Other	4,278	1,300	(527)
Total other income (expense), net	1,760	(162)	(540)
Income before income taxes and cumulative effect of change in accounting	50,925	59,663	69,870
Income tax provision	20,370	23,567	27,441
Net income before cumulative effect of change in accounting	30,555	36,096	42,429
Cumulative effect of change in accounting for income taxes	—	—	1,300
Net income	$ 30,555	$ 36,096	$ 43,729
Net income per share before cumulative effect of change in accounting	$0.89	$1.03	$1.18
Cumulative per share effect of change in accounting	—	—	0.04
Net income per share	$0.89	$1.03	$1.22

Lands' End, Inc. & Subsidiaries
Consolidated Balance Sheets (in Part)

(In thousands)	February 2, 1996	January 27, 1995
Total assets	$323,497	$297,612

A footnote from Lands' End 1996 annual report follows:

Note 7. Retirement Plan

The company has a retirement plan which covers most regular employees and provides for annual contributions at the discretion of the board of directors. Also included in the plan is a 401(k) feature that allows employees to make contributions, and the company matches a portion of those contributions. Total expense provided under this plan was $3.2 million, $3.5 million, and $3.7 million for the years ended February 2, 1996, January 27, 1995, and January 28, 1994, respectively.

As of October 1, 1995, the "Lands' End, Inc. Retirement Plan" was amended to allow certain participants to invest their elective contributions, employer matching contributions, and profit sharing contributions in a "Lands' End, Inc. Stock Fund" established primarily for investing in common stock of the company at the fair market value.

Note: Annual report courtesy of Lands' End, Inc.

Required
a. In general, what type of plan does Lands' End have?
b. Give your opinion as to the materiality of the pension plans.
c. Give your opinion as to the control of pension expense.

Case 7-7

Fair Value of Financial Instruments

MSC.Software included the following in its 2001 annual report:

MSC.Software Corporation

Fair Value of Financial Instruments—The following methods and assumptions were used by the Company in estimating its fair value disclosures for financial instruments:

Cash and Cash Equivalents, Trade Accounts Receivable and Accounts Payable—The carrying amount reported in the consolidated balance sheets for cash and cash equivalents, trade accounts receivable approximates their fair value.

Investments—The fair values for investments are based on quoted market prices.

Note Payable—The carrying amount reported in the consolidated balance sheets for the note payable approximates its fair value since the interest rate on the note payable is adjusted on a monthly basis.

Convertible Subordinated Debentures—The fair value of the convertible subordinated debentures outstanding was based on their quoted trading price.

Subordinated Notes Payable and Notes Payable to Shareholders—The fair value of the subordinated notes payable and notes payable to shareholders is based on the present value of their future cash flows using a discount rate that approximates the Company's current borrowing rate.

The carrying amounts and estimated fair values of the Company's financial instruments are as follows:

	December 31, 2001		December 31, 2000	
	Carrying Amount	**Estimated Fair Value**	Carrying Amount	Estimated Fair Value
Financial Instrument Assets:				
Cash and cash equivalents	$ 86,056,000	$ 86,056,000	$ 28,806,000	$ 28,806,000
Investments	$ 3,484,000	$ 3,484,000	$ 1,853,000	$ 1,853,000
Trade Accounts Receivable, Net	$ 82,276,000	$ 82,276,000	$ 45,950,000	$ 45,950,000
Financial Instrument Liabilities:				
Accounts Payable	$(22,289,000)	$(22,289,000)	$ (5,575,000)	$ (5,575,000)
Note Payable, including Current Portion	$ (1,333,000)	$ (1,333,000)	$ (4,533,000)	$ (4,533,000)
Convertible Subordinated Debentures	$ —	$ —	$(58,345,000)	$(51,237,000)
Notes Payable to Shareholders	$(24,178,000)	$(24,442,000)	$ —	$ —
Subordinated Notes Payable, including Current Portion	$ (9,185,000)	$(11,867,000)	$(12,110,000)	$(14,616,000)

Required   Give your opinion as to the fair value of financial instruments in relation to carrying amount.

Case 7-8

Communications

The Andrew Corporation presented this data as part of its 2001 annual report.

Consolidated Balance Sheets

Dollars in thousands	2001	2000	September 30 1999	1998	1997
Liabilities and Stockholders' Equity					
Current Liabilities					
Notes payable	$ 44,109	$ 45,771	$ 3,053	$ 13,897	$ 14,319
Accounts payable	59,225	58,538	43,105	32,867	37,237
Restructuring reserve	—	—	12,128	242	2,036
Accrued expenses and other liabilities	25,080	18,557	21,212	16,856	18,978
Compensation and related expenses	25,468	30,303	21,947	32,424	29,312
Income taxes	—	5,639	—	15,835	16,430
Liabilities related to discontinued operations	—	—	—	—	3,637
Current portion of long-term debt	25,546	15,215	8,205	4,568	5,144
Total Current Liabilities	179,428	174,023	109,650	116,689	127,093
Deferred Liabilities	37,433	25,132	18,602	14,044	10,239
Long-Term Debt, less current portion	39,905	65,843	48,760	38,031	35,693
Minority Interest	316	9,254	5,068	5,361	9,006
Stockholders' Equity					
Common stock	1,027	1,027	1,027	1,027	1,027
Additional paid-in capital	65,870	64,136	55,802	53,309	51,810
Accumulated other comprehensive income	(44,773)	(35,801)	(21,755)	(7,617)	(4,532)
Retained earnings	822,753	761,131	681,530	651,103	547,256
Treasury stock, at cost	(244,227)	(247,548)	(232,594)	(189,044)	(86,438)
	600,650	542,945	484,010	508,778	509,123
Total Liabilities and Stockholders' Equity	$ 857,732	$ 817,197	$ 666,090	$ 682,903	$691,154

Required

a. 1. Prepare a vertical common-size statement for 1997–2001. Use total liabilities and stockholders' equity as the base.
    2. Comment on the results in (1).

b. Compute these ratios for 1997–2001.
    1. Debt ratio
    2. Debt/equity ratio

c. Comment on the results in (b).

Web Case | **Thomson Analytics** *Business School Edition*

Please complete the web case that covers material covered in this chapter at http://gibson.swlearning.com. You'll be using Thomson Analytics Business School Edition, a version of the powerful tool used by Wall Street professionals, that combines a full range of fundamental financial information, earnings estimates, market data, and source documents for 500 publicly traded companies.

Endnotes

1. *Accounting Trends & Techniques* (Jersey City, NJ: American Institute of Certified Public Accountants, 2001), p. 326.
2. *Ibid.*
3. *Ibid.*
4. *Statement of Financial Accounting Standards No. 5*, "Accounting for Contingencies" (Stamford, CT: Financial Accounting Standards Board, 1975), paragraph 1.
5. *Statement of Financial Accounting Standards No. 5*, paragraph 8.
6. *Statement of Financial Accounting Standards No. 5*, paragraph 17.
7. *Statement of Financial Accounting Standards No. 105*, "Disclosure of Information About Financial Instruments with Off-Balance-Sheet Risk and Financial Instruments with Concentrations of Credit Risk" (Stamford, CT: Financial Accounting Standards Board, 1990), paragraph 17.
8. *Statement of Financial Accounting Standards No. 105*, paragraph 18.
9. *Statement of Financial Accounting Standards No. 107*, "Disclosure About Fair Value of Financial Instruments" (Stamford, CT: Financial Accounting Standards Board, 1991), paragraph 10.

8

PROFITABILITY

Profitability is the ability of the firm to generate earnings. Analysis of profit is of vital concern to stockholders since they derive revenue in the form of dividends. Further, increased profits can cause a rise in market price, leading to capital gains. Profits are also important to creditors because profits are one source of funds for debt coverage. Management uses profit as a performance measure.

In profitability analysis, absolute figures are less meaningful than earnings measured as a percentage of a number of bases: the productive assets, the owners' and creditors' capital employed, and sales.

PROFITABILITY MEASURES

The income statement contains several figures that might be used in profitability analysis. In general, the primary financial analysis of profit ratios should include only the types of income arising from the normal operations of the business. This excludes the following:

1. Discontinued operations
2. Extraordinary items
3. Cumulative effects of changes in accounting principles

Exhibit 4-3 in Chapter 4 illustrates an income statement with these items. Review this section on special income statement items in Chapter 4 before continuing with the discussion of profitability. Equity in earnings of nonconsolidated subsidiaries and the minority share of earnings are also important to the analysis of profitability. Chapter 4 covers these items, and Exhibits 4-5 and 4-9 illustrate the concepts.

Trend analysis should also consider only income arising from the normal operations of the business. An illustration will help justify this reasoning. XYZ Corporation had net income of $100,000 in Year 1 and $150,000 in Year 2. Year 2, however, included an extraordinary gain of $60,000. In reality, XYZ suffered a drop in profit from operating income.

Net Profit Margin

A commonly used profit measure is return on sales, often termed net profit margin. If a company reports that it earned 6% last year, this statistic usually means that its profit was 6% of sales. Calculate **net profit margin** as follows:

$$\text{Net Profit Margin} = \frac{\substack{\text{Net Income Before Minority Share of Earnings,} \\ \text{Equity Income and Nonrecurring Items}}}{\text{Net Sales}}$$

This ratio gives a measure of net income dollars generated by each dollar of sales. While it is desirable for this ratio to be high, competitive forces within an industry, economic conditions, use of debt financing, and operating characteristics such as high fixed costs will cause the net profit margin to vary between and within industries.

Exhibit 8-1 shows the net profit margin using the 2002 and 2001 figures for Nike. This analysis shows that Nike's net profit margin improved substantially.

Several refinements to the net profit margin ratio can make it more accurate than the ratio computation in this book. Numerator refinements include removing "other income" and "other expense" items from net income. These items do not relate to net sales (denominator). Therefore, they can cause a distortion in the net profit margin.

This book does not adjust the net profit margin ratio for these items because this often requires an advanced understanding of financial statements beyond the level intended. Also, this chapter covers operating income margin, operating asset turnover, and return on operating assets. These ratios provide a look at the firm's operations.

When working the problems in this book, do not remove "other income" or "other expense" when computing the net profit margin unless otherwise instructed by the problem. In other analyses, if you elect to refine a net profit margin computation by removing "other income" or "other ex-

EXHIBIT 8-1	**NIKE, INC.**		

Net Profit Margin

Years Ended May 31, 2002 and 2001

	2002	2001
	(in millions)	
Net income [A]	$ 668.3	$ 589.7
Net sales [B]	$9,893.0	$9,488.8
Net profit margin [A ÷ B]	6.76%	6.21%

pense" items from net income, remove them net of the firm's tax rate. This is a reasonable approximation of the tax effect.

If you do not refine a net profit margin computation for "other income" and "other expense" items, at least observe whether the company has a net "other income" or a net "other expense." A net "other income" distorts the net profit margin on the high side, while a net "other expense" distorts the profit margin on the low side.

The Nike statement can be used to illustrate the removal of other income. Exhibit 8-2 shows the net profit margin computed with the other income removed for 2002 and 2001. The adjusted computation results in the 2002 net profit margin being reduced by 0.03% and the 2001 net profit margin being reduced by 0.23%. Both of these reductions are likely to be considered immaterial.

Total Asset Turnover

Total asset turnover measures the activity of the assets and the ability of the firm to generate sales through the use of the assets. Compute **total asset turnover** as follows:

$$\text{Total Asset Turnover} = \frac{\text{Net Sales}}{\text{Average Total Assets}}$$

Exhibit 8-3 shows total asset turnover for Nike for 2002 and 2001. The total asset turnover decreased from 1.63 to 1.61. This decrease would be considered to be immaterial.

EXHIBIT 8-2   **NIKE, INC.**

Net Profit Margin (Revised Computation)

Years Ended May 31, 2002 and 2001

	2002	2001
	(in millions)	
Net income	$ 668.3	$ 589.7
Tax rate:		
Provision for income taxes [A]	349.0	331.7
Income before income taxes [B]	1,017.3	921.4
Tax rate [A ÷ B]*	34.31%	36.00%
Other income	3.0	34.1
Other income × (1 − tax rate)	1.97	21.82
Net income less net of tax other income [C]	666.33	567.88
Net sales [D]	$9,893.0	$9,488.8
Adjusted net profit margin [C ÷ D]	6.74%	5.98%

*The tax rate could also be determined from the income tax footnote.

EXHIBIT 8-3   **NIKE, INC.**

Total Asset Turnover

Years Ended May 31, 2002 and 2001

	2002	2001
	(in millions)	
Net sales [A]	$ 9,893.0	$ 9,488.8
Average total assets:		
Beginning of year	$ 5,819.6	$ 5,856.9
End of year	6,443.0	5,819.6
Total	$12,262.6	$11,676.5
Average [B]	$ 6,131.3	$5,838.25
Total asset turnover [A ÷ B]	1.61 times	1.63 times

The total asset turnover computation has refinements that relate to assets (denominator) but do not relate to net sales (numerator). Examples would be the exclusion of investments and construction in progress. This book does not make these refinements. This chapter covers operating income margin, operating asset turnover, and return on operating assets.

If the refinements are not made, observe the investment account, construction in progress, and other assets that do not relate to net sales. The presence of these accounts distorts the total asset turnover on the low side. (Actual turnover is better than the computation indicates.)

Return on Assets

Return on assets measures the firm's ability to utilize its assets to create profits by comparing profits with the assets that generate the profits. Compute the **return on assets** as follows:

$$\text{Return on Assets} = \frac{\text{Net Income Before Minority Share of Earnings and Nonrecurring Items}}{\text{Average Total Assets}}$$

Exhibit 8-4 shows the 2002 and 2001 return on assets for Nike. The return on total assets for Nike increased substantially in 2002.

Theoretically, the best average would be based on month-end figures, which are not available to the outside user. Computing an average based on beginning and ending figures provides a rough approximation that does not consider the timing of interim changes in assets. Such changes might be related to seasonal factors.

However, even a simple average based on beginning and ending amounts requires two figures. Ratios for two years require three years of balance sheet data. Since an annual report only contains two balance sheets, obtaining the data for averages may be a problem. If so, ending balance sheet figures may be used consistently instead of averages for ratio analysis. Similar comments could be made about other ratios that utilize balance sheet figures.

DuPont Return on Assets

The net profit margin, the total asset turnover, and the return on assets are usually reviewed together because of the direct influence that the net profit margin and the total asset turnover have on return on assets. This book reviews these ratios together. When these ratios are reviewed together, it is called the **DuPont return on assets**.

The rate of return on assets can be broken down into two component ratios: the net profit margin and the total asset turnover. These ratios allow for improved analysis of changes in the return on assets percentage. E. I. DuPont de Nemours and Company developed this method of separating the rate of return ratio into its component parts. Compute the DuPont return on assets as follows:

$$\frac{\text{Net Income Before Minority Share of Earnings and Nonrecurring Items}}{\text{Average Total Assets}} = \frac{\text{Net Income Before Minority Share of Earnings and Nonrecurring Items}}{\text{Net Sales}} \times \frac{\text{Net Sales}}{\text{Average Total Assets}}$$

EXHIBIT 8-4	NIKE, INC.

Return on Assets

Years Ended May 31, 2002 and 2001

	2002	2001
	(in millions)	
Net income [A]	$ 668.3	$ 589.7
Average total assets [B]	$6,131.3	$5,838.25
Return on assets [A ÷ B]	10.90%	10.10%

Exhibit 8-5 shows the DuPont return on assets for Nike for 2002 and 2001. Separating the ratio into the two elements allows for discussion of the causes for the increase in the percentage of return on assets. Exhibit 8-5 indicates that Nike's return on assets increased because of an increase in net profit margin. The increase in net profit margin was offset slightly be the reduction in total asset turnover.

Interpretation Through DuPont Analysis

The following examples help to illustrate the use of this analysis:

Example 1

	Return on Assets	=	Net Profit Margin	×	Total Asset Turnover
Year 1	10%	=	5%	×	2.0
Year 2	10%	=	4%	×	2.5

Example 1 shows how a more efficient use of assets can offset rising costs such as labor or materials.

Example 2

	Return on Assets	=	Net Profit Margin	×	Total Asset Turnover
Firm A					
Year 1	10%	=	4.0%	×	2.5
Year 2	8%	=	4.0%	×	2.0
Firm B					
Year 1	10%	=	4.0%	×	2.5
Year 2	8%	=	3.2%	×	2.5

Example 2 shows how a trend in return on assets can be better explained through the breakdown into two ratios. The two firms have identical returns on assets. Further analysis shows that Firm A suffers from a slowdown in asset turnover. It is generating fewer sales for the assets invested. Firm B suffers from a reduction in the net profit margin. It is generating less profit per dollar of sales.

Variation in Computation of DuPont Ratios Considering Only Operating Accounts

It is often argued that only operating assets should be considered in the return on asset calculation. Operating assets exclude construction in progress, long-term investments, intangibles, and the other assets category from total assets. Similarly, operating income—the profit generated by manufacturing, merchandising, or service functions—that equals net sales less the cost of sales and operating expenses should also be used instead of net income.

EXHIBIT 8-5 **NIKE, INC.**

DuPont Return on Assets

Years Ended May 31, 2002 and 2001

	Return on Assets*	=	Net Profit Margin	×	Total Asset Turnover
2002	10.90%	=	6.76%	×	1.61
2001	10.10%	=	6.21%	×	1.63

*There are some minor differences due to rounding.

The DuPont analysis, considering only operating accounts, requires a computation of operating income and operating assets. Exhibit 8-6 shows the computations of operating income and operating assets for Nike. This includes operating income for 2002 and 2001 and operating assets for 2002, 2001, and 2000.

The operating ratios may give significantly different results from net earnings ratios if a firm has large amounts of nonoperating assets. For example, if a firm has heavy investments in unconsolidated subsidiaries, and if these subsidiaries pay large dividends, then other income may be a large portion of net earnings. The profit picture may not be as good if these earnings from other sources are eliminated by analyzing operating ratios. Since earnings from investments are not derived from the primary business, the lower profit figures that represent normal earnings will typically be more meaningful.

Operating Income Margin

The **operating income margin** includes only operating income in the numerator. Compute the operating income margin as follows:

$$\text{Operating Income Margin} = \frac{\text{Operating Income}}{\text{Net Sales}}$$

Exhibit 8-7 indicates the operating income margin for Nike in 2002 and 2001. It shows a slight increase in 2002 in the operating income margin percentage.

EXHIBIT 8-6   **NIKE, INC.**

Operating Income and Operating Assets

Years Ended May 31, 2002 and 2001

	2002	2001	
	(in millions)		
Operating income:			
Net sales [A]	$9,893.0	$9,488.8	
Operating expenses:			
Cost of products sold	$6,004.7	$5,784.9	
Selling, general and administrative	2,820.4	2,689.7	
Total operating expenses [B]	$8,825.1	$8,474.6	
Operating income [A – B]	$1,067.9	$1,014.2	

	2002	2001	2000
Operating assets:			
Total assets [A]	$6,443.0	$5,819.6	$5,856.9
Less: Intangibles, deferred income taxes and			
other assets, and construction in progress [B]	743.2	746.5	1,125.4
Operating assets [A – B]	$5,699.8	$5,073.1	$4,731.5

EXHIBIT 8-7   **NIKE, INC.**

Operating Income Margin

Years Ended May 31, 2002 and 2001

	2002	2001
	(in millions)	
Operating Income [A]	$1,067.9	$1,014.2
Net sales [B]	$9,893.0	$9,488.8
Operating income margin [A ÷ B]	10.79%	10.69%

Operating Asset Turnover

This ratio measures the ability of operating assets to generate sales dollars. Compute operating asset turnover as follows:

$$\text{Operating Asset Turnover} = \frac{\text{Net Sales}}{\text{Average Operating Assets}}$$

Exhibit 8-8 shows the operating asset turnover for Nike in 2002 and 2001. It indicates a substantial decrease from 1.94 to 1.84. The decrease is substantially more than the decrease for total asset turnover.

Return on Operating Assets

Adjusting for nonoperating items results in the following formula for return on **operating assets**:

$$\text{Return on Operating Assets} = \frac{\text{Operating Income}}{\text{Average Operating Assets}}$$

Exhibit 8-9 shows the return on operating assets for Nike for 2002 and 2001. It indicates a decrease in the return on operating assets from 20.69% in 2001 to 19.83% in 2002.

The return on operating assets can be viewed in terms of the DuPont analysis that follows:

$$\begin{array}{c}\text{DuPont Return} \\ \text{on Operating Assets}\end{array} = \begin{array}{c}\text{Operating} \\ \text{Income} \\ \text{Margin}\end{array} \times \begin{array}{c}\text{Operating} \\ \text{Asset} \\ \text{Turnover}\end{array}$$

Exhibit 8-10 indicates the DuPont return on operating assets for Nike for 2002 and 2001. This figure supports the conclusion that an increase in operating income margin and a decrease in operating asset turnover resulted in a decrease in return on operating assets.

EXHIBIT 8-8   **NIKE, INC.**

Operating Asset Turnover

Years Ended May 31, 2002 and 2001

	2002	2001
	(in millions)	
Net sales [A]	$ 9,893.0	$9,488.8
Average operating assets		
Beginning of year	$ 5,073.1	$4,731.5
End of year	5,699.8	5,073.1
Total [B]	$10,772.90	$9,804.60
Average [B ÷ 2] = [C]	$ 5,386.45	$4,902.3
Operating asset turnover [A ÷ C]	1.84 times per year	1.94 times per year

---

EXHIBIT 8-9   **NIKE, INC.**

Return on Operating Assets

Years Ended May 31, 2002 and 2001

	2002	2001
	(in millions)	
Operating income [A]	$1,067.9	$1,014.2
Average operating assets [B]	$5,386.45	$4,902.3
Return on operating assets [A ÷ B]	19.83%	20.69%

EXHIBIT 8-10	NIKE, INC.

DuPont Analysis with Operating Accounts

Years Ended May 31, 2002 and 2001

	Return on Operating Assets*	=	Operating Income Margin	×	Operating Asset Turnover
2002	19.83%	=	10.79	×	1.84
2001	20.69%	=	10.69	×	1.94

*There are some differences due to rounding.

Sales to Fixed Assets

This ratio measures the firm's ability to make productive use of its property, plant, and equipment by generating sales dollars. Since construction in progress does not contribute to current sales, it should be excluded from net fixed assets. This ratio may not be meaningful because of old fixed assets or a labor-intensive industry. In these cases, the ratio is substantially higher because of the low fixed asset base. Compute the **sales to fixed assets** as follows:

$$\text{Sales to Fixed Assets} = \frac{\text{Net Sales}}{\text{Average Net Fixed Assets}}$$
$$\text{(Exclude Construction in Progress)}$$

Exhibit 8-11 shows the sales to fixed assets for Nike for 2002 and 2001. It declined substantially between 2001 and 2002. It appears that sales increases did not keep up with net fixed assets increases.

Return on Investment (ROI)

The **return on investment (ROI)** applies to ratios measuring the income earned on the invested capital. These types of measures are widely used to evaluate enterprise performance. Since return on investment is a type of return on capital, this ratio measures the ability of the firm to reward those who provide long-term funds and to attract providers of future funds. Compute the return on investment as follows:

$$\text{Return on Investment} = \frac{\begin{array}{c}\text{Net Income Before Minority Share of} \\ \text{Earnings and Nonrecurring Items} + \\ [(\text{Interest Expense}) \times (1 - \text{Tax Rate})]\end{array}}{\text{Average (Long-Term Liabilities} + \text{Equity)}}$$

EXHIBIT 8-11	NIKE, INC.

Sales to Fixed Assets (Exclude Construction in Progress)

Years Ended May 31, 2002 and 2001

	2002	2001
	(in millions)	
Net sales [A]	$9,893.0	$9,488.8
Net fixed assets: (Exclude Construction in Progress)		
Beginning of year	$1,447.8	$1,135.1
End of year	1,542.1	1,447.8
Total [B]	$2,989.9	$2,582.9
Average [(B) ÷ 2] = [C]	$1,494.95	$1,291.45
Sales to fixed assets [A ÷ C]	6.62 times per year	7.35 times per year

This ratio evaluates the earnings performance of the firm without regard to the way the investment is financed. It measures the earnings on investment and indicates how well the firm utilizes its asset base. Exhibit 8-12 shows the return on investment for Nike for 2002 and 2001. From 2001 to 2002, this ratio stayed the same between these two years.

Return on Total Equity

The **return on total equity** measures the return to both common and preferred stockholders. Compute the return on total equity as follows:

$$\text{Return on Total Equity} = \frac{\text{Net Income Before Nonrecurring Items} - \text{Dividends on Redeemable Preferred Stock}}{\text{Average Total Equity}}$$

Preferred stock subject to mandatory redemption is termed **redeemable preferred stock.** The SEC requires that redeemable preferred stock be categorized separately from other equity securities because the shares must be redeemed in a manner similar to the repayment of debt. Most companies do not have redeemable preferred stock. For those firms that do, the redeemable preferred is excluded from total equity and considered part of debt. Similarly, the dividends must be deducted from income. They have not been deducted on the income statement, despite the similarity to debt and interest, because they are still dividends and payable only if declared.

Exhibit 8-13 shows the return on total equity for Nike for 2002 and 2001. It increased moderately from 17.78% to 18.22%.

Return on Common Equity

This ratio measures the return to the common stockholder, the residual owner. Compute the **return on common equity** as follows:

$$\text{Return on Common Equity} = \frac{\text{Net Income Before Nonrecurring Items} - \text{Preferred Dividends}}{\text{Average Common Equity}}$$

EXHIBIT 8-12	NIKE, INC.

Return on Investment

Years Ended May 31, 2002 and 2001

	2002	2001
	(in millions)	
Interest expense [A]	$ 47.6	$ 58.7
Net income	$ 668.3	$ 589.7
Tax rate (see footnote)	34.3%	36.0%
1 – Tax rate [B]	65.7%	64.0%
(Interest expense) × (1 – Tax rate) [A × B]	$ 31.27	$ 37.57
Net income + [(Interest expense) × (1 – Tax rate)] [C]	$ 699.57	$ 627.27
Long-term liabilities and stockholders' equity		
Beginning of year:		
Long-term liabilities	$ 538.4	$ 580.9
Total stockholders' equity	3,494.5	3,136.0
End of year:		
Long-term liabilities	767.8	538.4
Total stockholders' equity	3,839.0	3,494.5
Total [D]	$8,639.7	$7,749.80
Average [D ÷ 2] = [E]	$4,319.85	$3,874.9
Return on investment [C ÷ E]	16.19%	16.19%

EXHIBIT 8-13	NIKE, INC.

Return on Total Equity

Years Ended May 31, 2002 and 2001

	2002	2001
	(in millions)	
Net income before cumulative effect of accounting change	$ 668.3	$ 589.7
Less: Redeemable preferred dividends	.3	.3
Adjusted income [A]	$ 668.0	$ 589.4
Total equity:		
Beginning of year	$3,494.5	$3,136.0
End of year	3,839.0	3,494.5
Total [B]	$7,333.5	$6,630.5
Average [B ÷ 2] = [C]	$3,666.75	$3,315.25
Return on total equity [A ÷ C]	18.22%	17.78%

The net income appears on the income statement. The preferred dividends appear most commonly on the statement of stockholders' equity. Common equity includes common capital stock and retained earnings less common treasury stock. This amount equals total equity minus the preferred capital and any minority interest included in the equity section.

Exhibit 8-14 shows the return on common equity for Nike for 2002 and 2001. Nike's return on common equity is the same as its return on total equity.

The Relationship Between Profitability Ratios

Technically, a ratio with a profit figure in the numerator and some type of "supplier of funds" figure in the denominator is a type of return on investment. Another frequently used measure is a variation of the return on total assets. Compute this return on total assets variation as follows:

$$\text{Return on Total Assets Variation} = \frac{\text{Net Income} + \text{Interest Expense}}{\text{Average Total Assets}}$$

This ratio includes the return to all suppliers of funds, both long- and short-term, by both creditors and investors. It differs from the return on assets ratio previously discussed because it adds back

EXHIBIT 8-14	NIKE, INC.

Return on Common Equity

Years Ended May 31, 2002 and 2001

	2002	2001
	(in millions)	
Net income before cumulative effect of accounting change	$ 668.3	$ 589.7
Less: Redeemable preferred dividends	.3	.3
Adjusted income [A]	$ 668.0	$ 589.4
Total common equity:		
Beginning of year	$3,494.5	$3,136.0
End of year	3,839.0	3,494.5
Total [B]	$7,333.5	$6,630.5
Average common equity [B ÷ 2] = [C]	$3,666.75	$3,315.25
Return on common equity [A ÷ C]	18.22%	17.78%

the interest. It differs from the return on investment in that it does not adjust interest for the income tax effect, it includes short-term funds, and it uses the average investment. It will not be discussed or utilized further here because it does not lend itself to DuPont analysis.

Rates of return have been calculated on a variety of bases. The interrelationship between these ratios is of importance in understanding the return to the suppliers of funds. Exhibit 8-15 displays a comparison of profitability measures for Nike.

The return on assets measures the return to all providers of funds since total assets equal total liabilities and equity. This ratio will usually be the lowest since it includes all of the assets. The return on investment measures the return to long-term suppliers of funds, and it is usually higher than the return on assets because of the relatively low amount paid for short-term funds. This is especially true of accounts payable.

The rate of return on total equity will usually be higher than the return on investment because the rate of return on equity measures return only to the stockholders. A profitable use of long-term sources of funds from creditors provides a higher return to stockholders than the return on investment. In other words, the profits made on long-term funds from creditors were greater than the interest paid for the use of the funds.

Common stockholders absorb the greatest degree of risk and, therefore, usually earn the highest return. For the return on common equity to be the highest, the return on funds obtained from preferred stockholders must be more than the funds paid to the preferred stockholders.

Gross Profit Margin

Gross profit equals the difference between net sales revenue and the cost of goods sold. The cost of goods sold is the beginning inventory plus purchases minus the ending inventory. It is the cost of the product sold during the period. Changes in the cost of goods sold, which represents such a large expense for merchandising and manufacturing firms, can have a substantial impact on the profit for the period. Comparing gross profit to net sales is termed the **gross profit margin**. Compute the gross profit margin as follows:

$$\text{Gross Profit Margin} = \frac{\text{Gross Profit}}{\text{Net Sales}}$$

This ratio should then be compared with industry data or analyzed by trend analysis. Exhibit 8-16 illustrates trend analysis. In this illustration, the gross profit margin has declined substantially over the three-year period. This could be attributable to a number of factors:

1. The cost of buying inventory has increased more rapidly than have selling prices.
2. Selling prices have declined due to competition.
3. The mix of goods has changed to include more products with lower margins.
4. Theft is occurring. If sales are not recorded, the cost of goods sold figure in relation to the sales figure is very high. If inventory is being stolen, the ending inventory will be low and the cost of goods sold will be high.

Gross profit margin analysis helps a number of users. Managers budget gross profit levels into their predictions of profitability. Gross profit margins are also used in cost control. Estimations utilizing gross profit margins can determine inventory levels for interim statements in the merchandising

EXHIBIT 8-15	NIKE, INC.		
Comparison of Profitability Measures			
Years Ended May 31, 2002 and 2001		**2002**	**2001**
Return on assets		10.90%	10.10%
Return on investment		16.19%	16.19%
Return on total equity		18.22%	17.78%
Return on common equity		18.22%	17.78%

| EXHIBIT 8-16 | EXAMPLE GROSS PROFIT MARGIN |

Years Ended May 31, 2002, 2001, and 2000

	2002	2001	2000
Net sales [B]	$5,000,000	$4,500,000	$4,000,000
Less: Cost of goods sold	3,500,000	2,925,000	2,200,000
Gross profit [A]	$1,500,000	$1,575,000	$1,800,000
Gross profit margin [A ÷ B]	30.00%	35.00%	45.00%

industries. Gross profit margins can also be used to estimate inventory involved in insured losses. In addition, gross profit measures are used by auditors and the Internal Revenue Service to judge the accuracy of accounting systems.

Gross profit margin analysis requires an income statement in multiple-step format. Otherwise the gross profit must be computed, which is the case with Nike. Exhibit 8-17 presents Nike's gross profit margin, which has decreased between 2000 and 2001. Comparing 2002 with 2000 there was a slight decrease.

TRENDS IN PROFITABILITY

Exhibit 8-18 shows profitability trends for manufacturing for the period 1965–2001. Operating profit compared with net sales declined substantially over this period. Net income compared with net sales fluctuated substantially. Notice the material decline in this ratio in 1992 and 2001. In general, there has been a decline in profitability. This decline in profitability probably occurred due to factors such as an increase in competition domestically and internationally. The decline in profitability indicates an increase in the risk of doing business.

SEGMENT REPORTING

A public business enterprise reports financial and descriptive information about reportable operating segments. Operating segments are segments about which separate financial information is available that is evaluated by the chief operating decision maker in deciding how to allocate resources and in assessing performance. It requires information about the countries in which the firm earns revenues and holds assets, and about major customers.

Descriptive information must be disclosed about the way the operating segments were determined. Disclosure is required for products and services by the operating segments. Disclosure is also required about the differences between the measurements used in reporting segment information and those used in the firm's general-purpose financial information.

Segment data can be analyzed both in terms of trends and ratios. Vertical and horizontal common-size analyses can be used for trends. Examples of ratios would be relating profits to sales or identifiable assets.

| EXHIBIT 8-17 | NIKE, INC. |

Gross Profit Margin

Years Ended May 31, 2002, 2001, and 2000

	2002	2001	2000
		(in millions)	
Net sales [B]	$9,893.0	$9,488.8	$8,995.1
Less: Cost of products sold	6,004.7	5,784.9	5,403.8
Gross profit [A]	$3,888.3	$3,703.9	$3,591.3
Gross profit margin [A ÷ B]	39.30%	39.03%	39.93%

EXHIBIT 8-18	TRENDS IN PROFITABILITY
	United States Manufacturing

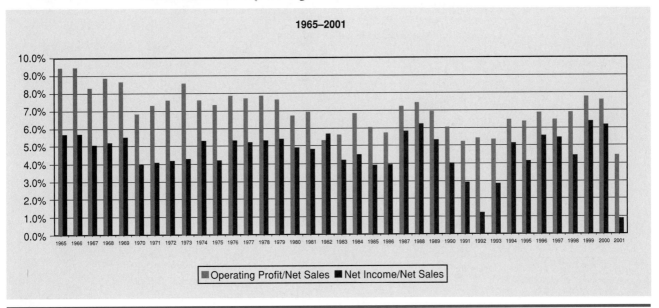

Source: Quarterly Financial Reports of Manufacturing, Mining, & Trading, Department of Commerce, Washington, DC: Government Printing Office.

Segment trends would be of interest to management and investors. The maximum benefits from this type of analysis come when analyzing a nonintegrated company in terms of product lines, especially with segments of relatively similar size.

Nike reported operating segments and related information in Note 16. Note 16 is partially included in Exhibit 8-19. This data should be reviewed, and consideration should be given to using vertical and horizontal analyses and to computing ratios that appear meaningful. This type of review is illustrated in Exhibits 8-20 and 8-21.

Exhibit 8-20 presents some Nike information in vertical common-size analysis. Net revenue, management pretax income, additions to long-lived assets, and property, plant and equipment, net, are included. Based on this analysis, the United States is the dominant segment, followed by Europe, Middle East, and Africa. The proportion of revenue coming from the United States has declined moderately, while the proportion of revenue coming from Europe, Middle East, and Africa has increased slightly.

Asia Pacific, Americas, and Other all had increases in proportion of net revenue. In total these increases would be considered to be moderate.

A review of Exhibit 8-21 (segment information—ratio analysis) on page 266 indicates that management pretax income to net revenue increased moderately for the United States and Europe, Middle East, and Africa. There was a material increase in Asia Pacific and the Americas, and material decrease in Other.

Exhibit 8-21 indicates material increases in Americas, Other, and corporate for additions to long-lived assets to property, plant and equipment, net.

SALES AND MARKETING

Exhibit 8-22 (page 266) has the sales and marketing table presented by Nike (in part).

Total U.S. revenues increased slightly, while international sales increased substantially. Footwear sales in the United States decreased, while equipment and other sales surged.

Europe, Middle East, and Africa sales increased moderately. In this region footwear sales increased substantially. Asia Pacific increased sales substantially. This was especially true of equipment and other sales.

| EXHIBIT 8-19 | NIKE, INC. |

Segment Information (in Part)

Years Ended May 31, 2002, 2001, and 2000

	2002	2001 (in millions)	2000
Net Revenue			
United States	$4,916.0	$4,819.0	$4,732.1
Europe, Middle East, and Africa	2,731.5	2,584.8	2,407.0
Asia Pacific	1,211.7	1,110.0	955.1
Americas	568.1	539.1	494.1
Other	465.7	435.9	406.8
	$9,893.0	$9,488.8	$8,995.1
Management Pre-tax Income			
United States	$ 977.6	$ 919.6	$ 924.3
Europe, Middle East, and Africa	445.4	386.3	376.9
Asia Pacific	238.7	206.1	146.0
Americas	92.9	81.6	63.7
Other	20.0	41.4	68.9
Corporate	(757.3)	(713.6)	(660.6)
	$1,017.3	$ 921.4	$ 919.2
Additions to Long-lived Assets			
United States	$ 33.4	$ 45.2	$ 29.0
Europe, Middle East, and Africa	27.2	26.2	46.1
Asia Pacific	22.1	52.9	269.7
Americas	4.8	5.1	4.8
Other	76.3	26.3	32.4
Corporate	115.2	161.9	146.8
	$ 279.0	$ 317.6	$ 528.8
Property, Plant and Equipment, Net			
United States	$ 244.4	$ 263.5	$ 271.7
Europe, Middle East, and Africa	212.2	208.2	240.4
Asia Pacific	378.4	403.5	426.4
Americas	12.4	15.4	18.1
Other	109.7	113.4	114.4
Corporate	657.4	614.8	512.4
	$1,614.5	$1,618.8	$1,583.4

Americas increased sales moderately. Equipment and other increased materially.

The increase in sales was led by equipment and other. This category increased materially in all regions, except for Europe, Middle East, and Africa.

GAINS AND LOSSES FROM PRIOR PERIOD ADJUSTMENTS

Prior period adjustments result from certain changes in accounting principles, the realization of income tax benefits of preacquisition operating loss carryforwards of purchased subsidiaries, a change in accounting entity, and corrections of errors in prior periods. Prior period adjustments are charged to retained earnings.

These items are a type of gain or loss but they never go through the income statement. They are not recognized on the income statement. If material, they should be considered in analysis. Current period ratios would not be revised because these items relate to prior periods.

A review of the retained earnings account presented in the statement of stockholders' equity will reveal prior period adjustments.

Exhibit 8-23 (page 267) presents a prior period adjustment from the 1998 annual report of the Nord Resources Corp. This prior period adjustment of $15,705,000 increased retained earnings.

EXHIBIT 8-20	NIKE, INC.

Segment Information—Vertical Common-Size Analysis

Years Ended May 31, 2002, 2001, and 2000

	2002	2001 (in millions)*	2000
Net Revenue			
United States	49.69%	50.79%	52.61%
Europe, Middle East, and Africa	27.61	27.24	26.76
Asia Pacific	12.25	11.70	10.62
Americas	5.74	5.68	5.49
Other	4.71	4.59	4.52
Total	100.00%	100.00%	100.00%
Management Pre-tax Income			
United States	96.10%	99.80%	100.55%
Europe, Middle East, and Africa	43.78	41.93	41.00
Asia Pacific	23.46	22.37	15.88
Americas	9.13	8.86	6.93
Other	1.97	4.49	7.50
Corporate	(74.44)	(77.43)	(71.87)
	100.00%	100.00%	100.00%
Additions to Long-lived Assets			
United States	11.97%	14.23%	5.48%
Europe, Middle East, and Africa	9.75	8.25	8.72
Asia Pacific	7.92	16.66	51.00
Americas	1.72	1.61	0.91
Other	27.35	8.28	6.13
Corporate	41.29	50.98	27.76
	100.00%	100.00%	100.00%
Property, Plant and Equipment, Net			
United States	15.14%	16.28%	17.16%
Europe, Middle East, and Africa	13.14	12.86	15.18
Asia Pacific	23.44	24.93	26.93
Americas	0.77	0.95	1.14
Other	6.79	7.01	7.22
Corporate	40.72	37.98	32.36
	100.00%	100.00%	100.00%

*There are some differences due to rounding.

COMPREHENSIVE INCOME

Chapter 4 explained that the categories within accumulated other income are: (1) foreign currency translation adjustments, (2) unrealized holding gains and losses on available-for-sale marketable securities, (3) changes to stockholder's equity resulting from additional minimum pension liability adjustments, and (4) unrealized gains and losses from derivative instruments. Chapter 4 also explained that there is considerable flexibility in reporting comprehensive income. One format uses a single income statement to report net income and comprehensive income. The second format reports comprehensive income in a separate statement of financial activity. The third format reports comprehensive income within the statement of changes in stockholders' equity.

Review the reporting of comprehensive income to determine which items are reported. Nike presents comprehensive income within the statement of changes in stockholders' equity. The only comprehensive income item reported by Nike is foreign currency translation adjustments.

Note that comprehensive income includes items not in net income. Our traditional profitability analysis includes items that related to net income. This excludes other comprehensive income items. Ratios in which you may want to consider including comprehensive income are: (1) return on assets, (2) return on investment, (3) return on total equity, and (4) return on common equity. For

EXHIBIT 8-21   **NIKE, INC.**

Segment Information—Ratio Analysis

Years Ended May 31, 2002, 2001, and 2000

	2002	2001	2000
Management pretax income to net revenue:			
United States	19.89%	19.08%	19.53%
Europe, Middle East, and Africa	16.31	14.95	15.66
Asia Pacific	19.70	18.57	15.29
Americas	16.35	15.14	12.89
Other	4.29	9.50	16.94
Additions to long-lived assets to property, plant and equipment, net:			
United States	13.67%	17.15%	10.67%
Europe, Middle East, and Africa	12.82	12.58	19.18
Asia Pacific	5.84	13.11	63.25
Americas	38.71	33.12	26.52
Other	69.55	23.19	28.32
Corporate	17.52	26.33	28.65

EXHIBIT 8-22   **NIKE, INC.**

Sales and Marketing (in Part)

The table below shows certain information regarding NIKE's United States and international (non-U.S.) revenues for the last three fiscal years.

May 31,	Fiscal 2002	Fiscal 2001	FY02 vs. FY01 % CHG (in millions)	Fiscal 2000	FY01 vs. FY00 % CHG
USA Region					
Footwear	$3,185.0	$3,208.9	(0.7)%	$3,351.2	(4.2)%
Apparel	1,305.3	1,260.3	3.6%	1,154.4	9.2%
Equipment and other	425.7	349.8	21.7%	226.5	54.4%
Total USA	4,916.0	4,819.0	2.0%	4,732.1	1.8%
Europe, Middle East and Africa (EMEA) Region					
Footwear	1,551.8	1,422.8	9.1%	1,309.4	8.7%
Apparel	989.5	976.3	1.4%	933.9	4.5%
Equipment and other	190.2	185.7	2.4%	163.7	13.4%
Total EMEA	2,731.5	2,584.8	5.7%	2,407.0	7.4%
Asia Pacific Region					
Footwear	657.7	632.4	4.0%	557.0	13.5%
Apparel	431.0	374.8	15.0%	321.0	16.8%
Equipment and other	123.0	102.8	19.6%	77.1	33.3%
Total Asia Pacific	1,211.7	1,110.0	9.2%	955.1	16.2%
Americas Region					
Footwear	359.2	355.2	1.1%	343.9	3.3%
Apparel	167.1	152.2	9.8%	137.7	10.5%
Equipment and other	41.8	31.7	31.9%	12.5	153.6%
Total Americas	568.1	539.1	5.4%	494.1	9.1%
Total NIKE brand	9,427.3	9,052.9	4.1%	8,588.3	5.4%
Other brands	465.7	435.9	6.8%	406.8	7.2%
Total Revenues	$9,893.0	$9,488.8	4.3%	$8,995.1	5.5%

EXHIBIT 8-23	**NORD RESOURCES CORP.—1998 ANNUAL REPORT** **Prior Period Adjustment**

Insurance Recovery

The Company had certain amounts of insurance to cover risk of loss on its investment in SRL due to political violence and expropriation of SRL's assets. Under an insurance policy provided by an agency of the United States government, $15,705,000 of coverage was provided for the Company's share of damage to property from political violence. This policy expired on December 31, 1995 and the insurer elected not to renew the coverage. The Company filed a claim under this policy for its 50% share of damage to mine assets resulting from events which began in January 1995. In September 1996, the Company received a $1,500,000 provisional payment from the insurer under this policy. A further claim for the full amount covered by the policy was filed in February 1998, and the balance of $14,205,000 was received in May 1998. These amounts totaling $15,705,000 were recorded as a prior period adjustment to retained earnings in the Company's financial statements as of January 1, 1996.

some firms, these ratios will change substantially. Exhibit 8-24 presents these ratios for Nike. For Nike, there was a moderate change in these profitability ratios.

PRO FORMA FINANCIAL INFORMATION

Pro forma financial information is a hypothetical or projected amount. Synonymous with "what if" analysis, pro forma data indicates what would have happened under specified circumstances.

Used properly, pro forma financial information makes a positive contribution to financial reporting—for example, what would be the net income if additional shares were issued?

Used improperly pro forma financial information can be a negative contribution to financial reporting. For example, releasing pro forma earnings can be misleading if not explained.

It became popular in the United States for companies to release pro forma earnings at approximately the time that financial results were released that used GAAP. Typically how the company arrived at the pro forma earnings was not adequately disclosed. It was inferred that this was the better number for investors to follow. Many investors did make decisions based on the pro forma earnings as opposed to the GAAP earnings.

The Sarbanes-Oxley Act required the Commission (SEC) to adopt rules requiring that if a company publicly discloses non-GAAP financial measures or includes them in a Commission filing:

1. the company must reconcile those non-GAAP financial measures to a company's financial condition and results of operations under GAAP.
2. that any public disclosure of a non-GAAP financial measure not contain an untrue statement of a material fact or omit to state a material fact necessary in order to make the non-GAAP financial measure, in light of circumstances under which it is presented, not misleading.[1]

EXHIBIT 8-24	**NIKE, INC.**

Selected Ratios Considering Comprehensive Income

Year Ended May 31, 2002

	2002	
Ratio	Prior Computation	Including Comprehensive Income
Return on assets	10.90%	10.16%
Return on investment	16.19%	15.15%
Return on total equity	18.22%	16.99%
Return on common equity	18.22%	16.99%

INTERIM REPORTS

Interim reports are an additional source of information on profitability. These are reports that cover fiscal periods of less than one year. The SEC requires that limited financial data be provided on Form 10-Q. The SEC also requires that these companies disclose certain quarterly information in notes to the annual report.

The same reporting principles used for annual reports should be employed for interim reports, with the intent that the interim reporting be an integral part of the annual report. For interim financial reports, timeliness of data offsets lack of detail. Some data included are:

1. Income statement amounts:
   a. Sales or gross revenues
   b. Provision for income taxes
   c. Extraordinary items and tax effect
   d. Cumulative effect of an accounting change
   e. Net income
2. Earnings per share
3. Seasonal information
4. Significant changes in income tax provision or estimate
5. Disposal of segments of business and unusual items material to the period
6. Contingent items
7. Changes in accounting principles or estimates
8. Significant changes in financial position

Interim reports contain more estimates in the financial data than in the annual reports. Interim reports are also unaudited. For these reasons, they are less reliable than annual reports.

Income tax expense is an example of a figure that can require considerable judgment and estimation for the interim period. The objective with the interim income tax expense is to use an annual effective tax rate, which may require considerable estimation. Some reasons for this are foreign tax credits and the tax effect of losses in an interim period.

Interim statements must disclose the seasonal nature of the activities of the firm. It is also recommended that firms that are seasonal in nature supplement their interim report by including information for 12-month periods ended at the interim date for the current and preceding years.

Interim statements can help the analyst determine trends and identify trouble areas before the year-end report is available. The information obtained (such as a lower profit margin) may indicate that trouble is brewing.

Nike included a section called "Selected Quarterly Financial Data" in its annual report. It indicates that the 4th quarter has the highest volume and is most profitable. This would be the months of March, April, and May. Revenue was up in each quarter compared with 2001, except the first quarter. Net income was up in each quarter compared with 2001, except the first quarter.

SUMMARY

Profitability is the ability of a firm to generate earnings. It is measured relative to a number of bases, such as assets, sales, and investment.

The ratios related to profitability covered in this chapter follow:

$$\text{Net Profit Margin} = \frac{\text{Net Income Before Minority Share of Earnings, Equity Income and Nonrecurring Items}}{\text{Net Sales}}$$

$$\text{Total Asset Turnover} = \frac{\text{Net Sales}}{\text{Average Total Assets}}$$

$$\text{Return on Assets} = \frac{\text{Net Income Before Minority Share of Earnings and Nonrecurring Items}}{\text{Average Total Assets}}$$

$$\frac{\text{Net Income Before Minority Share of Earnings and Nonrecurring Items}}{\text{Average Total Assets}} = \frac{\text{Net Income Before Minority Share of Earnings and Nonrecurring Items}}{\text{Net Sales}} \times \frac{\text{Net Sales}}{\text{Average Total Assets}}$$

$$\text{Operating Income Margin} = \frac{\text{Operating Income}}{\text{Net Sales}}$$

$$\text{Operating Asset Turnover} = \frac{\text{Net Sales}}{\text{Average Operating Assets}}$$

$$\text{Return on Operating Assets} = \frac{\text{Operating Income}}{\text{Average Operating Assets}}$$

$$\text{DuPont Return on Operating Assets} = \text{Operating Income Margin} \times \text{Operating Asset Turnover}$$

$$\text{Sales to Fixed Assets} = \frac{\text{Net Sales}}{\text{Average Net Fixed Assets (Exclude Construction in Progress)}}$$

$$\text{Return on Investment} = \frac{\text{Net Income Before Minority Share of Earnings and Nonrecurring Items} + [(\text{Interest Expense}) \times (1 - \text{Tax Rate})]}{\text{Average (Long-Term Liabilities + Equity)}}$$

$$\text{Return on Total Equity} = \frac{\text{Net Income Before Nonrecurring Items} - \text{Dividends on Redeemable Preferred Stock}}{\text{Average Total Equity}}$$

$$\text{Return on Common Equity} = \frac{\text{Net Income Before Nonrecurring Items} - \text{Preferred Dividends}}{\text{Average Common Equity}}$$

$$\text{Gross Profit Margin} = \frac{\text{Gross Profit}}{\text{Net Sales}}$$

To the Net

1. Go to the SEC site (http://www.sec.gov). Under Filings & Forms (Edgar), click on "Search for Company Filings." Click on "Search Companies and Filings." Under company name enter "Hershey Foods." Select the 10-K405 submitted March 15, 2002.
   a. Determine the consolidated statements of net income for the years ended December 31, 2001, 2000, and 1999.
   b. Determine the cash dividends paid per share—common stock—for the years ended December 31, 2001, 2000, and 1999.

2. Go to the SEC site (http://www.sec.gov). Under Filings & Forms (Edgar), click on "Search for Company Filings." Click on "Search for Companies and Filings." Under company name enter "General Electric." Select the 10-K405 filed March 8, 2002.
   a. What is the standard industrial classification for General Electric?
   b. Determine the earnings before accounting changes for the years ended December 31, 2001, 2000, and 1999.
   c. 1. Briefly describe the accounting change for the year ended December 31, 2001.
      2. Describe the inconsistency in reported earnings because of the accounting change.

3. a. Go to http://www.walmart.com. Determine the following for fiscal year ended January 31, 2002 and 2001 (in millions).

	Fiscal January 31, 2002	Fiscal January 31, 2001
Net sales		
Cost of sales		
Gross profit		

b. Go to the SEC site (http://www.sec.gov). Under Filings & Forms (Edgar), click on "Search for Company Filings." Click on "Search Companies and Filings." Under company name enter "Kmart." Select the 10-K submitted May 15, 2002. Determine the following for fiscal year ended January 30, 2002 and January 31, 2001 (in millions).

	Year Ended* January 31, 2002	Year Ended** January 31, 2001
Net sales		
Cost of sales		
Gross profit		

*Included 52 weeks
**Included 53 weeks

c. Which firm appears to have performed better? Comment.

Questions

Q 8-1. Profits might be compared to sales, assets, or stockholders' equity. Why might all three bases be used? Will trends in these ratios always move in the same direction?

Q 8-2. What is the advantage of segregating extraordinary items in the income statement?

Q 8-3. If profits as a percent of sales decline, what can be said about expenses?

Q 8-4. Would you expect the profit margin in a quality jewelry store to differ from that of a grocery store? Comment.

Q 8-5. The ratio return on assets has net income in the numerator and total assets in the denominator. Explain how each part of the ratio could cause return on assets to fall.

Q 8-6. What is DuPont analysis, and how does it aid in financial analysis?

Q 8-7. How does operating income differ from net income? How do operating assets differ from total assets? What is the advantage in removing nonoperating items from the DuPont analysis?

Q 8-8. Why are equity earnings usually greater than cash flow generated from the investment? How can these equity earnings distort profitability analysis?

Q 8-9. Explain how return on assets could decline, given an increase in net profit margin.

Q 8-10. How is return on investment different from return on total equity? How does return on total equity differ from return on common equity?

Q 8-11. What is return on investment? What are some of the types of measures for return on investment? Why is the following ratio preferred?

$$\frac{\text{Net Income Before Minority Share of Earnings and Nonrecurring Items} + [(\text{Interest Expense}) \times (1 - \text{Tax Rate})]}{\text{Average (Long-Term Debt} + \text{Equity)}}$$

Why is the interest multiplied by (1 – Tax Rate)?

Q 8-12. G. Herrich Company and Thomas, Inc. are department stores. For the current year, they reported a net income after tax of $400,000 and $600,000, respectively. Is Thomas, Inc. a more profitable company than G. Herrich Company? Discuss.

Q 8-13. Since interim reports are not audited, they are not meaningful. Comment.

Q 8-14. Speculate on why accounting standards do not mandate full financial statements in interim reports.

Q 8-15.   Why may comprehensive income fluctuate substantially more than net income?

Q 8-16.   Why can pro forma financial information be misleading?

Problems

P 8-1.   Ahl Enterprise lists the following data for 2004 and 2003:

	2004	2003
Net income	$ 52,500	$ 40,000
Net sales	1,050,000	1,000,000
Average total assets	230,000	200,000
Average common equity	170,000	160,000

Required   Calculate the net profit margin, return on assets, total asset turnover, and return on common equity for both years. Comment on the results. (For return on assets and total asset turnover, use end-of-year total assets; for return on common equity, use end-of-year common equity.)

P 8-2.   Income statement data for Starr Canning Corporation are as follows:

	2004	2003
Sales	$1,400,000	$1,200,000
Cost of goods sold	850,000	730,000
Selling expenses	205,000	240,000
General expenses	140,000	100,000
Income tax expense	82,000	50,000

Required   a.   Prepare an income statement in comparative form, stating each item for both years as a percent of sales (vertical common-size analysis).
b.   Comment on the findings in (a).

P 8-3.   The balance sheet for Schultz Bone Company at December 31, 2004, had the following account balances:

Total current liabilities (non-interest-bearing)	$450,000
Bonds payable, 6% (issued in 1982; due in 2010)	750,000
Preferred stock, 5%, $100 par	300,000
Common stock, $10 par	750,000
Premium on common stock	150,000
Retained earnings	600,000

Income before income tax was $200,000, and income taxes were $80,000 for the current year.

Required   Calculate each of the following:
a.   Return on assets (using ending assets)
b.   Return on total equity (using ending total equity)
c.   Return on common equity (using ending common equity)
d.   Times interest earned

P 8-4.   Revenue and expense data for Vent Molded Plastics and for the plastics industry as a whole follow.

	Vent Molded Plastics	**Plastics Industry**
Sales	$462,000	100.3%
Sales returns	4,500	.3
Cost of goods sold	330,000	67.1
Selling expenses	43,000	10.1
General expenses	32,000	7.9
Other income	1,800	.4
Other expense	7,000	1.3
Income tax	22,000	5.5

Required   Convert the dollar figures for Vent Molded Plastics into percentages based on net sales. Compare these with the industry average, and comment on your findings.

P 8-5.   Day Ko Incorporated presented the following comparative income statements for 2004 and 2003:

| | For the Years Ended | |
	2004	2003
Net sales	$1,589,150	$1,294,966
Other income	22,334	20,822
	1,611,484	1,315,788
Costs and expenses:		
Material and manufacturing costs of products sold	651,390	466,250
Research and development	135,314	113,100
General and selling	526,680	446,110
Interest	18,768	11,522
Other	15,570	7,306
	1,347,722	1,044,288
Earnings before income taxes and minority equity	263,762	271,500
Provision for income taxes	114,502	121,740
Earnings before minority equity	149,260	149,760
Minority equity in earnings	11,056	12,650
Net earnings	$ 138,204	$ 137,110

Other relevant financial information follows:

| | For the Years Ended | |
	2004	2003
Average common shares issued	29,580	29,480
Total long-term debt	$ 209,128	$ 212,702
Total stockholders' equity (all common)	810,292	720,530
Total assets	1,437,636	1,182,110
Operating assets	1,411,686	1,159,666
Dividends per share	1.96	1.86
Stock price (December 31)	53 3/4	76 1/8

Required   a.   How did 2004 net sales compare to 2003?
 b.   How did 2004 net earnings compare to 2003?
 c.   Calculate the following for 2004 and 2003:
   1. Net profit margin
   2. Return on assets (using ending assets)
   3. Total asset turnover (using ending assets)
   4. DuPont analysis
   5. Operating income margin
   6. Return on operating assets (using ending assets)
   7. Operating asset turnover (using ending assets)
   8. DuPont analysis with operating ratios
   9. Return on investment (using ending liabilities and equity)
   10. Return on equity (using ending common equity)
 d.   Based on the previous computations, summarize the trend in profitability for this firm.

P 8-6.   Dorex, Inc. presented the following comparative income statements for 2004, 2003, and 2002:

| | For the Years Ended | | |
	2004	2003	2002
Net sales	$1,600,000	$1,300,000	$1,200,000
Other income	22,100	21,500	21,000
	1,622,100	1,321,500	1,221,000
Costs and expenses:			
Material and manufacturing costs of products sold	740,000	624,000	576,000
Research and development	90,000	78,000	71,400
General and selling	600,000	500,500	465,000
Interest	19,000	18,200	17,040
Other	14,000	13,650	13,800
	1,463,000	1,234,350	1,143,240

| | For the Years Ended | | |
	2004	2003	2002
Earnings before income taxes and minority equity	$159,100	$87,150	$77,760
Provision for income taxes	62,049	35,731	32,659
Earnings before minority equity	97,051	51,419	45,101
Minority equity in earnings	10,200	8,500	8,100
Net earnings	86,851	42,919	37,001

| | For the Years Ended | | |
	2004	2003	2002
Other relevant financial information:			
Average common shares issued	29,610	29,100	28,800
Average long-term debt	$ 211,100	$ 121,800	$ 214,000
Average stockholders' equity (all common)	811,200	790,100	770,000
Average total assets	1,440,600	1,220,000	1,180,000
Average operating assets	1,390,200	1,160,000	1,090,000

Required a. Calculate the following for 2004, 2003, and 2002:
1. Net profit margin
2. Return on assets
3. Total asset turnover
4. DuPont analysis
5. Operating income margin
6. Return on operating assets
7. Operating asset turnover
8. DuPont analysis with operating ratios
9. Return on investment
10. Return on total equity

b. Based on the previous computations, summarize the trend in profitability for this firm.

P 8-7. Selected financial data for Squid Company are as follows:

	2004	2003	2002
Summary of operations:			
Net sales	$1,002,100	$980,500	$900,000
Cost of products sold	520,500	514,762	477,000
Selling, administrative, and general expenses	170,200	167,665	155,700
Nonoperating income	9,192	8,860	6,500
Interest expense	14,620	12,100	11,250
Earnings before income taxes	287,588	277,113	249,550
Provision for income taxes	116,473	113,616	105,560
Net earnings	171,115	163,497	143,990
Financial information:			
Working capital	$ 190,400	$189,000	$180,000
Average property, plant, and equipment	302,500	281,000	173,000
Average total assets	839,000	770,000	765,000
Average long-term debt	120,000	112,000	101,000
Average stockholders' equity	406,000	369,500	342,000

Required a. Compute the following for 2004, 2003, and 2002:
1. Net profit margin
2. Return on assets
3. Total asset turnover
4. DuPont analysis
5. Return on investment
6. Return on total equity
7. Sales to fixed assets

b. Discuss your findings in (a).

P 8-8. The D. H. Muller Company presented the following income statement in its 2004 annual report.

(Dollars in thousands except per-share amounts)	**For the Years Ended**		
	2004	**2003**	**2002**
Net sales	$297,580	$256,360	$242,150
Cost of sales	206,000	176,300	165,970
Gross profit	91,580	80,060	76,180
Selling, administrative, and other expenses	65,200	57,200	56,000
Operating earnings	26,380	22,860	20,180
Interest expense	(5,990)	(5,100)	(4,000)
Other deductions, net	(320)	(1,100)	(800)
Earnings before income taxes, minority interests, and extraordinary items	20,070	16,660	15,380
Income taxes	(8,028)	(6,830)	(6,229)
Net earnings of subsidiaries applicable to minority interests	(700)	(670)	(668)
Earnings before extraordinary items	11,342	9,160	8,483
Extraordinary items:			
Gain on sale of investment, net of federal and state income taxes of $520	—	1,050	—
Loss due to damages to South American facilities, net of minority interest of $430	—	(1,600)	—
Net earnings	$ 11,342	$ 8,610	$ 8,483

	2004	**2003**	**2002**
Earnings per common share:			
Earnings before extraordinary items	$2.20	$1.82	$1.65
Extraordinary items	—	(.06)	—
Net earnings	$2.20	$1.76	$1.65

The asset side of the balance sheet is summarized as follows:

(Dollars in thousands)	**2004**	**2003**	**2002**
Current assets	$ 89,800	$ 84,500	$ 83,100
Property, plant, and equipment	45,850	40,300	39,800
Other assets (including investments, deposits, deferred charges, and intangibles)	10,110	12,200	13,100
Total assets	$145,760	$137,000	$136,000

Required   a.   Based on these data, compute the following for 2004, 2003, and 2002:
  1. Net profit margin
  2. Return on assets (using total assets)
  3. Total asset turnover (using total assets)
  4. DuPont analysis
  5. Operating income margin
  6. Return on operating assets (using end-of-year operating assets)
  7. Operating asset turnover (using end-of-year operating assets)
  8. DuPont analysis with operating ratios
  9. Gross profit margin
  b.   Discuss your findings.

P 8-9.   The following financial information is for the A. Galler Company for 2004, 2003, and 2002:

	2004	**2003**	**2002**
Income before interest	$4,400,000	$4,000,000	$3,300,000
Interest expense	800,000	600,000	550,000
Income before tax	3,600,000	3,400,000	2,750,000
Tax	1,500,000	1,450,000	1,050,000
Net income	$2,100,000	$1,950,000	$1,700,000

	2004	2003	2002
Current liabilities	$ 2,600,000	$2,300,000	$2,200,000
Long-term debt	7,000,000	6,200,000	5,800,000
Preferred stock (14%)	100,000	100,000	100,000
Common equity	10,000,000	9,000,000	8,300,000

Required a. For 2004, 2003, and 2002, determine the following:
1. Return on assets (using end-of-year total assets)
2. Return on investment (using end-of-year long-term liabilities and equity)
3. Return on total equity (using ending total equity)
4. Return on common equity (using ending common equity)

b. Discuss the trend in these profit figures.

c. Discuss the benefit from the use of long-term debt and preferred stock.

P 8-10. The Dexall Company recently had a fire in its store. Management must determine the inventory loss for the insurance company. Since the firm did not have perpetual inventory records, the insurance company has suggested that it might accept an estimate using the gross profit test. The beginning inventory, as determined from the last financial statements, was $10,000. Purchase invoices indicate purchases of $100,000. Credit and cash sales during the period were $120,000. Last year, the gross profit for the firm was 40%, which was also the industry average.

Required a. Based on these data, estimate the inventory loss.

b. If the industry average gross profit was 50%, why might the insurance company be leery of the estimated loss?

P 8-11. Transactions affect various financial statement amounts.

	Net Profit	Retained Earnings	Total Stockholders' Equity
a. A stock dividend is declared and paid.	0	–	0
b. Merchandise is purchased on credit.	0	0	0
c. Marketable securities are sold above cost.	+	+	+
d. Accounts receivable are collected.	0	0	0
e. A cash dividend is declared and paid.	0	–	–
f. Treasury stock is purchased and recorded at cost.	0	0	–
g. Treasury stock is sold above cost.	0	+/0	+
h. Common stock is sold.	0	0	+
i. A fixed asset is sold for less than book value.	–	–	–
j. Bonds are converted into common stock.	+	+	+

Required Indicate the effects of the previous transactions on each of the following: net profit, retained earnings, total stockholders' equity. Use + to indicate an increase, – to indicate a decrease, and 0 to indicate no effect.

P 8-12. Consecutive five-year balance sheets and income statements of the Mary Lou Szabo Corporation are as follows:

MARY LOU SZABO CORPORATION
Balance Sheets
December 31, 2000, through December 31, 2004

(Dollars in thousands)	2004	2003	2002	2001	2000
Assets					
Current assets:					
Cash	$ 24,000	$ 25,000	$ 26,000	$ 24,000	$ 26,000
Accounts receivable, net	120,000	122,000	128,000	129,000	130,000
Inventories	135,000	138,000	141,000	140,000	137,000
Total current assets	279,000	285,000	295,000	293,000	293,000
Property, plant and equipment, net	500,000	491,000	485,000	479,000	470,000
Goodwill	80,000	85,000	90,000	95,000	100,000
Total assets	$ 859,000	$ 861,000	$ 870,000	$ 867,000	$ 863,000

Liabilities and Stockholders' Equity

Current liabilities:

	2004	2003	2002	2001	2000
Accounts payable	$ 180,000	$ 181,000	$ 181,500	$ 183,000	$ 184,000
Income taxes	14,000	14,500	14,000	12,000	12,500
Total current liabilities	194,000	195,500	195,500	195,000	196,500
Long-term debt	65,000	67,500	79,500	82,000	107,500
Redeemable preferred stock	80,000	80,000	80,000	80,000	—
Total liabilities	339,000	343,000	355,000	357,000	304,000
Stockholders' equity:					
Preferred stock	70,000	70,000	70,000	70,000	120,000
Common stock	350,000	350,000	350,000	350,000	350,000
Paid-in capital in excess of par, common stock	15,000	15,000	15,000	15,000	15,000
Retained earnings	85,000	83,000	80,000	75,000	74,000
Total stockholders' equity	520,000	518,000	515,000	510,000	559,000
Total liabilities and stockholders' equity	$ 859,000	$ 861,000	$ 870,000	$ 867,000	$ 863,000

MARY LOU SZABO CORPORATION
Statement of Earnings
Years Ended December 31, 2000–2004

(Dollars in thousands)	2004	2003	2002	2001	2000
Net sales	$ 980,000	$ 960,000	$ 940,000	$ 900,000	$ 880,000
Cost of goods sold	625,000	616,000	607,000	580,000	566,000
Gross profit	355,000	344,000	333,000	320,000	314,000
Selling and administrative expense	(240,000)	(239,000)	(238,000)	(239,000)	(235,000)
Interest expense	(6,500)	(6,700)	(8,000)	(8,100)	(11,000)
Earnings from continuing operations before income taxes	108,500	98,300	87,000	72,900	68,000
Income taxes	35,800	33,400	29,200	21,700	23,100
Earnings from continuing operations	72,700	64,900	57,800	51,200	44,900
Extraordinary loss, net of taxes	—	—	—	—	(30,000)
Net earnings	$ 72,700	$ 64,900	$ 57,800	$ 51,200	$ 14,900
Earnings (loss) per share:					
Continuing operations	$2.00	$1.80	$1.62	$1.46	$1.28
Extraordinary loss	—	—	—	—	(.85)
Net earnings per share	$2.00	$1.80	$1.62	$1.46	$ .43

Note: Dividends on preferred stock were as follows:

Redeemable preferred stock		Preferred stock	
2001–2004	$6,400	2001–2004	$6,300
		2000	$10,800

Required   a.   Compute the following for the years ended December 31, 2000–2004:
1. Net profit margin
2. Total asset turnover
3. Return on assets
4. DuPont return on assets
5. Operating income margin
6. Operating asset turnover
7. Return on operating assets
8. DuPont return on operating assets
9. Sales to fixed assets
10. Return on investment
11. Return on total equity

12. Return on common equity
13. Gross profit margin
   Note: For ratios that call for using average balance sheet figures, compute the rate using average balance sheet figures and year-end balance sheet figures.
b. Briefly comment on profitability and trends indicated in profitability. Also comment on the difference in results between using the average balance sheet figures and year-end figures.

Case 8-1 Jeff's Self-Service Station

John Dearden and his wife, Patricia, have been taking an annual vacation to Stowe, Vermont, each summer. They like the area very much and would like to retire someday in this vicinity. While in Stowe during the summer, they notice a "for sale" sign in front of a self-service station. John is 55 and is no longer satisfied with commuting to work in New York City. He decides to inquire about the asking price of the station. He is aware that Stowe is considered a good vacation area during the entire year, especially when the ski season is in progress.

On inquiry, John determines that the asking price of the station is $70,000, which includes two pumps, a small building, and 1/8 acre of land.

John asks to see some financial statements and is shown profit and loss statements for 2004 and 2003 that have been prepared for tax purposes by a local accountant.

JEFF'S SELF-SERVICE STATION
Statement of Earnings
For the Years Ended December 31, 2004 and 2003

	2004	2003
Revenue	$185,060	$175,180
Expenses:		
Cost of goods sold	160,180	153,280
Depreciation (a)	1,000	1,000
Real estate and property taxes	1,100	1,050
Repairs and maintenance	1,470	1,200
Other expenses	680	725
Total expenses	164,430	157,255
Profit	$ 20,630	$ 17,925

(a) Building and equipment cost	$30,000
Original estimated life	30 years
Depreciation per year	$1,000

John is also given an appraiser's report on the property. The land is appraised at $50,000, and the equipment and building are valued at $20,000. The equipment and building are estimated to have a useful life of 10 years.

The station has been operated by Jeff Szabo without additional help. He estimates that if help were hired to operate the station, it would cost $10,000 per year. John anticipates that he will be able to operate the station without additional help. John intends to incorporate. The anticipated tax rate is 50%.

Required
a. Determine the indicated return on investment if John Dearden purchases the station. Include only financial data that will be recorded on the books. Consider 2004 and 2003 to be representative years for revenue and expenses.
b. Determine the indicated return on investment if help were hired to operate the station.
c. Why is there a difference between the rates of return in part (a) and part (b)? Discuss.
d. Determine the cash flow for 2005 if John serves as the manager and 2005 turns out to be the same as 2004. Do not include the cost of the hired help. No inventory is on hand at the date of purchase, but an inventory of $10,000 is on hand at the end of the year. There are no receivables or liabilities.
e. Indicate some other considerations that should be analyzed.
f. Should John purchase the station?

Case 8-2

The Tale of the Segments

The segment information from the 2001 Annual Report of Johnson Controls, Inc. follows:

14 SEGMENT INFORMATION

Business Segments The Company has two operating segments, the Automotive Systems Group and the Controls Group, which also constitute its reportable segments. The Automotive Systems Group designs and manufactures products for motorized vehicles. The segment supplies interior systems and batteries for cars, light trucks and vans. The Controls Group installs and services facility control systems and provides broad-based management services for the non-residential buildings market.

The accounting policies applicable to the reportable segments are the same as those described in the Summary of Significant Accounting Policies. Management evaluates the performance of the segments based primarily on operating income. Operating revenues and expenses are allocated to business segments in determining segment operating income. Items excluded from the determination of segment operating income include interest income and expense, equity in earnings of partially-owned affiliates, gains and losses from sales of businesses and long-term assets, foreign currency gains and losses, and other miscellaneous expense. Unallocated assets are corporate cash and cash equivalents, investments in partially-owned affiliates and other non-operating assets.

Financial information relating to the Company's reportable segments is as follows:

In millions	Year ended September 30,		
	2001	2000	1999
Net Sales			
Automotive Systems Group	$13,620.5	$12,738.5	$12,075.1
Controls Group	4,806.7	4,416.1	4,064.3
Total	$18,427.2	$17,154.6	$16,139.4
Operating Income			
Automotive Systems Group	$ 720.5	$ 765.2	$ 682.4
Controls Group	240.6	199.8	172.5
Total	$ 961.1	$ 965.0	$ 854.9
Assets (Year-End)			
Automotive Systems Group	$ 7,429.1	$ 7,309.9	$ 6,430.5
Controls Group	1,880.0	1,621.0	1,610.2
Unallocated	602.4	497.1	573.5
Total	$ 9,911.5	$ 9,428.0	$ 8,614.2
Depreciation/Amortization			
Automotive Systems Group	$ 450.0	$ 400.1	$ 386.1
Controls Group	65.9	61.7	59.5
Total	$ 515.9	$ 461.8	$ 445.6
Capital Expenditures			
Automotive Systems Group	$ 549.6	$ 468.8	$ 438.0
Controls Group	71.9	77.9	76.0
Total	$ 621.5	$ 546.7	$ 514.0

The Company has significant sales to the automotive industry. DaimlerChrysler AG accounted for 14 percent of the Company's net sales in 2001 and 16 percent of the Company's net sales in 2000 and 1999; Ford Motor Company accounted for 11 percent in 2001 and 13 percent in 2000 and 1999; and General Motors Corporation accounted for 14 percent in 2001 and 2000 and 13 percent in 1999. Approximately 74 percent of the Company's 2001 net sales to these customers were based in North America, 23 percent were European sales and 3 percent were attributable to sales in other foreign markets. As of September 30, 2001, the Company had accounts receivable totaling $781 million from these customers.

Geographic Segments Financial information relating to the Company's operations by geographic area is as follows:

In millions	Year ended September 30,		
	2001	**2000**	**1999**
Net Sales			
North America	**$11,584.1**	$11,325.1	$10,465.4
Europe	**4,711.6**	4,799.7	4,872.3
Other foreign	**2,131.5**	1,029.8	801.7
Total	**$18,427.2**	$17,154.6	$16,139.4
Long-Lived Assets (Year-End)			
North America	**$ 1,510.3**	$ 1,389.1	$ 1,282.9
Europe	**610.9**	565.5	589.1
Other foreign	**258.6**	350.4	124.0
Total	**$ 2,379.8**	$ 2,305.0	$ 1,996.0

The Company's net sales in Europe declined during the three-year period presented above due to the negative effect of currency translation rates.

Net sales attributed to geographic locations are based on the location of the assets producing the sales. Long-lived assets by geographic location consist of net property, plant and equipment.

Required a. Non-geographic
   1. Prepare horizontal common-size analysis for net sales. Use 1999 as the base. Comment on the results.
   2. Prepare horizontal common-size analysis for operating income. Use 1999 as the base. Comment on the results.
   3. Prepare horizontal common-size analysis for capital expenditures. Use 1999 as the base. Comment on the results.
   4. Prepare vertical common-size analysis for net sales, 1999–2001. Use total as the base. Comment on the results.

   b. Use geographic segments
   1. Prepare horizontal common-size analysis for net sales. Use 1999 as the base. Comment on the results.
   2. Prepare vertical common-size analysis for net sales, 1999–2001. Use total as the base. Comment on the results.
   3. Prepare horizontal common-size analysis for long-lived assets. Use 1999 as the base. Comment on the results.
   4. Prepare vertical common-size analysis for long-lived assets, 1999–2001. Use total as the base. Comment on the results.

Case 8-3

The Story of Starbucks—In Segments

Starbucks presented the following note in their annual report:

Note 18: Segment Reporting

The Company is organized into a number of business units which correspond to the Company's operating segments.

The Company's North American retail business unit sells coffee and other beverages, whole bean coffees, complementary food, hardware and merchandise through Company-operated retail stores in the United States and Canada.

At the beginning of fiscal 2001, the Company combined its foodservice and domestic retail store licensing operations to form the Business Alliances business unit. As a result of this internal reorganization and the manner in which the operations of foodservice and domestic retail store licensing are measured and evaluated as one combined business unit, the Company's management determined that separate segment reporting of Business Alliances is appropriate under SFAS No. 131, "Disclosures about Segments of an Enterprise and Related Information." All prior period disclosures are restated as if Business Alliances had always been a separately reported segment.

The Company operates through several other business units, each of which is managed and evaluated independently. These operations include international retail store licensing agreements, grocery channel licensing agreements, warehouse club accounts, direct-to-consumer marketing channels, joint ventures, international Company-operated retail stores and other initiatives related to the Company's core businesses.

Revenues from these segments include both sales to unaffiliated customers and sales between segments, which are accounted for on a basis consistent with sales to unaffiliated customers. Intersegment revenues, consisting primarily of product sales to subsidiaries and equity method investees, and other intersegment transactions have been eliminated on the accompanying consolidated financial statements.

The accounting policies of the operating segments are the same as those described in the summary of significant accounting policies in Note 1. Operating income represents earnings before "Interest and other income, net," "Internet-related investment losses" and "Income taxes." No allocations of overhead, interest or income taxes are made to the segments. Identifiable assets by segment are those assets used in the Company's operations in each segment. General corporate assets include cash and investments, unallocated assets of the corporate headquarters and roasting facilities, deferred taxes and certain intangibles. Management evaluates performance of the segments based on direct product sales and operating costs.

The tables below present information by operating segment (in thousands):

Fiscal year ended	Sept. 30, 2001	Oct. 1, 2000	Oct.3, 1999
REVENUES:			
North American retail	$2,086,354	$1,734,929	$1,375,018
Business Alliances	193,574	160,812	126,888
All other business units	419,843	305,080	200,399
Intersegment revenues	(50,791)	(23,207)	(15,477)
Total revenues	$2,648,980	$2,177,614	$1,686,828
EARNINGS BEFORE INCOME TAXES:			
North American retail	$ 336,434	$ 249,924	$ 209,338
Business Alliances	50,165	43,777	33,098
All other business units	70,116	53,323	22,900
Unallocated corporate expenses	(174,288)	(134,902)	(107,460)
Intersegment eliminations	(1,333)	130	(1,165)
Operating income	281,094	212,252	156,711
Interest and other income, net	10,768	7,110	7,315
Internet-related investment losses	(2,940)	(58,792)	—
Earnings before income taxes	$ 288,922	$ 160,570	$ 164,026
DEPRECIATION AND AMORTIZATION:			
North American retail	$ 115,061	$ 94,312	$ 72,252
Business Alliances	5,278	3,547	2,561
All other business units	17,768	10,117	5,205
Unallocated corporate expenses	25,394	22,256	17,779
Total depreciation and amortization	$ 163,501	$ 130,232	$ 97,797
INCOME FROM EQUITY METHOD INVESTEES:			
All other business units	$ 17,556	$ 15,139	$ 2,318
Intersegment eliminations	11,059	5,161	874
Total income from equity method investees	$ 28,615	$ 20,300	$ 3,192

	Sept. 30, 2001	Oct. 1, 2000
IDENTIFIABLE ASSETS:		
North American retail	$ 873,306	$ 664,773
Business Alliances	57,578	52,596
All other business units	217,027	111,521
General corporate assets	703,128	662,656
Total assets	$1,851,039	$1,491,546

The following tables represent information by geographic area (in thousands):

	Sept. 30, 2001	Oct. 1, 2000	Oct. 3, 1999
REVENUES FROM EXTERNAL CUSTOMERS:			
United States	$2,301,013	$1,910,092	$1,467,410
Foreign countries	347,967	267,522	219,418
Total	$2,648,980	$2,177,614	$1,686,828

Revenues from foreign countries are based on the location of the customers and consist primarily of retail revenues from Canada and the United Kingdom as well as specialty revenues generated from product sales to its international licensees. No customer accounts for 10% or more of the Company's revenues.

	Sept. 30, 2001	Oct. 1, 2000
LONG-LIVED ASSETS:		
United States	$ 977,125	$ 819,200
Foreign countries	158,659	111,559
Total	$1,135,784	$ 930,759

Assets attributed to foreign countries are based on the country in which those assets are located.

Required

a. Using operating segment
1. Prepare horizontal common-size analysis for net sales. Use 1999 as the base. Comment on the results.
2. Prepare horizontal common-size analysis for earnings before income taxes. Use 1999 as the base (only include North American retail, business alliances, and all other business units). Comment on the results.
3. Relate depreciation and amortization to identifiable assets (use years 2000 and 2001). Comment on the results.

b. Using geographic area
1. Prepare horizontal common-size analysis of revenues from external customers. Use 1999 as the base. Comment on the results.
2. Prepare vertical common-size analysis of long-lived assets for 2000 and 2001. Use total as the base. Comment on the results.

Case 8-4 Tide, Pampers, and Etc.

The consolidated statements of earnings and balance sheets are presented for The Procter & Gamble Company and subsidiaries.

Consolidated Statements of Earnings

	Year ended June 30,		
Amounts in Millions Except Per Share Amounts	1998	1997	1996
Net Sales	$37,154	$35,764	$35,284
Cost of products sold	21,064	20,510	20,938
Marketing, research and administrative expenses	10,035	9,766	9,531
Operating Income	6,055	5,488	4,815
Interest expense	548	457	484
Other income, net	201	218	338
Earnings Before Income Taxes	5,708	5,249	4,669
Income taxes	1,928	1,834	1,623
Net Earnings	$ 3,780	$ 3,415	$ 3,046
Basic Net Earnings Per Common Share	$2.74	$2.43	$2.14
Diluted Net Earnings Per Common Share	$2.56	$2.28	$2.01
Dividends Per Common Share	$1.01	$.90	$.80

Consolidated Balance Sheets

Amounts in Millions Except Per Share Amounts	June 30, 1998	1997
ASSETS		
Current Assets		
Cash and cash equivalents	$ 1,549	$ 2,350
Investment securities	857	760
Accounts receivable	2,781	2,738
Inventories		
Materials and supplies	1,225	1,131
Work in process	343	228
Finished goods	1,716	1,728
Deferred income taxes	595	661
Prepaid expenses and other current assets	1,511	1,190
Total Current Assets	10,577	10,786
Property, Plant and Equipment		
Buildings	3,660	3,409
Machinery and equipment	15,953	14,646
Land	539	570
	20,152	18,625
Accumulated depreciation	(7,972)	(7,249)
Total Property, Plant and Equipment	12,180	11,376
Goodwill and Other Intangible Assets		
Goodwill	7,023	3,915
Trademarks and other intangible assets	1,157	1,085
	8,180	5,000
Accumulated depreciation	(1,169)	(1,051)
Total Goodwill and Other Intangible Assets	7,011	3,949
Other Non-Current Assets	1,198	1,433
Total Assets	$30,966	$27,544
LIABILITIES AND SHAREHOLDERS' EQUITY		
Current Liabilities		
Accounts payable	$ 2,051	$ 2,203
Accrued and other liabilities	3,942	3,802
Taxes payable	976	944
Debt due within one year	2,281	849
Total Current Liabilities	9,250	7,798
Long-Term Debt	5,765	4,143
Deferred Income Taxes	428	559
Other Non-Current Liabilities	3,287	2,998
Total Liabilities	18,730	15,498
Shareholders' Equity		
Convertible Class A preferred stock, stated value $1 per share (600 shares authorized)	1,821	1,859
Non-Voting Class B preferred stock, stated value $1 per share (200 shares authorized; none issued)	—	—
Common stock, stated value $1 per share (5,000 shares authorized; shares outstanding: 1998—1,337.4 and 1997—1,350.8)	1,337	1,351
Additional paid-in capital	907	559
Reserve for employee stock ownership plan debt retirement	(1,616)	(1,634)
Accumulated other comprehensive income	(1,357)	(819)
Retained earnings	11,144	10,730
Total Shareholders' Equity	12,236	12,046
Total Liabilities and Shareholders' Equity	$30,966	$27,544

Note: Preferred dividends, net of tax benefit, of $104 in 1998 and 1997.

Required   a.   Compute the following for 1998 and 1997:
1. Net profit margin
2. Total asset turnover (Use year-end assets.)
3. Return on assets (Use year-end assets.)
4. Operating income margin
5. Return on operating assets (Use year-end assets.)
6. Sales to fixed assets (Use year-end fixed assets.)
7. Return on investment (Use year-end balance sheets accounts.)
8. Return on total equity (Use year-end equity.)
9. Return on common equity (Use year-end common equity.)
10. Gross profit margin

b.   Comment on trends in (a).

Case 8-5   **Vehicles and Housing**

The consolidated statements of income and retained earnings and the balance sheet are presented for Coachmen Industries, Inc.

Consolidated Statements of Income and Retained Earnings

| | For the years ended December 31, | | |
	1998	1997	1996
Net sales	$756,029,526	$661,591,185	$606,474,128
Cost of goods sold	646,118,708	568,836,172	517,966,127
Gross profit	109,910,818	92,755,013	88,508,001
Operating expenses:			
Selling and delivery	35,973,828	31,605,666	27,719,131
General and administrative	28,009,137	25,889,028	21,116,814
	63,982,965	57,494,694	48,835,945
Operating income	45,927,853	35,260,319	39,672,056
Nonoperating income (expense):			
Interest expense	(1,738,608)	(2,544,021)	(1,572,092)
Investment income	4,831,102	4,975,360	1,615,442
Gain on sale of properties, net	46,302	137,246	726,023
Other income, net	1,223,959	996,720	1,041,401
	4,362,755	3,565,305	1,810,774
Income before income taxes and cumulative effect of accounting change	50,290,608	38,825,624	41,482,830
Income taxes	17,228,000	14,063,000	14,146,000
Income before cumulative effect of accounting change	33,062,608	24,762,624	27,336,830
Cumulative effect of accounting change for Company-owned life insurance policies	—	—	2,293,983
Net income	33,062,608	24,762,624	29,630,813
Retained earnings, beginning of year	115,984,289	94,670,593	67,824,816
Cash dividends (per common share: 1998—$.20, 1997—$.20 and 1996—$.185)	(3,432,903)	(3,448,928)	(2,785,036)
Retained earnings, end of year	$145,613,994	$115,984,289	$ 94,670,593
Earnings per common share:			
Income before cumulative effect of accounting change:			
Basic	$1.93	$1.44	$1.79
Diluted	1.92	1.42	1.76
Net income:			
Basic	1.93	1.44	1.94
Diluted	1.92	1.42	1.91

Consolidated Balance Sheets

| | December 31, | |
	1998	1997
ASSETS		
CURRENT ASSETS		
Cash and temporary cash investments	$ 23,009,502	$ 71,427,918
Marketable securities	31,279,433	15,852,718
Trade receivables, less allowance for doubtful receivables		
1998—$768,000 and 1997—$1,354,000	27,584,551	25,212,595
Other receivables	1,838,171	2,980,257
Refundable income taxes	3,741,000	1,761,000
Inventories	93,349,453	68,416,006
Prepaid expenses and other	1,341,175	1,247,973
Deferred income taxes	3,268,000	3,040,000
Total current assets	185,411,285	189,938,467
PROPERTY AND EQUIPMENT, at cost		
Land and improvements	11,016,684	9,041,817
Buildings and improvements	53,761,414	39,950,161
Machinery and equipment	19,712,798	16,874,788
Transportation equipment	11,175,667	10,159,168
Office furniture and fixtures	8,850,146	5,712,961
	104,516,709	81,738,895
Less accumulated depreciation	41,444,585	35,137,268
	63,072,124	46,601,627
OTHER ASSETS		
Real estate held for sale	2,622,218	4,188,063
Rental properties	1,371,915	2,000,218
Intangibles, less accumulated amortization		
1998—$516,913 and 1997—$516,469	4,553,105	4,927,807
Deferred income taxes	579,000	569,000
Other	10,866,639	10,836,844
	19,992,877	22,521,932
TOTAL ASSETS	$268,476,286	$259,062,026

| | December 31, | |
	1998	1997
LIABILITIES AND SHAREHOLDERS' EQUITY		
CURRENT LIABILITIES		
Current maturities of long-term debt	$ 2,125,175	$ 2,258,519
Accounts payable, trade	18,997,193	22,818,303
Accrued wages, salaries and commissions	4,357,878	4,876,790
Accrued dealer incentives	3,783,628	3,226,255
Accrued warranty expense	6,138,081	6,013,528
Accrued income taxes	1,509,429	1,529,543
Accrued insurance	1,862,811	2,319,518
Other accrued liabilities	6,943,999	6,633,762
Total current liabilities	45,718,194	49,676,218
LONG-TERM DEBT	10,191,476	12,591,144
OTHER	7,108,956	6,658,872
Total liabilities	63,018,626	68,926,234
COMMITMENTS AND CONTINGENCIES (Note 11)		
SHAREHOLDERS' EQUITY		
Common shares, without par value: authorized 60,000,000 shares; issued 1998—20,842,568 shares and 1997—20,689,214 shares	89,105,324	87,519,740
Additional paid-in capital	3,866,398	3,012,596
Retained earnings	145,613,994	115,984,289
Treasury shares, at cost, 1998—4,257,985 shares and 1997—3,387,648 shares	(33,128,056)	(16,380,833)
Total shareholders' equity	205,457,660	190,135,792
TOTAL LIABILITIES AND SHAREHOLDERS' EQUITY	$268,476,286	$259,062,026

Required

a. Compute the following for 1998 and 1997:
   1. Net profit margin
   2. Total asset turnover (Use year-end total assets.)
   3. Return on assets (Use year-end total assets.)
   4. Operating income margin
   5. Return on operating assets (Use year-end operating assets.)
   6. Sales to fixed assets (Use year-end fixed assets.)
   7. Return on investment (Use year-end long-term liabilities + equity.)
   8. Return on total equity (Use year-end total equity.)
   9. Gross profit margin
b. Comment on trends in (a).

Case 8-6   Cars, Trucks, Etc.

The Ford Motor Company presented this summary of vehicle unit sales with its 2001 annual report.

ELEVEN-YEAR FINANCIAL SUMMARY

SUMMARY OF VEHICLE UNIT SALES*

(in thousands)

	2001	2000	1999	1998	1997	1996	1995	1994	1993	1992	1991
NORTH AMERICA											
United States											
Cars	**1,427**	1,775	1,725	1,563	1,614	1,656	1,767	2,036	1,925	1,820	1,588
Trucks	**2,458**	2,711	2,660	2,425	2,402	2,241	2,226	2,182	1,859	1,510	1,253
Total United States	**3,885**	4,486	4,385	3,988	4,016	3,897	3,993	4,218	3,784	3,330	2,841
Canada	**245**	300	288	279	319	258	254	281	256	237	259
Mexico	**162**	147	114	103	97	67	32	92	91	126	112
Total North America	**4,292**	4,933	4,787	4,370	4,432	4,222	4,279	4,591	4,131	3,693	3,212
EUROPE											
Britain	**637**	476	518	498	466	516	496	520	464	420	471
Germany	**383**	320	353	444	460	436	409	386	340	407	501
Italy	**249**	222	209	205	248	180	193	179	172	266	301
Spain	**178**	180	180	155	155	155	160	163	117	165	128
France	**163**	158	172	171	153	194	165	180	150	194	190
Other countries	**551**	526	528	377	318	339	286	281	250	270	296
Total Europe	**2,161**	1,882	1,960	1,850	1,800	1,820	1,709	1,709	1,493	1,722	1,887
OTHER INTERNATIONAL											
Brazil	**125**	134	117	178	214	190	201	164	151	117	137
Australia	**115**	125	125	133	132	138	139	125	120	105	104
Taiwan	**53**	63	56	77	79	86	106	97	122	119	107
Argentina	**29**	49	60	97	147	64	48	54	49	49	26
Japan	**18**	26	32	25	40	52	57	50	53	64	83
Other countries	**198**	212	83	93	103	81	67	63	65	71	67
Total other international	**538**	609	473	603	715	611	618	553	560	525	524
Total worldwide vehicle unit sales	**6,991**	7,424	7,220	6,823	6,947	6,653	6,606	6,853	6,184	5,940	5,623

*Vehicle unit sales generally are reported worldwide on a "where sold" basis and include sales of all Ford Motor Company-badged units, as well as units manufactured by Ford and sold to other manufacturers.

Required
    a.   Prepare a horizontal common-size statement for the period 1995–2001. Use 1995 as the base.
    b.   Comment on results in (a).

Case 8-7

Shoes, Shoes, Shoes

Shoe Carnival, Inc. presented this data with its selected financial data as part of its 2001 annual report.

Selected Financial Data
Shoe Carnival, Inc.

(In thousands, except share and operating data)

Fiscal years	2001	2000	1999	1998	1997
Income Statement Data					
Net sales	$476,556	$418,164	$339,929	$280,157	$246,520
Cost of sales (including buying, distribution and occupancy costs)	341,425	298,233	238,097	196,141	173,953
Gross profit	135,131	119,931	101,832	84,016	72,567
Selling, general and administrative expenses	112,736	100,692	80,888	66,464	59,438
Operating income	22,395	19,239	20,944	17,552	13,129
Interest expense	2,275	3,168	1,010	507	912
Income before income taxes	20,120	16,071	19,934	17,045	12,217
Income tax expense	7,545	6,348	7,973	6,818	4,826
Net income	$ 12,575	$ 9,723	$ 11,961	$ 10,227	$ 7,391

Required

a. 1. Prepare a vertical common-size statement for 1997–2001. Use net sales as a base and include all items through net income.
   2. Comment on the results in (1).

b. 1. Prepare a horizontal common-size statement for 1997–2001. Use 1997 as the base.
   2. Comment on the results in (1).

Web Case

Thomson Analytics *Business School Edition*

Please complete the web case that covers material covered in this chapter at http://gibson.swlearning.com. You'll be using Thomson Analytics Business School Edition, a version of the powerful tool used by Wall Street professionals, that combines a full range of fundamental financial information, earnings estimates, market data, and source documents for 500 publicly traded companies.

Endnotes

1. Release No. 33-8176, January 22, 2003, Conditions for Use of Non-GAAP Financial Measures Release Nos.: 34-47226; FR-65. http://www.sec.gov/, "Regulatory Actions, Final Rule Releases."

CHAPTER 9

FOR THE INVESTOR

Certain types of analysis particularly concern investors. While this chapter is not intended as a comprehensive guide to investment analysis, it will introduce certain types of analysis useful to the investor. In addition to the analysis covered in this chapter, an investor would also be interested in the liquidity, debt, and profitability ratios covered in prior chapters.

LEVERAGE AND ITS EFFECTS ON EARNINGS

The use of debt, called *financial leverage*, has a significant impact on earnings. The existence of fixed operating costs, called *operating leverage*, also affects earnings. The higher the percentage of fixed operating costs, the greater the variation in income as a result of a variation in sales (revenue).

This book does not compute a ratio for operating leverage because it cannot be readily computed from published financial statements. This book does compute financial leverage because it is readily computed from published financial statements.

The expense of debt financing is interest, a fixed charge dependent on the amount of financial principal and the rate of interest. Interest is a contractual obligation created by the borrowing agreement. In contrast to dividends, interest must be paid regardless of whether the firm is in a highly profitable period. An advantage of interest over dividends is its tax deductibility. Because the interest is subtracted to calculate taxable income, income tax expense is reduced.

Definition of Financial Leverage and Magnification Effects

The use of financing with a fixed charge (such as interest) is termed **financial leverage**. Financial leverage is successful if the firm earns more on the borrowed funds than it pays to use them. It is not successful if the firm earns less on the borrowed funds than it pays to use them. Using financial leverage results in a fixed financing charge that can materially affect the earnings available to the common shareholders.

Exhibit 9-1 illustrates financial leverage and its magnification effects. In this illustration, earnings before interest and tax for the Dowell Company are $1,000,000. Further, the firm has interest expense of $200,000 and a tax rate of 40%. The statement illustrates the effect of leverage on the return to the common stockholder. At earnings before interest and tax (EBIT) of $1,000,000, the net income is $480,000. If EBIT increases by 10% to $1,100,000, as in the exhibit, the net income rises by 12.5%. This magnification is caused by the fixed nature of interest expense. While earnings available to pay interest rise, interest remains the same, thus leaving more for the residual owners. Note that since the tax rate remains the same, earnings before tax change at the same rate as earnings after tax. Hence, this analysis could be made with either profit figure.

If financial leverage is used, a rise in EBIT will cause an even greater rise in net income, and a decrease in EBIT will cause an even greater decrease in net income. Looking again at the statement for the Dowell Company in Exhibit 9-1, when EBIT declined 20%, net income dropped from $480,000 to $360,000—a decline of $120,000, or 25%, based on the original $480,000. The use of financial leverage, termed **trading on the equity**, is only successful if the rate of earnings on borrowed funds exceeds the fixed charges.

| EXHIBIT 9-1 | | | | |

DOWELL COMPANY
Financial Leverage
Partial Income Statement to Illustrate Magnification Effects

	Base Year Figures	20% Decrease in Earnings Before Interest and Tax	10% Increase in Earnings Before Interest and Tax
Earnings before interest and tax	$1,000,000	$ 800,000	$1,100,000
Interest	(200,000)	(200,000)	(200,000)
Earnings before tax	800,000	600,000	900,000
Income tax (40%)	(320,000)	(240,000)	(360,000)
Net income	$ 480,000	$ 360,000	$ 540,000
Percentage change in net income [A]		25.0%	12.5%
Percentage change in earnings before interest and tax [B]		20.0%	10.0%
Degree of financial leverage [A ÷ B]		1.25	1.25

Computation of the Degree of Financial Leverage

The degree of financial leverage is the multiplication factor by which the net income changes as compared to the change in EBIT. One way of computing it follows:

$$\frac{\text{\% Change Net Income}}{\text{\% Change EBIT}}$$

For the Dowell Company:

$$\frac{12.5\%}{10.0\%} = 1.25, \quad = \frac{25.0\%}{20.0\%} = 1.25$$

The degree of financial leverage is 1.25. From a base EBIT of $1,000,000, any change in EBIT will be accompanied by 1.25 times that change in net income. If net income before interest and tax rises 4%, earnings to the stockholder will rise 5%. If net income before interest and tax falls 8%, earnings to the stockholder will decline 10%. The degree of financial leverage (DFL) can be computed more easily as follows:

$$\text{Degree of Financial Leverage} = \frac{\text{Earnings Before Interest and Tax}}{\text{Earnings Before Tax}}$$

Again referring to the Dowell Company:

$$\frac{\text{Degree of Financial Leverage at Earnings}}{\text{Before Interest and Tax on \$1,000,000}} = \frac{\$1,000,000}{\$800,000} = 1.25$$

Note that the degree of financial leverage represents a particular base level of income. The degree of financial leverage may differ for other levels of income or fixed charges.

The degree of financial leverage formula will not work precisely when the income statement includes any of the following items:

1. Minority share of earnings
2. Equity income
3. Nonrecurring items
   a. Discontinued operations
   b. Extraordinary items
   c. Cumulative effect of change in an accounting principle

When any of these items are included, they should be eliminated from the numerator and denominator. The all-inclusive formula follows:

$$\text{Degree of Financial Leverage} = \frac{\begin{array}{c}\text{Earnings Before Interest, Tax, Minority}\\ \text{Share of Earnings, Equity Income,}\\ \text{and Nonrecurring Items}\end{array}}{\begin{array}{c}\text{Earnings Before Tax, Minority}\\ \text{Share of Earnings, Equity Income,}\\ \text{and Nonrecurring Items}\end{array}}$$

This formula results in the ratio by which earnings before interest, tax, minority share of earnings, equity income, and nonrecurring items will change in relation to a change in earnings before tax, minority share of earnings, equity income, and nonrecurring items. In other words, it eliminates the minority share of earnings, equity income, and nonrecurring items from the degree of financial leverage.

Exhibit 9-2 shows the degree of financial leverage for 2002 and 2001 for Nike. The degree of financial leverage is 1.05 for 2002 and 1.06 for 2001. This is a very low degree of financial leverage. Therefore, the financial leverage at the end of 2002 indicates that as earnings before interest changes, net income will change by 1.05 times that amount. If earnings before interest increases, the financial leverage will be favorable. If earnings before interest decreases, the financial leverage will be unfavorable. In periods of relatively low interest rates or declining interest rates, financial leverage looks more favorable than in periods of high interest rates or increasing interest rates.

| EXHIBIT 9-2 | **NIKE, INC.** |

Degree of Financial Leverage

Base Years 2002 and 2001

	2002	2001
	(in millions)	
Income before income taxes and cumulative effect of accounting change [B]	$1,017.3	$921.4
Interest	47.6	58.7
Earnings before interest and tax [A]	1,064.9	980.1
Degree of financial leverage [A ÷ B]	1.05	1.06

Summary of Financial Leverage

Two things are important in looking at financial leverage as part of financial analysis. First, how high is the degree of financial leverage? This is a type of risk (or opportunity) measurement from the viewpoint of the stockholder. The higher the degree of financial leverage, the greater the multiplication factor. Second, does the financial leverage work for or against the owners?

EARNINGS PER COMMON SHARE

Earnings per share—the amount of income earned on a share of common stock during an accounting period—applies only to common stock and to corporate income statements. Nonpublic companies, because of cost-benefit considerations, do not have to report earnings per share. Because earnings per share receives much attention from the financial community, investors, and potential investors, it will be described in some detail.

Fortunately, we do not need to compute earnings per share. A company is required to present it at the bottom of the income statement. Per-share amounts for discontinued operations, extraordinary items, and the cumulative effect of an accounting change must be presented on the face of the income statement or in the notes to the financial statements. Earnings per share for recurring items is the most significant for primary analysis.

Computing earnings per share initially involves net income, preferred stock dividends declared and accumulated, and the weighted average number of shares outstanding, as follows:

$$\text{Diluted Earnings per Common Share} = \frac{\text{Net Income} - \text{Preferred Dividends}}{\substack{\text{Weighted Average Number of} \\ \text{Common Shares Outstanding}}}$$

Since earnings pertain to an entire period, they should be related to the common shares outstanding during the period. Thus, the denominator of the equation is the weighted average number of common shares outstanding.

To illustrate, assume that a corporation had 10,000 shares of common stock outstanding at the beginning of the year. On July 1, it issued 2,000 shares, and on October 1, it issued another 3,000 shares. The weighted average number of shares outstanding would be computed as follows:

Months Shares Are Outstanding	Shares Outstanding	×	Fraction of Year Outstanding	=	Weighted Average
January–June	10,000		6/12		5,000
July–September	12,000		3/12		3,000
October–December	15,000		3/12		3,750
					11,750

When the common shares outstanding increase as a result of a stock dividend or stock split, retroactive recognition must be given to these events for all comparative earnings per share presentations. Stock dividends and stock splits do not provide the firm with more funds; they only change the number of outstanding shares. Earnings per share should be related to the outstanding common stock after the stock dividend or stock split. In the weighted average common shares illustration, if we assume that a 2-for-1 stock split took place on December 31, the denominator of the earnings per share computation becomes 23,500 (11,750 × 2). The denominator of prior years' earnings per share computations would also be doubled. If we assume that net income is $100,000 and preferred dividends total $10,000 in this illustration, then the earnings per common share would be $3.83 [($100,000 − $10,000)/23,500].

The current earnings per share guidelines call for the presentation of basic earnings per share and diluted earnings per share. Basic earnings per share is computed by dividing net income less preferred dividends by the weighted average number of shares of common stock outstanding during the period. Diluted earnings per share is computed by dividing net income less preferred dividends by the weighted average number of shares of common stock outstanding plus the dilutive effect of potentially dilutive securities. Potentially dilutive securities are convertible securities, warrants, options, or other rights that upon conversion or exercise could in the aggregate dilute earnings per common share.

Exhibit 9-3 presents the earnings per share of Nike for the years 2000, 2001, and 2002. There was a material increase in earnings per share.

PRICE/ EARNINGS RATIO

The **price/earnings (P/E) ratio** expresses the relationship between the market price of a share of common stock and that stock's current earnings per share. Compute the P/E ratio as follows:

$$\text{Price/Earnings Ratio} = \frac{\text{Market Price per Share}}{\substack{\text{Diluted Earnings per Share,} \\ \text{before Nonrecurring Items}}}$$

Using diluted earnings per share results in a higher price/earnings ratio, a conservative computation of the ratio. Ideally, the P/E ratio should be computed using diluted earnings per share for continuing earnings per share. This gives an indication of what is being paid for a dollar of recurring earnings.

P/E ratios are available from many sources, such as *The Wall Street Journal* and *Standard & Poor's Industry Surveys*. Exhibit 9-4 shows the P/E ratio for Nike for 2002 and 2001. The P/E ratio was 21.85 at the end of 2002 and 19.03 at the end of 2001. This indicates that the stock has been selling for about 22 times earnings. You can get a perspective on this ratio by comparing it to competitors, average P/E for the industry, and an average for all of the stocks on an exchange, such as the New York Stock Exchange. These averages will vary greatly over several years.

Investors view the P/E ratio as a gauge of future earning power of the firm. Companies with high growth opportunities generally have high P/E ratios; firms with low growth tend to have lower P/E ratios. However, investors may be wrong in their estimates of growth potential. One fundamental of investing is to be wiser than the market. An example would be buying a stock that has a relatively low P/E ratio when the prospects for the company are much better than reflected in the P/E ratio.

EXHIBIT 9-3	NIKE, INC.

Earnings Per Share

Years Ended May 31, 2002, 2001, and 2000

	2002	2001	2000
Basic earnings per common share—before accounting change	$2.50	$2.18	$2.10
Diluted earnings per common share—before accounting change	$2.46	$2.16	$2.07

EXHIBIT 9-4	NIKE, INC.

Price/Earnings Ratio

May 31, 2002 and 2001

	2002	2001
Market price per common share (May 31, close) [A]	$ 53.75	$41.10
Diluted Earnings per share before nonrecurring items [B]	$ 2.46	$ 2.16
Price/earnings ratio [A ÷ B]	21.85	19.03

P/E ratios do not have any meaning when a firm has abnormally low profits in relation to the asset base or when a firm has losses. The P/E ratio in these cases would be abnormally high or negative.

PERCENTAGE OF EARNINGS RETAINED

The proportion of current earnings retained for internal growth is computed as follows:

$$\text{Percentage of Earnings Retained} = \frac{\text{Net Income before Nonrecurring Items} - \text{All Dividends}}{\text{Net Income before Nonrecurring Items}}$$

The percentage of earnings retained is better for trend analysis if nonrecurring items are removed. This indicates what is being retained of recurring earnings. Determine dividends from the statement of cash flows.

A problem occurs because the percentage of earnings retained implies that earnings represent a cash pool for paying dividends. Under accrual accounting, earnings do not represent a cash pool. Operating cash flow compared with cash dividends gives a better indication of the cash from operations and the dividends paid. Chapter 10 introduces this ratio.

Many firms have a policy on the percentage of earnings that they want retained—for example, between 60% and 75%. In general, new firms, growing firms, and firms perceived as growth firms will have a relatively high percentage of earnings retained. Many new firms, growing firms, and firms perceived as growing firms do not pay dividends.

In the *Almanac of Business and Industrial Financial Ratios*, the percentage of earnings retained is called the *ratio of retained earnings to net income*. The phrase *retained earnings* as used in the ratio in the *Almanac* is a misnomer. Retained earnings in this ratio does not mean accumulated profits, but rather that portion of income retained in a single year. Hence, this ratio has two different names.

Exhibit 9-5 shows the percentage of earnings retained by Nike, using 2002 and 2001 figures. Nike retains a substantial proportion of its profits for internal use.

EXHIBIT 9-5	NIKE, INC.

Percentage of Earnings Retained

Years Ended May 31, 2002 and 2001

	2002	2001
	(in millions)	
Net income before nonrecurring items [B]	$668.3	$589.7
Less: Dividends	128.9	129.7
Earnings retained [A]	$539.4	$460.0
Percentage of earnings retained [A ÷ B]	80.71%	78.01%

DIVIDEND PAYOUT

The **dividend payout ratio** measures the portion of current earnings per common share being paid out in dividends. Compute the dividend payout ratio as follows:

$$\text{Dividend Payout} = \frac{\text{Dividends per Common Share}}{\text{Diluted Earnings per Share before Nonrecurring Items}}$$

Earnings per share are diluted in the formula because this is the most conservative viewpoint. Ideally, diluted earnings per share should not include nonrecurring items since directors normally look at recurring earnings to develop a stable dividend policy.

The dividend payout ratio has a similar problem as the percentage of earnings retained. Investors may assume that dividend payout implies that earnings per share represent cash. Under accrual accounting, earnings per share do not represent a cash pool.

Most firms hesitate to decrease dividends since this tends to have adverse effects on the market price of the company's stock. No rule of thumb exists for a correct payout ratio. Some stockholders prefer high dividends; others prefer to have the firm reinvest the earnings in hopes of higher capital gains. In the latter case, the payout ratio would be a relatively smaller percentage.

Exhibit 9-6 presents Nike's 2002 and 2001 dividend payout ratios, which decreased from 22.22% in 2001 to 19.51% in 2002. These are conservative payout ratios. Often, to attract the type of stockholder who looks favorably on a low dividend payout ratio, a company must have a good return on common equity.

Industry averages of dividend payout ratios are available in *Standard & Poor's Industry Surveys*. Although no correct payout exists, even within an industry, the outlook for the industry often makes the bulk of the ratios in a particular industry similar.

In general, new firms, growing firms, and firms perceived as growth firms have a relatively low dividend payout. Nike would be considered a growing firm.

DIVIDEND YIELD

The **dividend yield** indicates the relationship between the dividends per common share and the market price per common share. Compute the dividend yield as follows:

$$\text{Dividend Yield} = \frac{\text{Dividends per Common Share}}{\text{Market Price per Common Share}}$$

For this ratio, multiply the fourth quarter dividend declared by 4. This indicates the current dividend rate. Exhibit 9-7 shows the dividend yield for Nike for 2002 and 2001. The dividend yield has been relatively low.

Since total earnings from securities include both dividends and price appreciation, no rule of thumb exists for dividend yield. The yield depends on the firm's dividend policy and the market price. If the firm successfully invests the money not distributed as dividends, the price should rise. If the firm holds the dividends at low amounts to allow for reinvestment of profits, the dividend yield is likely to be low. A low dividend yield satisfies many investors if the company has a record of above average return on common equity. Investors that want current income prefer a high dividend yield.

EXHIBIT 9-6   **NIKE, INC.**

Dividend Payout

Years Ended May 31, 2002 and 2001

	2002	2001
Dividends per share [A]	$ .48	$ .48
Diluted earnings per share before nonrecurring items [B]	$2.46	$2.16
Dividend payout ratio [A ÷ B]	19.51%	22.22%

| EXHIBIT 9-7 | NIKE, INC. |

Dividend Yield

May 31, 2002 and 2001

	2002	2001
Dividends per share [A]	$ .48	$ .48
Market price per share [B]	$53.75	$41.10
Dividend yield [A ÷ B]	.89%	1.17%

BOOK VALUE PER SHARE

A figure frequently published in annual reports is book value per share, which indicates the amount of stockholders' equity that relates to each share of outstanding common stock. The formula for book value per share follows:

$$\text{Book Value per Share} = \frac{\text{Total Stockholders' Equity} - \text{Preferred Stock Equity}}{\text{Number of Common Shares Outstanding}}$$

Preferred stock equity should be stated at liquidation price, if other than book, because the preferred stockholders would be paid this value in the event of liquidation. Liquidation value is sometimes difficult to locate in an annual report. If this value cannot be found, the book figure that relates to preferred stock may be used in place of liquidation value. Exhibit 9-8 shows the book value per share for Nike for 2002 and 2001. The book value increased from $13.01 in 2001 to $14.43 in 2002.

The market price of the securities usually does not approximate the book value. These historical dollars reflect past unrecovered cost of the assets. The market value of the stock, however, reflects the potential of the firm as seen by the investor. For example, land will be valued at cost, and this asset value will be reflected in the book value. If the asset were purchased several years ago and is now worth substantially more, however, the market value of the stock may recognize this potential.

Book value is of limited use to the investment analyst since it is based on the book numbers. When market value is below book value, investors view the company as lacking potential. A market value above book value indicates that investors view the company as having enough potential to be worth more than the book numbers. Note that Nike was selling materially above book value (Market 2002, $53.75).

When investors are pessimistic about the prospects for stocks, the stocks sell below book value. On the other hand, when investors are optimistic about stock prospects, the stocks sell above book value. There have been times when the majority of stocks sold below book value. There have also been times when the majority of stocks sold at a multiple of 5 or 6 times book value.

| EXHIBIT 9-8 | NIKE, INC. |

Book Value per Share

May 31, 2002 and 2001

	2002	2001
	(in millions)	
Shareholders' equity	$3,839.0	$3,494.5
Less:		
Preferred stock*	—	—
Adjusted shareholders' equity [A]	$3,839.0	$3,494.5
Shares outstanding [B]	266.1	268.6
Book value per share [A ÷ B]	$ 14.43	$ 13.01

*Redeemable preferred stock classified above shareholders' equity.

STOCK OPTIONS (STOCK-BASED COMPENSATION)

Corporations frequently provide stock options for employees and officers of the company. Setting aside shares for options has become increasingly popular in the United States. A substantial majority of public companies have employee stock-option programs.[1]

When stock options are exercised, the additional funds improve the short-run liquidity of the firm and its long-term debt position. Any improvements are almost always immaterial, however, because of the relatively small amount of funds involved.

A basic understanding of stock option accounting is needed in order to assess the stock option disclosure of a company. Employers are allowed to account for stock option plans under either APB Opinion No. 25, "Accounting for Stock Issued to Employees," or under SFAS No. 123, "Accounting for Stock-Based Compensation." (Both APB Opinion No. 25 and SFAS No. 123 were amended by SFAS No. 148 in December 2002.)

APB Opinion No. 25 Firms

Under APB Opinion No. 25, a stock option plan is either a noncompensatory plan or a compensatory plan. A *noncompensatory* plan attempts to raise capital or encourage wide spread ownership of the corporation's stock among officers and employees. Because the officers and employees purchase the stock at only a slight discount from the market price, there is not a substantial dilution of the position of existing stockholders or a substantial compensation issue. For these plans, no compensation expense is recognized under APB Opinion No. 25. When these options are exercised, the shares are issued slightly below the market price.

A *compensatory* plan is available only to select individuals, such as officers of the company. These plans typically provide the potential for purchasing stock at a bargain rate.

The company records compensation only to the extent that the option price was below market price on the date the option was granted. This would be rare. Thus, when the option price is at the market price (or above the market price) on the date of grant, no compensation is recorded. Thus, many accountants feel that compensation from stock option plans under APB Opinion No. 25 is understated because the individual purchases the stock substantially below market at date of exercise (the date that the options and cash are exchanged for stock). The APB Opinion No. 25 approach is referred to as the intrinsic value method.

SFAS No. 123 amended APB Opinion No. 25 to require firms reporting under APB Opinion No. 25 to disclose the impact on income and earnings per share based on the fair value at the grant date. This footnote disclosure included reported net income and pro forma net income with the options expense included. It also included earnings per share (diluted), based on reported income and pro forma income.

Nike elected to use APB Opinion No. 25 and make pro forma disclosures of net income and earnings per share, as if the fair value-based method of accounting defined in SFAS No. 123 had been applied.

Exhibit 9-9 presents the Nike presentation for its 2002 annual report. Exhibit 9-9 also includes a computation of the materiality of option expense. For Nike the impact from options would likely be considered substantial.

The format used by Nike was an acceptable format prior to SFAS No. 148. SFAS No. 148 requires a new standard format for firms reporting under APB Opinion No. 25. The new format was effective for financial statements for fiscal years ending after December 15, 2002. This new format presentation must be in the "Summary of Significant Accounting Policies" or its equivalent, along with a statement of the method used. This presentation is also required for interim periods.

Exhibit 9-10 illustrates APB No. 25 following SFAS No. 148 format requirements, using International Business Machines Corporation.

SFAS No. 123 Firms

SFAS No. 123 introduced a fair value-based method of determining the options expense. Fair value is determined using an option-pricing model that considers the stock price at the grant date, the exercise price, the expected life of the option, the volatility of the underlying stock and the expected dividends on it, and the risk-free interest rate over the expected life of the option.

EXHIBIT 9-9   **NIKE, INC.**

If the company had accounted for options issued to employees in accordance with SFAS No. 123.

| | Year Ended May 31, | | | | | | | | |
| | 2002 | | | 2001 | | | 2000 | | |
	Net Income	Diluted EPS	Basic EPS	Net Income	Diluted EPS	Basic EPS	Net Income	Diluted EPS	Basic EPS
	(In millions, except per share data)								
As reported	$663.3	$2.44	$2.48	$589.7	$2.16	$2.18	$579.1	$2.07	$2.10
Pro Forma	627.2	2.30	2.34	559.0	2.05	2.07	551.2	1.97	2.00

Materiality of option compensation expense: (Added by author)

	2002*	2001	2000
Pro forma/Reported net income	93.85	94.79	95.18
Pro forma/Reported earnings per share	93.50	94.91	95.17

*Excluded nonrecurring item

This standard treats both the compensation and noncompensatory options similarly: compensation cost is measured by the estimated fair value at the grant date. Compensation cost is only recognized for the number of instruments that are actually vested.

The impact of SFAS No. 123 can be substantial, resulting in lower net income and earning per share. It can have a particularly material impact on high-tech companies that are rewarding employees with substantial stock-based compensation.

Firms that elected to use SFAS No. 123 usually disclosed only, as only a few firms elected to expense. For firms disclosing only the analysis would be similar to the analysis of firms under APB Opinion No. 25.

As of December 31, 2001, the Boeing Company was one of the few companies electing to report under SFAS No. 123 and expense stock options. A detailed description of the option programs was disclosed by the Boeing Company.

EXHIBIT 9-10   **APB OPINION NO. 25 FOLLOWING SFAS NO. 148 FORMAT REQUIREMENTS**

International Business Machines Corporation December 31, 2002
A. Significant Accounting Policies (in Part)
Stock-Based Compensation (in Part)
(Dollars in Millions Except Per Share Amounted)

	2002	2001	2000
Net income applicable to common stockholders, as reported	$3,579	$7,713	$8,073
Add: stock-based employee compensation expense included in reported net income, net of related tax effects	112	104	82
Deduct: Total stock-based employee compensation expense determined under fair value method for all awards, net of related tax effects	1,315	1,343	972
Pro forma net income	$2,376	$6,474	$7,183
Earnings per share:			
Basic—as reported	$ 2.10	$ 4.45	$ 4.58
Basic—pro forma	$ 1.40	$ 3.74	$ 4.07
Assuming dilution—as reported	$ 2.06	$ 4.35	$ 4.44
Assuming dilution—pro forma	$ 1.39	$ 3.69	$ 3.99

The Trend

In 2002 several additional companies announced that they would start expensing stock options with their 2002 annual report. These companies were responding to the public concern relating to financial reporting.

Warren E. Buffett, one of the world's richest persons, and likely the world's most famous investor, has been very critical of firms not recognizing option expense on the income statement. His view is that option expense needs to be considered when evaluating the performance of a company.

When stock prices decline, is there a value to holding stock options? A decline in stock prices could make the existing stock options worthless. But many companies rewrite the options with a lower option price when the stock declines. Thus, for the holders of the options it becomes a situation of "Tales I Win, Heads I Win." Warren E. Buffet tells this story relating to stock options.

A gorgeous woman slinks up to a CEO at a party and through moist lips purrs, "I'll do anything—anything—you want. Just tell me what you would like." With no hesitation, he replies, "Reprice my options."[2]

SFAS No. 148 permits two additional transition methods for entities that elect the fair value method. The original SFAS No. 123 prospective method of transition for changes to the fair value-based method is not permitted for changes to the fair value-based method in fiscal years beginning after December 15, 2003.

SFAS No. 148 prescribes tabular format presentation to be disclosed in the "Summary of Significant Accounting Policies" or its equivalent. These firms are also required to include this presentation in financial reports for interim periods.

Exhibit 9-11 illustrates SFAS No. 123 using the Boeing Company. Boeing elected to show stock-based compensation in the body of the income statement.

Options—Concluding Comments

Accounting for options can be complicated, but from the analysis view the situation has been substantially clarified. We want to know the impact of option expense on net income before nonrecurring items. This can now be determined using the income statement and the footnote requirements.

To assist in determining the materiality of options use the following ratio.

$$\text{Materiality of Options} = \frac{\begin{pmatrix}\text{Net Income before}\\\text{Nonrecurring Items}\\\text{Not Including Option}\\\text{Expense}\end{pmatrix} - \begin{pmatrix}\text{Net Income before}\\\text{Nonrecurring Items}\\\text{Including Option}\\\text{Expense}\end{pmatrix}}{\begin{pmatrix}\text{Net Income before Nonrecurring Items}\\\text{Not Including Option Expense}\end{pmatrix}}$$

Using Exhibit 9-10 that illustrates International Business Machines Corporation the materiality of options is computed as follows for 2002.

$$\frac{(\$3,579,000,000 + \$112,000,000) - \$2,376,000,000}{(\$3,579,000,000 + \$112,000,000)} = 35.63\%$$

For the International Business Corporation stock option expense appears to be material for 2002.

STOCK APPRECIATION RIGHTS

Some firms grant key employees **stock appreciation rights** instead of stock options or in addition to stock options. Stock appreciation rights give the employee the right to receive compensation in cash or stock (or a combination of these) at some future date, based on the difference between the market price of the stock at the date of exercise over a preestablished price.

The accounting for stock appreciation rights directs that the compensation expense recognized each period be based on the difference between the quoted market value at the end of each period and the option price. This compensation expense is then reduced by previously recognized

EXHIBIT 9-11   **SFAS NO. 123 FOLLOWING SFAS NO. 148 REQUIREMENTS**

The Boeing Company and Subsidiaries
Consolidated Statements of Operations
(Dollars in millions)

Year Ended December 31,	2002	2001	2000
Sales and other operating revenues	$54,069	$58,198	$51,321
Cost of products and services	45,499	48,778	43,712
	8,570	9,420	7,609
Income/(loss) from operating investments, net	(128)	93	64
General and administrative expense	2,534	2,389	2,335
Research and development expense	1,639	1,936	1,441
In-process research and development expense			557
Gain on dispositions, net	44	21	34
Share-based plans expense	42	378	316
Impact of September 11, 2001, charges/(recoveries)	(2)	935	
Earnings from operations	3,868	3,896	3,058
Other income/(expense), net	42	318	386
Interest and debt expense	(730)	(650)	(445)
Earnings before income taxes	3,180	3,564	2,999
Income taxes	861	738	871
Net earnings before cumulative effect of accounting change	2,319	2,826	2,128
Cumulative effect of accounting change, net of tax	(1,827)	1	
Net earnings	$ 492	$ 2,827	$ 2,128
Basic earnings per share before cumulative effect **of accounting change**	$ 2.90	$ 3.46	$ 2.48
Cumulative effect of accounting change, net of tax	(2.28)		
Basic earnings per share	$ 0.62	$ 3.46	$ 2.48
Diluted earnings per share before cumulative effect **of accounting change**	$ 2.87	$ 3.41	$ 2.44
Cumulative effect of accounting change, net of tax	(2.26)		
Diluted earnings per share	$ 0.61	$ 3.41	$ 2.44

Note 1—Summary of Significant Accounting Policies (In Part)

Share-based compensation

The Company uses a fair value based method of accounting for stock-based compensation provided to its employees in accordance with Statement of Financial Accounting Standards (SFAS) No. 123, *Accounting for Stock-Based Compensation*. The Company values stock options issued based upon an option-pricing model and recognizes this value as an expense over the period in which the options vest. Potential distributions from the Share Value Trust described in Note 17 have been valued based upon an option-pricing model, with the related expense recognized over the life of the trust. Share-based expense associated with Performance Shares described in Note 17 is determined based on the market value of the Company's stock at the time of the award applied to the maximum number of shares contingently issuable based on stock price and is amortized over a five-year period.

compensation expense on the stock appreciation right. For example, assume that the option price is $10.00 and the market value is $15.00 at the end of the first period of the stock appreciation right. Compensation expense would be recognized at $5.00 ($15.00 – $10.00) per share included in the plan. If 100,000 shares are in the plan, then the expense to be charged to the income statement would be $500,000 ($5.00 × 100,000 shares). If the market value is $12.00 at the end of the second period of the stock appreciation right, expenses are reduced by $3.00 per share. This is because the total compensation expense for the two years is $2.00 ($12.00 – $10.00). Since $5.00 of expense was recognized in the first year, $3.00 of negative compensation is considered in the second year in order to total $2.00 of expense. With 100,000 shares, the reduction to expenses in the second year would be $300,000 ($3.00 × 100,000 shares). Thus, stock appreciation rights can have a material influence on income, dictated by changing stock prices.

A company with outstanding stock appreciation rights describes them in a footnote to the financial statements. If the number of shares is known, a possible future influence on income can be computed, based on assumptions made regarding future market prices. For example, if the footnote discloses that the firm has 50,000 shares of stock appreciation rights outstanding, and the stock market price was $10.00 at the end of the year, the analyst can assume a market price at the end of next year and compute the compensation expense for next year. With these facts and an assumed market price of $15.00 at the end of next year, the compensation expense for next year can be computed to be $250,000 [($15.00 – $10.00) × 50,000 shares]. This potential charge to earnings should be considered as the stock is evaluated as a potential investment.

Stock appreciation rights tied to the future market price of the stock can represent a material potential drain on the company. Even a relatively small number of stock appreciation rights outstanding could be material. This should be considered by existing and potential stockholders. Some firms have placed limits on the potential appreciation in order to control the cost of appreciation rights.

Forbes reported the following in a May 17, 1999 article, "Safe Haven."

> According to the Company's latest filing with the SEC, both the Daimler-Benz and the Chrysler compensation systems disappeared when the merger was consummated. The Daimler bonus and the Chrysler option plan was replaced with performance-based stock appreciation rights.

The General Electric Company 2001 annual report indicated that "at year-end 2001, there were 131 thousand SARs outstanding at an average exercise price of $7.68." The General Electric Company stock price during 2001 ranged from a low of $28.25 to a high of $52.90.

Apparently stock appreciation rights were not outstanding as of May 31, 2002 for Nike.

SUMMARY

This chapter has reviewed certain types of analysis that particularly concern investors. Ratios relevant to this analysis include the following:

$$\text{Degree of Financial Leverage} = \frac{\text{Earnings Before Interest and Tax}}{\text{Earnings Before Tax}}$$

$$\text{All-Inclusive Degree of Financial Leverage} = \frac{\text{Earnings Before Interest, Tax, Minority Share of Earnings, Equity Income, and Nonrecurring Items}}{\text{Earnings Before Tax, Minority Share of Earnings, Equity Income, and Nonrecurring Items}}$$

$$\text{Diluted Earnings per Common Share} = \frac{\text{Net Income} - \text{Preferred Dividends}}{\text{Weighted Average Number of Common Shares Outstanding}}$$

$$\text{Price/Earnings Ratio} = \frac{\text{Market Price per Share}}{\text{Diluted Earnings per Share, before Nonrecurring Items}}$$

$$\text{Percentage of Earnings Retained} = \frac{\text{Net Income before Nonrecurring Items} - \text{All Dividends}}{\text{Net Income before Nonrecurring Items}}$$

$$\text{Dividend Payout} = \frac{\text{Dividends per Common Share}}{\text{Diluted Earnings per Share before Nonrecurring Items}}$$

$$\text{Dividend Yield} = \frac{\text{Dividends per Common Share}}{\text{Market Price per Common Share}}$$

$$\text{Book Value per Share} = \frac{\text{Total Stockholders' Equity} - \text{Preferred Stock Equity}}{\text{Number of Common Shares Outstanding}}$$

$$\text{Materiality of Options} = \frac{\begin{array}{c}\text{Net Income Before}\\\text{Nonrecurring Items}\\\text{Not Including Option}\\\text{Expense}\end{array} - \begin{array}{c}\text{Net Income Before}\\\text{Nonrecurring Items}\\\text{Including Option}\\\text{Expense}\end{array}}{\begin{array}{c}\text{Net Income Before Nonrecurring Items}\\\text{Not Including Option Expense}\end{array}}$$

To the Net

1. Go to the SEC site (http://www.sec.gov). Under Filings & Forms (Edgar), click on "Search for Company Filings." Click on "Search Companies and Filings." Under company name enter "Wendy's." Select the DEF14A (proxy), filed March 12, 2002.

    For the years ended December 30, 2001, December 31, 2000, and January 2, 2000, compute or find the following:
    a.   Earnings per common share. (basic and diluted)
    b.   Price/earnings ratio.
    c.   Percentage of earnings retained.
    d.   Dividend payout.
    e.   Dividend yield.

    Note: Seldom does a firm include the year-end market price in their financial report. The year-end market price usually needs to be obtained from other sources.

2. Go to the SEC site (http://www.sec.gov). Under Filings & Forms (Edgar), click on "Search for Company Filings." Click on "Search Companies and Filings." Under company name enter "Motorola, Inc." Select the DEF14A (proxy) filed March 29, 2002.

    Review the consolidated statements of operations for years ended December 31, 2001, 2000, and 1999. In your opinion what line item(s) makes it difficult to form an opinion on the results of Motorola, Inc.?

3. Go to the SEC site (http://www.sec.gov). Under Filings & Forms (Edgar), click on "Search for Company Filings." Click on "Search Companies and Filings." Under company name enter "Boeing." Select the 10-K filed March 8, 2002.

    For the years ended December 31, 2001, 2000, and 1999, compute the following:
    a.   Earnings per common share.
    b.   Price/earnings ratio.
    c.   Percentage of earnings retained.
    d.   Dividend payout.
    e.   Dividend yield.

    Note: Year-end market price December 31, 2001 ($38.78); December 31, 2000 ($66.00); and December 31, 1999 ($41.44).

4. Go to the SEC site (http://www.sec.gov). Under Filings & Forms (Edgar), click on "Search for Company Filings." Click on "Search Companies and Filings." Under company name enter "Microsoft." Select the 10-K filed September 6, 2002.

    For the years ended June 30, 2001 and 2002, find the following:
    a.   Total assets.
    b.   Shareholders' equity.
    c.   Common stock shares issued and outstanding.
    d.   Compute the total capitalization at June 30, 2001 and June 30, 2002.
    e.   Why is the total capitalization different than the total shareholders' equity?

    Note: The Microsoft market price was $73.00 June 30, 2001; and $54.70 June 30, 2002.

Questions

Q 9-1.   Give a simple definition of *earnings per share*.

Q 9-2.   Assume that the corporation is a nonpublic company. Comment on the requirement for this firm to disclose earnings per share.

Q 9-3.   Keller & Fink, a partnership, engages in the wholesale fish market. How would this company disclose earnings per share?

Q 9-4.   Dividends on preferred stock total $5,000 for the current year. How would these dividends influence earnings per share?

Q 9-5.   The denominator of the earnings per share computation includes the weighted average number of common shares outstanding. Why use the weighted average instead of the year-end common shares outstanding?

Q 9-6.   Preferred dividends decreased this year because some preferred stock was retired. How would this influence the earnings per share computation this year?

Q 9-7.   Retroactive recognition is given to stock dividends and stock splits on common stock when computing earnings per share. Why?

Q 9-8.   Why do many firms try to maintain a stable percentage of earnings retained?

Q 9-9.   Define financial leverage. What is its effect on earnings? When is the use of financial leverage advantageous and disadvantageous?

Q 9-10.   Given a set level of earnings before interest and tax, how will a rise in interest rates affect the degree of financial leverage?

Q 9-11.   Why is the price/earnings ratio considered a gauge of future earning power?

Q 9-12.   Why does a relatively new firm often have a low dividend payout ratio? Why does a firm with a substantial growth record and/or substantial growth prospects often have a low dividend payout ratio?

Q 9-13.   Why would an investor ever buy stock in a firm with a low dividend yield?

Q 9-14.   Why is book value often meaningless? What improvements to financial statements would make it more meaningful?

Q 9-15.   Why should an investor read the footnote concerning stock options? How might stock options affect profitability?

Q 9-16.   Why can a relatively small number of stock appreciation rights prove to be a material drain on future earnings and cash of a company?

Q 9-17.   Explain how outstanding stock appreciation rights could increase reported income in a particular year.

Problems

P 9-1.   McDonald Company shows the following condensed income statement information for the current year:

Revenue from sales		$ 3,500,000
Cost of products sold		(1,700,000)
Gross profit		1,800,000
Operating expenses:		
Selling expenses	$425,000	
General expenses	350,000	(775,000)
Operating income		1,025,000
Other income		20,000
Interest		(70,000)
Operating income before income taxes		975,000
Taxes related to operations		(335,000)
Income from operations		640,000
Extraordinary loss (less applicable income taxes of $40,000)		(80,000)
Income before minority interest		560,000
Minority share of earnings		(50,000)
Net income		$ 510,000

Required   Calculate the degree of financial leverage.

P 9-2.   A firm has earnings before interest and tax of $1,000,000, interest of $200,000, and net income of $400,000 in Year 1.

Required   a.   Calculate the degree of financial leverage in base Year 1.

b.   If earnings before interest and tax increase by 10% in Year 2, what will be the new level of earnings, assuming the same tax rate as in Year 1?

c.   If earnings before interest and tax decrease to $800,000 in Year 2, what will be the new level of earnings, assuming the same tax rate as in Year 1?

P 9-3.   The following information was in the annual report of the Rover Company:

	2003	2002	2001
Earnings per share	$1.12	$1.20	$1.27
Cash dividends per share (common)	$.90	$.85	$.82
Market price per share	$12.80	$14.00	$16.30
Total common dividends	$21,700,000	$19,500,000	$18,360,000
Shares outstanding, end of year	24,280,000	23,100,000	22,500,000
Total assets	$1,280,100,000	$1,267,200,000	$1,260,400,000
Total liabilities	$800,400,000	$808,500,000	$799,200,000
Nonredeemable preferred stock	$15,300,000	$15,300,000	$15,300,000
Preferred dividends	$910,000	$910,000	$910,000
Net income	$31,200,000	$30,600,000	$29,800,000

Required   a.   Based on these data, compute the following for 2003, 2002, and 2001:
1.   Percentage of earnings retained
2.   Price/earnings ratio
3.   Dividend payout
4.   Dividend yield
5.   Book value per share

b.   Discuss your findings from the viewpoint of a potential investor.

P 9-4.   The following data relate to the Edger Company:

	2003	2002	2001
Earnings per share	$2.30	$3.40	$4.54
Dividends per share	$1.90	$1.90	$1.90
Market price, end of year	$41.25	$35.00	$29.00
Net income	$9,100,000	$13,300,000	$16,500,000
Total cash dividends	$6,080,000	$5,900,000	$6,050,000
Order backlog at year-end	$5,490,800,000	$4,150,200,000	$3,700,100,000
Net contracts awarded	$2,650,700,000	$1,800,450,000	$3,700,100,000

Note: The stock was selling at 120.5%, 108.0%, and 105.0% of book value in 2003, 2002, and 2001, respectively.

Required   a.   Compute the following for 2003, 2002, and 2001:
1.   Percentage of earnings retained
2.   Price/earnings ratio
3.   Dividend payout
4.   Dividend yield
5.   Book value per share

b.   Comment on your results from (a). Include in your discussion the data on backlog and new contracts awarded.

P 9-5.   The Dicker Company has the following pattern of financial data for Years 1 and 2:

	Year 1	Year 2
Net income	$40,000	$42,000
Preferred stock (5%)	$450,000	$550,000
Weighted average number of common shares outstanding	38,000	38,000

Required   Calculate earnings per share and comment on the trend.

P 9-6. Assume the following facts for the current year:

> Common shares outstanding on January 1, 50,000 shares
> July 1, 2-for-1 stock split
> October 1, a stock issue of 10,000 shares

Required Compute the denominator of the earnings per share computation for the current year.

P 9-7. The XYZ Corporation reported earnings per share of $2.00 in 2002. In 2003, the XYZ Corporation reported earnings per share of $1.50. On July 1, 2003, and December 31, 2003, 2-for-1 stock splits were declared.

Required Present the earnings per share for a two-year comparative income statement that includes 2003 and 2002.

P 9-8. The Cook Company shows the following condensed income statement information for the year ended December 31, 2003:

Income before extraordinary gain	$30,000
Plus: Extraordinary gain, net of tax expense of $2,000	5,000
Net income	$35,000

The company declared dividends of $3,000 on preferred stock and $5,000 on common stock. At the beginning of 2003, 20,000 shares of common stock were outstanding. On July 1, 2003, the company issued 1,000 additional common shares. The preferred stock is not convertible.

Required
a. Compute the earnings per share.
b. How much of the earnings per share appears to be recurring?

P 9-9. Assume the following facts for the current year:

Net income	$200,000
Common dividends	$20,000
Preferred dividends (The preferred stock is not convertible.)	$10,000
Common shares outstanding on January 1	20,000 shares
Common stock issued on July 1	5,000 shares
2-for-1 stock split on December 31	

Required
a. Compute the earnings per share for the current year.
b. Earnings per share in the prior year was $8.00. Use the earnings per share computed in part (a) and present a two-year earnings per share comparison for the current year and the prior year.

P 9-10. Smith and Jones, Inc. is primarily engaged in the worldwide production, processing, distribution, and marketing of food products. The following information is from its 2003 annual report:

	2003	2002
Earnings per share	$1.08	$1.14
Cash dividends per common share	$.80	$.76
Market price per common share	$12.94	$15.19
Common shares outstanding	25,380,000	25,316,000
Total assets	$1,264,086,000	$1,173,924,000
Total liabilities	$823,758,000	$742,499,000
Nonredeemable preferred stock	$16,600,000	$16,600,000
Preferred dividends	$4,567,000	$930,000
Net income	$32,094,000	$31,049,000

Required
a. Based on these data, compute the following for 2003 and 2002:
  1. Percentage of earnings retained
  2. Price/earnings ratio
  3. Dividend payout
  4. Dividend yield
  5. Book value per share
b. Discuss your findings from the viewpoint of a potential investor.

P 9-11. On December 31, 2003, Farley Camera, Inc. issues 5,000 stock appreciation rights to its president to entitle her to receive cash for the difference between the market price of its stock and a preestablished price of $20. The date of exercise is December 31, 2006, and the required service period is the entire three years. The market price fluctuates as follows: 12/31/04—$23.00; 12/31/05—$21.00; 12/31/06—$26.00. Farley Camera accrued the following compensation expense:

2004	$15,000	2005	$(10,000)	2006	$25,000

Required   a.   What is the executive's main advantage of receiving stock appreciation rights over stock options?
b.   In 2004, a $15,000 expense is recorded. What is the offsetting account?
c.   What is the financial impact on the company of the exercise of the stock appreciation rights in 2006? How does this impact affect financial statement analysis?

P 9-12a.   A company has only common stock outstanding.

Required   Answer the following multiple-choice question. Total stockholders' equity minus preferred stock equity divided by the number of shares outstanding represents the:
1.   Return on equity.
2.   Stated value per share.
3.   Book value per share.
4.   Price/earnings ratio.

P 9-12b.   Maple Corporation's stockholders' equity at June 30, 2003, consisted of the following:

Preferred stock, 10%, $50 par value; liquidating value, $55 per share; 20,000 shares issued and outstanding	$1,000,000
Common stock, $10 par value; 500,000 shares authorized; 150,000 shares issued and outstanding	1,500,000
Retained earnings	500,000

Required   Answer the following multiple-choice question. The book value per share of common stock is:
1. $10.00.
2. $12.67.
3. $13.33.
4. $17.65.

P 9-13.   Consecutive five-year balance sheets and income statements of the Donna Szabo Corporation are shown below and on the following page.

Required   a.   Compute or determine the following for the years 1999–2003.
1.   Degree of financial leverage
2.   Earnings per common share
3.   Price/earnings ratio
4.   Percentage of earnings retained
5.   Dividend payout
6.   Dividend yield
7.   Book value per share
8.   Materiality of options (use stock options outstanding)
b.   Comment from the perspective of an investor.

Donna Szabo Corporation
Balance Sheets
December 31, 1999 through December 31, 2003

(dollars in thousands)	2003	2002	2001	2000	1999
Assets					
Current assets:					
Cash	$ 26,000	$ 27,000	$ 29,000	$ 28,000	$ 27,000
Accounts receivable, net	125,000	126,000	128,000	130,000	128,000
Inventories	140,000	143,000	145,000	146,000	144,000
Total current assets	291,000	296,000	302,000	304,000	299,000
Property, plant, and equipment, net	420,000	418,000	417,000	418,000	415,000
Total assets	$ 711,000	$ 714,000	$ 719,000	$ 722,000	$ 714,000

Liabilities and Stockholders' Equity

Current liabilities:

Accounts payable	$ 120,000	$ 122,000	$ 122,500	$ 124,000	$ 125,000
Income taxes	12,000	13,000	13,500	13,000	12,000
Total current liabilities	132,000	135,000	136,000	137,000	137,000
Long-term debt	90,000	65,000	67,000	68,000	69,000

Stockholders' equity:

Preferred stock	49,000	76,000	80,000	82,000	75,000
Common stock	290,000	290,000	290,000	290,000	290,000
Paid-in capital in excess of par, common stock	70,000	70,000	70,000	70,000	70,000
Retained earnings	80,000	78,000	76,000	75,000	73,000
Total stockholders' equity	489,000	514,000	516,000	517,000	508,000
Total liabilities and stockholders' equity	$ 711,000	$ 714,000	$ 719,000	$ 722,000	$ 714,000

Donna Szabo Corporation
Statement of Earnings
Years Ended December 31, 1999–2003

(in thousands, except per share)	2003	2002	2001	2000	1999
Net sales	$ 890,000	$ 870,000	$ 850,000	$ 935,000	$ 920,000
Cost of goods sold	(540,000)	(530,700)	(522,750)	(579,000)	(570,000)
Gross profit	350,000	339,300	327,250	356,000	350,000
Selling and administrative expense	(230,000)	(225,000)	(220,000)	(225,000)	(224,000)
Interest expense	(9,500)	(6,600)	(6,800)	(6,900)	(7,000)
Earnings from continuing operations before income taxes	110,500	107,700	100,450	124,100	119,000
Income taxes	(33,000)	(33,300)	(32,100)	(30,400)	(37,400)
Earnings from continuing operations	77,500	74,400	68,350	93,700	81,600
Extraordinary gains, net of taxes	20,000	—	—	—	—
Net earnings	$ 97,500	$ 74,400	$ 68,350	$ 93,700	$ 81,600
Earnings per share:					
Continuing operations	$2.67	$2.57	$2.36	$3.23	$2.81
Extraordinary gain	.69	—	—	—	—
Net earnings per share	$3.36	$2.57	$2.36	$3.23	$2.81

Note: Additional data:

1. Preferred stock dividends (in thousands):

2003	$3,920
2002	$6,100
2001	$6,400
2000	$6,600
1999	$6,000

2. Common shares outstanding, 29,000,000 (actual) (1999–2003)
3. Stock options outstanding, 1,000,000 (actual) (1999–2003)
4. Dividends per common share (actual):

2003	$3.16
2002	$2.29
2001	$2.10
2000	$2.93
1999	$2.80

5. Market price per common share (actual):

2003 $24.00
2002 $22.00
2001 $21.00
2000 $37.00
1999 $29.00

Case 9-1

Why the Change?

USBANCOR presented the following with its 1998 annual report from the consolidated statement of income.

Year ended December 31	1998	1997	1996
	(in thousands, except per share data)		
Income before income taxes	$28,799	$32,800	$27,263
Provision for income taxes	7,655	9,303	7,244
Net income	$21,144	$23,497	$20,019
Per common share data:[1]			
Basic:			
Net income	$1.51	$1.56	$1.28
Average number of shares outstanding	14,011,893	15,043,128	15,586,092
Diluted:			
Net income	$1.48	$1.54	$1.28
Average number of shares outstanding	14,257,557	15,274,272	15,694,761
Cash dividends declared	$.60	$.53	$.46

(1) All per share and share data have been adjusted to reflect a 3-for-1 split effected in the form of a 200% stock dividend that was distributed on July 31, 1998, to shareholders of record on July 16, 1998.

From consolidated balance sheet:

At December 31	1998	1997
	(in thousands)	
Stockholders' equity[1]		
Preferred stock, no par value; 2,000,000 shares authorized: there were no shares issued and outstanding on December 31, 1998, and 1997	—	—
Common stock, par value $2.50 per share; 24,000,000 shares authorized; 17,350,136 shares issued and 13,512,317 outstanding on December 31, 1998; 17,282,028 shares issued and 14,681,154 shares outstanding on December 31, 1997	$ 43,375	$ 14,402
Treasury stock at cost, 3,837,819 shares on December 31, 1998, and 2,600,874 shares on December 1997	(61,521)	(31,175)
Surplus	65,495	93,934
Retained earnings	91,737	78,866
Accumulated other comprehensive income	2,584	2,153
Total stockholders' equity	141,670	158,180
Total liabilities and stockholders' equity	$2,377,081	$2,239,110

(1) All share data has been adjusted to reflect a 3-for-1 stock split effected in the form of a 200% stock dividend that was distributed on July 31, 1998, to shareholders of record on July 16, 1998.

Per the 1998 annual report the market price for the common stock was $19.88 for 1998 and $24.33 for 1997.

Required   a.   1.   How many shares of common stock were outstanding at December 31, 1998?
2.   What was the weighted average common shares for the year ended December 31, 1998?
3.   Which share number is used to compute earnings per share?
4.   Why did the outstanding shares decrease between 1997 and 1998?

b.   When computing the price/earnings ratio, should the basic or diluted earnings per share be used? Why?

c.   1.   For the 1997 annual report, would the net income have been $23,497,000? Explain.
2.   For the 1997 annual report, would the diluted earnings per share have been $1.54 for 1997? Explain.

d.   1.   Compute the book value for 1998 and 1997.
2.   Considering the earnings per share and the cash dividends per share for 1998, why did the book value decrease?

e.   Compute the dividend payout for 1998, 1997, and 1996.

Case 9-2

Stock Split Revisited

Selected data from the 1995 annual report of Lands' End, Inc. follows:

Lands' End, Inc. & Subsidiaries
Consolidated Statements of Operations (in Part)

	For the Period Ended		
(in thousands, except per-share data)	January 27, 1995	January 28, 1994	January 29, 1993
Net income	$ 36,096	$ 43,729	$ 33,500
Net income per share before cumulative effect of change in accounting	$ 1.03	$ 1.18	$ 0.92
Cumulative effect of change in accounting	—	.04	—
Net income per share	$ 1.03	$ 1.22	$ 0.92

Consolidated Balance Sheets (in Part)

(in thousands)	January 27, 1995	January 28, 1994
Shareholders' investment:		
Common stock, 40,221 and 20,110 shares issued, respectively	$ 402	$ 201
Donated capital	8,400	8,400
Paid-in capital	25,817	24,888
Deferred compensation	(1,421)	(2,001)
Currency translation adjustment	284	246
Retained earnings	229,554	193,460
Treasury stock, 5,395 and 2,154 shares at cost, respectively	(73,908)	(47,909)
Total shareholders' investment	$189,128	$177,285

Consolidated Statements of Shareholders' Investment

	For the Period Ended		
(in thousands)	January 27, 1995	January 28, 1994	January 29, 1993
Common Stock:			
Beginning balance	$ 201	$ 201	$ 201
2-for-1 stock split	201	—	—
Ending balance	$ 402	$ 201	$ 201
Donated Capital Balance	$ 8,400	$ 8,400	$ 8,400

(in thousands)	For the Period Ended		
	January 27, 1995	January 28, 1994	January 29, 1993
Paid-In Capital:			
Beginning balance	$ 24,888	$ 24,857	$ 23,782
Tax benefit of stock options exercised	1,130	31	1,075
2-for-1 stock split	(201)	—	—
Ending balance	$ 25,817	$ 24,888	$ 24,857
Deferred Compensation:			
Beginning balance	$ (2,001)	$ (1,680)	$ (886)
Issuance of treasury stock	—	(564)	(985)
Amortization of deferred compensation	580	243	191
Ending balance	$ (1,421)	$ (2,001)	$ (1,680)
Foreign Currency Translation:			
Beginning balance	$ 246	$ —	$ —
Adjustment for the year	38	246	—
Ending balance	$ 284	$ 246	$ —
Retained Earnings:			
Beginning balance	$193,460	$153,324	$123,418
Net income	36,096	43,729	33,500
Cash dividends paid	—	(3,592)	(3,589)
Issuance of treasury stock	(2)	(1)	(5)
Ending balance	$229,554	$193,460	$153,324
Treasury Stock:			
Beginning balance	$ (47,909)	$ (45,714)	$ (28,283)
Purchase of treasury stock	(27,979)	(2,861)	(20,972)
Issuance of treasury stock	1,980	666	3,541
Ending balance	$ (73,908)	$ (47,909)	$ (45,714)
Total Stockholders' Equity	$189,128	$177,285	$139,388

Consolidated Statement of Cash Flows (in Part)

(in thousands)	For the Period Ended		
	January 27, 1995	January 28, 1994	January 29, 1993
Cash flows (used for) from financing activities:			
Proceeds from short-term and long-term debt	$ 7,539	$ 80	—
Payment of short-term and long-term debt	(40)	—	$ (16,349)
Tax effect of exercise of stock options	1,130	31	1,075
Purchase of treasury stock	(27,979)	(2,861)	(20,972)
Issuance of treasury stock	1,978	101	2,551
Cash dividends paid to common shareholders	—	(3,592)	(3,589)
Net cash flows used for financing activities	$ (17,372)	$ (6,241)	$ (37,284)

Note 1. Summary of significant accounting policies (in Part)

Net income per share

Net income per share is computed by dividing net income by the weighted average number of common shares outstanding during each period. After the 2-for-1 stock split, the weighted average common shares outstanding were 35.2 million, 35.9 million, and 36.3 million (see Note 2) for fiscal years 1995, 1994, and 1993, respectively. Common stock equivalents include awards, grants, and stock options issued by the company. The common stock equivalents do not significantly dilute basic earnings per share.

Note 2. Shareholders' investment (in Part)

Capital Stock

Pursuant to shareholder approval in May 1994, the company increased its authorized common stock from 30 million shares of $0.01 par value to 160 million shares. Also, the company is authorized to issue 5 million shares of preferred stock, $0.01 par value. The company's board of directors has the authority to issue shares and to fix dividend, voting and conversion rights, redemption provisions, liquidation preferences, and other rights and restrictions of the preferred stock.

Ten-Year Consolidated Financial Summary (unaudited) (in Part)

(in thousands, except per share data)	1995	1994[2]	1993	1992
Per share of common stock:[1]				
Net income per share before cumulative effect of change in accounting	$1.03	$1.18	$0.92	$0.77
Cumulative effect of change in accounting	—	$0.04	—	—
Net income per share	$1.03	$1.22	$0.92	$0.77
Cash dividends per share	—	$0.10	$0.10	$0.10
Common shares outstanding	34,826	35,912	36,056	36,944

(1) Net income per share (pro forma 1986 and 1987) was computed after giving retroactive effect to the 108-for-1 stock split in August 1986, the 2-for-1 stock split in August 1987, the 2-for-1 stock split in May 1994, and assuming that the shares sold in the October 1986 initial public offering were issued at the beginning of fiscal 1986.

(2) Effective January 30, 1993, the company adopted Statement of Financial Accounting Standards (SFAS) No. 109, "Accounting for Income Taxes," which was recorded as a change in accounting principle at the beginning of fiscal 1994, with an increase to net income of $1.3 million or $0.04 per share.

Selected data from the 1993 annual report of Lands' End, Inc. follows:

Consolidated Balance Sheets (in Part)

(in thousands)	January 29, 1993	January 31, 1992
Shareholders' investment:		
Common stock, 20,110,294 shares issued	$ 201	$ 201
Donated capital	8,400	8,400
Paid-in capital	24,857	23,782
Deferred compensation	(1,680)	(886)
Retained earnings	153,324	123,418
Treasury stock, 2,082,035 and 1,638,840 shares at cost, respectively	(45,714)	(28,283)
Total shareholders' investment	$139,388	$126,632

Consolidated Statement of Operations (in Part)

(dollars in thousands, except per-share data)	January 29, 1993	January 31, 1992	January 31, 1991
Net income	$33,500	$28,732	$14,743
Net income per share	1.85	1.53	0.75

Note: Annual report courtesy of Lands' End, Inc.

Required   a.   The 1995 annual report discloses net income for the period ended January 29, 1993 of $33,500,000 and net income per share of $0.92 for this same period. The 1993 annual report discloses net income for the period ended January 29, 1993 of $33,500,000 and net income per share of $1.85 for this same period. Speculate on why the net income per share has changed.

b.   1.   How many shares have been sold and paid for as of January 27, 1995?
   2.   How many shares have been bought back and not retired as of January 27, 1995?
   3.   How many shares are outstanding as of January 27, 1995?

    c.   Indicate the total cash dividend paid for the period ended:
        1.   January 27, 1995.
        2.   January 28, 1994.
        3.   January 29, 1993.
    d.   Indicate the amount paid for the purchase of treasury stock:
        1.   For the period ended January 27, 1995.
        2.   For the period ended January 28, 1994.
        3.   For the period ended January 29, 1993.
    e.   Indicate the total paid to stockholders for the period ended:
        1.   January 27, 1995.
        2.   January 28, 1994.
        3.   January 29, 1993.
    f.   What common share number was used to compute earnings per share for 1995?
    g.   What is the par value of common stock?

Case 9-3   Stock Option Plans (Stock-Based Compensation)

Reebok International Ltd. Vs. Motorola Inc. and Subsidiaries

Reebok International Ltd.
10-K (for year ended December 31, 2002) (in Part)

Item 1: Business
    General
    Reebok International Ltd. is a global company that designs and markets sports and fitness products, including footwear, apparel and accessories. . . We also design and market casual footwear, apparel and accessories for non-athletic use.

Reebok International Ltd. (year ended December 31, 2002)
Summary of Significant Accounting Policies (in Part)
Accounting for Stock-Based Compensation

    At December 31, 2002 the Company has stock-based employee compensation plans which are described in Note 8 to the consolidated financial statements. The Company accounts for those plans under the recognition and measurement principles of Accounting Principles Board Opinion No. 25, "Accounting for Stock Issued to Employees," and related interpretations. No stock-based employee compensation cost is reflected in net income, as all options granted under those plans has an exercise price equal to the market value of the underlying common stock on the date of grant. The Company provides pro forma disclosures of the compensation expense determined under the fair value provisions of Financial Accounting Standards Board Statement No. 123, "Accounting for Stock-Based Compensation." See Note 8 to the consolidated financial statements.

Note 8 Stock Plans (in Part)

"For purposes of pro forma disclosures, the estimated fair value of the options is amortized to expense over the options' vesting period. The Company's pro forma information follows (in thousands except for earnings per share information):

	2002	2001	2000
Net income before cumulative effect of accounting change	$131,528	$102,726	$80,878
Deduct: Total stock-based employee compensation expense determined under fair value based method for all awards, net of related tax effect	7,031	6,111	5,953
Pro forma net income before cumulative effect of accounting change	$124,497	$ 96,615	$74,925

	2002	2001	2000
Basic earnings per share before cumulative effect of accounting change:			
As reported	$2.21	$1.75	$1.42
Pro forma	$2.15	$1.70	$1.37
Diluted earnings per share before cumulative effect of accounting change:			
As reported	$2.04	$1.66	$1.40
Pro forma	$1.99	$1.61	$1.35
Net income as reported	$126,458	$102,726	$80,878
Deduct: Total stock based employee compensation employee compensation expense determined under the fair value based method for all awards, net of related tax effect	7,031	6,111	5,953
Pro forma net income	$119,427	$ 96,615	$74,925
Basic earnings per share:			
As reported	$2.12	$1.75	$1.42
Pro forma	$2.06	$1.70	$1.37
Diluted earnings per share:			
As reported	$1.97	$1.66	$1.40
Pro forma	$1.91	$1.61	$1.35

Motorola Inc. and Subsidiaries
10-K (for year ended December 31, 2002) (in Part)

Item 1: Business

General

Motorola is a global leader in providing integrated communications and embedded electronic solutions.

Item 8: Financial Statements and Supplementary Data Incorporates by reference to Motorola's Proxy Statement for the 2003 annual meet of stockholders.

Proxy (in Part)

Notes to consolidated Financial Statements Motorola Inc. and Subsidiaries (dollars in millions, except as noted) (in Part)

Stock Compensation Costs (in Part)

"The Company measures compensation cost for stock options and restricted stock using the intrinsic value-based method."

"The Company has evaluated the pro forma effects of using the fair-value-based method of accounting and as such, net earnings (loss), basic earnings (loss) per common share and diluted earnings (loss) per common share would have been as follows:

Year Ended December 31	2002	2001	2000
Net earnings (loss);			
Net earnings (loss) as reported	$ (2,485)	$ (3,937)	$ 1,318
Add: Stock-based employee compensation expense included in reported net earnings (loss), net of related tax effects	28	33	32
Deduct: Stock-based employee compensation expense determined under fair value-based method for all awards, net of related tax effects	(319)	(373)	(208)
Pro forma	$ (2,776)	$ (4,277)	$ 1,142

	2002	2001	2000
Basic earnings (loss) per common share:			
As reported	$(1.09)	$(1.78)	$0.61
Pro forma	$(1.22)	$(1.93)	$0.53
Diluted earnings (loss) per common share:			
As reported	$(1.09)	$(1.78)	$0.58
Pro forma	$(1.22)	$(1.93)	$0.51

Required

a. Considering the nature of the industries that these firms operate in would you expect a difference in the use of options?

b. Comment on the materiality of stock-based compensation for Reebok International Ltd.

c. Comment on the materiality of stock-based compensation for Motorola Inc.

Case 9-4

Food, Food, Food

Selected data from the 2002 annual report of Frisch's Restaurants, Inc. follow:

Consolidated Balance Sheet

ASSETS

June 2, 2001 and June 3, 2001

	2002	2001
Current Assets		
Cash	$ 670,726	$ 280,460
Receivables		
Trade	858,524	1,048,983
Other	309,723	415,592
Inventories	3,585,239	3,601,508
Prepaid expenses and sundry deposits	993,366	1,018,741
Prepaid and deferred income taxes	1,069,381	600,164
Total current assets	7,486,959	6,965,448
Property and Equipment		
Land and improvements	38,859,285	29,381,174
Buildings	63,069,041	54,099,186
Equipment and fixtures	62,677,482	55,967,327
Leasehold improvements and buildings on leased land	14,692,924	13,263,779
Capitalized leases	7,388,580	7,343,935
Construction in progress	6,790,095	6,959,407
	193,477,407	167,014,808
Less accumulated depreciation and amortization	85,757,893	78,595,507
Net property and equipment	107,719,514	88,419,301
Other Assets		
Goodwill	740,644	740,644
Other intangible assets	998,549	980,423
Investments in land	945,217	1,340,492
Property held for sale	2,045,972	1,801,747
Long-term receivables	2,383,479	856,342
Net cash surrender value—life insurance policies	4,571,067	4,367,384
Deferred income taxes	87,086	762,035
Other	2,356,446	2,076,200
Total other assets	14,128,460	12,925,267
	$129,334,933	$108,310,016

LIABILITIES AND SHAREHOLDERS' EQUITY

June 2, 2002 and June 3, 2001

	2002	2001
Current Liabilities		
Long-term obligations due within one year		
Long-term debt	$ **4,099,770**	$ 1,605,318
Obligations under capitalized leases	**466,123**	413,824
Self insurance	**1,418,040**	838,321
Accounts payable	**9,357,584**	8,870,147
Accrued expenses	**6,674,742**	5,994,499
Income taxes	**334,556**	210,290
Total current liabilities	**22,350,815**	17,932,399
Long-Term Obligations		
Long-term debt	**35,904,960**	23,678,748
Obligations under capitalized leases	**4,245,504**	4,503,891
Self insurance	**2,877,412**	2,964,549
Other	**2,726,314**	2,784,388
Total long-term obligations	**45,754,190**	33,931,576
Commitments	**—**	—
Shareholders' Equity		
Capital stock		
Preferred stock—authorized, 3,000,000 shares		
without par value; none issued	**—**	—
Common stock—authorized, 12,000,000 shares		
without par value; issued 7,385,107 and 7,362,279		
shares—stated value—$1	**7,385,107**	7,362,279
Additional contributed capital	**60,496,396**	60,257,601
	67,881,503	67,619,880
Retained earnings	**26,487,596**	20,243,357
	94,369,099	87,863,237
Less cost of treasury stock (2,474,347 and 2,350,685 shares)	**33,139,171**	31,417,196
Total shareholders' equity	**61,229,928**	56,446,041
	$129,334,933	$108,310,016

Consolidated Statement of Earnings

Three years ended June 2, 2002˙

	2002	2001*	2000
Revenue			
Sales	**$210,434,433**	$187,464,958	$165,846,505
Other	**1,324,023**	2,564,642	1,353,295
Total revenue	**211,758,456**	190,029,600	167,199,800
Costs and expenses			
Cost of sales			
Food and paper	**69,994,741**	62,696,341	54,621,455
Payroll and related	**73,811,585**	64,825,646	57,286,588
Other operating costs	**42,236,535**	38,074,381	34,230,261
	186,042,861	165,596,368	146,138,304
Administrative and advertising	**11,061,466**	10,285,259	9,224,978
Impairment of long-lived assets	**—**	1,549,171	—
Interest	**2,420,370**	2,606,747	2,410,443
Total costs and expenses	**199,524,697**	180,037,545	157,773,725
Earnings from continuing operations before income taxes	**12,233,759**	9,992,055	9,426,075
Income taxes			
Current			
Federal	**3,225,283**	2,693,855	3,194,952
Less tax credits	**(347,911)**	(318,457)	(239,750)
State and municipal	**680,212**	482,035	577,307
Deferred	**704,794**	577,661	(181,580)
	4,262,378	3,435,094	3,350,929
Earnings from continuing operations	**7,971,381**	6,556,961	6,075,146
Income from discontinued operations (net of applicable tax)	**—**	430,023	70,395
Gain on disposal of discontinued operations (net of applicable tax)	**—**	698,809	—
Earnings from discontinued operations	**—**	1,128,832	70,395
NET EARNINGS	**$ 7,971,381**	$ 7,685,793	$ 6,145,541
Earnings per share (EPS) of common stock:			
Basic EPS—continuing operations	**$1.61**	$1.28	$1.08
Basic EPS—discontinued operations	**—**	.22	.01
Basic net earnings per share	**$1.61**	$1.50	$1.09
Diluted EPS—continuing operations	**$1.59**	$1.27	$1.08
Diluted EPS—discontinued operations	**—**	.22	.01
Diluted net earnings per share	**$1.59**	$1.49	$1.09

*Indicates 53-week period.

Required

a. Compute the following for 2002 and 2001.
1. Degree of financial leverage
2. Price/earnings ratio
3. Percentage of earnings retained
4. Dividend yield
5. Book value per share

b. Comment on the ratios computed under (a).

Other selected data:

| | Year Ended | |
	June 2, 2002	June 3, 2001
1. Market price per common share	$19.90	$12.80
2. Dividends paid in total	$1,727,142	$1,639,185
3. Dividends paid per share	$.35	$.32

Case 9-5

Connecting

The Gannett Co., Inc. presented this data as part of its 2001 annual report.

5-YEAR SUMMARY (Part of 5-Year Summary, which is part of 11-year summary)

In thousands of dollars, except per share amounts

	2001	2000	1999	1998	1997
Net operating revenues					
Newspaper advertising	$4,119,773	$3,972,936	$3,115,250	$2,773,247	$2,479,828
Newspaper circulation	1,233,106	1,120,991	971,114	958,456	903,309
Broadcasting	662,652	788,767	728,642	721,298	703,558
All other	328,714	339,624	280,356	256,030	221,470
Total (Notes a and b, see page 50)	6,344,245	6,222,318	5,095,362	4,709,031	4,308,165
Operating expenses					
Costs and expenses	4,310,633	4,029,147	3,252,170	3,069,754	2,812,218
Depreciation	202,456	195,428	169,460	163,776	152,964
Amortization of intangible assets	241,321	180,487	110,631	89,687	80,741
Total	4,754,410	4,405,062	3,532,261	3,323,217	3,045,923
Operating income	1,589,835	1,817,256	1,563,101	1,385,814	1,262,242
Non-operating (expense) income					
Interest expense	(221,854)	(219,228)	(94,619)	(79,412)	(98,242)
Other	2,616	10,812	58,705(11)	305,323	(9,047)
Income before income taxes	1,370,597	1,608,840	1,527,187	1,611,725	1,154,953
Provision for income taxes	539,400	636,900	607,800	645,300	473,600
Income from continuing operations	831,197	971,940	919,387(11)	966,425	681,353
Discontinued operations:					
Income from the operation of discontinued businesses (net of income taxes) (12)		2,437	38,541	33,488	31,326
Gain on sale of discontinued businesses (net of income taxes) (13)	—	744,700	—	—	—
Total	—	747,137	38,541	33,488	31,326
Net income	$ 831,197	$1,719,077	$ 957,928	$ 999,913	$ 712,679

Other:

Market price per share:

December 30, 2001	67.93
December 31, 2000	63.06
December 26, 1999	79.31

Total dividends declared:

2001	$238,301,000
2000	228,212,000
1999	228,781,000

Required   a. 1. For net operating revenues prepare a horizontal common-size analysis for 1997–2001. Use 1997 as the base.
2. Comment on the results in (1).
b. 1. For net operating revenues prepare a vertical common-size analysis for 1997–2001. Use total net operating revenues as the base.
2. Comment on the results in (1).
c. Based on these data compute the following for 1999–2001.
1. Degree of financial leverage
2. Percentage of earnings retained
d. Comment on the results in (c).

Web Case   # Thomson Analytics *Business School Edition*

Please complete the web case that covers material covered in this chapter at http://gibson.swlearning.com. You'll be using Thomson Analytics Business School Edition, a version of the powerful tool used by Wall Street professionals, that combines a full range of fundamental financial information, earnings estimates, market data, and source documents for 500 publicly traded companies.

Endnotes

1. Justin Fox, "The Next Best Thing to Free Money (Silicon Valley's Stock-Options Culture)," *Fortune* (July 7, 1997), p. 54.
2. Copyrighted material—reproduced with permission of the author.

CHAPTER

10

STATEMENT OF CASH FLOWS

Considering the importance of cash, it is not surprising that the statement of cash flows has become one of the primary financial statements. The statement of cash flows allow managers, equity analysts, commercial lenders, and investment bankers a thorough explanation of the changes that occurred in the firm's cash balances.

The statement of cash flows provides an explanation of the changes that occurred in the firm's cash balances for a specific period. Cash is considered to be the lifeblood of the firm. Understanding the flow of cash is critical to having a handle on the pulse of the firm.

Quote the Banker, "Watch Cash Flow

Once upon a midnight dreary as I pondered weak and weary
Over many a quaint and curious volume of accounting lore,
Seeking gimmicks (without scruple) to squeeze through some new tax loophole,
Suddenly I heard a knock upon my door,
    Only this, and nothing more.

Then I felt a queasy tingling and I heard the cash a-jingling
As a fearsome banker entered whom I'd often seen before.
His face was money-green and in his eyes there could be seen
Dollar-signs that seemed to glitter as he reckoned up the score.
    "Cash flow," the banker said, and nothing more.

I had always thought it fine to show a jet black bottom line,
But the banker sounded a resounding, "No,
Your receivables are high, mounting upward toward the sky;
Write-offs loom. What matters is cash flow."
    He repeated, "Watch cash flow."

Then I tried to tell the story of our lovely inventory
Which, though large, is full of most delightful stuff.
But the banker saw its growth, and with a mighty oath
He waved his arms and shouted, "Stop! Enough!
    Pay the interest, and don't give me any guff!"

Next I looked for non-cash items which could add ad infinitum
To replace the ever-outward flow of cash,
But to keep my statement black I'd held depreciation back,
And my banker said that I'd done something rash.
    He quivered, and his teeth began to gnash.

When I asked him for a loan, he responded, with a groan,
That the interest rate would be just prime plus eight,
And to guarantee my purity he'd insist on some security—
All my assets plus the scalp upon my pate.
    Only this, a standard rate.

Though my bottom line is black, I am flat upon my back.
My cash flows out and customers pay slow.
The growth of my receivables is almost unbelievable;
The result is certain—unremitting woe!
And I hear the banker utter an ominous low mutter,
    "Watch cash flow."

—Herbert S. Bailey, Jr.
Reprinted with permission

**BASIC
ELEMENTS
OF THE
STATEMENT OF
CASH FLOWS**

The statement of cash flows is prepared using a concept of cash that includes not only cash itself but also short-term, highly liquid investments. This is referred to as the "cash and cash equivalent" focus. The category cash and cash equivalents includes cash on hand, cash on deposit, and investments in short-term, highly liquid investments. The cash flow statement analysis explains the change in these focus accounts by examining all the accounts on the balance sheet other than the focus accounts.

Management may use the statement of cash flows to determine dividend policy, cash generated by operations, and investing and financing policy. Outsiders, such as creditors or investors, may use it to determine such things as the firm's ability to increase dividends, its ability to pay debt with cash from operations, and the percentage of cash from operations in relation to the cash from financing.

The statement of cash flows must report all transactions affecting cash flow. A company will occasionally have investing and/or financing activities that have no direct effect on cash flow. For example, a company may acquire land in exchange for common stock. This is an investing transaction (acquiring the land) and a financing transaction (issuing the common stock). The conversion of long-term bonds into common stock involves two financing activities with no effect on cash flow. Since transactions such as these will have future effects on cash flows, these transactions are to be disclosed in a separate schedule presented with the statement of cash flows.

The statement of cash flows classifies cash receipts and cash payments into operating, investing, and financing activities.[1] In brief, operating activities involve income statement items. Investing activities generally result from changes in long-term asset items. Financing activities generally relate to long-term liability and stockholders' equity items. A description of these activities and typical cash flows are as follows:

1. **Operating activities.** Operating activities include all transactions and other events that are not investing or financing activities. Cash flows from operating activities are generally the cash effects of transactions and other events that enter into the determination of net income.
    Typical cash inflows:
    > From sale of goods or services
    > From return on loans (interest)
    > From return on equity securities (dividends)

    Typical cash outflows:
    > Payments for acquisitions of inventory
    > Payments to employees
    > Payments to governments (taxes)
    > Payments of interest expense
    > Payments to suppliers for other expenses

2. **Investing activities.** Investing activities include lending money and collecting on those loans and acquiring and selling investments and productive long-term assets.
    Typical cash inflows:
    > From receipts from loans collected
    > From sales of debt or equity securities of other corporations
    > From sale of property, plant, and equipment

    Typical cash outflows:
    > Loans to other entities
    > Purchase of debt or equity securities of other entities
    > Purchase of property, plant, and equipment

3. **Financing activities.** Financing activities include cash flows relating to liability and owners' equity.
    Typical cash inflows:
    > From sale of equity securities
    > From sale of bonds, mortgages, notes, and other short- or long-term borrowings

    Typical cash outflows:
    > Payment of dividends
    > Reacquisition of the firm's capital stock
    > Payment of amounts borrowed

The statement of cash flows presents cash flows from operating activities first, followed by investing activities and then financing activities. The individual inflows and outflows from investing and financing activities are presented separately. The operating activities section can be presented using the *direct method* or the *indirect method*. (The indirect method is sometimes referred to as the *reconciliation method*.) The direct method essentially presents the income statement on a cash basis, instead of an accrual basis. The indirect method adjusts net income for items that affected net income but did not affect cash.

SFAS No. 95 encouraged enterprises to use the direct method to present cash flows from operating activities. However, if a company uses the direct method, the standard requires a reconciliation of net income to net cash provided by operating activities in a separate schedule. If a firm uses the indirect method, it must make a separate disclosure of interest paid and income taxes paid during the period. Exhibit 10–1 presents skeleton formats of a statement of cash flows using the direct method and the indirect method.

The 1986 SFAS Exposure Draft, "Statement of Cash Flows," indicates that:

> The principal advantage of the direct method is that it shows the operating cash receipts and payments. Knowledge of where operating cash flows came from and how cash was used in past periods

EXHIBIT 10-1	**JONES COMPANY EXAMPLE** **Statement of Cash Flows—Comparison of Presentation** **of Direct Method and Indirect Method** **For Year Ended December 31, 20XX**

Direct Method	
Cash flows from operating activities:	
Cash received from customers	$ 370,000
Cash paid to suppliers and employees	(310,000)
Interest received	10,000
Interest paid (net of amount capitalized)	(4,000)
Income taxes paid	(15,000)
Net cash provided by operations	51,000
Cash flows from investing activities:	
Capital expenditures	(30,000)
Proceeds from property, plant, and equipment disposals	6,000
Net cash used in investing activities	(24,000)
Cash flows from financing activities:	
Net proceeds from repayment of commercial paper	(4,000)
Proceeds from issuance of long-term debt	6,000
Dividends paid	(5,000)
Net cash used in financing activities	(3,000)
Net increase in cash and cash equivalents	24,000
Cash and cash equivalents at beginning of period	8,000
Cash and cash equivalents at end of period	$ 32,000
Reconciliation of net earnings to cash provided by operating activities:	
Net earnings	$ 40,000
Provision for depreciation	6,000
Provision for allowance for doubtful accounts	1,000
Deferred income taxes	1,000
Loss on property, plant, and equipment disposals	2,000
Changes in operating assets and liabilities:	
Receivables increase	(2,000)
Inventories increase	(4,000)
Accounts payable increase	5,000
Accrued income taxes increase	2,000
Net cash provided by operating activities	$ 51,000
Supplemental schedule of noncash investing and financing activities:	
Land acquired (investing) by issuing bonds (financing)	$ 10,000

EXHIBIT 10-1

JONES COMPANY EXAMPLE
Statement of Cash Flows—Comparison of Presentation
of Direct Method and Indirect Method
For Year Ended December 31, 20XX (*continued*)

Indirect Method

Operating activities:	
Net earnings	$ 40,000
Provision for depreciation	6,000
Provision for allowance for doubtful accounts	1,000
Deferred income taxes	1,000
Loss on property, plant, and equipment disposals	2,000
Changes in operating assets and liabilities:	
Receivables increase	(2,000)
Inventories increase	(4,000)
Accounts payable increase	5,000
Accrued income taxes increase	2,000
Net cash provided by operating activities	$ 51,000
Cash flows from investing activities:	
Capital expenditures	(30,000)
Proceeds from property, plant, and equipment disposals	6,000
Net cash used in investing activities	(24,000)
Cash flows from financing activities:	
Net proceeds from repayment of commercial paper	(4,000)
Proceeds from issuance of long-term debt	6,000
Dividends paid	(5,000)
Net cash used in financing activities	(3,000)
Net increase in cash and cash equivalents	24,000
Cash and cash equivalents at beginning of period	8,000
Cash and cash equivalents at end of period	$ 32,000
Supplemental disclosure of cash flow information:	
Interest paid	$ 500
Income taxes paid	10,000
Supplemental schedule of noncash investing and financing activities:	
Land acquired (investing) and issuing bonds (financing)	$ 10,000

may be useful in estimating future cash flows. The indirect method of reporting has the advantage of focusing on the differences between income and cash flow from operating activities.[2]

Exhibit 10–2 presents the 2002 Nike Statement of Cash Flows. This statement presents cash from operations, using the indirect method. The statement closely follows the standard format.

In addition to reviewing the flow of funds on a yearly basis, reviewing a flow of funds for a three-year period may be helpful. This can be accomplished by adding a total column to the statement that represents the total of each item for the three-year period. This has been done for Nike in Exhibit 10-2.

Some observations on the 2002 Nike Statement of Cash Flows, considering the three-year period ended May 31, 2002, follow:

1. Net cash provided by operating activities was the major source of cash.
2. Net cash used in investing activities, specifically additions to property, plant, and equipment, was the major use of cash for investing activities.
3. Repurchase of stock was the major financing use of cash.
4. Cash dividends were approximately 16.07% of net cash provided by operating activities.

EXHIBIT 10-2   NIKE, INC.

Consolidated Statements of Cash Flows, with Three-Year Total

	Total	Year Ended May 31, 2002	2001	2000
		(in millions)		
Cash provided (used) by operations:				
Net income	$ 1,832.1	$ 663.3	$ 589.7	$ 579.1
Income charges not affecting cash:				
Depreciation	608.9	223.5	197.4	188.0
Deferred income taxes	131.8	15.2	79.8	36.8
Amortization and other	105.4	53.1	16.7	35.6
Income tax benefit from exercise of stock options	61.2	13.9	32.4	14.9
Changes in certain working capital components:				
Increase in accounts receivable	(359.2)	(135.2)	(141.4)	(82.6)
Decrease (increase) in inventories	(273.1)	55.4	(16.7)	(311.8)
Decrease in other current assets and income taxes receivable	156.1	16.9	78.0	61.2
Increase (decrease) in accounts payable, accrued				
liabilities and income taxes payable	174.4	175.4	(179.4)	178.4
Cash provided by operations	2,437.6	1,081.5	656.5	699.6
Cash provided (used) by investing activities:				
Additions to property, plant and equipment and other	(1,020.3)	(282.8)	(317.6)	(419.9)
Disposals of property, plant and equipment	53.6	15.6	12.7	25.3
Increase in other assets	(132.9)	(39.1)	(42.5)	(51.3)
Increase in other liabilities	14.5	3.5	5.1	5.9
Cash used by investing activities	(1,085.1)	(302.8)	(342.3)	(440.0)
Cash provided (used) by financing activities:				
Proceeds from long-term debt issuance	329.9	329.9	—	—
Reductions in long-term debt, including current portion	(132.3)	(80.3)	(50.3)	(1.7)
(Decrease) increase in notes payable	4.7	(431.5)	(68.9)	505.1
Proceeds from exercise of stock options and other stock issuances	139.4	59.5	56.0	23.9
Repurchase of stock	(1,030.2)	(226.9)	(157.0)	(646.3)
Dividends—common and preferred	(391.7)	(128.9)	(129.7)	(133.1)
Cash used by financing activities	(1,080.2)	(478.2)	(349.9)	(252.1)
Effect of exchange rate changes	105.1	(29.0)	85.4	48.7
Net increase in cash and equivalents	377.4	271.5	49.7	56.2
Cash and equivalents, beginning of year	198.1	304.0	254.3	198.1
Cash and equivalents, end of year	$ 575.5	$ 575.5	$ 304.0	$ 254.3
Supplemental disclosure of cash flow information:				
Cash paid during the year for:				
Interest	$ 167.7	$ 54.2	$ 68.5	$ 45.0
Income taxes	636.2	262.0	173.1	221.1
Non-cash investing and financing activity:				
Assumption of long-term debt to acquire property, plant and equipment	$ 108.9	—	—	$ 108.9

Exhibit 10–3 presents the 2001 cash flow statement of Rowe Furniture, with a total column for the three-year period. This firm presented the cash flows from operating activities using the direct method. Note the following with regard to Exhibit 10–3:

1. Net cash provided by operations represented a major source of cash.
2. Capital expenditures represented the largest outflow from investing activities.
3. Payments to acquire businesses represented a major outflow from investing activities.
4. The net proceeds from issuance of long-term debt represented the major inflow from financing activities.

Exhibit 10–4 restates the 2001 cash flows for Rowe Furniture, viewing inflows and outflows separately. Some observations regarding Exhibit 10–4 follow:

EXHIBIT 10-3	THE ROWE COMPANIES Consolidated Statement of Cash Flows, with Three-Year Total

	Total	12/2/01 (52 weeks)	Year Ended 12/3/00 (53 weeks)	11/28/99 (52 weeks)
		(in thousands)		
Increase (Decrease) in Cash				
Cash flows from operating activities:				
Cash received from customers	$1,004,646	$ 329,683	$ 379,400	$ 295,563
Cash paid to suppliers and employees	(958,388)	(328,948)	(354,570)	(274,870)
Income taxes paid, net of refunds	(13,324)	585	(6,183)	(7,726)
Interest paid	(13,021)	(4,642)	(5,693)	(2,686)
Interest received	927	480	288	159
Other receipts—net	3,949	1,109	1,156	1,684
Net cash and cash equivalents provided by (used in) operating activities	24,789	(1,733)	14,398	12,124
Cash flows from investing activities:				
Proceeds from sale of property and equipment	1,096	1,056	21	19
Capital expenditures	(21,302)	(3,317)	(9,155)	(8,830)
Payments to acquire businesses (Note 2)	(14,052)	—	(5,160)	(8,892)
Net cash used in investing activities	(34,258)	(2,261)	(14,294)	(17,703)
Cash flows from financing activities:				
Net borrowings (payments) under line of credit	7,275	5,368	(164)	2,071
Proceeds from issuance of long-term debt	45,017	6,865	13,020	25,132
Payments to reduce long-term debt	(30,265)	(3,821)	(11,922)	(14,522)
Proceeds from loans against life insurance policies	3,014	3,014	—	—
Proceeds from issuance of common stock	538	27	51	460
Dividends paid	(4,942)	(1,379)	(1,849)	(1,714)
Purchase of treasury stock	(4,191)	(16)	(951)	(3,224)
Net cash provided by (used in) financing activities	16,446	10,058	(1,815)	8,203
Net increase (decrease) in cash and cash equivalents	6,977	6,064	(1,711)	2,624
Cash at beginning of year	2,480	3,393	5,104	2,480
Cash at end of year	$ 9,457	$ 9,457	$ 3,393	$ 5,104

(continued)

1. Approximately 95% of the total cash inflows came from operations.
2. Approximately 98% of total cash outflows related to operations.
3. There were no material inflows and outflows other than (1) or (2).

FINANCIAL RATIOS AND THE STATEMENT OF CASH FLOWS

Financial ratios that relate to the statement of cash flows were slow in being developed. This was related to several factors. For one thing, most financial ratios traditionally related an income statement item(s) to a balance sheet item(s). This became the normal way of approaching financial analysis, and the statement of cash flows did not become a required statement until 1987. Thus, it took a while for analysts to become familiar with the statement.

Ratios have now been developed that relate to the cash flow statement. Some of these ratios are as follows:

1. Operating cash flow/current maturities of long-term debt and current notes payable
2. Operating cash flow/total debt
3. Operating cash flow per share
4. Operating cash flow/cash dividends

EXHIBIT 10-3	**THE ROWE COMPANIES**

Reconciliation of Net Earnings (Loss) to Net Cash Provided by (Used in) Operating Activities, with Three-Year Total (*continued*)

	Total	12/2/01 (52 weeks)	Year Ended 12/3/00 (53 weeks)	11/28/99 (52 weeks)
			(in thousands)	
Net earnings (loss)	$ 11,256	$ (6,189)	$ 3,544	$ 13,901
Adjustments to reconcile net earnings (loss) to net cash provided by (used in) operating activities, net of acquisition and disposition of businesses:				
Loss on disposition of Wexford	5,455	—	5,455	—
Depreciation and amortization	23,315	8,569	8,581	6,165
Provision for deferred compensation	2,072	173	816	1,083
Payments made for deferred compensation	(1,292)	(813)	(160)	(319)
Deferred income taxes	(1,570)	1,001	(2,099)	(472)
Provision for losses on accounts receivable	6,319	4,421	1,485	413
Loss (gain) on disposition of assets	48	15	29	4
Change in operating assets and liabilities net of effects of acquisition and disposition of businesses:				
Decrease (increase) in accounts receivable	834	4,649	5,564	(9,379)
Decrease (increase) in inventories	(6,297)	227	(832)	(5,692)
Decrease (increase) in prepaid expenses and other	(3)	1,679	(887)	(795)
Decrease (increase) in other assets	(1,090)	(352)	472	(1,210)
Increase (decrease) in accounts payable	(11,197)	(10,277)	(4,750)	3,830
Increase (decrease) in accrued expenses	(3,978)	(4,433)	(1,715)	2,170
Increase (decrease) in customer deposits	917	(403)	(1,105)	2,425
Total adjustments	13,533	4,456	10,854	(1,777)
Net cash provided by (used in) operating activities	$ 24,789	$ (1,733)	$ 14,398	$ 12,124
Supplemental Disclosures of Cash Flows:				
Fair value of assets acquired other than cash				$ 37,272
Liabilities assumed				(28,380)
Payments to acquire businesses				$ 8,892

Operating Cash Flow/Current Maturities of Long-Term Debt and Current Notes Payable

The **operating cash flow/current maturities of long-term debt and current notes payable** is a ratio that indicates a firm's ability to meet its current maturities of debt. The higher this ratio, the better the firm's ability to meet its current maturities of debt. The higher this ratio, the better the firm's liquidity. This ratio relates to the liquidity ratios discussed in Chapter 6.

The formula for this ratio is:

$$\frac{\text{Operating Cash Flow}}{\text{Current Maturities of Long-Term Debt and Current Notes Payable}}$$

It is computed for Nike for 2002 and 2001 in Exhibit 10–5. For Nike, this ratio substantially improved in 2002.

Operating Cash Flow/Total Debt

The **operating cash flow/total debt** indicates a firm's ability to cover total debt with the yearly operating cash flow. The higher the ratio, the better the firm's ability to carry its total debt. From a debt standpoint, this is considered to be important. It relates to the debt ratios presented in Chap-

EXHIBIT 10-4

ROWE FURNITURE CORPORATION
Statement of Cash Flows (Inflows and Outflows by Activity)
Year Ended December 2, 2001

(in thousands)	Inflows	Outflows	Percent Inflow	Percent Outflow
Cash flows for operating activities:				
Cash received from customers	$329,683		94.68	
Cash paid to suppliers and employees		$328,948		96.15
Income taxes paid, net of refunds	585		.17	
Interest paid		4,642		1.36
Interest received	480		.14	
Other receipts—net	1,109		.32	
Net cash and cash equivalents provided by (used) in operating activities	331,857	333,590	95.31	97.51
Cash flows from investing activities:				
Proceeds from sale of property and equipment	1,056		.30	
Capital expenditures		3,317		.96
Payments to acquire businesses	—	—	—	—
Net cash used in investing activities	1,056	3,317	.30	.96
Cash flows from financing activities:				
Net borrowings (payments) under line of credit	5,368		1.54	
Proceeds from issuance of long-term debt	6,865		1.97	
Payments to reduce long-term debt		3,821		1.12
Proceeds from loans against life insurance policies	3,014		.87	
Proceeds from issuance of common stock	27		.01	
Dividends paid		1,379		.40
Purchase of treasury stock		16		.01
Net cash provided by (used in) financing activities	15,274	5,216	4.39	1.53
Total cash inflows/outflows	348,187	$342,123		
Total cash outflows	342,123		100.00	100.00
Net increase in cash	$ 6,064			

EXHIBIT 10-5	**NIKE, INC.**

Operating Cash Flow/Current Maturities of
Long-Term Debt and Current Notes Payable

Years Ended May 31, 2002 and 2001

	2002	2001
	(in millions)	
Operating cash flow [A]	$1,081.5	$656.5
Current maturities of long-term debt and current notes payable [B]	$ 480.5	$860.7
Operating cash flow/current maturities of long-term debt and current notes payable [A ÷ B]	2.25 times	.76 times

ter 7. It is a type of income view of debt, except that operating cash flow is the perspective instead of an income figure.

The operating cash flow is the same cash flow amount that is used for the operating cash flow/current maturities of long-term debt and current notes payable. The total debt figure is the same total debt amount that was computed in Chapter 7 for the debt ratio and the debt/equity ratio. For the primary computation of the operating cash flow/total debt ratio, all possible balance sheet debt items are included, as was done for the debt ratio and the debt/equity ratio. This is the more conservative approach to computing the ratio. In practice, many firms are more selective in what is included in debt. Some include only short-term liabilities and long-term items, such as bonds payable. The formula for operating cash flow/total debt is as follows:

$$\frac{\text{Operating Cash Flow}}{\text{Total Debt}}$$

The operating cash flow/total debt ratio is computed in Exhibit 10–6 for Nike for the years ended May 31, 2002 and 2001. It indicates that cash flow is significant in relation to total debt in both years, especially in 2002.

Operating Cash Flow per Share

Operating cash flow per share indicates the funds flow per common share outstanding. It is usually substantially higher than earnings per share because depreciation has not been deducted.

In the short run, operating cash flow per share is a better indication of a firm's ability to make capital expenditure decisions and pay dividends than is earnings per share. This ratio should not be viewed as a substitute for earnings per share in terms of a firm's profitability. For this reason, firms are prohibited from reporting cash flow per share on the face of the statement of cash flows or elsewhere in its financials. However, it is a complementary ratio that relates to the ratios of relevance to investors (discussed in Chapter 9).

The operating cash flow per share formula is as follows:

$$\frac{\text{Operating Cash Flow} - \text{Preferred Dividends}}{\text{Diluted Weighted Average Common Shares Outstanding}}$$

The operating cash flow amount is the same figure that was used in the two previous cash flow formulas in this chapter. For common shares outstanding, use the shares that were used for the purpose of computing earnings per share on the most diluted basis. This figure is available when doing internal analysis. It is also in a firm's 10-K annual report. Some companies disclose these shares in the annual report. This share number cannot be computed from information in the annual report, except for very simple situations.

When these share amounts are not available, use the outstanding shares of common stock. This will result in an approximation of the operating cash flow per share. The advantage of using the number of shares used for earnings per share is that this results in an amount that can be compared to earnings per share, and it avoids distortions.

Operating cash flow per share is computed for Nike for 2002 and 2001 in Exhibit 10–7. Operating cash flow per share was significantly more than earnings per share in both 2002 and 2001. Operating cash flow per share significantly increased in 2002.

| EXHIBIT 10-6 | NIKE, INC. |

Operating Cash Flow/Total Debt

Years Ended May 31, 2002 and 2001

	2002	2001
	(in millions)	
Operating cash flow [A]	$1,081.5	$ 656.5
Total debt [B]	$2,604.0	$2,325.1
Operating cash flow/total debt [A ÷ B]	41.53%	28.24%

EXHIBIT 10-7	NIKE, INC.

Operating Cash Flow per Share

Years Ended May 31, 2002 and 2001

	2002	2001
	(in millions)	
Operating cash flow	$1,081.5	$656.5
Less: Redeemable preferred dividends	.3	.3
Operating cash flow after preferred dividends [A]	$1,081.2	$656.2
Diluted weighted average common shares outstanding [B]	272.2	273.3
Operating cash flow per share [A ÷ B]	$ 3.97	$ 2.40

Operating Cash Flow/Cash Dividends

The **operating cash flow/cash dividends** indicates a firm's ability to cover cash dividends with the yearly operating cash flow. The higher the ratio, the better the firm's ability to cover cash dividends. This ratio relates to the investor ratios discussed in Chapter 9.

The operating cash flow/cash dividends formula is as follows:

$$\frac{\text{Operating Cash Flow}}{\text{Cash Dividends}}$$

The operating cash flow amount is the same figure that was used in the three previous formulas in this chapter. Operating cash flow/cash dividends is computed for Nike for 2002 and 2001 in Exhibit 10–8. It indicates material coverage of cash dividends in both 2002 and 2001.

ALTERNATIVE CASH FLOW

There is no standard definition of cash flow in the financial literature. Often, cash flow is used to mean net income plus depreciation expense. This definition of cash flow could be used to compute the cash flow amount for the formulas introduced in this chapter. However, this is a narrow definition of cash flow, and it is considered less useful than the net cash flow from operating activities.

EXHIBIT 10-8	NIKE, INC.

Operating Cash Flow/Cash Dividends

Years Ended May 31, 2002 and 2001

	2002	2001
	(in millions)	
Operating cash flow [A]	$1,081.5	$656.5
Cash dividends [B]	$ 128.9	$129.7
Operating cash flow/cash dividends [A ÷ B]	8.39 times per year	5.06 times per year

PROCEDURES
FOR
DEVELOPMENT
OF THE
STATEMENT OF
CASH FLOWS

Cash inflows and outflows are determined by analyzing all balance sheet accounts other than the cash and cash equivalent accounts. The following account balance changes indicate cash inflows:

1. Decreases in assets (e.g., the sale of land for cash)
2. Increases in liabilities (e.g., the issuance of long-term bonds)
3. Increases in stockholders' equity (e.g., the sale of common stock)

Cash outflows are indicated by the following account balance changes:

1. Increases in assets (e.g., the purchase of a building for cash)
2. Decreases in liabilities (e.g., retirement of long-term debt)
3. Decreases in stockholders' equity (e.g., the payment of a cash dividend)

Transactions within any individual account may result in both a source and a use of cash. For example, the land account may have increased, but analysis may indicate that there was both an acquisition and a disposal of land.

Exhibit 10–9 contains the data needed for preparing a statement of cash flows for ABC Company for the year ended December 31, 2003. These data will be used to illustrate the preparation of the statement of cash flows.

Three techniques may be used to prepare the statement of cash flows: (1) the visual method, (2) the T-account method, and (3) the worksheet method. The visual method can be used only when the financial information is not complicated. When the financial information is complicated, either the T-account method or the worksheet method must be used. This book illustrates only the visual method because of the emphasis on using financial accounting information, not on preparing financial statements. For an explanation of the T-account method and the worksheet method, consult an intermediate accounting textbook.

Following the steps in developing the statement of cash flows, first compute the change in cash and cash equivalents. For ABC Company, this is the increase of $600 in the cash account—the net increase in cash.

For the second step, compute the net change in each balance sheet account other than the cash account. The changes in the balance sheet accounts for ABC Company follow:

Assets:

Accounts receivable decrease	$ 100	Operating
Inventories increase	1,000	Operating
Land increase	9,500	Investing
Equipment increase	1,000	Investing
Accumulated depreciation increase	4,500	Operating
(contra-asset—a change would be		
similar to a change in liabilities)		

Liabilities:

Accounts payable decrease	1,100	Operating
Taxes payable increase	400	Operating
Bonds payable increase	5,000	Financing

Stockholders' equity:

Common stock increase	3,000	Financing
Retained earnings increase	200	*

*This is a combination of operating, financing, and investing activities.

For the third step, consider the changes in the balance sheet accounts along with the income statement for the current period and the supplementary information. The cash flows are segregated into cash flows from operating activities, cash flows from investing activities, and cash flows from financing activities. Noncash investing and/or financing activities should be shown in a separate schedule with the statement of cash flows.

To illustrate the direct and indirect methods of presenting operating activities, the ABC Company income statement is used, along with the relevant supplemental information and balance sheet accounts. For the direct approach, the income statement is adjusted to present the revenue and ex-

EXHIBIT 10-9	**ABC COMPANY**
	Financial Information for Statement of Cash Flows

Balance Sheet Information

Accounts	Balances December 31, 2002	December 31, 2003	Category
Assets:			
Cash	$ 2,400	$ 3,000	Cash
Accounts receivable, net	4,000	3,900	Operating
Inventories	5,000	6,000	Operating
Total current assets	11,400	12,900	
Land	10,000	19,500	Investing
Equipment	72,000	73,000	Investing
Accumulated depreciation	(9,500)	(14,000)	Operating
Total assets	$83,900	$ 91,400	
Liabilities:			
Accounts payable	$ 4,000	$ 2,900	Operating
Taxes payable	1,600	2,000	Operating
Total current liabilities	5,600	4,900	
Bonds payable	35,000	40,000	Financing
Stockholders' Equity:			
Common stock, $10 par	36,000	39,000	Financing
Retained earnings	7,300	7,500	*
Total liabilities and stockholders' equity	$83,900	$ 91,400	

Income Statement Information
For the Year Ended December 31, 2003

		Category
Sales	$ 22,000	Operating
Operating expenses	17,500	Operating
Operating income	4,500	
Gain on sale of land	1,000	Investing
Income before tax expense	5,500	
Tax expense	2,000	Operating
Net income	$ 3,500	

Supplemental Information

	Category
(a) Dividends declared and paid are $3,300.	Financing
(b) Land was sold for $1,500.	Investing
(c) Equipment was purchased for $1,000.	Investing
(d) Bonds payable were retired for $5,000.	Financing
(e) Common stock was sold for $3,000.	Financing
(f) Operating expenses include depreciation expense of $4,500.	Operating
(g) The land account and the bonds payable account increased by $10,000 because of a noncash exchange.	Investing and Financing

*Retained earnings is decreased by cash dividends, $3,300 (financing), and increased by net income, $3,500. Net income can be a combination of operating, investing, and financing activities. In this exhibit, all of the net income relates to operating activities, except for the gain on sale of land (investing).

pense accounts on a cash basis. Exhibit 10–10 illustrates the accrual basis income statement adjusted to a cash basis. Exhibit 10–11 shows the statement of cash flows for ABC Company, using the direct approach for presenting cash flows from operations.

When the cash provided by operations is presented using the direct approach, the income statement accounts are usually described in terms of receipts or payments. For example, "sales" on the accrual basis income statement is usually described as "receipts from customers" when presented on a cash basis.

EXHIBIT 10-10

ABC COMPANY
Schedule of Change from Accrual Basis to Cash Basis Income Statement

	Accrual Basis	Adjustments*	Add (Subtract)	Cash Basis
Sales	$22,000	Decrease in receivables	100	$22,100
Operating expenses	17,500	Depreciation expense	(4,500)	
		Increase in inventories	1,000	
		Decrease in accounts payable	1,100	15,100
Operating income	4,500			7,000
Gain on sale of land	1,000	This gain is related to investing activities.	(1,000)	—
Income before tax expense	5,500			7,000
Tax expense	2,000	Increase in taxes payable	(400)	1,600
Net income	$ 3,500			$ 5,400

*Adjustments are for noncash flow items in the income statement, changes in balance sheet accounts related to cash flow from operations, and the removal of gains and losses on the income statement that are related to investing or financing activities.

The noncash flow items in the income statement are removed from the account. For example, depreciation expense may be in the cost of goods sold, and this expense would be removed from the cost of goods sold.

Changes in balance sheet accounts related to cash flow from operations are adjusted to the related income statement account as follows:

Revenue accounts	$ XXX
Add decreases in asset accounts and increases in liability accounts	+ XXX
Deduct increases in asset accounts and decreases in liability accounts	– XXX
Cash inflow	$ XXX
Expense accounts	
Add increases in asset accounts and decreases in liability accounts	+ XXX
Deduct decreases in asset accounts and increases in liability accounts	– XXX
Cash outflow	$ XXX

Exhibit 10–12 shows the statement of cash flows for ABC Company, using the indirect approach. To compute cash flows from operations, we start with net income and add back or deduct adjustments necessary to change the income on an accrual basis to income on a cash basis, after eliminating gains or losses that relate to investing or financing activities. Notice on the ABC Company schedule of change from accrual to cash basis income statement (Exhibit 10-10) that the adjustments include noncash flow items on the income statement, changes in balance sheet accounts related to operations, and gains and losses on the income statement related to investing or financing activities.

For the indirect approach, follow these directions when adjusting the net income (or loss) to net cash flows from operating activities:

Net income (loss)	$ XXX
Noncash flow items:	
Add expense	+ XXX
Deduct revenues	– XXX
Changes in balance sheet accounts related to operations:*	
Add decreases in assets and increases in liabilities	+ XXX
Deduct increases in assets and decreases in liabilities	– XXX
Gains and losses on the income statement that	
are related to investing or financing activities:	
Add losses	+ XXX
Deduct gains	– XXX
Net cash provided by operating activities	$ XXX

*These are usually the current asset and current liability accounts.

EXHIBIT 10-11	**ABC COMPANY**

Direct Approach for Presenting Cash Flows from Operations
Statement of Cash Flows
For the Year Ended December 31, 2003

Cash flows from operating activities:		
Receipts from customers	$ 22,100	
Payments to suppliers	(15,100)	
Income taxes paid	(1,600)	
Net cash provided by operating activities		$ 5,400
Cash flows from investing activities:		
Proceeds from sale of land	1,500	
Purchase of equipment	(1,000)	
Net cash provided by investing activities		500
Cash flows from financing activities:		
Dividends declared and paid	(3,300)	
Retirement of bonds payable	(5,000)	
Proceeds from common stock	3,000	
Net cash used for financing activities		(5,300)
Net increase in cash		$ 600
Reconciliation of net income to net cash provided by operating activities:		
Net income		$ 3,500
Adjustments to reconcile net income to net cash provided		
by operating activities:		
Decrease in accounts receivable		100
Depreciation expense		4,500
Increase in inventories		(1,000)
Decrease in accounts payable		(1,100)
Gain on sale of land		(1,000)
Increase in taxes payable		400
Net cash provided by operating activities		$ 5,400
Supplemental schedule of noncash investing and financing activities:		
Land acquired by issuing bonds		$10,000

The remaining changes in balance sheet accounts (other than those used to compute cash provided by operating activities) and the remaining supplemental information are used to determine the cash flows from investing activities and cash flows from financing activities. These accounts are also used to determine noncash investing and/or financing.

Some observations on the ABC Company statement of cash flows follow:

1.	Net cash provided by operating activities	$5,400
2.	Net cash provided by investing activities	$500
3.	Net cash used for financing activities	$5,300
4.	Net increase in cash	$600

As previously indicated, when the operations section has been presented using the direct method, additional observations can be determined by preparing the statement of cash flows to present inflows and outflows separately. This has been done in Exhibit 10–13. Some observations from the summary of cash flows in Exhibit 10–13 follow:

Inflows:

1. Receipts from customers represent approximately 83% of total cash flow.
2. Proceeds from common stock sales approximate 11% of total cash inflow.
3. Proceeds from sales of land approximate 6% of total cash inflow.

Outflows:

1. Payments to suppliers represent approximately 58% of total cash outflow.
2. Retirement of bonds payable approximates 19% of total cash outflow.
3. Dividends paid approximate 13% of total cash outflow.

EXHIBIT 10-12

ABC COMPANY
Indirect Approach for Presenting Cash Flows from Operations
Statement of Cash Flows
For the Year Ended December 31, 2003

Cash flows from operating activities:		
Net income		$ 3,500
Add (deduct) items not affecting operating activities:		
Depreciation expense		4,500
Decrease in accounts receivable		100
Increase in inventories		(1,000)
Decrease in accounts payable		(1,100)
Increase in taxes payable		400
Gain on sale of land		(1,000)
Net cash provided by operating activities		$ 5,400
Cash flows from investing activities:		
Proceeds from sale of land	1,500	
Purchase of equipment	(1,000)	
Net cash provided by investing activities		500
Cash flows from financing activities:		
Dividends declared and paid	(3,300)	
Retirement of bonds payable	(5,000)	
Proceeds from common stock	3,000	
Net cash used for financing activities		(5,300)
Net increase in cash		$ 600
Supplemental disclosure of cash flow information:		
Cash paid during the year for:		
Interest net of amount capitalized		$ 0
Income taxes		1,600
Supplemental schedule of noncash investing and financing activities:		
Land acquired by issuing bonds		$10,000

EXHIBIT 10-13

ABC COMPANY
Statement of Cash Flows
For the Year Ended December 31, 2003
(Inflows and Outflows, by Activity—Inflows Presented on Direct Basis)

	Inflows	Outflows	Inflow Percent	Outflow Percent
Operating activities:				
Receipts from customers	$22,100		83.1%	
Payments to suppliers		$15,100		58.1%
Income taxes paid		1,600		6.2
Cash flow from operating activities	22,100	16,700	83.1	64.3
Investing activities:				
Proceeds from sale of land	1,500		5.6	
Purchase of equipment		1,000		3.8
Cash flow from investing activities	1,500	1,000	5.6	3.8
Financing activities:				
Dividends declared and paid		3,300		12.7
Retirement of bonds payable		5,000		19.2
Proceeds from common stock	3,000		11.3	
Cash flow from financing activities	3,000	8,300	11.3	31.9
Total cash inflows/outflows	26,600	$26,000	100.0%	100.0%
Total cash outflows	26,000			
Net increase in cash	$ 600			

SUMMARY

The statement of cash flows provides cash flow information that is critical for users to make informed decisions. The statement of cash flows should be reviewed for several time periods in order to determine the major sources of cash and the major uses of cash.

The ratios related to the statement of cash flows are the following:

$$\text{Operating Cash Flow/Current Maturities of Long-Term Debt and Current Notes Payable} = \frac{\text{Operating Cash Flow}}{\text{Current Maturities of Long-Term Debt and Current Notes Payable}}$$

$$\text{Operating Cash Flow/Total Debt} = \frac{\text{Operating Cash Flow}}{\text{Total Debt}}$$

$$\text{Operating Cash Flow per Share} = \frac{\text{Operating Cash Flow} - \text{Preferred Dividends}}{\text{Diluted Weighted Average Common Shares Outstanding}}$$

$$\text{Operating Cash Flow/Cash Dividends} = \frac{\text{Operating Cash Flow}}{\text{Cash Dividends}}$$

To the Net

1. Go to the SEC site (http://www.sec.gov). Under Filings & Forms (Edgar), click on "Search for Company Filings." Click on "Search Companies and Filings." Under company name enter "Northrop Grumman." Select the 10-K/A filed March 8, 2002.
   a. Determine the standard industrial classification.
   b. Review the consolidated statements of cash flows. Under what method is the operating activities presented? What advantage does this presentation have over the alternative presentation?

2. Go to the SEC site (http://www.sec.gov). Under Filings & Forms (Edgar), click on "Search for Company Filings." Click on "Search Companies and Filings." Under company name enter "Dell Computers." Select the 10-K filed May 1, 2002.
   a. Determine the standard industrial classification.
   b. Determine the numbers for the following:

	February 1, 2002	February 2, 2001
	(in millions)	
Accounts receivable, net		
Inventories		
Accounts payable		

   c. Perform a horizontal common-size analysis of (b) with February 2, 2001 as the base.
   d. Determine the numbers for the following:

	Fiscal Year Ended	
	February 1, 2002	February 2, 2001
	(in millions)	
Net revenue		
Net income		
Net cash provided by operating activities		

   e. Perform a horizontal common-size analysis of (d) with February 2, 2001 as the base.
   f. Comment on the material (b)–(e), paying particular attention to cash flow.

3. Go to the SEC site (http://www.sec.gov). Under Filings & Forms (Edgar), click on "Search for Company Filings." Click on "Search Companies and Filings." Under company name enter "Coors Adolph." Select the 10-K filed March 29, 2002.
   a. Determine the standard industrial classification.
   b. Determine the numbers for the following:

	December 30, 2001	December 31, 2000
Current maturities of long-term debt and current notes payable		
Total debt		
Common shares outstanding		

c. Determine the numbers for the following:

	Fiscal Year Ended	
	December 30, 2001	December 31, 2000
	(in thousands)	
Operating Cash Flow		
Preferred Dividends		
Total Cash Dividends		

d. Compute the following for 2001 and 2000:
   1. Operating cash flow.
   2. Current maturities of long-term debt and current notes payable.
   3. Operating cash flow/total debt.
   4. Operating cash flow per share.
   5. Operating cash flow/cash dividends.

e. Comment on the ratios computed.

Questions

Q 10-1. If a firm presents an income statement and a balance sheet, why is it necessary that a statement of cash flows also be presented?

Q 10-2. Into what three categories are cash flows segregated on the statement of cash flows?

Q 10-3. Using the descriptions of assets, liabilities, and stockholders' equity, summarize the changes to these accounts for cash inflows and changes to these accounts for cash outflows.

Q 10-4. The land account may be used only to explain a use of cash, but not a source of cash. Comment.

Q 10-5. Indicate the three techniques that may be used to complete the steps in developing the statement of cash flows.

Q 10-6. There are two principal methods of presenting cash flow from operating activities—the direct method and the indirect method. Describe these two methods.

Q 10-7. Depreciation expense, amortization of patents, and amortization of bond discount are examples of items that are added to net income when using the indirect method of presenting cash flows from operating activities. Amortization of premium on bonds and a reduction in deferred taxes are examples of items that are deducted from net income when using the indirect method of presenting cash flows from operating activities. Explain why these adjustments to net income are made to compute cash flows from operating activities.

Q 10-8. What is the meaning of the term cash in the statement of cash flows?

Q 10-9. What is the purpose of the statement of cash flows?

Q 10-10. Why is it important to disclose certain noncash investing and financing transactions, such as exchanging common stock for land?

Q 10-11. Would a write-off of uncollectible accounts against allowance for doubtful accounts be disclosed on a cash flow statement? Explain.

Q 10-12. Fully depreciated equipment costing $60,000 was discarded, with no salvage value. What effect would this have on the statement of cash flows?

Q 10-13. For the current year, a firm reported net income from operations of $20,000 on its income statement and an increase of $30,000 in cash from operations on the statement of cash flows. Explain some likely reasons for the greater increase in cash from operations than net income from operations.

Q 10-14. A firm owed accounts payable of $150,000 at the beginning of the year and $250,000 at the end of the year. What influence will the $100,000 increase have on cash from operations?

Q 10-15. A member of the Board of Directors is puzzled by the fact that the firm has had a very profitable year but does not have enough cash to pay its bills on time. Explain to the director how a firm can be profitable, yet not have enough cash to pay its bills and dividends.

Q 10-16. Depreciation is often considered a major source of funds. Do you agree? Explain.

Q 10-17. Pickerton started the year with $50,000 in accounts receivable. The firm ended the year with $20,000 in accounts receivable. How did this decrease influence cash from operations?

Q 10-18. The Aerco Company acquired equipment in exchange for $50,000 in common stock. Should this transaction be on the statement of cash flows?

Q 10-19. Operating cash flow per share is a better indicator of profitability than is earnings per share. Do you agree? Explain.

Q 10-20. The Hornet Company had operating cash flow of $60,000 during a year in which it paid dividends of $11,000. What does this indicate about Hornet's dividend-paying ability?

Problems

P 10-1. The following material relates to the Darrow Company:

| Data | Cash Flows Classification | | | Effect on Cash | | Noncash Trans-actions |
	Operating Activity	Investing Activity	Financing Activity	Increase	Decrease	
a. Net loss	X				X	
b. Increase in inventory	X				X	
c. Decrease in receivables	X			X		
d. Increase in prepaid insurance	X				X	
e. Issuance of common stock			X	X		
f. Acquisition of land, using notes payable		X				X
g. Purchase of land, using cash		X			X	
h. Paid cash dividend			X		X	
i. Payment of income taxes	X				X	
j. Retirement of bonds, using cash			X		X	
k. Sale of equipment for cash		X		X		

Required Place an X in the appropriate columns for each of the situations.

P 10-2.

| Data | Cash Flows Classification | | | Effect on Cash | | Noncash Trans-actions |
	Operating Activity	Investing Activity	Financing Activity	Increase	Decrease	
a. Net income						
b. Paid cash dividend						

		Cash Flows Classification			Effect on Cash		Noncash Trans- actions
	Data	Operating Activity	Investing Activity	Financing Activity	Increase	Decrease	
c.	Increase in receivables	___	___	___	___	___	___
d.	Retirement of debt—paying cash	___	___	___	___	___	___
e.	Purchase of treasury stock	___	___	___	___	___	___
f.	Purchase of equipment	___	___	___	___	___	___
g.	Sale of equipment	___	___	___	___	___	___
h.	Decrease in inventory	___	___	___	___	___	___
i.	Acquisition of land, using common stock	___	___	___	___	___	___
j.	Retired bonds, using common stock	___	___	___	___	___	___
k.	Decrease in accounts payable	___	___	___	___	___	___

Required   Place an X in the appropriate columns for each of the situations.

P 10-3.   The BBB Company balance sheet and income statement follow:

BBB COMPANY
Balance Sheet
December 31, 2005 and 2004

	December 31	
	2005	2004
Assets		
Cash	$ 4,500	$ 4,000
Marketable securities	2,500	2,000
Accounts receivable	6,800	7,200
Inventories	7,500	8,000
Total current assets	21,300	21,200
Land	11,000	12,000
Equipment	24,000	20,500
Accumulated depreciation—equipment	(3,800)	(3,000)
Building	70,000	70,000
Accumulated depreciation—building	(14,000)	(12,000)
Total assets	$108,500	$108,700
Liabilities and Stockholders' Equity		
Accounts payable	$ 7,800	$ 7,000
Wages payable	1,050	1,000
Taxes payable	500	1,500
Total current liabilities	9,350	9,500
Bonds payable	30,000	30,000
Common stock, $10 par	32,000	30,000
Additional paid-in capital	21,000	19,200
Retained earnings	16,150	20,000
Total liabilities and stockholders' equity	$108,500	$108,700

BBB COMPANY
Income Statement
For Year Ended December 31, 2005

Sales		$38,000
Operating expenses:		
Depreciation expense	$ 2,800	
Other operating expenses	35,000	37,800
Operating income		200
Gain on sale of land		800
Income before tax expense		1,000
Tax expense		500
Net income		$ 500

Supplemental information:	
Dividends declared and paid	$ 4,350
Land sold for cash	1,800
Equipment purchased for cash	3,500
Common stock sold for cash	3,800

Required   a.   Prepare a statement of cash flows for the year ended December 31, 2005. (Present the cash flows from operations, using the indirect method.)

           b.   Comment on the statement of cash flows.

P 10-4.   The income statement and other selected data for the Frish Company follow:

FRISH COMPANY
Income Statement
For Year Ended December 31, 2005

Net sales	$640,000
Expenses:	
Cost of goods sold	360,000
Selling and administrative expense	43,000
Other expense	2,000
Total expenses	405,000
Income before income tax	235,000
Income tax	92,000
Net income	$143,000

Other data:

a. Cost of goods sold, including
   depreciation expense of $15,000

b. Selling and administrative expense, including
   depreciation expense of $5,000

c. Other expense, representing amortization
   of patent, $3,000, and amortization
   of bond premium, $1,000

d. Increase in accounts receivable	$ 27,000
e. Increase in accounts payable	15,000
f. Increase in inventories	35,000
g. Decrease in prepaid expenses	1,000
h. Increase in accrued liabilities	3,000
i. Decrease in income taxes payable	10,000

Required   a.   Prepare a schedule of change from accrual basis to cash basis income statement.

           b.   Using the schedule of change from accrual basis to cash basis income statement computed in (a), present the cash provided by operations, using (1) the direct approach and (2) the indirect approach.

P 10-5.   The income statement and other selected data for the Boyer Company follow:

BOYER COMPANY
Income Statement
For Year Ended December 31, 2005

Sales		$19,000
Operating expenses:		
Depreciation expense	$ 2,300	
Other operating expenses	12,000	14,300
Operating income		4,700
Loss on sale of land		1,500
Income before tax expense		3,200
Tax expense		1,000
Net income		$ 2,200

Supplemental information:

a. Dividends declared and paid	$ 800
b. Land purchased	3,000
c. Land sold	500
d. Equipment purchased	2,000
e. Bonds payable retired	2,000
f. Common stock sold	1,400
g. Land acquired in exchange for common stock	3,000
h. Increase in accounts receivable	400
i. Increase in inventories	800
j. Increase in accounts payable	500
k. Decrease in income taxes payable	400

Required   a. Prepare a schedule of change from an accrual basis to a cash basis income statement.

               b. Using the schedule of change from accrual basis to cash basis income statement computed in (a), present the cash provided by operations, using (1) the direct approach and (2) the indirect approach.

P 10-6.   Sampson Company's balance sheet for December 31, 2005, as well as the income statement for the year ended December 31, 2005, are shown below and on the following page.

Required   a. Prepare the statement of cash flows for the year ended December 31, 2005, using the indirect method for net cash flow from operating activities.

               b. Prepare the statement of cash flows for the year ended December 31, 2005, using the direct method for net cash flow from operating activities.

               c. Comment on significant items disclosed in the statement of cash flows.

SAMPSON COMPANY
Balance Sheet
December 31, 2005 and 2004

	2005	2004
Assets		
Cash	$ 38,000	$ 60,000
Net receivables	72,000	65,000
Inventory	98,000	85,000
Plant assets	195,000	180,000
Accumulated depreciation	(45,000)	(35,000)
Total assets	$358,000	$355,000
Liabilities and Stockholders' Equity		
Accounts payable	$ 85,000	$ 80,000
Accrued liabilities (related to cost of sales)	44,000	61,000
Mortgage payable	11,000	—
Common stock	180,000	174,000
Retained earnings	38,000	40,000
Total liabilities and stockholders' equity	$358,000	$355,000

SAMPSON COMPANY
Income Statement
For Year Ended December 31, 2005

Net sales	$145,000
Cost of sales	108,000
Gross profit	37,000
Other expenses	6,000
Profit before taxes	31,000
Tax expense	12,000
Net income	$ 19,000

Other data:
1. Dividends paid in cash during 2005 were $21,000.
2. Depreciation is included in the cost of sales.
3. The change in the accumulated depreciation account is the depreciation expense for the year.

P 10-7.   The Arrowbell Company is a growing company. Two years ago, it decided to expand in order to increase its production capacity. The company anticipates that the expansion program can be completed in another two years. Financial information for Arrowbell are shown below and on the following page.

Required   a.   Comment on the short-term debt position, including computations of current ratio, acid-test ratio, cash ratio, and operating cash flow/current maturities of long-term debt and current notes payable.

b.   If you were a supplier to this company, what would you be concerned about?

c.   Comment on the long-term debt position, including computations of the debt ratio, debt/equity, debt to tangible net worth, and operating cash flow/total debt. Review the statement of operating cash flows.

d.   If you were a banker, what would you be concerned about if this company approached you for a long-term loan to continue its expansion program?

e.   What should management consider doing at this point in regard to the company's expansion program?

ARROWBELL COMPANY
Sales and Net Income

Year	Sales	Net Income
2001	$2,568,660	$145,800
2002	2,660,455	101,600
2003	2,550,180	52,650
2004	2,625,280	86,800
2005	3,680,650	151,490

ARROWBELL COMPANY
Balance Sheet
December 31, 2005 and 2004

	2005	2004
Assets		
Current assets:		
Cash	$ 250,480	$ 260,155
Accounts receivable (net)	760,950	690,550
Inventories at lower-of-cost-or-market	725,318	628,238
Prepaid expenses	18,555	20,250
Total current assets	1,755,303	1,599,193
Plant and equipment:		
Land, buildings, machinery, and equipment	3,150,165	2,646,070
Less: Accumulated depreciation	650,180	525,650
Net plant and equipment	2,499,985	2,120,420
Other assets:		
Cash surrender value of life insurance	20,650	18,180
Other	40,660	38,918
Total other assets	61,310	57,098
Total assets	$4,316,598	$3,776,711

(continued)

Liabilities and Stockholders' Equity	2005	2004
Current liabilities:		
Notes and mortgages payable, current portion	$ 915,180	$ 550,155
Accounts payable and accrued liabilities	1,160,111	851,080
Total current liabilities	2,075,291	1,401,235
Long-term notes and mortgages payable, less current portion above	550,000	775,659
Total liabilities	2,625,291	2,176,894
Stockholders' equity:		
Capital stock, par value $1.00; authorized, 800,000; issued and outstanding, 600,000 (2005 and 2004)	600,000	600,000
Paid in excess of par	890,000	890,000
Retained earnings	201,307	109,817
Total stockholders' equity	1,691,307	1,599,817
Total liabilities and stockholders' equity	$4,316,598	$3,776,711

ARROWBELL COMPANY
Statement of Cash Flows
For Years Ended December 31, 2005 and 2004

	2005	2004
Cash flows from operating activities:		
Net income	$ 151,490	$ 86,800
Noncash expenses, revenues, losses, and gains included in income:		
Depreciation	134,755	102,180
Increase in accounts receivable	(70,400)	(10,180)
Increase in inventories	(97,080)	(15,349)
Decrease in prepaid expenses in 2005, increase in 2004	1,695	(1,058)
Increase in accounts payable and accrued liabilities	309,031	15,265
Net cash provided by operating activities	429,491	177,658
Cash flows from investing activities:		
Proceeds from retirement of property, plant, and equipment	10,115	3,865
Purchases of property, plant, and equipment	(524,435)	(218,650)
Increase in cash surrender value of life insurance	(2,470)	(1,848)
Other	(1,742)	(1,630)
Net cash used for investing activities	(518,532)	(218,263)
Cash flows from financing activities:		
Retirement of long-term debt	(225,659)	(50,000)
Increase in notes and mortgages payable	365,025	159,155
Cash dividends	(60,000)	(60,000)
Net cash provided by financing activities	79,366	49,155
Net increase (decrease) in cash	$ (9,675)	$ 8,550

P 10-8. The balance sheet for December 31, 2005, income statement for the year ended December 31, 2005, and the statement of cash flows for the year ended December 31, 2005, of the Bernett Company are shown on the following two pages.

The president of the Bernett Company cannot understand why Bernett is having trouble paying current obligations. He notes that business has been very good, as sales have more than doubled, and the company achieved a profit of $69,000 in 2005.

Required

a. Comment on the statement of cash flows.

b. Compute the following liquidity ratios for 2005:
1. Current ratio
2. Acid-test ratio
3. Operating cash flow/current maturities of long-term debt and current notes payable
4. Cash ratio

c. Compute the following debt ratios for 2005:
1. Times interest earned
2. Debt ratio
3. Operating cash flow/total debt

d. Compute the following profitability ratios for 2005:
1. Return on assets (using average assets)
2. Return on common equity (using average common equity)

e. Compute the following investor ratio for 2005: Operating cash flow/cash dividends.

f. Give your opinion as to the liquidity of Bernett.

g. Give your opinion as to the debt position of Bernett.

h. Give your opinion as to the profitability of Bernett.

i. Give your opinion as to the investor ratio.

j. Give your opinion of the alternatives Bernett has in order to ensure that it can pay bills as they come due.

BERNETT COMPANY
Balance Sheet
December 31, 2005 and 2004

	2005	2004
Assets		
Cash	$ 5,000	$ 28,000
Accounts receivable, net	92,000	70,000
Inventory	130,000	85,000
Prepaid expenses	4,000	6,000
Land	30,000	10,000
Building	170,000	30,000
Accumulated depreciation	(20,000)	(10,000)
Total assets	$411,000	$219,000
Liabilities and Stockholders' Equity		
Accounts payable	$ 49,000	$ 44,000
Income taxes payable	5,000	4,000
Accrued liabilities	6,000	5,000
Bonds payable (current $10,000 at 12/31/05)	175,000	20,000
Common stock	106,000	96,000
Retained earnings	70,000	50,000
Total liabilities and stockholders' equity	$411,000	$219,000

BERNETT COMPANY
Income Statement
For Year Ended December 31, 2005

Sales	$ 500,000
Less expenses:	
Cost of goods sold (includes depreciation of $4,000)	310,000
Selling and administrative expenses (includes depreciation of $6,000)	80,000
Interest expense	11,000
Total expenses	401,000
Income before taxes	99,000
Income tax expense	30,000
Net income	$ 69,000

BERNETT COMPANY
Statement of Cash Flows
For the Year Ended December 31, 2005

Net cash flow from operating activities:		
Net income	$ 69,000	
Noncash expenses, revenues, losses, and gains		
included in income:		
Depreciation	10,000	
Increase in receivables	(22,000)	
Increase in inventory	(45,000)	
Decrease in prepaid expenses	2,000	
Increase in accounts payable	5,000	
Increase in income taxes payable	1,000	
Increase in accrued liabilities	1,000	
Net cash flow from operating activities		$ 21,000
Cash flows from investing activities:		
Increase in land	$ (20,000)	
Increase in buildings	(140,000)	
Net cash used by investing activities		(160,000)
Cash flows from financing activities:		
Bond payable increase	$ 155,000	
Common stock increase	10,000	
Cash dividends paid	(49,000)	
Net cash provided by financing activities:		116,000
Net decrease in cash		$ (23,000)

P 10-9. The Zaro Company's balance sheet for December 31, 2005, income statement for the year ended December 31, 2005, and the statement of cash flows for the year ended December 31, 2005, follow:

ZARO COMPANY
Balance Sheet
December 31, 2005 and 2004

	2005	2004
Assets		
Cash	$ 30,000	$ 15,000
Accounts receivable, net	75,000	87,000
Inventory	90,000	105,000
Prepaid expenses	3,000	2,000
Land	25,000	25,000
Building and equipment	122,000	120,000
Accumulated depreciation	(92,000)	(80,000)
Total assets	$253,000	$274,000
Liabilities and Stockholders' Equity		
Accounts payable	$ 25,500	$ 32,000
Income taxes payable	2,500	3,000
Accrued liabilities	5,000	5,000
Bonds payable (current $20,000 at 12/31/05)	90,000	95,000
Common stock	85,000	85,000
Retained earnings	45,000	54,000
Total liabilities and stockholders' equity	$253,000	$274,000

ZARO COMPANY
Income Statement
For Year Ended December 31, 2005

Sales	$400,000
Less expense:	
Cost of goods sold (includes depreciation of $5,000)	$280,000
Selling and administrative expenses (includes depreciation expenses of $7,000)	78,000
Interest expense	8,000
Total expenses	$366,000
Income before taxes	34,000
Income tax expense	14,000
Net income	$ 20,000

ZARO COMPANY
Statement of Cash Flows
For Year Ended December 31, 2005

Net cash flow from operating activities:		
Net income		$ 20,000
Noncash expenses, revenues, losses, and		
gains included in income:		
Depreciation	12,000	
Decrease in accounts receivable	12,000	
Decrease in inventory	15,000	
Increase in prepaid expenses	(1,000)	
Decrease in accounts payable	(6,500)	
Decrease in income taxes payable	(500)	
Net cash flow from operating activities		$ 51,000
Cash flows from investing activities:		
Increase in buildings and equipment	$ (2,000)	
Net cash used by investing activities		(2,000)
Cash flows from financing activities:		
Decrease in bonds payable	$ (5,000)	
Cash dividends paid	(29,000)	
Net cash used for financing activities:		(34,000)
Net increase in cash		$ 15,000

The president of the Zaro Company cannot understand how the company was able to pay cash dividends that were greater than net income and at the same time increase the cash balance. He notes that business was down slightly in 2005.

Required
a. Comment on the statement of cash flows.
b. Compute the following liquidity ratios for 2005:
   1. Current ratio
   2. Acid-test ratio
   3. Operating cash flow/current maturities of long-term debt and current notes payable
   4. Cash ratio
c. Compute the following debt ratios for 2005:
   1. Times interest earned
   2. Debt ratio
d. Compute the following profitability ratios for 2005:
   1. Return on assets (using average assets)
   2. Return on common equity (using average common equity)
e. Give your opinion as to the liquidity of Zaro.
f. Give your opinion as to the debt position of Zaro.

g. Give your opinion as to the profitability of Zaro.
h. Explain to the president how Zaro was able to pay cash dividends that were greater than net income and at the same time increase the cash balance.

P 10-10.   The Ladies Store presented the following statement of cash flows for the year ended December 31, 2005.

THE LADIES STORE
Statement of Cash Flows
For Year Ended December 31, 2005

Cash received:	
From sales to customers	$150,000
From sales of bonds	100,000
From issuance of notes payable	40,000
From interest on bonds	5,000
Total cash received	295,000
Cash payments:	
For merchandise purchases	110,000
For purchase of truck	20,000
For purchase of investment	80,000
For purchase of equipment	45,000
For interest	2,000
For income taxes	15,000
Total cash payments	272,000
Net increase in cash	$ 23,000

Note: Depreciation expense was $15,000.

Required   a. Prepare a statement of cash flows in proper form.
           b. Comment on the major flows of cash.

P 10-11.   Answer the following multiple-choice questions:
           a. Which of the following could lead to cash flow problems?
               1. Tightening of credit by suppliers
               2. Easing of credit by suppliers
               3. Reduction of inventory
               4. Improved quality of accounts receivable
               5. Selling of bonds
           b. Which of the following would not contribute to bankruptcy of a profitable firm?
               1. Substantial increase in inventory
               2. Substantial increase in receivables
               3. Substantial decrease in accounts payable
               4. Substantial decrease in notes payable
               5. Substantial decrease in receivables
           c. Which of the following current asset or current liability accounts is not included in the computation of cash flows from operating activities?
               1. Change in accounts receivable
               2. Change in inventory
               3. Change in accounts payable
               4. Change in accrued wages
               5. Change in notes payable to banks
           d. Which of the following items is not included in the adjustment of net income to cash flows from operating activities?
               1. Increase in deferred taxes
               2. Amortization of goodwill
               3. Depreciation expense for the period
               4. Amortization of premium on bonds payable
               5. Proceeds from selling land

e. Which of the following represents an internal source of cash?
1. Cash inflows from financing activities
2. Cash inflows from investing activities
3. Cash inflows from selling land
4. Cash inflows from operating activities
5. Cash inflows from issuing stock
f. How would revenue from services be classified?
1. Investing inflow
2. Investing outflow
3. Operating inflow
4. Operating outflow
5. Financing outflow
g. What type of account is inventory?
1. Investing
2. Financing
3. Operating
4. Noncash
5. Sometimes operating and sometimes investing
h. How would short-term investments in marketable securities be classified?
1. Operating activities
2. Financing activities
3. Investing activities
4. Noncash activities
5. Cash and cash equivalents

P 10-12. The Szabo Company presented the following data with the 2005 financial statements:

SZABO COMPANY
Statements of Cash Flows
Years Ended December 31, 2005, 2004, and 2003

	2005	2004	2003
Increase (Decrease) in Cash:			
Cash flows from operating activities:			
Cash received from customers	$ 173,233	$ 176,446	$ 158,702
Cash paid to suppliers and employees	(150,668)	(157,073)	(144,060)
Interest received	132	105	89
Interest paid	(191)	(389)	(777)
Income taxes paid	(6,626)	(4,754)	(845)
Net cash provided by operations	15,880	14,335	13,109
Cash flows from investing activities:			
Capital expenditures	(8,988)	(5,387)	(6,781)
Proceeds from property, plant, and equipment disposals	1,215	114	123
Net cash used in investing activities	(7,773)	(5,273)	(6,658)
Cash flows from financing activities:			
Net increase (decrease) in short-term debt	—	5,100	7,200
Increase in long-term debt	4,100	3,700	5,200
Dividends paid	(6,050)	(8,200)	(8,000)
Purchase of common stock	(8,233)	(3,109)	(70)
Net cash used in financing activities	(10,183)	(2,509)	4,330
Net increase (decrease) in cash and cash equivalents	(2,076)	6,553	10,781
Cash and cash equivalents at beginning of year	24,885	18,332	7,551
Cash and cash equivalents at end of year	$ 22,809	$ 24,885	$ 18,332

Reconciliation of Net Income to Net Cash Provided by Operating Activities

	2005	2004	2003
Net income	$ 7,610	$ 3,242	$ 506
Provision for depreciation and amortization	12,000	9,700	9,000
Provision for losses on accounts receivable	170	163	140
Gain on property, plant, and equipment disposals	(2,000)	(1,120)	(1,500)
Changes in operating assets and liabilities:			
Accounts receivable	(2,000)	(1,750)	(1,600)
Inventories	(3,100)	(2,700)	(2,300)
Other assets	—	—	(57)
Accounts payable	—	5,100	7,200
Accrued income taxes	1,200	—	—
Deferred income taxes	2,000	1,700	1,720
Net cash provided by operating activities	$15,880	$14,335	$13,109

Required
a. Prepare a statement of cash flows with a three-year total column for 2003–2005.
b. Comment on significant trends you detect in the statement prepared in (a).
c. Prepare a statement of cash flows, with inflow/outflow for the year ended December 31, 2005.
d. Comment on significant trends you detect in the statement prepared in (c).

P 10-13. Consider the following data for three different companies:

	($000 Omitted)		
	Owens	Arrow	Alpha
Net cash provided (used) by:			
Operating activities	$(2,000)	$2,700	$(3,000)
Investing activities	(6,000)	(600)	(400)
Financing activities	9,000	(400)	(2,600)
Net increase (decrease) in cash	$ 1,000	$1,700	$(6,000)

The patterns of cash flows for these firms differ. One firm is a growth firm that is expanding rapidly, another firm is in danger of bankruptcy, while another firm is an older firm that is expanding slowly.

Required Select the growth firm, the firm in danger of bankruptcy, and the firm that is the older firm expanding slowly. Explain your selection.

P 10-14. The following information was taken from the 2005 financial statements of the Jones Corporation:

Accounts receivable, January 1, 2005	$ 30,000
Accounts receivable, December 31, 2005	40,000
Sales (all credit sales)	480,000

Note: No accounts receivable were written off or recovered during the year.

Required
a. Determine the cash collected from customers by the Jones Corporation in 2005.
b. Comment on why cash collected from customers differed from sales.

P 10-15. Webster Corporation's statement of cash flows for the year ended December 31, 2005, was prepared using the indirect method, and it included the following items:

Net income	$100,000
Noncash adjustments:	
Depreciation expense	20,000
Decrease in accounts receivable	8,000
Decrease in inventory	25,000
Increase in accounts payable	10,000
Net cash flows from operating activities	$163,000

Note: Webster Corporation reported revenues from customers of $150,000 in its 2005 income statement.

Required
a. What amount of cash did Webster receive from customers during the year ended December 31, 2005?
b. Did depreciation expense provide cash inflow? Comment.

Case 10-1	**The Big . Com**

The data in this case comes from the financial reports of Amazon.com, Inc.

Selected Consolidated Balance Sheet Items
(in thousands)

	December 31,		
	2001	**2000**	**1999**
Total current assets	$ 1,207,920	$ 1,361,129	$1,006,477
Total assets	1,637,547	2,135,169	2,465,850
Total current liabilities	921,414	974,956	733,234
Long-term debt and other	2,156,133	2,127,464	1,466,338
Stockholders' deficit	(1,440,000)	(967,251)	266,278

Note: The 10-K listed an aggregate market value of voting stock held by nonaffiliates of the registrant as of January 10, 2002 of $2,859,000,000.

Selected Consolidated Statements of Operations Items
(in thousands)

	Year Ended December 31,			
	2001	**2000**	**1999**	**1998**
Net sales	$3,122,433	$ 2,761,983	$1,639,839	$ 609,819
Gross profit	798,558	655,777	290,645	133,664
Total operating expenses	1,210,815	1,519,657	896,400	242,719
Loss from operations	(412,257)	(863,880)	(605,755)	(109,055)
Interest expense	139,232	130,921	84,566	26,639
Loss before equity in losses of equity-market investees	(526,427)	(1,106,677)	(643,199)	(121,641)
Equity in losses of equity—method investees, net	(30,327)	(304,596)	(76,968)	(2,905)
Loss before change in accounting principle	(556,754)	(1,411,273)	(719,968)	(124,546)
Cumulative effect of change in accounting principle	10,523	—	—	—
Net loss	(567,277)	(1,411,273)	(719,968)	(124,546)

Selected Consolidated Statements of Cash Flows Items (in part)
(in thousands)

| | Year Ended December 31, | | | |
	2001	2000	1999	1998
Net cash (used) in operating activities	$ (119,782)	$ (130,442)	$ (90,875)	$ 31,035
Investing activities:				
Sales and maturities of marketable securities	370,377	545,724	2,064,101	227,789
Purchases of marketable securities	(567,152)	(184,455)	(2,359,398)	(504,435)
Purchase of fixed assets, including internal use software and Web site development	(50,321)	(134,758)	(287,055)	(28,333)
Investment in equity-method investees	(6,198)	(62,533)	(369,607)	(19,019)
Net cash provided by (used in) investing activities	(253,294)	163,978	(931,959)	(323,998)
Financing activities:				
Proceeds from exercise of stock options and other	16,625	44,697	64,469	14,366
Proceeds from issuance of common stock, net of issuance costs	99,831	—	—	—
Proceeds from long-term debt and other	10,000	681,499	1,263,639	325,987
Repayment of long-term debt and other	(19,575)	(16,927)	(188,886)	(78,108)
Financing costs	—	(16,122)	(35,151)	(7,783)
Net cash provided by financing activities	106,881	693,147	1,104,071	254,462
Effect of exchange–rate changes on cash and cash equivalents	(15,958)	(37,557)	489	(35)
Net increase (decrease) in cash and cash equivalents	(282,153)	689,126	61,726	(38,536)
Cash and cash equivalents, End of Period	$ 540,282	$ 822,435	$ 133,309	$ 71,583

Required   a.   Comment on the investment in equity-method investees and the related equity in losses of equity-method investees, net.

b.   Comment on net cash (used) in operating activities.

c.   From where did the bulk of the funds come?

d.   In your opinion where should Amazon try to obtain or generate funds in the near future?

e.   Why is the market capitalization materially more than the stockholders' deficit?

Case 10-2   Watch the Cash

The Arden Group, Inc. presented these statements of cash flows in its 1998 annual report:

Fiscal Year

The Company operates on a fiscal year ending on the Saturday closest to December 31. Fiscal years for the financial statements included herein ended on January 2, 1999 (52 weeks), January 3, 1998 (53 weeks) and December 28, 1996 (52 weeks).

Statements of Cash Flows

(In Thousands)	1998	1997	1996
Cash flows from operating activities:			
Cash received from customers	$ 296,751	$ 274,683	$ 252,482
Cash paid to suppliers and employees	(278,213)	(254,622)	(242,869)
Sales (purchases) of trading securities, net		8,851	(1,311)
Interest and dividends received	1,449	1,683	1,678
Interest paid	(751)	(705)	(878)
Income taxes paid	(6,689)	(3,831)	(2,694)
Net cash provided by operating activities	12,547	26,059	6,408
Cash flows from investing activities:			
Capital expenditures	(4,244)	(7,896)	(12,841)
Deposits for property in escrow			2,664
Transfer to discontinued operations		(2,575)	(456)
Purchases of available-for-sale securities	(3,793)	(3,202)	
Sales of available-for-sale securities	268	1,380	
Proceeds from the sale of property, plant and equipment, liquor licenses and leasehold interests	3,171	163	2,338
Payments received on notes from the sale of property, plant and equipment and liquor licenses		53	3
Net cash used in investing activities	(4,598)	(12,077)	(8,292)
Cash flows from financing activities:			
Purchase and retirement of stock		(13,966)	(1,613)
Principal payments on long-term debt	(1,188)	(799)	(752)
Principal payments under capital lease obligations	(230)	(205)	(325)
Loan payments received from officer/director	40	114	
Proceeds from equipment financing		2,500	
Purchase of Company debentures	(23)		(55)
Net cash used in financing activities	(1,401)	(12,356)	(2,745)
Net increase (decrease) in cash	6,548	1,626	(4,629)
Cash at beginning of year	7,099	5,473	10,102
Cash at end of year	$ 13,647	$ 7,099	$ 5,473

Reconciliation of Net Income to Net Cash Provided
by Operating Activities:

	1998	1997	1996
Net income	$10,081	$ 5,959	$ 3,523
Adjustments to reconcile net income to net cash provided by operating activities:			
Loss from discontinued operations		2,738	456
Depreciation and amortization	5,618	5,111	4,686
Unrealized loss on trading securities			151
Provision for losses on accounts and notes receivable	92	62	55
Deferred income taxes	(865)	270	578
Net loss (gain) from the disposal of property, plant and equipment, liquor licenses and early lease terminations	(409)	731	(556)
Realized gains on marketable securities, net	(408)	(605)	
Gain on purchase of 7% debentures	(2)		(5)
Change in assets and liabilities net of effects from noncash investment and financing activities:			
(Increase) decrease in assets:			
Marketable securities		8,851	(1,347)
Accounts and notes receivable	794	1,639	8
Inventories	756	(824)	(556)
Other current assets	(239)	(274)	(456)
Other assets	(103)	(90)	(548)
Increase (decrease) in liabilities:			
Accounts payable and other accrued expenses	(2,611)	3,847	492
Deferred income taxes on unrealized gains		(275)	
Other liabilities	(157)	(1,081)	(73)
Net cash provided by operating activities	$12,547	$26,059	$ 6,408

Required

a. Prepare the statement of cash flows, with a total column for the three-year period ended January 2, 1999. Do not include reconciliation of net income to net cash provided by operating activities.

b. Comment on significant cash flow items in the statement prepared in (a).

c. Prepare the statement of cash flows for 1998, with inflows separated from outflows. Present the data in dollars and percentages. Do not include reconciliation of net income to net cash provided by operating activities.

d. Comment on significant cash flow items in the statement prepared in (c).

Case 10-3

Rapidly Expanding

The data for this case was extracted from the 1996 Annual Report of Best Buy Co., Inc.

Future Growth

Fiscal 1997 promises to be a challenging year for all retailers. A more cautious consumer outlook and higher levels of consumer debt may signal a softer retail environment during the first half of this fiscal year. Also, increased competition in the PC industry and the anticipated slowdown of personal computer sales will mean additional pressure on sales and margins. The initiatives we have implemented in major appliances and ESP sales will help offset this anticipated slowdown.

In addition, we intend to moderate overall new store growth and open 20 to 25 new retail locations. Half of these stores are expected to open in the new markets of Philadelphia, Pennsylvania, and Tampa, Florida. The remainder will increase our presence in existing markets where we have established advertising, administrative, regional management and distribution leverage. We intend to finance this expansion with internally generated funds.

This more conservative store expansion will allow us to refine our stores' operations and focus our retail efforts on our four major categories of product specialization. Our plan is to simplify our retail procedures while improving our level of customer service. We will strengthen the training programs for our retail personnel to prepare them for the challenges ahead. A well-trained sales force will help us attract and retain customers while enhancing our market position. Our store teams will be more actively engaged in the presentation of new product technologies, technical services, appropriate product accessories, ESPs and classroom training. This will enhance consumers' knowledge and their shopping experience. We intend to improve overall product in-stock by establishing improved standards of inventory management.

Our Strategy

We believe that our retail strategy is right for today's consumer and expect to improve our execution in all our product categories. Fiscal 1996 was a challenging year for retail, and we thank our employees, shareholders and vendor partners for their continued commitment and support. We are confident that the initiatives we are implementing will result in strengthened execution of our retail strategy and market-leading position as we enter our 30th year of business.

Richard M. Schulze
Founder, Chairman & CEO

Bradbury H. Anderson
President & COO

Selected Consolidated Financial and Operating Data
(Dollars in thousands, except per share amounts)

Fiscal Period	1996[1]	1995	1994[2]	1993	1992
Statement of Earnings Data					
Revenues	$7,217,448	$5,079,557	$3,006,534	$1,619,978	$929,692
Gross profit	936,571	690,393	456,925	284,034	181,062
Selling, general and administrative expenses	813,988	568,466	379,747	248,126	162,286
Operating income	122,583	121,927	77,178	35,908	18,776
Earnings before cumulative effect of accounting change	48,019	57,651	41,710	19,855	9,601
Net earnings	48,019	57,651	41,285	19,855	9,601
Per-Share Data					
Earnings before cumulative effect of accounting change	$1.10	$1.33	$1.01	$.57	$.33
Net earnings	1.10	1.33	1.00	.57	.33
Common stock price: High	29 5/8	45 1/4	31 7/16	15 23/32	11 25/32
Low	12 3/4	22 1/8	10 27/32	4 23/32	2 21/32
Weighted average shares outstanding (000s)	43,640	43,471	41,336	34,776	28,848
Operating and Other Data					
Comparable stores sales increase[3]	5.5%	19.9%	26.9%	19.4%	14.0%
Number of stores (end of period)	251	204	151	111	73
Average revenues per store[4]	$31,100	$28,400	$22,600	$17,600	$14,300
Gross profit percentage	13.0%	13.6%	15.2%	17.5%	19.5%
Selling, general and administrative expense percentage	11.3%	11.2%	12.6%	15.3%	17.5%
Operating income percentage	1.7%	2.4%	2.6%	2.2%	2.0%
Inventory turns[5]	4.8x	4.7x	5.0x	4.8x	5.1x

Balance Sheet Data (at period end)	1996	1995	1994	1993	1992
Working capital	$ 585,855	$ 609,049	$362,582	$118,921	$126,817
Total assets	1,890,832	1,507,125	952,494	439,142	337,218
Long-term debt, including current portion	229,855	240,965	219,710	53,870	52,980
Convertible preferred securities	230,000	230,000	—	—	—
Shareholders' equity	431,614	376,122	311,444	182,283	157,568

This table should be read in conjunction with Management's Discussion and Analysis of Financial Condition and Results of Operations and the Consolidated Financial Statements and Notes thereto.

(1)   Fiscal 1996 contained 53 weeks. All other periods presented contained 52 weeks.
(2)   During fiscal 1994, the Company adopted FAS 109, resulting in a cumulative effect adjustment of ($425) or ($.01) per share.
(3)   Comparable stores are stores open at least 14 full months.
(4)   Average revenues per store are based upon total revenues for the period divided by the weighted average number of stores open during such period.
(5)   Inventory turns are calculated based upon a rolling 12-month average of inventory balances.

Management's Discussion & Analysis of Financial Condition and Results of Operations (In Part)

Liquidity and Capital Resources

The Company has funded the retail growth and the increase in distribution capacity in the last two years through a combination of long-term financing, working capital and cash flow from operations. In fiscal 1995, the Company issued $230 million of 6 1/2% monthly income convertible preferred securities which mature in November 2024. The Company also entered into a master lease facility which has provided over $125 million in financing for retail store and distribution center development in fiscal 1995 and 1996. The funds from these two long-term financings and the increase in the Company's credit facility to $550 million in fiscal 1996 have supported the Company's growth. The proceeds from the $150 million note offering in October 1993 were also used to support much of the Company's expansion and growth in fiscal 1995. In fiscal 1994, the $86 million in proceeds from a Common Stock offering and the proceeds of the 1993 note offering were used to provide the financing necessary for business expansion that year. Cash flow from operations, before changes in working capital, improved to over $100 million in fiscal 1996, an increase from the $97 million in fiscal 1995 and $65 million in fiscal 1994.

Over the past two fiscal years, the Company has developed 50 new and relocated stores in order to secure the desired store locations and assure timely completion of the stores. The Company also built two of the brown goods distribution centers opened in the last two years, including the Company's newest 780,000-square-foot distribution center in Findlay, Ohio, opened in September 1995. Interim financing for these properties was provided either through working capital or the Company's master lease agreement. The Company's practice is to lease rather than own real estate, and for those sites developed using working capital, it is the Company's intention to enter into sale/leaseback transactions and recover the cost of development. The costs of this development are classified in the balance sheet as recoverable costs from developed properties. Proceeds from the sale of properties were nearly $90 million in fiscal 1996 and $43 million in fiscal 1995. In fiscal 1994, the Company sold 17 store locations for an aggregate of $44 million in a single sale/leaseback transaction. At fiscal 1996 year end, the Company had approximately $125 million in recoverable costs related to developed properties. A difficult credit market for retail real estate has delayed the sale of certain of these properties, the majority of which were opened late in fiscal 1996. These properties are expected to be sold and leased back during fiscal 1997.

Current assets increased to $1.6 billion at March 2, 1996, compared to $1.2 billion at February 25, 1995, primarily as a result of the increased inventory levels necessary to support the larger stores and higher sales volumes. The 47 new stores added approximately $160 million in inventory. Inventory turns were 4.8 times in fiscal 1996, comparable to the prior year. Increases in trade payables and secured inventory financing arrangements at year end supported most of the increase in inventory. Higher business volumes in February 1996 as compared to February 1995 resulted in higher year-end receivables. The Company sells the receivables from sales on the Company's private label credit card, without recourse, to an unrelated third party. An increase in recoverable costs from developed properties also contributed to the increase in current assets.

The Company's revolving credit facility provides for borrowings of $250 million throughout the year and an increase to $550 million on a seasonal basis from July through December. Borrowings under the facility are unsecured and are limited to certain percentages of inventories. The underlying agreement requires that the maximum balance outstanding be reduced to $50 million for a period of 45 days, following the holiday season. This facility expires in June 1998. The Company also has $185 million available, increasing to $310 million on a seasonal basis, under an inventory financing facility provided by a commercial credit corporation.

The Company's expansion plans for fiscal 1997 reflect management's expectations for a slowing economy and the Company's desire to fund growth with internally generated funds. The Company plans to open approximately 20 to 25 new stores, including entry into the new major markets of Philadelphia, Pennsylvania in May and Tampa, Florida in the third quarter. The remainder of the new stores opened will be in existing markets. The Company also intends to remodel or relocate ten stores to larger facilities during fiscal 1997. Only six of the new and relocated stores are expected to be developed by the Company. Management believes the Company's existing distribution facilities are adequate to support the planned expansion and operations in fiscal 1997.

Each new store requires approximately $3.0 to $4.0 million in working capital for merchandise inventory (net of vendor financing), fixtures and leasehold improvements. Management expects that there will be adequate funds available, including funds generated from the sale of developed property owned at the end of fiscal 1996, to finance the $80 million in planned capital expenditures in addition to the anticipated property development in fiscal 1997.

Management believes that funds available from the Company's revolving credit facility, inventory financing programs and expected vendor terms, along with cash on hand and anticipated cash flow from operations, will be sufficient to support planned store expansion and the increased assortment in the appliance category in the coming year.

Consolidated Balance Sheets
(Dollars in thousands, except per-share amounts)

	March 2 1996	February 25 1995
Assets		
Current Assets:		
Cash and cash equivalents	$ 86,445	$ 144,700
Receivables	121,438	84,440
Recoverable costs from developed properties	126,237	86,222
Merchandise inventories	1,201,142	907,677
Deferred income taxes	20,165	15,022
Prepaid expenses	5,116	2,606
Total current assets	1,560,543	1,240,667
Property and Equipment:		
Land and buildings	16,423	13,524
Leasehold improvements	131,289	93,889
Furniture, fixtures and equipment	266,582	191,084
Property under capital leases	29,421	27,096
	443,715	325,593
Less accumulated depreciation and amortization	132,676	88,116
Net property and equipment	311,039	237,477
Other Assets:		
Deferred income taxes	7,204	9,223
Other assets	12,046	19,758
Total other assets	19,250	28,981
Total Assets	$1,890,832	$1,507,125

(continued)

	March 2 1996	February 25 1995
Liabilities and Shareholders' Equity		
Current Liabilities:		
Accounts payable	$ 673,852	$ 395,337
Obligations under financing arrangements	93,951	81,755
Accrued salaries and related expenses	26,890	23,785
Accrued liabilities	125,582	77,102
Deferred service plan revenue and warranty reserve	30,845	24,942
Accrued income taxes		14,979
Current portion of long-term debt	23,568	13,718
Total current liabilities	974,688	631,618
Deferred service plan revenue and warranty reserve, long-term	48,243	42,138
Long-term debt	206,287	227,247
Convertible preferred securities of subsidiary	230,000	230,000
Shareholders' equity:		
Preferred stock, $1.00 par value:		
Authorized—400,000 shares; Issued		
and outstanding—none	—	—
Common stock, $.10 par value:		
Authorized—120,000,000 shares; Issued		
and outstanding—42,842,000		
and 42,216,000 shares, respectively	4,284	4,221
Additional paid-in capital	236,392	228,982
Retained earnings	190,938	142,919
Total shareholders' equity	431,614	376,122
Total Liabilities and Shareholders' Equity	$1,890,832	$1,507,125

Consolidated Statement of Earnings
(Dollars in thousands, except per-share amounts)

For The Fiscal Years Ended	March 2, 1996	February 25, 1995	February 26, 1994
Revenues	$7,217,448	$5,079,557	$3,006,534
Cost of goods sold	6,280,877	4,389,164	2,549,609
Gross profit	936,571	690,393	456,925
Selling, general and administrative expenses	813,988	568,466	379,747
Operating income	122,583	121,927	77,178
Interest expense, net	43,594	27,876	8,800
Earnings before income taxes and cumulative effect of change in accounting principle	78,989	94,051	68,378
Income taxes	30,970	36,400	26,668
Earnings before cumulative effect of change in accounting principle	48,019	57,651	41,710
Cumulative effect of change in accounting for income taxes	—	—	(425)
Net Earnings	$ 48,019	$ 57,651	$ 41,285
Earnings per Share:			
Earnings before cumulative effect of change in accounting principle	$1.10	$1.33	$1.01
Cumulative effect of change in accounting for income taxes			(.01)
Net Earnings per Share	$1.10	$1.33	$1.00
Weighted Average Common Shares Outstanding (000)	43,640	43,471	41,336

Consolidated Statements of Cash Flows
(Dollars in thousands, except per-share amounts)

For The Fiscal Years Ended	March 2, 1996	February 25, 1995	February 26, 1994
Operating Activities:			
Net earnings	$ 48,019	$ 57,651	$ 41,285
Charges to earnings not affecting cash:			
Depreciation and amortization	54,862	38,570	22,412
Loss on disposal of property and equipment	1,267	760	719
Cumulative effect of change in accounting for income taxes	—	—	425
	104,148	96,981	64,841
Changes in operating assets and liabilities:			
Receivables	(36,998)	(31,496)	(14,976)
Merchandise inventories	(293,465)	(269,727)	(387,959)
Deferred income taxes and prepaid expenses	(5,634)	(5,929)	(5,234)
Accounts payable	278,515	106,920	175,722
Other current liabilities	40,946	46,117	33,014
Deferred service plan revenue and warranty reserve	12,008	19,723	8,393
Total cash provided by (used in) operating activities	99,520	(37,411)	(126,199)
Investing Activities:			
Additions to property and equipment	(126,201)	(118,118)	(101,412)
Recoverable costs from developed properties	(40,015)	(86,222)	—
Decrease (increase) in other assets	7,712	(11,676)	(6,592)
Proceeds form sale/leasebacks	—	24,060	44,506
Total cash used in investing activities	(158,504)	(191,956)	(63,498)
Financing Activities:			
Long-term debt payments	(14,600)	(10,199)	(6,977)
Increase in obligations under financing arrangements	12,196	70,599	6,285
Common stock issued	3,133	2,366	86,513
Proceeds from issuance of convertible preferred securities	—	230,000	—
Long-term debt borrowings	—	21,429	160,310
Payments on revolving credit line, net	—	—	(3,700)
Total cash provided by financing activities	729	314,195	242,431
Increase (Decrease) in Cash and Cash Equivalents	(58,255)	84,828	52,734
Cash & Cash Equivalents at Beginning of Period	144,700	59,872	7,138
Cash & Cash Equivalents at End of Period	$ 86,445	$ 144,700	$ 59,872

Required

a. Prepare the following liquidity ratios for 1996 and 1995:
   1. Current ratio
   2. Acid-test ratio
b. Prepare the following long-term debt-paying ratios for 1996 and 1995:
   1. Times interest earned
   2. Debt ratio
   3. Operating cash flow/total debt
c. Prepare the following profitability ratios for 1996 and 1995:
   1. Total asset turnover (using year-end total assets)
   2. Return on assets (using year-end total assets)
   3. Return on total equity (using year-end total equity)
   4. Operating cash flow per share (using weighted average shares outstanding)

d. Prepare the following investor analysis ratios for 1996 and 1995:
    1. Degree of financial leverage
    2. Price earnings ratio (the high and low market price for the year—two computations)
    3. Percentage of earnings retained
    4. Book value
e. Using the Selected Consolidated Financial and Operating Data, compute horizontal common-size analysis for 1992–1996 for the following items:
    1. Revenues
    2. Gross profit
    3. Selling, general, and administrative expenses
    4. Operating income
    5. Net earnings
    6. Number of stores
    7. Average revenue per store
    8. Total assets
    9. Shareholders' equity
f. Prepare an executive summary relating to liquidity, debt, profitability, and investor analysis. Consider data computed and data disclosed in the case.

Case 10-4	**The Retail Mover**

This case represents an actual retail company. The dates and format have been changed.

Required

a. Compute and comment on the following for 1997, 1998, and 2001:
    1. working capital
    2. current ratio
b. Comment on the difference between net income and net cash outflow from operating activities for the year ended December 31, 1998 and December 31, 2001.
c. This company reported a loss of $177,340,000 for 2002. Reviewing the balance sheet data, speculate on major reasons for this loss.
d. Considering (a), (b), and (c), comment on the wisdom of the short-term bank loan in 2002. (Consider the company's perspective and the bank's perspective.)

a.

	December 31, 1998	December 31, 1997
Selected Balance Sheet Data		
Total current assets	$719,478,441	$628,408,895
Total current liabilities	$458,999,682	$366,718,656

The Retail Mover
Statement of Cash Flows
Year Ended December 31, 1998

Net cash flow from operating activities:	
Net income	$ 39,577,000
Noncash expenses, revenues, losses, and gains	
included in income:	
Increase in equity in Zeller's Limited	(2,777,000)
Depreciation and amortization	9,619,000
Net increase in reserves	74,000
Increase in deferred federal income taxes	232,000
Net increase in receivables	(51,463,995)
Net increase in inventories	(38,364,709)
Net increase in prepaid taxes, rents, etc.	(209,043)
Increase in accounts payable	9,828,348
Increase in salaries, wages, and bonuses	470,054
Increase in taxes withheld from employees' compensation	301,035
Decrease in taxes other than federal income taxes	(659,021)
Increase in federal income taxes payable	4,007,022
Increases in deferred credits, principally income	
taxes related to installment sales (short-term)	14,045,572
Rounding difference in working capital	520
Net cash outflow from operating activities	(15,319,217)
Cash flows from investing activities:	
Investment in properties, fixtures, and improvements	(16,141,000)
Investment in Zeller's Limited	(436,000)
Increase in sundry accounts (net)	(48,000)
Net cash outflow from investing activities	(16,625,000)
Cash flows from financing activities:	
Sales of common stock to employees	5,219,000
Dividends to stockholders	(20,821,000)
Purchase of treasury stock	(13,224,000)
Purchase of preferred stock for cancellation	(948,000)
Retirement of 4 3/4% sinking fund debentures	(1,538,000)
Increase in short-term notes payable	56,323,016
Increase in bank loans	7,965,000
Net cash inflow from financing activities	32,976,016
Net increase in cash and short-term securities	$ 1,031,799

b.

	December 31, 2001
Selected Balance Sheet Data	
Total current assets	$1,044,689,000
Total current liabilities	661,058,000

The Retail Mover
Statement of Cash Flows
Year Ended December 31, 2001

Net cash flow from operating activities:	
Net income	$ 10,902,000
Noncash expenses, revenues, losses, and gains included in income:	
Undistributed equity in net earnings of unconsolidated subsidiaries	(3,570,000)
Depreciation and amortization of properties	13,579,000
Increase in deferred federal income taxes—non-current	2,723,000
Decrease in deferred contingent compensation and other liabilities	(498,000)
Net receivables increase	(52,737,000)
Merchandise inventories increase	(51,104,000)
Other current assets increase	(8,935,000)
Accounts payable for merchandise decrease	(2,781,000)
Salaries, wages and bonuses decrease	(3,349,000)
Other accrued expenses increase	3,932,000
Taxes withheld from employees increase	2,217,000
Sales and other taxes increase	448,000
Federal income taxes payable decrease	(8,480,000)
Increase in deferred income taxes related to installment sales	4,449,000
Net cash flow from operating activities	(93,204,000)
Cash flows from investing activities:	
Investments on properties, fixtures and improvements	(23,143,000)
Increase in other assets—net	(642,000)
Investment in Granjewel Jewelers & Distributors, Inc.	(5,700,000)
Net cash outflow from investing activities	(29,485,000)
Cash flows from financing activities:	
Increase in short-term notes payable to banks	100,000,000
Receipts from employees under stock purchase contracts	2,584,000
Short-term commercial notes	73,063,000
Cash dividends to stockholders	(21,122,000)
Decrease in long-term debt	(6,074,000)
Purchase of cumulative preferred stock, for cancellation	(618,000)
Purchase of treasury common stock	(136,000)
Bank loans decreased	(10,000,000)
Net cash inflow from financing activities	137,697,000
Net increase in cash	$ 15,008,000

c.

Income Statement Data related to 2001 and 2002 (in Part)

	2002	2001
Net earnings (loss)	$(177,340,000)	$10,902,000

Balance Sheet Data related to 2001 and 2002 (in Part)

	December 31, 2002	December 31, 2001
Assets		
Current assets:		
Cash notes	$ 79,642,000	$ 45,951,000
Customers' installment		
accounts receivable	518,387,000	602,305,000
Less:		
Allowance for doubtful accounts	(79,510,000)	(16,315,000)
Unearned credit insurance premiums	(1,386,000)	(4,923,000)
Deferred finance income	(37,523,000)	(59,748,000)
	399,968,000	521,319,000
Merchandise inventories	407,357,000	450,637,000
Other accounts receivable, refundable taxes and claims	31,223,000	19,483,000
Prepaid expenses	6,591,000	7,299,000
Total current assets	$924,781,000	$1,044,689,000
Liabilities		
Current liabilities:		
Bank loans	$600,000,000	—
Short-term commercial notes	—	453,097,000
Current portion of long-term debt	995,000	
Accounts payable for merchandise	50,067,000	58,192,000
Salaries, wages and bonuses	10,808,000	14,678,000
Other accrued expenses	49,095,000	14,172,000
Taxes withheld from employees	1,919,000	4,412,000
Sales and other taxes	17,322,000	13,429,000
Federal income taxes payable	17,700,000	—
Deferred income taxes related to installment sales	2,000,000	103,078,000
Total current liabilities	749,906,000	661,058,000
Other liabilities		
Long-term debt	216,341,000	220,336,000
Deferred federal income taxes	—	14,649,000
Deferred contingent compensation and other liabilities	2,183,000	4,196,000
Total other liabilities	218,524,000	239,181,000
Total liabilities	$968,430,000	$ 900,239,000

Case 10-5

Non-Cash Charges

Owens Corning Fiberglass Corporation

For Immediate Release (February 6, 1992)

Owens Corning Takes $800 Million Non-Cash Charge to Accrue For Future Asbestos Claims

"This action demonstrates our desire to put the asbestos situation behind us," new chairman and CEO Glen H. Hiner says.

Toledo, Ohio, February 6, 1992—Owens Corning Fiberglass Corp. (NYSE:OCF) today announced that its results for the fourth quarter and year ended December 31, 1991, include a special non-cash charge of $800 million to accrue for the estimated uninsured cost of future asbestos claims the Company may receive through the balance of the decade. "This action demonstrates our desire to put the asbestos situation behind us," said Glen Hiner, Owens Corning's new chairman and chief executive officer. "After a thorough review of the situation with outside consultants, we believe this accrual will be sufficient to cover the company's uninsured costs for cases received until the year 2000. We will, of course, make adjustments to our reserves if that becomes appropriate, but this is our best estimate of these uninsured costs. With this action," Mr. Hiner continued, "everyone can now focus once again on the fundamental strengths of the Company. We generate considerable amounts of cash, our operating divisions are leaders in every market they serve throughout the world, and we have taken a number of steps in the last few years to strengthen our competitive position even further."

#

Owens Corning Fiberglass Corporation

For Immediate Release (June 20, 1996)

Owens Corning Initiates Federal Lawsuit, Records
Post-1999 Asbestos Provisions and Announces Dividend

NEW YORK, New York, June 20, 1996 — A Federal lawsuit aimed at fraudulent testing procedures for asbestos-related illnesses, involving tens of thousands of pending cases, was filed yesterday by Owens Corning. The Company also announced the quantification of liabilities related to post-1999 asbestos claims, the reinstatement of an annual dividend and a sales goal of $5 billion by 1999.

The specific announcements are as follows:

- A lawsuit, alleging falsified medical test results in tens of thousands of asbestos claims, was filed on June 19, 1996, in the U.S. District Court for the Eastern District of Louisiana against the owners and operators of three pulmonary function testing laboratories. Overall, a total of 40,000 cases may be impacted by the investigation for fraudulent testing procedures. The lawsuit is the subject of a separate press release also disseminated this morning.
- A net, after-tax charge of $545 million, or $9.56 per fully diluted share for asbestos claims—received after 1999—will be recorded in the second quarter of 1996, as detailed in a Form 8-K filed this morning with the SEC. Cash payments associated with this charge will begin after the year 2000 and will be spread over 15 years or more.
- The Board of Directors has approved an annual dividend policy of 25 cents per share and declared a quarterly dividend of 6-1/4 cents per share payable on October 15, 1996, to shareholders of record as of September 30, 1996.
- The company expects to reach its sales goal of $5 billion in 1999 — a full year ahead of the original goal.

"The asbestos charge quantifies what we expect to be the cost to Owens Corning of post-1999 claims," stated Glen H. Hiner, chairman and chief executive officer. "We further believe that the present value of the Owens Corning asbestos liability, including the current charge, is less than the current discount in our stock price."

In addition to these developments, Owens Corning announced it is engaged in substantive discussions with 30 of the principal plaintiff law firms in an effort to obtain further resolution of its asbestos liability. These discussions have encompassed the possibility of global as well as individual law firm settlements.

"These meetings are by mutual consent," stated Hiner. "The discussions will continue and we expect to know by year end whether we can achieve further agreement. Plaintiff attorneys involved in the talks stated they will not serve any more non-malignancy claims on Owens Corning while negotiations continue."

In reference to the dividend, Hiner stated, "we were able to initiate this action because debt has been reduced to target levels and cash flow from operations will be in excess of internal funding requirements.

"We are delighted to be able to reward our shareholders with a dividend," said Hiner. "Reinstating the dividend has been a priority of mine since joining the company and I am pleased that we now are in a position to set the date."

The Toledo-based company had 1995 sales of $3.6 billion and employs 18,000 people in more than 30 countries.

#

Owens Corning
Consolidated Statement of Cash Flows (in Part)

For the years ended December 31, 1997, 1996 and 1995 (in millions of dollars)

	1997	1996	1995
Net Cash Flow from Operations			
Net income (loss)	$ 47	$(284)	$ 231
Reconciliation of net cash provided by operating activities:			
Noncash items:			
Provision for asbestos litigation claims (Note 22)	—	875	—
Cumulative effect of accounting change (Note 6)	15		—
Provision for depreciation and amortization	173	141	132
Provision (credit) for deferred income taxes (Note 11)	110	(258)	142
Other (Note 4)	49	(2)	(2)
(Increase) decrease in receivables (Note 13)	57	20	36
(Increase) decrease in inventories	60	(71)	(15)
Increase (decrease) in accounts payable and accrued liabilities	(60)	103	(50)
Disbursements (funding) of VEBA trust	19	45	(64)
Proceeds from insurance for asbestos litigation claims, excluding Fibreboard (Note 22)	97	101	251
Payments for asbestos litigation claims, excluding Fibreboard (Note 22)	(300)	(267)	(308)
Other	(136)	(68)	(68)
Net cash flow from operations	131	335	285

April 29, 1998

Owens Corning opened a new front in its battle to avoid being swamped by tens of thousands of damage claims filed by people who say they got sick from exposure to asbestos-containing insulation produced by the company. Owens Corning charged in U.S. District Court in Toledo, Ohio, that Allstate Insurance Co. is guilty of breach of contract by failing to provide coverage.

Owens Corning announced in March 1998 that it might have to spend more than expected to resolve asbestos claims because of growing damage awards to people with a severe form of asbestos-linked cancer called mesothelioma.

Required
a. In the long run, cash receipts from operations is equal to revenue from operations. Comment.
b. February 6, 1992—Owens Corning announced a special noncash charge of $800 million to accrue for the estimated uninsured cost of future asbestos claims the company may receive through the balance of the decade. How much will the noncash charge reduce gross earnings in 1992? Over what period of time is the expected outflow?
c. June 20, 1996—Owens Corning announced a net, after-tax charge of $545 million for asbestos claims received after 1999. How much will this charge reduce net income in 1996? Over what period of time is the cash outflow expected?
d. Assume Owens Corning receives money related to the federal lawsuit alleging falsified medical tests. In what period will the cash inflow be recorded? When will the related revenue be recorded?
e. April 29, 1998—Owens Corning filed suit against Allstate Insurance Co. related to asbestos exposure coverage. What are the apparent implications if Owens Corning does not win the suit?

f.   Owens Corning announced in March 1998 that it might have to spend more than expected to resolve asbestos claims. What does this imply as to future expenses and cash outflow related to asbestos claims?

g.   Owens Corning, Consolidated Statement of Cash Flows, for the years ended December 31, 1997, 1996, and 1995.
   1.   What year has a charge for asbestos litigation claims?
   2.   What years have cash inflow from proceeds from insurance for asbestos litigation claims?
   3.   What years have payments for asbestos litigation claims?

Case 10-6

Sorry—Give it Back*

Owens Corning went into Chapter 11 bankruptcy in 2000. In October 2002, it claimed that it was insolvent for four years before filing for bankruptcy (1996–2000). Apparently the major issue was asbestos cases.

Because of the insolvent condition, it claims dividends paid were invalid during the period 1996–2000. Owens Corning is only pursuing holders who received more than $100,000. This amounts to millions of dollars.

Required   Comment on implications to investors if firms in bankruptcy can claim dividends paid years after receipt.

---

*Source: Carrie Coolidge, "The Great Dividend Heist," *Forbes* (November 11, 2002), pp. 46–47.

Case 10-7

Cash Movements and Periodic Income Determination

"The estimating of income, under conditions of uncertainty as well as of certainty, requires that the accountant trace carefully the relation between income flows and cash movements."

"While it is true that there may not be an equality between the amount of revenue and the amount of cash receipts for any period less than the duration of enterprise existence, receipts are the elements with which we construct all measures of revenue. A dollar is received at some time during the life of the enterprise for each dollar of revenue exhibited during the fiscal period. The sum of the annual revenues for all fiscal periods is equal to the amount of ultimate total revenue. There may be no equality between the amount of expense and the amount of cash disbursements for the fiscal period and yet the two sums are equal for the life of the enterprise. A dollar is disbursed at some time during the enterprise existence for each dollar exhibited as expense of the fiscal period."*

"The accountant's problem is essentially one of reconciling cash receipts with revenues and cash disbursements with expenses. That is, for every revenue recognized but not received in cash during the current period, an asset of equal value must be recorded (or a liability must be amortized); for every expense recognized but not paid in cash in the current period, a liability of equal value must be recognized but not paid in cash in the current period, a liability of equal value must be recognized (or an asset must be amortized)."

Required   a.   Income determination is an exact science. Comment.
   b.   Cash flow must be estimated. Comment.
   c.   In the long run, cash receipts from operations is equal to revenue from operations. Comment.
   d.   Assume that a firm has a negative cash flow from operations in the short run. How could this negative cash flow from operations be compensated for in the short run? Discuss.
   e.   Assume that the reported operating income has been substantially more than the cash flow from operations for the past two years. Comment on what will need to happen to future cash flow from operations in order for the past reported income to hold up.

---

* Edward G. Nelson, "The Relationship between the Balance Sheet and the Profit and Loss Statement," *The Accounting Review*, Vol. XVIII (April 1942), p. 133.
NOTE: This case includes excerpts from "Cash Movements And Periodic Income Determination," Reed K. Storey, *The Accounting Review*, Vol. XXXV, No. 3 (July 1960), pp. 449–454.

Thomson Analytics *Business School Edition*

Please complete the web case that covers material covered in this chapter at http://gibson.swlearning.com. You'll be using Thomson Analytics Business School Edition, a version of the powerful tool used by Wall Street professionals, that combines a full range of fundamental financial information, earnings estimates, market data, and source documents for 500 publicly traded companies.

Endnotes

1. The effect of exchange rate changes on cash is presented separately at the bottom of the statement.
2. *Exposure Draft*, "Statement of Cash Flows" (Stamford, CT: Financial Accounting Standards Board, 1986), p. 21.

SUMMARY ANALYSIS
NIKE, INC.
(INCLUDES 2002
FINANCIAL STATEMENTS)

Users must be able to apply and understand financial statement analysis. They must study ratio and trend analysis for meaning. This analysis is the difficult aspect of interpreting financial statements. Chapters 6 through 10 have illustrated the technique of calculating ratios for the analysis of Nike, Inc.

This summary analysis brings together the analysis in Chapters 6 through 10 relating to Nike. It adds information on a selected competitor and the industry. It also adds some common-size analysis.

NIKE— BACKGROUND INFORMATION

Bill Bowerman, head track coach, University of Oregon, teamed up with Philip Knight a former student, to form Blue Ribbon Sports in 1964. Blue Ribbon Sports became Nike in 1972. The name "Nike" was chosen because Nike was the Greek goddess of victory.

Nike specialized in athletic footwear until 1979. In 1979 the Nike apparel line appeared. In 1996 the Nike equipment division formed.

By 1999 Nike was the world's largest supplier of athletic footwear and one of the world's largest suppliers of athletic apparel. Nike products are sold in over 100 countries. Nike is about the only sports footwear and apparel company with the infrastructure to sell extensively worldwide.

Bill Bowerman retired from the Board in June 1999, and passed away in December 1999. Philip Knight is the chairman of the Board and chief executive officer of Nike.

For considerable information relating to Nike, go to http://www.nike.com.

Management Discussion and Analysis (See Annual Report) (in Part)

Results of Operations—Fiscal 2002 Highlights

- Revenues increased 4.3% to $9.9 billion, compared to $9.5 billion in fiscal 2001.
- Income before the cumulative effect of an accounting change increased to $668.3 million from $587.7 million in the prior year, an increase of 13.3%. After the effect of the accounting change, net income rose 12.5%.
- Diluted earnings per share before the effect of the accounting change increased by 13.9%, from $2.16 to $2.46. After the effect of the accounting change, diluted earnings per share rose 13.0%.
- Gross margins increased as a percentage of revenues to 39.3% from 39.0% in fiscal 2001.
- Selling and administrative expenses increased as a percentage of revenues to 28.5% from 28.3% in fiscal 2001.

Vertical Common-Size Statement of Income (Exhibit 1)

Highlights

There were no substantial changes, using vertical common-size statement of income, from 2000 to 2002. This is significant resulting in the increased revenue (Exhibit 2), being carried through to net income.

EXHIBIT 1   **NIKE, INC.**

Vertical Common-Size Statement of Income

Year Ended May 31

	2002	2001	2000
Revenues	100.00%	100.00%	100.00%
Costs and expenses:			
Costs of sales	60.70	60.97	60.07
Selling and administrative	28.51	28.35	28.98
Interest expense	.48	.62	.50
Other income/expense, net	.03	.36	.23
Total costs and expenses	89.72	90.29	89.78
Income before income taxes and cumulative effect of accounting change	10.28	9.71	10.22
Income taxes	(3.53)	(3.50)	(3.78)
Income before cumulative effect of accounting change	6.76	6.21	6.44
Cumulative effect of accounting change, net of income taxes of $3.0	(.05)	—	—
Net income	6.70	6.21	6.44

Note: There are some rounding differences.

Horizontal Common-Size Statement of Income (Exhibit 2)

Highlights

- Revenues increased approximately 10% between 2000 and 2002.
- Costs of sales increased approximately 11% between 2000 and 2002.
- Selling and administrative expenses increased approximately 8% between 2000 and 2002.
- The combined increase in costs of sales and selling and administrative expenses approximately equaled the increase in revenues.
- Interest expense and other income/expense, net fluctuated substantially, but these expenses were immaterial in relation to costs of sales and selling and administrative.
- Income taxes increased substantially less than income before income taxes and cumulative effect accounting change. This resulted in income before cumulative effect of accounting change increasing substantially more than revenue.

Three-Year Comparison (Exhibit 3)

The use of ratios can be very helpful in analysis, but caution must be exercised in drawing conclusions from the absolute numbers. Many potential problems were discussed in previous chapters. Keep these potential problems in mind when using ratios. Nike uses a year ended May 31, and has somewhat of a seasonal business. This could influence some of its ratios, particularly liquidity ratios.

Liquidity

- Days' sales in receivables increased slightly, which would be a negative. Turnover of receivables increased in 2001, but ended in 2002 at approximately the same as 2000.
- Days' sales in inventory decreased substantially, which would be a positive. Merchandise inventory turnover times per period increased moderately, which would be a positive.

EXHIBIT 2   **NIKE, INC.**

Horizontal Common-Size Statement of Income

Year Ended May 31

	2002	2001	2000
Revenues	109.98%	105.49%	100.00%
Costs and expenses:			
Costs of sales	111.12	107.05	100.00
Selling and administrative	108.21	103.20	100.00
Interest expense	105.78	130.44	100.00
Other income/expense, net	14.49	164.73	100.00
Total costs and expenses	109.90	106.09	100.00
Income before income taxes and cumulative effect of accounting change	110.67	100.24	100.00
Income taxes	102.62	97.53	100.00
Income before cumulative effect on accounting change	115.40	101.83	100.00
Cumulative effect on accounting change, net of income taxes of $3.0	N/A	N/A	N/A
Net income	114.54	101.83	100.00
Basic earnings per common share—			
before accounting change	119.05	103.81	100.00
Cumulative effect of accounting change	N/A	N/A	N/A
	118.10	103.81	100.00
Diluted earnings per common share—			
before accounting change	118.84	104.35	100.00
Cumulative effect of accounting change	N/A	N/A	N/A
	117.87	104.35	100.00

| EXHIBIT 3 | **NIKE, INC.** |

Three-Year Ratio Comparison

Liquidity	Unit	2002	2001	2000
Days' sales in receivables	Days	69.54	65.13	66.25
Accounts receivable turnover	Times per period	5.53	5.70	5.54
Accounts receivable turnover	Days	66.01	64.01	65.86
Days' sales in inventory	Days	83.51	89.85	97.68
Merchandise inventory turnover	Times per period	4.29	4.03	4.13
Inventory turnover	Days	85.04	90.54	88.37
Operating cycle	Days	151.05	154.55	154.23
Working capital (in millions)		2,321.50	1,838.60	1,456.40
Current ratio	N/A	2.26	2.03	1.68
Acid-test ratio	N/A	1.30	1.08	0.85
Cash ratio	N/A	0.31	0.17	0.12
Sales to working capital	Times per period	4.76	5.76	5.49
Operating cash flow/current maturities of long-term debt and notes payable	Times per period	2.25	0.76	0.78
Long-term debt-paying ability:				
Times interest earned	Times per period	21.60	14.61	19.31
Fixed charge coverage	Times per period	10.90	8.75	10.28
Debt ratio	%	40.42	39.95	46.46
Debt/equity	%	67.83	66.54	86.76
Debt to tangible net worth	%	76.56	75.07	99.85
Operating cash flow/total debt	%	41.53	28.24	27.93
Profitability:				
Net profit margin	%	6.76	6.21	6.41
Total asset turnover	Times per period	1.61	1.63	1.62
Return on assets	%	10.90	10.10	10.43
Operating income margin	%	10.79	10.69	10.95
Operating asset turnover	Times per period	1.84	1.94	2.01
Return on operating assets	%	19.83	20.69	22.05
Sales to fixed assets	Times per period	6.62	7.35	8.69
Return on investment	%	16.19	16.19	16.16
Return on total equity	%	18.22	17.78	17.89
Return on common equity	%	18.22	17.78	17.89
Gross profit margin	%	39.30	39.03	39.93
Investor analysis:				
Degree of financial leverage	N/A	1.05	1.06	1.05
Earnings per share	$	2.46	2.16	2.07
Price/earnings ratio	N/A	21.85	19.03	20.71
Percentage of earnings retained	%	80.71	78.01	77.02
Dividend payout ratio	%	19.51	22.22	23.19
Dividend yield	%	0.89	1.17	1.12
Book value per share	$	14.43	13.01	11.63
Materiality of option compensation expense:				
Pro forma/Reported net income	%	93.85	94.79	95.18
Pro forma/Reported earnings per share	%	93.50	94.91	95.17
Operating cash flow per share	$	3.97	2.40	2.50
Operating cash flow/cash dividends	Times per year	8.39	5.06	5.26
Year-end market price	$	53.75	41.10	42.87

- The operating cycle decreased slightly, which would be a positive.
- Working capital increased materially. This would be considered positive from a liquidity view.
- The current ratio increased materially. This would be considered positive from a liquidity view.
- The acid-test ratio increased materially. This would be considered positive from a liquidity view.
- The cash ratio increased materially. This would be considered positive from a liquidity view.
- Sales to working capital decreased materially. This would be considered a negative. Sales did not keep up with the working capital increase.

- Operating cash flow/current maturities of long-term debt and notes payable increased materially. This would be considered positive.

Summary

In general, liquidity improved substantially and appears to be very good.

Long-term debt-paying ability

- Times interest earned and fixed charge coverage both increased moderately. Both appear to be very good.
- Debt ratio and debt/equity both improved substantially. This would be considered a positive.
- Debt to intangible net worth improved substantially. This would be considered a positive.
- Operating cash flow/total debt improved materially. This would be considered a positive.

Summary

Long-term debt-paying ability improved substantially and appears to be very good.

Profitability

- Net profit margin improved moderately. This would be considered a positive.
- Total asset turnover was steady.
- Return on assets improved moderately. This would be considered a positive.
- Operating income margin decreased slightly. This would be a negative.
- Operating asset turnover decreased slightly. This would be considered a negative.
- Return on operating assets decreased slightly. This would be considered a negative.
- Sales to fixed assets decreased materially. This would be considered a negative.
- Return on investment improved slightly. This would be considered a positive.
- Return on total equity and return on common equity improved slightly. This would be considered a positive.
- Gross profit margin decreased slightly. This would be considered a negative.

Summary

In general profitability improved slightly between 2000 and 2002. This was particularly true considering return on assets, return on investment, return on total equity, and return on common equity. Operating ratios decreased slightly in this period.

Investor Analysis

- The degree of financial leverage is moderate. This represents a conservative position when it comes to debt.
- Earnings per share increased materially. This would be very important to investors.
- The price/earnings ratio increased slightly. This would be very positive because the price/earnings ratio declined in the total market in this period of time.
- Percentage of earnings retained and dividend payout ratio indicate that approximately 20% of earnings are paid out in dividends. This would be considered a moderate amount.
- The dividend yield was approximately 1%. Investors in Nike would be expecting most of their gains in market appreciation.
- The book value per share increased moderately. This would be expected since the percentage of earnings retained was moderate.
- Materiality of option compensation expense increased slightly. Option compensation expense was moderate.
- Operating cash flow per share increased materially. Operating cash flow was materially greater than earnings per share each year.
- The year-end market price increased substantially between 2000 and 2002. This is particularly impressive considering that the overall market conditions were poor during this period.

Summary

In general the investor analysis is positive. This is particularly influenced by the earnings per share increase.

Reebok was selected as a competitor for ratio comparison. Both Nike and Reebok are United States companies that are in the athletic shoe and apparel business. Nike is also in the equipment business, while Reebok apparently is not in the equipment business.

Reebok is somewhat smaller than Nike as indicted by revenue and assets. Nike is the dominant company in the athletic shoe and apparel business.

Revenue:
Nike	$9,893,000,000 (Year ended May 31, 2002)
Reebok	$2,992,878,000 (Year ended December 31, 2001)

Total Assets:
Nike	$6,443,000,000 (May 31, 2002)
Reebok	$1,543,173,000 (December 31, 2001)

Again, caution must be exercised in drawing conclusions from the absolute numbers. Keep potential problems in mind when drawing conclusions. Some of the potential problems on this comparison are the different year-ends, somewhat seasonal business, and different size of firms. This could influence some of the ratios, particularly liquidity ratios.

Liquidity

- In the receivables area Reebok appears to be ahead of Nike. About half the difference can likely be accounted for as a seasonal difference.
- In the inventory area Reebok appears to be ahead of Nike. About half the difference can likely be accounted for as a seasonal difference.
- Reebok has much higher current ratio, acid-test ratio, and cash ratio than these ratios for Nike. Much of this difference comes from the cash and cash equivalent area. Reebok may have more cash and cash equivalents that they want for the long run. Both firms appear to have very good liquidity as indicated by these ratios.
- Nike has a better sales to working capital than Reebok.
- Reebok has a very high operating cash flow/current maturities of long-term debt and notes payable.

Summary

Reebok's liquidity position appears to be substantially better than Nike's. Reebok's position may be better than they want in the long run. Nike's liquidity position appears to be good.

Long-term debt-paying ability

- Nike has a superior debt position, as indicated by the times interest earned and the fixed charge coverage.
- Nike has a superior debt position, as indicated by the debt ratio, debt/equity, and debt to tangible net worth.
- Nike's operating cash flow/total debt is materially better than Reebok's.

Summary

Nike's debt indicators appear to be materially better than Reebok's.

Profitability

- Most of the profitability ratios are substantially better for Nike than for Reebok. This includes net profit margin, total asset turnover, return on assets, operating income margin, return on operating assets, return on investment, return on total equity, return on common equity, and gross profit margin.
- Reebok has a better operating asset turnover and sales to fixed assets.

Summary

Nike's profitability appears to be materially better than the profitability of Reebok.

Ratio Comparison with Selected Competitor (Exhibit 4)

EXHIBIT 4   **NIKE, INC.**

Ratio Comparison with Selected Competitor
Year Ended May 31, 2002 (Nike),
Year Ended December 31, 2001 (Reebok)

	Unit	Nike 2002	Reebok 2001
Liquidity:			
Days' sales in receivables	Days	69.54	53.49
Accounts receivable turnover	Times per period	5.53	6.57
Accounts receivable turnover	Days	66.01	55.52
Days' sales in inventory	Days	83.51	69.92
Merchandise inventory turnover	Times per period	4.29	5.01
Inventory turnover	Days	85.04	72.88
Operating cycle	Days	151.05	128.40
Working capital (in millions)	$	2,321.50	845.30
Current ratio	N/A	2.26	2.88
Acid-test ratio	N/A	1.30	1.77
Cash ratio	N/A	0.31	0.92
Sales to working capital	Times per period	4.76	3.54
Operating cash flow/current maturities of long-term debt and notes payable	Times per period	2.25	14.84
Long-term debt-paying ability:			
Times interest earned	Times per period	21.60	9.84
Fixed charge coverage	Times per period	10.90	5.29
Debt ratio	%	40.42	53.35
Debt/equity	%	67.83	114.35
Debt to tangible net worth	%	76.56	127.98
Operating cash flow/total debt	%	41.53	21.41
Profitability:			
Net profit margin	%	6.76	3.59
Total asset turnover	Times per period	1.61	1.00
Return on assets	%	10.90	7.15
Operating income margin	%	10.79	6.16
Operating asset turnover	Times per period	1.84	2.14
Return on operating assets	%	19.83	13.19
Sales to fixed assets	Times per period	6.62	21.70
Return on investment	%	16.19	11.57
Return on total equity	%	18.22	15.47
Return on common equity	%	18.22	15.47
Gross profit margin	%	39.30	36.70
Investor analysis:			
Degree of financial leverage	N/A	1.05	1.11
Earnings per share	$	2.46	1.66
Price/earnings ratio	N/A	21.85	15.96
Percentage of earnings retained	%	80.71	100.00
Dividend payout ratio	%	19.51	0.00
Dividend yield	%	0.89	0.00
Book value per share	$	14.43	26.14
Materiality of option compensation expense:			
Pro forma/Reported net income	%	93.85	94.05
Pro forma/Reported earnings per share	%	93.50	96.99
Operating cash flow per share	$	3.97	2.99
Operating cash flow/cash dividends	Times per year	8.39	No dividends
Year-end market price	$	53.75	26.50

Investor Analysis
- Degree of financial leverage is low for Nike and somewhat higher for Reebok.
- Earnings per share is somewhat higher for Nike.
- The price/earnings ratio is much higher for Nike than Reebok. This could be reflecting the higher profitability of Nike.
- Percentage of earnings retained is relatively high for Nike. Reebok does not pay a dividend.
- Dividend payout ratio is relatively low for Nike. Reebok does not pay a dividend.
- Book value per share is substantially higher for Reebok.
- Materiality of option compensation expense is somewhat higher for Nike.
- Operating cash flow per share is very good for both firms in relation to earnings per share.
- Operating cash flow/cash dividends is very good for Nike. Reebok does not pay a dividend.
- Year-end market price is materially higher for Nike than for Reebok.

Summary
In general the investor analysis appears to be better for Nike than for Reebok.

Ratio Comparison with Industry (Exhibit 5)

Comparison with the industry is frequently a problem as to the quality of the comparison. The companies in the industry will typically be using different accounting methods. An example would be costing of inventory, with some companies using LIFO, some using FIFO, and some using an average. Industry ratios frequently do not address issues such as income statement unusual or infrequent items, equity earnings, discontinued operations, extraordinary items, or minority earnings.

A problem with using industry data at a library is that commercial publications sometimes send the material to a library several months after general distribution. This brings a time issue to be considered. The U.S. Department of Commerce Quarterly Financial report is online and represents relatively recent data.

The industry ratios available are frequently of a broader industry coverage than the ideal. Nike is under SIC Rubber & Plastics Footwear (3021). Robert Morris Associates Annual Statement studies publishes some industry material using SIC 3052 Manufacturing Rubber and Plastics, Hose and Belting. The U.S. Department of Commerce publishes Quarterly Financial Report for Manufacturing, Mining and Trade Corporations. They have dropped SIC in favor of NAICS. The NAICS 316 is cross-referenced to SIC Major Group 30. For Nike the NAICS is 316211, Rubber and Plastics Footwear Manufacturing.

Although there are problems with using industry comparisons, the effort is usually beneficial. It is necessary to be cautious when drawing conclusions. You may want to review "Caution in Using Industry Averages" in Chapter 5.

Liquidity
- Nike's receivables appear to be substantially less liquid than the industry. Part of this can likely be explained by the May 31 year-end for Nike. The difference between the Nike ratios and the industry are so material that it is likely that most firms in the industry are using shorter credit terms.
- Nike's inventory appears to be substantially less liquid than the industry. Part of this likely can be explained by the May 31 year-end for Nike. Possibly many firms in the industry are using a different inventory costing method than the method used by Nike.
- The operating cycle of Nike is substantially longer than the operating cycle for the industry. This is the result of less liquid receivables and inventory.
- The current ratio and acid-test ratio are much better for Nike than the industry. This would be influenced by a less liquid receivables and inventory.
- The cash ratio is much better for Nike than for the industry.
- Sales to working capital is much better for the industry than for Nike.

Summary
We likely do not have good industry comparisons with Nike in the liquidity area.

EXHIBIT 5	NIKE, INC.

Ratio Comparison with Industry

			Industry	
	Unit	Nike	Ratio	Source
Liquidity:				
Days' sales in receivables	Days	69.54	41.68	DC
Accounts receivable turnover	Times per period	5.53	8.61	DC
Accounts receivable turnover	Days	66.01	42.42	DC
Days' sales in inventory	Days	83.51	61.00	RMA
Merchandise inventory turnover	Times per period	4.29	6.00	RMA
Inventory turnover	Days	85.04	61.00	RMA
Operating cycle	Days	151.05	103.42	RMA + DC
Working capital (in millions)	$	2,321.50	—	N/A
Current ratio	N/A	2.26	1.75	DC
Acid-test ratio	N/A	1.30	0.68	DC
Cash ratio	N/A	0.31	0.16	DC
Sales to working capital	Times per period	4.76	6.46	DC
Operating cash flow/current maturities of long-term debt and notes payable	Times per period	2.25	—	Not available
Long-term debt-paying ability:				
Times interest earned	Times per period	21.60	2.50	RMA
Fixed charge coverage	Times per period	10.90	—	Not available
Debt ratio	$	40.42	64.51	DC
Debt/equity	$	67.83	181.74	DC
Debt to tangible net worth	$	76.56	—	Not available
Operating cash flow/total debt	$	41.53	—	Not available
Profitability:				
Net profit margin	$	6.76	Negative	DC
Total asset turnover	Times per period	1.61	1.24	DC
Return on assets	$	10.90	Negative	DC
Operating income margin	$	10.79	4.34	DC
Operating asset turnover	Times per period	1.84	1.60	DC
Return on operating assets	$	19.83	6.43	DC
Sales to fixed assets	Times per period	6.62	3.35	DC
Return on investment	$	16.19	—	Not available
Return on total equity	$	18.22	2.49	DC
Return on common equity	$	18.22	—	Not available
Gross profit margin	$	39.30	30.20	IN
Investor analysis:				
Degree of financial leverage	N/A	1.05	6.43	DC
Earnings per share	$	2.46	—	Not available
Price/earnings ratio	N/A	21.85	21.89	S&P
Percentage of earnings retained	%	80.71	Negative	DC
Dividend payout ratio	%	19.51	—	Not available
Dividend yield	%	0.89	1.33	S&P
Book value per share	$	14.43	—	N/A
Materiality of option compensation				
Pro forma/Reported net income	%	93.85	—	Not available
Pro forma/Reported earnings per share	%	93.50	—	Not available
Operating cash flow per share	$	3.97	—	N/A
Operating cash flow/cash dividends	Times per year	8.39	—	Not available
Year-end market price	$	53.75	—	N/A

Index: Industry statistics are directly from or computed from the following sources:

DC = U.S. Department of Commerce—Quarterly Financial Report for Manufacturing, Mining, and Trade Corporations NAIC 316
IN = Dun & Bradstreet—Industry Norm & Key Business Ratios, SIC Major Group 30
RMA = Robert Morris Associates, Annual Statement studies, SIC 3052, NAICS 32622
S&P = Standard & Poor's, The Outlook, Super Composite 1,500

Long-term debt-paying ability

- The times interest earned is materially better for Nike than the industry.
- The debt ratio and debt/equity are materially better for Nike than the industry.

Summary

Nike's long-term debt-paying ability appears to be materially better than the industry.

Profitability

All of the profitability ratios were materially better for Nike than the industry.

Summary

The industry apparently had many firms with low profits and some with losses. Nike had a very good profit year.

Investor Analysis

- The degree of financial leverage is much lower for Nike than for the industry.
- The price/earnings ratio is approximately the same for Nike as for the Super Composite 1500. This appears to be very favorable to Nike considering the ratios of Nike, especially the profitability ratios.
- Nike had a percentage of earnings retained of approximately 80%. The industry had a negative percentage of earnings retained.
- Dividend yield is slightly less for Nike than the industry.

Summary

Only a few comparisons were possible in the investor area. The comparisons are very favorable toward Nike.

OTHER

Two areas reviewed in Chapter 8, Profitability, appear to be particularly significant. They are management pretax income to net profit (Exhibit 8-21) and sales and marketing (Exhibit 8-22).

Exhibit 8-21 indicates that management pretax income to net profit was the highest for the United States and increased moderately. Foreign pretax income to net profit increased much faster than for the United States. Foreign sales are also increasing much faster than United States sales. It appears that foreign sales have hit a critical mass and that future increases will increase profits at an even faster rate. This could be very positive.

Sales and marketing (Exhibit 8-22) total U.S. revenues increased slightly, while international sales increased substantially. In 1996 the Nike equipment division was formed. Sales of equipment and other have increased materially (Exhibit 8-22).

SUMMARY

In general, the years 2000–2002 appear to be good for Nike in terms of liquidity. The debt position appears to be very good. This appears to be the case from an income statement view and a balance sheet view. Profitability appears to be very good.

Nike appears to be a good company to sell products to on credit (liquidity would be particularly important) and to lend money to (liquidity and debt position would be particularly important). Nike's liquidity and debt position should also be considered when investing, but investors tend to pay a great deal of attention to profitability. Profit was very good when compared with a competitor and the industry.

NIKE 2002 FINANCIAL STATEMENTS

Included here are the 2002 financials of Nike, reprinted with the permission of Nike, Inc.

SECURITIES AND EXCHANGE COMMISSION
Washington, D.C. 20549

Form 10-K

(Mark One)

☑   **ANNUAL REPORT PURSUANT TO SECTION 13 OR 15(d) OF THE SECURITIES EXCHANGE ACT OF 1934**

For the fiscal year ended May 31, 2002

or

☐   **TRANSITION REPORT PURSUANT TO SECTION 13 OR 15(d) OF THE SECURITIES EXCHANGE ACT OF 1934**

For the transition period from   to   .

Commission File No. 1-10635

NIKE, Inc.
(Exact name of Registrant as specified in its charter)

Oregon	**93-0584541**
(State or other jurisdiction of incorporation)	*(IRS Employer Identification No.)*
One Bowerman Drive **Beaverton, Oregon 97005-6453**	**(503) 671-6453**
(Address of principal executive offices) (Zip Code)	*(Registrant's Telephone Number, Including Area Code)*

Securities registered pursuant to Section 12(b) of the Act:

Class B Common Stock	New York Stock Exchange
(Title of each class)	*(Name of each exchange on which registered)*

Securities registered pursuant to Section 12(g) of the Act:
None

Indicate by check mark whether the Registrant (1) has filed all reports required to be filed by Section 13 or 15(d) of the Securities Exchange Act of 1934 during the preceding 12 months (or for such shorter period that the Registrant was required to file such reports), and (2) has been subject to such filing requirements for the past 90 days.   Yes ☑   No ☐

As of July 25, 2002, the aggregate market value of the Registrant's Class A Common Stock held by nonaffiliates of the Registrant was $170,452,457 and the aggregate market value of the Registrant's Class B Common Stock held by nonaffiliates of the Registrant was $8,037,948,759.

As of July 25, 2002, the number of shares of the Registrant's Class A Common Stock outstanding was 98,095,361 and the number of shares of the Registrant's Class B Common Stock outstanding was 168,763,188.

DOCUMENTS INCORPORATED BY REFERENCE:

Parts of Registrant's Proxy Statement for the annual meeting of shareholders to be held on September 18, 2002 are incorporated by reference into Part III of this Report.

Indicate by check mark if disclosure of delinquent filers pursuant to Item 405 of Regulation S-K (229.405 of this chapter) is not contained herein, and will not be contained to the best of Registrant's knowledge, in definitive proxy or information statements incorporated by reference in Part III of this Form 10-K or any amendment to this Form 10-K.   ☐

NIKE, INC.
ANNUAL REPORT ON FORM 10-K
TABLE OF CONTENTS

PART I

Item 1. *Business*

General

NIKE, Inc. was incorporated in 1968 under the laws of the state of Oregon. As used in this report, the terms "we", "us", "NIKE" and the "Company" refer to NIKE, Inc. and its predecessors, subsidiaries and affiliates, unless the context indicates otherwise.

Our principal business activity involves the design, development and worldwide marketing of high quality footwear, apparel, equipment, and accessory products. NIKE is the largest seller of athletic footwear and athletic apparel in the world. We sell our products to approximately 18,000 retail accounts in the United States and through a mix of independent distributors, licensees and subsidiaries in approximately 140 countries around the world. Virtually all of our products are manufactured by independent contractors. Virtually all footwear products are produced outside the United States, while apparel products are produced both in the United States and abroad.

Products

NIKE's athletic footwear products are designed primarily for specific athletic use, although a large percentage of the products are worn for casual or leisure purposes. We place considerable emphasis on high quality construction and innovative design. Running, basketball, children's, cross-training and women's shoes are currently our top-selling product categories and we expect them to continue to lead in product sales in the near future. However, we also market shoes designed for outdoor activities, tennis, golf, soccer, baseball, football, bicycling, volleyball, wrestling, cheerleading, aquatic activities, hiking, and other athletic and recreational uses.

We sell active sports apparel covering most of the above categories, athletically inspired lifestyle apparel, as well as athletic bags and accessory items. NIKE apparel and accessories are designed to complement our athletic footwear products, feature the same trademarks and are sold through the same marketing and distribution channels. We often market footwear, apparel and accessories in "collections" of similar design or for specific purposes. We also market apparel with licensed college and professional team and league logos.

We sell a line of performance equipment under the NIKE brand name, including sport balls, timepieces, eyewear, skates, bats, gloves, and other equipment designed for sports activities. We also have agreements for licensees to produce and sell NIKE brand swimwear, women's sports bras, cycling apparel, children's clothing, posters, school supplies, timepieces, and electronic media devices. We also sell small amounts of various plastic products to other manufacturers through our wholly-owned subsidiary, NIKE IHM, Inc.

We sell a line of dress and casual footwear and accessories for men, women and children under the brand name Cole Haan® through our wholly-owned subsidiary, Cole Haan Holdings, Inc., headquartered in Yarmouth, Maine.

Our wholly-owned subsidiary, Bauer NIKE Hockey Inc., headquartered in Greenland, New Hampshire, manufactures and distributes ice skates, skate blades, in-line roller skates, protective gear, hockey sticks, and hockey jerseys and accessories under the Bauer® and NIKE® brand names. Bauer also offers a full selection of products for street, roller and field hockey.

In April 2002, we acquired Hurley International LLC, headquartered in Costa Mesa, California, which designs and distributes a line of action sports apparel (for surfing, skateboarding, and snowboarding) and youth lifestyle apparel under the Hurley brand name.

Sales and Marketing

The table below shows certain information regarding NIKE's United States and international (non-U.S.) revenues for the last three fiscal years.

May 31,	Fiscal 2002	Fiscal 2001	FY02 vs. FY01 % CHG (In millions)	Fiscal 2000	FY01 vs. FY00 % CHG
USA Region					
Footwear	$3,185.0	$3,208.9	(0.7)%	$3,351.2	(4.2)%
Apparel	1,305.3	1,260.3	3.6%	1,154.4	9.2%
Equipment and other	425.7	349.8	21.7%	226.5	54.4%
Total USA	4,916.0	4,819.0	2.0%	4,732.1	1.8%
Europe, Middle East and Africa (EMEA) Region					
Footwear	1,551.8	1,422.8	9.1%	1,309.4	8.7%
Apparel	989.5	976.3	1.4%	933.9	4.5%
Equipment and other	190.2	185.7	2.4%	163.7	13.4%
Total EMEA	2,731.5	2,584.8	5.7%	2,407.0	7.4%
Asia Pacific Region					
Footwear	657.7	632.4	4.0%	557.0	13.5%
Apparel	431.0	374.8	15.0%	321.0	16.8%
Equipment and other	123.0	102.8	19.6%	77.1	33.3%
Total Asia Pacific	1,211.7	1,110.0	9.2%	955.1	16.2%
Americas Region					
Footwear	359.2	355.2	1.1%	343.9	3.3%
Apparel	167.1	152.2	9.8%	137.7	10.5%
Equipment and other	41.8	31.7	31.9%	12.5	153.6%
Total Americas	568.1	539.1	5.4%	494.1	9.1%
Total NIKE brand	9,427.3	9,052.9	4.1%	8,588.3	5.4%
Other brands	465.7	435.9	6.8%	406.8	7.2%
Total Revenues	$9,893.0	$9,488.8	4.3%	$8,995.1	5.5%

Financial information about geographic and segment operations appears in Note 16 of the consolidated financial statements on page 51.

We experience moderate fluctuations in aggregate sales volume during the year. However, the mix of product sales may vary considerably from time to time as a result of changes in seasonal and geographic demand for particular types of footwear, apparel, and equipment.

Because NIKE is a consumer products company, the relative popularity of various sports and fitness activities and changing design trends affect the demand for our products. We must therefore respond to trends and shifts in consumer preferences by adjusting the mix of existing product offerings, developing new products, styles and categories, and influencing sports and fitness preferences through aggressive marketing. This is a continuing risk. Failure to timely and adequately respond could have a material adverse affect on our sales and profitability.

United States Market

During fiscal 2002, sales in the United States accounted for approximately 53 percent of total revenues, compared to 54 percent in fiscal 2001 and 56 percent in fiscal 2000. We sell to approximately 18,000 retail accounts in the United States. The NIKE brand domestic retail account base includes a mix of footwear stores, sporting goods stores, athletic specialty stores, department stores, skate, tennis and golf shops, and other retail accounts. During fiscal year 2002, our three largest customers accounted for approximately 28 percent of NIKE brand sales in the United States, and 26 percent of total sales in the United States.

We make substantial use of our "futures" ordering program, which allows retailers to order five to six months in advance of delivery with the guarantee that 90 percent of their orders will be delivered within a set time period at a fixed price. In fiscal year 2002, 92 percent of our U.S. footwear shipments (excluding Cole Haan, Bauer and Hurley) were made under the futures program, compared to 86 percent in fiscal 2001 and 90 percent in fiscal 2000. In fiscal 2002, 77 percent of our U.S. apparel shipments were made under the futures program, compared to 78 percent in fiscal 2001, and 82 percent in 2000.

We utilize 18 NIKE sales offices to solicit sales in the United States. We also utilize 15 independent sales representatives to sell specialty products for golf, cycling, water sports and outdoor activities. In addition, we operate the following retail outlets in the United States:

Retail Stores	Number
NIKE factory stores (which carry primarily B-grade and close-out merchandise)	78
NIKE stores (including NIKE Goddess Stores)	4
NIKETOWNs (designed to showcase NIKE products)	13
Employee-only stores	4
Cole Haan stores (including factory and employee stores)	61
Total..	160

NIKE's domestic distribution centers for footwear are located in Beaverton, Oregon, Wilsonville, Oregon, Memphis, Tennessee, and Greenland, New Hampshire. Apparel products are shipped from our Memphis distribution center. Cole Haan footwear and Bauer NIKE Hockey products are distributed primarily from Greenland, New Hampshire, and Hurley products are shipped from Costa Mesa, California.

International Markets

We currently market our products in approximately 140 countries outside of the United States through independent distributors, licensees, subsidiaries and branch offices. Non-U.S. sales accounted for 47 percent of total revenues in fiscal 2002, compared to 46 percent in fiscal 2001 and 44 percent in fiscal 2000. We operate 19 distribution centers in Europe, Asia, Australia, Latin America, and Canada, and also distribute through independent distributors and licensees. We estimate that our products are sold through more than 30,000 retail accounts outside the United States. In many countries and regions, including Japan, Canada, Asia, Latin America, and Europe, we have a futures ordering program for retailers similar to the United States futures program described above. NIKE's three largest customers outside of the U.S. accounted for approximately 9 percent of non-U.S. sales.

We operate 162 retail outlets outside the United States, which are comprised of NIKETOWNs, factory stores, employee stores, and Cole Haan stores.

International branch offices and subsidiaries of NIKE are located in Argentina, Australia, Austria, Belgium, Brazil, Canada, Chile, Croatia, Czech Republic, Denmark, Finland, France, Germany, Hong Kong, Hungary, Indonesia, India, Ireland, Israel, Italy, Japan, Korea, Malaysia, Mexico, New Zealand, The Netherlands, Norway, Peoples Republic of China, The Philippines, Poland, Portugal, Singapore, Slovakia, Slovenia, South Africa, Spain, Sweden, Switzerland, Taiwan, Thailand, Turkey, the United Kingdom, and Vietnam.

Significant Customers

Foot Locker, Inc., which operates a chain of retail stores specializing in athletic footwear and apparel, accounted for approximately 11 percent of global net sales of NIKE brand products during fiscal 2002. No other customer accounted for 10 percent or more of our net sales during fiscal 2002.

Orders

As of May 31, 2002, our worldwide futures orders for NIKE brand athletic footwear and apparel totaled $4.6 billion, compared to $4.4 billion as of May 31, 2001. These orders are scheduled for delivery from June through November of 2002. Based upon historical data, we expect that approximately 95 percent of these orders will be filled in that time period, although the orders may be cancelable.

Product Research and Development

We believe that our research and development efforts are a key factor in our past and future success. Technical innovation in the design of footwear, apparel, and athletic equipment receive continued emphasis as NIKE strives to produce products that reduce or eliminate injury, aid athletic performance and maximize comfort.

In addition to NIKE's own staff of specialists in the areas of biomechanics, exercise physiology, engineering, industrial design and related fields, we also utilize research committees and advisory boards made up of athletes, coaches, trainers, equipment managers, orthopedists, podiatrists and other experts who consult with us and review designs, materials and concepts for product improvement. Employee athletes wear-test and evaluate products during the design and development process.

Manufacturing

In fiscal 2002, approximately 5 percent of total NIKE brand apparel production for sale to the United States market was manufactured in the United States by independent contract manufacturers, most of which are located in the southern states. The remainder was manufactured by independent contractors located in 28 countries. Most of this apparel production occurred in Bangladesh, Bulgaria, China, Hong Kong, India, Indonesia, Malaysia, Mexico, Pakistan, The Philippines, Sri Lanka, Taiwan, Thailand, and Turkey. Substantially all of our apparel production for sale to the international market was manufactured outside the U.S. Our largest single apparel supplier accounted for approximately 8 percent of total fiscal 2002 apparel production.

Virtually all of our footwear is produced outside of the United States. In fiscal 2002, contract suppliers in the following countries manufactured the following percentages of total NIKE brand footwear:

Country	Percent
People's Republic of China	38
Indonesia	30
Vietnam	15
Thailand	14
Italy	1
Taiwan	1
South Korea	1

We also have manufacturing agreements with independent factories in Argentina, Brazil, India, Mexico, South Africa, and Zimbabwe, to manufacture footwear for sale within those countries. Our largest single footwear supplier accounted for approximately 6 percent of total fiscal 2002 footwear production.

The principal materials used in our footwear products are natural and synthetic rubber, plastic compounds, foam cushioning materials, nylon, leather, canvas, and polyurethane films used to make AIR-SOLE cushioning components. NIKE IHM, Inc., a wholly-owned subsidiary of NIKE, is our sole supplier of the AIR-SOLE cushioning components used in footwear. The principal materials used in our apparel products are natural and synthetic fabrics and threads, plastic and metal hardware, and specialized performance fabrics designed to repel rain, retain heat, or efficiently transport body moisture. NIKE and its contractors and suppliers buy raw materials in bulk. Most raw materials are available in the countries where manufacturing takes place. We have thus far experienced little difficulty in satisfying our raw material requirements.

Our international operations are subject to the usual risks of doing business abroad, such as possible revaluation of currencies, export duties, quotas, restrictions on the transfer of funds and, in certain parts of the world, political instability. See "Trade Legislation" below. We have not, to date, been materially affected by any such risk, but cannot predict the likelihood of such developments occurring. We believe that we have the ability to develop, over a period of time, adequate alternative sources of supply for the products obtained from our present suppliers outside of the United States. If events prevented us from acquiring products from our suppliers in a particular country, our footwear operations could be temporarily disrupted and we could experience an adverse financial impact. However, we believe that we could eliminate any such disruption within a period of no more than 12 months, and that any adverse impact would, therefore, be of a short-term nature. We believe that our principal competitors are subject to similar risks.

All of our products manufactured overseas and imported into the United States and other countries are subject to customs duties collected by customs authorities. Customs information submitted by us is routinely subject to review by customs authorities. We are unable to predict whether additional customs duties, quotas or other restrictions may be imposed on the importation of our products in the future. The enactment of any such duties, quotas or restrictions could result in increases in the cost of our products generally and might adversely affect the sales or profitability of NIKE and the imported footwear and apparel industry as a whole.

Since 1972, Nissho Iwai American Corporation ("NIAC"), a subsidiary of Nissho Iwai Corporation, a large Japanese trading company, has performed significant import-export financing services for us. Currently, NIAC provides such financing services with respect to at least 80 percent of the NIKE products sold outside of the United States, Europe and Japan. Any failure of NIAC to provide these services could disrupt our ability to acquire products from our suppliers and to deliver products to our customers outside of the United States, Europe and Japan. Such a disruption could result in cancelled orders that would adversely affect sales and profitability. However, we believe that any such disruption would be short term in duration due to the ready availability of alternative sources of financing at competitive rates. Our current agreements with NIAC expire on May 31, 2003.

Trade Legislation

Our non-U.S. operations are subject to the usual risks of doing business abroad, such as the imposition of import quotas or anti-dumping duties. In 1994, the European Union ("EU") Commission imposed quotas on certain types of footwear manufactured in China. These quotas replaced national quotas that had previously been in effect in several Member States. Footwear designed for use in sporting activities, meeting certain technical criteria and having a CIF (cost, insurance and freight) price above 9 euros ("Special Technology Athletic Footwear" or "STAF"), is excluded from the quotas. As a result of the STAF exclusion, and the amount of quota made available to us, the quotas have not, to date, had a material effect on our business.

In 1995, the EU Commission, at the request of European footwear manufacturers, initiated two anti-dumping investigations covering footwear imported from the People's Republic of China, Indonesia and Thailand. As a result, in 1997 the Commission imposed definitive anti-dumping duties on certain textile upper footwear imported from China and Indonesia. In 1998, the Commission imposed definitive anti-dumping duties on certain synthetic and leather upper footwear originating in China, Indonesia and Thailand. In the case of textile upper footwear, the anti-dumping duties do not cover sports footwear. In the case of synthetic and leather upper footwear, the anti-dumping duties do not cover footwear meeting the STAF technical criteria nor footwear with a CIF price above 5.7 euros. As the anti-dumping duties for synthetic and leather uppers only affect some low cost footwear, these measures have no impact for us. While the exclusions are subject to some interpretation by customs authorities, we believe that most of our footwear sourced in the target countries for sale in the EU fits within the exclusions. We have also shifted the production of these types of footwear to other countries. Accordingly, the anti-dumping duties have not had a material effect on our business. The EU Commission has announced the impending expiration of these anti-dumping cases, subject to possible review requests by the European footwear manufacturers. Such reviews may result in the renewal of the anti-dumping regulations.

The EU Commission in June 2000 issued an amendment to the explanatory notes to the EU's customs nomenclature ("CN"). The amendment, which is not legally binding, interprets some of the technical criteria for the STAF exclusion and the footwear types that can be classified as for use in sporting activity. The amendment restricts somewhat the scope of the STAF exclusion from the quotas and also the sports footwear exclusions from the two EU anti-dumping measures. To date, the large majority of our footwear models fall within the exclusions provided for under the CN. Our innovative footwear designs may stretch the traditional concepts of athletic or sports footwear reflected in the technical criteria. We anticipate that the majority of these new designs will fall within the exclusions. NIKE is an active participant in discussions to revise the technical criteria to reflect technologically advanced designs.

If the EU trade measures become substantially more restrictive we would consider shifting the production of such footwear to other countries in order to maintain competitive pricing. We believe that we are prepared to deal effectively with any such change of circumstances and that any adverse impact would be of a temporary nature. We continue to closely monitor international restrictions and maintain our multi-country sourcing strategy and contingency plans. We believe that our major competitors stand in much the same position regarding these trade measures.

We currently source footwear and apparel products from factories in Vietnam. In July 2000, the United States and Vietnam signed an historic, comprehensive bilateral trade agreement, which, among other things, provides reciprocal, non-discriminatory Normal Trade Relations ("NTR") between the two countries. In September 2001, that agreement was approved by Congress and then ratified by the Vietnamese National Assembly. Once approved, the United States granted an annual extension of NTR to Vietnam. Under current U.S. law, the President must renew this grant annually with the opportunity for review by the Congress. In June 2002, President Bush renewed NTR for Vietnam for an additional year and in July 2002, the Congress supported the President's decision. We currently believe that, absent unforeseen circumstances, the President will continue his annual extensions of NTR to Vietnam and that Congress will support the President's decisions. Ongoing NTR trading status for Vietnam will allow us to expand our production and marketing opportunities in Vietnam and allow for Vietnamese-sourced product to enter the United States at NTR tariff rates.

Competition

The athletic footwear, apparel and equipment industry is keenly competitive in the United States and on a worldwide basis. We compete internationally with an increasing number of athletic and leisure shoe companies, athletic and leisure apparel companies, sports equipment companies, and large companies having diversified lines of athletic and leisure shoes, apparel and equipment, including Reebok, Adidas and others. The intense competition and the rapid changes in technology and consumer preferences in the markets for athletic and leisure footwear and apparel, and athletic equipment, constitute significant risk factors in our operations.

NIKE is the largest seller of athletic footwear and athletic apparel in the world. Performance and reliability of shoes, apparel, and equipment, new product development, price, product identity through marketing and promotion, and customer support and service are important aspects of competition in the athletic footwear, apparel and equipment industry. To help market our products, we contract with prominent and influential athletes, coaches, teams, colleges, and sports leagues to endorse our brands and use our products, and we actively sponsor sporting events and clinics. We believe that we are competitive in all of these areas.

Trademarks and Patents

We utilize trademarks on nearly all of our products and believe that having distinctive marks that are readily identifiable is an important factor in creating a market for our goods, in identifying the Company, and in distinguishing our goods from the goods of others. We consider our NIKE® and Swoosh Design® trademarks to be among our most valuable assets and we have registered these trademarks in over 100 countries. In addition, we own many other trademarks which we utilize in marketing our products. We continue to vigorously protect our trademarks against infringement.

NIKE has an exclusive, worldwide license to make and sell footwear using patented "Air" technology. The process utilizes pressurized gas encapsulated in polyurethane. Some of the early NIKE AIR® patents have expired, which may enable competitors to use certain types of like technology. Subsequent NIKE AIR patents will not expire for several years. We also have a number of patents covering components and features used in various athletic and leisure shoes. We believe that our success depends primarily upon skills in design, research and development, production and marketing rather than upon our patent position. However, we have followed a policy of filing applications for United States and foreign patents on inventions, designs and improvements that we deem valuable.

Employees

We had approximately 22,700 employees at May 31, 2002. Management considers its relationship with employees to be excellent. With the exception of Bauer NIKE Hockey Inc., our employees are not represented by a union. Of Bauer NIKE Hockey's North American employees, approximately 65 percent, or fewer than 450, are covered by three union collective bargaining agreements with three separate bargaining units, and all of Bauer NIKE Hockey's approximately 150 non-immigrant employees in Italy are covered by three collective bargaining agreements. The collective bargaining agreements expire on various dates from 2002 through 2003. There has never been a material interruption of operations due to labor disagreements.

Executive Officers of the Registrant

The executive officers of NIKE as of July 25, 2002 are as follows:

Philip H. Knight, Chief Executive Officer, Chairman of the Board, and President — Mr. Knight, 64, a director since 1968, is a co-founder of NIKE and, except for the period from June 1983 through September 1984, served as its President from 1968 to 1990, and from June 2000 to present. Prior to 1968, Mr. Knight was a certified public accountant with Price Waterhouse and Coopers & Lybrand and was an Assistant Professor of Business Administration at Portland State University.

Donald W. Blair, Vice President and Chief Financial Officer — Mr. Blair, 44, joined NIKE in November 1999. Prior to joining NIKE, he held a number of financial management positions with Pepsico, Inc., including Vice President, Finance of Pepsi-Cola Asia, Vice President, Planning of PepsiCo's Pizza Hut Division, and Senior Vice President, Finance of The Pepsi Bottling Group, Inc. Prior to joining Pepsico, Mr. Blair was a certified public accountant with Deloitte, Haskins, and Sells.

Thomas E. Clarke, President of New Ventures — Dr. Clarke, 51, a director since 1994, joined the Company in 1980. He was appointed divisional Vice President in charge of marketing in 1987, elected corporate Vice President in 1989, appointed General Manager in 1990, and served as President and Chief Operating Officer from 1994 to 2000. Dr. Clarke previously held various positions with the Company, primarily in research, design, development and marketing. Dr. Clarke holds a doctorate degree in biomechanics.

Charles D. Denson, President of the NIKE Brand — Mr. Denson, 46, has been employed by NIKE since February 1979. Mr. Denson held several positions within the Company, including his appointments as Director of USA Apparel Sales in 1994, divisional Vice President, US Sales in 1994, divisional Vice President European Sales in 1997, divisional Vice President and General Manager, NIKE Europe in 1998, Vice President and General Manager of NIKE USA in June 2000, and President of the NIKE Brand in March 2001.

Gary M. DeStefano, President of USA Operations — Mr. DeStefano, 45, has been employed by NIKE since 1982, with primary responsibilities in sales and regional administration. Mr. DeStefano was appointed Director of Domestic Sales in 1990, divisional Vice President in charge of domestic sales in 1992, Vice President of Global Sales in 1996, Vice President and General Manager of Asia Pacific in March 1997, and President of USA Operations in March 2001.

Mindy F. Grossman, Vice President of Global Apparel — Ms. Grossman, 44, joined NIKE in October 2000. Prior to joining NIKE, she was President and Chief Executive Officer of Polo Jeans Company/Ralph Lauren, a division of Jones Apparel Group, Inc. from 1995 to 2000. Prior to that, Ms. Grossman was Vice President of New Business Development at Polo Ralph Lauren Corp. from 1994 to 1995, President of The Warnaco Group Inc. Chaps Ralph Lauren division, and Senior Vice President of The Warnaco Group Inc. Menswear division from 1991 to 1994.

P. Eunan McLaughlin, Vice President, Asia Pacific — Mr. McLaughlin, 44, joined NIKE as Vice President, Sales, NIKE Europe in February 1999, was appointed Vice President Commercial Sales and Retail in February 2000, and became Vice President, Asia Pacific in June 2001. Prior to joining NIKE, he was Partner and Vice President of Consumer & Retail Practices Division, Korn/Ferry International from 1996 to 1999. From 1985 to 1996 Mr. McLaughlin held the following positions with Mars, Inc.: Finance Director, Sales Director, and Managing Director of Germany Drink Division; Operations Director of Pedigree Pet Foods; and European Sales & Marketing Director. Mr. McLaughlin also worked for Reynolds McCarron (formerly Ernst & Young) in Ireland.

D. Scott Olivet, Vice President, NIKE Subsidiaries and New Business Development — Mr Olivet, 40, joined NIKE in August 2001. Prior to joining NIKE, he was a Senior Vice President of Gap Inc., responsible for real estate, store design, and construction across Gap, Banana Republic, and Old Navy brands from 1998 to 2001. Prior to that, Mr. Olivet was employed by Bain & Company, an international strategic consulting firm from 1984 to 1998 (a Partner from 1993 to 1998). In addition to direct client work, Mr. Olivet was the leader of the firm's worldwide practice in organizational effectiveness and change management.

Mark G. Parker, President of the NIKE Brand — Mr. Parker, 45, has been employed by NIKE since 1979 with primary responsibilities in product research, design and development. Mr. Parker was appointed divisional Vice President in charge of development in 1987, corporate Vice President in 1989, General Manager in 1993, Vice President of Global Footwear in 1998, and President of the NIKE Brand in March 2001.

Eric D. Sprunk, Vice President, Global Footwear — Mr. Sprunk, 38, joined the Company in 1993. He was appointed Finance Director and General Manager of the Americas in 1994, Finance Director, NIKE Europe in 1995, Regional General Manager, NIKE Europe Footwear in 1998, and Vice President & General Manager of the Americas in 2000. Mr. Sprunk was appointed corporate Vice President, Global Footwear in June 2001.

Lindsay D. Stewart, Vice President and Chief of Staff, and Assistant Secretary — Mr. Stewart, 55, joined NIKE as Assistant Corporate Counsel in 1981. Mr. Stewart became Corporate Counsel in 1983. He was appointed Vice President and General Counsel in 1991, and Chief of Staff in March 2001. Prior to joining NIKE, Mr. Stewart was in private practice and an attorney for Georgia-Pacific Corporation.

Frits D. van Paasschen, Vice President and General Manager, NIKE Europe — Mr. van Paasschen, 42, has been employed by NIKE since 1997. He served as Vice President, Strategic Planning, and was appointed Vice President and General Manager, The Americas and Africa in 1998, and corporate Vice President and General Manager, NIKE Europe in 2000. Mr. van Paasschen was formerly Vice President, Finance & Planning, Disney Consumer Products, The Walt Disney Company.

Roland P. Wolfram, Vice President, Global Operations & Technology — Mr. Wolfram, 42, joined NIKE as Vice President, Strategic Planning in November 1998, and was appointed Vice President, Global Operations & Technology in February 2002. Prior to NIKE, Mr. Wolfram was Vice President and General Manager of Pacific Bell Video Services. From 1992 to 1993 he was director of the desktop products group for Compression Labs, Inc.

Item 2.   *Properties*

Following is a summary of principal properties owned or leased by NIKE. Our leases expire at various dates through the year 2017.

U.S. Administrative Offices:
Beaverton, Oregon (10 locations) — 9 leased
Memphis, Tennessee (2 locations) — 1 leased
Yarmouth, Maine
Charlotte, North Carolina — leased
Greenland, New Hampshire — leased
Costa Mesa, California — leased

International Administrative Offices:
Europe (23 locations) — leased
Africa (1 location) — leased
Asia Pacific (16 locations) — leased
Canada (2 locations) — leased
Latin America (2 locations) — leased

Sales Offices and Showrooms:
United States (22 locations) — leased
Europe (63 locations) — leased
Africa (1 location) — leased
Asia Pacific (24 locations) — leased
Canada (3 locations) — leased
Latin America (2 locations) — leased

Distribution Facilities:
Greenland, New Hampshire — leased
Wilsonville, Oregon
Forest Park, Georgia
Memphis, Tennessee (2 locations) — 1 leased
Costa Mesa, California — leased
Europe (5 locations) — 4 leased
Asia Pacific (11 locations) — 9 leased
Canada (2 locations) — leased
Latin America (2 locations) — leased

International Production Offices:
Europe (3 locations) — leased
Latin America (2 locations) — leased
Asia Pacific (24 locations) — leased

Manufacturing Facilities:
United States (3 locations) — 1 leased
Canada (3 locations) — 2 leased
Europe (2 locations) — leased
Asia Pacific (1 location)

Retail Outlets:
United States (160 locations) — 157 leased
Europe (40 locations) — leased
Asia Pacific (99 locations) — leased
Latin America (16 locations) — leased
Canada (7 locations) — leased

Item 3.   *Legal Proceedings*

Except as described below, there are no material pending legal proceedings, other than ordinary routine litigation incidental to our business, to which we are a party or of which any of our property is the subject.

The Company and certain of its officers and directors were named as defendants in four substantially identical securities class actions filed in the U.S. District Court for the District of Oregon on March 9, 14, 20, and April 4, 2001. On July 23, 2001, the cases were consolidated as In re NIKE, Inc. Securities Litigation, CV-01-332-K. The consolidated amended complaint sought unspecified damages on behalf of a purported class consisting of purchasers of the Company's stock during the period December 20, 2000 through February 26, 2001. Plaintiffs allege that the defendants made false and misleading statements about the Company's actual and expected business and financial performance in violation of federal securities laws. Plaintiffs further allege that certain individual defendants sold Company stock while in possession of material non-public information. In January 2002, the Court dismissed this action with leave to amend. On February 25, 2002, plaintiffs filed an amended complaint extending the purported class period to June 29, 2000 through February 26, 2001 and containing the same allegations. Based on the available information we do not currently anticipate that the action will have a material financial impact. We believe the claims are without merit, and we intend to vigorously defend against them.

A related shareholder derivative lawsuit, Metivier v. Denunzio, et al., 0104-04339, was filed in the Multnomah County Circuit Court of the State of Oregon on April 26, 2001. The state derivative suit was brought by certain Company shareholders, allegedly on behalf of the Company, against certain directors and officers of the Company. The derivative plaintiffs allege that these officers and directors breached their fiduciary duties to the Company by making or causing to be made alleged misstatements about the Company's actual and expected financial performance while certain officers and directors sold Company stock and by allowing the Company to be sued in the shareholder class action. The derivative plaintiffs seek compensatory and other damages, and disgorgement of compensation received. On July 25, 2001, the Court entered a stipulation and order abating the action until further notice.

Another related shareholder derivative lawsuit, Lendman v. Knight, et al., CV-01-1153-AS, was filed in the U.S. District Court for the District of Oregon on July 26, 2001. The federal derivative suit is not materially different from the state derivative action. It alleges substantially similar causes of action and seeks substantially similar remedies. The federal derivative action was served on the Company and the individual defendants on December 13, 2001 and was also stayed pending the outcome of In re NIKE, Inc. Securities Litigation on December 13, 2001.

In accordance with the Company's Articles of Incorporation and Bylaws, and in accordance with indemnity agreements between the Company and the directors and officers named in the above legal actions, the Company has agreed to indemnify these individuals and assume their defense in the actions.

The Company and certain of its officers were named as defendants in an lawsuit, Kasky v. NIKE, Inc. et al., No. 994446, filed in 1998 in San Francisco County Superior Court. Plaintiff brought the action under the California Business and Professions Code alleging that statements made by the Company in response to criticism about labor practices in factories making its products were false or misleading. Plaintiff seeks injunctive relief and restitution of profits earned from the alleged violations of the California Code. The claims were dismissed by the Superior Court, with the court concluding that the alleged statements, if made, were protected speech as part of a public debate under the First Amendment to the United States Constitution. Plaintiff appealed the Superior Court ruling to the California Court of Appeals, which court affirmed the ruling of the lower court. Plaintiff sought review in the California Supreme Court, which, on May 2, 2002, overturned the lower court rulings by a four to three vote. The California Supreme Court made no ruling on the merits of plaintiff's contention that the Company had made false or misleading statements, but concluded that the alleged statements were commercial speech and not entitled to the full protection of the First Amendment of the United States Constitution. The Company filed a petition for rehearing before the California Supreme Court, which was denied on July 31, 2002. The case has been remanded to the lower California state courts for further proceedings. We have announced our intention to seek review by the United States Supreme Court and have engaged additional counsel for that specific purpose. Since the litigation is in a preliminary stage, we do not currently anticipate that the action will have a material financial impact. We believe that the claims are without merit and we intend to vigorously defend against them.

Item 4.   *Submission of Matters to a Vote of Security Holders*

No matter was submitted during the fourth quarter of the 2002 fiscal year to a vote of security holders, through the solicitation of proxies or otherwise.

PART II

Item 5.   *Market for Registrant's Common Equity and Related Stockholder Matters*

NIKE's Class B Common Stock is listed on the New York Stock Exchange and the Pacific Stock Exchange and trades under the symbol NKE. At July 25, 2002, there were approximately 19,200 holders of record of our Class B Common Stock and 26 holders of record of our Class A Common Stock. These figures do not include beneficial owners who hold shares in nominee name. The Class A Common Stock is not publicly traded but each share is convertible upon request of the holder into one share of Class B Common Stock.

We refer to the table entitled "Selected Quarterly Financial Data" in Item 6, which lists, for the periods indicated, the range of high and low closing sales prices on the New York Stock Exchange. That table also describes the amount and frequency of all cash dividends declared on our common stock for the 2002 and 2001 fiscal years.

Item 6. *Selected Financial Data*

Financial History

	2002	2001	2000	1999	1998	1997	1996	1995	1994	1993	1992
	(In millions, except per share data, financial ratios and number of shareholders)										
Year Ended May 31,											
Revenues	$9,893.0	$9,488.8	$8,995.1	$8,776.9	$9,553.1	$9,186.5	$6,470.6	$4,760.8	$3,789.7	$3,931.0	$3,405.2
Gross margin	3,888.3	3,703.9	3,591.3	3,283.4	3,487.6	3,683.5	2,563.9	1,895.6	1,488.2	1,544.0	1,316.1
Gross margin %	39.3%	39.0%	39.9%	37.4%	36.5%	40.1%	39.6%	39.8%	39.3%	39.3%	38.7%
Restructuring charge, net	—	0.1	(2.5)	45.1	129.9	—	—	—	—	—	—
Income before accounting change	668.3	589.7	579.1	451.4	399.6	795.8	553.2	399.7	298.8	365.0	329.2
Cumulative effect of change in accounting principle	5.0	—	—	—	—	—	—	—	—	—	—
Net income	663.3	589.7	579.1	451.4	399.6	795.8	553.2	399.7	298.8	365.0	329.2
Basic earnings per common share:											
Income before accounting change	2.50	2.18	2.10	1.59	1.38	2.76	1.93	1.38	1.00	1.20	1.09
Cumulative effect of change in accounting principle	0.02	—	—	—	—	—	—	—	—	—	—
Net income	2.48	2.18	2.10	1.59	1.38	2.76	1.93	1.38	1.00	1.20	1.09
Diluted earnings per common share:											
Income before accounting change	2.46	2.16	2.07	1.57	1.35	2.68	1.88	1.36	0.99	1.18	1.07
Cumulative effect of change in accounting principle	0.02	—	—	—	—	—	—	—	—	—	—
Net income	2.44	2.16	2.07	1.57	1.35	2.68	1.88	1.36	0.99	1.18	1.07
Average common shares outstanding	267.7	270.0	275.7	283.3	288.7	288.4	286.6	289.6	298.6	302.9	301.7
Diluted average common shares outstanding	272.2	273.3	279.4	288.3	295.0	297.0	293.6	294.0	301.8	308.3	306.4
Cash dividends declared per common share	0.48	0.48	0.48	0.48	0.46	0.38	0.29	0.24	0.20	0.19	0.15
Cash flow from operations	1,081.5	656.5	699.6	941.4	517.5	323.1	339.7	254.9	576.5	265.3	435.8
Price range of common stock											
High	63.99	59.438	64.125	65.500	64.125	76.375	52.063	20.156	18.688	22.563	19.344
Low	40.81	35.188	26.563	31.750	37.750	47.875	19.531	14.063	10.781	13.750	8.781
At May 31,											
Cash and equivalents	$ 575.5	$ 304.0	$ 254.3	$ 198.1	$ 108.6	$ 445.4	$ 262.1	$ 216.1	$ 518.8	$ 291.3	$ 260.1
Inventories	1,373.8	1,424.1	1,446.0	1,170.6	1,396.6	1,338.6	931.2	629.7	470.0	593.0	471.2
Working capital	2,321.5	1,838.6	1,456.4	1,818.0	1,828.8	1,964.0	1,259.9	938.4	1,208.4	1,165.2	964.3
Total assets	6,443.0	5,819.6	5,856.9	5,247.7	5,397.4	5,361.2	3,951.6	3,142.7	2,373.8	2,186.3	1,871.7
Long-term debt	625.9	435.9	470.3	386.1	379.4	296.0	9.6	10.6	12.4	15.0	69.5
Redeemable Preferred Stock	0.3	0.3	0.3	0.3	0.3	0.3	0.3	0.3	0.3	0.3	0.3
Shareholders' equity	3,839.0	3,494.5	3,136.0	3,334.6	3,261.6	3,155.9	2,431.4	1,964.7	1,740.9	1,642.8	1,328.5
Year-end stock price	53.75	41.100	42.875	60.938	46.000	57.500	50.188	19.719	14.750	18.125	14.500
Market capitalization	14,302.5	11,039.5	11,559.1	17,202.2	13,201.1	16,633.0	14,416.8	5,635.2	4,318.8	5,499.3	4,379.6
Financial Ratios:											
Return on equity	18.2%	17.8%	17.9%	13.7%	12.5%	28.5%	25.2%	21.6%	17.7%	24.5%	27.9%
Return on assets	10.9%	10.1%	10.4%	8.5%	7.4%	17.1%	15.6%	14.5%	13.1%	18.0%	18.4%
Inventory turns	4.3	4.0	4.1	4.3	4.4	4.8	5.0	5.2	4.3	4.5	3.9
Current ratio at May 31	2.3	2.0	1.7	2.3	2.1	2.1	1.9	1.8	3.2	3.6	3.3
Price/Earnings ratio at May 31 (Diluted)	21.8	19.0	20.7	38.8	34.1	21.5	26.6	14.5	14.9	15.3	13.5
Geographic Revenues:											
United States	$5,258.8	$5,144.2	$5,017.4	$5,042.6	$5,460.0	$5,538.2	$3,964.7	$2,997.9	$2,432.7	$2,528.8	$2,270.9
Europe	2,731.5	2,584.8	2,407.0	2,293.8	2,096.1	1,789.8	1,334.3	980.4	927.3	1,085.7	919.8
Asia/Pacific	1,211.7	1,110.0	955.1	844.5	1,253.9	1,241.9	735.1	515.6	283.4	178.2	75.7
Americas (exclusive of United States)	691.0	649.8	615.6	596.0	743.1	616.6	436.5	266.9	146.3	138.3	138.8
Total Revenues	$9,893.0	$9,488.8	$8,995.1	$8,776.9	$9,553.1	$9,186.5	$6,470.6	$4,760.8	$3,789.7	$3,931.0	$3,405.2

12

All per common share data has been adjusted to reflect the 2-for-1 stock splits paid October 23, 1996 and October 30, 1995. The Company's Class B Common Stock is listed on the New York and Pacific Exchanges and trades under the symbol NKE. At May 31, 2002, there were approximately 126,000 shareholders of Class A and Class B common stock.

Financial Highlights

	Year Ended May 31,		
	2002	**2001**	**% CHG**
	(In millions, except per share data and financial ratios)		
Revenues	$9,893.0	$9,488.8	4.3%
Gross margin	3,888.3	3,703.9	5.0%
Gross margin %	39.3%	39.0%	
Income before accounting change	668.3	589.7	13.3%
Basic earnings per common share before accounting change	2.50	2.18	14.7%
Diluted earnings per common share before accounting change	2.46	2.16	13.9%
Return on equity	18.2%	17.8%	
Stock price at May 31	53.75	41.10	30.8%

Selected Quarterly Financial Data

	1st Quarter		2nd Quarter		3rd Quarter		4th Quarter	
	2002	**2001**	**2002**	**2001**	**2002**	**2001**	**2002**	**2001**
	(Unaudited) (In millions, except per share data and financial ratios)							
Revenues	$2,613.7	$2,636.7	$2,336.8	$2,198.7	$2,260.3	$2,170.1	$2,682.2	$2,483.3
Gross margin...........	1,028.9	1,067.5	895.4	871.4	883.5	828.6	1,080.5	936.4
Gross margin %	39.4%	40.5%	38.3%	39.6%	39.1%	38.2%	40.3%	37.7%
Income before accounting change	204.2	210.2	129.3	119.4	126.3	97.4	208.5	162.7
Basic earnings per common share before accounting change	0.74	0.78	0.48	0.44	0.47	0.36	0.78	0.60
Diluted earnings per common share before accounting change	0.73	0.77	0.48	0.44	0.46	0.35	0.77	0.60
Net income	199.2	210.2	129.3	119.4	126.3	97.4	208.5	162.7
Average common shares outstanding	268.6	269.9	268.1	269.8	268.4	270.9	266.9	269.3
Diluted average common shares outstanding	271.6	273.8	271.6	273.2	273.4	274.6	272.0	271.5
Cash dividends declared per common share	0.12	0.12	0.12	0.12	0.12	0.12	0.12	0.12
Price range of common stock								
High................	51.28	48.00	53.55	44.50	61.00	59.44	63.99	45.09
Low	40.81	35.19	42.26	36.38	52.31	39.05	52.75	36.30

Item 7. *Management's Discussion and Analysis of Financial Condition and Results of Operations*

Critical Accounting Policies

Our discussion and analysis of our financial condition and results of operations following are based upon our consolidated financial statements, which have been prepared in accordance with accounting principles generally accepted in the United States. The preparation of these financial statements requires us to make estimates and judgments that affect the reported amounts of assets, liabilities, revenues and expenses, and related disclosure of contingent assets and liabilities.

We believe that the estimates, assumptions and judgments involved in the accounting policies described below have the greatest potential impact on our financial statements, so we consider these to be our critical accounting policies. Because of the uncertainty inherent in these matters, actual results could differ from the estimates we use in applying the critical accounting policies. Certain of these critical accounting policies affect working capital account balances, including the policies for revenue recognition, the reserve for uncollectible accounts receivable, inventory reserves, and contingent payments under endorsement contracts. These policies require that we make estimates in the preparation of our financial statements as of a given date. However, since our business cycle is relatively short, actual results related to these estimates are generally known within the six-month period following the financial statement date. Thus, these policies generally affect only the timing of reported amounts across two to three quarters.

Within the context of these critical accounting policies, we are not currently aware of any reasonably likely events or circumstances which would result in materially different amounts being reported.

Revenue Recognition

We record wholesale revenues when title passes and the risks and rewards of ownership have passed to the customer, based on the terms of sale. Title passes generally upon shipment or upon receipt by the customer depending on the country of the sale and the agreement with the customer. Retail store revenues are recorded at the time of sale.

In some instances, we ship product directly from our supplier to the customer. In these cases, we recognize revenue when the product is delivered to the customer. Our revenues may fluctuate in cases when our customers delay accepting shipment of product for periods up to several weeks.

In certain countries outside of the U.S., precise information regarding the date of receipt by the customer is not readily available. In these cases, we estimate the date of receipt by the customer based upon historical delivery times by geographic location. On the basis of our tests of actual transactions, we have no indication that these estimates have been materially inaccurate historically.

As part of our revenue recognition policy, we record estimated sales returns and miscellaneous claims from customers as reductions to revenues at the time revenues are recorded. We base our estimates on historical rates of product returns and claims, and specific identification of outstanding claims and outstanding returns not yet received from customers. In the past, actual returns and claims have not exceeded our reserves. However, actual returns and claims in any future period are inherently uncertain and thus may differ from our estimates. If actual or expected future returns and claims were significantly greater or lower than the reserves we had established, we would record a reduction or increase to net revenues in the period in which we made such determination.

Reserve for Uncollectible Accounts Receivable

We make ongoing estimates relating to the collectibility of our accounts receivable and maintain a reserve for estimated losses resulting from the inability of our customers to make required payments. In determining the amount of the reserve, we consider our historical level of credit losses and make judgments about the creditworthiness of significant customers based on ongoing credit evaluations. Historically, losses from uncollectible accounts have not exceeded our reserves. Since we cannot predict future changes in the financial stability of our customers, actual future losses from uncollectible accounts may differ from our estimates. If the financial condition of our customers were to deteriorate, resulting in their inability to make payments, a larger reserve might be required. In the event we determined that a smaller or larger reserve was appropriate, we would record a credit or a charge to selling and administrative expense in the period in which we made such a determination.

Inventory Reserves

We also make ongoing estimates relating to the market value of inventories, based upon our assumptions about future demand and market conditions. If we estimate that the net realizable value of our inventory is less than the cost of the inventory recorded on our books, we record a reserve equal to the difference between the cost of the inventory and the estimated market value. This reserve is recorded as a charge to cost of sales. If changes in market conditions result in reductions in the estimated market value of our inventory below our previous estimate, we would increase our reserve in the period in which we made such a determination and record a charge to cost of sales.

Contingent Payments under Endorsement Contracts

A significant portion of our demand creation (advertising and promotion) expense relates to payments under endorsement contracts. In general, endorsement payments are expensed uniformly over the term of the contract. However, certain contract elements may be accounted for differently, based upon the facts and circumstances of each individual contract.

Certain contracts provide for contingent payments to endorsers based upon specific achievements in their sports (e.g. winning a championship). We record selling and administrative expense for these amounts when the endorser achieves the specific goal.

Certain contracts provide for payments based upon endorsers maintaining a level of performance in their sport over an extended period of time (e.g. maintaining a top ranking in a sport for a year). These amounts are reported in selling and administrative expense when we determine that it is probable that the specified level of performance will be maintained throughout the period. In these instances, to the extent that actual payments to the endorser differ from our estimate due to changes in the endorser's athletic performance, increased or decreased selling and administrative expense may be reported in a future period.

Certain contracts provide for royalty payments to endorsers based upon a predetermined percentage of sales of particular products. We expense these payments in cost of sales as the related sales are made. In certain contracts, we offer minimum guaranteed royalty payments. For contractual obligations for which we estimate that we will not meet the minimum guaranteed amount of royalty fees through sales of product, we record in selling and administrative expense the minimum guaranteed payment amount uniformly over the remaining royalty term.

Property, Plant and Equipment and Other Long-lived Assets

Property, plant and equipment, including buildings, equipment, and computer hardware and software is recorded at cost (including, in some cases, the cost of internal labor) and is depreciated over its estimated useful life. Changes in circumstances (such as technological advances or changes to our business operations) can result in differences between the actual and estimated useful lives. In those cases where we determine that the useful life of a long-lived asset should be shortened, we increase depreciation expense over the remaining useful life to depreciate the asset's net book value to its salvage value.

Under current accounting standards, when events or circumstances indicate that the carrying value of a long-lived asset may be impaired, we estimate the future undiscounted cash flows to be derived from the asset to determine whether or not a potential impairment exists. If the carrying value exceeds our estimate of future undiscounted cash flows, we then calculate the impairment as the excess of the carrying value of the asset over our estimate of its fair market value. Any impairment charges are recorded as other expense. We estimate future undiscounted cash flows using assumptions about our expected future operating performance. Our estimates of undiscounted cash flows may differ from actual cash flows due to, among other things, technological changes, economic conditions, or changes to our business operations. For fiscal 2002, no significant impairment related to the carrying value of our long-lived assets (including property, plant, and equipment, goodwill, and other intangible assets) has been recorded under current accounting standards. However, as of June 1, 2002, we will adopt Statement of Financial Accounting Standards (SFAS) No. 142, "Goodwill and Other Intangible Assets." We expect to record an impairment charge related to the goodwill and other intangible assets of our subsidiaries Bauer NIKE Hockey, Inc. and Cole-Haan Holdings, Inc. in the first quarter of fiscal 2003. See "Recently Issued Accounting Standards" below.

Hedge Accounting for Derivatives

We use forward exchange contracts and option contracts to hedge certain anticipated foreign currency exchange transactions, as well as any resulting receivable or payable balance. When specific criteria required by SFAS No. 133, "Accounting for Derivative Instruments and Hedging Activities," have been met, changes in fair values of hedge contracts relating to anticipated transactions are recorded in other comprehensive income rather than current earnings until the underlying hedged transaction affects current earnings. In most cases, this results in gains and losses on hedge derivatives being released from other comprehensive income into current earnings some time after the maturity of the derivative. One of the criteria for this accounting treatment is that the forward exchange contract amount should not be in excess of specifically identified anticipated transactions. By their very nature, our estimates of anticipated transactions may fluctuate over time and may ultimately vary from actual transactions. When anticipated transaction estimates or actual transaction amounts decrease below hedged levels, or when the timing of transactions changes significantly, we are required to reclassify at least a portion of the cumulative changes in fair values of the related hedge contracts from other comprehensive income to other income/expense during the quarter in which such changes occur. Once an anticipated transaction estimate or actual transaction amount decreases below hedged levels, we make adjustments to the related hedge contract in order to reduce the amount of the hedge contract to that of the revised anticipated transaction.

Taxes

We record valuation allowances against our deferred tax assets, when necessary, in accordance with SFAS No. 109, "Accounting for Income Taxes." Realization of deferred tax assets (such as net operating loss carryforwards) is dependent on future taxable earnings and is therefore uncertain. At least quarterly, we assess the likelihood that our deferred tax asset balance will be recovered from future taxable income. To the extent we believe that recovery is not likely, we establish a valuation allowance against our deferred tax asset, increasing our income tax expense in the period such determination is made.

In addition, we have not recorded U.S. income tax expense for foreign earnings that we have declared as indefinitely reinvested offshore, thus reducing our overall income tax expense. The amount of earnings designated as indefinitely reinvested offshore is based upon the actual deployment of such earnings in our offshore assets and our expectations of the future cash needs of our U.S. and foreign entities. Income tax considerations are also a factor in determining the amount of foreign earnings to be repatriated.

In the event actual cash needs of our U.S. entities exceed our current expectations or the actual cash needs of our foreign entities are less than expected, we may need to repatriate foreign earnings which have been designated as indefinitely reinvested offshore. This would result in additional income tax expense being recorded.

We take a conservative approach in determining the amount of foreign earnings to declare as reinvested offshore. As required by U.S. generally accepted accounting principles, the presumption is that such earnings will be repatriated in the future. In order to overcome this presumption, we carefully review all factors which drive the ultimate disposition of such foreign earnings, and apply stringent standards to overcoming the presumption of repatriation. Despite this conservative approach, because the determination involves our future plans and expectations of future events, there is a possibility that amounts declared as indefinitely reinvested offshore may ultimately be repatriated. Conversely, this conservative approach may result in accumulated foreign earnings (for which U.S. income taxes have been provided) being determined in the future to be indefinitely reinvested offshore. In this latter case, our income tax expense would be reduced in the year of such determination.

On an interim basis, we estimate what our effective tax rate will be for the full fiscal year and record a quarterly income tax provision in accordance with the anticipated annual rate. As the fiscal year progresses, we continually refine our estimate based upon actual events and earnings by jurisdiction during the year. This continual estimation process periodically results in a change to our expected effective tax rate for the fiscal year. When this occurs, we adjust the income tax provision during the quarter in which the change in estimate occurs so that the year-to-date provision equals the expected annual rate.

Other Contingencies

In the ordinary course of business, we are involved in legal proceedings involving contractual and employment relationships, product liability claims, trademark rights, and a variety of other matters. We record contingent liabilities resulting from claims against us when it is probable that a liability has been incurred and the amount of the loss is reasonably estimable. We disclose contingent liabilities when there is a reasonable possibility that the ultimate loss will exceed the recorded liability. Estimating probable losses requires analysis of multiple factors, in some cases including judgments about the potential actions of third party claimants and courts. Therefore, actual losses in any future period are inherently uncertain. Currently, we do not believe that any of our pending legal proceedings or claims will have a material impact on our financial position or results of operations. However, if actual or estimated probable future losses exceed our recorded liability for such claims, we would record additional charges as other expense during the period in which the actual loss or change in estimate occurred.

Results of Operations

Fiscal 2002 Highlights

- Revenues increased 4.3% to $9.9 billion, compared to $9.5 billion in fiscal 2001.

- Income before the cumulative effect of an accounting change increased to $668.3 million from $589.7 million in the prior year, an increase of 13.3%. After the effect of the accounting change, net income rose 12.5%.

- Diluted earnings per share before the effect of the accounting change increased by 13.9%, from $2.16 to $2.46. After the effect of the accounting change, diluted earnings per share rose 13.0%.

- Gross margins increased as a percentage of revenues to 39.3% from 39.0% in fiscal 2001.

- Selling and administrative expenses increased as a percentage of revenues to 28.5% from 28.3% in fiscal 2001.

Fiscal 2002 Compared to Fiscal 2001

Net income increased 13.3% over fiscal 2001, from $589.7 million to $668.3 million (excluding an after-tax loss of $5.0 million related to the cumulative effect of the adoption of SFAS No. 133, "Accounting for Derivative Instruments and Hedging Activities"). Diluted earnings per share before the effect of the accounting change improved 13.9%, from $2.16 to $2.46. These increases reflected a 10.4% increase in income before income taxes and a 1.7 point decrease in our effective income tax rate. The increase in income before income taxes was due to increased revenues, improved gross margins and lower interest and other expenses, partially offset by a slight increase in selling and administrative expenses as a percentage of revenues.

Fiscal 2002 revenues were the highest in our history, reflecting increased NIKE brand sales in all of our geographic regions. In the U.S., NIKE brand revenues increased 2.0% for the fiscal year, driven by increased sales of apparel and equipment. The increased sales in apparel reflected higher demand for in-line products, particularly for NIKE brand and Brand Jordan basketball apparel, more than offsetting the effect of the expiration of our apparel license agreement with the National Football League last year. In equipment, our rapidly growing golf business drove a 21.7% increase for the year.

U.S. footwear revenues declined 0.7% versus fiscal 2001. While in-line sales of footwear increased compared to last year, particularly in the mid-range price segment, close-out sales decreased significantly. The reduction in close-out sales reflected both our efforts to limit the availability of close-out products in the marketplace (in order to build overall profitability) and relatively high levels of close-out sales in the last half of fiscal 2001 due to supply chain system disruptions discussed further below in the *Fiscal 2001 Compared to*

Fiscal 2000 section. As in the apparel business, sales of NIKE brand and Brand Jordan basketball footwear products were the primary drivers of increased wholesale sales of in-line footwear during the year.

In fiscal 2002, NIKE brand revenues from our international regions continued to grow versus the prior year, both as a percentage of total company revenues and in total dollars. These revenues represented 45.6% of total company revenues as compared to 44.6% in fiscal 2001. Revenues from our international regions were $4.5 billion as compared to $4.2 billion in fiscal 2001, a 6.6% increase. Had the U.S. dollar remained constant with the prior year, these international revenues would have increased 12.4%, and consolidated revenues would have increased 6.9% (compared to 4.3% growth as reported).

Increased revenues in each of our international regions resulted from higher demand for products in all NIKE brand businesses: footwear, apparel, and equipment. Revenues in our Europe, Middle East, and Africa (EMEA) region increased for the eighth consecutive year. Fiscal 2002 reported revenues in EMEA increased by 5.7% over fiscal 2001, a 9.6% increase in constant dollars. In our Asia Pacific region, reported revenues grew 9.2%, a 19.3% increase in constant dollars. The Americas region grew reported revenues 5.4%, an 11.9% increase in constant dollars, despite a drop-off in sales in Argentina during the second half of the year due to that country's economic crisis.

In fiscal 2002, other revenue, which primarily includes revenues from Bauer NIKE Hockey, Cole Haan, and Hurley, increased 6.8% to $465.7 million.

Foot Locker, Inc. is our largest single customer and represented 10.9% of our worldwide revenues in fiscal 2002. Foot Locker has expressed its intention to reduce the emphasis of its U.S. business on higher-priced, premium footwear and place more focus on moderately-priced offerings. Due to this change in strategy, Foot Locker's futures orders in the U.S. for the holiday season (scheduled for delivery from September through November 2002) decreased significantly versus the same period in the previous year. In spite of the reduction in orders from Foot Locker, total U.S. futures orders for the September to November period are down only 2.3% versus the prior year and worldwide futures orders for the same period increased 3.0% versus fiscal 2002.

The impact of lower orders from Foot Locker for the September to November period was largely included in the June to November futures orders reported in our June 27, 2002 press release. However, additional changes in November orders from Foot Locker reduced the overall growth of worldwide futures for the six-month period by approximately 30 basis points to 6.3%.

Although we expect Foot Locker to continue to be an important retail partner for NIKE, second half U.S. footwear orders from this customer will likely be significantly below the prior year. We are aggressively pursuing incremental sales across our business as we work to offset these declines and achieve our worldwide revenue growth goals for the year. We believe there continues to be strong consumer demand for high-end, performance footwear; this segment has always been central to the success of the NIKE brand. Therefore, we will continue to work aggressively with those retailers who are focused on serving this market. While the success of these efforts over the next few quarters is uncertain, we remain confident in the long-term strength of our brand and our business.

Worldwide futures (advance) orders for NIKE brand athletic footwear and apparel scheduled for delivery from June through November 2002 were 6.3% higher than such orders booked in the comparable period of fiscal 2002. The percentage growth in futures orders is not necessarily indicative of our expectation of revenue growth in subsequent periods. This is because the mix of orders can shift between advance/futures and at-once orders. In addition, exchange rate fluctuations as well as differing levels of order cancellations can cause differences in the comparisons between future orders and actual revenues. Finally, a significant portion of our revenues are not derived from futures orders, including wholesale sales of equipment, U.S. licensed team apparel, Bauer NIKE Hockey, Cole Haan, Hurley, and retail sales across all brands. In the first quarter of fiscal 2003, we expect that revenue growth will lag futures order growth, reflecting lower close-out sales versus the first quarter of fiscal 2002 and lower retail sales versus the same period last year as U.S. retail sales have remained at relatively low levels since the terrorist attacks of September 11, 2001.

The breakdown of revenues follows:

May 31,	Fiscal 2002	Fiscal 2001	FY02 vs. FY01 % CHG (In millions)	Fiscal 2000	FY01 vs. FY00 % CHG
USA Region					
Footwear	$3,185.0	$3,208.9	(0.7)%	$3,351.2	(4.2)%
Apparel	1,305.3	1,260.3	3.6%	1,154.4	9.2%
Equipment and other	425.7	349.8	21.7%	226.5	54.4%
Total USA	4,916.0	4,819.0	2.0%	4,732.1	1.8%
EMEA Region					
Footwear	1,551.8	1,422.8	9.1%	1,309.4	8.7%
Apparel	989.5	976.3	1.4%	933.9	4.5%
Equipment and other	190.2	185.7	2.4%	163.7	13.4%
Total EMEA	2,731.5	2,584.8	5.7%	2,407.0	7.4%
Asia Pacific Region					
Footwear	657.7	632.4	4.0%	557.0	13.5%
Apparel	431.0	374.8	15.0%	321.0	16.8%
Equipment and other	123.0	102.8	19.6%	77.1	33.3%
Total Asia Pacific	1,211.7	1,110.0	9.2%	955.1	16.2%
Americas Region					
Footwear	359.2	355.2	1.1%	343.9	3.3%
Apparel	167.1	152.2	9.8%	137.7	10.5%
Equipment and other	41.8	31.7	31.9%	12.5	153.6%
Total Americas	568.1	539.1	5.4%	494.1	9.1%
Total NIKE brand	9,427.3	9,052.9	4.1%	8,588.3	5.4%
Other	465.7	435.9	6.8%	406.8	7.2%
Total Revenues	$9,893.0	$9,488.8	4.3%	$8,995.1	5.5%

Our gross margin percentage improved 30 basis points, from 39.0% in fiscal 2001 to 39.3% in fiscal 2002. Factors contributing to the improved gross margin percentage versus the prior year were as follows:

(1) Higher in-line pricing margins in EMEA, due to the effect of higher prices effective at the beginning of the fiscal year and sourcing and warehousing efficiencies, partially offset by the effect of weaker euro/U.S. dollar currency hedge rates relative to fiscal 2001.

(2) Higher footwear margins in the U.S. due in part to lower product costs and lower transportation costs, as a result of both effective negotiations with shippers and lower air freight costs incurred. Relatively higher air freight costs were incurred in fiscal 2001 due to supply chain problems discussed following.

(3) A higher mix of in-line sales versus close-out sales of U.S. footwear, reflecting increased demand for in-line footwear and lower close-out sales as compared to fiscal 2001 as discussed above.

Selling and administrative expenses increased as a percentage of revenues from 28.3% in fiscal 2001 to 28.5% in fiscal 2002. Operating overhead increased 6.0% during fiscal 2002 largely as a result of our continued investment in initiatives intended to generate future revenues and profits. Significant drivers of the increased operating overhead included increased investment in our supply chain initiative, additional headcount to support our growing golf and European businesses, additional expense for compensation programs tied to our profitability and stock performance, and costs for additional retail stores primarily in our EMEA and Asia Pacific regions.

The supply chain initiative refers to our on-going development of systems and processes supporting our worldwide supply chain. This initiative is intended to improve revenue (by increasing our ability to respond to market conditions), margins (by lowering close-outs and distribution costs) and cash flow (by reducing inventories). The ultimate level of benefit to revenues, margins, and cash flows, if any, will not be known until the new systems and processes have been implemented worldwide over the next few years. During fiscal 2002, we implemented new systems and processes for certain global functions and for our U.S. business, and we plan on implementing new systems and processes in EMEA during fiscal 2003. In fiscal 2003, we will continue to invest in the implementation of the new systems worldwide and support our existing system infrastructure for those businesses where we have not yet implemented the new systems.

Demand creation expense was $1,027.9 million in fiscal 2002 versus $998.2 million in fiscal 2001, which was consistent between years as a percentage of revenues. Our fiscal 2002 demand creation expense reflected incremental spending for our World Cup 2002 marketing campaign, which occurred primarily in our international regions. In fiscal 2003, we expect demand creation expense to grow slightly faster than revenues, reflecting the continuation of the World Cup 2002 campaign into the first quarter of fiscal 2003. In addition, we have entered into a long-term license and endorsement agreement with Manchester United, one of the premier soccer clubs in the world, which begins in August 2002. Payments under this contract will result in additional demand creation expense.

Interest expense decreased 18.9%, from $58.7 million to $47.6 million in fiscal 2002, due to lower interest rates in the current year and lower average debt levels, as we used operating free cash flow to reduce debt.

Other income/expense was a net expense of $3.0 million versus a net expense of $34.1 million in fiscal 2001. Consistent with previous years, other income/expense included interest income, profit sharing expense, goodwill amortization, certain foreign currency conversion gains and losses, and asset disposal gains/losses. Net other expense decreased between years as the fiscal 2001 amount included charges for contractual settlements that did not recur in fiscal 2002. In addition, fiscal 2002 other income/expense included credits related to the favorable resolution of some outstanding claims.

Our fiscal 2002 effective tax rate was 34.3% as compared to 36.0% in fiscal 2001. As required by U.S. generally accepted accounting principles, we do not accrue for U.S. tax liability on foreign earnings permanently invested offshore. The lower effective tax rate in fiscal 2002 is primarily the result of a larger amount of foreign earnings permanently invested offshore in fiscal 2002 than in fiscal 2001.

Fiscal 2001 Compared to Fiscal 2000

Net income increased 1.8% over fiscal 2000, from $579.1 million to $589.7 million. Although consolidated revenues increased 5.5% over fiscal 2000, income before income taxes was essentially flat as pretax profit margins decreased due to a lower gross margin percentage, higher interest expense, and increased other expenses, partially offset by lower selling and administrative expenses as a percentage of revenues. Despite flat income before income taxes, net income increased due to a lower effective tax rate. Diluted earnings per share increased 4.3%, from $2.07 to $2.16. The percentage increase in earnings per share was higher than that of net income primarily due to share repurchases in fiscal years 2000 and 2001.

NIKE brand revenues in the U.S. region increased 1.8% as compared to fiscal 2000, while NIKE brand revenues in our international regions increased 9.8%. Had the U.S. dollar remained constant with the prior year, these international revenues would have increased 18.6%, and consolidated revenues would have advanced 9.3%. In the U.S. region, our largest market segment, the 1.8% increase in revenues reflected a 9.2% increase in apparel sales and a 54.4% increase in equipment sales, offset by a 4.2% decrease in footwear sales. The increases in apparel and equipment reflected stronger demand for in-line products. The increase in the equipment product line reflected increases in a variety of sports equipment categories, including golf, football, and baseball products as well as socks, bags and eyewear. The decrease in footwear reflected lower demand, particularly in the mid-range price segment, and supply chain disruptions resulting from the implementation of a new global demand and supply planning system. The supply chain disruptions resulted in product excesses as well as product shortages and late deliveries in the second half of the fiscal 2001.

Revenues from our international regions were $4.2 billion as compared to $3.9 billion in fiscal 2000. Fiscal 2001 revenues in EMEA increased over fiscal 2000 by 7.4% to $2,584.8 million, a 19.3% increase in constant dollars. In our Asia Pacific region, revenues grew 16.2%, a 20.8% increase in constant dollars. The Americas region grew revenues 9.1%, an 11.4% increase in constant dollars.

In fiscal 2001, other revenue increased 7.2% to $435.9 million.

Our gross margin percentage declined 90 basis points, from 39.9% in fiscal 2000 to 39.0% in fiscal 2001. Factors contributing to the lower gross margin percentage were as follows:

(1) The effect of the change in foreign exchange rates, most notably the weakening of the euro against the U.S. dollar relative to fiscal 2000.

(2) A higher mix of close-out sales as well as lower margins achieved on close-outs, primarily in footwear and licensed team apparel in the U.S. In footwear, the higher mix of close-outs and lower close-out margins were due in part to the supply chain disruptions discussed above. Higher close-outs and lower margins in U.S. licensed team apparel resulted primarily from the liquidation of National Football League ("NFL") team apparel, due to the termination of our NFL license agreement.

(3) Product recalls of certain footwear models in the United States, which resulted in product returns and write-offs.

Selling and administrative expenses decreased as a percentage of revenues from 29.0% to 28.3%. Demand creation expense decreased as a percentage of revenues from 10.8% to 10.5%. Fiscal 2001 demand creation expense was $998.2 million versus $974.1 million in fiscal 2000. The overall decrease in selling and administrative expenses as a percentage of revenues reflected cost containment measures, both in marketing and operational areas. While implementing these measures to control selling and administrative expense growth, we also continued to invest in operational initiatives designed to create future revenues and profits. These initiatives included the expansion of NIKE-owned retail outlets, the development of e-commerce applications, and systems and processes supporting our worldwide supply chain. Our level of investment in these areas in fiscal 2001 was comparable to our level of investment in fiscal 2000.

Interest expense increased 30.4%, from $45.0 million to $58.7 million, due to higher average debt levels in fiscal 2001 versus fiscal 2000. During fiscal 2000, we increased debt to fund capital expenditures and higher working capital requirements, and to repurchase common stock. Although our debt balance decreased during fiscal 2001, the average debt balance for fiscal 2001 remained above the prior year.

Other income/expense was a net expense of $34.1 million versus a net expense of $20.7 million in fiscal 2000. Significant amounts included in other income/expense were interest income, profit sharing expense, goodwill amortization, certain foreign currency conversion gains and losses, asset disposal gains and losses, and charges for contractual settlements.

Our fiscal 2001 effective tax rate was 36.0% as compared to 37.0% in fiscal 2000. As discussed above, we do not accrue for U.S. tax liability on foreign earnings permanently invested offshore. The lower effective tax rate in fiscal 2001 was primarily the result of lower taxes on a larger amount of foreign earnings that were permanently invested offshore in fiscal 2001 than in fiscal 2000 as well as additional research tax credits.

Recently Issued Accounting Standards

In July 2001, the Financial Accounting Standards Board (FASB) issued SFAS No. 141, "Business Combinations" (FAS 141) and SFAS No. 142, "Goodwill and Other Intangible Assets" (FAS 142). FAS 141 requires the purchase method of accounting to be used for all business combinations initiated after June 30, 2001. FAS 141 also requires a more rigorous identification of intangible assets which must be recognized and reported separately from goodwill. The adoption of FAS 141 will not have a material effect on our results of operations or financial position.

FAS 142 requires that goodwill and intangible assets with indefinite lives no longer be amortized but instead be measured for impairment at least annually, or when events indicate that an impairment exists. Our adoption date is June 1, 2002. As of that date, amortization of outstanding goodwill and other indefinite-lived intangible assets will cease. As a result of the elimination of this amortization, other expense will decrease by approximately $13 million annually beginning in fiscal 2003.

As required by FAS 142, we will perform impairment tests on goodwill and other indefinite-lived intangible assets as of the adoption date. Thereafter, we will perform impairment tests annually and whenever events or circumstances indicate that the value of goodwill or other indefinite-lived intangible assets might be impaired. In connection with the FAS 142 indefinite-lived intangible asset impairment test, we will utilize the required one-step method to determine whether an impairment exists as of the adoption date. The test will consist of a comparison of the estimated fair values of indefinite-lived assets with the carrying amounts. If the carrying amount of an intangible asset exceeds our estimate of its fair value, we will recognize an impairment loss in an amount equal to that excess.

In connection with the FAS 142 transitional goodwill impairment test, we will utilize the required two-step method for determining goodwill impairment as of the adoption date. To accomplish this, we will identify our reporting units and determine the carrying value of each reporting unit by assigning our assets and liabilities, including the existing goodwill and intangible assets, to those reporting units as of the adoption date. We will then estimate the fair value of each reporting unit and compare it to the carrying amount of the reporting unit. To the extent the carrying amount of a reporting unit exceeds our estimate of the fair value of the reporting unit, we then will perform the second step of the transitional impairment test.

Where necessary, in the second step, we will compare the implied fair value of the reporting unit goodwill with the carrying amount of the reporting unit goodwill, both of which will be measured as of the adoption date. The implied fair value of goodwill will be determined by allocating the estimated fair value of the reporting unit to all of the assets (recognized and unrecognized) and liabilities of the reporting unit in a manner similar to a purchase price allocation, in accordance with FAS 141. The residual fair value after this allocation will be the implied fair value of the reporting unit goodwill. We will record a transitional impairment loss for any excess of the carrying value of goodwill allocated to the reporting unit over the implied fair value.

We have estimated that we will likely incur a transitional impairment loss of approximately $270 million related to our Bauer NIKE Hockey and Cole Haan subsidiaries, reflecting that the fair values we have estimated for these subsidiaries are less than the carrying values including goodwill. This expected transitional impairment loss will be recognized as the cumulative effect of a change in accounting principle in our consolidated statement of income during the first quarter of fiscal 2003.

In October 2001, the FASB issued SFAS No. 144, "Accounting for the Impairment or Disposal of Long-Lived Assets" (FAS 144). This statement supersedes SFAS No. 121, "Accounting for the Impairment of Long-Lived Assets and for Long-Lived Assets to be Disposed Of" (FAS 121), and amends Accounting Principles Board Statement No. 30, "Reporting the Effects of Disposal of a Segment of a Business, and Extraordinary, Unusual and Infrequently Occurring Events and Transactions" (APB 30). FAS 144 requires that long-lived assets that are to be disposed of by sale be measured at the lower of book value or fair value less costs to sell. FAS 144 retains the fundamental provisions of FAS 121 for (a) recognition and measurement of the impairment of long-lived assets to be held and used and (b) measurement of long-lived assets to be disposed of by sale. This statement also retains APB 30's requirement that companies report discontinued operations separately from continuing operations. All provisions of this statement will be effective for us on June 1, 2003. We do not expect that the adoption of FAS 144 will have any impact on our consolidated financial position or results of operations.

Liquidity and Capital Resources

Fiscal 2002 Cash Flow Activity

Cash provided by operations was $1,081.5 million in fiscal 2002, compared to $656.5 million in fiscal 2001. Our primary source of operating cash flow was net income earned during the year of $663.3 million. Operating cash flow increased significantly over the prior year due to reduced investment in certain working capital components during fiscal 2002, which generated positive operating cash flow.

Cash used by investing activities during fiscal 2002 was $302.8 million, compared to $342.3 million invested during fiscal 2001. The total for fiscal 2002 related primarily to capital expenditures for computer equipment and software, driven by our supply chain initiative, and investments in new retail outlets. In addition, we acquired all of the assets and substantially all of the liabilities of Hurley International LLC, a teen lifestyle brand company. During fiscal 2003, we will continue to incur expenditures related to systems improvements (most notably the supply chain initiative), retail expansion, and investments in our worldwide warehouse facilities.

Cash used by financing activities in fiscal 2002 was $478.2 million, up from $349.9 million in the prior year. This amount included uses of cash for dividends to shareholders, a net reduction in debt, and share repurchases. These uses of cash were partially offset by proceeds from the exercise of employee stock options.

The share repurchases were part of a $1.0 billion share repurchase program that began in fiscal 2001, after completion of a four-year, $1.0 billion program in fiscal 2000. In fiscal 2002, we repurchased 4.3 million shares of NIKE's Class B common stock for $237.7 million. To date, under the current program, we have purchased a total of 8.3 million shares of NIKE's Class B common stock for $394.7 million. We expect to fund the current program from operating cash flow. The timing and the amount of shares purchased will be dictated by our capital needs and stock market conditions.

Long-term Financial Obligations and Other Commercial Commitments

Our significant long-term contractual obligations as of May 31, 2002 are as follows:

Description of Commitment	Cash Payments Due During the Year Ended May 31,						
	2003	2004	2005	2006	2007	Thereafter	Total
				(In millions)			
Operating Leases	$158.2	143.4	119.1	95.3	98.2	288.0	$ 902.2
Long-term Debt	55.3	205.3	5.5	5.5	254.7	154.9	681.2
Endorsement Contracts	274.2	220.3	166.1	133.5	92.7	208.1	1,094.9

The amounts listed for endorsement contracts represent approximate amounts of base compensation and minimum guaranteed royalty fees we are obligated to pay athlete and sport team endorsers of our products. Actual payments under some contracts are likely be higher than the amounts listed as these contracts provide for bonuses to be paid to the endorsers based upon athletic achievements in future periods. Actual payments under some contracts may also be lower as a limited number of contracts include provisions for reduced payments if athlete performance declines in future periods.

In addition to the cash payments disclosed above, we are obligated to furnish the endorsers with NIKE products for their use. It is not possible to determine how much we will spend on this product on an annual basis as the contracts do not stipulate a specific amount of cash to be spent on the product. The amount of product provided to the endorsers will depend on many factors including general playing conditions, the number of sporting events in which they participate, and our own decisions regarding product and marketing initiatives. In addition, the costs to design, develop, source, and purchase the products furnished to the endorsers are incurred over a period of time and are not necessarily tracked separately from similar costs incurred for products sold to customers.

An outsourcing contractor provides us with information technology operations management services through 2006. The amount of the payments in future years depends on our level of monthly use of the different elements of the contractor's services. If we were to terminate the entire contract as of May 31, 2002, we would be required to provide the contractor with four months notice and pay a termination liability of $22.6 million. Our monthly payments to the contractor currently are approximately $6 million.

We also have the following outstanding short-term debt obligations as of May 31, 2002. Please refer to the accompanying *Notes to Consolidated Financial Statements (Note 4 — Short-term Borrowings and Credit Lines)* for further description and interest rates related to the below short-term debt obligations.

	Outstanding as of May 31, 2002
	(In millions)
Commercial paper outstanding and other notes payable for U.S. operations, all original maturities ninety-five days or less	$339.2
Notes payable for non-U.S. operations, due at a mutually agreed-upon dates, generally ninety days from issuance or on demand	86.0
Payable to Nissho Iwai American Company (NIAC) for the purchase of inventories, generally due sixty days after shipment of goods from a foreign port	36.3

As of May 31, 2002, letters of credit of $808.4 million were outstanding for the purchase of inventories. All letters of credit generally expire within one year.

Capital Resources

We have an effective shelf registration statement on file with the Securities and Exchange Commission (SEC) under which $1.0 billion in debt securities are available to be issued. On May 29, 2002, we commenced a medium-term note program under the shelf registration that allows us to issue up to $500.0 million in medium-term notes, as our capital needs dictate. We entered into this program to provide additional liquidity to meet our working capital and general corporate cash requirements. As of May 31, 2002, we had not issued any debt securities under the shelf registration.

Subsequent to May 31, 2002, we issued a total of $90 million in notes under the medium-term note program. The notes have coupon rates that range from 4.80% to 5.66%. The maturities range from July 9, 2007 to August 7, 2012. For $75 million of the notes, we simultaneously entered into interest rate swap agreements whereby we receive fixed interest payments at the same rate as the notes and pay variable interest payments based on the six-month London Inter Bank Offering Rate (LIBOR) plus a spread. Each swap has the same notional amount and maturity date as its respective note. After issuance of these notes, $910.0 million remains available to be issued under our shelf registration. We may issue additional notes under the shelf registration in fiscal 2003 depending on working capital and general corporate needs.

As of May 31, 2001, we had a $750.0 million, 364-day committed credit facility and a $500.0 million, multi-year committed credit facility in place with a group of banks. In November 2001, we renewed the 364-day facility in the amount of $600.0 million. Thus, our current total availability under these two bank facilities is $1.1 billion. We currently have no amounts outstanding under these facilities. The $600.0 million facility matures on November 15, 2002 and can be extended 364 days on each maturity date. The $500.0 million facility matures on November 17, 2005, and once a year, it can be extended for one additional year. Based on our current long-term senior unsecured debt ratings of A and A2 from Standard and Poor's Corporation and Moody's Investor Services, respectively, the interest rate charged on any outstanding borrowings on the $600.0 million facility would be the prevailing LIBOR plus 0.24%, and the interest rate charged on any outstanding borrowings on the $500.0 million facility would be the prevailing LIBOR plus 0.22%. The facility fees for the $600.0 million and the $500.0 million facilities are 0.06% and 0.08%, respectively, of the total commitment.

If our long-term debt rating were to decline, the facility fees and interest rates under our committed credit facilities would increase. Conversely, if our long-term debt rating improves, the facility fees and interest rates would decrease. Changes in our long-term debt rating would not trigger acceleration of maturity of any then outstanding borrowings or any future borrowings under the committed credit facilities. However, under these committed credit facilities, we have agreed to various covenants. These covenants include limits on our disposal of fixed assets and the amount of debt secured by liens we may incur, and set a minimum ratio of net worth to indebtedness. In the event we were to have any borrowings outstanding under these facilities, failed to meet any covenant, and were unable to obtain a waiver from a majority of the banks, any borrowings would become immediately due and payable. As of May 31, 2002, we were in full compliance with each of these covenants and believe it is unlikely we will fail to meet any of these covenants in the future.

Liquidity is also provided by our commercial paper program, under which there was $338.3 million and $710.0 million outstanding at May 31, 2002 and May 31, 2001, respectively. We currently have short-term debt ratings of A1 and P1 from Standard and Poor's Corporation and Moody's Investor Services, respectively.

We currently believe that cash generated by operations, together with access to external sources of funds as described above, will be sufficient to meet our operating and capital needs.

Dividends per share of common stock for fiscal 2002 were $0.48, the same as in fiscal 2001. We have paid a dividend every quarter since February 1984. We review our dividend policy from time to time; however, based upon current projected earnings and cash flow requirements, we anticipate continuing to pay a quarterly dividend.

Item 7A. *Quantitative and Qualitative Disclosures about Market Risk*

In the normal course of business and consistent with established policies and procedures, we employ a variety of financial instruments to manage exposure to fluctuations in the value of foreign currencies and interest rates. It is our policy to utilize these financial instruments only where necessary to finance our business and manage such exposures; we do not enter into these transactions for speculative purposes.

We are exposed to foreign currency fluctuation as a result of our international sales, production and funding activities. Our foreign currency risk management objective is to reduce the variability of local entity cash flows as a result of exchange rate movements. We use forward exchange contracts and options to hedge certain anticipated but not yet firmly committed transactions as well as certain firm commitments and the related receivables and payables, including third party or intercompany transactions.

When we begin hedging exposures depends on the nature of the exposure and market conditions. Generally, all anticipated and firmly committed transactions that are hedged are to be recognized within twelve months, although at May 31, 2002 we had forward contracts hedging anticipated transactions that will be recognized in as many as 24 months. The majority of the contracts expiring in more than twelve months relate to the anticipated purchase of inventory by our Japanese subsidiary. We use forward contracts and cross-currency swaps to hedge foreign currency denominated payments under intercompany loan agreements. When intercompany loans are hedged, it is typically for their expected duration, which in some circumstances may be in excess of five years. Hedged transactions are principally denominated in European currencies, Japanese yen, Canadian dollars, Korean won, Mexican pesos, Australian dollars and new Taiwan dollars.

Our earnings are also exposed to movements in short and long-term market interest rates. Our objective in managing this interest rate exposure is to limit the impact of interest rate changes on earnings and cash flows, and to reduce overall borrowing costs. To achieve these objectives, we maintain a mix of medium and long-term fixed rate debt, commercial paper, and bank loans and have entered into interest rate swaps under which we receive fixed interest and pay variable interest.

Market Risk Measurement

We monitor foreign exchange risk, interest rate risk and related derivatives using a variety of techniques including a review of market value, sensitivity analysis, and Value-at-Risk (VaR). Our market-sensitive derivative and other financial instruments, as defined by the SEC, are foreign currency forward contracts, foreign currency option contracts, cross-currency swaps, interest rate swaps, intercompany loans denominated in foreign currencies, fixed interest rate U.S. dollar denominated debt, and fixed interest rate Japanese yen denominated debt.

We use VaR to monitor the foreign exchange risk of our foreign currency forward and foreign currency option derivative instruments only. The VaR determines the maximum potential one-day loss in the fair value of these foreign exchange rate-sensitive financial instruments. The VaR model estimates assume normal market conditions and a 95% confidence level. There are various modeling techniques that can be used in the VaR computation. Our computations are based on interrelationships between currencies and interest rates (a "variance/co-variance" technique). These interrelationships are a function of foreign exchange currency market changes and interest rate changes over the preceding one year. The value of foreign currency options does not change on a one-to-one basis with changes in the underlying currency rate. We adjusted the potential loss in option value for the estimated sensitivity (the "delta" and "gamma") to changes in the underlying currency rate. This calculation reflects the impact of foreign currency rate fluctuations on the derivative instruments only, and hence does not include the impact of such rate fluctuations on the underlying based transactions that are anticipated transactions, firm commitments, cash balances and accounts and loans receivable and payable denominated in foreign currencies from the VaR calculation, including those which are hedged by these instruments.

The VaR model is a risk analysis tool and does not purport to represent actual losses in fair value that we will incur, nor does it consider the potential effect of favorable changes in market rates. It also does not represent the full extent of the possible loss that may occur. Actual future gains and losses will differ from those estimated because of changes or differences in market rates and interrelationships, hedging instruments and hedge percentages, timing and other factors.

The estimated maximum one-day loss in fair value on our foreign currency sensitive financial instruments, derived using the VaR model, was $13.7 million and $18.9 million at May 31, 2002 and May 31, 2001, respectively. The reduction in VaR as of May 31, 2002 occurred due to the effect of currency volatility on existing trades on the May 31, 2002 VaR computation versus the effect of currency volatility on existing trades on the May 31, 2001 VaR computation. Such a hypothetical loss in fair value of our derivatives would be offset by increases in the value of the underlying transactions being hedged. The average monthly change in the fair values of foreign currency forward and foreign currency option derivative instruments was $42.9 million and $22.4 million for fiscal 2002 and fiscal 2001, respectively.

Details of other market-sensitive financial instruments and derivative financial instruments not included in the VaR calculation above, are provided in the table below except the interest rate swaps which are described in the last paragraph of this section. These instruments include intercompany loans denominated in foreign currencies, fixed interest rate Japanese yen denominated debt, fixed interest rate U.S. dollar denominated debt, cross-currency swaps, and interest rate swaps. For debt obligations, the table presents principal cash flows and related weighted average interest rates by expected maturity dates. We have excluded the cross-currency swaps from the foreign exchange risk category because these instruments eliminate all foreign currency exposure in the cash flows of a euro denominated intercompany loan. We have included these cross-currency swaps in the interest rate risk category but excluded the related intercompany loan from this category because the intercompany interest eliminates in consolidation. For the cross-currency swaps the table presents both the euro swap payable and U.S. dollar swap receivable and the respective pay and receive interest rates. All information is presented in U.S. dollar equivalents, in millions, except interest rates.

Intercompany loans and related interest amounts eliminate in consolidation. Intercompany loans are generally hedged against foreign exchange risk through the use of forward contracts and swaps with third parties.

The fixed interest rate Japanese yen denominated debts were issued by and are accounted for by two of our Japanese subsidiaries. Accordingly, the monthly remeasurement of these instruments due to changes in foreign exchange rates is recognized in accumulated other comprehensive loss upon the consolidation of these subsidiaries.

There was not a significant change in debt or cross-currency swap market risks during fiscal 2002. The U.S. dollar fair values of intercompany loans denominated in foreign currencies was $647.2 million at May 31, 2001, which is the same as the carrying values of the loans prior to their elimination. The U.S. dollar fair value of the fixed rate Japanese yen denominated debt that was outstanding at May 31, 2001 was $181.1 million versus a carrying value of $191.0 million at that date. The U.S. dollar fair values of the fixed rate U.S. dollar denominated debt, the euro swap payable and the U.S. dollar swap receivable as of May 31, 2001 were $256.2 million, $179.4 million and $266.4 million, respectively, versus carrying values of $249.6 million, $172.6 million and $250.0 million, respectively, at that date.

In August 2001, we issued a $250 million corporate bond maturing in August 2006, with a fixed interest rate of 5.5%. In November 2001, we entered into receive-fixed pay-variable interest rate swap agreements to hedge the interest rate exposure related to this bond. The interest rate swaps have an aggregate notional amount of $250 million maturing in August 2006. The receive-fixed rates on the swaps match the fixed rate on the bond, and the pay-variable rates are based on the three-month LIBOR rates plus a spread. As a result of the interest rate swap agreements, our effective interest rate on the $250 million corporate bond was 3.3% as of May 31, 2002. The difference between the carrying amounts and fair value of the corporate bond and related interest rate swaps was $1.8 million at May 31, 2002.

Expected Maturity Date
Year Ended May 31,

	2003	2004	2005	2006	2007	Thereafter	Total	Fair Value
			(In millions, except interest rates)					
Foreign Exchange Risk								
Euro Functional Currency								
Intercompany loan — U.S. dollar denominated — Fixed rate								
Principal payments	$131.4	—	—	—	—	—	$131.4	$131.4
Average interest rate	2.2%	—	—	—	—	—	2.2%	
U.S. Dollar Functional Currency								
Intercompany loans — Euro denominated — Fixed rate								
Principal payments	$135.1	147.4	—	—	—	—	$282.5	$282.5
Average interest rate	5.5%	5.6%	—	—	—	—	5.6%	
Intercompany loan — Japanese yen denominated — Fixed rate								
Principal payments	$161.3	—	—	—	—	—	$161.3	$161.3
Average interest rate	0.4%	—	—	—	—	—	0.4%	
Intercompany loan — Canadian dollar denominated — Fixed rate								
Principal payments	$ 29.3	—	—	—	—	—	$ 29.3	$ 29.3
Average interest rate	2.6%	—	—	—	—	—	2.6%	
Argentine peso Functional Currency								
Intercompany loan — U.S. dollar denominated — Fixed rate								
Principal payments	$ 44.9	—	—	—	—	—	$ 44.9	$ 44.9
Average interest rate	2.3%	—	—	—	—	—	2.3%	
Japanese Yen Functional Currency								
Long-term Japanese yen debt-Fixed rate								
Principal payments	$ 5.3	5.3	5.3	5.3	5.3	$154.9	$181.4	$207.4
Average interest rate	3.3%	3.3%	3.3%	3.4%	3.4%	3.7%	3.6%	

| | **Expected Maturity Date** Year Ended May 31, | | | | | | | |
	2003	2004	2005	2006	2007	Thereafter	Total	Fair Value
	(In millions, except interest rates)							
Interest Rate Risk								
Japanese Yen Functional Currency								
Long-term Japanese yen debt-Fixed rate Principal payments	$ 5.3	5.3	5.3	5.3	5.3	$154.9	$181.4	$207.4
Average interest rate	3.3%	3.3%	3.3%	3.4%	3.4%	3.7%	3.6%	
U.S. Dollar Functional Currency								
Long-term U.S. dollar debt-Fixed rate Principal payments	$ 50.0	199.8	—	—	250.0	—	$499.8	$516.5
Average interest rate	5.9%	5.8%	5.5%	5.5%	5.5%	—	5.7%	
Fixed euro for fixed U.S. dollar cross-currency swap Euro swap payable	$ 41.4	147.4	—	—	—	—	$188.8	$196.2
U.S. dollar swap receivable	$ 50.0	200.0	—	—	—	—	$250.0	$267.9
Average pay rate (euro)	5.6%	5.6%	—	—	—	—	5.6%	
Average receive rate (U.S. dollars)	6.5%	6.5%	—	—	—	—	6.5%	

Special Note Regarding Forward-Looking Statements and Analyst Reports

Certain written and oral statements, other than purely historical information, including estimates, projections, statements relating to NIKE's business plans, objectives and expected operating results, and the assumptions upon which those statements are based, made or incorporated by reference from time to time by NIKE or its representatives in this report, other reports, filings with the Securities and Exchange Commission, press releases, conferences, or otherwise, are "forward-looking statements" within the meaning of the Private Securities Litigation Reform Act of 1995 and Section 21E of the Securities Exchange Act of 1934. Forward-looking statements include, without limitation, any statement that may predict, forecast, indicate, or imply future results, performance, or achievements, and may contain the words "believe," "anticipate," "expect," "estimate," "project," "will be," "will continue," "will likely result," or words or phrases of similar meaning. Forward-looking statements involve risks and uncertainties which may cause actual results to differ materially from the forward-looking statements. The risks and uncertainties are detailed from time to time in reports filed by NIKE with the SEC, including Forms 8-K, 10-Q, and 10-K, and include, among others, the following: international, national and local general economic and market conditions; the size and growth of the overall athletic footwear, apparel, and equipment markets; intense competition among designers, marketers, distributors and sellers of athletic footwear, apparel, and equipment for consumers and endorsers; demographic changes; changes in consumer preferences; popularity of particular designs, categories of products, and sports; seasonal and geographic demand for NIKE products; difficulties in anticipating or forecasting changes in consumer preferences, consumer demand for NIKE products, and the various market factors described above; difficulties in implementing, operating, and maintaining NIKE's increasingly complex information systems and controls, including, without limitation, the systems related to demand and supply planning, and inventory control; interruptions in data and communications systems; fluctuations and difficulty in forecasting operating results, including, without limitation, the fact that advance "futures" orders may not be indicative of future revenues due to the changing mix of futures and at-once orders; the ability of NIKE to sustain, manage or forecast its growth and inventories; the size, timing and mix of purchases of NIKE's products; new product development and introduction; the ability to secure and protect trademarks, patents, and other intellectual property; performance and reliability of products; customer service; adverse publicity; the loss of significant customers or suppliers; dependence on distributors; business disruptions; increased costs of freight and transportation to meet delivery deadlines; increases in borrowing costs due to any decline in our debt ratings; changes in business strategy or development plans; general risks associated with doing business outside the United States, including without limitation, import duties, tariffs, quotas and political and economic instability; changes in government regulations; liability and other claims asserted against NIKE; the ability to attract and retain qualified personnel; and other factors referenced or incorporated by reference in this report and other reports.

The risks included here are not exhaustive. Other sections of this report may include additional factors which could adversely affect NIKE's business and financial performance. Moreover, NIKE operates in a very competitive and rapidly changing environment. New risk factors emerge from time to time and it is not possible for management to predict all such risk factors, nor can it assess the impact of all such risk factors on NIKE's business or the extent to which any factor, or combination of factors, may cause actual results to differ materially from those contained in any forward-looking statements. Given these risks and uncertainties, investors should not place undue reliance on forward-looking statements as a prediction of actual results.

Investors should also be aware that while NIKE does, from time to time, communicate with securities analysts, it is against NIKE's policy to disclose to them any material non-public information or other confidential commercial information. Accordingly, shareholders should not assume that NIKE agrees with any statement or report issued by any analyst irrespective of the content of the statement or report. Furthermore, NIKE has a policy against issuing or confirming financial forecasts or projections issued by others. Thus, to the extent that reports issued by securities analysts contain any projections, forecasts or opinions, such reports are not the responsibility of NIKE.

Item 8.   *Financial Statements and Supplemental Data*

Management of NIKE, Inc. is responsible for the information and representations contained in this report. The financial statements have been prepared in conformity with the generally accepted accounting principles we considered appropriate in the circumstances and include some amounts based on our best estimates and judgments. Other financial information in this report is consistent with these financial statements.

Our accounting systems include controls designed to reasonably assure that assets are safeguarded from unauthorized use or disposition and which provide for the preparation of financial statements in conformity with generally accepted accounting principles. These systems are supplemented by the selection and training of qualified financial personnel and an organizational structure providing for appropriate segregation of duties.

An Internal Audit department reviews the results of its work with the Audit Committee of the Board of Directors, presently consisting of three outside directors. The Audit Committee is responsible for recommending to the Board of Directors the appointment of the independent accountants and reviews with the independent accountants, management and the internal audit staff, the scope and the results of the annual examination, the effectiveness of the accounting control system and other matters relating to the financial affairs of NIKE as they deem appropriate. The independent accountants and the internal auditors have full access to the Committee, with and without the presence of management, to discuss any appropriate matters.

REPORT OF INDEPENDENT ACCOUNTANTS

To the Board of Directors and
Shareholders of NIKE, Inc.

In our opinion, the consolidated financial statements listed in the index appearing under Item 14(A)(1) on page 55 present fairly, in all material respects, the financial position of NIKE, Inc. and its subsidiaries at May 31, 2002 and 2001, and the results of their operations and their cash flows for each of the three years in the period ended May 31, 2002 in conformity with accounting principles generally accepted in the United States of America. In addition, in our opinion, the financial statement schedule listed in the index appearing under Item 14(A)(2) on page 55 presents fairly, in all material respects, the information set forth therein when read in conjunction with the related consolidated financial statements. These financial statements and financial statement schedule are the responsibility of the Company's management; our responsibility is to express an opinion on these financial statements and financial statement schedule based on our audits. We conducted our audits of these statements in accordance with auditing standards generally accepted in the United States of America, which require that we plan and perform the audit to obtain reasonable assurance about whether the financial statements are free of material misstatement. An audit includes examining, on a test basis, evidence supporting the amounts and disclosures in the financial statements, assessing the accounting principles used and significant estimates made by management, and evaluating the overall financial statement presentation. We believe that our audits provide a reasonable basis for our opinion.

As discussed in Note 1 to the consolidated financial statements, effective June 1, 2001, the Company changed its method of accounting for derivative instruments in accordance with Statement of Financial Accounting Standards No. 133 "Accounting for Derivative Instruments and Hedging Activities" and Statement of Financial Accounting Standards No. 138, "Accounting for Certain Derivative Instruments and Certain Hedging Activities."

/s/   PRICEWATERHOUSECOOPERS LLP

Portland, Oregon
June 27, 2002

NIKE, INC.

CONSOLIDATED STATEMENTS OF INCOME

	Year Ended May 31,		
	2002	**2001**	**2000**
	(In millions, except per share data)		
Revenues	$9,893.0	$9,488.8	$8,995.1
Costs and expenses:			
Cost of sales	6,004.7	5,784.9	5,403.8
Selling and administrative	2,820.4	2,689.7	2,606.4
Interest expense (Notes 4 and 5)	47.6	58.7	45.0
Other income/expense, net (Notes 1, 10 and 11)	3.0	34.1	20.7
Total costs and expenses	8,875.7	8,567.4	8,075.9
Income before income taxes and cumulative effect accounting change....	1,017.3	921.4	919.2
Income taxes (Note 6)	349.0	331.7	340.1
Income before cumulative effect of accounting change................	668.3	589.7	579.1
Cumulative effect of accounting change, net of income taxes of $3.0 (Note 1)	5.0	—	—
Net income	$ 663.3	$ 589.7	$ 579.1
Basic earnings per common share — before accounting change (Notes 1 and 9)	$ 2.50	$ 2.18	$ 2.10
Cumulative effect of accounting change	0.02	—	—
	$ 2.48	$ 2.18	$ 2.10
Diluted earnings per common share — before accounting change (Notes 1 and 9)...	$ 2.46	$ 2.16	$ 2.07
Cumulative effect of accounting change	0.02	—	—
	$ 2.44	$ 2.16	$ 2.07

The accompanying notes to consolidated financial statements are an integral part of this statement.

31

NIKE, INC.

CONSOLIDATED BALANCE SHEETS

	May 31,	
	2002	**2001**
	(In millions)	

ASSETS

Current Assets:

	2002	2001
Cash and equivalents	$ 575.5	$ 304.0
Accounts receivable, less allowance for doubtful accounts of $77.4 and $72.1	1,807.1	1,621.4
Inventories (Note 2)	1,373.8	1,424.1
Deferred income taxes (Notes 1 and 6)	140.8	113.3
Prepaid expenses and other current assets (Note 1)	260.5	162.5
Total current assets	4,157.7	3,625.3
Property, plant and equipment, net (Note 3)	1,614.5	1,618.8
Identifiable intangible assets and goodwill, net (Note 1)	437.8	397.3
Deferred income taxes and other assets (Notes 1 and 6)	233.0	178.2
Total assets	$6,443.0	$5,819.6

LIABILITIES AND SHAREHOLDERS' EQUITY

Current Liabilities:

	2002	2001
Current portion of long-term debt (Note 5)	$ 55.3	$ 5.4
Notes payable (Note 4)	425.2	855.3
Accounts payable (Note 4)	504.4	432.0
Accrued liabilities (Note 15)	768.3	472.1
Income taxes payable	83.0	21.9
Total current liabilities	1,836.2	1,786.7
Long-term debt (Notes 5 and 14)	625.9	435.9
Deferred income taxes and other liabilities (Notes 1 and 6)	141.6	102.2
Commitments and contingencies (Notes 13 and 15)	—	—
Redeemable Preferred Stock (Note 7)	0.3	0.3

Shareholders' Equity:

Common Stock at stated value (Note 8):

	2002	2001
Class A convertible — 98.1 and 99.1 shares outstanding	0.2	0.2
Class B — 168.0 and 169.5 shares outstanding	2.6	2.6
Capital in excess of stated value	538.7	459.4
Unearned stock compensation	(5.1)	(9.9)
Accumulated other comprehensive loss	(192.4)	(152.1)
Retained earnings	3,495.0	3,194.3
Total shareholders' equity	3,839.0	3,494.5
Total liabilities and shareholders' equity	$6,443.0	$5,819.6

The accompanying notes to consolidated financial statements are an integral part of this statement.

32

NIKE, INC.

CONSOLIDATED STATEMENTS OF CASH FLOWS

	Year Ended May 31,		
	2002	2001	2000
		(In millions)	
Cash provided (used) by operations:			
Net income	$ 663.3	$ 589.7	$ 579.1
Income charges not affecting cash:			
Depreciation	223.5	197.4	188.0
Deferred income taxes	15.2	79.8	36.8
Amortization and other	53.1	16.7	35.6
Income tax benefit from exercise of stock options	13.9	32.4	14.9
Changes in certain working capital components:			
Increase in accounts receivable	(135.2)	(141.4)	(82.6)
Decrease (increase) in inventories	55.4	(16.7)	(311.8)
Decrease in other current assets and income taxes receivable	16.9	78.0	61.2
Increase (decrease) in accounts payable, accrued liabilities and income taxes payable	175.4	(179.4)	178.4
Cash provided by operations	1,081.5	656.5	699.6
Cash provided (used) by investing activities:			
Additions to property, plant and equipment and other	(282.8)	(317.6)	(419.9)
Disposals of property, plant and equipment	15.6	12.7	25.3
Increase in other assets	(39.1)	(42.5)	(51.3)
Increase in other liabilities	3.5	5.1	5.9
Cash used by investing activities	(302.8)	(342.3)	(440.0)
Cash provided (used) by financing activities:			
Proceeds from long-term debt issuance	329.9	—	—
Reductions in long-term debt including current portion	(80.3)	(50.3)	(1.7)
(Decrease) increase in notes payable	(431.5)	(68.9)	505.1
Proceeds from exercise of stock options and other stock issuances	59.5	56.0	23.9
Repurchase of stock	(226.9)	(157.0)	(646.3)
Dividends — common and preferred	(128.9)	(129.7)	(133.1)
Cash used by financing activities	(478.2)	(349.9)	(252.1)
Effect of exchange rate changes	(29.0)	85.4	48.7
Net increase in cash and equivalents	271.5	49.7	56.2
Cash and equivalents, beginning of year	304.0	254.3	198.1
Cash and equivalents, end of year	$ 575.5	$ 304.0	$ 254.3
Supplemental disclosure of cash flow information:			
Cash paid during the year for:			
Interest	$ 54.2	$ 68.5	$ 45.0
Income taxes	262.0	173.1	221.1
Non-cash investing and financing activity:			
Assumption of long-term debt to acquire property, plant and equipment	—	—	$ 108.9

The accompanying notes to consolidated financial statements are an integral part of this statement.

33

NIKE, INC.

CONSOLIDATED STATEMENTS OF SHAREHOLDERS' EQUITY

	Common Stock				Capital in Excess of Stated Value	Unearned Stock Compensation	Accumulated Other Comprehensive Loss	Retained Earnings	Total
	Class A		Class B						
	Shares	Amount	Shares	Amount					
					(In millions, except per share data)				
Balance at May 31, 1999	100.7	0.2	181.6	2.7	334.1	—	(68.9)	3,066.5	3,334.6
Stock options exercised			1.3		38.7				38.7
Conversion to Class B Common Stock	(1.5)		1.5						
Repurchase of Class B Common Stock			(14.5)	(0.1)	(17.3)			(627.1)	(644.5
Dividends on Common stock ($.48 per share)								(131.5)	(131.5
Issuance of shares to employees			0.5		13.5	(13.5)			—
Amortization of unearned compensation						1.8			1.8
Comprehensive income:									
Net income								579.1	579.1
Foreign currency translation (net of tax expense of $1.2)							(42.2)		(42.2
Comprehensive income							(42.2)	579.1	536.9
Balance at May 31, 2000	99.2	0.2	170.4	2.6	369.0	(11.7)	(111.1)	2,887.0	3,136.0
Stock options exercised			2.9		91.0				91.0
Conversion to Class B Common Stock	(0.1)		0.1						—
Repurchase of Class B Common Stock			(4.0)		(4.8)			(152.2)	(157.0
Dividends on Common stock ($.48 per share)								(129.6)	(129.6
Issuance of shares to employees			0.1		6.7	(6.7)			—
Amortization of unearned compensation						7.3			7.3
Forfeiture of shares from employees					(2.5)	1.2		(0.6)	(1.9)
Comprehensive income:									
Net income								589.7	589.7
Foreign currency translation and other (net of tax benefit of $2.4)							(41.0)		(41.0)
Comprehensive income							(41.0)	589.7	548.7
Balance at May 31, 2001	99.1	$0.2	169.5	$ 2.6	$459.4	$ (9.9)	$(152.1)	$3,194.3	3,494.5
Stock options exercised			1.7		72.9				72.9
Conversion to Class B Common Stock	(1.0)		1.0						
Repurchase of Class B Common Stock			(4.3)		(5.2)			(232.5)	(237.7)
Dividends on Common stock ($.48 per share)								(128.6)	(128.6)
Issuance of shares to employees and others			0.2		13.2	(1.9)			11.3
Amortization of unearned compensation						6.5			6.5
Forfeiture of shares from employees			(0.1)		(1.6)	0.2		(1.5)	(2.9)
Comprehensive income (Note 12):									
Net income								663.3	663.3
Other comprehensive income (net of tax benefit of $17.4):									
Foreign currency translation							(1.5)		(1.5)
Cumulative effect of change in accounting principle (Note 1)							56.8		56.8
Adjustment for fair value of hedge derivatives							(95.6)		(95.6)
Comprehensive income							(40.3)	663.3	623.0
Balance at May 31, 2002	98.1	$0.2	168.0	$ 2.6	$538.7	$ (5.1)	$(192.4)	$3,495.0	$3,839.0

The accompanying notes to consolidated financial statements are an integral part of this statement.

NIKE, INC.

NOTES TO CONSOLIDATED FINANCIAL STATEMENTS

Note 1 — Summary of Significant Accounting Policies

Basis of Consolidation

The consolidated financial statements include the accounts of NIKE, Inc. and its subsidiaries (the Company). All significant intercompany transactions and balances have been eliminated.

Recognition of Revenues

Wholesale revenues are recognized when title passes and the risks and rewards of ownership have passed to the customer, based on the terms of sale. Title passes generally upon shipment or upon receipt by the customer depending on the country of the sale and the agreement with the customer. Retail store revenues are recorded at the time of sale. Provisions for sales discounts and returns are made at the time of sale.

Shipping and Handling Costs

Shipping and handling costs are expensed as incurred and included in cost of sales.

Advertising and Promotion

Advertising production costs are expensed the first time the advertisement is run. Media (TV and print) placement costs are expensed in the month the advertising appears. A significant amount of the Company's promotional expenses result from payments under endorsement contracts. Accounting for endorsement payments is based upon specific contract provisions. Generally, endorsement payments are expensed uniformly over the term of the contract after giving recognition to periodic performance compliance provisions of the contracts. Prepayments made under contracts are included in Prepaid expenses and other current assets or Other assets depending on the length of the contract. Through cooperative advertising programs, we reimburse our retail customers for certain of their costs of advertising our products. We record these costs in selling and administrative expense at the point in time when we are obligated to our customers for the costs. This obligation may arise prior to the related advertisement being run. Total advertising and promotion expenses were $1,027.9 million, $998.2 million and $974.1 million for the years ended May 31, 2002, 2001 and 2000, respectively. Included in Prepaid expenses and other current assets and Other assets was $113.2 million and $122.3 million at May 31, 2002 and 2001, respectively, relating to prepaid advertising and promotion expenses.

Cash and Equivalents

Cash and equivalents represent cash and short-term, highly liquid investments with original maturities of three months or less.

Inventory Valuation

Inventories are stated at the lower of cost or market. Inventories are valued on a first-in, first-out (FIFO) or moving-average cost basis.

Property, Plant and Equipment and Depreciation

Property, plant and equipment are recorded at cost. Depreciation for financial reporting purposes is determined on a straight-line basis for buildings and leasehold improvements over 2 to 40 years and principally on a declining balance basis for machinery and equipment over 2 to 15 years. Computer software is depreciated on a straight-line basis over 3 to 10 years.

NIKE, INC.

NOTES TO CONSOLIDATED FINANCIAL STATEMENTS — (Continued)

Identifiable Intangible Assets and Goodwill

At May 31, 2002 and 2001, the Company had patents, trademarks and other identifiable intangible assets recorded at a cost of $264.2 million and $218.6 million, respectively. The Company's excess of purchase cost over the fair value of net assets of businesses acquired (goodwill) was $333.6 million and $322.5 million at May 31, 2002 and 2001, respectively.

Identifiable intangible assets and goodwill are being amortized over their estimated useful lives on a straight-line basis over five to forty years. Accumulated amortization was $160.0 million and $143.8 million at May 31, 2002 and 2001, respectively. Amortization expense, which is included in other income/expense, was $15.7 million, $15.6 million and $18.5 million for the years ended May 31, 2002, 2001 and 2000, respectively.

Impairment of Long-Lived Assets

When events or circumstances indicate the carrying value of a long-lived asset may be impaired, the Company estimates the future undiscounted cash flows to be derived from the asset to assess whether or not a potential impairment exists. If the carrying value exceeds our estimate of future undiscounted cash flows, we then calculate the impairment as the excess of the carrying value of the asset over our estimate of its fair market value.

Foreign Currency Translation and Foreign Currency Transactions

Adjustments resulting from translating foreign functional currency financial statements into U.S. dollars are included in the foreign currency translation adjustment, a component of accumulated other comprehensive loss in shareholders' equity.

Transaction gains and losses generated by the effect of foreign exchange on recorded assets and liabilities denominated in a currency different from the functional currency of the applicable Company entity are recorded in other income/expense currently.

Net foreign currency transaction gains, which include transaction gains and losses referred to above as well as hedge results captured in revenues, cost of sales, selling and administrative expense and other income/expense, were $45.1 million, $129.6 million, and $36.1 million for the years ended May 31, 2002, 2001, and 2000 respectively.

Adoption of FAS 133

The Company adopted Statement of Financial Accounting Standards ("SFAS") No. 133, "Accounting for Derivative Instruments and Hedging Activities," as amended by SFAS No. 138, "Accounting for Certain Derivative Instruments and Certain Hedging Activities" (FAS 133) on June 1, 2001.

In accordance with the transition provisions of FAS 133, the Company recorded a one-time transition adjustment as of June 1, 2001 on both the consolidated statement of income and the consolidated balance sheet. The transition adjustment on the consolidated statement of income was a charge of $5.0 million, net of tax effect. This amount related to an investment that was adjusted to fair value in accordance with FAS 133. The transition adjustment on the consolidated balance sheet represented the initial recognition of the fair values of hedge derivatives outstanding on the adoption date and realized gains and losses on effective hedges for which the underlying exposure had not yet affected earnings. The transition adjustment on the consolidated balance sheet was an increase in current assets of $116.4 million, an increase in noncurrent assets of $87.0 million, an increase in current liabilities of $151.6 million, and an increase in other comprehensive income of approximately $56.8 million, net of tax effect. The majority of the $56.8 million recorded in other comprehensive income as of June 1, 2001 related to outstanding derivatives at that date. Because exchange rates on the transition date were different from those on the maturity dates of these derivatives and because

NIKE, INC.

NOTES TO CONSOLIDATED FINANCIAL STATEMENTS — (Continued)

some contracts maturing during the year ended May 31, 2002 were entered into after the transition date, amounts ultimately reclassified to earnings during the year ended May 31, 2002, as described in note 12, are significantly different from this amount.

Accounting for Derivatives and Hedging Activities

The purpose of the Company's foreign currency hedging activities is to protect the Company from the risk that the eventual cash flows resulting from transactions in foreign currencies, including revenues, product costs, selling and administrative expenses, and intercompany transactions, including intercompany borrowings, will be adversely affected by changes in exchange rates. The Company does not hold or issue derivatives for trading purposes. It is the Company's policy to utilize derivatives to reduce foreign exchange risks where internal netting strategies cannot be effectively employed. Fluctuations in the value of hedging instruments are offset by fluctuations in the value of the underlying exposures being hedged.

Derivatives used by the Company to hedge the risks described above are forward exchange contracts, options and cross-currency swaps. These instruments protect against the risk that the eventual net cash inflows and outflows from foreign currency denominated transactions will be adversely affected by changes in exchange rates. The cross-currency swaps are used to hedge foreign currency denominated payments related to intercompany loan agreements. Hedged transactions are denominated primarily in European currencies, Japanese yen, Canadian dollars, Korean won, Mexican pesos, Australian dollars, and new Taiwan dollars. The Company hedges up to 100% of anticipated exposures typically twelve months in advance but has hedged as much as 32 months in advance. When intercompany loans are hedged, it is typically for their expected duration, which in some circumstances may be in excess of five years.

The Company is also exposed to the risk of changes in the fair value of certain fixed-rate debt attributable to changes in interest rates. Derivatives currently used by the Company to hedge this risk are receive-fixed, pay-variable interest rate swaps. See Note 5.

All derivatives are recognized on the balance sheet at their fair value. Unrealized gain positions are recorded as other current assets or other non-current assets. Unrealized loss positions are recorded as accrued liabilities or other non-current liabilities.

The fair values of the interest rate swap agreements are recorded as other non-current assets or other non-current liabilities. The unrealized gain or loss on the interest rate swaps is exactly offset by an unrealized loss or gain on the underlying long-term debt.

Substantially all foreign currency derivatives entered into by the Company qualify for and are designated as foreign-currency cash flow hedges, including those hedging foreign currency denominated firm commitments.

The interest rate swap agreements are designated as fair value hedges of the related long-term debt and meet the shortcut method requirements under FAS 133. Accordingly, interest expense on the related long-term debt is recorded based on the variable rates paid under the interest rate swap agreements, and changes in the fair values of the interest rate swap agreements exactly offset changes in the fair value of the long-term debt.

The Company considers whether any provisions in non-derivative contracts represent "embedded" derivative instruments as described in FAS 133. For the period ended May 31, 2002 the Company has concluded that no "embedded" derivative instruments warrant separate fair value accounting under FAS 133.

Changes in fair values of outstanding cash flow hedge derivatives that are highly effective are recorded in other comprehensive income, until earnings are affected by the variability of cash flows of the hedged transaction. In most cases amounts recorded in other comprehensive income will be released to earnings some time after the maturity of the related derivative. The consolidated statement of income classification of

NIKE, INC.

NOTES TO CONSOLIDATED FINANCIAL STATEMENTS — (Continued)

effective hedge results is the same as that of the underlying exposure. Results of hedges of revenue and product costs are recorded in revenue and cost of sales, respectively, when the underlying hedged transaction affects earnings. Results of hedges of selling and administrative expense are recorded together with those costs when the related expense is recorded. Results of hedges of anticipated intercompany transactions are recorded in other income/expense when the transaction occurs. Hedges of recorded balance sheet positions are recorded in other income/expense currently together with the transaction gain or loss from the hedged balance sheet position. Unrealized derivative gains and losses recorded in current and non-current assets and liabilities and amounts recorded in other comprehensive income are non-cash items and therefore are taken into account in the preparation of the consolidated statement of cash flows based on their respective balance sheet classifications.

The critical terms of the company's outstanding interest rate swap agreements exactly match the critical terms of the underlying debt. Therefore, under the shortcut provisions of FAS 133, the swaps are considered perfectly effective.

The Company formally documents all relationships between hedging instruments and hedged items, as well as its risk-management objective and strategy for undertaking hedge transactions. This process includes linking all derivatives that are designated as foreign-currency cash flow hedges to either specific assets and liabilities on the balance sheet or specific firm commitments or forecasted transactions. The Company also formally assesses, both at the hedge's inception and on an ongoing basis, whether the derivatives that are used in hedging transactions have been highly effective in offsetting changes in the cash flows of hedged items and whether those derivatives may be expected to remain highly effective in future periods. When it is determined that a derivative is not, or has ceased to be, highly effective as a hedge, the Company discontinues hedge accounting prospectively, as discussed below.

The Company discontinues hedge accounting prospectively when (1) it determines that the derivative is no longer highly effective in offsetting changes in the cash flows of a hedged item (including hedged items such as firm commitments or forecasted transactions); (2) the derivative expires or is sold, terminated, or exercised; (3) it is no longer probable that the forecasted transaction will occur; or (4) management determines that designating the derivative as a hedging instrument is no longer appropriate.

When the Company discontinues hedge accounting because it is no longer probable that the forecasted transaction will occur in the originally expected period, the gain or loss on the derivative remains in accumulated other comprehensive income and is reclassified into earnings when the forecasted transaction affects earnings. However, if it is probable that a forecasted transaction will not occur by the end of the originally specified time period or within an additional two-month period of time thereafter, the gains and losses that were accumulated in other comprehensive loss will be recognized immediately in earnings. In all situations in which hedge accounting is discontinued and the derivative remains outstanding, the Company will carry the derivative at its fair value on the balance sheet, recognizing future changes in the fair value in current-period earnings. Any hedge ineffectiveness is recorded in current-period earnings. Effectiveness is assessed based on forward rates.

Premiums paid on options are initially recorded as deferred charges. The Company assesses effectiveness on options based on the total cash flows method and records total changes in the options' fair value to other comprehensive income to the degree they are effective.

Income Taxes

United States income taxes are provided currently on financial statement earnings of non-U.S. subsidiaries expected to be repatriated. The Company determines annually the amount of undistributed non-U.S. earnings to invest indefinitely in its non-U.S. operations. The Company accounts for income taxes using the asset and liability method. This approach requires the recognition of deferred tax assets

NIKE, INC.

NOTES TO CONSOLIDATED FINANCIAL STATEMENTS — (Continued)

and liabilities for the expected future tax consequences of temporary differences between the carrying amounts and the tax bases of other assets and liabilities. See Note 6 for further discussion.

Earnings Per Share

Basic earnings per common share is calculated by dividing net income by the weighted average number of common shares outstanding during the year. Diluted earnings per common share is calculated by adjusting weighted average outstanding shares, assuming conversion of all potentially dilutive stock options and awards. See Note 9 for further discussion.

Management Estimates

The preparation of financial statements in conformity with generally accepted accounting principles requires management to make estimates, including estimates relating to assumptions that affect the reported amounts of assets and liabilities and disclosure of contingent assets and liabilities at the date of financial statements and the reported amounts of revenues and expenses during the reporting period. Actual results could differ from these estimates.

Reclassifications

Certain prior year amounts have been reclassified to conform to fiscal year 2002 presentation. These changes had no impact on previously reported results of operations or shareholders' equity.

Recently Issued Accounting Standards

The Company will adopt SFAS No. 142, "Goodwill and Other Intangible Assets" (FAS 142) on June 1, 2002. FAS 142 requires that goodwill and intangible assets with indefinite lives no longer be amortized but instead be measured for impairment at least annually, or when events indicate that an impairment exists. As of the adoption date, amortization of outstanding goodwill and other indefinite-lived intangible assets will cease. As a result of the elimination of this amortization, other expense will decrease by approximately $13 million annually beginning in the quarter ended August 31, 2002.

As required by FAS 142, we will perform impairment tests on goodwill and other indefinite-lived intangible assets as of the adoption date. Thereafter, we will perform impairment tests annually and whenever events or circumstances indicate that the value of goodwill or other indefinite-lived intangible assets might be impaired. In connection with the FAS 142 indefinite-lived intangible asset impairment test, we will utilize the required one-step method to determine whether an impairment exists as of the adoption date. In connection with the FAS 142 transitional goodwill impairment test, we will utilize the required two-step method for determining goodwill impairment as of the adoption date.

We have estimated that we will likely incur a transitional impairment loss of approximately $270 million related to our Bauer NIKE Hockey and Cole Haan subsidiaries, reflecting that the fair values we have estimated for these subsidiaries are less than the carrying values including goodwill. This expected transitional impairment loss will be recognized as a cumulative effect of a change in accounting principle in our consolidated statement of income during the quarter ended August 31, 2002.

In October 2001, the FASB issued SFAS No. 144, "Accounting for the Impairment or Disposal of Long-Lived Assets" (FAS 144). This statement supersedes SFAS No. 121, "Accounting for the Impairment of Long-Lived Assets and for Long-Lived Assets to be Disposed Of" (FAS 121), and amends Accounting Principles Board Statement No. 30, "Reporting the Effects of Disposal of a Segment of a Business, and Extraordinary, Unusual and Infrequently Occurring Events and Transactions" (APB 30). FAS 144 requires that long-lived assets that are to be disposed of by sale be measured at the lower of book value or fair value less costs to sell. FAS 144 retains the fundamental provisions of FAS 121 for (a) recognition and measurement of

NIKE, INC.

NOTES TO CONSOLIDATED FINANCIAL STATEMENTS — (Continued)

the impairment of long-lived assets to be held and used and (b) measurement of long-lived assets to be disposed of by sale. This statement also retains APB 30's requirement that companies report discontinued operations separately from continuing operations. All provisions of this statement will be effective for the Company on June 1, 2003. It is not expected that the adoption of FAS 144 will have any impact on the Company's consolidated financial position or results of operations.

Note 2 — Inventories

Inventories by major classification are as follows:

	May 31,	
	2002	2001
	(In millions)	
Finished goods	$1,348.2	$1,399.9
Work-in-progress	13.0	15.1
Raw materials	12.6	9.1
	$1,373.8	$1,424.1

Note 3 — Property, Plant and Equipment

Property, plant and equipment includes the following:

	May 31,	
	2002	2001
	(In millions)	
Land	$ 178.3	$ 177.2
Buildings	739.9	695.4
Machinery and equipment	1,356.9	1,117.3
Leasehold improvements	394.2	391.9
Construction in process	72.4	171.0
	2,741.7	2,552.8
Less accumulated depreciation	1,127.2	934.0
	$1,614.5	$1,618.8

Capitalized interest expense incurred was $1.7 million, $8.4 million and $4.8 million for the years ended May 31, 2002, 2001 and 2000, respectively.

NIKE, INC.

NOTES TO CONSOLIDATED FINANCIAL STATEMENTS — (Continued)

Note 4 — Short-Term Borrowings and Credit Lines:

Commercial paper outstanding, notes payable to banks, and interest-bearing accounts payable to Nissho Iwai American Corporation (NIAC) are summarized below:

| | May 31, | | | |
| | 2002 | | 2001 | |
	Borrowings (In millions)	Interest Rate	Borrowings (In millions)	Interest Rate
Notes payable and commercial paper:				
U.S. operations	$339.2	1.82%	$710.0	4.07%
Non-U.S. operations	86.0	6.61%	145.3	6.50%
	$425.2		$855.3	
NIAC	36.3	2.62%	30.4	5.14%

At May 31, 2002 there was $338.3 million outstanding and at May 31, 2001 there was $710.0 million outstanding under our commercial paper program.

The Company purchases through NIAC certain athletic footwear and apparel it acquires from non-U.S. suppliers. These purchases are for the Company's operations outside of the U.S., Europe, and Japan. Accounts payable to NIAC are generally due up to 60 days after shipment of goods from the foreign port. The interest rate on such accounts payable is the 60 day London Interbank Offered Rate (LIBOR) as of the beginning of the month of the invoice date, plus 0.75%.

The Company has a $600.0 million, 364-day committed credit facility and a $500.0 million, multi-year committed credit facility in place with a group of banks under which no amounts are outstanding. The $600.0 million facility matures on November 15, 2002 and can be extended 364 days on each maturity date. The $500.0 million facility matures on November 17, 2005, and once a year, it can be extended for one additional year. Based on the Company's current senior unsecured debt ratings, the interest rate charged on any outstanding borrowings on the $600.0 million facility would be the prevailing LIBOR plus 0.24%, and the interest rate charged on any outstanding borrowings on the $500.0 million facility would be the prevailing LIBOR plus 0.22%. The facility fees for the $600.0 million and the $500.0 million facilities are 0.06% and 0.08%, respectively, of the total commitment. Under these agreements, the Company must maintain, among other things, certain minimum specified financial ratios with which the Company was in compliance at May 31, 2002.

NIKE, INC.

NOTES TO CONSOLIDATED FINANCIAL STATEMENTS — (Continued)

Note 5 — Long-Term Debt

Long-term debt includes the following:

	May 31,	
	2002	2001
	(In millions)	
6.69% Medium term note, payable June 17, 2002	$ 50.0	$ 50.0
6.375% Corporate Bond, payable December 1, 2003	199.8	199.8
5.5% Corporate Bond, payable August 15, 2006	248.2	—
4.3% Japanese yen note, payable June 26, 2011	83.4	85.3
2.6% Japanese yen note, maturing August 20, 2001 through November 20, 2020	67.8	73.2
2.0% Japanese yen note, maturing August 20, 2001 through November 20, 2020	30.2	32.5
Other	1.8	.5
Total	681.2	441.3
Less current maturities	55.3	5.4
	$625.9	$435.9

The 6.69% medium term note, due June 17, 2002, was repaid subsequent to May 31, 2002.

In February 1999, the Company filed a shelf registration with the U.S. Securities and Exchange Commission ("SEC") for the sale of up to $500.0 million in debt securities. In August 2001, we issued a $250.0 million corporate bond under this shelf registration, maturing in August 2006, with an interest rate of 5.5%. With the proceeds, we reduced the amount of commercial paper outstanding. In November 2001 the Company entered into interest rate swap agreements totaling $250 million and maturing August 2006, whereby the Company receives fixed interest payments at 5.5% and pays variable interest payments based on the three-month LIBOR plus a spread. At May 31, 2002, the interest rates payable on the swap agreements were approximately 3.3%.

We have an effective shelf registration statement with the Securities and Exchange Commission for $1 billion of debt securities. As of May 31, 2002, we had not issued any debt under the registration statement. Subsequent to May 31, 2002, we issued a total of $90.0 million in notes under the medium term note program of the shelf registration. The notes have coupon rates that range from 4.80% to 5.66%. The maturities range from July 9, 2007 to August 7, 2012. For $75 million of the notes, we simultaneously entered into interest rate swap agreements whereby we receive fixed interest payments at the same rate as the notes and pay variable interest payments based on the six-month LIBOR plus a spread. Each swap has the same notional amount and maturity date as the corresponding note. After issuance of these notes, $910.0 million remains available to be issued under our shelf registration. We may issue further notes under the shelf registration during the year ended May 31, 2003 depending on working capital and general corporate needs.

In June 1996, one of the Company's Japanese subsidiaries borrowed 10,500 million Japanese yen in a private placement with a maturity of June 26, 2011. Interest is paid semi-annually. The agreement provides for early retirement after year ten.

In July 1999, another of the Company's Japanese subsidiaries assumed 13,000 million in Japanese yen loans as part of its agreement to purchase a distribution center in Japan, which serves as collateral for the loans. These loans mature in equal quarterly installments during the period August 20, 2001 through November 20, 2020. Interest is also paid quarterly.

NIKE, INC.

NOTES TO CONSOLIDATED FINANCIAL STATEMENTS — (Continued)

Amounts of long-term debt maturities in each of the years ending May 31, 2003 through 2007 are $55.3 million, $205.3 million, $5.5 million, $5.5 million and $254.7 million, respectively.

Note 6 — Income Taxes

Income before income taxes and cumulative effect of accounting change is as follows:

	Year Ended May 31,		
	2002	2001	2000
	(In millions)		
Income before income taxes and cumulative effect of accounting change:			
United States	$ 511.2	$470.7	$530.4
Foreign	506.1	450.7	388.8
	$1,017.3	$921.4	$919.2

The provision for income taxes is as follows:

	Year Ended May 31,		
	2002	2001	2000
	(In millions)		
Current:			
United States			
Federal	$156.5	$158.5	$205.0
State	32.0	31.6	30.6
Foreign	147.7	76.2	58.8
	336.2	266.3	294.4
Deferred:			
United States			
Federal	(3.3)	64.2	32.7
State	3.3	2.6	1.6
Foreign	12.8	(1.4)	11.4
	12.8	65.4	45.7
	$349.0	$331.7	$340.1

NIKE, INC.

NOTES TO CONSOLIDATED FINANCIAL STATEMENTS — (Continued)

Deferred tax (assets) and liabilities are comprised of the following:

	May 31,	
	2002	2001
	(In millions)	
Deferred tax assets:		
Allowance for doubtful accounts	(14.5)	(16.3)
Inventory reserves	(17.4)	(17.2)
Sales return reserves	(22.1)	(18.4)
Deferred compensation	(49.0)	(40.1)
Reserves and accrued liabilities	(38.5)	(40.1)
Tax basis inventory adjustment	(16.0)	(16.8)
Property, plant, and equipment	(23.4)	(25.7)
Foreign loss carryforwards	(39.9)	(34.6)
Hedges	(26.7)	—
Other	(22.7)	(21.5)
Total deferred tax assets	(270.2)	(230.7)
Deferred tax liabilities:		
Undistributed earnings of foreign subsidiaries	$ 22.0	$ 53.9
Property, plant and equipment	59.6	18.4
Hedges	13.7	—
Other	26.7	20.5
Total deferred tax liabilities	122.0	92.8
Net deferred tax asset before valuation allowance	(148.2)	(137.9)
Valuation allowance	13.2	1.4
Net deferred tax asset	$(135.0)	$(136.5)

A reconciliation from the U.S. statutory federal income tax rate to the effective income tax rate follows:

	Year Ended May 31,		
	2002	2001	2000
Federal income tax rate	35.0%	35.0%	35.0%
State taxes, net of federal benefit	2.2	2.4	2.3
Foreign earnings	(3.1)	(1.8)	(1.5)
Other, net	0.2	0.4	1.2
Effective income tax rate	34.3%	36.0%	37.0%

The Company has indefinitely reinvested approximately $361.1 million of the cumulative undistributed earnings of certain foreign subsidiaries, of which $150.0 million was earned during the year ended May 31, 2002. Such earnings would be subject to U.S. taxation if repatriated to the U.S. The amount of unrecognized deferred tax liability associated with the permanently reinvested cumulative undistributed earnings was approximately $91.5 million.

Deferred tax assets at May 31, 2002 and 2001 were reduced by a valuation allowance relating to tax benefits attributable to net operating losses of certain foreign subsidiaries where local tax laws limit the utilization of such net operating losses.

NIKE, INC.

NOTES TO CONSOLIDATED FINANCIAL STATEMENTS — (Continued)

A benefit was recognized for foreign loss carryforwards of $80.1 million at May 31, 2002. Such losses expire as follows (millions):

Year Ended May 31,	2004	2005	2006	2007	2008	Indefinite
Expiration Amount..........................	4.1	4.4	24.8	8.4	9.0	29.4

During the years ended May 31, 2002, 2001, and 2000 income tax benefits attributable to employee stock option transactions of $13.9 million, $32.4 million, and $14.9 million, respectively, were allocated to shareholders' equity.

Note 7 — Redeemable Preferred Stock

NIAC is the sole owner of the Company's authorized Redeemable Preferred Stock, $1 par value, which is redeemable at the option of NIAC or the Company at par value aggregating $0.3 million. A cumulative dividend of $0.10 per share is payable annually on May 31 and no dividends may be declared or paid on the common stock of the Company unless dividends on the Redeemable Preferred Stock have been declared and paid in full. There have been no changes in the Redeemable Preferred Stock in the three years ended May 31, 2002. As the holder of the Redeemable Preferred Stock, NIAC does not have general voting rights but does have the right to vote as a separate class on the sale of all or substantially all of the assets of the Company and its subsidiaries, on merger, consolidation, liquidation or dissolution of the Company or on the sale or assignment of the NIKE trademark for athletic footwear sold in the United States.

Note 8 — Common Stock

The authorized number of shares of Class A Common Stock no par value and Class B Common Stock no par value are 110 million and 350 million, respectively. Each share of Class A Common Stock is convertible into one share of Class B Common Stock. Voting rights of Class B Common Stock are limited in certain circumstances with respect to the election of directors.

In 1990, the Board of Directors adopted, and the shareholders approved, the NIKE, Inc. 1990 Stock Incentive Plan (the "1990 Plan"). The 1990 Plan provides for the issuance of up to 37.5 million shares of Class B Common Stock in connection with stock options and other awards granted under such plan. The 1990 Plan authorizes the grant of incentive stock options, non-statutory stock options, stock appreciation rights, stock bonuses and the sale of restricted stock. The exercise price for incentive stock options may not be less than the fair market value of the underlying shares on the date of grant. The exercise price for non-statutory stock options, stock appreciation rights and the purchase price of restricted stock may not be less than 75% of the fair market value of the underlying shares on the date of grant. No consideration will be paid for stock bonuses awarded under the 1990 Plan. A committee of the Board of Directors administers the 1990 Plan. The committee has the authority to determine the employees to whom awards will be made, the amount of the awards, and the other terms and conditions of the awards. As of May 31, 2002, the committee has granted substantially all non-statutory stock options at 100% of fair market value on the date of grant under the 1990 Plan.

From time to time, the Company grants restricted stock and unrestricted stock to key employees under the 1990 plan. The number of shares granted to employees during the years ended May 31, 2002 and May 31, 2001 was not material. During the year ended May 31, 2000, the Company granted 427,000 shares of restricted stock at a market value of $27.69 per share. The restrictions lapse and recipients of the restricted shares become vested in the shares over a three-year period from the date of grant. The shares are subject to partial forfeiture if employment terminates within the three-year period. Recipients of restricted shares are entitled to cash dividends and to vote their respective shares. The value of all of the restricted shares was established by the market price on the date of grant. Unearned compensation was charged for the market value of the restricted shares. The unearned compensation is shown as a reduction of shareholders' equity and

NIKE, INC.

NOTES TO CONSOLIDATED FINANCIAL STATEMENTS — (Continued)

is being amortized ratably over the vesting period. During the years ended May 31, 2002, 2001, and 2000, respectively, the Company recognized $4.3 million, $4.3 million and $1.0 million in selling and administrative expense related to the grants, net of forfeitures.

During the years ended May 31, 2002, 2001 and 2000, the Company also granted shares of restricted stock under the Long-Term Incentive Plan ("LTIP"), adopted by the Board of Directors and approved by shareholders in September 1997. Under the LTIP, awards are made to certain executives based on performance targets established over varying time periods. Once performance targets are achieved, the shares of stock are issued and, for certain plan years, remain restricted for an additional three years. In other plan years the shares are immediately vested upon issuance. Unvested shares are subject to forfeiture if the executive's employment terminates within that period. Plan participants are entitled to cash dividends and to vote their respective shares. The value of the restricted shares is established by the market price on the date of issuance. Unearned compensation is charged for the market value of the restricted shares. The unearned compensation is shown as a reduction of shareholders' equity and is being amortized ratably over the service and vesting periods. Under the LTIP a total of 38,000 restricted shares with an average price of $49.50 were issued during the year ended May 31, 2002, 115,000 restricted shares with an average market value of $47.56 were issued during the year ended May 31, 2001, and 33,000 restricted shares with an average market value of $51.06 were issued during the year ended May 31, 2000. Related to the LTIP, the Company recognized $9.0 million, $2.3 million and $2.0 million of selling and administrative expense in the years ending May 31, 2002, 2001 and 2000, respectively, net of forfeitures.

SFAS No. 123, "Accounting for Stock-Based Compensation," (FAS 123) defines a fair value method of accounting for employee stock compensation and encourages, but does not require, all entities to adopt that method of accounting. Entities electing not to adopt the fair value method of accounting must make pro forma disclosures of net income and earnings per share, as if the fair value based method of accounting defined in this statement had been applied.

The Company has elected not to adopt the fair value method; however, as required by FAS 123, the Company has computed for pro forma disclosure purposes, the fair value of options granted during the years ended May 31, 2002, 2001 and 2000 using the Black-Scholes option pricing model. The weighted average assumptions used for stock option grants for each of these years were a dividend yield of 1%, expected volatility of the market price of the Company's common stock of 38%, 39% and 37% for the years ended May 31, 2002, 2001 and 2000, respectively; a weighted-average expected life of the options of approximately five years; and interest rates of 4.8% and 5.4% for the years ended May 31, 2002 and 2001, respectively, and 5.8%, 6.2% and 6.6% for the year ended May 31, 2000. These interest rates are reflective of option grant dates throughout the year.

Options were assumed to be exercised over the 5 year expected life for purposes of this valuation. Adjustments for forfeitures are made as they occur. For the years ended May 31, 2002, 2001 and 2000, the total value of the options granted, for which no previous expense has been recognized, was computed as approximately $73.4 million, $5.0 million and $129.8 million, respectively, which would be amortized on a straight line basis over the vesting period of the options. The weighted average fair value per share of the options granted in the years ended May 31, 2002, 2001 and 2000 are $16.02, $17.27 and $15.81, respectively.

NIKE, INC.

NOTES TO CONSOLIDATED FINANCIAL STATEMENTS — (Continued)

If the Company had accounted for these stock options issued to employees in accordance with FAS 123, the Company's pro forma net income and pro forma earnings per share (EPS) would have been reported as follows:

	Year Ended May 31,								
	2002			2001			2000		
	Net Income	Diluted EPS	Basic EPS	Net Income	Diluted EPS	Basic EPS	Net Income	Diluted EPS	Basic EPS
	(In millions, except per share data)								
As reported	$663.3	$2.44	$2.48	$589.7	$2.16	$2.18	$579.1	$2.07	$2.10
Pro Forma	627.2	2.30	2.34	559.0	2.05	2.07	551.2	1.97	2.00

The pro forma effects of applying FAS 123 may not be representative of the effects on reported net income and earnings per share for future years since options vest over several years and additional awards are made each year.

The following summarizes the stock option transactions under plans discussed above (adjusted for all applicable stock splits):

| | Shares | Weighted Average Option Price |
	(In thousands)	
Options outstanding May 31, 1999	11,865	$34.97
Exercised...	(1,237)	18.23
Surrendered	(852)	52.86
Granted	8,294	40.94
Options outstanding May 31, 2000	18,070	38.02
Exercised...	(2,944)	19.24
Surrendered	(1,302)	44.80
Granted	341	40.71
Options outstanding May 31, 2001	14,165	41.28
Exercised...	(1,687)	33.62
Surrendered	(724)	44.43
Granted	4,687	42.68
Options outstanding May 31, 2002	16,441	$42.31
Options exercisable at May 31,		
2000...	6,655	$28.72
2001...	6,626	39.70
2002...	7,590	42.30

NIKE, INC.

NOTES TO CONSOLIDATED FINANCIAL STATEMENTS — (Continued)

The following table sets forth the exercise prices, the number of options outstanding and exercisable and the remaining contractual lives of the Company's stock options at May 31, 2002:

	Options Outstanding			Options Exercisable	
Exercise Price	Number of Options Outstanding	Weighted Average Exercise Price	Weighted Average Contractual Life Remaining	Number of Options Exercisable	Weighted Average Exercise Price
	(In thousands)		(Years)	(In thousands)	
$11.25-$27.69	4,253	$25.07	6.33	2,486	$23.21
28.13- 40.63	368	39.65	7.56	186	39.93
40.69- 42.36	4,378	42.34	9.09	31	40.95
42.50- 52.06	3,291	48.00	5.89	2,414	48.01
52.44- 74.88	4,151	55.65	6.66	2,473	56.11

In September 2001, the Company's shareholders approved the establishment of an Employee Stock Purchase Plan (the "ESPP") under which 3,000,000 shares of Class B Stock are reserved for issuance to employees. The plan qualifies as a noncompensatory employee stock purchase plan under Section 423 of the Internal Revenue Code. Employees are eligible to participate through payroll deductions in amounts ranging from 1% to 10% of their compensation. At the end of each six-month offering period, shares are purchased by the participants at 85% of the lower of the fair market value at the beginning or the end of the offering period. Under the ESPP, 78,000 shares were issued during the year ended May 31, 2002.

Note 9 — Earnings Per Share

The following represents a reconciliation from basic earnings per share to diluted earnings per share. Options to purchase 4.2 million, 8.3 million, and 9.7 million shares of common stock were outstanding at May 31, 2002, 2001, and 2000, respectively, but were not included in the computation of diluted earnings per share because the options' exercise prices were greater than the average market price of the common shares and, therefore, the effect would be antidilutive.

	Year Ended May 31,		
	2002	2001	2000
	(In millions, except per share data)		
Determination of shares:			
Average common shares outstanding	267.7	270.0	275.7
Assumed conversion of dilutive stock options and awards	4.5	3.3	3.7
Diluted average common shares outstanding	272.2	273.3	279.4
Basic earnings per common share — before cumulative effect of accounting change	$ 2.50	$ 2.18	$ 2.10
Cumulative effect of accounting change	0.02	—	—
	$ 2.48	$ 2.18	$ 2.10
Diluted earnings per common share — before cumulative effect of accounting change	$ 2.46	$ 2.16	$ 2.07
Cumulative effect of accounting change	0.02	—	—
	$ 2.44	$ 2.16	$ 2.07

NIKE, INC.

NOTES TO CONSOLIDATED FINANCIAL STATEMENTS — (Continued)

Note 10 — Benefit Plans

The Company has a profit sharing plan available to substantially all U.S.-based employees. The terms of the plan call for annual contributions by the Company as determined by the Board of Directors. Contributions of $14.4 million, $13.1 million and $15.7 million to the plan are included in other income/expense in the consolidated financial statements for the years ended May 31, 2002, 2001 and 2000, respectively. The Company has a voluntary 401(k) employee savings plan. The Company matches a portion of employee contributions with common stock. Plan changes during the year ended May 31, 2001 included a larger Company match percentage and a change to immediate vesting of the Company match, compared to a previous vesting schedule over 5 years. Company contributions to the savings plan were $13.7 million, $12.7 million and $6.7 million for the years ended May 31, 2002, 2001 and 2000, respectively, and are included in selling and administrative expenses.

Note 11 — Interest Income

Included in other income/expense for the years ended May 31, 2002, 2001, and 2000, was interest income of $13.6 million, $13.9 million and $13.6 million, respectively.

Note 12 — Comprehensive Income

Comprehensive income is as follows:

	Year Ended May 31,		
	2002	2001	2000
	(In millions)		
Net income	$663.3	$589.7	$579.1
Other comprehensive income:			
Change in cumulative translation adjustment and other (net tax expense/(benefit) of $(2.2) in 2002, $(2.4) in 2001, $1.2 in 2000)	(1.5)	(41.0)	(42.2)
Recognition in net income of previously deferred unrealized loss on securities, due to accounting change (net of tax benefit of $2.2)	3.4	—	—
Changes due to cash flow hedging instruments (Note 1):			
Initial recognition of net deferred gain as of June 1, due to accounting change (net of tax expense of $28.7)	53.4	—	—
Loss on hedge derivatives (net of tax benefit of $31.5)	(73.3)	—	—
Reclassification to net income of previously deferred gains related to hedge derivative instruments (net of tax benefit of $10.2)	(22.3)	—	—
Other comprehensive income	(40.3)	(41.0)	(42.2)
Total comprehensive income	$623.0	$548.7	$536.9

The components of accumulated other comprehensive loss are as follows:

	Year Ended May 31,	
	2002	2001
	(In millions)	
Cumulative translation adjustment and other	$(150.2)	$(152.1)
Net deferred loss on hedge derivatives	(42.2)	—
	$(192.4)	$(152.1)

49

NIKE, INC.

NOTES TO CONSOLIDATED FINANCIAL STATEMENTS — (Continued)

Note 13 — Commitments and Contingencies

The Company leases space for certain of its offices, warehouses and retail stores under leases expiring from one to fifteen years after May 31, 2002. Rent expense was $159.9 million, $152.0 million and $145.5 million for the years ended May 31, 2002, 2001 and 2000, respectively. Amounts of minimum future annual rental commitments under non-cancelable operating leases in each of the five years ending May 31, 2003 through 2007 are $158.2 million, $143.4 million, $119.1 million, $95.3 million, $98.2 million, respectively, and $288.0 million in later years.

As of May 31, 2002 and 2001, the Company had letters of credit outstanding totaling $808.4 million and $851.8 million, respectively. These letters of credit were issued for the purchase of inventory.

In the ordinary course of its business, the Company is involved in legal proceedings involving contractual and employment relationships, product liability claims, trademark rights, and a variety of other matters. The Company does not believe there are any pending legal proceedings that will have a material impact on the Company's financial position or results of operations.

Note 14 — Fair Value of Financial Instruments

The carrying amounts reflected in the consolidated balance sheet for cash and equivalents and notes payable approximate fair value due to the short maturities. The fair value of long-term debt is estimated using discounted cash flow analyses, based on the Company's incremental borrowing rates for similar types of borrowing arrangements. The fair value of the Company's long-term debt, including current portion, is approximately $723.9 million, compared to a carrying value of $681.2 million at May 31, 2002 and $437.8 million, compared to a carrying value of $441.3 million at May 31, 2001.

Note 15 — Financial Risk Management and Derivatives

As of May 31, 2002, $50.9 million of deferred net losses (net of tax) on both outstanding and matured derivatives accumulated in other comprehensive income are expected to be reclassified to earnings during the next twelve months as a result of underlying hedged transactions also being recorded in earnings. Actual amounts ultimately reclassified to earnings are dependent on the exchange rates in effect when derivative contracts that are currently outstanding mature. As of May 31, 2002, the maximum term over which the Company is hedging exposures to the variability of cash flows for all forecasted and recorded transactions is 24 months.

For the year ended May 31, 2002 the Company recorded in other expense an insignificant loss representing the total ineffectiveness of all derivatives. Net income for the year ended May 31, 2002 was not materially affected due to discontinued hedge accounting.

At May 31, 2002, the fair values of derivatives in a gain position and recorded in Prepaid expenses and other current assets and Deferred income taxes and other assets were $60.3 million and $70.0 million, respectively. At this same date, the fair values of derivatives in a loss position and recorded in Accrued liabilities and Deferred income taxes and other liabilities were $123.8 million and $8.1 million, respectively.

Prior to the adoption of FAS 133 carrying values of derivatives recorded on the balance sheet were different from fair values. Accordingly, the aggregate notional principle amounts, carrying values and fair

NIKE, INC.

NOTES TO CONSOLIDATED FINANCIAL STATEMENTS — (Continued)

values of the Company's derivative financial instruments as of May 31, 2001 are provided in the following table:

| | May 31, 2001 | | |
| | Notional Principal Amounts | Carrying Values | Fair Values |
		(In millions)	
Currency Swaps..	$ 250.0	$ 77.4	$ 87.0
Forward Contracts.....................................	2,428.3	17.8	51.7
Purchased Options	727.5	17.7	20.4
Total	$3,405.8	$112.9	$159.1

Carrying values primarily represent amounts recognized for unrealized gains and losses on contracts which did not meet the criteria for deferral accounting and unamortized premiums paid on option contracts. The net fair value of outstanding forward contracts of $51.7 million as of May 31, 2001 was comprised of unrealized fair value losses of $22.9 million and unrealized fair value gains of $74.6 million.

The Company is exposed to credit-related losses in the event of non-performance by counterparties to hedging instruments. The counterparties to all derivative transactions are major financial institutions with investment grade credit ratings. However, this does not eliminate the Company's exposure to credit risk with these institutions. This credit risk is generally limited to the unrealized gains in such contracts should any of these counterparties fail to perform as contracted. To manage this risk, the Company has established strict counterparty credit guidelines which are continually monitored and reported to senior management according to prescribed guidelines. The Company utilizes a portfolio of financial institutions either headquartered or operating in the same countries the Company conducts its business. As a result of the above considerations, the Company considers the risk of counterparty default to be minimal.

In addition to hedging instruments, the Company is subject to concentrations of credit risk associated with cash and equivalents and accounts receivable. The Company places cash and equivalents with financial institutions with investment grade credit ratings and, by policy, limits the amount of credit exposure to any one financial institution. The Company considers its concentration risk related to accounts receivable to be mitigated by the Company's credit policy, the significance of outstanding balances owed by each individual customer at any point in time and the geographic dispersion of these customers.

Note 16 — Operating Segments and Related Information

Operating Segments. The Company's major operating segments are defined by geographic regions for subsidiaries participating in NIKE brand sales activity. "Other" as shown below represents activity for Cole-Haan Holdings, Inc., Bauer NIKE Hockey, Inc., NIKE IHM, Inc., and Hurley International LLC, which are immaterial for individual disclosure. Where applicable, "Corporate" represents items necessary to reconcile to the consolidated financial statements, which generally include corporate activity and corporate eliminations. The segments are evidence of the structure of the Company's internal organization. Each NIKE brand geographic segment operates predominantly in one industry: the design, production, marketing and selling of sports and fitness footwear, apparel, and equipment.

Net revenues as shown below represent sales to external customers for each segment. Intercompany revenues have been eliminated and are immaterial for separate disclosure. The Company evaluates performance of individual operating segments based on management pre-tax income. On a consolidated basis, this amount represents income before income taxes and cumulative effect of accounting change as shown in the Consolidated Statements of Income. Reconciling items for management pre-tax income represent corporate

NIKE, INC.

NOTES TO CONSOLIDATED FINANCIAL STATEMENTS — (Continued)

costs that are not allocated to the operating segments for management reporting, and intercompany eliminations for specific income statement items.

Additions to long-lived assets as presented following represent capital expenditures and additions to identifiable intangibles and goodwill. Generally, amortization of identifiable intangible assets and goodwill is considered a corporate expense and is not attributable to any specific operating segment. See Note 1 for further discussion on identifiable intangible assets and goodwill. Additions to other long-lived assets are not significant and are comprised of additions to miscellaneous corporate assets not attributable to any specific operating segment.

Accounts receivable, inventory and property, plant and equipment for operating segments are regularly reviewed by management and are therefore provided below.

	Year Ended May 31,		
	2002	2001	2000
	(In millions)		
Net Revenue			
United States	$4,916.0	$4,819.0	$4,732.1
Europe, Middle East, and Africa	2,731.5	·2,584.8	2,407.0
Asia/Pacific	1,211.7	1,110.0	955.1
Americas	568.1	539.1	494.1
Other	465.7	435.9	406.8
	$9,893.0	$9,488.8	$8,995.1
Management Pre-tax Income			
United States	$ 977.6	$ 919.6	$ 924.3
Europe, Middle East, and Africa	445.4	386.3	376.9
Asia/Pacific	238.7	206.1	146.0
Americas	92.9	81.6	63.7
Other	20.0	41.4	68.9
Corporate	(757.3)	(713.6)	(660.6)
	$1,017.3	$ 921.4	$ 919.2
Additions to Long-lived Assets			
United States	$ 33.4	$ 45.2	$ 29.0
Europe, Middle East, and Africa	27.2	26.2	46.1
Asia/Pacific	22.1	52.9	269.7
Americas	4.8	5.1	4.8
Other	76.3	26.3	32.4
Corporate	115.2	161.9	146.8
	$ 279.0	$ 317.6	$ 528.8
Depreciation			
United States	$ 51.2	$ 51.2	$ 50.8
Europe, Middle East, and Africa	35.2	38.9	39.9
Asia/Pacific	38.4	20.5	19.4
Americas	5.3	6.3	7.1
Other	22.4	23.5	23.7
Corporate	71.0	57.0	47.1
	$ 223.5	$ 197.4	$ 188.0
Accounts Receivable, net			
United States	$ 759.8	$ 622.5	$ 564.7
Europe, Middle East, and Africa	570.8	512.5	529.9
Asia/Pacific	189.6	194.8	200.8
Americas	125.3	144.7	123.0
Other	142.8	118.6	121.0
Corporate	18.8	28.3	30.0
	$1,807.1	$1,621.4	$1,569.4

NIKE, INC.

NOTES TO CONSOLIDATED FINANCIAL STATEMENTS — (Continued)

	Year Ended May 31,		
	2002	2001	2000
	(In millions)		
Inventory, net			
United States	$ 681.5	$ 744.2	$ 736.5
Europe, Middle East, and Africa	339.3	298.3	357.4
Asia/Pacific	159.8	125.8	115.9
Americas	62.9	72.4	65.5
Other	119.9	156.4	141.4
Corporate	10.4	27.0	29.3
	$1,373.8	$1,424.1	$1,446.0
Property, Plant and Equipment, net			
United States	$ 244.4	$ 263.5	$ 271.7
Europe, Middle East, and Africa	212.2	208.2	240.4
Asia/Pacific	378.4	403.5	426.4
Americas	12.4	15.4	18.1
Other	109.7	113.4	114.4
Corporate	657.4	614.8	512.4
	$1,614.5	$1,618.8	$1,583.4

Revenues by Major Product Lines. Revenues to external customers for NIKE brand products are attributable to sales of footwear, apparel, and equipment. Other revenues to external customers primarily include external sales by Cole Haan Holdings, Inc., Bauer NIKE Hockey Inc. and Hurley International LLC.

	Year Ended May 31,		
	2002	2001	2000
	(In millions)		
Footwear	$5,753.7	$5,619.3	$5,561.5
Apparel	2,892.9	2,763.6	2,547.0
Equipment	780.7	670.0	479.8
Other	465.7	435.9	406.8
	$9,893.0	$9,488.8	$8,995.1

Revenues and Long-Lived Assets by Geographic Area. Geographical area information is similar to that shown previously under operating segments with the exception that Other activity is derived predominantly from activity in the U.S. and Americas. Revenues derived in the U.S. were $5,258.8 million $5,144.2 million, $5,017.4 million, during the years ended May 31, 2002, 2001, and 2000, respectively. Our largest concentrations of long-lived assets are in the U.S. and Japan. Long-lived assets attributable to operations in the U.S., which are primarily comprised of net property, plant & equipment and net identifiable intangible assets and goodwill, were $1,217.7 million, $1,165.3 million, and $1,187.0 million at May 31, 2002, 2001, and 2000, respectively. Long-lived assets attributable to operations in Japan were $321.6 million, $339.1 million, and $355.5 million at May 31, 2002, 2001, and 2000, respectively.

Major Customers. During the years ended May 31, 2002, 2001 and 2000, revenues derived from Foot Locker, Inc. represented 10.9%, 11.8% and 12.4%, respectively of the Company's consolidated revenues. Sales to this customer are included in all segments of the Company participating in NIKE brand sales activity.

Item 9. *Changes In and Disagreements with Accountants on Accounting and Financial Disclosure*

There has been no change of accountants nor any disagreements with accountants on any matter of accounting principles or practices or financial statement disclosure required to be reported under this Item.

PART III

Item 10. *Directors and Executive Officers of the Registrant*

The information required by Item 401 of Regulation S-K regarding directors is included under "Election of Directors" in the definitive Proxy Statement for our 2002 Annual Meeting of Shareholders and is incorporated herein by reference. The information required by Item 401 of Regulation S-K regarding executive officers is included under "Executive Officers of the Registrant" in Item 1 of this Report. The information required by Item 405 of Regulation S-K is included under "Section 16(a) Beneficial Ownership Reporting Compliance" in the definitive Proxy Statement for our 2002 Annual Meeting of Shareholders and is incorporated herein by reference.

Item 11. *Executive Compensation*

The information required by this Item is included under "Director Compensation and Retirement Plan," "Executive Compensation" (but excluding the Performance Graph), "Personnel Committee Interlocks and Insider Participation" and "Employment Contracts and Termination of Employment and Change-in-Control Arrangements" in the definitive Proxy Statement for our 2002 Annual Meeting of Shareholders and is incorporated herein by reference.

Item 12. *Security Ownership of Certain Beneficial Owners and Management*

The information required by this Item is included under "Stock Holdings of Certain Owners and Management" and under "Equity Compensation Plans" in the definitive Proxy Statement for our 2002 Annual Meeting of Shareholders and is incorporated herein by reference.

Item 13. *Certain Relationships and Related Transactions*

The information required by this Item is included under "Certain Transactions and Business Relationships" and "Indebtedness of Management" in the definitive Proxy Statement for our 2002 Annual Meeting of Shareholders and is incorporated herein by reference.

PART IV

Item 14. *Exhibits, Financial Statement Schedule, and Reports on Form 8-K*

(A) The following documents are filed as part of this report:

	Form 10-K Page No.
1. FINANCIAL STATEMENTS:	
Report of Independent Accountants	30
Consolidated Statements of Income for each of the three years ended May 31, 2002	31
Consolidated Balance Sheets at May 31, 2002 and 2001	32
Consolidated Statements of Cash Flows for each of the three years ended May 31, 2002	33
Consolidated Statements of Shareholders' Equity for each of the three years ended May 31, 2002	34
Notes to Consolidated Financial Statements	35
2. FINANCIAL STATEMENT SCHEDULE:	
II — Valuation and Qualifying Accounts	F-1

All other schedules are omitted because they are not applicable or the required information is shown in the financial statements or notes thereto.

3. EXHIBITS:

3.1   Restated Articles of Incorporation, as amended (incorporated by reference from Exhibit 3.1 to the Company's Quarterly Report on Form 10-Q for the fiscal quarter ended August 31, 1995).

3.2   Third Restated Bylaws, as amended (incorporated by reference from Exhibit 3.2 to the Company's Quarterly Report on Form 10-Q for the fiscal quarter ended August 31, 1995).

4.1   Restated Articles of Incorporation, as amended (see Exhibit 3.1).

4.2   Third Restated Bylaws, as amended (see Exhibit 3.2).

4.3   Indenture between the Company and The First National Bank of Chicago, as Trustee (incorporated by reference from Exhibit 4.01 to Amendment No. 1 to Registration Statement No. 333-15953 filed by the Company on November 26, 1996).

4.4   Form of Officers' Certificate relating to the Company's 6.375% Notes and form of 6.375% Note (incorporated by reference to Exhibits 4.1 and 4.2 of the Company's Form 8-K dated December 10, 1996).

4.5   Form of Officers' Certificate relating to the Company's 5.5% Notes and form of 5.5% Note (incorporated by reference to Exhibits 4.2 and 4.3 of the Company's Form 8-K dated August 17, 2001).

4.6   Form of Officers' Certificate relating to the Company's Fixed Rate Medium-Term Notes and the Company's Floating Rate Medium-Term Notes, form of Fixed Rate Note and form of Floating Rate Note (incorporated by reference to Exhibits 4.2, 4.3 and 4.4 of the Company's Form 8-K dated May 29, 2002).

10.1   Credit Agreement dated as of November 17, 2000 among NIKE, Inc., Bank of America, N.A., individually and as Agent, and the other banks party thereto (incorporated by reference from Exhibit 10.1 to the Company's Quarterly Report on Form 10-Q for the fiscal quarter ended November 30, 2000).

10.2   First Amendment to Credit Agreement dated as of November 16, 2001 (incorporated by reference from Exhibit 10.2 to the Company's Quarterly Report on Form 10-Q for the fiscal quarter ended November 30, 2001).

10.3   Form of non-employee director Stock Option Agreement (incorporated by reference from Exhibit 10.2 to the Company's Quarterly Report on Form 10-Q for the fiscal quarter ended November 30, 2000).*

10.4   Form of Indemnity Agreement entered into between the Company and each of its officers and directors (incorporated by reference from the Company's definitive proxy statement filed in connection with its annual meeting of shareholders held on September 21, 1987).

10.5   NIKE, Inc. 1990 Stock Incentive Plan.*

10.6   NIKE, Inc. Executive Performance Sharing Plan (incorporated by reference from the Company's definitive proxy statement filed in connection with its annual meeting of shareholders held on September 18, 2000).*

10.7   NIKE, Inc. Long-Term Incentive Plan (incorporated by reference from the Company's definitive proxy statement filed in connection with its annual meeting of shareholders held on September 22, 1997).*

10.8   Collateral Assignment Split-Dollar Agreement between NIKE, Inc. and Philip H. Knight dated March 10, 1994 (incorporated by reference from Exhibit 10.7 to the Company's Annual Report on Form 10-K for the fiscal year ended May 31, 1994).*

10.9   Covenant Not To Compete And Non-Disclosure Agreement between NIKE, Inc. and Thomas E. Clarke dated August 31, 1994 (incorporated by reference from Exhibit 10.8 to the Company's Quarterly Report on Form 10-Q for the fiscal quarter ended August 31, 2001).*

10.10   Covenant Not To Compete And Non-Disclosure Agreement between NIKE, Inc. and Mark G. Parker dated October 6, 1994 (incorporated by reference from Exhibit 10.9 to the Company's Quarterly Report on Form 10-Q for the fiscal quarter ended August 31, 2001).*

10.11   NIKE, Inc. Deferred Compensation Plan dated January 1, 2000 (incorporated by reference from Exhibit 10.10 to the Company's Quarterly Report on Form 10-Q for the fiscal quarter ended August 31, 2001).*

10.12   Employment Agreement, and Covenant Not To Compete And Non-Disclosure Agreement between NIKE, Inc. and Mindy F. Grossman dated September 6, 2000.*

12.1   Computation of Ratio of Earnings to Fixed Charges.

21   Subsidiaries of the Registrant.

23   Consent of PricewaterhouseCoopers LLP, independent accountants (set forth on page F-2 of this Annual Report on Form 10-K).

---

* Management contract or compensatory plan or arrangement.

The exhibits filed herewith do not include certain instruments with respect to long-term debt of NIKE and its subsidiaries, inasmuch as the total amount of debt authorized under any such instrument does not exceed 10% of the total assets of NIKE and its subsidiaries on a consolidated basis. NIKE agrees, pursuant to Item 601(b)(4)(iii) of Regulation S-K, that it will furnish a copy of any such instrument to the SEC upon request.

Upon written request to Investor Relations, NIKE, Inc., One Bowerman Drive, Beaverton, Oregon 97005-6453, NIKE will furnish shareholders with a copy of any Exhibit upon payment of $.10 per page, which represents our reasonable expenses in furnishing Exhibits.

(B) The following reports on Form 8-K were filed by NIKE during the last quarter of fiscal 2002:

Date	Item	Subject
May 29, 2002	Item 5. Other Events & Item 7. Financial Statements & Exhibits	Medium-Term Note

SCHEDULE II

VALUATION AND QUALIFYING ACCOUNTS

Description	Balance at Beginning of Period	Charged to Costs and Expenses	Charged to Other Accounts	Write-Offs Net of Recoveries	Balance at End of Period
			(In millions)		
For the year ended May 31, 2000:					
Allowance for doubtful accounts	$73.2	$26.0	$1.8	$(35.6)	$65.4
For the year ended May 31, 2001:					
Allowance for doubtful accounts	$65.4	$32.7	$2.8	$(28.8)	$72.1
For the year ended May 31, 2002:					
Allowance for doubtful accounts	$72.1	$23.7	$1.2	$(19.6)	$77.4

CONSENT OF INDEPENDENT ACCOUNTANTS

We hereby consent to the incorporation by reference in the documents listed below of our report dated June 27, 2002 relating to the financial statements and financial statement schedule of NIKE, Inc., which appears in this Form 10-K:

1. Registration Statement on Form S-8 (No. 2-81419) of NIKE, Inc.;

2. Registration Statement on Form S-3 (No. 33-43205) of NIKE, Inc.;

3. Registration Statement on Form S-3 (No. 33-48977) of NIKE, Inc.;

4. Registration Statement on Form S-3 (No. 33-41842) of NIKE, Inc.;

5. Registration Statement on Form S-8 (No. 33-63995) of NIKE, Inc.;

6. Registration Statement on Form S-3 (No. 333-15953) of NIKE, Inc.;

7. Registration Statement on Form S-8 (No. 333-63581) of NIKE, Inc.;

8. Registration Statement on Form S-8 (No. 333-63583) of NIKE, Inc.;

9. Registration Statement on Form S-3 (No. 333-71975) of NIKE, Inc.;

10. Registration Statement on Form S-8 (No. 333-68864) of NIKE, Inc.;

11. Registration Statement on Form S-8 (No. 333-68886) of NIKE, Inc.;

12. Registration Statement on Form S-8 (No. 333-71660) of NIKE, Inc.; and

13. Registration Statement on Form S-3 (No. 333-71324) of NIKE, Inc.

/s/   PRICEWATERHOUSECOOPERS LLP

Portland, Oregon
August 14, 2002

SIGNATURES

Pursuant to the requirements of Section 13 or 15(d) of the Securities Exchange Act of 1934, the registrant has duly caused this report to be signed on its behalf by the undersigned, thereunto duly authorized.

NIKE, INC.

BY: /s/   PHILIP H. KNIGHT

Philip H. Knight
*Chairman of the Board, Chief Executive Officer
and President*

Date: August 14, 2002

Pursuant to the requirements of the Securities Exchange Act of 1934, this report has been signed below by the following persons on behalf of the registrant and in the capacities and on the dates indicated.

Signature	Title	Date
Principal Executive Officer and Director:		
/s/ PHILIP H. KNIGHT Philip H. Knight	Chairman of the Board, Chief Executive Officer, and President	August 14, 2002
Principal Financial and Accounting Officer:		
/s/ DONALD W. BLAIR Donald W. Blair	Chief Financial Officer	August 14, 2002
Directors:		
/s/ THOMAS E. CLARKE Thomas E. Clarke	Director	August 14, 2002
/s/ JILL K. CONWAY Jill K. Conway	Director	August 14, 2002
/s/ RALPH D. DENUNZIO Ralph D. DeNunzio	Director	August 14, 2002
/s/ RICHARD K. DONAHUE Richard K. Donahue	Director	August 14, 2002
/s/ DELBERT J. HAYES Delbert J. Hayes	Director	August 14, 2002
/s/ DOUGLAS G. HOUSER Douglas G. Houser	Director	August 14, 2002

Signature	Title	Date
/s/ JEANNE P. JACKSON Jeanne P. Jackson	Director	August 14, 2002
/s/ JOHN E. JAQUA John E. Jaqua	Director	August 14, 2002
/s/ CHARLES W. ROBINSON Charles W. Robinson	Director	August 14, 2002
/s/ A. MICHAEL SPENCE A. Michael Spence	Director	August 14, 2002
/s/ JOHN R. THOMPSON, JR. John R. Thompson, Jr.	Director	August 14, 2002

EXHIBIT 12.1

NIKE, INC. COMPUTATION OF RATIO OF EARNINGS TO FIXED CHARGES

	Year Ended May 31,		
	2002	2001	2000
		(In millions)	
Net income	$ 663.3	$ 589.7	$ 579.1
Income taxes	349.0	331.7	340.1
Cumulative change in accounting principle	5.0	—	—
Income before income taxes and cumulative change	1,017.3	921.4	919.2
Add fixed charges			
Interest expense(A)	49.3	67.1	49.8
Interest component of leases(B)	53.3	50.7	48.5
Total fixed charges	102.6	117.8	98.3
Earnings before income taxes and fixed charges(C)	$1,118.2	$1,030.8	$1,012.7
Ratio of earnings to total fixed charges	10.90	8.75	10.30

(A) Interest expense includes interest both expensed and capitalized.

(B) Interest component of leases includes one-third of rental expense, which approximates the interest component of operating leases.

(C) Earnings before income taxes and fixed charges is exclusive of capitalized interest.

(This page intentionally left blank)

EXHIBIT 21

SUBSIDIARIES OF THE REGISTRANT

NIKE, Inc. has 38 wholly-owned subsidiaries, 7 of which operate in the United States, and 31 of which operate in foreign countries. All of the subsidiaries, except for NIKE IHM, Inc., Triax Insurance, Inc., and NIKE Suzhou Sports Co. Ltd. carry on the same line of business, namely the design, marketing, distribution and sale of athletic and leisure footwear, apparel, accessories, and equipment. NIKE IHM, Inc., a Missouri corporation, manufactures plastics and Air-Sole shoe cushioning components. Triax Insurance, Inc., a Hawaii corporation, is a captive insurance company that insures the Company for certain risks. NIKE Suzhou Sports Co. Ltd., a Chinese corporation, manufactures footwear in the People's Republic of China.

(This page intentionally left blank)

11

EXPANDED ANALYSIS

This chapter reviews special areas related to the usefulness of ratios and financial analyses. These special areas are as follows: (1) financial ratios as perceived by commercial loan departments, (2) financial ratios as perceived by corporate controllers, (3) financial ratios as perceived by certified public accountants, (4) financial ratios as perceived by chartered financial analysts, (5) financial ratios used in annual reports, (6) degree of conservatism and quality of earnings, (7) forecasting financial failure, (8) analytical review procedures, (9) management's use of analysis, (10) use of LIFO reserves, (11) graphing financial information, (12) management of earnings.

FINANCIAL RATIOS AS PERCEIVED BY COMMERCIAL LOAN DEPARTMENTS

Financial ratios can be used by a commercial loan department to aid the loan officers in deciding whether to grant a commercial loan and in maintaining control of a loan once it is granted.[1] In order to gain insights into how commercial loan departments view financial ratios, a questionnaire was sent to the commercial loan departments of the 100 largest banks in the United States. Usable responses were received from 44% of them.

A list of 59 financial ratios was drawn from financial literature, textbooks, and published industry data for this study. The study set three objectives: (1) the significance of each ratio, in the opinion of commercial loan officers, (2) how frequently each ratio is included in loan agreements, and (3) what a specific financial ratio primarily measures, in the opinion of commercial loan officers. For the primary measure, the choices were liquidity, long-term debt-paying ability, profitability, or other. Exhibit 11-1 lists the ratios included in this study.

Most Significant Ratios and Their Primary Measure

Exhibit 11-2 displays the 10 financial ratios given the highest significance rating by the commercial loan officers, as well as the primary measure of these ratios. The highest rating is a 9, and the lowest rating is a 0.

Most of the ratios given a high significance rating were regarded primarily as measures of liquidity or debt. Only 2 of the top 10 ratios measure profitability, 5 measure debt, and 3 measure liq-

---

EXHIBIT 11-1   RATIOS RATED BY COMMERCIAL LOAN OFFICERS

Ratio	Ratio
Cash ratio	Sales/fixed assets
Accounts receivable turnover in days	Sales/working capital
Accounts receivable turnover—times per year	Sales/net worth
Days' sales in receivables	Cash/sales
Quick ratio	Quick assets/sales
Inventory turnover in days	Current assets/sales
Inventory turnover—times per year	Return on assets:
Days' sales in inventory	before interest and tax
Current debt/inventory	before tax
Inventory/current assets	after tax
Inventory/working capital	Return on operating assets
Current ratio	Return on total invested:
Inventory/current assets	before tax
Inventory/working capital	after tax
Current ratio	Return on equity:
Net fixed assets/tangible net worth	before tax
Cash/total assets	after tax
Quick assets/total assets	Net profit margin:
Current assets/total assets	before tax
Retained earnings/total assets	after tax
Debt/equity ratio	Retained earnings/net income
Total debt as a % of net working capital	Cash flow/current maturities of long-term debt
Total debt/total assets	Cash flow/total debt
Short-term debt as a % of total invested capital	Times interest earned
Long-term debt as a % of total invested capital	Fixed charge coverage
Funded debt/working capital	Degree of operating leverage
Total equity/total assets	Degree of financial leverage
Fixed assets/equity	Earnings per share
Common equity as a % of total invested capital	Book value per share
Current debt/net worth	Dividend payout ratio
Net worth at market value/total liabilities	Dividend yield
Total asset turnover	Price/earnings ratio
Sales/operating assets	Stock price as a % of book value

EXHIBIT 11-2

EXHIBIT 11-2   **COMMERCIAL LOAN DEPARTMENTS**
Most Significant Ratios and Their Primary Measures

Ratio	Significance Rating	Primary Measure
Debt/equity	8.71	Debt
Current ratio	8.25	Liquidity
Cash flow/current maturities of long-term debt	8.08	Debt
Fixed charge coverage	7.58	Debt
Net profit margin after tax	7.56	Profitability
Times interest earned	7.50	Debt
Net profit margin before tax	7.43	Profitability
Degree of financial leverage	7.33	Debt
Inventory turnover in days	7.25	Liquidity
Accounts receivable turnover in days	7.08	Liquidity

uidity. The two profitability ratios were two different computations of the net profit margin: (1) net profit margin after tax and (2) net profit margin before tax. Two of the top three ratios were measures of debt, and the other was a measure of liquidity. The debt/equity ratio was given the highest significance rating, with the current ratio second highest. We can assume that the financial ratios rated most significant by commercial loan officers would have the greatest influence on a loan decision.

Ratios Appearing Most Frequently in Loan Agreements

A commercial bank may elect to include a ratio as part of a loan agreement. This would be a way of using ratios to control an outstanding loan. Exhibit 11-3 contains a list of the 10 financial ratios that appear most frequently in loan agreements, along with an indication of what each ratio primarily measures. For the two ratios that do not have a primary measure indicated, there was no majority opinion as to what the ratio primarily measured. Six of the ratios that appear most frequently in loan agreements primarily measure debt, two primarily measure liquidity, and none primarily measure profitability.

The two top ratios, debt/equity and current ratio, were given the highest significance rating. The dividend payout ratio was the third most likely ratio to appear in loan agreements, but it was

EXHIBIT 11-3   **COMMERCIAL LOAN DEPARTMENTS**
Ratios Appearing Most Frequently in Loan Agreements

Ratio	Percentage of Banks Including Ratio in 26% or More of Their Loan Agreements	Primary Measure
Debt/equity	92.5	Debt
Current ratio	90.0	Liquidity
Dividend payout ratio	70.0	*
Cash flow/current maturities of long-term debt	60.3	Debt
Fixed charge coverage	55.2	Debt
Times interest earned	52.6	Debt
Degree of financial leverage	44.7	Debt
Equity/assets	41.0	*
Cash flow/total debt	36.1	Debt
Quick ratio	33.3	Liquidity

*No majority primary measure indicated in this survey.

not rated as a highly significant ratio. Logically, this ratio appears in loan agreements as a means of controlling outflow of cash for dividends.

FINANCIAL RATIOS AS PERCEIVED BY CORPORATE CONTROLLERS	To get the views of corporate controllers on important issues relating to financial ratios, a questionnaire was sent to the controllers of the companies included in the *Fortune 500* list of the largest industrials.[2] The study excluded companies 100% owned or controlled by another firm. The survey received a usable response rate of 19.42%. The questionnaire used the same ratios used for the commercial loan department survey. Three objectives of this study were the determination of: (1) the significance of a specific ratio as perceived by controllers, (2) which financial ratios are included as corporate objectives, and (3) the primary measure of each ratio.

Most Significant Ratios and Their Primary Measure

Exhibit 11-4 displays the 10 financial ratios given the highest significance rating by the corporate controllers, along with the primary measure of these ratios. The highest rating is a 9 and the lowest is a 0.

The financial executives gave the profitability ratios the highest significance ratings. The highest rated debt ratio was debt/equity, while the highest rated liquidity ratio was the current ratio. In comparing the responses of the commercial loan officers and the controllers, the controllers rate the profitability ratios as having the highest significance, while the commercial loan officers rate the debt and liquidity ratios highest.

Key Financial Ratios Included as Corporate Objectives

Many firms have selected key financial ratios to be included as part of their corporate objectives. The next section of the survey was designed to determine what ratios the firms used in their corporate objectives. Exhibit 11-5 lists the 10 ratios most likely to be included in corporate objectives according to the controllers. Nine of the ratios included in Exhibit 11-5 were also included in Exhibit 11-4. One ratio, accounts receivable turnover in days, appears in the top 10 ratios in relation to corporate objectives but not in the top 10 significant ratios. One ratio, the price/earnings ratio, appears in the top 10 ratios in relation to significance but not in the top 10 ratios used for corporate objectives.

Logically, there would be a high correlation between the ratios rated as highly significant and those included in corporate objectives. The debt/equity ratio and the current ratio are rated higher

EXHIBIT 11-4	**CORPORATE CONTROLLERS** Most Significant Ratios and Their Primary Measures

Ratio	Significance Rating	Primary Measure
Earnings per share	8.19	Profitability
Return on equity after tax	7.83	Profitability
Net profit margin after tax	7.47	Profitability
Debt/equity ratio	7.46	Debt
Net profit margin before tax	7.41	Profitability
Return on total invested capital after tax	7.20	Profitability
Return on assets after tax	6.97	Profitability
Dividend payout ratio	6.83	Other*
Price/earnings ratio	6.81	Other*
Current ratio	6.71	Liquidity

*Primary measure indicated to be other than liquidity, debt, or profitability. The ratios rated this way tend to be related to stock analysis.

EXHIBIT 11-5	**Ratios Appearing in Corporate Objectives and Their Primary Measures**

Ratio	Percentage of Firms Indicating That the Ratio Was Included in Corporate Objectives	Primary Measure
Earnings per share	80.6	Profitability
Debt/equity ratio	68.8	Debt
Return on equity after tax	68.5	Profitability
Current ratio	62.0	Liquidity
Net profit margin after tax	60.9	Profitability
Dividend payout ratio	54.3	Other
Return on total invested capital after tax	53.3	Profitability
Net profit margin before tax	52.2	Profitability
Accounts receivable turnover in days	47.3	Liquidity
Return on assets after tax	47.3	Profitability

on the objectives list than on the significance list. This makes sense since a firm has to have some balance in its objectives between liquidity, debt, and profitability.

FINANCIAL RATIOS AS PERCEIVED BY CERTIFIED PUBLIC ACCOUNTANTS

A research study performed in 1984 dealt with financial ratios as perceived by certified public accountants (CPAs).[3] A questionnaire was sent to one-third of the members of The Ohio Society of Certified Public Accountants who were registered as a partner in a CPA firm. A total of 495 questionnaires were sent and the usable response rate was 18.8%.

This questionnaire used the same ratios as were used for the commercial loan department and corporate controllers. The specific objectives of this study were to determine the following from the viewpoint of the CPA:

1. The specific financial ratios that CPAs view primarily as a measure of liquidity, debt, and profitability.
2. The relative importance of the financial ratios viewed as a measure of liquidity, debt, or profitability.

Exhibit 11-6 displays the 10 financial ratios given the highest significance rating by the CPAs and the primary measure of these ratios. The highest rating is a 9 and the lowest is a 0.

EXHIBIT 11-6	**CPAs** **Most Significant Ratios and Their Primary Measures**

Ratio	Significance Rating	Primary Measure
Current ratio	7.10	Liquidity
Accounts receivable turnover in days	6.94	Liquidity
After-tax return on equity	6.79	Profitability
Debt/equity ratio	6.78	Debt
Quick ratio (acid test)	6.77	Liquidity
Net profit margin after tax	6.67	Profitability
Net profit margin before tax	6.63	Profitability
Return on assets after tax	6.39	Profitability
Return on total invested capital after tax	6.30	Profitability
Inventory turnover in days	6.09	Liquidity

The CPAs gave the highest significance rating to two liquidity ratios—the current ratio and the accounts receivable turnover in days. The highest rated profitability ratio was after-tax return on equity, and the highest rated debt ratio was debt/equity.

FINANCIAL RATIOS AS PERCEIVED BY CHARTERED FINANCIAL ANALYSTS[4]

Exhibit 11-7 displays the 10 financial ratios given the highest significance rating by chartered financial analysts (CFAs) and the primary measure of these ratios. Again, the highest rating is a 9 and the lowest rating is a 0.

The surveyed CFAs gave the highest significance ratings to profitability ratios, with the exception of the price/earnings ratio. Return on equity after tax received the highest significance by a wide margin. Four of the next five most significant ratios were also profitability ratios—earnings per share, net profit margin after tax, return on equity before tax, and net profit margin before tax.

The price/earnings ratio—categorized by the analysts as an "other" measure—received the second highest significance rating. CFAs apparently view profitability and what is being paid for those profits before turning to liquidity and debt.

The two highest rated debt ratios were fixed charge coverage and times interest earned, rated seventh and tenth, respectively. Both of these ratios indicate a firm's ability to carry debt. The highest rated debt ratio relating to the balance sheet was the debt/equity ratio, rated as the eleventh most significant. Surprisingly, more significance was placed on debt ratios relating to the ability to carry debt than on those relating to the ability to meet debt obligations.

The highest rated liquidity ratio was the acid-test ratio, rated eighth. The second highest liquidity ratio was the current ratio, rated twentieth.[5]

FINANCIAL RATIOS USED IN ANNUAL REPORTS

Financial ratios are used to interpret and explain financial statements.[6] Used properly, they can be effective tools in evaluating a company's liquidity, debt position, and profitability. Probably no tool is as effective in evaluating where a company has been financially and projecting its financial future as the proper use of financial ratios.

A firm can use its annual report effectively to relate financial data by the use of financial ratios. To determine how effectively firms use ratios to communicate financial data, the annual reports of 100 firms identified in the *Fortune 500* industrial companies were reviewed. The 100 firms represented the first 20 of each 100 in the *Fortune 500* list. The objective of this research project was to determine (1) which financial ratios were frequently reported in annual reports, (2) where the ratios were disclosed in the annual reports, and (3) what computational methodology was used to compute these ratios.

| EXHIBIT 11-7 | **CHARTERED FINANCIAL ANALYSTS**
Most Significant Ratios and Their Primary Measures |

Ratio	Significance Rating	Primary Measure
Return on equity after tax	8.21	Profitability
Price/earnings ratio	7.65	*
Earnings per share	7.58	Profitability
Net profit margin after tax	7.52	Profitability
Return on equity before tax	7.41	Profitability
Net profit margin before tax	7.32	Profitability
Fixed charge coverage	7.22	Debt
Quick ratio (acid test)	7.10	Liquidity
Return on assets after tax	7.06	Profitability
Times interest earned	7.06	Debt

*Primary measure indicated to be other than liquidity, debt, or profitability. The ratios rated this way tend to be related to stock analysis.

Exhibit 11-8 indicates the ratios disclosed most frequently in the annual reports reviewed and the section of the annual report where the ratios were located. The locations were the president's letter, management discussion, management highlights, financial review, and financial summary. In many cases, the same ratio was located in several sections, so the numbers under the sections in Exhibit 11-8 do not add up to the total number of annual reports where the ratio was included.

Seven ratios appeared more than 50% of the time in one section or another. These ratios and the number of times found were earnings per share (100), dividends per share (98), book value per share (84), working capital (81), return on equity (62), profit margin (58), and effective tax rate (50). The current ratio was found 47 times, and the next ratio in order of disclosure, the debt/capital ratio, appeared 23 times. From this listing, we can conclude that profitability ratios and ratios related to investing were the most popular. Exhibit 11-8 excludes ratios not disclosed at least five times.

Logically, profitability ratios and ratios related to investing were the most popular for inclusion in the annual report. Including ratios related to investing in the annual report makes sense because one of the annual report's major objectives is to inform stockholders.

A review of the methodology used indicated that wide differences of opinion exist on how some of the ratios should be computed. This is especially true of the debt ratios. The two debt ratios most frequently disclosed were the debt/capital ratio and the debt/equity ratio. This book does not cover the debt/capital ratio. It is similar to the debt/equity ratio, except that the denominator includes sources of capital, in addition to stockholders' equity.

The annual reports disclosed the debt/capital ratio 23 times and used 11 different formulas. One firm used average balance sheet amounts between the beginning and the end of the year, while 22 firms used ending balance sheet figures. The debt/equity ratio was disclosed 19 times, and 6 different formulas were used. All firms used the ending balance sheet accounts to compute the debt/equity ratio.

In general, no major effort is being made to explain financial results by the disclosure of financial ratios in annual reports. Several financial ratios that could be interpreted as important were not disclosed or were disclosed very infrequently. This is particularly important for ratios that cannot be reasonably computed by outsiders because of a lack of data such as accounts receivable turnover.

At present, no regulatory agency such as the SEC or the FASB accepts responsibility for determining either the content of financial ratios or the format of presentation for annual reports, except

EXHIBIT 11-8	Ratios Disclosed Most Frequently in Annual Reports*					
	Number Included	President's Letter	Management Discussion	Management Highlights	Financial Review	Financial Summary
Earnings per share	100	66	5	98	45	93
Dividends per share	98	53	10	85	49	88
Book value per share	84	10	3	53	18	63
Working capital	81	1	1	50	23	67
Return on equity	62	28	3	21	23	37
Profit margin	58	10	3	21	23	35
Effective tax rate	50	2	1	2	46	6
Current ratio	47	3	1	16	12	34
Debt/capital	23	9	0	4	14	23
Return on capital	21	6	2	8	8	5
Debt/equity	19	5	0	3	8	8
Return on assets	13	4	1	2	5	10
Dividend payout	13	3	0	0	6	6
Gross profit	12	0	1	0	11	3
Pretax margin	10	2	0	3	6	6
Total asset turnover	7	1	0	0	4	4
Price/earnings ratio	7	0	0	0	1	6
Operating margin	7	1	0	2	6	1
Labor per hour	5	0	2	2	2	2

*Numbers represent both absolute numbers and percentages, since a review was made of the financial statements of 100 firms.

for the ratio earnings per share. Many practical and theoretical issues relate to the computation of financial ratios. As long as each firm can exercise its opinion as to the practical and theoretical issues, there will be a great divergence of opinion on how a particular ratio should be computed.

DEGREE OF CONSERVATISM AND QUALITY OF EARNINGS	A review of financial statements, including the footnotes, indicates their conservatism in regard to accounting policies. Accounting policies that result in the slowest reporting of income are the most conservative. When a firm has conservative accounting policies, it is said that its earnings are of high quality. This section reviews a number of areas that often indicate a firm's degree of conservatism in reporting income.

Inventory

Under inflationary conditions, the matching of current cost against the current revenue results in the lowest income for a period of time. The LIFO inventory method follows this procedure. FIFO, the least conservative method, uses the oldest costs and matches them against revenue. Other inventory methods fall somewhere between the results of LIFO and FIFO.

For a construction firm that has long-term contracts, the two principal accounting methods that relate to inventory are the completed-contract method and the percentage-of-completion method. The conservative completed-contract method recognizes all of the income when the contract is completed; the percentage-of-completion method recognizes income as work progresses on the contract.

Fixed Assets

Two accounting decisions related to fixed assets can have a significant influence on income: the method of depreciation and the period of time selected to depreciate an asset.

The conservative methods, sum-of-the-years'-digits and declining-balance, recognize a large amount of depreciation in the early years of the asset's life. The straight-line method, the least conservative method, recognizes depreciation in equal amounts over each year of the asset's life.

Sometimes a material difference in the asset's life used for depreciation occurs between firms. Comparing the lives used for depreciation for similar firms can be a clue as to how conservative the firms are in computing depreciation. The shorter the period of time used, the lower the income.

Intangible Assets

Intangible assets include goodwill, patents, and copyrights. Research and development (R&D) costs are a type of intangible asset, but they are expensed as incurred. The shorter the period of time used to recognize the cost of the intangible asset, the more conservative the accounting. (Goodwill is not amortized.)

Some firms spend very large sums on R&D, and others spend little or nothing. Because of the requirement that R&D costs be expensed in the period incurred, the income of a firm that does considerable research is reduced substantially in the period that the cost is incurred. This results in more conservative earnings.

Pensions

Two points relating to pensions should be examined when the firm has a defined benefit plan. One is the assumed discount rate used to compute the actuarial present value of the accumulated benefit obligation and the projected benefit obligation. The higher the interest rate used, the lower the present value of the liability and the lower the immediate pension cost. The other item is the rate of compensation increase used in computing the projected benefit obligations. If the rate is too low, the projected benefit obligation is too low. If the rate is too high, the projected benefit obligation is too high.

FORECASTING
FINANCIAL
FAILURE

There have been many academic studies on the use of financial ratios to forecast financial failure. Basically, these studies try to isolate individual ratios or combinations of ratios that can be observed as trends that may forecast failure.

A reliable model that can be used to forecast financial failure can also be used by management to take preventive measures. Such a model can aid investors in selecting and disposing of stocks. Banks can use it to aid in lending decisions and in monitoring loans. Firms can use it in making credit decisions and in monitoring accounts receivable. In general, many sources can use such a model to improve the allocation and control of resources. A model that forecasts financial failure can also be valuable to an auditor. It can aid in the determination of audit procedures and in making a decision as to whether the firm will remain as a going concern.

Financial failure can be described in many ways. It can mean liquidation, deferment of payments to short-term creditors, deferment of payments of interest on bonds, deferment of payments of principal on bonds, or the omission of a preferred dividend. One of the problems in examining the literature on forecasting financial failure is that different authors use different criteria to indicate failure. When reviewing the literature, always determine the criteria used to define financial failure.

This book reviews two of the studies that deal with predicting financial failure. Based on the number of references to these two studies in the literature, they appear to be particularly significant on the subject of forecasting financial failure.

Univariate Model

William Beaver reported his univariate model in a study published in *The Accounting Review* in October 1968.[7] A univariate model uses a single variable. Such a model would use individual financial ratios to forecast financial failure. The Beaver study classified a firm as failed when any one of the following events occurred in the 1954–1964 period: bankruptcy, bond default, an overdrawn bank account, or nonpayment of a preferred stock dividend.

Beaver paired 79 failed firms with a similar number of successful firms drawn from *Moody's Industrial Manuals*. For each failed firm in the sample, a successful one was selected from the same industry. The Beaver study indicated that the following ratios were the best for forecasting financial failure (in the order of their predictive power):

1. Cash flow/total debt
2. Net income/total assets (return on assets)
3. Total debt/total assets (debt ratio)

Beaver speculated as to the reason for these results:

My interpretation of the finding is that the cash flow, net income, and debt positions cannot be altered and represent permanent aspects of the firm. Because failure is too costly to all involved, the permanent, rather than the short-term, factors largely determine whether or not a firm will declare bankruptcy or default on a bond payment.[8]

Assuming that the ratios identified by Beaver are valid in forecasting financial failure, it would be wise to pay particular attention to trends in these ratios when following a firm. Beaver's reasoning for seeing these ratios as valid in forecasting financial failure appears to be very sound.

These three ratios for Nike for 2002 have been computed earlier. Cash flow/total debt was 41.53%, which appears to be very good. Net income/total assets (return on assets) was 10.90%, which appears to be good. The debt ratio was 40.42%, which is very good. Thus, Nike appears to have minimal risk of financial failure.

The Beaver study also computed the mean values of 13 financial statement items for each year before failure. Several important relationships were indicated among the liquid asset items.[9]

1. Failed firms have less cash but more accounts receivable.
2. When cash and receivables are added together, as they are in quick assets and current assets, the differences between failed and successful firms is obscured because the cash and receivables differences are working in opposite directions.
3. Failed firms tend to have less inventory.

These results indicate that particular attention should be paid to three current assets when forecasting financial failure: cash, accounts receivable, and inventory. The analyst should be alert for low cash and inventory and high accounts receivable.

Multivariate Model

Edward I. Altman developed a multivariate model to predict bankruptcy.[10] His model uses five financial ratios weighted in order to maximize the predictive power of the model. The model produces an overall discriminant score, called a **Z score**. The Altman model is as follows:

$$Z = .012\, X_1 + .014\, X_2 + .033\, X_3 + .006\, X_4 + .010\, X_5$$
$$X_1 = \text{Working Capital/Total Assets}$$

This computation is a measure of the net liquid assets of the firm relative to the total capitalization.

$$X_2 = \text{Retained Earnings (balance sheet)/Total Assets}$$

This variable measures cumulative profitability over time.

$$X_3 = \text{Earnings Before Interest and Taxes/Total Assets}$$

This variable measures the productivity of the firm's assets, abstracting any tax or leverage factors.

$$X_4 = \text{Market Value of Equity/Book Value of Total Debt}$$

This variable measures how much the firm's assets can decline in value before the liabilities exceed the assets and the firm becomes insolvent. Equity is measured by the combined market value of all shares of stock, preferred and common, while debt includes both current and long-term debts.

$$X_5 = \text{Sales/Total Assets}$$

This variable measures the sales-generating ability of the firm's assets.

When computing the Z score, the ratios are expressed in absolute percentage terms. Thus, X_1 (working capital/total assets) of 25% is noted as 25.

The Altman model was developed using manufacturing companies whose asset size was between $1 million and $25 million. The original sample by Altman and the test samples used the period 1946–1965. The model's accuracy in predicting bankruptcies in more recent years (1970–1973) was reported in a 1974 article.[11] Not all of the companies included in the test were manufacturing companies, although the model was initially developed by using only manufacturing companies.

With the Altman model, the lower the Z score, the more likely that the firm will go bankrupt. By computing the Z score for a firm over several years, it can be determined if the firm is moving toward a more likely or less likely position in regard to bankruptcy. In a later study that covered the period 1970–1973, a Z score of 2.675 was established as a practical cutoff point. Firms that scored below 2.675 are assumed to have characteristics similar to those of past failures.[12] Current GAAP recognizes more liabilities than the GAAP used at the time of this study. Thus, we would expect firms to score somewhat less than in the time period 1970–1973. The Altman model is substantially less significant if there is no firm market value for the stock (preferred and common), because variable X_4 in the model requires that the market value of the stock be determined.

The Z score for Nike for 2002 follows:

$$
\begin{aligned}
Z = \; & .012 \text{ (working capital/total assets)} \\
+ \; & .014 \text{ (retained earnings [balance sheet]/total assets)} \\
+ \; & .033 \text{ (earnings before interest and taxes/total assets)} \\
+ \; & .006 \text{ (market value of equity/book value of total debt)} \\
+ \; & .010 \text{ (sales/total assets)}
\end{aligned}
$$

$$Z = .012\ (\$4{,}157.7 - \$1{,}836.2)$$
$$Z = .012\ ([\$4{,}157{,}700{,}000 - \$1{,}836{,}200{,}000]/\$6{,}443{,}000{,}000)$$
$$+ .014\ (\$3{,}495{,}000{,}000/\$6{,}443{,}000{,}000)$$
$$+ .033\ ([\$1{,}017{,}300{,}000 + \$47{,}600{,}000])/\$6{,}443{,}000{,}000)$$
$$+ .006\ ([\$266{,}000{,}000 \times \$53.75]/\$2{,}604{,}000{,}000)$$
$$+ .010\ (\$9{,}893{,}000{,}000/\$6{,}443{,}000{,}000)$$
$$Z = .012\ (36.03)$$
$$+ .014\ (54.24)$$
$$+ .033\ (16.53)$$
$$+ .006\ (549.06)$$
$$+ .010\ (153.55)$$
$$Z = .43 + .76 + .55 + 3.29 + 1.54$$
$$Z = 6.57$$

The Z score for Nike for 2002 was 6.57. Considering that higher scores are better and that companies with scores below 2.675 are assumed to have characteristics similar to those of past failures, Nike is a very healthy company.

There are many academic studies on the use of ratios to forecast financial failure. These studies help substantiate that firms with weak ratios are more likely to go bankrupt than firms with strong ratios. Since no conclusive model has yet been developed, the best approach is probably an integrated one. As a supplemental measure, it may also be helpful to compute some of the ratios that appear useful in forecasting financial failure.

ANALYTICAL REVIEW PROCEDURES

Statement of Auditing Standards No. 23, "Analytical Review Procedures," provides guidance for the use of such procedures in audits. The objective of analytical review procedures is to isolate significant fluctuations and unusual items in operating statistics.

Analytical review procedures may be performed at various times, including the planning stage, during the audit itself, and near the completion of the audit. Some examples of analytical review procedures that may lead to special audit procedures follow.

1. Horizontal common-size analysis of the income statement may indicate that an item, such as selling expenses, is abnormally high for the period. This could lead to a close examination of the selling expenses.
2. Vertical common-size analysis of the income statement may indicate that cost of goods sold is out of line in relation to sales, in comparison with prior periods.
3. A comparison of accounts receivable turnover with the industry data may indicate that receivables are turning over much slower than is typical for the industry. This may indicate that receivables should be analyzed closely.
4. Cash flow in relation to debt may have declined significantly, indicating a materially reduced ability to cover debt from internal cash flow.
5. The acid-test ratio may have declined significantly, indicating a materially reduced ability to pay current liabilities with current assets less inventories.

When the auditor spots a significant trend in a statement or ratio, follow-up procedures should be performed to determine the reason. Such an investigation can lead to significant findings.

MANAGEMENT'S USE OF ANALYSIS

Management can use financial ratios and common-size analysis as aids in many ways. Analysis can indicate the relative liquidity, debt, and profitability of a firm. Analysis can also indicate how investors perceive the firm and can help detect emerging problems and strengths in a firm. As indicated previously, financial ratios can also be used as part of the firm's corporate objectives. Using financial ratios in conjunction with the budgeting process can be particularly helpful. An objective of the budgeting process is the determination of the firm's game plan. The budget can consist of an overall comprehensive budget and many separate budgets, such as a production budget.

The comprehensive budget relating to financial statements indicates how a firm plans to get from one financial position (balance sheet) to another. The income statement details how the firm changed internally from one balance sheet position to another in terms of revenue and expenses. The statement of cash flows indicates how the firm's cash changed from one balance sheet to another.

A proposed comprehensive budget should be compared with financial ratios that have been agreed upon as part of the firm's corporate objectives. For example, if corporate objectives include a current ratio of 2:1, a debt equity of 40%, and a return on equity of 15%, then the proposed comprehensive budget should be compared with these corporate objectives before accepting the budget as the firm's overall game plan. If the proposed comprehensive budget will not result in the firm achieving its objectives, management should attempt to change the game plan in order to achieve its objectives. If management cannot change the proposed comprehensive budget satisfactorily to achieve the corporate objectives, they should know this when the comprehensive budget is accepted.

USE OF LIFO RESERVES

A firm that uses LIFO usually discloses a LIFO reserve account in a footnote or on the face of the balance sheet. If a LIFO reserve account is not disclosed, there is usually some indication of an amount that approximates current cost. Nike did not have the LIFO reserve for its 1999 financial statement. Therefore, the Union Carbide Corporation was selected to illustrate LIFO reserve analysis.

In its 1998 annual report, Union Carbide disclosed in a footnote that "It is estimated that if inventories had been valued at current costs they would have been approximately $224 million and $348 million higher than reported at December 31, 1998 and 1997, respectively."

This information can be used to improve the analysis of inventory and (in general) the analysis of liquidity, debt, and profitability. Supplemental analysis using this additional inventory information can be particularly significant when there is a substantial LIFO reserve and/or a substantial change in the reserve.

For Union Carbide, an approximation of the increase or decrease in income if inventory is at approximate current costs could be computed by comparing the change in inventory, net of any tax effect. For 1998, compute the approximation of the income if the inventory were at approximate current costs as follows:

1998 net income		$403,000,000
Net decrease in inventory reserve:		
1998	$224,000,000	
1997	348,000,000	
(a)	$124,000,000	
(b) Effective tax rate	31.5%	
(c) Change in taxes [a × b] =	$39,060,000	
(d) Net decrease in income [a – c] ($124,000,000 – $39,060,000)		84,940,000
Approximate income for 1998 if inventory had been		
valued at approximate current cost for 1998 and 1997		$318,060,000

This type of computation can be made for each year. The approximate new income figures can then be considered and reviewed over a series of years to obtain an idea of what net income would have been if inventory had been computed using a method that approximated inventory costs closer to current costs. Some analysts would consider this adjusted income amount to be more realistic than the unadjusted amount.

Specific liquidity and debt ratios can be recomputed, taking into consideration the adjusted inventory figure. To make these computations, add the gross inventory reserve to the inventory disclosed in current assets. Add the approximate additional taxes to the current liabilities.

Estimate the additional tax figure by multiplying the gross LIFO reserve by the effective tax rate. This tax figure relates to the additional income that would have been reported in the current year and all prior years if the higher inventory amounts had been reported. The additional tax amount is a deferred tax amount that is added to current liabilities, to be conservative. The difference between the additional inventory amount and the additional tax amount is added to retained earnings because it represents the total prior influence on net income. The adjusted figures for Union Carbide at the end of 1998 follow.

Inventory:	
As disclosed on the balance sheet	$ 667,000,000
Increase in inventory	224,000,000
	$ 891,000,000
Deferred current tax liability:	
Effective tax rate (31.5%) × increase in inventory	
($224,000,000)	$ 70,560,000
Retained earnings:	
As disclosed on the balance sheet	$3,357,000,000
Increase in retained earnings	
($224,000,000 − $70,560,000)	153,440,000
	$3,510,440,000

An adjusted cost of goods sold can also be estimated, using the change in the inventory reserve. A net increase in the inventory reserve would reduce the cost of goods sold. A net decrease in inventory reserve would increase the cost of goods sold.

Union Carbide reported cost of goods sold of $4,294,000,000 and a decrease in inventory reserve of $124,000,000 in 1998. The decrease in inventory reserve is added to the cost of goods sold, resulting in an adjusted cost of goods sold of $4,418,000,000. The adjusted cost of goods sold could be used when computing several ratios, such as days' sales in inventory. This refinement of the cost of goods sold usually has an immaterial influence on the ratios because the change in inventory reserve is usually immaterial in relation to the cost of goods sold figure. Therefore, this refinement to the cost of goods sold is not used in the illustrations and problems in this book.

Exhibit 11-9 displays selected liquidity, debt, and profitability ratios for Union Carbide, comparing the adjusted ratio with the prior computation. For some of these ratios, there is a material

---

EXHIBIT 11-9

UNION CARBIDE
Selected Liquidity, Debt, and Profitability Considering
LIFO Disclosure for the Year Ended December 31, 1998

	1998 Considering LIFO Disclosure	1998 Normal Computations
Liquidity:		
Days' sales in inventory	73.61 days	56.70 days
Inventory turnover	4.79 times per year	6.76 times per year
Inventory turnover in days	76.13 days	54.02 days
Operating cycle	129.08 days	106.97 days
Working capital	$589,440,000	$436,000,000
Current ratio	1.38	1.30
Acid-test ratio	.64	.67
Cash ratio	.032	.033
Debt:		
Debt ratio	65.37%	66.41%
Debt/equity	188.77%	197.71%
Times interest earned*	5.96	7.04
Profitability:		
Net profit margin	6.84%	8.34%
Total asset turnover	.76 times per year	.79 times per year
Return on assets	4.33%	5.70%
Return on total equity	12.24%	16.80%

*Capitalized interest not determined. Capitalized interest would lower the coverage.

difference. The ratios that relate to inventory are not as favorable when considering the LIFO disclosure as when not considering the LIFO disclosure. Working capital is more favorable, and the current ratio is more favorable. The acid-test and cash ratios are less favorable. The balance sheet-related debt ratios (debt ratio and debt/equity) are slightly more favorable when considering the LIFO disclosure. The income statement-related debt ratio of times interest earned is less favorable. The profitability ratios are less favorable when considering the LIFO disclosure.

The adjusted liquidity, debt, and profitability ratios could possibly be considered to be more realistic than the prior computations because of the use of a realistic inventory amount. For many of the ratios, we cannot generalize about whether the ratio will improve or decline when the LIFO reserve is used. For example, if the current ratio is above 2.00, then it may not improve when the LIFO reserve is considered, especially if the firm has a high tax rate. When the current ratio is low and/or the tax rate is low, then the current ratio will likely improve.

GRAPHING FINANCIAL INFORMATION

It has become very popular to use graphs in annual reports to present financial information. Graphs make it easier to grasp key financial information. Graphs can be a better communicative device than a written report or a tabular presentation because they communicate by means of pictures and, thus, create more immediate mental images.

There are many forms of graphs. Some popular forms used by accountants are line, column, and pie graphs. These forms will be briefly described here, but a detailed description of these and other forms can be found in reference books and articles.[13]

The **line graph** uses a set of points connected by a line to show change over time. It is important for the vertical axis to start at zero and that it not be broken. Not starting the vertical axis at zero and/or breaking the vertical axis can result in a very misleading presentation. Exhibit 11-10 illustrates a line graph.

A **column graph** has vertical columns. As in a line graph, it is important that the vertical axis start at zero and that it not be broken. A column graph is often the best form of graph for presenting accounting data. Exhibit 11-11 presents a column graph.

A **pie graph** is divided into segments. This type of graph makes a comparison of the segments, which must add up to a total or to 100%. A pie graph can mislead if it creates an optical illusion. Also, some accounting data do not fit on a pie graph. Exhibit 11-12 illustrates a pie graph.

MANAGEMENT OF EARNINGS

In Chapter 1 the cash basis is described as recognizing revenue when cash is received and recognizing expenses when cash is paid. It was indicated that the cash basis usually does not provide rea-

---

EXHIBIT 11-10   **GENTEX CORPORATION**
Line Graph
2001 Annual Report

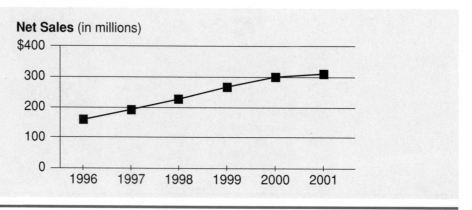

Source: Gentex Corporation, Zealand, MI.

| EXHIBIT 11-11 | **SMITH INTERNATIONAL, INC.**
Column Graph
2001 Annual Report |

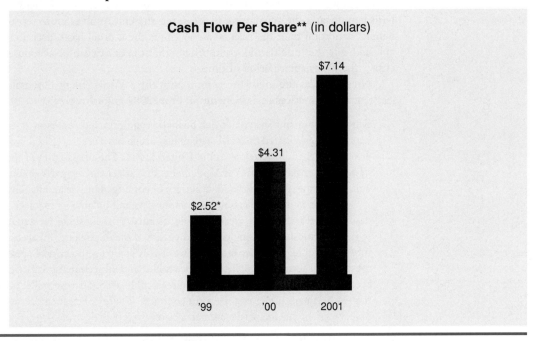

*Excludes impact of non-recurring items recorded in 1999.
**Cash flow per share consists of earnings before interest, taxes, depreciation and amortization earned by the company after reduction for minority interests.

| EXHIBIT 11-12 | **JLG INDUSTRIES, INC.**
Pie Graph
2001 Annual Report |

Geographic Mix
(as % of total sales)

□ United States—**74%**

▨ Europe—**19%**

■ Other International—**7%**

sonable information about the earning capability of the entity in the short run. Because of the short-comings of the cash basis, the accrual basis has been adopted for income reporting for most firms.

With the accrual basis, revenue is recognized when realized (realization concept), and expenses are recognized when incurred (matching concept). As indicated in Chapter 1, the use of the accrual basis complicates the accounting process, but the end result is more representative of an entity's financial condition than the cash basis. Without the accrual basis, accountants would not usually be able to make the time period assumption—that the entity can be accounted for with reasonable accuracy for a particular period of time.

Nike includes the following comment in their Management Discussion and Analysis of Financial Condition and Results of Operation in its 2002 annual report.

> Our discussion and analysis of our financial condition and results of operations following are based upon our consolidated financial statements, which have been prepared in accordance with accounting principles generally accepted in the United States. The preparation of these financial statements requires us to make estimates and judgments that affect the reported amounts of assets, liabilities, revenues and expenses, and related disclosure of contingent assets and liabilities.
>
> We believe that the estimates, assumptions and judgments involved on the accounting policies described below have the greatest potential impact on our financial statements, so we consider these to be our critical accounting policies. Because of the uncertainty inherent in these matters, actual results could differ from the estimates we use in applying the critical accounting policies. Certain of these critical accounting policies affect working capital accounting balances, including the policies for revenue recognition, the reserve for uncollectible accounts receivable, inventory reserves, and contingent payments under endorsement contracts. These policies require that we make estimates in the preparation of our financial statements as of given date.

Thus, Nike describes the proper use of estimates and judgments to prepare their financial statements under generally accepted accounting principles.

Some firms have used estimates and judgments to improperly manipulate their financial statements. Other firms have deliberately made errors to manipulate their financial statements. This results in financial statements that are not a proper representation of financial condition and results of operations. This became a substantial problem during the 1990s. The chairman of the Securities and Exchange Commission, Arthur Levitt, had this to say as part of his address entitled the "Numbers Game," at the New York University Center for Law and Business on September 28, 1998:

> Increasingly, I have become concerned that the motivation to meet Wall Street earnings expectations may be overriding common sense business practices. Too many corporate managers, auditors, and analysts are participants in a game of nods and winks. In the zeal to satisfy consensus earnings estimates and project a smooth earnings path, wishful thinking may be winning the day over faithful representation.
>
> As a result, I fear that we are witnessing an erosion in the quality of earnings, and therefore, the quality of financial reporting. Managing may be giving way to manipulations; integrity may be losing out to illusion.
>
> Many in corporate America are just as frustrated and concerned about this trend as we, at the SEC, are. They know how difficult it is to hold the line on good practices when their competitors operate in the gray area between legitimary and outright fraud.
>
> A gray area where the Accounting is being perverted; where managers are cutting corners; and, where earnings reports reflect the desires of management rather than the underlying financial performance of the company.[14]

Thus, there was concern of the chairman of the Securities and Exchange Commission and the financial community as to the apparent increase in the inappropriate management of earnings during the 1990s. We can speculate on why there was an increase in the improper management of earnings during the 1990s. Some of the reasons likely were (1) conviction that the capital markets would pay more for a stock that represented smooth earnings rather than peaks and valleys of earnings, (2) increase in the awarding of stock options as a means of compensation as opposed to cash, (3) substantial negative market reaction when a company would not meet its numbers, and (4) possibly an all-time high in greed.

The general public did not appear to be overly concerned with the increase in the improper management of earnings until the Enron situation developed in 2001. A possible reason for this was the substantial increase in stock prices during the 1990s. Starting in 2000, stock prices had substantial declines. These declines in stock prices likely influenced the general public to be concerned about the improper management of earnings.

There are many ways to improperly manage earnings. We don't know of all the possibilities. The ways that we do know would require a separate book to describe. We do know that revenue recognition is often involved in the manipulation of financial reports. The General Accounting Office, Congress's investigative arm, reported in an October 2002 report to the Senate Banking Committee that earnings restatements cost investors $100 billion in the prior five years. Earnings restatements rose by about 145% from 1997 through June 2002. Revenue-recognition issues arose in 38% of the cases studied.[15]

Revenue-recognition often also involves inventory, accounts receivable, and cash flow. For example, early recognition of revenue could involve moving inventory from the balance sheet to cost of goods sold on the income statement, the booking of accounts receivable, and lack of cash flow. An understanding of financial reporting and analysis would help in detecting the problem.

Enron and WorldCom substantially influenced financial reporting in the United States. These cases crystallized views of the U.S. House and Senate that resulted in the Sarbanes-Oxley Act of 2002. Hopefully, the Sarbanes-Oxley Act leads to constructive improvement in financial reporting.

Enron was one of the largest corporations in the world. It announced in October 2001 that it was reducing after-tax net income by approximately $500 million and shareholders' equity by $1.2 billion. In November it announced that it was restating reported net income for the years 1997–2000. In December 2001 Enron filed for bankruptcy.

There were many financial reporting issues in the Enron situation. Many of these issues were poorly disclosed or not disclosed. Some of the issues were accounting for investments in subsidiaries and special-purpose entities, sales of investments to special-purpose entities, revenue for fees, and fair value of investments.[16] The Enron financial statements, including the footnotes, were complicated and difficult to comprehend. The lesson here is if a reasonable understanding of financial reporting and analysis is not adequate to understand the financial report, then consider this when investing.

WorldCom announced in June 2002 that it had inflated profits by $3.8 billion over the previous five quarters. This was the largest corporate accounting fraud in history. Soon after this announcement, WorldCom declared bankruptcy.[17] In November 2002 a special bankruptcy court examiner reported that the improper accounting would exceed $7.2 billion.[18]

The WorldCom fraud was uncovered by three accountants working in the internal auditing department. Their findings were communicated to the audit committee of the board, and later the entire board was informed. The internal discovery and reporting of the fraud represents a positive aspect of the WorldCom fraud.[19]

The WorldCom problem apparently started in 2000 when business declined. Initially WorldCom moved funds from reserve accounts to hold up profits. When this was no longer sufficient, they then turned to shifting operating costs to capital accounts. Shifting operating costs (expenses on the income statement) to capital accounts (assets on the balance sheet) would make the company look more profitable in the short run. As capital expenditures, these costs would be depreciated in subsequent years. Apparently, WorldCom had planned a write-down. This would remove these accounts from the balance sheet. Hopefully Wall Street would overlook the write-down when looking to the future.[20]

Although the WorldCom fraud was discovered by internal auditors, the Securities and Exchange Commission sent a "Request for Information" to WorldCom on March 7, 2002. The Securities and Exchange Commission apparently thought that the WorldCom profit figures were suspicious, considering that WorldCom's closest competitors, including AT&T Corp., were losing money throughout 2001. A lesson from WorldCom is that if the numbers look too good, that may be because they *are* too good.[21]

SUMMARY

This chapter reviewed special areas related to financial statements. It was noted that commercial loan departments give a high significance rating to selected ratios that primarily measure liquidity or debt. The debt/equity ratio received the highest significance rating, and the current ratio was the second highest rated by the commercial loan officers. A commercial bank may elect to include a ratio as part of a loan agreement. The two ratios most likely to be included in a loan agreement are the debt/equity and the current ratio.

Financial executives give the profitability ratios the highest significance ratings. They rate earnings per share and return on investment the highest. Many firms have selected key financial ratios, such as profitability ratios, to be included as part of their corporate objectives.

Certified public accountants give the highest significance rating to two liquidity ratios: the current ratio and the accounts receivable turnover in days. The highest rated profitability ratio was the after-tax net profit margin, while the highest rated debt ratio was debt/equity.

A firm could use its annual report to relate financial data effectively by the use of financial ratios. In general, no major effort is being made to explain financial results by the disclosure of financial ratios in annual reports. A review of the methodology used to compute the ratios disclosed in annual reports indicated that wide differences of opinion exist on how many of the ratios should be computed.

A review of the financial statements, including the footnotes, indicates the conservatism of the statements in terms of accounting policies. When a firm has conservative accounting policies, it is said that its earnings are of high quality.

There have been many academic studies on the use of financial ratios to forecast financial failure. No conclusive model has yet been developed to forecast financial failure.

Auditors use financial analysis as part of their analytical review procedures. By using financial analysis, they can detect significant fluctuations and unusual items in operating statistics. This can result in a more efficient and effective audit.

Management can use financial analysis in many ways to manage a firm more effectively. A particularly effective use of financial analysis is to integrate ratios that have been accepted as corporate objectives into comprehensive budgeting.

It has become very popular to use graphs in annual reports to present financial information. Graphs make it easier to grasp key financial information. Graphs can communicate better than a written report or a tabular presentation.

The improper management of earnings has become a very hot topic. Hopefully this improper manipulation of earnings is under control.

To the Net

1. Go to the Cooper Tire & Rubber Company site (http://www.coopertires.com). Determine:
   a.

	December 31	
	2001	**2000**
The inventory reserve at December 31.		

   b. 2001 effective tax rate.
   c. 2001 net income.
   d. The approximate income for 2001 if inventory had been valued at approximate current cost.

2. Go to the Albertsons Inc. site (http://www.albertsons.com).
   a. What was the net earnings for the 52 weeks ending January 31, 2002?
   b. During 2001 and 2000 inventory quantities were reduced. These reductions resulted in a liquidation of LIFO inventory quantities carried at lower costs prevailing in price years as compared with the cost of 2001 and 2000 purchases. This increased net earnings in 2001 by what amount?

Questions

Q 11-1.   Commercial loan officers regard profitability financial ratios as very significant. Comment.

Q 11-2.   Which two financial ratios do commercial loan officers regard as the most significant? Which two financial ratios appear most frequently in loan agreements?

Q 11-3.   The commercial loan officers did not list the dividend payout ratio as a highly significant ratio, but they indicated that the dividend payout ratio was a ratio that appeared frequently in loan agreements. Speculate on the reason for this apparent inconsistency.

Q 11-4.   Corporate controllers regard profitability financial ratios as very significant. Comment.

Q 11-5.   List the top five financial ratios included in corporate objectives according to the study reviewed in this book. Indicate what each of these ratios primarily measures.

Q 11-6.   CPAs regard which two financial ratios as the most significant? The highest rated profitability ratio? The highest debt ratio?

Q 11-7.   Financial ratios are used extensively in annual reports to interpret and explain financial statements. Comment.

Q 11-8.   List the sections of annual reports where ratios are most frequently located, in order of use.

Q 11-9.   According to a study of annual reports reviewed in this chapter, what type or types of financial ratios are most likely to be included in annual reports? Speculate on the probable reason for these ratios appearing in annual reports.

Q 11-10.   The study of annual reports reviewed in this chapter showed that earnings per share was disclosed in every annual report. Why?

Q 11-11.   The study of annual reports reviewed in this chapter indicated that wide differences of opinion exist on how many ratios should be computed. Comment.

Q 11-12.   What type of accounting policies are described as conservative?

Q 11-13.   Indicate which of the following accounting policies are conservative by placing an *X* under *Yes* or *No*. Assume inflationary conditions exist.

	Conservative	
	Yes	**No**
a. LIFO inventory	———	———
b. FIFO inventory	———	———
c. Completed-contract method	———	———
d. Percentage-of-completion method	———	———
e. Accelerated depreciation method	———	———
f. Straight-line depreciation method	———	———
g. A relatively short estimated life for a fixed asset	———	———
h. Short period for expensing intangibles	———	———
i. Amortization of patent over 5 years	———	———
j. High interest rate used to compute the present value of accumulated benefit obligation	———	———
k. High rate of compensation increase used in computing the projected benefit obligation	———	———

Q 11-14.   All firms are required to expense R&D costs incurred each period. Some firms spend very large sums on R&D, while others spend little or nothing on this area. Why is it important to observe whether a firm has substantial or immaterial R&D expenses?

Q 11-15.   Indicate some possible uses of a reliable model that can be used to forecast financial failure.

Q 11-16.   Describe what is meant by a firm's *financial failure*.

Q 11-17.   According to the Beaver study, which ratios should be watched most closely, in order of their predictive power?

Q 11-18.   According to the Beaver study, three current asset accounts should be paid particular attention in order to forecast financial failure. List each of these accounts and indicate whether they should be abnormally high or low.

Q 11-19.   What does a Z score below 2.675 indicate, according to the Altman model?

Q 11-20.   Indicate a practical problem with computing a Z score for a closely held firm.

Q 11-21.   No conclusive model has been developed to forecast financial failure. This indicates that financial ratios are not helpful in forecasting financial failure. Comment.

Q 11-22.   You are the auditor of Piedmore Corporation. You determine that the accounts receivable turnover has been much slower this period than in prior periods and that it is also materially lower than the industry average. How might this situation affect your audit plan?

Q 11-23.   You are in charge of preparing a comprehensive budget for your firm. Indicate how financial ratios can help determine an acceptable, comprehensive budget.

Q 11-24.   List three popular forms of graphs used by accountants.

Q 11-25.   List two things that can make a line graph misleading.

Q 11-26.   Indicate two possible problems with a pie graph for accounting data.

Q 11-27.   The surveyed CFAs gave the highest significance rating to which type of financial ratio?

Q 11-28.   CFAs gave liquidity ratios a high significance rating. Comment.

Q 11-29   Describe a proper management of earnings. Describe an improper management of earnings.

Problems

P 11-1.
Required   Answer the following multiple-choice questions.
   a.   Footnotes to financial statements are beneficial in meeting the disclosure requirements of financial reporting. The footnotes should not be used to
       1.   Describe significant accounting policies.
       2.   Describe depreciation methods employed by the company.
       3.   Describe principles and methods peculiar to the industry in which the company operates when these principles and methods are predominately followed in that industry.
       4.   Disclose the basis of consolidation for consolidated statements.
       5.   Correct an improper presentation in the financial statements.
   b.   Which one of the following would be a source of funds under a cash concept of funds, but would not be listed as a source under the working capital concept?
       1.   Sale of stock
       2.   Sale of machinery
       3.   Sale of treasury stock
       4.   Collection of accounts receivable
       5.   Proceeds from long-term bank borrowing
   c.   The concept of conservatism is often considered important in accounting. The application of this concept means that in the event some doubt occurs as to how a transaction should be recorded, it should be recorded so as to
       1.   Understate income and overstate assets.
       2.   Overstate income and overstate assets.
       3.   Understate income and understate assets.
       4.   Overstate income and understate assets.
       5.   Overstate cash and overstate assets.
   d.   Early in a period in which sales were increasing at a modest rate and plant expansion and start-up costs were occurring at a rapid rate, a successful business would likely experience
       1.   Increased profits and increased financing requirements because of an increasing cash shortage.
       2.   Increased profits and decreased financing requirements because of an increasing cash surplus.
       3.   Increased profits and no change in financing requirements.
       4.   Decreased profits and increased financing requirements because of an increasing cash shortage.
       5.   Decreased profits and decreased financing requirements because of an increasing cash surplus.
   e.   Which of the following ratios would best disclose effective management of working capital by a given firm relative to other firms in the same industry?
       1.   A high rate of financial leverage relative to the industry average
       2.   A high number of days' sales uncollected relative to the industry average
       3.   A high turnover of net working capital relative to the industry average
       4.   A high number of days' sales in inventory relative to the industry average
       5.   A high proportion of fixed assets relative to the industry average
   f.   Stock options are frequently provided to officers of companies. Exercised stock options would
       1.   Improve the debt/equity ratio.
       2.   Improve earnings per share.

3.   Improve the ownership interest of existing stockholders.
4.   Improve the total asset turnover.
5.   Improve the net profit margin.

P 11-2.
Required   Answer the following multiple-choice questions.
a.   If business conditions are stable, a decline in the number of days' sales outstanding from one year to the next (based on a company's accounts receivable at year-end) might indicate
1.   A stiffening of the company's credit policies.
2.   That the second year's sales were made at lower prices than the first year's sales.
3.   That a longer discount period and a more distant due date were extended to customers in the second year.
4.   A significant decrease in the volume of sales of the second year.
b.   Trading on the equity (financial leverage) is likely to be a good financial strategy for stockholders of companies having
1.   Cyclical high and low amounts of reported earnings.
2.   Steady amounts of reported earnings.
3.   Volatile fluctuation in reported earnings over short periods of time.
4.   Steadily declining amounts of reported earnings.
c.   The ratio of total cash, trade receivables, and marketable securities to current liabilities is
1.   The acid-test ratio.
2.   The current ratio.
3.   Significant if the result is 2-to-1 or below.
4.   Meaningless.
d.   The times interest earned ratio is a primary measure of
1.   Liquidity.
2.   Long-term debt-paying ability.
3.   Activity.
4.   Profitability.
e.   The calculation of the number of times bond interest is earned involves dividing
1.   Net income by annual bond interest expense.
2.   Net income plus income taxes by annual bond interest expense.
3.   Net income plus income taxes and bond interest expense by annual bond interest expense.
4.   Sinking fund earnings by annual bond interest expense.

P 11-3.   The Thorpe Company is a wholesale distributor of professional equipment and supplies. The company's sales have averaged about $900,000 annually for the three-year period 2002–2004. The firm's total assets at the end of 2004 amounted to $850,000.

The president of the Thorpe Company has asked the controller to prepare a report that summarizes the financial aspects of the company's operations for the past three years. This report will be presented to the board of directors at its next meeting.

In addition to comparative financial statements, the controller has decided to present a number of relevant financial ratios that can assist in the identification and interpretation of trends. At the request of the controller, the accounting staff has calculated the following ratios for the three-year period 2002–2004:

Ratio	2002	2003	2004
Current ratio	2.00	2.13	2.18
Acid-test (quick) ratio	1.20	1.10	0.97
Accounts receivable turnover	9.72	8.57	7.13
Inventory turnover	5.25	4.80	3.80
Percent of total debt to total assets	44.00%	41.00%	38.00%
Percent of long-term debt to total assets	25.00%	22.00%	19.00%
Sales to fixed assets (fixed asset turnover)	1.75	1.88	1.99
Sales as a percent of 2002 sales	100.00%	103.00%	106.00%
Gross profit percentage	40.0%	33.6%	38.5%
Net income to sales	7.8%	7.8%	8.0%
Return on total assets	8.5%	8.6%	8.7%
Return on stockholders' equity	15.1%	14.6%	14.1%

In preparing his report, the controller has decided first to examine the financial ratios independently of any other data to determine if the ratios themselves reveal any significant trends over the first three-year period.

Required   a. The current ratio is increasing, while the acid-test (quick) ratio is decreasing. Using the ratios provided, identify and explain the contributing factor(s) for this apparently divergent trend.

b. In terms of the ratios provided, what conclusion(s) can be drawn regarding the company's use of financial leverage during the 2002–2004 period?

c. Using the ratios provided, what conclusion(s) can be drawn regarding the company's net investment in plant and equipment?

CMA Adapted

P 11-4.   L. Konrath Company is considering extending credit to D. Hawk Company. L. Konrath estimated that sales to D. Hawk Company would amount to $2,000,000 each year. L. Konrath Company, a wholesaler, sells throughout the Midwest. D. Hawk Company, a retail chain operation, has a number of stores in the Midwest. L. Konrath Company has had a gross profit of approximately 60% in recent years and expects to have a similar gross profit on the D. Hawk Company order. The D. Hawk Company order is approximately 15% of L. Konrath Company's present sales. Data from recent statements of D. Hawk Company follow.

(in millions)	2002	2003	2004
Assets			
Current assets:			
Cash	$ 2.6	$ 1.8	$ 1.6
Government securities (cost)	.4	.2	—
Accounts and notes receivable (net)	8.0	8.5	8.5
Inventories	2.8	3.2	2.8
Prepaid assets	.7	.6	.6
Total current assets	14.5	14.3	13.5
Property, plant, and equipment (net)	4.3	5.4	5.9
Total assets	$18.8	$19.7	$19.4
Liabilities and Equities			
Current liabilities	$ 6.9	$ 8.5	$ 9.3
Long-term debt, 6%	3.0	2.0	1.0
Total liabilities	9.9	10.5	10.3
Shareholders' equity	8.9	9.2	9.1
Total liabilities and equities	$18.8	$19.7	$19.4
Income			
Net sales	$24.2	$24.5	$24.9
Cost of goods sold	16.9	17.2	18.0
Gross margin	7.3	7.3	6.9
Selling and administrative expenses	6.6	6.8	7.3
Earnings (loss) before taxes	.7	.5	(.4)
Income taxes	.3	.2	(.2)
Net income	$ .4	$ .3	$ (.2)

Required   a. Calculate the following for D. Hawk Company for 2004:
1. Rate of return on total assets
2. Acid-test ratio
3. Return on sales
4. Current ratio
5. Inventory turnover

b. As part of the analysis to determine whether L. Konrath should extend credit to D. Hawk, assume the ratios were calculated from D. Hawk Company statements. For each ratio, indicate whether it is a favorable, unfavorable, or neutral statistic in the decision to grant D. Hawk credit. Briefly explain your choice in each case.

Ratio	2002	2003	2004
Rate of return on total assets	1.96%	1.12%	(.87)%
Return on sales	1.69%	.99%	(.69)%
Acid-test ratio	1.73	1.36	1.19
Current ratio	2.39	1.92	1.67
Inventory turnover (times per year)	4.41	4.32	4.52

Equity relationships:			
Current liabilities	36.0%	43.0%	48.0%
Long-term liabilities	16.0	10.5	5.0
Shareholders' equity	48.0	46.5	47.0
	100.0%	100.0%	100.0%
Asset relationships:			
Current assets	77.0%	72.5%	69.5%
Property, plant, and equipment	23.0	27.5	30.5
	100.0%	100.0%	100.0%

c. Would you grant credit to D. Hawk Company? Support your answer with facts given in the problem.

d. What additional information, if any, would you want before making a final decision?

CMA Adapted

P 11-5. Your company is considering the possible acquisition of Growth Inc. Financial statements of Growth Inc. follow.

GROWTH INC.
Balance Sheet
December 31, 2004 and 2003

	2004	2003
Assets		
Current assets:		
Cash	$ 64,346	$ 11,964
Accounts receivable, less allowance		
of $750 for doubtful accounts	99,021	83,575
Inventories, FIFO	63,414	74,890
Prepaid expenses	834	1,170
Total current assets	227,615	171,599
Investments and other assets	379	175
Property, plant, and equipment:		
Land and land improvements	6,990	6,400
Buildings	63,280	59,259
Machinery and equipment	182,000	156,000
	252,270	221,659
Less: Accumulated depreciation	110,000	98,000
Net property, plant, and equipment	142,270	123,659
Total assets	$370,264	$295,433
Liabilities and Stockholders' Equity		
Current liabilities:		
Accounts payable	$ 32,730	$ 26,850
Federal income taxes	5,300	4,800
Accrued liabilities	30,200	24,500
Current portion of long-term debt	5,500	5,500
Total current liabilities	73,730	61,650
Long-term debt	76,750	41,900
Other long-term liabilities	5,700	4,300
Deferred federal income taxes	16,000	12,000
Total liabilities	172,180	119,850
Stockholders' equity:		
Capital stock	44,000	43,500
Retained earnings	154,084	132,083
Total stockholders' equity	198,084	175,583
Total liabilities and stockholders' equity	$370,264	$295,433

GROWTH INC.
Statement of Income
Years Ended December 31, 2004, 2003, and 2002

	2004	2003	2002
Revenues	$578,530	$523,249	$556,549
Costs and expenses:			
Cost of products sold	495,651	457,527	482,358
Selling, general, and administrative	35,433	30,619	29,582
Interest and debt expense	4,308	3,951	2,630
	535,392	492,097	514,570
Income before income taxes	43,138	31,152	41,979
Provision for income taxes	20,120	12,680	17,400
Net income	$ 23,018	$ 18,472	$ 24,579
Net income per share	$ 2.27	$ 1.85	$ 2.43

Partial footnotes: Under the LIFO method, inventories have been reduced by approximately $35,300 and $41,100 at December 31, 2004 and 2003, respectively, from current cost, which would be reported under the first-in, first-out method.

The effective tax rates were 36.6%, 30.7%, and 31.4%, respectively, for the years ended December 31, 2004, 2003, and 2002.

Required   a.   Compute the following for 2004, without considering the LIFO reserve:

Liquidity
1.   Days' sales in inventory
2.   Merchandise inventory turnover
3.   Inventory turnover in days
4.   Operating cycle
5.   Working capital
6.   Current ratio
7.   Acid-test ratio
8.   Cash ratio

Debt
1.   Debt ratio
2.   Debt/equity ratio
3.   Times interest earned

Profitability
1.   Net profit margin
2.   Total asset turnover
3.   Return on assets
4.   Return on total equity

b.   Compute the ratios in part (a), considering the LIFO reserve.

c.   Comment on the apparent liquidity, debt, and profitability, considering both sets of ratios.

P 11-6.

Required   For each of the following numbered items, you are to select the lettered item(s) that indicate(s) its effect(s) on the corporation's statements. If more than one effect is applicable to a particular item, be sure to indicate *all* applicable letters. (Assume that the state statutes do not permit declaration of nonliquidating dividends except from earnings.)

Item	Effect
1. Declaration of a cash dividend due in one month on noncumulative preferred stock.	a. Reduces working capital
	b. Increases working capital
2. Declaration and payment of an ordinary stock dividend.	c. Reduces current ratio
	d. Increases current ratio
3. Receipt of a cash dividend, not previously recorded, on stock of another corporation.	e. Reduces the dollar amount of total capital stock

Item	Effect
4. Passing of a dividend on cumulative preferred stocks.	f. Increases the dollar amount of total capital stock
5. Receipt of preferred shares as a dividend on stock held as a temporary investment. This was not a regularly recurring dividend.	g. Reduces total retained earnings
	h. Increases total retained earnings
	i. Reduces equity per share of common stock
6. Payment of dividend mentioned in 1.	j. Reduces equity of each common stockholder
7. Issue of new common shares in a 5-for-1 stock split.	

P 11-7.   Argo Sales Corporation has in recent years maintained the following relationships among the data on its financial statements:

Gross profit rate on net sales	40%
Net profit rate on net sales	10%
Rate of selling expenses to net sales	20%
Accounts receivable turnover	8 per year
Inventory turnover	6 per year
Acid-test ratio	2-to-1
Current ratio	3-to-1
Quick-asset composition: 8% cash, 32% marketable securities, 60% accounts receivable	
Asset turnover	2 per year
Ratio of total assets to intangible assets	20-to-1
Ratio of accumulated depreciation to cost of fixed assets	1-to-3
Ratio of accounts receivable to accounts payable	1.5-to-1
Ratio of working capital to stockholders' equity	1-to-1.6
Ratio of total debt to stockholders' equity	1-to-2

The corporation had a net income of $120,000 for 2004, which resulted in earnings of $5.20 per share of common stock. Additional information includes the following.

Capital stock authorized, issued (all in 1970), and outstanding:
   Common, $10 per share par value, issued at 10% premium.
   Preferred, 6% nonparticipating, $100 per share par value, issued at a 10% premium.
Market value per share of common at December 31, 2004: $78.
Preferred dividends paid in 2004: $3,000.
Times interest earned in 2004: 33.
The amounts of the following were the same at December 31, 2004, as at January 1, 2004: inventory, accounts receivable, 5% bonds payable—due 2013, and total stockholders' equity.
All purchases and sales were on account.

Required   a.   Prepare in good form the condensed balance sheet and income statement for the year ending December 31, 2004, presenting the amounts you would expect to appear on Argo's financial statements (ignoring income taxes). Major captions appearing on Argo's balance sheet are current assets, fixed assets, intangible assets, current liabilities, long-term liabilities, and stockholders' equity. In addition to the accounts divulged in the problem, you should include accounts for prepaid expenses, accrued expenses, and administrative expenses. Supporting computations should be in good form.
   b.   Compute the following for 2004. (Show your computations.):
   1.   Rate of return on stockholders' equity
   2.   Price/earnings ratio for common stock
   3.   Dividends paid per share of common stock
   4.   Dividends paid per share of preferred stock
   5.   Yield on common stock

CMA Adapted

P 11-8.   Warford Corporation was formed five years ago through a public subscription of common stock. Lucinda Street, who owns 15% of the common stock, was one of the organizers of Warford and is its current president. The company has been successful but currently is experiencing a shortage of funds. On June 10, Street approached Bell National Bank, asking for a 24-month extension on two $30,000 notes, which are due on June 30, 2004, and September 30, 2004. Another note of $7,000 is due on December 31, 2004, but

Street expects no difficulty in paying this note on its due date. Street explained that Warford's cash flow problems are due primarily to the company's desire to finance a $300,000 plant expansion over the next two fiscal years through internally generated funds.

The commercial loan officer of Bell National Bank requested financial reports for the last two fiscal years. These reports follow.

WARFORD CORPORATION
Statement of Financial Position
March 31, 2003 and 2004

	2003	2004
Assets:		
Cash	$ 12,500	$ 16,400
Notes receivable	104,000	112,000
Accounts receivable (net)	68,500	81,600
Inventories (at cost)	50,000	80,000
Plant and equipment (net of depreciation)	646,000	680,000
Total assets	$881,000	$970,000
Liabilities and Owners' Equity:		
Accounts payable	$ 72,000	$ 69,000
Notes payable	54,500	67,000
Accrued liabilities	6,000	9,000
Common stock (60,000 shares, $10 par)	600,000	600,000
Retained earnings*	148,500	225,000
Total liabilities and owners' equity	$881,000	$970,000

*Cash dividends were paid at the rate of $1.00 per share in fiscal year 2003 and $1.25 per share in fiscal year 2004.

WARFORD CORPORATION
Income Statement
For the Fiscal Years Ended March 31, 2003 and 2004

	2003	2004
Sales	$2,700,000	$3,000,000
Cost of goods sold*	1,720,000	1,902,500
Gross profit	980,000	1,097,500
Operating expenses	780,000	845,000
Net income before taxes	200,000	252,500
Income taxes (40%)	80,000	101,000
Income after taxes	$ 120,000	$ 151,500

*Depreciation charges on the plant and equipment of $100,000 and $102,500 for fiscal years ended March 31, 2003 and 2004, respectively, are included in cost of goods sold.

Required a. Calculate the following items for Warford Corporation:
1. Current ratio for fiscal years 2003 and 2004
2. Acid-test (quick) ratio for fiscal years 2003 and 2004
3. Inventory turnover for fiscal year 2004
4. Return on assets for fiscal years 2003 and 2004
5. Percentage change in sales, cost of goods sold, gross profit, and net income after taxes from fiscal year 2003 to 2004

b. Identify and explain what other financial reports and/or financial analyses might be helpful to the commercial loan officer of Bell National Bank in evaluating Street's request for a time extension on Warford's notes.

c. Assume that the percentage changes experienced in fiscal year 2004, as compared with fiscal year 2003 for sales, cost of goods sold, gross profit, and net income after taxes, will be repeated in each of the next two years. Is Warford's desire to finance the plant expansion from internally generated funds realistic? Explain.

d. Should Bell National Bank grant the extension on Warford's notes, considering Street's statement about financing the plant expansion through internally generated funds? Explain.

CMA Adapted

P 11-9. The following data apply to items (a) through (g):

JOHANSON COMPANY
Statement of Financial Position
December 31, 2003 and 2004

(in thousands)	2003	2004
Assets		
Current assets:		
Cash and temporary investments	$ 380	$ 400
Accounts receivable (net)	1,500	1,700
Inventories	2,120	2,200
Total current assets	4,000	4,300
Long-term assets:		
Land	500	500
Building and equipment (net)	4,000	4,700
Total long-term assets	4,500	5,200
Total assets	$ 8,500	$9,500
Liabilities and Equities		
Current liabilities:		
Accounts payable	$ 700	$1,400
Current portion of long-term debt	500	1,000
Total current liabilities	1,200	2,400
Long-term debt	4,000	3,000
Total liabilities	5,200	5,400
Stockholders' equity:		
Common stock	3,000	3,000
Retained earnings	300	1,100
Total stockholders' equity	3,300	4,100
Total liabilities and equities	$ 8,500	$9,500

JOHANSON COMPANY
Statement of Income and Retained Earnings
For the Year Ended December 31, 2004

(in thousands)		
Net sales		$28,800
Less: Cost of goods sold	$15,120	
Selling expenses	7,180	
Administrative expenses	4,100	
Interest	400	
Income taxes	800	27,600
Net income		1,200
Retained earnings, January 1		300
Subtotal		1,500
Cash dividends declared and paid		400
Retained earnings, December 31		$ 1,100

Required Answer the following multiple-choice questions.

  a. The acid-test ratio for 2004 is

    1. 1.1-to-1.

    2. .9-to-1.

      3.   1.8-to-1.
      4.   .2-to-1.
      5.   .17-to-1.

b.   The average number of days' sales outstanding in 2004 is
      1.   18 days.
      2.   360 days.
      3.   20 days.
      4.   4.4 days.
      5.   80 days.

c.   The times interest earned ratio for 2004 is
      1.   3.0 times.
      2.   1.0 times.
      3.   72.0 times.
      4.   2.0 times.
      5.   6.0 times.

d.   The asset turnover in 2004 is
      1.   3.2 times.
      2.   1.7 times.
      3.   .4 times.
      4.   1.1 times.
      5.   .13 times.

e.   The inventory turnover in 2004 is
      1.   13.6 times.
      2.   12.5 times.
      3.   .9 times.
      4.   7.0 times.
      5.   51.4 times.

f.   The operating income margin in 2004 is
      1.   2.7%.
      2.   91.7%.
      3.   52.5%.
      4.   95.8%.
      5.   8.3%.

g.   The dividend payout ratio in 2004 is
      1.   100%.
      2.   36%.
      3.   20%.
      4.   8.8%.
      5.   33.3%.

CMA Adapted

P 11-10.   The statement of financial position for Paragon Corporation at November 30, 2004, the end of its current fiscal year, follows. The market price of the company's common stock was $4 per share on November 30, 2004.

Assets   *(in thousands)*

Current assets:

Cash		$ 6,000
Accounts receivable	$ 7,000	
Less: Allowance for doubtful accounts	400	6,600
Merchandise inventory		16,000
Supplies on hand		400
Prepaid expenses		1,000
Total current assets		$30,000
Property, plant, and equipment:		
Land		27,500
Building	$36,000	
Less: Accumulated depreciation	13,500	22,500
Total property, plant, and equipment		50,000
Total assets		$80,000

Liabilities and Stockholders' Equity

Current liabilities:

Accounts payable	$ 6,400	
Accrued interest payable	800	
Accrued income taxes payable	2,200	
Accrued wages payable	600	
Deposits received from customers	2,000	
Total current liabilities		$12,000

Long-term debt:

Bonds payable—20-year, 8% convertible debentures due December 1, 2010 (Note 7)	20,000	
Less: Unamortized discount	200	19,800
Total liabilities		31,800

Stockholders' equity:

Common stock—authorized 40,000,000 shares of $1 par value; 20,000,000 shares issued and outstanding	20,000	
Paid-in capital in excess of par value	12,200	
Total paid-in capital	32,200	
Retained earnings	16,000	
Total stockholders' equity		48,200
Total liabilities and stockholders' equity		$80,000

All items are to be considered independent of one another, and any transactions given in the items are to be considered the only transactions to affect Paragon Corporation during the just-completed current or coming fiscal year. Average balance sheet account balances are used in computing ratios involving income statement accounts. Ending balance sheet account balances are used in computing ratios involving only balance sheet items.

Required Answer the following multiple-choice questions.

a. If Paragon paid back all of the deposits received from customers, its current ratio would be
   1. 2.50-to-1.00.
   2. 2.80-to-1.00.
   3. 2.33-to-1.00.
   4. 3.00-to-1.00.
   5. 2.29-to-1.00.

b. If Paragon paid back all of the deposits received from customers, its quick (acid-test) ratio would be
   1. 1.06-to-1.00.
   2. 1.00-to-1.00.
   3. 0.88-to-1.00.
   4. 1.26-to-1.00.
   5. 1.20-to-1.00.

c. A 2-for-1 common stock split by Paragon would
   1. Result in each $1,000 bond being convertible into 600 new shares of Paragon common stock.
   2. Decrease the retained earnings due to the capitalization of retained earnings.
   3. Not affect the number of common shares outstanding.
   4. Increase the total paid-in capital.
   5. Increase the total stockholders' equity.

d. Paragon Corporation's building is being depreciated using the straight-line method, salvage value of $6,000,000, and life of 20 years. The number of years the building has been depreciated by Paragon as of November 30, 2004, is
   1. 7.5 years.
   2. 12.5 years.
   3. 9.0 years.
   4. 15.0 years.
   5. None of these.

e. Paragon's book value per share of common stock as of November 30, 2004, is
   1. $4.00.
   2. $1.61.
   3. $1.00.

4. $2.41.
5. None of these.

f. If, during the current fiscal year ending November 30, 2004, Paragon had sales of $90,000,000 with a gross profit of 20% and an inventory turnover of five times per year, the merchandise inventory balance on December 1, 2003, was
   1. $14,400,000.
   2. $12,800,000.
   3. $18,000,000.
   4. $20,000,000.
   5. $16,000,000.

g. If Paragon has a payout ratio of 80% and declared and paid $4,000,000 of cash dividends during the current fiscal year ended November 30, 2004, the retained earnings balance on December 1, 2003, was
   1. $20,000,000.
   2. $17,000,000.
   3. $15,000,000.
   4. $11,000,000.
   5. None of these.

CMA Adapted

P 11-11. The Calcor Company has been a wholesale distributor of automobile parts for domestic automakers for 20 years. Calcor has suffered through the recent slump in the domestic auto industry, and its performance has not rebounded to the levels of the industry as a whole.

Calcor's single-step income statement for the year ended November 30, 2004, follows.

CALCOR COMPANY
Income Statement
For the Year Ended November 30, 2004 (thousands omitted)

Net sales	$8,400
Expenses:	
Cost of goods sold	6,300
Selling expense	780
Administrative expense	900
Interest expense	140
Total	8,120
Income before income taxes	280
Income taxes	112
Net income	$ 168

Calcor's return on sales before interest and taxes was 5% in fiscal 2004 compared to the industry average of 9%. Calcor's turnover of average assets of four times per year and return on average assets before interest and taxes of 20% are both well below the industry average.

Joe Kuhn, president of Calcor, wishes to improve these ratios and raise them nearer to the industry averages. He established the following goals for Calcor Company for fiscal 2005:

Return on sales before interest and taxes	8%
Turnover of average assets	5 times per year
Return on average assets before interest and taxes	30%

For fiscal 2005, Kuhn and the rest of Calcor's management team are considering the following actions, which they expect will improve profitability and result in a 5% increase in unit sales:

1. Increase selling prices 10%.
2. Increase advertising by $420,000 and hold all other selling and administrative expenses at fiscal 2004 levels.
3. Improve customer service by increasing average current assets (inventory and accounts receivable) by a total of $300,000, and hold all other assets at fiscal 2004 levels.
4. Finance the additional assets at an annual interest rate of 10% and hold all other interest expense at fiscal 2004 levels.

5. Improve the quality of products carried; this will increase the units of goods sold by 4%.
6. Calcor's 2005 effective income tax rate is expected to be 40%—the same as in fiscal 2004.

Required   a. Prepare a single-step pro forma income statement for Calcor Company for the year ended November 30, 2005, assuming that Calcor's planned actions would be carried out, and that the 5% increase in unit sales would be realized.
b. Calculate the following ratios for Calcor Company for the 2004–2005 fiscal year and state whether Kuhn's goal would be achieved:
   1. Return on sales before interest and taxes
   2. Turnover of average assets
   3. Return on average assets before interest and taxes
c. Would it be possible for Calcor Company to achieve the first two of Kuhn's goals without achieving his third goal of a 30% return on average assets before interest and taxes? Explain your answer.

CMA Adapted

P 11-12.   The following data are for the A, B, and C Companies.

	Company		
Variables	**A**	**B**	**C**
Current assets	$150,000	$170,000	$180,000
Current liabilities	$60,000	$50,000	$30,000
Total assets	$300,000	$280,000	$250,000
Retained earnings	$80,000	$90,000	$60,000
Earnings before interest and taxes	$70,000	$60,000	$50,000
Market price per share	$20.00	$18.75	$16.50
Number of shares outstanding	9,000	9,000	9,000
Book value of total debt	$30,000	$50,000	$80,000
Sales	$430,000	$400,000	$200,000

Required   a. Compute the Z score for each company.
b. According to the Altman model, which of these firms is most likely to experience financial failure?

P 11-13.   The General Company financial statements for 2004 follow here and on the following pages:

GENERAL COMPANY
Statement of Income
Years Ended December 31, 2004, 2003, and 2002

	2004	2003	2002
Net sales	$860,000	$770,000	$690,000
Cost and expenses:			
Cost of products sold	730,000	630,000	580,000
Selling, general, and administrative	46,000	40,000	38,000
Interest and debt expense	4,000	3,900	6,500
	780,000	673,900	624,500
Income before income taxes	80,000	96,100	65,500
Provision for income taxes	33,000	24,000	21,000
Net income	$ 47,000	$ 72,100	$ 44,500
Net income per share	$ 2.67	$ 4.10	$ 2.54

Required   a. Compute the Z score of the General Company at the end of 2004.
b. According to the Altman model, does the Z score of the General Company indicate a high probability of financial failure?

GENERAL COMPANY
Statement of Cash Flows
Years Ended December 31, 2004, 2003, and 2002

	2004	2003	2002
Operating activities:			
Net income	$ 47,000	$ 72,100	$ 44,500
Adjustments to reconcile net income to net cash provided by operating activities:			
Depreciation and amortization	21,000	20,000	19,000
Deferred taxes	3,800	2,500	2,000
Increase in accounts receivable	(4,000)	(3,000)	(3,000)
Decrease (increase) in inventories	(3,000)	(2,500)	1,000
Decrease (increase) in prepaid expenses	(300)	(200)	100
Increase (decrease) in accounts payable	6,000	5,000	(1,000)
Increase (decrease) in income taxes	100	300	(100)
Increase (decrease) in accrued liabilities	6,000	3,000	(1,000)
Net cash provided by operating activities	76,600	97,200	61,500
Investing activities:			
Additions to property, plant, and equipment	(66,500)	(84,400)	(52,500)
Financing activities:			
Payment on long-term debt	(1,000)	(2,000)	(1,500)
Issuance of other long-term liabilities	9,200	1,000	(1,000)
Issuance of capital stock	1,000	—	—
Dividend paid	(10,300)	(9,800)	(9,500)
Net cash used in financing activities	(1,100)	(10,800)	(12,000)
Increase (decrease) in cash	9,000	2,000	(3,000)
Cash at beginning of year	39,000	37,000	40,000
Cash at end of year	$ 48,000	$ 39,000	$ 37,000

GENERAL COMPANY
Balance Sheet
December 31, 2004

	2004	2003
Assets		
Current assets:		
Cash	$ 48,000	$ 39,000
Accounts receivable, less allowance for doubtful accounts of $2,000 in 2004 and $1,400 in 2003	125,000	121,000
Inventories	71,000	68,000
Prepaid expenses	2,500	2,200
Total current assets	246,500	230,200
Property, plant, and equipment:		
Land and land improvements	12,000	10,500
Buildings	98,000	89,000
Machinery and equipment	303,000	247,000
	413,000	346,500
Less: Accumulated depreciation	165,000	144,000
Net property, plant and equipment	248,000	202,500
Total assets	$494,500	$432,700

Liabilities and Stockholders' Equity

Current liabilities:

Accounts payable	$ 56,000	$ 50,000
Income taxes	3,700	3,600
Accrued liabilities	34,000	28,000
Total current liabilities	93,700	81,600
Long-term debt	63,000	64,000
Other long-term liabilities	16,000	6,800
Deferred federal income taxes	27,800	24,000
Total liabilities	200,500	176,400
Stockholders' equity:		
Capital stock	46,000	45,000
Retained earnings	248,000	211,300
Total stockholders' equity	294,000	256,300
Total liabilities and stockholders' equity	$494,500	$ 432,700

Note: The market price of the stock at the end of 2004 was $30.00 per share. There were 23,000 common shares outstanding at December 31, 2004.

P 11-14.

LIFO reserves: Rhodes Company
Reported year for analysis, 2004

2004 net income as reported	$ 90,200,000
2004 inventory reserve	50,000,000
2003 inventory reserve	46,000,000
2004 income taxes	55,000,000
2004 income before income taxes	145,200,000

Required Compute the approximate income if inventory had been valued at approximate current cost.

P 11-15.

LIFO reserves: Lion Company
Reported year for analysis, 2003

2003 net income as reported	$45,000,000
2003 inventory reserve	20,000,000
2002 inventory reserve	28,000,000
2003 income taxes	14,000,000
2003 income before income taxes	59,000,000

Required Compute the approximate income if inventory had been valued at approximate current cost.

P 11-16. An airline presented this graph with its annual report:

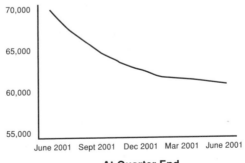

Staffing Levels
Full-Time Equivalent Employees

At Quarter End

Required Indicate the misleading feature in this graph.

Case 11-1

What Position?

Seaway Food Town, Inc. presented this data in its 1995 annual report:

SEAWAY FOOD TOWN, INC.
CONSOLIDATED STATEMENTS OF INCOME
Years Ended August 26, 1995, August 27, 1994, and August 28, 1993
(Dollars in thousands, except per share data)

	1995	1994	1993
Net sales	$ 559,244	$ 546,193	$ 566,883
Cost of merchandise sold	418,128	409,305	428,478
Gross profit	141,116	136,888	138,405
Selling, general and administrative expenses	131,267	129,921	133,175
Operating profit	9,849	6,967	5,230
Interest expense	(4,469)	(4,410)	(4,660)
Other income—net	1,815	1,169	1,133
Income before income taxes, extraordinary item and cumulative effect	7,195	3,726	1,703
Provision for income taxes	2,715	1,288	580
Income before extraordinary item and cumulative effect	4,480	2,438	1,123
Extraordinary item—losses from early extinguishment of debt, less applicable income taxes of $63 (Note 2)	—	(123)	—
Cumulative effect of change in accounting for income taxes (Note 3)	—	(256)	—
Net income	$ 4,480	$ 2,059	$ 1,123
Per common share:			
Income before extraordinary item and cumulative effect	$ 2.04	$ 1.06	$ .48
Extraordinary item	—	(.06)	—
Cumulative effect of change in accounting for income taxes	—	(.11)	—
Net income	$ 2.04	$ .89	$ .48

SEAWAY FOOD TOWN, INC.
CONSOLIDATED BALANCE SHEETS
August 26, 1995 and August 27, 1994
(Dollars in thousands, except per share data)

Assets	1995	1994
Current assets		
Cash and cash equivalents	$ 7,402	$ 7,137
Income tax recoverable	—	600
Notes and accounts receivable, less allowance of		
$450 for doubtful accounts	6,587	5,627
Merchandise inventories	44,064	44,749
Prepaid expenses	1,371	1,272
Deferred income taxes	4,211	4,036
Total current assets	63,635	63,421
Other assets	6,366	6,436
Property and equipment, at cost		
Land	4,160	4,202
Buildings and improvements	65,983	62,453
Leasehold improvements	28,921	26,005
Equipment	89,356	92,165
	188,420	184,825
Less accumulated depreciation and amortization	104,420	99,479
Net property and equipment	84,000	85,346
	$154,001	$ 155,203
Liabilities and Shareholders' Equity		
Current liabilities		
Accounts payable—trade	$ 38,889	$ 36,318
Income taxes	1,027	407
Accrued liabilities:		
Insurance	5,521	5,027
Payroll	2,994	2,766
Taxes, other than income	2,352	2,434
Other	3,213	4,191
	14,080	14,418
Long-term debt due within one year	3,553	3,341
Total current liabilities	57,549	54,484
Long-term debt	48,399	55,060
Deferred income taxes	5,276	5,495
Deferred other	2,046	2,579
Total liabilities	113,270	117,618
Shareholders' equity		
Serial preferred stock, without par value:		
300,000 shares authorized, none issued	—	—
Common stock, without par value (stated value		
$2 per share): 6,000,000 shares authorized		
2,193,352 shares outstanding (2,242,373 in 1994)	4,387	4,485
Capital in excess of stated value	680	434
Retained earnings	35,664	32,666
Total shareholders' equity	40,731	37,585
Total liabilities and shareholders' equity	$154,001	$ 155,203

1. Significant Accounting Policies (in Part)

Inventories—Meat, produce, and drug inventories are valued at the lower of cost, using the first-in, first-out (FIFO) method, or market. All other merchandise inventories are valued at the lower of cost, using the last-in, first-out (LIFO) method, or market. Inventories have been reduced by $18,157,000 and

$17,576,000 at August 26, 1995 and August 27, 1994, respectively, from amounts which would have been reported under the FIFO method (which approximates current cost).

During 1995 and 1994, merchandise inventory quantities were reduced. These reductions resulted in liquidations of the LIFO inventory quantities carried at lower costs prevailing in prior years as compared with costs of 1995 and 1994 purchases, the effect of which increased consolidated net income by approximately $89,000 ($.04 per share) in 1995 and $75,000 ($.03 per share) in 1994.

Other data:
a. Net cash provided by operating activities, $19,829,000, $16,183,000, and $16,534,000 for 1995, 1994, and 1993, respectively.
b. Market price of common stock:
   1. August 26, 1995, $16.25
   2. August 27, 1994, $10.50

Required
a. LIFO inventory liquidation increased income in 1995 and 1994. Determine the amount by which income was increased in 1995 and 1994 because of LIFO inventory.
b. Determine the change in net income, in comparison with the reported net income, if FIFO had been used for all inventory.
c. Compute the following for 1995, with no adjustment for LIFO reserve:
   1. Days' sales in inventory
   2. Working capital
   3. Current ratio
   4. Acid-test ratio
   5. Debt ratio
d. Compute the measures in (c), considering the LIFO reserve. (Eliminate the LIFO reserve.)
   1. Days' sales in inventory
   2. Working capital
   3. Current ratio
   4. Acid-test ratio
   5. Debt ratio
e. Comment on the different results of the ratios computed in (c) and (d).
f. Compute the following for 1995 (use the financial statements as published):
   1. Cash flow/total debt
   2. Net income/total assets
   3. Debt ratio
   Assuming that these ratios are valid in forecasting financial failure, give your opinion as to the financial position of this company.
g. Compute the Z score for 1995. Comment.

Case 11-2   Accounting Hocus-Pocus

This case is an excerpt from a presentation given by Chairman Arthur Levitt, Securities and Exchange Commission, the "Numbers Game," to New York University Center for Law and Business, September 28, 1998.

Accounting Hocus-Pocus

Our accounting principles weren't meant to be a straitjacket. Accountants are wise enough to know they cannot anticipate every business structure or every new and innovative transaction, so they develop principles that allow for flexibility to adapt to changing circumstances. That's why the highest standards of objectivity, integrity and judgment can't be the exception. They must be the rule.

Flexibility in accounting allows it to keep pace with business innovations. Abuses such as earnings management occur when people exploit this pliancy. Trickery is employed to obscure actual financial volatility. This, in turn, masks the true consequences of management's decisions. These practices aren't limited to smaller companies struggling to gain investor interest. It's also happening in companies whose products we know and admire.

So what are these illusions? Five of the more popular ones I want to discuss today are "big bath" restructuring charges, creative acquisition accounting, "cookie jar reserves," "immaterial" misapplications of accounting principles and the premature recognition of revenue.

"Big-Bath" Charges

Let me first deal with "Big Bath" restructuring charges.

Companies remain competitive by regularly assessing the efficiency and profitability of their operations. Problems arise, however, when we see large charges associated with companies restructuring. These charges help companies "clean up" their balance sheet—giving them a so-called "big bath."

Why are companies tempted to overstate these charges? When earnings take a major hit, the theory goes Wall Street will look beyond a one-time loss and focus only on future earnings.

And if these charges are conservatively estimated with a little extra cushioning, that so-called conservative estimate is miraculously reborn as income when estimates change or future earnings fall short.

When a company decides to restructure, management and employees, investors and creditors, customers and suppliers all want to understand the expected effects. We need, of course, to ensure that financial reporting provides this information. But this should not lead to flushing all the associated costs—and maybe a little extra—through the financial statements.

Creative Acquisition Accounting

Let me turn now to the second gimmick.

In recent years, whole industries have been remade through consolidations, acquisitions and spin-offs. Some acquirers, particularly those using stock as an acquisition currency, have used this environment as an opportunity to engage in another form of "creative accounting." I call it "merger magic."

I am not talking tonight about the pooling versus purchase problem. Some companies have no choice but to use purchase accounting—which can result in lower future earnings. But that's a result some companies are unwilling to tolerate.

So what do they do? They classify an ever-growing portion of the acquisition price as "in-process" Research and Development, so—you guessed it—the amount can be written off in a "one-time" charge—removing any future earnings drag. Equally troubling is the creation of large liabilities for future operating expenses to protect future earnings—all under the mask of an acquisition.

Miscellaneous "Cookie Jar Reserves"

A third illusion played by some companies is using unrealistic assumptions to estimate liabilities for such items as sales returns, loan losses or warranty costs. In doing so, they stash accruals in cookie jars during the good times and reach into them when needed in the bad times.

I'm reminded of one U.S. company who took a large one-time loss to earnings to reimburse franchisees for equipment. That equipment, however, which included literally the kitchen sink, had yet to be bought. And, at the same time, they announced that future earnings would grow an impressive 15 percent per year.

"Materiality"

Let me turn now to the fourth gimmick—the abuse of materiality—a word that captures the attention of both attorneys and accountants. Materiality is another way we build flexibility into financial reporting. Using the logic of diminishing returns, some items may be so insignificant that they are not worth measuring and reporting with exact precision.

But some companies misuse the concept of materiality. They intentionally record errors within a defined percentage ceiling. They then try to excuse that fib by arguing that the effect on the bottom line is too small to matter. If that's the case, why do they work so hard to create these errors? Maybe because the effect can matter, especially if it picks up that last penny of the consensus estimate. When either management or the outside auditors are questioned about these clear violations of GAAP, they answer sheepishly . . . "It doesn't matter. It's immaterial."

In markets where missing an earnings projection by a penny can result in a loss of millions of dollars in market capitalization, I have a hard time accepting that some of these so-called non-events simply don't matter.

Revenue Recognition

Lastly, companies try to boost earnings by manipulating the recognition of revenue. Think about a bottle of fine wine. You wouldn't pop the cork on that bottle before it was ready. But some companies are doing this with their revenue—recognizing it before a sale is complete, before the product is delivered to a customer, or at a time when the customer still has options to terminate, void or delay the sale.

Required
   a. "Big Bath"—Comment on how a "Big Bath" would have enabled WorldCom to cover up its fraud.

   b. Why would writing off "in-process" Research and Development be similar to a "Big Bath"?

c. How could a company use "allowance for doubtful accounts" as "Cookie Jar Reserves"?
d. Speculate on how a company could use "Materiality" or disregard or partially disregard a specific accounting standard.

Case 11-3

Turn a Cheek

June 1996, *New York Times* columnist Bob Herbert wrote a pair of opinion editorials accusing Nike Corp. of cruelly exploiting cheap Asian labor. Nike CEO Philip Knight replied in a letter to the editor, which the *Times* published. Some of the information in the Knight letter included that Nike has, on average paid double the minimum was as defined in countries where its products are produced under contract.[22]

In 1998, Marc Kasky, a resident of California, sued Nike alleging that the Knight letter violated California's consumer protection laws against deceptive advertising and unfair business practices.[23] In effect the position was that the *New York Times* editorials were under the First Amendment, but that the Nike reply was under the Fifth Amendment. The First Amendment covers freedom of speech, while the Fifth Amendment covers commercial speech.

The California Supreme Court ruled in May 2002 that the Nike reply had to be viewed under the Fifth Amendment. The Supreme Court stated it was "commercial speech because it is both more readily verifiable by its speaker and more hardy than noncommercial speech, can be effectively regulated to suppress false and actually or inherently misleading messages without undue risk of chilling public debate."[24]

Nike is appealing the decision to the United States Supreme Court.

Required

a. Write a position paper on why the Nike reply should be viewed under the First Amendment.
b. Write a position paper on why the Nike reply should be viewed under the Fifth Amendment.

Note: Good reference materials for this case are:

Roger Parloff, "Can We Talk," *Fortune* (September 2, 2002), pp. 102–104, 106, 108, 110.

Kasky v. Nike, Inc. Cite as 45 p. 3d (Cal 2002).

Nike web site http://www.Nike.com.

Web Case

Thomson Analytics Business School Edition

Please complete the web case that covers material covered in this chapter at http://gibson.swlearning.com. You'll be using Thomson Analytics Business School Edition, a version of the powerful tool used by Wall Street professionals, that combines a full range of fundamental financial information, earnings estimates, market data, and source documents for 500 publicly traded companies.

Endnotes

1. C.H. Gibson, "Financial Ratios as Perceived by Commercial Loan Officers," *Akron Business and Economic Review* (Summer 1983), pp. 23–27.
2. The basis of the comments in this section is a study by Dr. Charles Gibson in 1981. The research was done under a grant from the Deloitte Haskins & Sells Foundation.
3. C.H. Gibson, "Ohio CPA's Perceptions of Financial Ratios," *The Ohio CPA Journal* (Autumn 1985), pp. 25–30. © 1985. Reprinted with permission of *The Ohio CPA Journal*.
4. C.H. Gibson, "How Chartered Financial Analysts View Financial Ratios," *Financial Analysts Journal* (May–June 1987), pp. 74–76.
5. *Ibid.*
6. C.H. Gibson, "Financial Ratios in Annual Reports," *The CPA Journal* (September 1982), pp. 18–29.
7. W.H. Beaver, "Alternative Accounting Measures as Predictors of Failure," *The Accounting Review* (January 1968), pp. 113–122.
8. *Ibid.*, p. 117.
9. *Ibid.*, p. 119.
10. E.I. Altman, "Financial Ratios, Discriminant Analysis and the Prediction of Corporate Bankruptcy," *Journal of Finance* (September 1968), pp. 589–609.

11. Edward I. Altman and Thomas P. McGough, "Evaluation of a Company as a Going Concern," *The Journal of Accountancy* (December 1974), pp. 50–57.

12. *Ibid.*, p. 52.

13. Suggested reference sources:

Anker V. Andersen, "Graphing Financial Information: How Accountants Can Use Graphs to Communicate," *National Association of Accountants* (1983), p. 50.

Edward Bloches, Robert P. Moffie, and Robert W. Smud, "How Best to Communicate Numerical Data," *The Internal Auditor* (February 1985), pp. 38–42.

Deanna Qxender Burgess, "Graphical Sleight of Hand: How Can Auditors Spot Altered Exhibits that Appear in Annual Reports?" *Journal of Accountancy* (February 2002), pp. 45–50.

Charles H. Gibson and Nicholas Schroeder, "Improving Your Practice—Graphically," *The CPA Journal* (August 1990), pp. 28–37.

Johnny R. Johnson, Richard R. Rice, and Roger A. Roemmich, "Pictures That Lie: The Abuse of Graphs in Annual Reports," *Management Accounting* (October 1980), pp. 50–56.

Robert Lefferts, *How to Prepare Charts and Graphs for Effective Reports* (New York: Barnes & Noble Books, 1982), p. 166.

David Lynch and Steven Galen, "Got the Picture? CPAs Can Use Some Simple Principles to Create Effective Charts and Graphs for Financial Reports and Presentations," *Journal of Accountancy* (May 2002), pp. 183–187.

Calvin F. Schmid and Stanton E. Schmid, *Handbook of Graphic Presentation*, 2nd ed. (New York: Ronald Press, 1979), p. 308.

14. http://www.sec.gov.

15. "Restatements of Profits Prove Costly to Investors," *The Wall Street Journal* (October 24, 2002), p. D2.

16. George J. Benoton and Al L. Hartgraves, "Enron: What Happened and What We Can Learn from It," *Journal of Accounting and Public Policy* (August 2002), pp. 105–127.

17. Susan Pulliam and Deborah Solomon, "How Three Unlikely Sleuths Discovered Fraud at World-Com," *The Wall Street Journal* (October 30, 2002), p. A6.

18. Jared Sandberg and Susan Pulliam, "Report by WorldCom Examiner Finds New Fraudulent Activities," *The Wall Street Journal* (November 5, 2002), p. 1.

19. Pullman and Solomon, "How Three Unlikely Sleuths Discovered Fraud at WorldCom."

20. *Ibid.*

21. *Ibid.*

22. Roger Parloff, "Can We Talk," *Fortune* (September 2, 2002), pp. 102–103.

23. *Ibid.*, p. 103.

24. *Kasky v. Nike, Inc.* Cite as 45 p. 3d 243 (Cal 2002).

SPECIAL INDUSTRIES: BANKS, UTILITIES, OIL AND GAS, TRANSPORTATION, INSURANCE, REAL ESTATE COMPANIES

The preceding chapters covered material most applicable to manufacturing, retailing, wholesaling, and service industries. This chapter covers six specialized industries: banks, electric utilities, oil and gas, transportation, insurance, and real estate companies. The chapter notes the differences in statements and suggests changes or additions to analysis.

BANKS

Banks operate under either a federal or state charter. National banks are required to submit uniform accounting statements to the Comptroller of the Currency. State banks are controlled by their state banking departments. In addition, the Federal Deposit Insurance Corporation and the Board of Governors of the Federal Reserve System receive financial and operating statements from all members of the Federal Reserve System. Member banks are required to keep reserves with their district Federal Reserve bank. State banking laws also dictate the geographical area within which a bank may function. The range runs from within one county to interstate.

Banking systems usually involve two types of structures: individual banks and bank holding companies. **Bank holding companies** consist of a parent that owns one or many banks. Additionally, the holding company may own bank-related financial services and nonfinancial subsidiaries. In financial report analysis, we must determine the extent of the business generated by banking services. In order for the specific industry ratios to be meaningful, a large proportion of the services should be bank related.

Exhibit 12-1 presents part of the 2001 annual report of National City. Located in Cleveland, Ohio, National City owns and operates seven commercial banks with offices in Ohio, Kentucky, Illinois, Indiana, Michigan, and Pennsylvania.

Balance Sheet

The balance sheet of a commercial bank is sometimes termed the *report of condition.* Two significant differences exist between the traditional balance sheet and that of a bank. First, the accounts of banks may seem the opposite of those of other types of firms. Checking accounts or demand deposits are liabilities to a bank, since it owes the customers money in these cases. Similarly, loans to customers are assets—receivables. Further, the balance sheet accounts are not subdivided into current and noncurrent accounts.

Some banks provide a very detailed disclosure of their assets and liabilities. Other banks provide only general disclosure. The quality of review that can be performed can be no better than the disclosure.

Representative assets of a bank may include cash on hand or due from other banks, investment securities, loans, bank premises, and equipment. Closely review the disclosure of a bank's assets. This review may indicate risk or opportunity. For example, a review of the assets may indicate that the bank has a substantial risk if interest rates increase. The general rule is that for 20-year fixed obligations, a gain or loss of 8% of principal arises when interest rates change by 1%. Thus, an investment of $100,000,000 in 20-year bonds would lose approximately $32,000,000 in principal if interest rates increased by 4%. A similar example would be a bank that holds long-term fixed-rate mortgages. The value of these mortgages could decline substantially if interest rates increased. Many bank annual reports do not disclose the amount of fixed-rate mortgages.

Review the stockholders' equity section of the balance sheet to determine if significant accumulated comprehensive income (losses) exist. For National City, accumulated comprehensive income was $60,577,000 and $72,277,000 at the end of 2000 and 2001, respectively. Major changes were a decline of $25,995,000 from a change in accounting principle and a gain of $41,207,000 from a change in unrealized gains and losses on securities, net of reclassification adjustment for net gains included in net income.

In recent years, Less Developed Country (LDC) loans have become a national issue. In general, LDC loans are perceived as being more risky than domestic loans. National City apparently did not have international loans at the end of both 2001 and 2000.

As part of the review of assets, review the disclosure that describes related-party loans. Observe the materially and the trend of these loans. National City apparently did not have related-party loans at the end of 2001 and 2000.

Review the disclosure of allowance for loan losses. It may indicate a significant change and/or significant losses charged. National City disclosed net charge-offs of $462.6 million in 2001 and $286.3 million in 2000, respectively.

Review the footnotes and Management's Discussion and Analysis for disclosure of nonperforming assets. In general, **nonperforming assets** are those for which the bank is not receiving income or is receiving reduced income. The categories of nonperforming assets are nonaccrual loans,

EXHIBIT 12-1   NATIONAL CITY
Selected Data from 2001 Annual Report

Consolidated Financial Statements

Consolidated Balance Sheets

(Dollars in Thousands, Except Per Share Amounts)	December 31, 2001	2000
Assets		
Loans:		
Commercial	$ 26,752,115	$26,703,622
Real estate—commercial	7,281,268	6,511,018
Real estate—residential	14,763,546	13,357,438
Consumer	11,548,785	12,100,567
Credit card	1,867,053	2,152,445
Home equity	5,827,879	4,779,359
Total loans	68,040,646	65,604,449
Allowance for loan losses	(997,331)	(928,592)
Net loans	67,043,315	64,675,857
Loans held for sale or securitization:		
Commercial loans held for sale	50,959	—
Mortgage loans held for sale	15,553,297	3,030,672
Automobile loans held for securitization	824,434	—
Credit card loans held for securitization	402,305	407,900
Total loans held for sale or securitization	16,830,995	3,438,572
Securities available for sale, at fair value	9,858,868	9,904,533
Federal funds sold and security resale agreements	171,498	81,040
Other investments	432,861	687,732
Cash and demand balances due from banks	4,403,962	3,535,186
Properties and equipment	1,084,106	1,071,637
Accrued income and other assets	5,991,095	5,140,052
Total Assets	**$105,816,700**	**$88,534,609**
Liabilities		
Deposits:		
Noninterest bearing deposits	$ 14,823,277	$11,500,026
NOW and money market accounts	19,501,137	17,262,587
Savings accounts	2,608,565	2,883,763
Consumer time deposits	14,962,150	15,816,422
Other deposits	5,332,874	4,072,308
Foreign deposits	5,901,929	3,721,316
Total deposits	63,129,932	55,256,422
Federal funds borrowed and security repurchase agreements	6,593,388	5,677,643
Borrowed funds	8,578,742	903,725
Long-term debt	17,136,232	17,964,800
Corporation obligated mandatorily redeemable capital securities of subsidiary trusts holding solely debentures of the Corporation	180,000	180,000
Accrued expenses and other liabilities	2,817,183	1,782,198
Total Liabilities	**98,435,477**	**81,764,788**
Stockholders' Equity		
Preferred stock, stated value $50 per share, authorized 5,000,000 shares, outstanding 13,969 shares in 2001 and 599,365 shares in 2000	698	29,968
Common stock, par value $4 per share, authorized 1,400,000,000 shares, outstanding 607,354,729 shares in 2001 and 609,188,668 shares in 2000	2,429,419	2,436,755
Capital surplus	908,780	837,444
Retained earnings	3,970,049	3,405,077
Accumulated other comprehensive income	72,277	60,577
Total Stockholders' Equity	**7,381,223**	**6,769,821**
Total Liabilities and Stockholders' Equity	**$105,816,700**	**$88,534,609**

(continued)

EXHIBIT 12-1   **NATIONAL CITY**
Selected Data from 2001 Annual Report (*continued*)

Consolidated Statements of Income

(Dollars in Thousands, Except Per Share Amounts)	For the Calendar Year		
	2001	2000	1999
Interest Income			
Loans	$5,863,785	$ 5,790,093	$4,938,372
Securities:			
Taxable	433,115	641,406	826,332
Exempt from Federal income taxes	39,800	43,450	48,000
Dividends	45,201	54,852	47,918
Federal funds sold and security resale agreements	4,317	18,854	37,862
Other investments	28,534	17,928	14,125
Total interest income	6,414,752	6,566,583	5,912,609
Interest Expense			
Deposits	1,777,731	1,937,034	1,635,533
Federal funds borrowed and security repurchase agreements	297,374	395,935	368,061
Borrowed funds	63,987	164,716	144,232
Long-term debt and capital securities	836,811	1,110,536	764,761
Total interest expense	2,975,903	3,608,221	2,912,587
Net Interest Income	3,438,849	2,958,362	3,000,022
Provision for Loan Losses	605,295	286,795	249,674
Net interest income after provision for loan losses	2,833,554	2,671,567	2,750,348
Noninterest Income			
Deposit service charges	469,326	442,753	420,448
Item processing revenue	464,627	439,440	441,657
Trust and investment management fees	319,825	334,627	325,856
Mortgage banking revenue	199,244	478,954	389,292
Card-related fees	169,453	161,028	166,802
Ineffective hedge and other derivative gains, net	362,937	18,190	17,824
Other	547,609	552,390	480,530
Total fees and other income	2,533,021	2,427,382	2,242,409
Securities gains, net	144,802	56,852	138,360
Total noninterest income	2,677,823	2,484,234	2,380,769
Noninterest Expense			
Salaries, benefits and other personnel	1,710,309	1,627,260	1,558,403
Equipment	238,956	229,476	209,774
Net occupancy	212,780	209,229	202,077
Third-party services	203,762	197,485	193,148
Other	979,069	920,459	819,102
Total noninterest expense	3,344,876	3,183,909	2,982,504
Income before income tax expense	2,166,501	1,971,892	2,148,613
Income tax expense	778,393	669,515	743,128
Net Income	$1,388,108	$ 1,302,377	$1,405,485
Net Income Per Common Share			
Basic	$2.30	$2.14	$2.25
Diluted	2.27	2.13	2.22
Average Common Shares Outstanding			
Basic	603,611,073	607,378,801	623,623,811
Diluted	611,936,906	612,625,349	632,452,146

(continued)

renegotiated loans, and other real estate. *Nonaccrual loans* are loans for which payments have fallen significantly behind, so that the bank has stopped accruing interest income on these loans. *Renegotiated loans* are loans that the bank has renegotiated with a customer because the customer has had trouble meeting the terms of the original loan. For example, a loan in the amount of $10,000,000

NATIONAL CITY
Selected Data from 2001 Annual Report (*continued*)

Consolidated Statements of Changes in Stockholders' Equity (in Part)

(Dollars in Thousands, Except Per Share Amounts)	Preferred Stock	Common Stock	Capital Surplus	Retained Earnings	Accumulated Other Comprehensive Income (Loss)	Total
Balance, December 31, 2000	$ 29,968	$ 2,436,755	$ 837,444	$ 3,405,077	$ 60,577	$ 6,769,821
Comprehensive Income:						
Net income				1,388,108		1,388,108
Other comprehensive income, net of tax:						
Cumulative effect of change in accounting principle					(25,995)	(25,995)
Change in unrealized gains and losses on securities, net of reclassification adjustment for gains included in net income					41,207	41,207
Change in unrealized gains and losses on derivative instruments used in cash flow hedging relationships, net of reclassification adjustment for net losses included in net income					(7,384)	(7,384)
Change in unrealized gains and losses on retained interests in the securitized credit card, trust, net of reclassification adjustment for net gains included in net income					3,872	3,872
Total comprehensive income						1,399,808
Common dividends declared, $1.16 per share				(699,848)		(699,848)
Preferred dividends declared				(1,016)		(1,016)
Issuances of 5,709,641 common shares under stock-based compensation plans, including related tax effects		22,838	55,866			78,704
Repurchase of 9,316,800 common shares		(37,267)	(6,707)	(122,272)		(166,246)
Conversion of 585,396 shares of preferred stock to 1,773,220 common shares	(29,270)	7,093	22,177			—
Balance, December 31, 2001	$ 698	$ 2,429,419	$ 908,780	$ 3,970,049	$ 72,277	$ 7,381,223

and 10% interest may come due. The customer who cannot pay may be allowed to renegotiate the loan with the bank, reducing the principal to $8,000,000 and the interest rate to 6% and gaining a five-year extension. Under current GAAP, no immediate loss will be taken by the bank on the renegotiated loan if the projected cash flow under the renegotiated loan will cover the current book value of the loan. In the example, the projected cash flow comes to $10,400,000 ($8,000,000 in principal and $480,000 in interest each year for five years). Since this covers the current book figure of $10,000,000, no immediate loss will be recognized. In addition to other factors, banks should consider renegotiated loans when they adjust the loan loss reserve.

Other real estate usually consists of real estate the bank has taken when it foreclosed on a loan. For example, the bank may have made a loan to a company for a hotel and accepted a mortgage on the hotel as collateral. If the bank must foreclose on the loan, it may take possession of the hotel. The bank would want to sell the hotel, but it may be necessary to hold and operate the hotel for a relatively long period of time before a buyer can be found.

The amount and trend of nonperforming assets should be observed closely. This can be an early indication of troubles to come. For example, a significant increase in nonperforming assets late in the year may have had an insignificant effect on the past year's profits, but it could indicate a significant negative influence on the future year's profits.

National City discloses nonperforming assets at the end of 2001 and 2000 as $658.3 million and $402.3 million, respectively. This is a negative trend.

Typical liabilities of a bank include savings, time and demand deposits, loan obligations, and long-term debt. Closely review the disclosure of liabilities for favorable or unfavorable trends. For example, a decreasing amount in savings deposits would indicate that the bank is losing one of its cheapest sources of funds. There was a significant increase in liabilities in 2001. This included a significant increase in deposits, which appears to be positive, especially the non-interest bearing deposits. The material increase in long-term debt would not be positive.

As part of the review of liabilities, look for a footnote that describes commitments and contingent liabilities. This footnote may reveal significant commitments and contingent liabilities. National City discloses significant commitments at the end of 2001 and 2000. There appears to have been an increase in the commitments and contingent liabilities in 2001.

The stockholders' equity of a bank resembles that of other types of firms, except that the total stockholders' equity is usually very low in relation to total assets. A general guide for many years was that a bank's stockholders' equity should be approximately 10% of total assets, but very few banks in recent years have had that much stockholders' equity. Currently, stockholders' equity of 6–7%, would probably be considered favorable. National City had approximately 7.5% stockholders' equity at the end of 2001. In general, the lower the proportion of stockholders' equity in relation to total assets, the greater the risk of failure. A higher stockholders' equity in relation to total assets would probably improve safety, but the bank would perhaps be less profitable because of the additional capital requirement.

As part of the analysis of stockholders' equity, review the statement of stockholders' equity and the related footnotes for any significant changes. National City had significant changes from a stock dividend and repurchase of common stock.

The current approach by bank regulators is not only to view the adequacy of stockholders' equity in relation to total assets, but also to view capital in relation to risk-adjusted assets. National City discloses that it has consistently maintained regulatory capital rates at or above the "well capitalized" standards.

Income Statement

A bank's principal revenue source is usually interest income from loans and investment securities. The principal expense is usually interest expense on deposits and other debt. The difference between interest income and interest expense is termed *net interest income* or *net interest margin*.

The net interest margin is important to the profitability of a bank. Usually, falling interest rates are positive for a bank's interest margin because the bank will be able to reduce the interest rate that it pays for deposits before the average rate of return earned on loans and investments declines. Increasing interest rates are usually negative for a bank's interest margin because the bank will need to increase the interest rate on deposits, which is usually done before rates on loans and investments are adjusted.

Bank income statements include a separate section for other income. Typical other income includes trust department fees, service charges on deposit accounts, trading account profits (losses), and securities transactions.

The importance of other income has substantially increased for banks. For example, service charges have increased in importance in recent years since many banks have set service charges at a level to make the service profitable. This has frequently been the result of improved cost analysis. In addition, banks have been adding nontraditional sources of income, such as mortgage banking, sales of mutual funds, sales of annuities, and computer services for other banks and financial institutions.

National City had net interest income after provision for loan losses of $2,833,554,000 and $2,671,567,000, respectively, for 2001 and 2000. The non-interest income increased from $2,484,234,000 to $2,677,823,000, respectively. Total non-interest expense increased from $3,183,909,000 to $3,344,876,000.

Ratios for Banks

Because of the vastly different accounts and statement formats, few of the traditional ratios are appropriate for banks. Exceptions include return on assets, return on equity, and most of the investment-related ratios. The following sections present meaningful ratios for bank analysis, but this is not a comprehensive treatment. The investment firm of Keefe, Bruyette & Woods, Inc., in its *Bankbook Report on Performance*, lists 21 financial ratios. This is an excellent source of industry averages for banks.

Earning Assets to Total Assets

Earning assets includes loans, leases, investment securities, and money market assets. It excludes cash and nonearning deposits plus fixed assets. This ratio shows how well bank management puts bank assets to work. High-performance banks have a high ratio.

Banks typically present asset data on an average annual basis. National City provides a schedule of average balances in its annual report. This schedule is used for the average total assets in computing earning assets to total assets. Exhibit 12-2 presents National City's earning assets to total assets ratio, which has increased slightly between 2000 and 2001.

Interest Margin to Average Earning Assets

This is a key determinant of bank profitability, for it provides an indication of management's ability to control the spread between interest income and interest expense. Exhibit 12-3 presents this ratio for National City and indicates an increase in profitability.

Loan Loss Coverage Ratio

The loan loss coverage ratio, computed by dividing pretax income plus provision for loan losses by net charge-offs, helps determine the asset quality and the level of protection of loans. Exhibit 12-4 presents this ratio for National City. This ratio decreased materially in 2001.

Equity Capital to Total Assets

This ratio, also called funds to total assets, measures the extent of equity ownership in the bank. This ownership provides the cushion against the risk of using debt and leverage. Exhibit 12-5 presents this ratio, computed by using average figures, for National City. This ratio increased in 2001 to 7.51% from 7.18% in 2000. Both of these ratios appear to be good.

Deposits Times Capital

The ratio of deposits times capital concerns both depositors and stockholders. To some extent, it is a type of debt/equity ratio, indicating a bank's debt position. More capital implies a greater

---

EXHIBIT 12-2   **NATIONAL CITY**
Earning Assets to Total Assets 2001 and 2000

(in millions of dollars)	2001	2000
Average Earning Assets [A]	$84,837	$77,782
Average Total Assets [B]	$93,110	$85,550
Earnings Assets to Total Assets [A ÷ B]	91.11%	90.92%

EXHIBIT 12-3   **NATIONAL CITY**
Interest Margin to Average Earning Assets
For the Years Ended December 31, 2001 and 2000

(in thousands of dollars)	2001	2000
Interest margin [A]	$3,438,849	$2,958,362
Average earning assets [B]	$84,837,000	$77,782,000
Interest margin to average earning assets [A ÷ B]	4.05%*	3.80%*

---

*The annual report has 4.09% and 3.85% for 2001 and 2000, respectively.

| EXHIBIT 12-4 | **NATIONAL CITY**
Loan Loss Coverage Ratio
For the Years Ended December 31, 2001 and 2000 |

(in thousands of dollars)	2001	2000
Pretax income	$2,166,501	$1,971,892
Provision for loan losses [A]	$ 605,300	$ 286,800
	$2,771,801	$2,258,692
Net charge-offs [B]	$ 462,600	$ 286,300
Loan loss coverage ratio [A ÷ B]	5.99 times	7.89 times

| EXHIBIT 12-5 | **NATIONAL CITY**
Equity Capital to Total Assets
For the Years Ended December 31, 2001 and 2000 |

(in millions of dollars)	2001	2000
Average equity [A]	$6,991	$6,140
Average total assets [B]	$93,110	$85,550
Equity capital to total assets [A ÷ B]	7.51%	7.18%

margin of safety, while a larger deposit base gives a prospect of higher return to stockholders, since more money is available for investment purposes. Exhibit 12-6 presents this ratio for National City, based on average figures. Deposits times capital decreased in 2001 to 8.28 from 8.48 in 2000.

Loans to Deposits

Average total loans to average deposits is a type of asset to liability ratio. Loans make up a large portion of the bank's assets, and its principal obligations are the deposits that can be withdrawn on request—within time limitations. This is a type of debt coverage ratio, and it measures the position of the bank with regard to taking risks. Exhibit 12-7 shows this ratio for National City. Loans to deposits increased moderately in 2001, indicating an increase in risk from a debt standpoint.

REGULATED UTILITIES

Regulated utilities render a unique service on which the public depends. Regulated utilities are basically monopolies subject to government regulation, including rate regulation. In recent years, laws have been enacted that greatly reduce the monopoly aspect.

Uniformity of accounting is prescribed by the Federal Energy Regulatory Commission for interstate electric and gas companies and by the Federal Communications Commission for telephone and telegraph companies, as well as by state regulatory agencies.

| EXHIBIT 12-6 | **NATIONAL CITY**
Deposits Times Capital
For the Years Ended December 31, 2001 and 2000 |

(in millions of dollars)	2001	2000
Average deposits [A]	$57,908	$52,069
Average stockholders' equity [B]	$6,991	$6,140
Deposits times capital [A ÷ B]	8.28 times	8.48 times

| EXHIBIT 12-7 | **NATIONAL CITY**
Loans to Deposits
For the Years Ended December 31, 2001 and 2000 |

(in millions of dollars)	2001	2000
Average total loans [A]	$75,605	$65,325
Average deposits [B]	$57,908	$52,069
Loans to deposits [A ÷ B]	130.56%	125.46%

This section includes comments on regulated utilities. In recent years most utilities have added nonregulated businesses. In many cases the nonregulated businesses have become more than the regulated businesses. These utilities usually do not present financial reports like a regulated utility, especially the form of the balance sheet. These balance sheets may appear like a normal balance sheet. The ratios introduced in this section may not be feasible to be computed for utilities with substantial nonregulated businesses.

Financial Statements

Balance sheets for utilities differ from business balance sheets mainly in the order that accounts for utilities are presented. Plant and equipment are the first assets listed, followed by investments and other assets, current assets, and deferred charges. Under liabilities and equity, the first section is capitalization. The capitalization section usually includes all sources of long-term capital, such as common stock, preferred stock, and long-term debt. The capitalization section is followed by current liabilities, and then deferred credits and other.

The income statement for utilities is set up by operating revenues, less operating expenses to arrive at net operating income. Net operating income is adjusted by other income (deductions) to arrive at income before interest charges. Interest charges are then deducted to arrive at net income.

Exhibit 12-8 presents a part of the 2001 annual report of Southwest Gas Corporation. Review Exhibit 12-8 to become familiar with the form of utility financial statements.

Inventories are not a problem for electric utilities. Traditionally, receivables have not been a problem because the services are essential and could be cut off for nonpayment and because often a prepayment is required of the customer. In recent years, receivables have been a problem for some utilities because some utility commissions have ruled that services could not be cut off during the winter.

A few accounts on the financial statements of a utility are particularly important to the understanding of the statements. On the balance sheet, many utilities have a construction work in progress account. Exhibit 12-8 discloses that Southwest Gas had construction work in progress of $50,491,000 and $41,727,000 in 2001 and 2000, respectively.

Utilities that have substantial construction work in progress are usually viewed as being more risky investments than utilities that do not. Most utility commissions allow no construction work in progress or only a small amount in the rate base. Therefore, the utility rates essentially do not reflect the construction work in progress.

The utility intends to have the additional property and plant considered in the rate base when the construction work is completed. However, the utility commission may not allow all of this property and plant in the rate base. If the commission rules that inefficiency caused part of the cost, it may disallow the cost. The commission may also disallow part of the cost on the grounds that the utility used bad judgment and provided for excess capacity. Costs disallowed are in effect charged to the stockholders, as future income will not include a return on disallowed cost. In the long run, everybody pays for inefficiency and excess capacity because disallowed costs are a risk that can drive the stock price down and interest rates up for the utility. This increases the cost of capital for the utility, which in turn may force utility rates up.

For the costs allowed, the risk exists that the utility commission will not allow a reasonable rate of return. It is important to observe what proportion of total property and plant is represented by construction work in progress. Also, be familiar with the political climate of the utility commission that will be ruling on the construction work in progress costs.

EXHIBIT 12-8	**SOUTHWEST GAS CORPORATION** **Selected Financial Data**

CONSOLIDATED BALANCE SHEETS

December 31	2001	2000
(Thousands of dollars, except par value)		
Assets		
Utility plant:		
Gas plant	$2,561,937	$2,369,697
Less: accumulated depreciation	(789,751)	(728,466)
Acquisition adjustments, net	2,894	3,124
Construction work in progress	50,491	41,727
Net utility plant (Note 2)	1,825,571	1,686,082
Other property and investments	92,511	91,685
Current assets:		
Cash and cash equivalents	32,486	19,955
Accounts receivable, net of allowances (Note 3)	155,382	135,609
Accrued utility revenue	63,773	57,873
Taxes receivable, net	26,697	13,394
Deferred purchased gas costs (Note 4)	83,501	92,064
Prepaids and other current assets (Note 4)	38,310	84,334
Total current assets	400,149	403,229
Deferred charges and other assets (Note 4)	51,381	51,341
Total assets	$2,369,612	$2,232,337
Capitalization and Liabilities		
Capitalization:		
Common stock, $1 par (authorized—45,000,000 shares; issued and outstanding—32,492,832 and 31,710,004 shares)	$ 34,123	$ 33,340
Additional paid-in capital	470,410	454,132
Retained earnings	56,667	45,995
Total common equity	561,200	533,467
Company-obligated mandatorily redeemable preferred securities of the Company's subsidiary, Southwest Gas Capital I, holding solely $61.8 million principal amount of 9.125% subordinated notes of the Company due 2025 (Note 5)	60,000	60,000
Long-term debt, less current maturities (Note 6)	796,351	896,417
Total capitalization	1,417,551	1,489,884
Commitments and contingencies (Note 8)		
Current liabilities:		
Current maturities of long-term debt (Note 6)	307,641	8,139
Short-term debt (Note 7)	93,000	131,000
Accounts payable	109,167	194,679
Customer deposits	30,288	29,039
Accrued taxes	32,069	—
Accrued interest	20,423	15,702
Deferred income taxes (Note 10)	24,154	48,965
Other current liabilities	36,299	54,006
Total current liabilities	653,041	481,530
Deferred income taxes and other credits:		
Deferred income taxes and investment tax credits (Note 10)	217,804	204,168
Other deferred credits (Note 4)	81,216	56,755
Total deferred income taxes and other credits	299,020	260,923
Total capitalization and liabilities	$2,369,612	$2,232,337

(continued)

EXHIBIT 12-8	**SOUTHWEST GAS CORPORATION**
	Selected Financial Data (*continued*)

CONSOLIDATED STATEMENTS OF INCOME

Year Ended December 31	2001	2000	1999
(in thousands, except per share amounts)			
Operating revenues:			
Gas operating revenues	$1,193,102	$ 870,711	$791,155
Construction revenues	203,586	163,376	145,711
Total operating revenues	1,396,688	1,034,087	936,866
Operating expenses:			
Net cost of gas sold	677,547	394,711	330,031
Operations and maintenance	253,026	231,175	221,258
Depreciation and amortization	118,448	106,640	98,525
Taxes other than income taxes	32,780	29,819	27,610
Construction expenses	180,904	143,112	128,230
Total operating expenses	1,262,705	905,457	805,654
Operating income	133,893	128,630	131,212
Other income and (expenses):			
Net interest deductions	(80,731)	(70,671)	(63,202)
Preferred securities distributions (Note 5)	(5,475)	(5,475)	(5,475)
Other income (deductions)	8,964	(545)	(1,580)
Total other income and (expenses)	(77,242)	(76,691)	(70,257)
Income before income taxes	56,741	51,939	60,955
Income tax expense (Note 10)	19,585	13,628	21,645
Net income	$ 37,156	$ 38,311	$ 39,310
Basic earnings per share (Note 12)	$1.16	$1.22	$1.28
Diluted earnings per share (Note 12)	$1.15	$1.21	$1.27
Average number of common shares outstanding	32,122	31,371	30,690
Average shares outstanding (assuming dilution)	32,398	31,575	30,965

NOTES TO CONSOLIDATED FINANCIAL STATEMENTS (in Part)

Allowance for Funds Used During Construction (AFUDC). AFUDC represents the cost of both debt and equity funds used to finance utility construction. AFUDC is capitalized as part of the cost of utility plant. The Company capitalized $2.5 million in 2001, $1.6 million in 2000, and $2.3 million in 1999 of AFUDC related to natural gas utility operations. The debt portion of AFUDC is reported in the consolidated statements of income as an offset to net interest deductions and the equity portion is reported as other income. Utility plant construction costs, including AFUDC, are recovered in authorized rates through depreciation when completed projects are placed into operation, and general rate relief is requested and granted.

The income statement accounts—allowance for equity funds and allowance for borrowed funds used during construction—relate to construction work in progress costs on the balance sheet. Both of these accounts, sometimes jointly referred to as the allowance for funds used during construction, have been added to construction work in progress costs.

The account allowance for equity funds used during construction represents an assumed rate of return on equity funds used for construction. The account allowance for borrowed funds used during construction represents the cost of borrowed funds that are used for construction.

By increasing the balance sheet account, construction work in progress, for an assumed rate of return on equity funds, the utility builds into the cost base an amount for an assumed rate of return on equity funds. As explained previously, the utility commission may not accept this cost base. The costs that have been added into the cost base have also been added to income, through the allowance for equity funds. Sometimes the account allowance for equity funds used during construction represents a significant portion of the utility's net income.

The income statement account, allowance for borrowed funds used during construction, charges to the balance sheet account, construction in progress, the interest on borrowed funds used for construction in progress. Thus, this interest is added to the cost base.

Utilities with substantial construction work in progress can have significant cash flow problems. Their reported net income can be substantially higher than the cash flow related to the income statement. Sometimes these utilities issue additional bonds and stocks to obtain funds to pay interest and dividends.

Exhibit 12-8 discloses that Southwest Gas had relatively immaterial construction work in progress at the end of 2001. Exhibit 12-8 also shows a relatively immaterial allowance for equity funds used during construction and allowance for borrowed funds used during construction throughout 2001. This indicates that the company's quality of earnings have not been substantially impacted by construction work in progress.

Ratios for Regulated Utilities

Because of the vastly different accounts and statement formats, few of the traditional ratios are appropriate for regulated utilities. Exceptions are the return on assets, return on equity, debt/equity, and times interest earned. Investor-related ratios are also of value in analyzing utilities. For example, the cash flow per-share ratio can be a particularly important indicator of the utility's ability to maintain and increase dividends. Standard & Poor's *Industry Survey* is a good source for composite industry data on utilities.

Operating Ratio

The operating ratio measures efficiency by comparing operating expenses to operating revenues. A profitable utility holds this ratio low. A vertical common-size analysis of the income statement will aid in conclusions regarding this ratio. Exhibit 12-9 presents the operating ratio for Southwest Gas. This ratio increased in 2001, thus having a negative influence on profitability.

Funded Debt to Operating Property

A key ratio, the comparison of funded debt to net fixed operating property, is sometimes termed LTD (long-term debt) to *net property* because funded debt is long-term debt. Operating property consists of property and plant less the allowance for depreciation and any allowance for nuclear fuel amortization. Construction in progress is included since it has probably been substantially funded by debt. This ratio measures debt coverage and indicates how funds are supplied. It resembles debt to total assets, with only specialized debt and the specific assets that generate the profits to cover the debt charges. Exhibit 12-10 presents funded debt to operating property for Southwest Gas. This ratio increased in 2001, indicating a more risky debt position.

Percent Earned on Operating Property

This ratio, sometimes termed *earnings on net property*, relates net earnings to the assets primarily intended to generate earnings—net property and plant. Exhibit 12-11 presents this ratio for Southwest Gas. Note that this ratio decreased in 2001, which is an unfavorable trend.

EXHIBIT 12-9   **SOUTHWEST GAS CORPORATION**
Operating Ratio
For the Years Ended December 31, 2001 and 2000

(in thousands of dollars)	2001	2000
Operating expenses* [A]	$1,081,801	$762,345
Operating revenues* [B]	$1,193,102	$870,711
Operating ratio [A ÷ B]	90.67%	87.55%

*Did not include construction revenues or construction expenses.

EXHIBIT 12-10	**SOUTHWEST GAS CORPORATION** **Funded Debt to Operating Property** **For the Years Ended December 31, 2001 and 2000**

(in thousands of dollars)	2001	2000
Funded debt* [A]	$1,103,992	$904,556
Operating property [B]	$1,825,571	$1,686,082
Funded debt to operating property [A ÷ B]	60.47%	53.65%

*Included long-term debt and current maturities of long-term debt.

EXHIBIT 12-11	**SOUTHWEST GAS CORPORATION** **Percent Earned on Operating Property** **For the Years Ended December 31, 2001 and 2000**

(in thousands of dollars)	2001	2000
Net income [A]	$37,156	$38,311
Operating property* [B]	$1,775,080	$1,644,355
Percent earned on operating property [A ÷ B]	2.09%	2.33%

*Excluded construction work in progress.

Operating Revenue to Operating Property

This ratio is basically an operating asset turnover ratio. In public utilities, the fixed plant is often much larger than the expected annual revenue, and this ratio will be less than 1. Exhibit 12-12 presents this ratio for Southwest Gas, which indicates an increase in the operating revenue to operating property and represents a favorable trend.

OIL AND GAS

Oil and gas companies' financial statements are affected significantly by the method they choose to account for costs associated with exploration and production. The method chosen is some variation of the successful-efforts or full-costing methods, which will be explained along with their effects on the financial statements. The financial statements of oil and gas companies are also unique because they are required to disclose, in a footnote, supplementary information on oil and gas exploration, development, and production activities. This requirement will be explained in this section.

EXHIBIT 12-12	**SOUTHWEST GAS CORPORATION** **Operating Revenue to Operating Property** **For the Years Ended December 31, 2001 and 2000**

(in thousands of dollars)	2001	2000
Operating revenues* [A]	$1,193,102	$870,711
Operating property** [B]	$1,775,080	$1,644,355
Operating revenue to operating property [A ÷ B]	67.21%	52.95%

*Removed construction revenues.
**Removed construction work in progress.

Cash flow is important to all companies, but particularly to oil and gas companies. Therefore, cash flow must be part of the analysis of an oil or a gas company. In addition, most of the traditional financial ratios apply to oil and gas companies. This section will not cover special ratios that relate to oil and gas companies.

The 2001 financial statements of Conoco will be used to illustrate oil and gas financial statements. Conoco is an integrated international energy company.

Successful-Efforts Versus Full-Costing Methods

A variation of one of two costing methods is used by an oil or a gas company to account for exploration and production costs: the successful-efforts method and the full-costing method.

The **successful-efforts method** places only exploration and production costs of successful wells on the balance sheet under property, plant, and equipment. Exploration and production costs of unsuccessful (or dry) wells are expensed when it is determined that there is a dry hole. With the **full-costing method,** exploration and production costs of all the wells (successful and unsuccessful) are placed on the balance sheet under property, plant, and equipment.

Under both methods, exploration and production costs placed on the balance sheet are subsequently amortized as expense to the income statement. Amortization costs that relate to natural resources are called *depletion expense.*

The costing method used for exploration and production can have a very significant influence on the balance sheet and the income statement. Under both methods, exploration and production costs are eventually expensed, but a significant difference exists in the timing of the expense.

In theory, the successful-efforts method takes the position that a direct relationship exists between costs incurred and specific reserves discovered. These costs should be placed on the balance sheet. Costs associated with unsuccessful efforts are a period expense and should be charged to expense. In theory, the full-costing method takes the position that the drilling of all wells, successful and unsuccessful, is part of the process of finding successful wells. Therefore, all of the cost should be placed on the balance sheet.

In practice, the decision to use the successful-efforts method or the full-costing method is probably not significantly influenced by theory, but by practicalities. Most relatively small oil and gas companies select a variation of the full-costing method. This results in a much larger balance sheet. In the short run, it also usually results in higher reported profits. Small oil companies speculate that the larger balance sheet and the increased reported profits can be used to influence some banks and limited partners, which the small companies tend to use as sources of funds.

Large oil and gas companies tend to select a variation of the successful-efforts method. This results in a lower balance sheet amount and lower reported income in the short run. The large companies usually depend on bonds and stock as their primary sources of outside capital. Investors in bonds and stock are not likely to be influenced by the larger balance sheet and higher income that results from capitalizing dry wells.

The method used can have a significant influence on the balance sheet and the income statement. The successful-efforts method is more conservative. Review Exhibit 12-13 for a description of Conoco's method of accounting for exploration and production costs.

Supplementary Information on Oil and Gas Exploration, Development, and Production Activities

As part of your review of an oil or a gas company, note the supplemental oil and gas information. Review Exhibit 12-14 for a brief summary of the supplementary information presented by Conoco.

Cash Flow

Monitoring cash flow can be particularly important when following an oil or a gas company. The potential for a significant difference exists between the reported income and cash flow from operations. One reason is that large sums can be spent for exploration and development, years in advance of revenue from the found reserves. The other reason is that there can be significant differ-

| EXHIBIT 12-13 | **CONOCO**
Note 1 to Consolidated Financial Statements (in Part)
Depletion and Amortization—2001 Annual Report |

Oil and Gas Properties

We follow the successful efforts method of accounting. Under successful efforts, the costs of property acquisitions, successful exploratory wells, development wells and related support equipment and facilities are capitalized. The costs of producing properties are amortized at the field level on a unit-of-production method.

Unproved properties that are individually significant are periodically assessed for impairment. The impairment of individually insignificant properties is recorded by amortizing the costs based on past experience and the estimated holding period. Ex-

ploratory well costs are expensed in the period a well is determined to be unsuccessful. All other exploration costs, including geological and geophysical costs, production costs and overhead costs, are expensed in the period incurred.

The estimated costs of dismantlement and removal of oil- and gas-related facilities, well plugging and abandonment, and other site restoration costs are accrued over the properties' productive lives using the unit-of-production method and recognized as a liability as the amortization expense is recorded. See note 21 for further details.

| EXHIBIT 12-14 | **CONOCO**
Supplemental Oil and Gas Information (in Part)
2001 Annual Report |

Conoco presented Supplemental Petroleum Data (unaudited) using seven pages in their 2001 annual report. The title of the tables follow:

- Results of operations for oil and gas producing activities and syncrude mining operations.
- Costs incurred in oil and gas property acquisition, exploration and development activities and syncrude mining operation.
- Capitalized costs relating to oil and gas producing activities and syncrude mining operations.

- Estimated proved reserves of oil, gas and syncrude in millions of barrels-of-oil-equivalent (MMOE).
- Proved developed reserves in millions of barrels.
- Estimated proved reserves of gas in billion cubic feet (bcf)
- Proved developed reserves in billion cubic feet.
- Standardized measure of discounted future net cash flows relating to proved oils and gas reserves.
- Summary of changes in standardized measure of discounted future net cash flows relating to proved oil and gas reserves.

ences between when expenses are deducted on the financial statements and when they are deducted on the tax return. Therefore, observe the operating cash flow.

Cash from operating activities for a three-year period will be disclosed on the statement of cash flows. For Conoco, net cash provided by operating activities was $3,141,000,000, $3,438,000,000, and $2,216,000,000 for 2001, 2000, and 1999, respectively. Net income for Conoco was $1,589,000,000, $1,902,000,000, and $744,000,000 for 2001, 2000, and 1999, respectively.

TRANSPORTATION

Three components of the transportation industry will be discussed: air carriers, railroads, and the motor carrier industry. The Civil Aeronautics Board, which requires the use of a uniform system of accounts and reporting, regulates interstate commercial aviation. The Interstate Commerce Commission, which also has control over a uniform system of accounts and reporting, regulates interstate railroads. The Interstate Commerce Commission also regulates interstate motor carriers whose principal business is transportation services.

Financial Statements

The balance sheet format for air carriers, railroads, and motor carriers resembles that for manufacturing or retailing firms. As in a heavy manufacturing firm, property and equipment make up a large portion of assets. Also, supplies and parts comprise the basic inventory items. The income statement format resembles that of a utility. The system of accounts provides for the grouping of all revenues and expenses in terms of both major natural objectives and functional activities. There is no cost of goods sold calculation; rather, there is operating income: revenue (categorized) minus operating expenses. In essence, the statements are a prescribed, categorized form of single-step income statement. They cannot be converted to multiple-step format.

Ratios

Most of the traditional ratios also apply in the transportation field. Exceptions are inventory turnovers (because there is no cost of goods sold) and gross profit margin. The ratios discussed in the subsections that follow are especially suited to transportation. They are derived from the 2001 statement of income and balance sheet for Delta Air Lines, Inc., presented in Exhibit 12-15.

EXHIBIT 12-15	**DELTA AIR LINES, INC.** **Air Transportation** **Selected Financial Data**

Consolidated Balance Sheets
December 31, 2001 and 2000

Assets *in millions*	**2001**	**2000**
Current Assets:		
Cash and cash equivalents	$ 2,210	$ 1,364
Short-term investments	5	243
Accounts receivable, net of allowance for uncollectible accounts of		
$43 at December 31, 2001 and $31 at December 31, 2000	368	406
Expendable parts and supplies inventories, net of an allowance for obsolescence		
of $139 at December 31, 2001 and $124 at December 31, 2000	181	170
Deferred income taxes	518	345
Fuel hedge contracts, at fair market value	55	319
Prepaid expenses and other	230	358
Total current assets	3,567	3,205
Property and Equipment:		
Flight equipment	19,427	17,371
Less: Accumulated depreciation	5,730	5,139
Flight equipment, net	13,697	12,232
Flight equipment under capital leases	382	484
Less: Accumulated amortization	262	324
Flight equipment under capital leases, net	120	160
Ground property and equipment	4,412	4,371
Less: Accumulated depreciation	2,355	2,313
Ground property and equipment, net	2,057	2,058
Advance payment for equipment	223	390
Total property and equipment, net	16,097	14,840
Other Assets:		
Investments in debt and equity securities	96	339
Investments in associated companies	180	222
Cost in excess of net assets acquired, net of accumulated amortization		
of $253 at December 31, 2001 and $196 at December 31, 2000	2,092	2,149
Operating rights and other intangibles, net of accumulated amortization		
of $246 at December 31, 2001 and $236 at December 31, 2000	94	102
Restricted investments for Boston airport terminal project	475	—
Other noncurrent assets	1,004	1,074
Total other assets	3,941	3,886
Total assets	$23,605	$21,931

(continued)

EXHIBIT 12-15	**DELTA AIR LINES, INC.**

Air Transportation
Selected Financial Data (*continued*)

Liabilities and Shareowners' Equity
in millions, except share data

	2001	2000
Current Liabilities:		
Current maturities of long-term debt	$ 260	$ 62
Short-term obligations	765	—
Current obligations under capital leases	31	40
Accounts payable and miscellaneous accrued liabilities	1,617	1,634
Air traffic liability	1,224	1,442
Income and excise taxes payable	1,049	614
Accrued salaries and related benefits	1,121	1,170
Accrued rent	336	283
Total current liabilities	6,403	5,245
Noncurrent Liabilities:		
Long-term debt	7,781	5,797
Long-term debt issued by Massachusetts Port Authority	498	—
Capital leases	68	99
Postretirement benefits	2,292	2,026
Accrued rent	781	721
Deferred income taxes	465	1,220
Other	464	388
Total noncurrent liabilities	12,349	10,251
Deferred Credits:		
Deferred gain on sale and leaseback transactions	519	568
Manufacturers' and other credits	310	290
Total deferred credits	829	858
Commitments and Contingencies (Notes 3, 4, 5, 8, 10 and 11)		
Employee Stock Ownership Plan Preferred Stock:		
Series B ESOP Convertible Preferred Stock, $1.00 par value, $72.00 stated and liquidation value; 6,278,210 shares issued and outstanding at December 31, 2001, and 6,405,563 shares issued and outstanding at December 31, 2000	452	460
Unearned compensation under employee stock ownership plan	(197)	(226)
Total Employee Stock Ownership Plan Preferred Stock	255	234
Shareowners' Equity:		
Common stock, $1.50 par value; 450,000,000 shares authorized; 180,890,356 shares issued at December 31, 2001 and 180,764,057 shares issued at December 31, 2000	271	271
Additional paid-in capital	3,267	3,264
Retained earnings	2,930	4,176
Accumulated other comprehensive income	25	360
Treasury stock at cost, 57,644,690 shares at December 31, 2001 and 57,750,685 shares at December 31, 2000	(2,724)	(2,728)
Total shareowners' equity	3,769	5,343
Total liabilities and shareowners' equity	$23,605	$21,931

(continued)

The traditional sources of industry averages cover transportation. The federal government accumulates numerous statistics for regulated industries, including transportation. An example is the Interstate Commerce Commission's *Annual Report* on transport statistics in the United States.

For the motor carrier industry, a particularly good source of industry data is the annual publication *Financial Analysis of the Motor Carrier Industry*, published by the American Trucking Association, Inc., 1616 P Street, NW, Washington, DC 20036. This publication includes an economic and industry overview, distribution of revenue by carrier type, and industry issues. It also includes definitions of terminology that relate to the motor carrier industry.

EXHIBIT 12-15	**DELTA AIR LINES, INC.** **Air Transportation** **Selected Financial Data** (*continued*)

Consolidated Statement of Operations
For the years ended December 31, 2001, 2000, and 1999

in millions, except per share data	**2001**	**2000**	**1999**
Operating Revenues:			
Passenger	**$12,964**	$15,657	$13,949
Cargo	**506**	583	561
Other, net	**409**	501	373
Total operating revenues	**13,879**	16,741	14,883
Operating Expenses:			
Salaries and related costs	**6,124**	5,971	5,194
Aircraft fuel	**1,817**	1,969	1,421
Depreciation and amortization	**1,283**	1,187	1,057
Other selling expenses	**616**	688	626
Passenger commissions	**540**	661	784
Contracted services	**1,016**	966	824
Landing fees and other rents	**780**	771	723
Aircraft rent	**737**	741	622
Aircraft maintenance materials and outside repairs	**801**	723	594
Passenger service	**466**	470	498
Asset writedowns and other nonrecurring items	**1,119**	108	469
Stabilization Act compensation	**(634)**	—	—
Other	**816**	849	753
Total operating expenses	**15,481**	15,104	13,565
Operating Income (Loss)	**(1,602)**	1,637	1,318
Other Income (Expense):			
Interest expense, net	**(410)**	(257)	(126)
Net gain from sale of investments	**127**	301	927
Miscellaneous income (expense), net	**(47)**	27	(26)
Fair value adjustments of SFAS 133 derivatives	**68**	(159)	—
Total other income (expense)	**(262)**	(88)	775
Income (Loss) Before Income Taxes and Cumulative Effect of Change in Accounting Principle	**(1,864)**	1,549	2,093
Income tax benefit (provision)	**648**	(621)	(831)
Net Income (Loss) Before Cumulative Effect of Change in Accounting Principle, Net of Tax	**(1,216)**	928	1,262
Cumulative Effect of Change in Accounting Principle, Net of Tax of $64 Million in 2000 and $35 Million in 1999	**—**	(100)	(54)
Net Income (Loss)	**(1,216)**	828	1,208
Preferred Stock Dividends	**(14)**	(13)	(12)
Net Income (Loss) Available to Common Shareowners	**$ (1,230)**	$ 815	$ 1,196
Basic Earnings (Loss) per Share Before Cumulative Effect of Changes in Accounting Principles	**$(9.99)**	$7.39	$9.05
Basic Earnings (Loss) per Share	**$(9.99)**	$6.58	$8.66
Diluted Earnings (Loss) per Share Before Cumulative Effect of Changes in Accounting Principles	**$(9.99)**	$7.05	$8.52
Diluted Earnings (Loss) per Share	**$(9.99)**	$6.28	$8.15

There are hundreds of motor carrier firms, most of which are relatively small. The American Trucking Association compiles data by composite carrier groups. For example, Group A includes composite data for several hundred general freight carriers with annual revenues of less than $5 million. One of the groups includes composite data for the publicly held carriers of general freight.

The very extensive composite data in the American Trucking Association publication include industry total dollars for the income statement and balance sheet. It also includes vertical common-size analyses for the income statement and the balance sheet. This publication also includes approximately 36 ratios and other analytical data, such as total tons.

Operating Ratio

The operating ratio is computed by comparing operating expense to operating revenue. It measures cost and should be kept low, but external conditions, such as the level of business activity, may affect this ratio. Operating revenues vary from year to year because of differences in rates, classification of traffic, volume of traffic carried, and the distance traffic is transported. Operating expenses change because of variations in the price level, traffic carried, the type of service performed, and the effectiveness of operating and maintaining the properties. Common-size analysis of revenues and expenses is needed to explain changes in the operating ratio.

Exhibit 12-16 presents the operating ratio for Delta Air Lines, Inc. The operating ratio for Delta increased from 90.22% in 2000 to 111.54% in 2001. The operating ratio can dramatically affect the profitability of a carrier. In fact, Delta went from an operating income in 2000 of $1,637,000,000 to an operating loss in 2001 of $1,602,000,000.

Long-Term Debt to Operating Property

Because of the transportation companies' heavy investment in operating assets, such as equipment, the long-term ratios increase in importance. Long-term borrowing capacity is also a key consideration. The ratio of long-term debt to operating property ratio gives a measure of the sources of funds with which property is obtained. It also measures borrowing capacity. Operating property is defined as long-term property and equipment. Exhibit 12-17 presents this ratio for Delta Air Lines. For Delta, the long-term debt to operating property ratio increased in 2001 to 51.85% from 39.73%. This represents a major negative trend.

Operating Revenue to Operating Property

This ratio measures turnover of operating assets. The objective is to generate as many dollars in revenue per dollar of property as possible. Exhibit 12-18 presents this ratio for Delta Air Lines. The operating revenue to operating property decreased substantially between 2001 and 2000.

EXHIBIT 12-16   **DELTA AIR LINES, INC.**
Operating Ratio
For the Years Ended December 31, 2001 and 2000

(in millions)	2001	2000
Operating expenses [A]	$15,481	$15,104
Operating revenues [B]	$13,879	$16,741
Operating ratio [A ÷ B]	111.54%	90.22%

EXHIBIT 12-17   **DELTA AIR LINES, INC.**
Long-Term Debt to Operating Property
For the Years Ended December 31, 2001 and 2000

(in millions)	2001	2000
Long-term debt	$ 7,781	$ 5,797
Long-term debt issued by Massachusetts Port Authority	498	—
Capital leases	68	99
[A]	$ 8,347	$ 5,896
Operating property [B]	$16,097	$14,840
Long-term debt to operating property [A ÷ B]	51.85%	39.73%

EXHIBIT 12-18	**DELTA AIR LINES, INC.** **Operating Revenue to Operating Property** **For the Years Ended December 31, 2001 and 2000**

(in millions)	2001	2000
Operating revenue [A]	$13,879	$16,741
Operating property [B]	$16,097	$14,840
Operating revenue to operating property [A ÷ B]	86.22%	112.81%

Per-Mile, Per-Person, and Per-Ton Passenger Load Factors

For transportation companies, additional insight can be gained by looking at revenues and expenses on a per unit of usage basis. Examples would be per mile of line or per 10 miles for railroads, or a per passenger mile for air carriers. Although this type of disclosure is not required, it is often presented in highlights.

This type of disclosure is illustrated in Exhibit 12-19, which shows statistics for Delta Air Lines. Statistics in Exhibit 12-19 are available for revenue passengers enplaned, available seat miles, revenue passenger miles, operating revenue per available seat mile, passenger mile yield, operating cost per available seat mile, passenger load factor, breakeven passenger load factor, available ton miles, revenue ton miles, and operating cost per available ton mile.

EXHIBIT 12-19	**DELTA AIR LINES, INC.** **Other Financial and Statistical Data** **For the Years Ended December 31, 2001–1998***

	2001[1]	2000[2]	1999[3]	1998
Total assets (millions)	$23,605	$21,931	$19,942	$14,727
Long-term debt and capital leases (excluding current maturities) (millions)	$8,347	$5,896	$4,303	$1,720
Shareowners' equity (millions)	$3,769	$5,343	$4,908	$4,077
Shares of Common Stock outstanding at year-end[10]	123,245,666	123,013,372	132,893,470	141,514,262
Revenue passengers enplaned (thousands)	104,943	119,930	110,083	105,304
Available seat miles (millions)	147,837	154,974	147,073	142,154
Revenue passenger miles (millions)	101,717	112,998	106,165	103,342
Operating revenue per available seat mile	9.39¢	10.80¢	10.12¢	10.07¢
Passenger mile yield	12.74¢	13.86¢	13.14¢	12.99¢
Operating cost per available seat mile	10.47¢	9.75¢	9.22¢	8.80¢
Passenger load factor	68.80%	72.91%	72.18%	72.70%
Breakeven passenger load factor	77.31%	65.29%	65.37%	62.94%
Available ton miles (millions)	22,282	22,925	21,245	20,312
Revenue ton miles (millions)	11,752	13,058	12,227	12,052
Operating cost per available ton miles	69.48¢	65.88¢	63.85¢	61.58¢

[1] Includes $299 million in pretax unusual charges, net ($1.53 diluted loss per share). See Management's Discussion and Analysis, page 14.

[2] Includes $51 million in pretax unusual gains, net ($0.25 basic and $0.24 diluted earnings per share), excluding the cumulative effect of a change in accounting principle. See Management's Discussion and Analysis, page 14.

[3] Includes $418 million in pretax unusual gains, net ($1.85 basic and $1.73 diluted earnings per share), excluding the cumulative effect of a change in accounting principle. See Management's Discussion and Analysis, page 16.

[10] All share and earnings per share amounts for years prior to 1999 have been restated to reflect the two-for-one common stock split that became effective on November 2, 1998.

*This time period represents four years out of a 10-year presentation.

INSURANCE   Insurance companies provide two types of services. One is an identified contract service—mortality protection or loss protection. The second is investment management service.

There are basically four types of insurance organizations:

1. **Stock companies.** A stock company is a corporation organized to earn profits for its stockholders. The comments in this insurance section relate specifically to stock companies. Many of the comments are also valid for the other types of insurance organizations.
2. **Mutual companies.** A mutual company is an incorporated entity, without private ownership interest, operating for the benefit of its policyholders and their beneficiaries.
3. **Fraternal benefit societies.** A fraternal benefit society resembles a mutual insurance company in that, although incorporated, it does not have capital stock, and it operates for the benefit of its members and beneficiaries. Policyholders participate in the earnings of the society and the policies stipulate that the society has the power to assess them in case the legal reserves become impaired.
4. **Assessment companies.** An assessment company is an organized group with similar interests, such as a religious denomination.

The regulation of insurance companies started at the state level. Beginning in 1828, the state of New York required that annual reports be filed with the state controller. Subsequently, other states followed this precedent, and all 50 states have insurance departments that require annual statements of insurance companies. The reports are filed with the state insurance departments in accordance with statutory accounting practices (SAP). The National Association of Insurance Commissioners (NAIC), a voluntary association, has succeeded in achieving near uniformity among the states, so there are no significant differences in SAP among the states.[1]

Statutory accounting emphasizes the balance sheet. In its concern for protecting policyholders, statutory accounting focuses on the financial solvency of the insurance corporation. After the annual reports are filed with the individual state insurance departments, a testing process is conducted by the NAIC. This process is based on ratio calculations concerning the financial position of a company. If a company's ratio is outside the prescribed limit, the NAIC brings that to the attention of the state insurance department.

A.M. Best Company publishes *Best's Insurance Reports*, which are issued separately for life-health companies and property-casualty companies. *Best's Insurance Reports* evaluate the financial condition of more than 3,000 insurance companies. The majority of companies are assigned a Best's Rating, ranging from A+ (Superior) to C– (Fair). The other companies are classified as "Not Assigned." The "Not Assigned" category has 10 classifications to identify why a company has not been assigned a Best's Rating.

Some of the items included in Best's data include a balance sheet, summary of operations, operating ratios, profitability ratios, leverage ratios, and liquidity ratios. Most of the ratios are industry-specific. It is not practical to describe and explain them in this book. It should be noted that the financial data, including the ratios, are based on the data submitted to the state insurance departments and are thus based on SAP. Generally accepted accounting principles (GAAP) for insurance companies developed much later than SAP. The annual reports of insurance companies are based on GAAP.

The 1934 Securities and Exchange Act established national government regulation, in addition to the state regulation of insurance companies. Stock insurance companies with assets of $1 million and at least 500 stockholders must register with the SEC and file the required forms, such as the annual Form 10-K. Reports filed with the SEC must conform with GAAP.

Exhibit 12-20 contains the income statement and balance sheet from the 2001 annual report of The Chubb Corporation. These statements were prepared using GAAP. Review them to observe the unique nature of insurance company financial statements.

Balance Sheet Under GAAP

The balance sheet for an insurance company is not classified by current assets and current liabilities (nonclassified balance sheet). Instead, its basic sections are assets, liabilities, and shareholders' equity.

EXHIBIT 12-20   **THE CHUBB CORPORATION**
Consolidated Statement of Income and Balance Sheets
2001 Annual Report

Consolidated Statements of Income

	In Millions Years Ended December 31		
Revenues	**2001**	**2000**	**1999**
Premiums Earned	$6,656.4	$6,145.9	$5,652.0
Investment Income	982.8	957.2	893.4
Real Estate and Other Revenues	114.0	96.9	96.8
Realized Investment Gains	.8	51.5	87.4
TOTAL REVENUES	7,754.0	7,251.5	6,729.6
Claims and Expenses			
Insurance Claims and Claim Expenses	5,357.4	4,127.7	3,942.0
Amortization of Deferred Policy Acquisition Costs	1,771.4	1,645.4	1,529.7
Other Insurance Operating Costs and Expenses	483.4	448.6	375.1
Real Estate and Other Expenses	110.1	87.9	100.3
Investment Expenses	14.1	13.7	13.7
Corporate Expenses	83.6	77.2	58.7
TOTAL CLAIMS AND EXPENSES	7,820.0	6,400.5	6,019.5
INCOME (LOSS) BEFORE FEDERAL AND FOREIGN INCOME TAX	(66.0)	851.0	710.1
Federal and Foreign Income Tax (Credit)	(177.5)	136.4	89.0
NET INCOME	$ 111.5	$ 714.6	$ 621.1
Net Income Per Share			
Basic	$.65	$4.10	$3.70
Diluted	.63	4.01	3.66

(continued)

Assets

The asset section starts with investments, a classification where most insurance companies maintain the majority of their assets. Many of the investments have a high degree of liquidity, so that prompt payment can be assured in the event of a catastrophic loss. The majority of the investments are typically in bonds, with stock investments being much lower. Real estate investments are usually present for both property-casualty insurance companies and for life insurance companies. Because liabilities are relatively short term for property-casualty companies, the investment in real estate for these companies is usually immaterial. For life insurance companies, the investment in real estate may be much greater than for property-casualty companies because of the generally longer-term nature and predictability of their liabilities.

For debt and equity investments, review the disclosure to determine if there are significant differences between the fair value and the cost or amortized cost. Also review the stockholders' equity section of the balance sheet to determine if there is significant unrealized appreciation of investments (gains or losses).

Assets—Other than Investments

A number of asset accounts other than investments may be on an insurance company's balance sheet. Some of the typical accounts are described in the paragraphs that follow.

Real estate used in operations is reported at cost, less accumulated depreciation. Under SAP, real estate used in operations is expensed.

Deferred policy acquisition costs represent the cost of obtaining policies. Under GAAP, these costs are deferred and charged to expense over the premium-paying period. This is one of the major differences between GAAP reporting and SAP reporting. Under SAP reporting, these costs are charged to expense as they are incurred.

EXHIBIT 12-20	**THE CHUBB CORPORATION** **Consolidated Balance Sheets** **2001 Annual Report** (*continued*)

Consolidated Balance Sheets

(Millions, except share and per-share data)

	In Millions December 31 2001	2000
Assets		
Invested Assets		
Short-Term Investments	$ 956.8	$ 605.6
Fixed Maturities		
Held-to-Maturity—Tax Exempt (market $1,282.5 and $1,564.7)	1,218.5	1,496.1
Available-for-Sale		
Tax Exempt (cost $8,053.8 and $8,053.8)	8,372.9	8,380.5
Taxable cost ($6,408.2 and $5,666.6)	6,525.3	5,687.8
Equity Securities (cost $757.9 and $839.8)	710.4	830.6
TOTAL INVESTED ASSETS	17,783.9	17,000.6
Cash	25.8	22.4
Securities Lending Collateral	417.5	451.1
Accrued Investment Income	247.7	246.8
Premiums Receivable	1,692.8	1,409.8
Reinsurance Recoverable on Unpaid Claims and Claim Expenses	4,505.2	1,853.3
Prepaid Reinsurance Premiums	340.8	246.0
Deferred Policy Acquisition Costs	928.8	842.0
Real Estate Assets	646.6	677.1
Investments in Partially Owned Companies	386.2	122.9
Deferred Income Tax	674.8	501.0
Goodwill	467.4	487.3
Other Assets	1,331.5	1,166.4
TOTAL ASSETS	$29,449.0	$25,026.7
Liabilities		
Unpaid Claims and Claim Expenses	$15,514.9	$11,904.6
Unearned Premiums	3,916.2	3,516.3
Securities Lending Payable	417.5	451.1
Short Term Debt	199.0	—
Long Term Debt	1,351.0	753.8
Dividend Payable to Shareholders	57.8	57.8
Accrued Expenses and Other Liabilities	1,467.3	1,361.4
TOTAL LIABILITIES	22,923.7	18,045.0
Commitments and Contingent Liabilities (Notes 9, 15 and 16)		
Shareholders' Equity		
Preferred Stock—Authorized 4,000,000 Shares;		
$1 Par Value; Issued—None	—	—
Common Stock—Authorized 600,000,000 Shares;		
$1 Par Value; Issued 180,131,238 and 178,833,278 Shares	180.1	178.8
Paid-In Surplus	527.0	466.0
Retained Earnings	6,369.3	6,492.6
Accumulated Other Comprehensive Income		
Unrealized Appreciation of Investments, Net of Tax	252.6	220.1
Foreign Currency Translation Losses, Net of Tax	(73.0)	(68.5)
Receivable from Employee Stock Ownership Plan	(48.9)	(62.5)
Treasury Stock, at Cost—10,059,857 and 3,914,105 Shares	(681.8)	(244.8)
TOTAL SHAREHOLDERS' EQUITY	6,525.3	6,981.7
TOTAL LIABILITIES AND SHAREHOLDERS' EQUITY	$29,449.0	$25,026.7

Goodwill is an intangible account resulting from acquiring other companies. The same account can be found on the balance sheet of companies other than insurance companies. Under GAAP, the goodwill account is accounted for as an asset. Under SAP, neither the goodwill account nor other intangibles are recognized.

Liabilities

Generally, the largest liability is for loss reserves. Reserving for losses involves estimating the ultimate value, considering the present value of the commitments. The quantification process is subject to a number of subjective estimates, including inflation, interest rates, and judicial interpretations. Mortality estimates are also important for life insurance companies. These reserve accounts should be adequate to pay policy claims under the terms of the insurance policies.

Another liability account found on an insurance company's balance sheet is policy and contract claims. This account represents claims that have accrued as of the balance sheet date. These claims are reported net of any portion that can be recovered.

Many other liability accounts, such as notes payable and income taxes payable, are found on an insurance company's balance sheet. These are typically reported in the same manner as other industries report them, except there is no current liability classification.

Stockholders' Equity

The stockholders' equity section usually resembles the stockholders' equity section for companies in other industries. The account net unrealized gains (losses) on securities can be particularly large for insurance companies because of the expanded use of this account as a result of standards for insurance companies and the material amount of investments that an insurance company may have. Pay close attention to changes in this account, since these unrealized gains or losses have not been recognized on the income statement.

Income Statement Under GAAP

The manner of recognizing revenue on insurance contracts is unique for the insurance industry. In general, the duration of the contract governs the revenue recognition.

For contracts of short duration, revenue is ordinarily recognized over the period of the contract in proportion to the amount of insurance protection provided. When the risk differs significantly from the contract period, revenue is recognized over the period of risk in proportion to the amount of insurance protection.[2]

Policies relating to loss protection typically fall under the short-duration contract. An example would be casualty insurance in which the insurance company retains the right to cancel the contract at the end of the policy term.

For long-duration contracts, revenue is recognized when the premium is due from the policyholder. Examples would be whole-life contracts and single-premium life contracts.[3] Likewise, acquisition costs are capitalized and expensed in proportion to premium revenue.

Long-duration contracts that do not subject the insurance enterprise to significant risks arising from policyholder mortality or morbidity are referred to as *investment contracts*. Amounts received on these contracts are not to be reported as revenues but rather as liabilities and accounted for in the same way as interest-bearing instruments.[4] The contracts are regarded as investment contracts since they do not incorporate significant insurance risk. Interestingly, many of the life insurance policies currently being written are of this type.

With the investment contracts, premium payments are credited to the policyholder balance. The insurance company assesses charges against this balance for contract services and credits the balance for income earned. The insurer can adjust the schedule for contract services and the rate at which income is credited.

Investment contracts generally include an assessment against the policyholder on inception of the contract and an assessment when the contract is terminated. The inception fees are booked as recoveries of capitalized acquisition costs, and the termination fees are booked as revenue at the time of termination.

In addition to their insurance activities, insurance companies are substantially involved with investments. Realized gains and losses from investments are reported in operations in the period incurred.

Ratios

As previously indicated, many of the ratios relating to insurance companies are industry-specific. An explanation of industry-specific ratios is beyond the scope of this book. The industry-specific ratios are frequently based on SAP financial reporting to the states, rather than the GAAP financial reporting that is used for the annual report and SEC requirements.

Ratios computed from the GAAP-based financial statements are often profitability- and investor-related. Examples of such ratios are return on common equity, price/earnings ratio, dividend payout, and dividend yield. These ratios are explained in other sections of this book.

Insurance companies tend to have a stock market price at a discount to the average market price (price/earnings ratio). This discount is typically 10 to 20%, but at times it is much more. There are likely many reasons for this relatively low market value. Insurance is a highly regulated industry that some perceive as having low growth prospects. It is also an industry with substantial competition. The regulation and the competition put pressure on the premiums that can be charged. The accounting environment likely also contributes to the relatively low market price for insurance company stocks. The existence of two sets of accounting principles, SAP and GAAP, contributes to the lack of understanding of insurance companies' financial statements. Also, many of the accounting standards are complex and industry-specific.

The nature of the insurance industry leads to standards that allow much subjectivity and possible manipulation of reported profit. For example, insurance companies are perceived to underreserve during tough years and overreserve during good years.

REAL ESTATE COMPANIES

Real estate companies typically construct and operate income-producing real properties. Examples of such properties are shopping centers, hotels, and office buildings. A typical project would involve selecting a site, arranging financing, arranging for long-term leases, construction, and subsequently operating and maintaining the property.

Real estate companies contend that conventional accounting—recognizing depreciation but not the underlying value of the property—misleads investors. In some cases, these companies have taken the drastic step of selling major parts or all of the companies' assets to realize greater benefits for stockholders. Some real estate companies have attempted to reflect value by disclosing current value in addition to the conventional accounting. Such a company is The Rouse Company. The Rouse Company arrives at current value using future income potential, assuming that the property is held for the long-term development and sales programs. This is an attempt to indicate annual progress and reflect how investors perceive real estate values.

In The Rouse Company 1998 annual report, the conventional balance sheet has net stockholders' equity of $628,926,000, which is $8.71 per common share. In the letter to stockholders, it discloses the current value stockholders' equity of $2,400,000,000, which is $33.15 per share.

SUMMARY

Financial statements vary among industries, and they are especially different for banks, utilities, transportation companies, and insurance companies. In each case, the accounting for these firms is subject to a uniform accounting system. Changes in analysis are necessitated by the differences in accounting presentation.

Oil and gas companies' financial statements are affected significantly by the method that they choose to account for costs associated with exploration and production. Another important aspect of the financial statements of oil and gas companies is the footnote requirement that relates to supplementary information on oil and gas exploration, development, and production activities. Cash flow is also particularly significant to oil and gas companies.

Real estate companies emphasize the underlying value of the property and earnings before depreciation and deferred taxes from operations.

Special industry ratios were reviewed in this chapter. The following ratios are helpful when analyzing a bank:

$$\text{Earning Assets to Total Assets} = \frac{\text{Average Earning Assets}}{\text{Average Total Assets}}$$

$$\text{Interest Margin to Average Earning Assets} = \frac{\text{Interest Margin}}{\text{Average Earning Assets}}$$

$$\text{Loan Loss Coverage Ratio} = \frac{\text{Pretax Income} + \text{Provision for Loan Losses}}{\text{Net Charge-Offs}}$$

$$\text{Equity Capital to Total Assets} = \frac{\text{Average Equity}}{\text{Average Total Assets}}$$

$$\text{Deposits Times Capital} = \frac{\text{Average Deposits}}{\text{Average Stockholders' Equity}}$$

$$\text{Loans to Deposit} = \frac{\text{Average Net Loans}}{\text{Average Deposits}}$$

The following ratios are helpful in analyzing utility performance:

$$\text{Operating Ratio} = \frac{\text{Operating Expense}}{\text{Operating Revenue}}$$

$$\text{Funded Debt to Operating Property} = \frac{\text{Funded Debt}}{\text{Operating Property}}$$

$$\text{Percent Earned on Operating Property} = \frac{\text{Net Income}}{\text{Operating Property}}$$

$$\text{Operating Revenue to Operating Property} = \frac{\text{Operating Revenue}}{\text{Operating Property}}$$

The ratios that follow are especially suited to transportation. Additional insight can be gained by looking at revenues and expenses on a per unit of usage basis.

$$\text{Operating Ratio} = \frac{\text{Operating Expense}}{\text{Operating Revenue}}$$

$$\text{Long-Term Debt to Operating Property} = \frac{\text{Long-Term Debt}}{\text{Operating Property}}$$

$$\text{Operating Revenue to Operating Property} = \frac{\text{Operating Revenue}}{\text{Operating Property}}$$

To the Net

1. Go to the SEC site (http://www.sec.gov). Under Filings & Forms (Edgar), click on "Search for Company Filings." Click on "Search Companies and Filings." Under company name enter "Independent Bank Corp (MS)." Select the 10-K filed March 6, 2002.
   a. Determine the Standard Industrial Classification.
   b. Determine the following data for nonperforming assets held by the bank at the dates indicated:

	(Dollars in Thousands) December 31		
	2001	2000	1999
Loans past due 90 days or more but still accruing			
Loans accounted for on a nonaccrued basis			
Other real estate owned			
Total nonperforming loans			
Restructured loans			
Nonperforming loans as a percent of gross loans			
Nonperforming assets as a percent of total assets			

   c. Comment on the trends in (b).

2. Go to the SEC site (http://www.sec.gov). Under Filings & Forms (Edgar), click on "Search for Company Filings." Click on "Search Companies and Filings." Under company name enter "Maine Public Service Company." Select the 10-K filed March 14, 2002.
   a. Determine the Standard Industrial Classification.
   b. Determine the following year ended December 31, 2001, 2000, and 1999.
      1. Allowance for equity funds used during construction.
      2. Allowance for borrowed funds used during construction.
      3. Net income available for common stock.
   c. Determine the accounting policy as to where allowance for equity funds and allowance for borrowed funds is charged.
   d. Does allowance for equity funds and borrowed funds used during construction appear to be material?

3. Go to the SEC site (http://www.sec.gov). Under Filings & Forms (Edgar), click on "Search for Company Filings." Click on "Search Companies and Filings." Under company name enter "Cabot Oil & Gas Corporation." Select the 10-K filed February 22, 2002.
   a. Determine the Standard Industrial Classification.
   b. Historical Reserves
      Complete the following table for estimated proved reserves for the periods indicated.

	Natural Gas (Mmcf)	Oil & Liquids (Mbbl)	Total* (Mmcfe)
December 21, 2000			
Revision of prior estimates			
Extensions, discoveries and other additions			
Production			
Purchases of reserves in place			
Sales of reserves in place			
December 31, 2001			

   c. Historical Reserves
      Complete the following table for proved developed reserves.

	Natural Gas (Mmcf)	Oil & Liquids (Mbbl)	Total* (Mmcfe)
December 31, 1998			
December 31, 1999			
December 31, 2000			
December 31, 2001			

   d. Comment on the trend reserves.

*Includes natural gas and natural gas equivalents by using the ratio of 6 Mcf of natural gas to Bbl of crude oil. Condensate or natural gas liquids.

Questions

Q 12-1.   What are the main sources of revenue for banks?

Q 12-2.   Why are loans, which are usually liabilities, treated as assets for banks?

Q 12-3.   Why are savings accounts liabilities for banks?

Q 12-4.   Why are banks concerned with their loans/deposits ratios?

Q 12-5.   To what agencies and other users of financial statements must banks report?

Q 12-6.   Why must the user be cautious in analyzing bank holding companies?

Q 12-7.   What is usually the biggest expense item for a bank?

Q 12-8.   What does the ratio total deposits times capital measure?

Q 12-9.   What ratios are used to indicate profitability for banks?

Q 12-10.   Why are banks concerned about the percentage of earning assets to total assets?

Q 12-11.   What does the loan loss coverage ratio measure?

Q 12-12.   What type of ratio is deposits times capital?

Q 12-13.   Give an example of why a review of bank assets may indicate risk or opportunity you were not aware of.

Q 12-14.   Why review the disclosure of the market value of investments versus the book amount of investments for banks?

Q 12-15.   Why review the disclosure of foreign loans for banks?

Q 12-16.   Why review the disclosure of allowance for loan losses for a bank?

Q 12-17.   Why review the disclosure of nonperforming assets for banks?

Q 12-18.   Why could a review of savings deposit balances be important when reviewing a bank's financial statements?

Q 12-19.   Why review the footnote that describes commitments and contingent liabilities for a bank?

Q 12-20.   Utilities are very highly leveraged. How is it that they are able to carry such high levels of debt?

Q 12-21.   How does demand for utilities differ from demand for other products or services?

Q 12-22.   Why are plant and equipment listed first for utilities?

Q 12-23.   Are inventory ratios meaningful for utilities? Why?

Q 12-24.   What does the funded debt to operating property ratio measure for a utility?

Q 12-25.   Is times interest earned meaningful for utilities? Why or why not?

Q 12-26.   Are current liabilities presented first in utility reporting? Comment.

Q 12-27.   For a utility, why review the account construction work in progress?

Q 12-28.   For a utility, describe the income statement accounts, allowance for equity funds used during construction, and allowance for borrowed funds used during construction.

Q 12-29.   Differentiate between successful-efforts and full-costing accounting as applied to the oil and gas industry.

Q 12-30.   Some industries described in this chapter are controlled by federal regulatory agencies. How does this affect their accounting systems?

Q 12-31.   When reviewing the financial statements of oil and gas companies, why is it important to note the method of costing (expensing) exploration and production costs?

Q 12-32.   Oil and gas companies must disclose quantity estimates for proved oil and gas reserves and the major factors causing changes in these resource estimates. Briefly indicate why this disclosure can be significant.

Q 12-33.   For oil and gas companies, there is the potential for a significant difference between the reported income and cash flows from operations. Comment.

Q 12-34.   Is it more desirable to have the operating ratios increasing or decreasing for utilities and transportation companies?

Q 12-35.   What type of ratio is operating revenue to operating property? Will it exceed 1:1 for a utility?

Q 12-36.   What is the most important category of assets for transportation firms?

Q 12-37.   Briefly describe the revenue section of the income statement for a transportation firm.

Q 12-38.   In a transportation firm, what types of things will change operating revenues? Operating expenses?

Q 12-39.   If a transportation firm shows a rise in revenue per passenger mile, what does this rise imply?

Q 12-40.   How is the passenger load factor of a bus company related to profitability?

Q 12-41.   Explain how the publication *Financial Analysis of the Motor Carrier Industry* could be used to determine the percentage of total revenue a firm has in relation to similar trucking firms.

Q 12-42.   Annual reports filed with state insurance departments are in accordance with what accounting standards?

Q 12-43.   Annual reports that insurance companies issue to the public are in accordance with what accounting standards?

Q 12-44.   Why could an insurance company with substantial investments in real estate represent a risk?

Q 12-45.   For an insurance company, describe the difference between GAAP reporting and SAP reporting of deferred policy acquisition costs.

Q 12-46.   Briefly describe the difference between accounting for intangibles for an insurance company under GAAP and under SAP.

Q 12-47.   Briefly describe the unique aspects of revenue recognition for an insurance company.

Q 12-48.   Insurance industry-specific financial ratios are usually prepared from financial statements prepared under what standards?

Q 12-49.   Insurance companies tend to have a stock market price at a discount to the average market price (price/earnings ratio). Indicate some perceived reasons for this relatively low price/earnings ratio.

Q 12-50.   Real estate companies contend that conventional accounting does not recognize the underlying value of the property and that this misleads investors. Discuss.

Problems

P 12-1.   The following are statistics from the annual report of McEttrick National Bank:

	2004	2003
Average loans	$16,000,000	$13,200,000
Average total assets	26,000,000	22,000,000
Average total deposits	24,000,000	20,000,000
Average total capital	1,850,000	1,600,000
Interest expenses	1,615,000	1,512,250
Interest income	1,750,000	1,650,000

Required   a.   Calculate the total deposits times capital for each year.
            b.   Calculate the loans to total deposits for each year.
            c.   Calculate the capital funds to total assets for each year.
            d.   Calculate the interest margin to average total assets for each year.
            e.   Comment on any trends found in the calculations of (a) through (d).

P 12-2.   The following are statistics from the annual report of Dover Bank:

	2004	2003	2002
Average earning assets	$50,000,000	$45,000,000	$43,000,000
Average total assets	58,823,529	54,216,867	52,000,000
Income before securities transactions	530,000	453,000	420,000
Interest margin	2,550,000	2,200,000	2,020,000
Pretax income before securities transactions	562,000	480,500	440,000
Provision for loan losses	190,000	160,000	142,000
Net charge-offs	180,000	162,000	160,000
Average equity	4,117,600	3,524,000	3,120,000
Average net loans	32,500,000	26,000,000	22,500,000
Average deposits	52,500,000	42,500,000	37,857,000

Required   a.   Calculate the following for 2004, 2003, and 2002:
               1.   Earning assets to total assets
               2.   Interest margin to average earning assets

3. Loan loss coverage ratio
4. Equity to total assets
5. Deposits times capital
6. Loans to deposits
b. Comment on trends found in the ratios computed in (a).

P 12-3.   Super Power Company reported the following statistics in its statements of income.

	2004	2003
Electric revenues:		
Residential	$11,800,000	$10,000,000
Commercial and industrial	10,430,000	10,000,000
Other	600,000	500,000
	22,830,000	20,500,000
Operating expenses and taxes*	20,340,000	18,125,000
Operating income	2,490,000	2,375,000
Other income	200,000	195,000
Income before interest deductions	2,690,000	2,570,000
Interest deductions	1,200,000	1,000,000
Net income	$ 1,490,000	$ 1,570,000

*Includes taxes of $3,200,000 in 2004 and $3,000,000 in 2003.

Required   a. Calculate the operating ratio and comment on the results.
b. Calculate the times interest earned and comment on the results.
c. Perform a vertical common-size analysis of revenues, using total revenue as the base, and comment on the relative size of the component parts.

P 12-4.   The following statistics relate to Michgate, an electric utility:

	2004	2003	2002
	(in thousands of dollars, except per share)		
Operating expenses	$ 850,600	$ 820,200	$ 780,000
Operating revenues	1,080,500	1,037,200	974,000
Earnings per share	3.00	2.90	2.60
Cash flow per share	3.40	3.25	2.30
Operating property	3,900,000	3,750,000	3,600,000
Funded debt (long-term)	1,500,000	1,480,000	1,470,000
Net income	280,000	260,000	230,000

Required   a. Calculate the following for 2004, 2003, and 2002:
1. Operating ratio
2. Funded debt to operating property
3. Percent earned on operating property
4. Operating revenue to operating property
b. Comment on trends found in the ratios computed in (a).
c. Comment on the trend between earnings per share and cash flow per share.

P 12-5.   Local Airways had the following results in the last two years:

	2004	2003
Operating revenues	$ 624,000	$ 618,000
Operating expenses	625,000	617,000
Operating property	365,000	360,000
Long-term debt	280,000	270,000
Estimated passenger miles	7,340,000	7,600,000

Required   Calculate the following for 2004 and 2003:
a. The operating ratio and comment on the trend.
b. The long-term debt to operating property ratio. What does this tell about debt use?
c. The operating revenue to operating property and comment on the trend.
d. The revenue per passenger mile. What has caused this trend?

P 12-6.   Chihi Airways had the following results for the last three years:

	2004	2003	2002
	(in thousands of dollars)		
Operating expenses	$1,550,000	$1,520,000	$1,480,000
Operating revenues	1,840,000	1,670,400	1,620,700
Long-term debt	910,000	900,500	895,000
Operating property	995,000	990,000	985,000
Passenger load factor	66.5%	59.0%	57.8%

Required   a.   Calculate the following for 2004, 2003, and 2002:
                 1.   Operating ratio
                 2.   Long-term debt to operating property
                 3.   Operating revenue to operating property
            b.   Comment on trends found in the ratios computed in (a).
            c.   Comment on the passenger load factor.

P 12-7.

Required   Answer the following multiple-choice questions related to insurance financial reporting.
            a.   Which of the following does not represent a basic type of insurance organization?
                 1.   Stock companies   4.   Fraternal benefit societies
                 2.   Bond companies   5.   Assessment companies
                 3.   Mutual companies
            b.   Which of these statements is not correct?
                 1.   The balance sheet is a classified balance sheet.
                 2.   The asset section starts with investments.
                 3.   The majority of the investments are typically in bonds.
                 4.   For life insurance companies, the investment in real estate may be much greater than that for property-casualty companies.
                 5.   Real estate investments are reported at cost less accumulated depreciation and an allowance for impairment in value.
            c.   Generally, the largest liability is for loss reserves. The quantification process is subject to a number of estimates. Which of the following would not be one of the estimates?
                 1.   Investment gains/losses   4.   Judicial interpretations
                 2.   Inflation rate   5.   Mortality estimates
                 3.   Interest rates
            d.   The manner of recognizing revenue on insurance contracts is unique for the insurance industry. Which of the following statements is not true?
                 1.   In general, the duration of the contract governs the revenue recognition.
                 2.   When the risk differs significantly from the contract period, revenue is recognized over the period of risk in proportion to the amount of insurance protection.
                 3.   For long-duration contracts, revenue is recognized when the premium is due from policyholders.
                 4.   Realized gains and losses from investments are reported in operations in the period incurred.
                 5.   For investment contracts, termination fees are booked as revenue over the period of the contract.
            e.   Which of the following statements is not true?
                 1.   Statutory accounting has emphasized the balance sheet in its concern for protecting the policyholders by focusing on the financial solvency of the insurance corporation.
                 2.   All 50 states have insurance departments that require annual statements of insurance companies. These annual reports are filed with the state insurance departments in accordance with Statutory Accounting Practices (SAP).
                 3.   After the annual reports are filed with the individual state insurance departments, a testing process is conducted by the NAIC. If a company's ratio is outside the prescribed limit, the NAIC brings that to the attention of the company.
                 4.   The A.M. Best Company publishes *Best's Insurance Reports*, which are published separately for life-health companies and property-casualty companies. The financial data, including the ratios, are based on the data submitted to the state insurance departments and are thus based on SAP.
                 5.   Many stock insurance companies must register with the Securities and Exchange Commission and file the required forms, such as the annual Form 10-K. Reports filed with the SEC must conform with GAAP.

Case 12-1

Allowance for Funds

The following financial information is from the New England Electric System and Subsidiaries 1994 annual report:

NEW ENGLAND ELECTRIC SYSTEM AND SUBSIDIARIES
Consolidated Statement of Income
Year ended December 31

	1994	1993	1992
	(Dollars in thousands, except per-share amounts)		
Operating Revenue	$2,243,029	$2,233,978	$2,181,676
Operating Expenses:			
Fuel for generation	220,956	227,182	237,161
Purchased electric energy	514,143	527,307	525,655
Other operation	494,741	492,079	423,330
Maintenance	161,473	146,219	162,974
Depreciation and amortization	301,123	296,631	302,217
Taxes, other than income taxes	125,840	120,493	114,027
Income taxes	128,257	121,124	110,761
Total operating expenses	1,946,533	1,931,035	1,876,125
Operating Income	296,496	302,943	305,551
Other Income:			
Allowance for equity funds used during construction	10,169	3,795	2,732
Equity in income of generating companies	9,758	11,016	13,052
Other income (expense) net	(3,856)	(1,154)	936
Operating and other income	312,567	316,600	322,271
Interest:			
Interest on long-term debt	93,500	100,777	114,182
Other interest	11,298	9,809	5,420
Allowance for borrowing funds used during construction	(7,793)	(2,816)	(2,204)
Total Interest	97,005	107,770	117,398
Income after interest	215,562	208,830	204,873
Preferred dividends of subsidiaries	8,697	10,585	10,572
Minority interests	7,439	8,022	9,264
Net Income	$ 199,426	$ 190,223	$ 185,037
Common shares outstanding	64,969,652	64,969,652	64,969,652
Per-share data:			
Net income	$3.07	$2.93	$2.85
Dividends declared	$2.285	$2.22	$2.14

NEW ENGLAND ELECTRIC SYSTEM AND SUBSIDIARIES
Consolidated Balance Sheet
Year ended December 31

	1994	1993
	(Dollars in thousands)	
Assets		
Utility plant, at original cost	$4,914,807	$4,661,612
Less accumulated provisions for depreciation and amortization	1,610,378	1,511,271
	3,304,429	3,150,341
Net investment in Seabrook 1 under rate settlement (Note C)	38,283	103,344
Construction work in progress	374,009	228,816
Net utility plant	3,716,721	3,482,501
Oil and gas properties, at cost (Note A)	1,248,343	1,220,110
Less accumulated provision for amortization	964,069	884,837
Net oil and gas properties	284,274	335,273
Investments:		
Nuclear power companies, at equity (Note D)	46,349	46,342
Other subsidiaries, at equity	42,195	44,676
Other investments	50,895	28,836
Total investments	139,439	119,854
Current assets:		
Cash	3,047	2,876
Accounts receivable, less reserves of $15,095 and $14,551	295,627	275,020
Unbilled revenues (Note A)	55,900	43,400
Fuel, materials, and supplies, at average cost	94,431	74,314
Prepaid and other current assets	76,718	69,004
Total current assets	525,723	464,614
Accrued Yankee Atomic cost (Note D)	122,452	103,501
Deferred charges and other assets (Note A)	296,232	290,135
	$5,084,841	$4,795,878
Capitalization and Liabilities		
Capitalization (see accompanying statements):		
Common share equity	$1,580,838	$1,529,868
Minority interests in consolidated subsidiaries	55,066	55,855
Cumulative preferred stock of subsidiaries	147,016	147,528
Long-term debt	1,520,488	1,511,589
Total capitalization	3,303,408	3,244,840
Current liabilities:		
Long-term debt due within one year	65,920	12,920
Short-term debt	233,970	71,775
Accounts payable	168,937	128,342
Accrued taxes	11,002	10,332
Accrued interest	25,193	23,278
Dividends payable	37,154	36,950
Other current liabilities (Note A)	93,251	153,812
Total current liabilities	635,427	437,409
Deferred federal and state income taxes	751,855	705,026
Unamortized investment tax credits	94,930	99,355
Accrued Yankee Atomic cost (Note D)	122,452	103,501
Other reserves and deferred credits	176,769	205,747
Commitments and contingencies (Note E)		
	$5,084,841	$4,795,878

Selected note to consolidated financial statements

3. Allowance for funds used during construction (AFDC)

The utility subsidiaries capitalized AFDC as part of construction costs. AFDC represents the composite interest and equity costs of capital funds used to finance that portion of construction cost not eligible for inclusion in the rate base. In 1994, an average of $30 million of construction work in progress was included in the rate base, all of which was attributable to the Manchester Street Station repowering project. AFDC is capitalized in "Utility plant," with offsetting noncash credits to "Other income" and "Interest." This method is in accordance with an established rate-making practice, under which a utility is permitted a return on, and the recovery of, prudently incurred capital costs through their ultimate inclusion in the rate base and in the provision for depreciation. The composite AFDC rates were 7.6 percent, 7.4 percent, and 8.6 percent, in 1994, 1993, and 1992, respectively.

Required
a. Describe the allowance for equity funds used during construction.
b. Describe the allowance for borrowing funds used during construction.
c. How does capitalizing interest on borrowed funds affect income in the year of capitalization versus not capitalizing this interest? Explain.
d. Would net income tend to be higher than cash flow if there is substantial capitalization of interest on the borrowed funds during the current period? Explain.
e. How does capitalizing the allowance for equity funds used during construction affect income in the year of capitalization versus not capitalizing these charges?
f. Would net income tend to be higher than cash flow if there is substantial capitalization of the allowance for equity funds used during construction for the current year?
g. Describe how a utility that has substantial construction work in progress could have a material cash flow problem in relation to the reported income.
h. Compute the following for 1994 and 1993. Comment on each.
   1. Operating ratio
   2. Funded debt to operating property
   3. Percent earned on operating property
   4. Operating revenue to operating property
   5. Times interest earned
i. Using the balances at December 31, 1994, compute the percentage relationship between construction work in progress and net utility plant. Comment.

Case 12-2   Results of Operations for Oil and Gas Producing Activities

Amerada Hess Corporation included the information in this case as part of The Supplementary Oil and Gas Data. This case only represents a small portion of the Supplementary Oil and Gas Data.

The results of operations for oil and gas producing activities shown below exclude sales of purchased natural gas, nonoperating income (including gains on sales of oil and gas properties), interest expense and gains and losses resulting from foreign currency exchange transactions. Therefore, these results are on a different basis than the net income from exploration and production operations reported in management's discussion and analysis of results of operations and in Note 17 to the financial statements.

Results of Operations for Oil and Gas Producing Activities

For the Years Ended December 31 (Millions of dollars)	Total	United States	Europe	Africa, Asia and other
2001				
Sales and other operating revenues				
Unaffiliated customers	$2,519	$ 378	$1,706	$435
Inter-company	1,032	856	176	—
Total revenues	3,551	1,234	1,882	435
Costs and expenses				
Production expenses, including related taxes	711	213	374	124
Exploration expenses, including dry holes and lease impairment	368	156	103	109
Other operating expenses	153	80	25	48
Depreciation, depletion and amortization	913	368	446	99
Total costs and expenses	2,145	817	948	380
Results of operations before income taxes	1,406	417	934	55
Provision for income taxes	523	143	320	60
Results of operations	$ 883	$ 274	$ 614	$ (5)
Share of equity investees' results of operations	$ 17	$ —	$ 12	$ 5

Required

a. Prepare a vertical common-size analysis for results of operations for oil and gas producing activities for 2001. Use total revenues as the base.

b. Prepare a horizontal common-size analysis for results of operations for oil and gas producing activities for 2001. Use total as the base.

c. Comment on the common-size analysis in (a) and (b).

Case 12-3

Summary of Loan Loss Experience

State Bancorp, Inc. included the following in its 2001 annual report:

STATE BANCORP, INC. AND SUBSIDIARY
SUMMARY OF LOAN LOSS EXPERIENCE

The determination of the balance of the allowance for probable loan losses is based upon a review and analysis of the Company's loan portfolio and reflects an amount which, in management's judgment, is adequate to provide for probable future losses. Management's review includes monthly analysis of past due and nonaccrual loans and detailed, periodic loan by loan analyses.

The principal factors considered by management in determining the adequacy of the allowance are the growth and composition of the loan portfolio, historical loss experience, the level of nonperforming loans, economic conditions, the value and adequacy of collateral and the current level of the allowance. While management utilizes all available information to estimate the adequacy of the allowance for probable loan losses, the ultimate collectibility of a substantial portion of the loan portfolio and the need for future additions to the allowance will be based upon changes in economic conditions and other relevant factors.

The following table presents an analysis of the Company's allowance for probable loan losses for each period (dollars in thousands):

	2001	2000	1999	1998	1997
Balance, January 1,	$9,207	$7,107	$5,788	$5,124	$5,009
Adjustments	542[1]	—	—	—	—
Charge-offs:					
Commercial and industrial	4,211	868	593	1,332	1,509
Real estate—mortgage	—	21	987	197	379
Real estate—construction	—	500	500	—	—
Loans to individuals	44	20	45	128	169
Total charge-offs	4,255	1,409	2,125	1,657	2,057
Recoveries:					
Commercial and industrial	143	237	204	214	189
Real estate—mortgage	4	8	223	297	23
Loans to individuals	14	14	17	10	10
Total recoveries	161	259	444	521	222
Net charge-offs	4,094	1,150	1,681	1,136	1,835
Additions charged to operations	3,600	3,250	3,000	1,800	1,950
Balance at end of period	$9,255	$9,207	$7,107	$5,788	$5,124
Ratio of net charge-offs during the period to average loans outstanding during the period	0.75%	0.24%	0.37%	0.29%	0.51%

(1) Opening balance of allowance for probable loan losses of acquired leasing company.

The following table presents the allocation of the Company's allowance for probable loan losses for each period (dollars in thousands):

	2001	Percent of Loans to Total Loans	2000	Percent of Loans to Total Loans	1999	Percent of Loans to Total Loans	1998	Percent of Loans to Total Loans	1997	Percent of Loans to Total Loans
Commercial and industrial	$5,938	47.9%	$6,355	46.1%	$3,725	45.2%	$3,320	47.0%	$2,210	45.7%
Real estate—mortgage	2,366	45.9	2,118	47.0	1,572	44.4	1,633	44.6	1,790	46.2
Real estate—construction	98	2.9	282	3.5	644	5.3	675	4.1	499	3.9
Loans to individuals	49	1.4	34	1.2	36	1.1	47	1.8	82	1.9
Tax-exempt and other	63	1.9	62	2.2	144	4.0	67	2.5	50	2.3
Unallocated	741	—	356	—	986	—	46	—	493	—
Total	$9,255	100.0%	$9,207	100.0%	$7,107	100.0%	$5,788	100.0%	$5,124	100.0%

Required   Give your opinion as to significant information in this summary of Loan Loss Experience.

Case 12-4	**You Can Bank on It**

The financial data included in this case are from selected parts of the 1998 annual report of Wells Fargo & Company and subsidiaries.

Wells Fargo & Company and Subsidiaries
Consolidated Statement of Income

	Year ended December 31,		
(in millions, except per share amounts)	1998	1997	1996
INTEREST INCOME			
Securities available for sale	$ 1,844	$ 2,063	$ 1,950
Mortgages held for sale	898	490	529
Loans held for sale	371	312	328
Loans	10,685	10,539	9,854
Other interest income	257	198	180
Total interest income	14,055	13,602	12,841
INTEREST EXPENSE			
Deposits	3,111	3,150	2,911
Short-term borrowings	777	610	562
Long-term debt	1,097	1,093	1,140
Guaranteed preferred beneficial interests in			
Company's subordinated debentures	80	101	6
Total interest expense	5,065	4,954	4,619
NET INTEREST INCOME			
Provision for loan losses	8,990	8,648	8,222
Net interest income after provision for loan losses	1,545	1,140	500
	7,445	7,508	7,722
NONINTEREST INCOME			
Service charges on deposit accounts	1,357	1,244	1,198
Trust and investment fees and commissions	1,068	954	775
Credit card fee revenue	520	448	350
Other fees and commissions	946	826	689
Mortgage banking	1,106	927	844
Insurance	348	336	280
Net venture capital gains	113	191	256
Net gains on securities available for sale	169	99	12
Other	800	650	365
Total noninterest income	6,427	5,675	4,769
NONINTEREST EXPENSE			
Salaries and benefits	4,416	3,811	3,624
Equipment	900	739	724
Net occupancy	764	719	688
Goodwill	421	433	339
Core deposit intangible	243	273	265
Net losses on dispositions of premises and equipment	325	76	45
Operating losses	152	374	189
Other	3,358	2,565	2,850
Total noninterest expense	10,579	8,990	8,724
INCOME BEFORE INCOME TAX EXPENSE	3,293	4,193	3,767
Income tax expense	1,343	1,694	1,539
NET INCOME	$ 1,950	$ 2,499	$ 2,228
NET INCOME APPLICABLE TO COMMON STOCK	$ 1,915	$ 2,456	$ 2,143
EARNINGS PER COMMON SHARE	$ 1.18	$ 1.50	$ 1.38
DILUTED EARNINGS PER COMMON SHARE	$ 1.17	$ 1.48	$ 1.36
DIVIDENDS DECLARED PER COMMON SHARE	$ .70	$ .615	$ .525

Selected data related to changes in the allowance for loan losses were as follows:

(in millions)	Year ended December 31 1998	1997
Provision for loan losses	$1,545	$1,140
Total net loan charge-offs	$1,617	$1,305

Wells Fargo & Company and Subsidiaries
Consolidated Balance Sheet

(in millions, except shares)	December 31 1998	1997
ASSETS		
Cash and due from banks	$ 12,731	$ 13,081
Federal funds sold and securities purchased under resale agreements	1,517	1,049
Securities available for sale	31,997	27,872
Mortgages held for sale	19,770	9,706
Loans held for sale	5,322	4,494
Loans	107,994	106,311
Allowance for loan losses	3,134	3,062
Net loans	104,860	103,249
Mortgage servicing rights	3,080	3,048
Premises and equipment, net	3,130	3,311
Core deposit intangible	1,510	1,737
Goodwill	7,664	8,062
Interest receivable and other assets	10,894	10,076
Total assets	$202,475	$185,685
LIABILITIES		
Noninterest-bearing deposits	$ 46,732	$ 40,206
Interest-bearing deposits	90,056	87,450
Total deposits	136,788	127,656
Short-term borrowings	15,897	13,381
Accrued expenses and other liabilities	8,537	6,236
Long-term debt	19,709	17,335
Guaranteed preferred beneficial interests in Company's subordinated debentures	785	1,299
STOCKHOLDERS' EQUITY		
Preferred stock	547	543
Unearned ESOP shares	(84)	(80)
Total preferred stock	463	463
Common stock—$1 2/3 par value, authorized 4,000,000,000 shares; issued 1,661,392,590 shares and 1,630,640,939 shares	2,769	2,718
Additional paid-in capital	8,673	8,126
Retained earnings	9,045	8,292
Cumulative other comprehensive income	463	464
Notes receivable from ESOP	(3)	(10)
Treasury stock—17,334,787 shares and 10,493,685 shares	(651)	(275)
Total stockholders' equity	20,759	19,778
Total liabilities and stockholders' equity	$202,475	$185,685

Required a. Prepare a horizontal common-size analysis for 1996, 1997, and 1998 for the following items from the statement of income. (Use 1996 as the base.):
1. Net interest income
2. Provision for loan losses
3. Net interest income after provision for loan losses
4. Total noninterest income
5. Total noninterest expense

b. Comment on the trends indicated in part (a).

c. Compute the following for 1998 and 1997 (use ending balance sheet accounts):
1. Earning assets to total assets
2. Interest margin to average earning assets (use year-end total earning assets)
3. Loan loss coverage ratio
4. Equity capital to total assets (use year-end numbers)
5. Deposits times capital (use year-end numbers)
6. Loans to deposits (for loans, use loans held for sale and net loans: use year-end numbers)

d. Comment on the trends indicated by the ratios computed in (c).

Case 12-5   **You're Covered**

Exhibit 12-20 on page 504 includes consolidated statement of income for The Chubb Corporation.

Required a. Prepare a horizontal common-size analysis of this statement. Use 1999 as the base.

b. Comment on trends found in (a).

Web Case   # Thomson Analytics *Business School Edition*

Please complete the web case that covers material covered in this chapter at http://gibson.swlearning.com. You'll be using Thomson Analytics Business School Edition, a version of the powerful tool used by Wall Street professionals, that combines a full range of fundamental financial information, earnings estimates, market data, and source documents for 500 publicly traded companies.

Endnotes

1. Arthur Andersen & Co., *Insurance* (Essex, England: Saffren Press Ltd., 1983), p. 87.
2. *Statement of Financial Accounting Standards No. 60*, "Accounting and Reporting by Insurance Enterprises" (Stamford, CT: Financial Accounting Standards Board, 1982), paragraph 13.
3. *Statement of Financial Accounting Standards No. 60*, paragraph 15.
4. *Statement of Financial Accounting Standards No. 97*, "Accounting and Reporting by Insurance Enterprises for Certain Long-Duration Contracts and for Realized Gains and Losses from the Sale of Investments" (Stamford, CT: Financial Accounting Standards Board, 1987), paragraph 15.

PERSONAL FINANCIAL STATEMENTS AND ACCOUNTING FOR GOVERNMENTS AND NOT-FOR-PROFIT ORGANIZATIONS

This chapter briefly covers three types of financial reporting that have not been discussed in previous chapters: (1) personal financial statements, (2) governments, and (3) not-for-profit organizations other than governments.

PERSONAL FINANCIAL STATEMENTS

Personal financial statements of individuals, husband and wife, or a larger family group are prepared for obtaining credit, income tax planning, retirement planning, and estate planning. *Statement of Position 82-1* (SOP 82-1) covers guidelines for the preparation of personal financial statements.[1] SOP 82-1 concludes that:

> The primary users of personal financial statements normally consider estimated current value information to be more relevant for their decisions than historical cost information. Lenders require estimated current value information to assess collateral, and most personal loan applications require estimated current value information. Estimated current values are required for estate, gift, and income tax planning, and estimated current value information about assets is often required in federal and state filings of candidates for public office.[2]

SOP 82-1 concludes that personal financial statements should present assets at their estimated current values and liabilities at their estimated current amounts at the date of the financial statements. This contrasts with commercial financial statements, which predominantly use historical cost information. SOP 82-1 provides guidelines for determining the estimated current value of an asset and the estimated current amount of a liability. Exhibit 13-1 presents these guidelines.[3]

EXHIBIT 13-1   Guidelines for Determining the Estimated Current Values of Assets and the Estimated Current Amounts of Liabilities

General

12. Personal financial statements should present assets at their estimated current values and liabilities at their estimated current amounts. The estimated current value of an asset in personal financial statements is the amount at which the item could be exchanged between a buyer and seller, each of whom is well informed and willing, and neither of whom is compelled to buy or sell. Costs of disposal, such as commissions, if material, should be considered in determining estimated current values.[A] The division recognizes that the estimated current values of some assets may be difficult to determine and the cost of obtaining estimated current values of some assets directly may exceed the benefits of doing so; therefore, the division recommends that judgment be exercised in determining estimated current values.

13. Recent transactions involving similar assets and liabilities in similar circumstances ordinarily provide a satisfactory basis for determining the estimated current value of an asset and the estimated current amount of a liability. If recent sales information is unavailable, other methods that may be used include the capitalization of past or prospective earnings, the use of liquidation values, the adjustment of historical cost based on changes in a specific price index, the use of appraisals, or the use of the discounted amounts of projected cash receipts and payments.

14. In determining the estimated current values of some assets (for example, works of art, jewelry, restricted securities, investments in closely held businesses, and real estate), the person may need to consult a specialist.

15. The methods used to determine the estimated current values of assets and the estimated current amounts of liabilities should be followed consistently from period to period unless the facts and circumstances dictate and change to different methods.

Receivables

16. Personal financial statements should present receivables at the discounted amounts of cash the person estimates will be collected, using appropriate interest rates at the date of the financial statements.

Marketable Securities

17. Marketable securities include both debt and equity securities for which market quotations are available. The estimated current values of such securities are their quoted market prices. The estimated current values of securities traded on securities exchanges are the closing prices of the securities on the date of the financial statements (valuation date) if the securities were traded on that date. If the securities were not traded on that date but published bid and asked prices are available, the estimated current values of the securities should be within the range of those prices.

18. For securities traded in the over-the-counter market, quotations of bid and asked prices are available from several sources, including the financial press, various quotation publications and financial reporting services, and individual broker-dealers. For those securities, the mean of the bid prices, of the bid and asked prices, or of the prices of a representative selection of broker-dealers quoting the securities may be used as the estimated current values.

19. An investor may hold a large block of the equity securities of a company. A large block of stock might not be salable at the price at which a small number of shares were recently sold or quoted. Further, a large minority interest may be difficult to sell despite isolated sales of a small number of shares. However, a controlling interest may be proportionately more valuable than minority interests that were sold. Consideration of those factors may require adjustments to the price at which the security recently sold. Moreover, restrictions on the transfer of a security may also suggest the need to adjust the recent market price in determining the estimated current value.[B]

Options

20. If published prices of options are unavailable, their estimated current values should be determined on the basis of the values of the assets subject to option, considering such factors as the exercise prices and length of the option periods.

[A] Paragraph 27 defines the estimated current amount of a liability.
[B] For further discussion on valuing marketable securities, see the AICPA Industry Audit Guide, *Audits of Investment Companies* (New York: AICPA, 1973), pp. 15–17.

(continued)

EXHIBIT 13-1	**Guidelines for Determining the Estimated Current Values of Assets and the Estimated Current Amounts of Liabilities** *(continued)*

Investment in Life Insurance

21. The estimated current value of an investment in life insurance is the cash value of the policy less the amount of any loans against it. The face amount of life insurance the individuals own should be disclosed.

Investments in Closely Held Businesses

22. The division recognizes that the estimated current values of investments in closely held businesses usually are difficult to determine. The problems relate to investments in closely held businesses in any form, including sole proprietorships, general and limited partnerships, and corporations. As previously stated, only the net investment in a business enterprise (not its assets and liabilities) should be presented in the statement of financial condition. The net investment should be presented at its estimated current value at the date of the financial statement. Since there is usually no established ready market for such an investment, judgment should be exercised in determining the estimated current value of the investment.

23. There is no one generally accepted procedure for determining the estimated current value of an investment in a closely held business. Several procedures or combinations of procedures may be used to determine the estimated current value of a closely held business, including a multiple of earnings, liquidation value, reproduction value, appraisals, discounted amounts of projected cash receipts and payments, or adjustments of book value or cost of the person's share of the equity of the business.[C] The owner of an interest in a closely held business may have entered into a buy-sell agreement that specifies the amount (or the basis of determining the amount) to be received in the event of withdrawal, retirement, or sale. If such an agreement exists, it should be considered, but it does not necessarily determine estimated current value. Whatever procedure is used, the objective should be to approximate the amount at which the investment could be exchanged between a buyer and a seller, each of whom is well informed and willing, and neither of whom is compelled to buy or sell.

Real Estate (Including Leaseholds)

24. Investments in real estate (including leaseholds) should be presented in personal financial statements at their estimated current values. Information that may be used in determining their estimated current values includes:
   a. Sales of similar property in similar circumstances.
   b. The discounted amounts of projected cash receipts and payments relating to the property or the net realizable value of the property, based on planned courses of action, including leaseholds whose current rental value exceeds the rent in the lease.
   c. Appraisals based on estimates of selling prices and selling costs obtained from independent real estate agents or brokers familiar with similar properties in similar locations.
   d. Appraisals used to obtain financing.
   e. Assessed value for property taxes, including consideration of the basis for such assessments and their relationship to market values in the area.

Intangible Assets

25. Intangible assets should be presented at the discounted amounts of projected cash receipts and payments arising from the planned use or sale of the assets if both the amounts and timing can be reasonably estimated. For example, a record of receipts under a royalty agreement may provide sufficient information to determine its estimated current value. The cost of a purchased intangible should be used if no other information is available.

Future Interests and Similar Assets

26. Nonforfeitable rights to receive future sums that have all the following characteristics should be presented as assets at their discounted amounts:
   - The rights are for fixed or determinable amounts.
   - The rights are not contingent on the holder's life expectancy or the occurrence of a particular event, such as disability or death.
   - The rights do not require future performance or service by the holder.

Nonforfeitable rights that may have those characteristics include:
   - Guaranteed minimum portions of pensions.
   - Vested interest in pensions or profit-sharing plans.
   - Deferred compensation contracts.
   - Beneficial interests in trusts.
   - Remainder interests in property subject to life estates.
   - Annuities.
   - Fixed amounts of alimony for a definite future period.

Payables and Other Liabilities

27. Personal financial statements should present payables and other liabilities at the discounted amounts of cash to be paid. The discount rate should be the rate implicit in the transaction in which the debt was incurred. If, however, the debtor is able to discharge the debt currently at a lower amount, the debt should be presented at the lower amount.[D]

Noncancellable Commitments

28. Noncancellable commitments to pay future sums that have all the following characteristics should be presented as liabilities at their discounted amounts:
   - The commitments are for fixed or determinable amounts.
   - The commitments are not contingent on others' life expectancies or the occurrence of a particular event, such as disability or death.
   - The commitments do not require future performance of service by others.

Noncancellable commitments that may have those characteristics include fixed amounts of alimony for a definite future period and charitable pledges.

Income Taxes Payable

29. The liability for income taxes payable should include unpaid income taxes for completed tax years and an estimated amount for income taxes accrued for the elapsed portion of the current tax year to the date of the financial statements. That estimate should be based on

[C] The book value or costs of a person's share of the equity of a business adjusted for appraisals of specific assets, such as real estate or equipment, is sometimes used as the estimated current value.
[D] For a further discussion of the setting of a discount rate for payables and other liabilities, see APB Opinion 21, *Interest on Receivables and Payables*, paragraph 13.

(continued)

EXHIBIT 13-1	Guidelines for Determining the Estimated Current Values of Assets and the Estimated Current Amounts of Liabilities *(continued)*

the relationship of taxable income earned to date to total estimated taxable income for the year, net of taxes withheld or paid with estimated income tax returns.

Estimated Income Taxes on the Differences Between the Estimated Current Values of Assets and the Estimated Current Amounts of Liabilities and Their Tax Bases

30. A provision should be made for estimated income taxes on the differences between the estimated current values of assets and the estimated current amounts of liabilities and their tax bases, including consideration of negative tax bases of tax shelters, if any. The provision should be computed as if the estimated current values of all assets had been realized and the estimated current amounts of all liabilities had been liquidated on the statement date, using applicable income tax laws and regulations, considering recapture provisions and available carryovers. The estimated income taxes should be presented between liabilities and net worth in the statement of financial condition. The methods and assumptions used to compute the estimated income taxes should be fully disclosed. Appendix B to this statement of position illustrates how to compute the provision.

Source: Statement of Position 82-1, "Accounting and Financial Reporting for Personal Financial Statements," Copyright © 1982 by the American Institute of Certified Public Accountants, Inc. Reprinted with permission.

Form of the Statements

The basic statement prepared for personal financial statements, a statement of financial condition, resembles a balance sheet. It states assets at estimated current values and liabilities at estimated current amounts. A tax liability is estimated on the difference between the stated amounts of the assets and liabilities and the tax basis of these assets and liabilities. For example, land may cost $10,000, which would be the tax basis, but may have an estimated current value of $25,000. The estimated tax liability on the difference between the $10,000 and the $25,000 would be estimated.

The difference between the total assets and total liabilities, designated net worth, is equivalent to the equity section in a commercial balance sheet. The statement of financial condition is prepared on the accrual basis. Assets and liabilities are presented in order of liquidity and maturity, without classification as current and noncurrent.

The optional statement of changes in net worth presents the major changes (sources of increases and decreases) in net worth. This statement combines income and other changes because of the mix of business and personal items. Examples of changes in net worth would be income, increases in the estimated current value of assets, and decreases in estimated income taxes. The statement of changes in net worth presents changes in terms of realized increases (decreases) and unrealized increases (decreases). Examples of realized increases (decreases) are salary, dividends, income taxes, and personal expenditures. Examples of unrealized increases (decreases) are an increase in the value of securities, an increase in the value of a residence, a decrease in the value of a boat, and estimated income taxes on the differences between the estimated current values of assets and the estimated current amounts of liabilities and their tax bases. Comparative financial statements may be more informative than statements of only one period.

For personal financial statements, the statement of changes in net worth replaces the income statement. SOP 82-1 includes guidelines on disclosure (Exhibit 13-1). These guidelines are not all-inclusive. Examples of disclosure include the methods used in determining current values of major assets, descriptions of intangible assets, and assumptions used to compute the estimated income taxes.

Most individuals do not maintain a complete set of records, so the necessary data must be gathered from various sources. These sources include brokers' statements, income tax returns, safe deposit boxes, insurance policies, real estate tax returns, checkbooks, and bank statements.

Suggestions for Reviewing the Statement of Financial Condition

1. Usually the most important figure, the net worth amount, indicates the level of wealth.
2. Determine the amount of the assets that you consider to be very liquid (cash, savings accounts, marketable securities, and so on). These assets are readily available.
3. Observe the due date of the liabilities. In general, we would prefer the liabilities to be relatively long-term. Long-term liabilities do not represent an immediate pressing problem.
4. When possible, compare specific assets with their related liabilities. This will indicate the net investment in the asset. For example, a residence with a current value of $90,000 and a $40,000 mortgage represents a net investment of $50,000.

Suggestions for Reviewing the Statement of Changes in Net Worth

1. Review realized increases in net worth. Determine the principal sources of realized net worth.
2. Review realized decreases in net worth. Determine the principal items in realized decreases in net worth.
3. Observe whether the net realized amount increased or decreased and by how much.
4. Review unrealized increases in net worth. Determine the principal sources of the increases.
5. Review unrealized decreases in net worth. Determine the principal sources of the decreases.
6. Observe whether the net unrealized amount increased or decreased and the amount.
7. Observe whether the net change increased or decreased and the amount.
8. Observe the net worth at the end of the year.

Illustration of Preparation of the Statement of Financial Condition

For Bill and Mary, assume that assets and liabilities, effective income tax rates, and the amount of estimated income taxes are as follows at December 31, 2004:

Account	Tax Bases	Estimated Current Value	Excess of Estimated Current Values over Tax Bases	Effective Income Tax Rates	Amount of Estimated Income Taxes
Cash	$ 8,000	$ 8,000	—	—	—
Savings accounts	20,000	20,000	—	—	—
Marketable securities	50,000	60,000	$10,000	28%	$ 2,800
Options	-0-	20,000	20,000	28%	5,600
Royalties	-0-	10,000	10,000	28%	2,800
Auto	15,000	10,000	(5,000)	—	—
Boat	12,000	8,000	(4,000)	—	—
Residence	110,000	130,000	20,000	28%	5,600
Furnishings	30,000	25,000	(5,000)	—	—
Mortgage payable	(60,000)	(60,000)	—	—	—
Auto loan	(5,000)	(5,000)	—	—	—
Credit cards	(5,000)	(4,000)	—	—	—
Total estimated income tax					$16,800

Bill and Mary
Statement of Financial Condition
December 31, 2004

Assets:	
Cash	$ 8,000
Savings accounts	20,000
Marketable securities	60,000
Options	20,000
Royalties	10,000
Auto	10,000
Boat	8,000
Residence	130,000
Furnishings	25,000
Total assets	$291,000

Liabilities:

Credit cards	$ 4,000
Auto loan	5,000
Mortgage payable	60,000
Total liabilities	69,000
Estimated income taxes on the difference between the estimated current values of assets and the estimated current amounts of liabilities and their tax bases	16,800
Net worth	205,200
Total liabilities and net worth	$291,000

Comments

1. Many would consider the net worth, $205,200, a relatively high amount.
2. Liquid assets total $88,000 (cash, $8,000; savings accounts, $20,000; and marketable securities, $60,000).
3. Most of the liabilities appear to be long-term (mortgage payable, $60,000).
4. Compare specific assets with related liabilities:

Auto:			Residence:	
Current value	$10,000		Current value	$130,000
Auto loan	5,000		Mortgage payable	60,000
Net investment	$ 5,000		Net investment	$ 70,000

Illustration of Preparation of the Statement of Changes in Net Worth

For Bill and Mary, the data relating to changes in net worth for the year ended December 31, 2004, follow:

Realized increases in net worth:	
Salary	$ 70,000
Dividend income	5,000
Interest income	6,000
Gain on sale of marketable securities	2,000
Realized decreases in net worth:	
Income taxes	20,000
Real estate taxes	2,000
Personal expenditures	28,000
Unrealized increases in net worth:	
Marketable securities	11,000
Residence	3,000
Unrealized decreases in net worth:	
Boat	2,000
Furnishings	4,000
Estimated income taxes on the differences between the estimated current values of assets and current amounts of liabilities and their tax bases	12,000
Net worth at the beginning of year	$176,200

Bill and Mary
Statement of Changes in Net Worth
For the Year Ended December 31, 2004

Realized increases in net worth:	
Salary	$ 70,000
Dividend income	5,000
Interest income	6,000
Gain on sale of marketable securities	2,000
	83,000
Realized decreases in net worth:	
Income taxes	20,000
Real estate taxes	2,000
Personal expenditures	28,000
	50,000
Net realized increase in net worth	33,000
Unrealized increases in net worth:	
Marketable securities	11,000
Residence	3,000
	14,000
Unrealized decreases in net worth:	
Boat	2,000
Furnishings	4,000
Estimated income taxes on the differences between the estimated current values of assets and the estimated current amounts of liabilities and their tax base	12,000
	18,000
Net unrealized decreases in net worth	4,000
Net increase in net worth	29,000
Net worth at the beginning of year	176,200
Net worth at the end of the year	$205,200

Comments

1. Most of the realized increase in net worth is salary ($70,000).
2. The major decreases in realized net worth are income taxes ($20,000) and personal expenditures ($28,000).
3. The net realized increase in net worth totaled $33,000.
4. The principal unrealized increase in net worth is marketable securities ($11,000).
5. The principal unrealized decreases in net worth are estimated income taxes on the differences between the estimated current value of assets and the estimated current amounts of liabilities and their tax bases ($12,000).
6. The net unrealized decreases in net worth totaled $4,000.
7. The net increase in net worth totaled $29,000.
8. The net worth at the end of the year totaled $205,200.

ACCOUNTING FOR GOVERNMENTS

The accounting terminology utilized by governments differs greatly from that used by profit-oriented enterprises. Governments use such terms as *appropriations* and *general fund*. Definitions of some of the terms that will be encountered follow:

- **Appropriations.** Provision for necessary resources and the authority for their disbursement.
- **Debt service.** Cash receipts and disbursements related to the payment of interest and principal on long-term debt.

- **Capital projects.** Cash receipts and disbursements related to the acquisition of long-lived assets.
- **Special assessments.** Cash receipts and disbursements related to improvements or services for which special property assessments have been levied.
- **Enterprises.** Operations that are similar to private businesses in which service users are charged fees.
- **Internal services.** Service centers that supply goods or services to other governmental units on a cost reimbursement basis.
- **General fund.** All cash receipts and disbursements not required to be accounted for in another fund.
- **Proprietary funds.** Funds whose purpose is to maintain the assets through cost reimbursement by users or partial cost recovery from users and periodic infusion of additional assets.
- **Fiduciary funds (nonexpendable funds).** Funds whose principal must remain intact (revenues earned may be distributed).
- **Encumbrances.** Future commitments for expenditures.

Thousands of state and local governments in the United States account for a large segment of the gross national product. State and local governments have a major impact on the citizens. No organization has had a clear responsibility for providing accounting principles for state and local governments. The American Institute of Certified Public Accountants (AICPA), the National Council on Governmental Accounting, and the Municipal Finance Officers Association have provided significant leadership in establishing accounting principles for state and local governments.

During the early 1980s, many thought that governmental accounting could benefit from the establishment of a board similar to the Financial Accounting Standards Board (FASB). A group of government accountants and CPAs organized a committee known as the Governmental Accounting Standards Board Organizing Committee. The Committee recommended the establishment of a separate standard-setting body for governmental accounting.

In April 1984, the Financial Accounting Foundation amended its articles of incorporation to accommodate a Governmental Accounting Standards Board (GASB). Thus, GASB became a branch of the Financial Accounting Foundation.

Governmental Accounting Standards Board Statement No. 1, Appendix B, addresses the jurisdictional hierarchy of the GASB and the FASB. It establishes the following priorities for governmental units:

1. Pronouncements of the Governmental Accounting Standards Board.
2. Pronouncements of the Financial Accounting Standards Board.
3. Pronouncements of bodies composed of expert accountants that follow a due process procedure, including broad distribution of proposed accounting principles for public comment, for the intended purpose of establishing accounting principles or describing existing practices that are generally accepted.
4. Practices or pronouncements that are widely recognized as being generally accepted because they represent prevalent practice in a particular industry or the knowledgeable application to specific circumstances of pronouncements that are generally accepted.
5. Other accounting literature.[4]

Governmental Accounting Standards Board Statement No. 1 also adopts the National Council on Governmental Accounting pronouncements and the American Institute of Certified Public Accountants audit guide entitled *Audits of State and Local Governmental Units* as the basis for currently existing GAAP for state and local governmental units.

State and local governments serve as stewards over public funds. This stewardship responsibility dominates state and local government accounting.

State and local government accounting revolves around fund accounting. A **fund** is defined as an:

Independent fiscal and accounting entity with a self-balancing set of accounts recording cash and/or other resources together with all related liabilities, obligations, reserves, and equities which are segregated for the purpose of carrying on specific activities or attaining certain objectives in accordance with special regulations, restrictions, or limitations.[5]

Government transactions are recorded in one or more funds designed to emphasize control and budgetary limitations. Examples of funds, established for a specific purpose, are highway maintenance, parks, debt repayment, endowment, and welfare. The number of funds utilized depends on the responsibilities of the particular state or local government and the grouping of these responsibilities. For example, highway maintenance and bridge maintenance may be grouped together.

Some governments do their accounting using a method that resembles a cash basis, others use a modified accrual basis, and some use an accrual basis. A single government unit may use more than one basis, depending on the fund. For example, the City of Toledo, Ohio, uses a modified accrual basis for the governmental and expendable trust funds and uses an accrual basis of accounting for the proprietary and nonexpendable trust funds. The trend is away from the cash basis and toward the modified accrual basis. Some states have passed a law requiring governments to use a modified accrual basis.

In 1999 the GASB passed *Statement 34*, "Basic Financial Statements—and Management's Discussion and Analysis—for State and Local Governments," integrating government-wide reporting and enhanced fund reporting. The new model is to be implemented by all state and local governments by the year 2004. Large state and local governments should implement by 2002.

GASB Statement No. 34 requires a management's discussion and analysis (MD&A). The MD&A must include:

- An objective discussion of the basic financial statements and condensed financial information comparing current and prior years.
- An analysis of the overall financial position and results of operations.
- Analysis of balances and transactions of individual funds.
- Analysis of significant variations between the original and final budget and the final budget and actual results for the general fund.
- A description of significant capital—asset and long-term debt activity during the year.
- Known facts, decisions or conditions expected to have a significant impact on financial position or results of operations.[6]

Review a governmental accounting book for a detailed discussion of state and local governments accounting.

State and local governments prepare a **budget**, a detailed plan of operations for each period. This includes an item-by-item estimate of expenditures. When the representatives of the citizens (city council, town meeting, and so on) approve the budget, then the individual expenditures become limits. An increase in an approved expenditure will require approval by the same representatives who set up a *legal* control over expenditures. This differs from the budget for a commercial business, which is merely a plan of future revenues and expenses.

A great variance exists in the quality of disclosure in the financial reporting of state and local governments. Some poorly reported items have been pension liabilities, marketable securities, inventories, fixed assets, and lease obligations.

The Government Finance Officers Association of the United States and Canada presents a Certificate of Achievement for Excellence in Financial Reporting to governmental units and public employee retirement systems whose comprehensive annual financial reports are judged to conform substantially to program standards. These standards are considered to be very rigorous.

The municipal bond rating of the governmental unit should also be determined. Standard & Poor's and Moody's evaluate and grade the quality of a bond relative to the probability of default. One rating is assigned to all general obligation bonds (backed by the full faith and credit of the governmental unit). Bonds not backed by the full faith and credit of the governmental unit, such as industrial revenue bonds, are rated individually. These ratings do not represent the probability of default by the governmental unit.

When reviewing the financial reporting of governmental units, visualize the reporting in a pyramid fashion. The funds are typically grouped into major categories, which are supported by individual funds that serve to account for each of the separate governmental activities. Exhibit 13-2 illustrates the pyramid concept of financial reporting for a governmental unit.

When reviewing a governmental unit, the following suggestions are helpful:

1. Determine if a Certificate of Achievement has been received.
2. Determine the municipal bond rating of the governmental unit.

EXHIBIT 13-2   **THE FINANCIAL REPORTING "PYRAMID"**

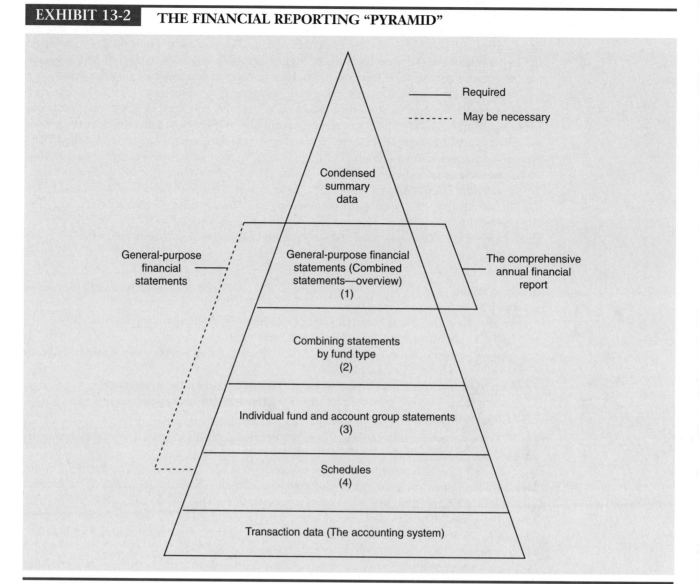

Source: Daniel L. Koulak, "Understanding Your Town's Financial Report," *Management Accounting* (December 1984), p. 54. Reprinted with permission.

3. Review the combined balance sheet.
4. Review the combined statement of revenues, expenditures, and changes in fund balances.
5. Review the disclosure of debt.
6. Review footnotes and other disclosures.
7. In addition to reviewing the absolute numbers, prepare selected common-size analyses.

The City of Toledo, Ohio, presents detailed financial statements and in recent years has been awarded Certificates of Achievement for Excellence in Financial Reporting. The total financial report consists of more than 100 pages. Selected parts follow.

1. Combined Balance Sheet—All Fund Types and Account Groups (Exhibit 13-3 on pages 534–537).
2. Combined Statement of Revenues, Expenditures, and Changes in Fund Balances—All Government Fund Types and Expendable Trust Funds (Exhibit 13-4 on page 538). (Notice that proceeds from debt are recorded on this statement as revenue. Principal retirement, interest, and fiscal charges are recorded as expenditures.)
3. Partial Footnote 1—Organization and Summary of Significant Accounting Policies (Exhibit 13-5 on page 539). (Notice that a modified accrual basis of accounting is utilized by the Governmental and Expendable Trust Funds, whereas an accrual basis of accounting is utilized by the

Proprietary and Nonexpendable Trust Funds. Agency Fund assets and liabilities are recognized on the modified accrual basis of accounting.)

4. Income Tax Revenues (Exhibit 13-6).
5. Ratio of Net General Bonded Debt to Assessed Value and Net Bonded Debt per Capita—Last Ten Years (Exhibit 13-7).

ACCOUNTING FOR NOT-FOR-PROFIT ORGANIZATIONS OTHER THAN GOVERNMENTS

Not-for-profit organizations account for a substantial portion of economic activity in the United States. There are over 20,000 not-for-profit organizations in the United States.[7] Examples of not-for-profit organizations include hospitals, religious institutions, professional organizations, universities, and museums.

Not-for-profit accounting principles were derived from numerous not-for-profit industry accounting manuals and audit guides. Examples were AICPA audit guides for Colleges and Universities, Audits of Voluntary Health and Welfare Organizations, and audits of providers of Health Care Services.

The FASB was concerned about the lack of uniformity in the accounting for not-for-profit organizations and the lack of overall quality of not-for-profit organizations' financial reporting. To address this concern, four accounting standards relating to not-for-profits were issued by the FASB. These standards are: (1) SFAS No. 93, "Recognition of Depreciation by Not-for-Profit Organizations," (2) SFAS No. 116, "Accounting for Contributions Received and Contributions Made," (3) SFAS No. 117, "Financial Statements of Not-for-Profit Organizations," and (4) SFAS No. 124, "Accounting for Certain Investments Held by Not-for-Profit Organizations." A brief description of these accounting standards and how they impact financial reports follows:

1. *SFAS No. 93*, "Recognition of Depreciation by Not-for-Profit Organizations"[8]

Prior to SFAS No. 93, most not-for-profit organizations did not recognize depreciation. SFAS No. 93 requires not-for-profit organizations to recognize depreciation on long-lived tangible assets. SFAS No. 93 includes these requirements relating to depreciation:

1. Disclose the amount of depreciation expense for each period.
2. Disclose depreciable assets by major classes as of the balance sheet date.
3. Disclose accumulated depreciation for each asset class or in total as of the balance sheet date.
4. Disclose the methods used to calculate depreciation.

SFAS No. 93 exempts individual works of art or historical treasures from the depreciation requirements. For this exemption, two requirements must be met:

1. The asset must have "cultural, aesthetic, or historical value that is worth preserving perpetually."
2. The organization that owns the artwork or historical treasure must be able to preserve the asset so that its potentially unlimited service potential will remain intact.

2. *SFAS No. 116*, "Accounting for Contributions Received and Contributions Made"[9]

SFAS No. 116 applies to *all not-for-profit organizations as well as to any entity that receives or makes contributions*. Some key aspects of SFAS No. 116 will be summarized.

Contributions Received
Contributions received are to be recognized as revenues or gains in the period received. In addition, these contributions are to be recognized as assets, decreases in liabilities, or as expenses in the same period. Contributions received are to be measured at their fair values and reported as restricted support or unrestricted support.

Contributed services received are to be recognized if one of the following conditions holds:

1. The service creates or enhances nonfinancial assets; or
2. These services involve specialized skills that would most likely be paid for, if they were not donated (i.e., electrical services, plumbing services, accounting services, etc.).

EXHIBIT 13-3

CITY OF TOLEDO, OHIO
Combined Balance Sheet, All Fund Types and Account Groups
December 31, 2001 (Amounts in thousands)

| | Governmental Fund Types | | | |
	General	Special Revenue	Debt Service	Capital Projects
Assets and Other Debits				
Equity in Pooled Cash	$ 1,094	$ 5,200	$ 495	$ —
Other Cash	144	1	—	—
Investments	—	3,669	—	—
Receivables (Net of Allowance for Uncollectible Accounts):				
Taxes	31,540	—	—	—
Accounts	1,943	5,532	—	600
Special Assessments	—	38,685	—	1,588
Notes	—	655	837	—
Interfund Receivable	—	—	—	23,374
Due From Other Governments	—	—	—	—
Prepaid Expenditures and Expenses	—	2	—	203
Inventory of Supplies	1,173	2,074	—	806
Restricted Assets:				
Equity in Pooled Cash	—	—	—	—
Other Cash	—	—	84	—
Investments	2,954	4,176	—	17,135
Accounts Receivable	—	—	—	—
Interfund Receivable	—	—	—	—
Property, Plant and Equipment (Net of Accumulated Depreciation)	—	—	—	—
Deferred Debt Issuance Cost	—	—	—	—
Amount Available in Debt Service Funds	—	—	—	—
Amount to be Provided for:				
Retirement of General Long-Term Obligations	—	—	—	—
Compensated Absences	—	—	—	—
Total Assets and Other Debits	$38,848	$59,994	$1,416	$43,706

(continued)

Contributed services recognized should be disclosed by nature and amount for the period. Service contributions are to be valued at the fair value of the services or the resulting increase in assets.

Under SFAS No. 116, donated works of art, historical treasures, or similar assets can be excluded if the following conditions are met:

1. Contributed items are held for public service purposes rather than for financial gain.
2. Contributed items must be protected, kept unencumbered, cared for, and preserved.
3. The organization must have a policy of using funds from the sales of collected items to purchase additional collection pieces.

Contributions received are to be segregated into permanent restrictions, temporary restrictions, and unrestricted support imposed by donors. Restricted contributions shall be reported as an increase in either permanently restricted net assets or temporarily restricted net assets. Unrestricted contributions received are to be reported as unrestricted support and increases in unrestricted net assets. Contributions received are to be measured at fair value.

Conditional promises are to be recognized in the financial statements when the condition(s) has been substantially met. If the nature of the conditional promise is ambiguous, it should be interpreted as conditional.

EXHIBIT 13-3

CITY OF TOLEDO, OHIO
Combined Balance Sheet, All Fund Types and Account Groups
December 31, 2001 (Amounts in thousands) *(continued)*

| | Proprietary Fund Types | | Fiduciary Fund Types | Account Groups | | Total (Memorandum Only) |
	Enterprise	Internal Service	Trust and Agency	General Fixed Assets	General Long-Term Obligations	
	$ 629	$32,781	$ 7,186	$ —	$ —	$ 47,385
	4	—	—	—	—	149
	69,357	—	1,748	—	—	74,774
	—	—	—	—	—	31,540
	5,897	52	153	—	—	14,177
	—	—	—	—	—	40,273
	22,664	—	—	—	—	24,156
	311	—	17,419	—	—	41,104
	94	—	—	—	—	94
	214	—	152	—	—	571
	2,911	766	—	—	—	7,730
	18,548	—	—	—	—	18,548
	264	—	—	—	—	348
	37,400	—	—	—	—	61,665
	7,084	—	—	—	—	7,084
	41,069	—	—	—	—	41,069
	382,620	14,143	—	95,210	—	491,973
	902	—	—	—	—	902
	—	—	—	—	579	579
	—	—	—	—	180,484	180,484
					34,111	34,111
	$589,968	$47,742	$26,658	$95,210	$215,174	$1,118,716

(continued)

Contributions Made

Contributions made are to be recognized as expenses in the period in which they are made. These contributions are to be reported as decreases in assets or increases in liabilities. Contributions made are to be measured at the fair value of the asset contributed or the liability discharged. Conditional promises to give are recognized when the conditions are substantially met.

3. *SFAS No. 117*, "Financial Statements of Not-for-Profit Organizations"[10]

Prior to SFAS No. 117, there were significant differences in the financial reports of not-for-profit organizations. The intent of SFAS No. 117 is to provide consistency in the financial statements of not-for-profit organizations. SFAS No. 117 addresses financial statements, the content of financial statements, and the classification of financial statement information.

Not-for-profit organizations are to present three aggregated financial statements. These include a statement of financial position, a statement of activities, and a statement of cash flows. SFAS No. 117 specifies the content of each of these required financial statements.

EXHIBIT 13-3	**CITY OF TOLEDO, OHIO**

Combined Balance Sheet, All Fund Types and Account Groups
December 31, 2001 (Amounts in thousands) *(continued)*

	Governmental Fund Types			
	General	**Special Revenue**	**Debt Service**	**Capital Projects**
Liabilities				
Accounts Payable	$ 1,185	$ 1,514	$ —	$ 2,123
Escrow	—	154	—	85
Retainages	34	—	—	460
Interfund Payable	510	10,274	—	361
Due to Other Governments	—	140	—	9
Deferred Revenue	15,728	38,685	837	1,588
Other Current Liabilities	1,754	8	—	—
Accrued Compensated Absences	—	—	—	—
Payable From Restricted Assets:				
Accounts Payable	—	—	—	—
Escrow	143	—	—	—
Retainages	—	—	—	—
Interfund Payable	—	—	—	—
Due to Other Governments	—	—	—	—
Other Current Liabilities	—	—	—	372
Debt:				
Notes Payable	—	32,000	—	1,580
General Obligation Bonds Payable	—	—	—	—
Police and Fire Pension General Obligation Bonds	—	—	—	—
Special Assessment Bonds Payable				
With Governmental Commitment	—	—	—	—
Revenue Bonds Payable	—	—	—	—
Capital Lease Obligation	—	—	—	—
Other Long-Term Debt	—	—	—	—
Landfill Closure and Postclosure Care	—	—	—	—
Total Liabilities	19,354	82,775	837	6,578
Fund Equity (Deficit) and Other Credits				
Contributed Capital	—	—	—	—
Investment in General Fixed Assets	—	—	—	—
Retained Earnings (Deficit):				
Reserved for Debt Service	—	—	—	—
Reserved for Replacement	—	—	—	—
Reserved for Improvement	—	—	—	—
Unreserved	—	—	—	—
Fund Balances (Deficit):				
Reserved for Encumbrances	926	8,718	—	8,342
Reserved for Inventory of Supplies	1,175	2,074	—	806
Reserved for Capital Improvements	—	—	—	16,721
Reserved for Long-Term Notes Receivable	—	751	—	—
Reserved for Debt Service	—	—	579	—
Reserved for Prepaid Expenditures	—	2	—	203
Reserved for Landfill Remediation	2,693	—	—	—
Reserved for Recycling	—	—	—	—
Reserved for Endowment	—	—	—	—
Unreserved:				
Designated for Subsequent Years Expenditures	302	221	—	—
Designated for Budget Stabilization	14,398	—	—	—
Undesignated	—	(34,547)	—	11,056
Total Fund Equity (Deficit) and Other Credits	19,494	(22,781)	579	37,128
Total Liabilities and Fund Equity (Deficit) and Other Credits	$38,848	$ 59,994	$1,416	$43,706

(continued)

EXHIBIT 13-3

CITY OF TOLEDO, OHIO
Combined Balance Sheet, All Fund Types and Account Groups
December 31, 2001 (Amounts in thousands) *(continued)*

| | Proprietary Fund Types | | Fiduciary Fund Types | Account Groups | | Total (Memorandum Only) |
	Enterprise	Internal Service	Trust and Agency	General Fixed Assets	General Long-Term Obligations	
	$ 882	$ 450	$ 197	$ —	$ —	$ 6,351
	27	—	977	—	—	1,243
	28	—	—	—	—	522
	62,747	2,167	14	—	—	76,073
	—	—	—	—	—	149
	—	—	—	—	—	56,838
	556	10,450	13,268	—	—	26,036
	—	—	7,224	—	34,111	41,335
	1,640	—	—	—	—	1,640
	4,621	—	—	—	—	4,764
	1,441	—	—	—	—	1,441
	6,100	—	—	—	—	6,100
	127	—	—	—	—	127
	1,527	—	—	—	—	1,899
	39,618	—	—	—	27,163	100,361
	28,601	7	—	—	117,601	146,218
	—	—	—	—	14,050	14,050
	—	—	—	—	542	542
	94,359	—	—	—	—	94,359
	11,445	—	—	—	10,454	21,899
	—	—	—	—	636	636
	—	—	—	—	10,608	10,608
	253,719	13,074	21,680	—	215,174	613,191
	23,869	80,931	—	—	—	104,800
	—	—	—	95,210	—	95,210
	18,319	—	—	—	—	18,319
	57,940	2,000	—	—	—	59,940
	57,514	—	—	—	—	57,514
	178,607	(48,263)	—	—	—	130,344
	—	—	—	—	—	17,986
	—	—	—	—	—	4,055
	—	—	—	—	—	16,721
	—	—	139	—	—	890
	—	—	—	—	—	579
	—	—	—	—	—	205
	—	—	—	—	—	2,693
	—	—	—	—	—	—
	—	—	739	—	—	739
	—	—	—	—	—	523
	—	—	—	—	—	14,398
	—	—	4,100	—	—	(19,391)
	336,249	34,668	4,978	95,210	—	505,525
	$589,968	$47,742	$26,658	$95,210	$215,174	$1,118,716

EXHIBIT 13-4	**CITY OF TOLEDO, OHIO**

Combined Statement of Revenues, Expenditures, and Changes in Fund Balances—All Governmental Fund Types and Expendable Trust Funds for the Year Ended December 31, 2001 (Amounts in thousands)

| | Governmental Fund Types | | | | Fiduciary Fund Types | |
	General	Special Revenue	Debt Service	Capital Projects	Expendable Trusts	Total (Memorandum Only)
Revenues:						
Income Taxes	$150,911	$ —	$ —	$ —	$ —	$150,911
Property Taxes	15,477	—	—	—	—	15,477
Special Assessments	—	19,883	229	225	—	20,337
Licenses and Permits	2,161	11	—	—	—	2,172
Intergovernmental Services	24,890	25,566	145	7,135	—	57,736
Charges for Services	11,323	808	—	96	136	12,363
Investment Earnings	5,305	665	20	1,302	242	7,534
Fines and Forfeitures	3,289	552	—	—	—	3,841
All Other Revenue	49	254	—	706	1,341	2,350
Total Revenues	213,405	47,739	394	9,464	1,719	272,721
Expenditures:						
Current:						
General Government	20,641	547	—	—	43	21,231
Public Service	1,875	25,638	—	—	—	27,513
Public Safety	135,391	2,026	—	—	619	138,036
Public Utilities	—	1,629	—	—	—	1,629
Community Environment	5,638	15,482	—	—	—	21,120
Health	14,578	2,272	—	—	—	16,850
Parks and Recreation	4,909	214	—	—	56	5,179
Capital Outlay	2,012	2,901	—	38,696	—	43,609
Debt Service:						
Principal Retirement	3,478	183	9,508	1,408	—	14,577
Interest and Fiscal Charges	2,803	2,046	5,283	1,975	—	12,107
Total Expenditures	191,325	52,938	14,791	42,079	718	301,851
Excess (Deficiency) of Revenues over Expenditures	22,080	(5,199)	(14,397)	(32,615)	1,001	(29,130)
Other Financing Sources (Uses):						
Operating Transfers In	5,698	2,179	13,821	38,718	645	61,061
Operating Transfers (Out)	(34,460)	(1,610)	—	(13,992)	(1,432)	(51,494)
Bond Proceeds	—	—	—	7,900	—	7,900
Note Proceeds	437	—	—	250	—	687
Premiums on Bond	—	—	—	4	—	4
Sale of Fixed Assets	50	—	—	—	—	50
Other Financing Sources (Uses)	370	183	—	193	2	748
Total Other Financing Sources and (Uses)	(27,905)	752	13,821	33,073	(785)	18,956
Excess (Deficiency) of Revenues and Other Financing Sources Over Expenditures and Other Financing Uses	(5,825)	(4,447)	(576)	458	216	(10,174)
Fund Balances (Deficit) at Beginning of Year	25,173	(19,225)	1,155	37,640	3,741	48,484
Residual Equity Transfers	—	(25)	—	(982)	—	(1,007)
Increase in Reserve for Inventory	146	916	—	12	—	1,074
Fund Balance (Deficit) at Year End	$ 19,494	$(22,781)	$ 579	$37,128	$3,957	$ 38,377

EXHIBIT 13-5   **Partial Footnote 1—Organization and Summary
of Significant Accounting Policies (in Part)**

C. Basis of Accounting

The modified accrual basis of accounting is utilized by the Governmental and Expendable Trust Funds. Under this method of accounting, the City recognizes revenue when it becomes both measurable and available to finance current City operations. Assistance awards made on the basis of entitlement are recorded as intergovernmental receivables and revenues when entitlement occurs. Revenues accrued at the end of the year include: individual income taxes during the fourth quarter that are received within 60 days after year-end, net of estimated refunds; property taxes for the budget year to which they apply where taxpayer liability has been established and such taxes are received during the year or within 60 days after year-end; property taxes levied in the current year to be collected in 2002, which are measurable, have been offset by a credit to deferred revenue since they are not available for appropriation and use until 2002; and intergovernmental revenues for the year which are received within 60 days after year-end or based on expenditures recognized where agreements stipulate funds must be expended for a specific purpose or project before any reimbursements will be made to the City. Expenditures are recorded when the related fund liability is incurred. Principal and interest on general long-term debt are recorded as fund liabilities when due or when amounts have been accumulated in the debt service fund for payments to be made early in the following year.

Concerning the statement of financial position, SFAS No. 117 directs that it is to include aggregated information about the assets, liabilities, and net assets. SFAS No. 117 requires the statement of activity to provide information concerning the effects of transactions on the amount and nature of net assets, the interrelationships between those transactions and other events, and how resources are used by the organization to provide services. The statement of activity is also to disclose the changes in the amounts of permanently restricted net assets, temporarily restricted net assets, and unrestricted net assets.

In regards to the content of the statement of cash flows, SFAS No. 117 requires that not-for-profit organizations comply with SFAS No. 95, "Statement of Cash Flows." In addition, SFAS No. 117 amends SFAS No. 95 concerning its description of financing activities. Financing activities now include receipts of donations restricted for acquiring, constructing, or improving long-lived assets or establishing or increasing permanent or term endowments.

For the statement of financial position, SFAS No. 117 requires that assets and liabilities should be reported in relatively homogenous groups. They should also be classified to provide information about their interrelationships, liquidity, and financial flexibility. New assets are to be classified as either permanently restricted, temporarily restricted, or unrestricted. Revenues, expenses, gains, and losses are to be separated into reasonably homogeneous groups for the statement of activities. They also are to be classified as affecting permanently restricted, temporarily restricted, or unrestricted net assets.

EXHIBIT 13-6   **CITY OF TOLEDO, OHIO
Income Tax Revenues—Last Ten Years
(Amounts in thousands)**

Fiscal Year	Tax Revenues	Tax Rate
1992	$110,423	2¼%
1993	115,755	2¼%
1994	124,975	2¼%
1995	129,789	2¼%
1996	138,487	2¼%
1997	142,701	2¼%
1998	144,505	2¼%
1999	150,170	2¼%
2000	153,830	2¼%
2001	150,911	2¼%

Source: City of Toledo Income Tax Department

EXHIBIT 13-7	**CITY OF TOLEDO, OHIO**

Ratio of Net General Bonded Debt to Assessed Value and Net Bonded Debt per Capita—Last Ten Years

Fiscal Year	Population[1]	Assessed Value[2]	Gross General Bonded Debt[2]	Less Balance in Debt Service Fund[2] & [3]	Net General Bonded Debt[2]	Ratio of Net Bonded Debt to Assessed Value	Net Bonded Debt per Capita
1992	332,943	$3,196,025	$ 68,995	$ 251	$ 68,744	2.2%	$206.75
1993	332,943	3,162,416	62,550	312	62,238	2.0%	186.93
1994	332,943	3,277,973	74,450	373	74,077	2.3%	222.50
1995	332,943	3,257,498	91,079	658	90,421	2.8%	271.58
1996	332,943	3,253,639	101,555	666	100,389	3.1%	301.52
1997	332,943	3,450,882	106,213	864	105,349	3.0%	312.51
1998	332,943	3,451,238	131,859	899	130,960	3.8%	393.34
1999	332,943	3,472,027	127,636	1,023	126,613	3.7%	380.28
2000	313,619	4,084,141	126,046	1,156	124,890	3.1%	398.22
2001	313,619	4,025,806	123,810	579	123,231	3.1%	392.93

(1) Source: U.S. Bureau of the Census

(2) Amounts shown in thousands of dollars. Source: Lucas County Auditor.

(3) The City has paid its general bonded debt service for the tax years shown from current income tax revenues. The amount required is transferred to the debt service funds from the capital improvement fund.

4. *SFAS No. 124*, "Accounting for Certain Investments Held by Not-for-Profit Organizations"[11]

This statement applies to investments in equity securities that have a readily determinable fair value and to all investments in debt securities. These investments are to be shown at their fair values in the statement of financial position. This statement does not apply to investments in equity securities that are accounted for under the equity method or to investments in consolidated subsidiaries. Disclosure requirements in the statement of financial position include the aggregate carrying value of investments by major categories and the basis for determining the carrying values of equity securities without readily determinable fair market values. Any shortfall in the fair value of donor-restricted endowment funds below the amount required by donor stipulations or by law must also be disclosed.

For the statement of activities, any realized or unrealized gains and losses are to be shown. Some of the disclosure requirements for the statement of activities include the composition of the investment return, which consists of investment income, realized gains and losses on investments not reported at fair value, and net gains and losses on investments that are reported at fair value.

Applicability of GAAP to Not-for-Profit Organizations

Some individuals were of the opinion that the applicability of GAAP to not-for-profit organizations was unclear. SOP 94-2 was issued to address the applicability of GAAP to not-for-profit organizations.[12]

SOP 94-2 concludes that not-for-profit organizations should follow the guidance in effective provisions of ARBs, APB Opinions, and FASB Statements and Interpretations unless the specific pronouncement explicitly exempts not-for-profit organizations or their subject matter precludes such applicability (SOP 94-2, paragraph .09).

Exhibit 13-8 contains major portions of the 1998 and 1997 financial statements of the Institute of Management Accountants. These statements are for the years ended June 30, 1998 and 1997.

Budgeting by Objectives and/or Measures of Productivity

Accounting for nonprofit institutions differs greatly from accounting for a profit-oriented enterprise. The accounting for a profit-oriented business centers on the entity concept and the effi-

EXHIBIT 13-8	THE INSTITUTE OF MANAGEMENT ACCOUNTANTS, INC.
	1998 Financial Report (in Part)

Institute of Management Accountants, Inc. and Affiliates
Combined Statement of Financial Position
June 30, 1998 and 1997
(Dollars in thousands)

	1998	1997
ASSETS		
Cash and cash equivalents	$ 1,766	$ 1,470
Marketable securities	20,199	19,000
Receivables, net allowance for doubtful accounts	685	814
Property, equipment and software, net	4,400	4,399
Other assets	1,226	1,208
Total assets	$28,276	$26,891
LIABILITIES, DEFERRED REVENUES AND NET ASSETS		
Accounts payable and accrued expenses	$ 2,686	$ 3,007
Bonds payable, net of discount	3,575	3,752
Total liabilities	6,261	6,759
Deferred revenues		
Membership dues	3,530	3,407
Other	510	964
Total deferred revenues	4,040	4,371
Net assets		
Unrestricted		
IMA		
Current Operating Fund	5,986	4,476
Reserve Fund	8,658	8,001
ICMA	201	867
IMAMEF		
Board Designated	100	100
Undesignated	3,030	2,367
IMAFAR	—	(50)
Total net assets	17,975	15,761
Total liabilities, deferred revenues and net assets	$28,276	$26,891

(continued)

ciency of the entity. The accounting for a nonprofit institution does not include an entity concept or efficiency. The accounting for a profit-oriented business has a bottom-line net income. The accounting for a nonprofit institution does not have a bottom line.

Some nonprofit institutions have added budgeting by objectives and/or measures of productivity to their financial reporting to incorporate measures of efficiency. The article, "Budgeting by Objectives: Charlotte's Experience," reported several objectives incorporated in the budget of Charlotte, North Carolina. Four primary objectives guided the budget: (1) the property tax rate should not increase, (2) continued emphasis should be placed on making the best use of city employees and the present computer capability, (3) any budget increase should be held to a minimum, and (4) a balanced program of services should be presented.[13]

This article also reports measures of productivity that Charlotte has used. These measures of productivity include: (1) customers served per $1,000 of sanitation expense, (2) number of tons of refuse per $1,000 expense, and (3) street miles flushed per $1,000 expense.[14]

Budgeting by objectives and/or measures of productivity could be added to the financial reporting of any nonprofit institution. The objectives and measures of productivity should be applicable to the particular nonprofit institution.

EXHIBIT 13-8

THE INSTITUTE OF MANAGEMENT ACCOUNTANTS, INC.
1998 Financial Report (in Part) *(continued)*

Institute of Management Accountants, Inc. and Affiliates
Combined Statement of Activities
Years Ended June 30, 1998 and 1997
(Dollars in thousands)

	1998	1997
REVENUES AND SUPPORT		
Membership dues and fees	$ 7,799	$ 8,114
Education programs	1,549	1,484
Annual conference	670	702
Advertising and sales of publications	2,399	2,310
CMA/CFM examination fees	1,205	1,516
Investment income	4,689	4,120
Other	785	1,046
Total revenues and support	19,096	19,292
EXPENSES		
Payments to chapters	1,020	1,044
Chapter and member services	1,959	2,056
Education programs	1,918	1,853
Marketing	509	492
Annual conference	588	543
Publications and information center	2,626	2,387
CMA/CFM program	1,564	1,935
Research expenditures	151	123
Administration and occupancy costs	5,788	6,413
Asset valuation charge	—	676
Other	759	1,044
Total expenses	16,882	18,566
Changes in net assets before cumulative effect of change in accounting principle	2,214	726
Cumulative effect of change in accounting principle:		
Marketable securities	—	4,750
Changes in net assets	2,214	5,476
Net assets, beginning of year	15,761	10,285
Net assets, end of year	$17,975	$15,761

(continued)

SUMMARY

This chapter reviewed financial reporting for personal financial statements and accounting for governments and other not-for-profit organizations. Accounting for these areas differs greatly from accounting for profit-oriented businesses. This difference has been narrowed substantially for not-for-profit organizations other than governments.

Statement of Position 82-1 presents guidelines for the preparation of personal financial statements. SOP 82-1 concludes that personal financial statements should present assets at their estimated current values and liabilities at their estimated current amounts at the date of the financial statements. This differs from commercial financial statements that predominantly use historical information.

The accounting for governments (state and local) revolves around fund accounting. Government transactions are recorded in one or more funds designed to emphasize control and budgetary limitations. Some governments do their accounting using a method that resembles a cash basis, others use a modified accrual basis, and some use an accrual basis.

Not-for-profit accounting for organizations, other than governments, has changed substantially. It now resembles accounting for profit organizations. A major difference is that not-for-profit organizations issue a statement of activities instead of an income statement.

Some nonprofit institutions have added budgeting by objectives and/or measures of productivity to their financial reporting to incorporate measures of efficiency.

EXHIBIT 13-8	**THE INSTITUTE OF MANAGEMENT ACCOUNTANTS, INC.** **1998 Financial Report (in Part)** *(continued)*

Institute of Management Accountants, Inc. and Affiliates
Combined Statement of Cash Flows
Years Ended June 30, 1998 and 1997
(Dollars in thousands)

	1998	1997
CASH FLOWS FROM OPERATING ACTIVITIES		
Changes in net assets	$ 2,214	$ 5,476
Adjustments to reconcile changes in net assets to		
net cash (used for) operating activities		
Depreciation, amortization and valuation allowances	567	711
Asset valuation charge	—	676
Realized gains on sales of marketable securities	(2,588)	(912)
Appreciation of marketable securities	(1,669)	(2,753)
Cumulative effect of change in accounting principle	—	(4,750)
Donated materials	(5)	(24)
Changes in assets and liabilities		
Decrease (increase) in receivables	98	(41)
(Increase) in other assets	(34)	(34)
(Decrease) increase in accounts payable and accrued expenses	(321)	1,030
(Decrease) in deferred revenues	(331)	(189)
Net cash (used for) operating activities	(2,069)	(810)
CASH FLOWS FROM INVESTING ACTIVITIES		
Capital expenditures	(513)	(512)
Purchases of marketable securities	(3,083)	(4,783)
Proceeds from sales of marketable securities	6,141	6,206
Net cash provided by investing activities	2,545	911
CASH FLOWS FROM FINANCING ACTIVITIES		
Repayment of current portion of bonds payable	(180)	(170)
Cash (used for) financing activities	(180)	(170)
Net increase (decrease) in cash and cash equivalents	296	(69)
Cash and cash equivalents		
Beginning of year	1,470	1,539
End of year	$ 1,766	$ 1,470

To the Net

1. Go to the Governmental Accounting Standards Board site (http://www.rutgers.edu/ Accounting/raw/gasb). What is the mission of the Governmental Accounting Standards Board?

2. Go to the Governmental Accounting Standards Board site (http://www.rutgers.edu/Accounting/raw/gasb). Select "Performance Measures." What does this page state about the use and reporting of performance measures for government services? Select "Performance Measures." Select "Introduction to Performance Measurement." Print "Introduction to Performance Measurement." Be prepared to discuss.

Questions

Q 13-1.   May personal financial statements be prepared only for an individual? Comment.

Q 13-2.   What is the basic personal financial statement?

Q 13-3. Is a statement of changes in net worth required when presenting personal financial statements?

Q 13-4. Are comparative financial statements required when presenting personal financial statements?

Q 13-5. When preparing a personal statement of financial condition, should assets and liabilities be presented on the basis of historical cost or estimated current value?

Q 13-6. In a personal statement of financial condition, what is the equity section called?

Q 13-7. What personal financial statement should be prepared when an explanation of changes in net worth is desired?

Q 13-8. Is the presentation of a personal income statement appropriate?

Q 13-9. GAAP as they apply to personal financial statements use the cash basis. Comment.

Q 13-10. Is the concept of working capital used with personal financial statements? Comment.

Q 13-11. List some sources of information that may be available when preparing personal financial statements.

Q 13-12. Give examples of disclosure in footnotes with personal financial statements.

Q 13-13. If quoted market prices are not available, a personal financial statement cannot be prepared. Comment.

Q 13-14. List some objectives that could be incorporated into the financial reporting of a professional accounting organization.

Q 13-15. Do not-for-profit organizations, other than governments, use fund accounting? Comment.

Q 13-16. The accounting for governments is centered on the entity concept and the efficiency of the entity. Comment.

Q 13-17. For governmental accounting, define the following types of funds:
1. General fund
2. Proprietary fund
3. Fiduciary fund

Q 13-18. How many funds will be used by a state or local government?

Q 13-19. The budget for a state or local government is not as binding as a budget for a commercial business. Comment.

Q 13-20. Which organization provides a service whereby it issues a certificate of conformance to governmental units with financial reports that meet its standards?

Q 13-21. The rating on an industrial revenue bond is representative of the probability of default of bonds issued with the full faith and credit of a governmental unit. Comment.

Q 13-22. The accounting for not-for-profit institutions does not typically include the concept of efficiency. Indicate how the concept of efficiency can be incorporated in the financial reporting of a not-for-profit institution.

Q 13-23. Could a profit-oriented enterprise use fund accounting practices? Comment.

Problems

P 13-1. For each of these situations, indicate the amount to be placed on a statement of financial condition at December 31, 2004.

a. Bill and Pat Konner purchased their home at 2829 Willow Road in Stow, Ohio, in August 1984 for $80,000. The unpaid mortgage is $20,000. Immediately after purchasing the home, Bill and Pat added several improvements totaling $10,000. Real estate prices in Stow have increased 40% since the time of purchase.

From the facts given, determine the estimated current value of the home.

b. Joe Best drives a Toyota, for which he paid $20,000 when it was new. Joe believes that since he maintains the car in good condition, he could sell it for $12,000. The average selling price for this model of Toyota is $9,000.

From the facts given, determine the estimated current value of Joe's car.

c.   Sue Bell is 40 years old and has an IRA with a balance of $20,000. The IRS penalty for early withdrawal is 10%. The marginal tax rate for Sue Bell is 30% (tax on gross amount).

   What is the estimated current value of the IRA and the estimated income taxes on the difference between the estimated current values of assets and the estimated current amounts of liabilities and their tax bases?

d.   Bill Kell guaranteed a loan of $8,000 for his girlfriend to buy a car. She is behind in payments on the car.

   What liability should be shown on Bill Kell's statement of financial condition?

e.   Dick Better bought a home in 1976 for $70,000. Currently the mortgage on the home is $45,000. Because of the current high interest rates, the bank has offered to retire the mortgage for $40,000.

   What is the estimated current value of this liability?

P 13-2.   For each of these situations, indicate the amount to be placed on a statement of financial condition at December 31, 2004.

a.   Raj Reel owns the following securities:

1,000 shares of Ree's

2,000 shares of Bell's

   Ree's is traded on the New York Stock Exchange. The prices from the most recent trade day follow:

Open 19

High 20½

Low   19

Close 20

   Bell's is a local company whose stock is sold by brokers on a workout basis. (The broker tries to find a buyer.) The most recent selling price was $8.

   What is the estimated current value of these securities? (Assume that the commission on Ree's would be $148 and the commission on Bell's would be $170.)

b.   Charlie has a certificate of deposit with a $10,000 balance. Accrued interest is $500. The penalty for early withdrawal would be $300.

   What is the estimated current value of the certificate of deposit?

c.   Jones has an option to buy 500 shares of ABC Construction at a price of $20 per share. The option expires in one year. ABC Construction shares are presently selling for $25.

   What is the estimated current value of these options?

d.   Carl Jones has a whole-life insurance policy with the face amount of $100,000, cash value of $50,000, and a loan outstanding against the policy of $20,000. Susan Jones is the beneficiary.

   What is the estimated current value of the insurance policy?

e.   Larry Solomon paid $60,000 for a home 10 years ago. The unpaid mortgage on the home is $30,000. Larry estimates the current value of the home to be $90,000. This estimate is partially based on the selling price of homes recently sold in the neighborhood. Larry's home is assessed for tax purposes at $50,000. Assessments in the area average one-half of market value. The house has not been inspected for assessment during the past two years. Larry would sell through a broker, who would charge 5% of the selling price.

   What is the estimated current value of the home?

P 13-3.   For Barb and Carl, the assets and liabilities and the effective income tax rates at December 31, 2004, follow:

Accounts	Tax Bases	Estimated Current Value	Excess of Estimated Current Values over Tax Bases	Effective Income Tax Rates	Amount of Estimated Income Taxes
Cash	$ 20,000	$ 20,000	—	—	_____
Marketable securities	45,000	50,000	5,000	28%	_____
Life insurance	50,000	50,000	—	—	_____
Residence	100,000	125,000	25,000	28%	_____
Furnishings	40,000	25,000	(15,000)	—	_____
Jewelry	20,000	20,000	—	—	_____
Autos	20,000	12,000	(8,000)	—	_____
Mortgage payable	(90,000)	(90,000)	—	—	_____
Note payable	(30,000)	(30,000)	—	—	_____
Credit cards	(10,000)	(10,000)	—	—	_____

Required   a. Compute the estimated tax liability on the differences between the estimated current value of the assets and liabilities and their tax bases.

b. Present a statement of financial condition for Barb and Carl at December 31, 2004.

c. Comment on the statement of financial condition.

P 13-4.   For Mary Lou and Ernie, the assets and liabilities and the effective income tax rates at December 31, 2004, follow:

Accounts	Tax Bases	Estimated Current Value	Excess of Estimated Current Values over Tax Bases	Effective Income Tax Rates	Amount of Estimated Income Taxes
Cash	$ 20,000	$ 20,000	—	—	_____
Marketable securities	80,000	100,000	20,000	28%	_____
Options	-0-	30,000	30,000	28%	_____
Residence	100,000	150,000	50,000	28%	_____
Royalties	-0-	20,000	20,000	28%	_____
Furnishings	40,000	20,000	(20,000)	—	_____
Auto	20,000	15,000	(5,000)	—	_____
Mortgage	(70,000)	(70,000)	—	—	_____
Auto loan	(10,000)	(10,000)	—	—	_____

Required   a. Compute the estimated tax liability on the differences between the estimated current value of the assets and liabilities and their tax bases.

b. Present a statement of financial condition for Mary Lou and Ernie at December 31, 2004.

c. Comment on the statement of financial condition.

P 13-5.   For Bob and Sue, the changes in net worth for the year ended December 31, 2004, follow:

Realized increases in net worth:	
Salary	$ 60,000
Dividend income	2,500
Interest income	2,000
Gain on sale of marketable securities	500
Realized decreases in net worth:	
Income taxes	20,000
Interest expense	6,000
Personal expenditures	29,000
Unrealized increases in net worth:	
Stock options	3,000
Land	7,000
Residence	5,000
Unrealized decreases in net worth:	
Boat	3,000
Jewelry	1,000
Furnishings	4,000
Estimated income taxes on the differences between the estimated current values of assets and the estimated current amounts of liabilities and their tax bases	15,000
Net worth at the beginning of year	150,000

Required   a. Prepare a statement of changes in net worth for the year ended December 31, 2004.

b. Comment on the statement of changes in net worth.

P 13-6.   For Jim and Carrie, the changes in net worth for the year ended December 31, 2004, are shown on the following page.

Required   a. Prepare a statement of changes in net worth for the year ended December 31, 2004.

b. Comment on the statement of changes in net worth.

Realized increases in net worth:	
Salary	$ 50,000
Interest income	6,000
Realized decreases in net worth:	
Income taxes	15,000
Interest expense	3,000
Personal property taxes	1,000
Real estate taxes	1,500
Personal expenditures	25,000
Unrealized increases in net worth:	
Marketable securities	2,000
Land	5,000
Residence	3,000
Stock options	4,000
Unrealized decreases in net worth:	
Furnishings	3,000
Estimated income taxes on the differences between the estimated current values of assets and the estimated current amounts of liabilities and their tax bases	12,000
Net worth at the beginning of year	130,000

P 13-7.   Use Exhibit 13-4, City of Toledo, Ohio, Combined Statement of Revenues, Expenditures, and Changes in Fund Balances—All Governmental Fund Types and Expendable Trust Funds.

Required   a.   Prepare a vertical common-size statement for Exhibit 13-4, using only total revenues and expenditures (memorandum only). Use total expenditures as the base.
b.   Comment on significant items in the vertical common-size analysis.

P 13-8.   Use Exhibit 13-6, City of Toledo, Ohio, Income Tax Revenues.

Required   a.   Prepare a horizontal common-size analysis of taxes collected. Use 1992 as the base.
b.   Comment on significant trends indicated in the horizontal common-size analysis prepared for (a).

P 13-9.   Use Exhibit 13-7, City of Toledo, Ohio, Ratio of Net General Bonded Debt to Assessed Value and Net Bonded Debt Per Capita.

Required   a.   How much has assessed value increased from 1992 to 2001?
b.   How much has net general bonded debt increased from 1992 to 2001?
c.   Give your opinion of the significance of the change in debt between 1992 and 2001.

P 13-10.   Use Exhibit 13-8, The Institute of Management Accountants financial report.

Required   a.   How much was the combined change in net assets between 1997 and 1998?
b.   Prepare a horizontal common-size analysis for total revenue and expenses for 1997 and 1998. (Use 1997 as the base.)
c.   Prepare a vertical common-size analysis for the combined revenues and expenses for 1997 and 1998. (Use total revenues as the base.)
d.   Comment on significant items in the horizontal and vertical common-size analyses.

Case 13-1

Governor Lucas—This is Your County

The 2001 Lucas County, Ohio, financial report contains approximately 200 pages, and has consistently received the Certificate of Achievement for Excellence in Financial Reporting. This case includes selected parts of that report.

LUCAS COUNTY, OHIO
STATEMENT OF NET ASSETS
DECEMBER 31, 2001
(Amounts in 000s)

| | Primary Government | | | |
	Governmental Activities	Business-type Activities	Total	Component Units
Assets:				
Pooled cash and cash equivalents	$ 54,905	$ 2,811	$ 57,716	$ 2,187
Pooled Investments	153,403	7,697	161,100	5,848
Segregated cash accounts	6,331		6,331	
Receivables (net of allowances for uncollectables)	137,383	4,020	141,403	1,721
Due from other funds	181		181	
Due from other governments	9,703		9,703	
Prepaid expenses			—	213
Inventory of materials and supplies	651	24	675	215
Capital assets (net of accumulated depreciation)	265,867	89,907	355,774	14,784
Total assets	628,424	104,459	732,883	24,968
Liabilities:				
Accounts payable	18,708	365	19,073	1,697
Accrued wages and benefits	29,288	679	29,967	382
Due to other funds	178	3	181	
Due to other governments	1,843		1,843	
Deposits	6,331		6,331	
Matured bonds payable	16		16	
Matured interest payable	17		17	
Deferred revenue	—		—	485
Claims payable	6,841		6,841	
Notes payable	10,740		10,740	
Long-term liabilities				
Due within one year	12,562	716	13,278	136
Due in more than one year	108,680	20,341	129,021	7,114
Total liabilities	195,204	22,104	217,308	9,814
Net assets:				
Invested in capital assets, net of related debt	144,625	68,850	213,475	
Restricted for:				
Capital projects	19,672		19,672	
Debt service	10,542		10,542	
Other purposes	101		101	
Unrestricted	258,280	13,505	271,785	15,154
Total net assets	$433,220	$ 82,355	$515,575	$15,154

LUCAS COUNTY, OHIO
NOTES TO THE FINANCIAL STATEMENTS (In Part)
DECEMBER 31, 2001

Note A—*Description of Lucas County and Basis of Presentation*

The County: Lucas County is a political subdivision of the State of Ohio. The County was formed by an act of the Ohio General Assembly in 1835. The three member **Board of County Commissioners** is the legislative and executive body of the County. The **County Auditor** is the chief fiscal officer. In addition, there are seven other elected administrative officials, each of whom are independent as set forth by Ohio law. These officials are: **Clerk of Courts**, **Coroner**, **Engineer**, **Prosecutor**, **Recorder**, **Sheriff**, and **Treasurer**. There are also ten **Common Pleas Court Judges**, two **Domestic Relations Court Judges**, two **Juvenile Court Judges**, one **Probate Court Judge** and five **Court of Appeals Judges** elected on a County-wide basis to oversee the County's judicial system.

The accompanying financial statements present the County (Primary Government) and its component units, which are legally separate organizations which the elected officials of the primary government are financially accountable. The financial data of the component units are included in the County's reporting entity because of the significance of their operational or financial relationships with the County. Blended component units, although legally separate entities, are, in substance, part of the government operations.

A discretely presented component unit is an entity that is legally separate from the County but for which the County is financially accountable, or its relationship with the County is such that exclusion would cause the County's financial statements to be misleading or incomplete.

The discretely presented component unit column in the combined financial statements include the County's component units. They are reported in a separate column to emphasize that they are legally separate from the county. A brief description of each component unit, and its relationships to the County follows:

Toledo Mud Hens Baseball Club, Inc. is organized to own, manage, and operate a professional baseball club. The board of this component unit is appointed by the Board of County Commissioners. The County receives rent from the Mud Hens that is substantially below market rate, which imposes a financial burden, as defined by GASB 14 on the County. For report purposes, the Mud Hens are a proprietary component unit. The Mud Hens are reported on a fiscal year ending October 31. Complete financial statements of the component unit can be obtained from its administrative office at Fifth Third Field, 406 Washington St., Toledo, OH 43604.

Lott Industries, Inc., is a nonprofit organization affiliated with the Lucas County Board of Mental Retardation and Developmental Disabilities (LCBMR/DD), a special revenue fund of the County. It provides employment for individuals with mental retardation and developmental disabilities by obtaining work competitively from the private and public sectors. A majority of the board of the component unit is appointed by the LCBMR/DD. The LCBMR/DD pays the salaries of the administrative staff, which is a financial obligation of the County, and the component unit exists solely to provide service to the LCBMR/DD. For report purposes, Lott Industries, Inc. is a governmental component unit. Complete financial statements of the component unit can be obtained from its administrative office at 2001 Collingwood, Toledo, Ohio 43620.

Preferred Properties, Inc. and Affiliates is a not-for-profit corporation organized to provide affordable and accessible housing to persons with disabilities. One third of the board of the component unit is appointed by the LCBMR/DD. Funds for the purchase of housing are received from the LCBMR/DD which come from board funds and pass through of funds from Community Assistance Projects administered by the Ohio Department of Mental Retardation and Developmental Disabilities. This imposes a financial obligation on the County. For report purposes, Preferred Properties, Inc. is a governmental component unit. Preferred Properties, Inc. is reported on a fiscal year ending June 30. Complete financial statements of the component unit can be obtained from its administrative office at 2001 Collingwood, Toledo, Ohio 43620.

Community Living Options, Inc. is a non-profit corporation that provides residential assistance and support services to individuals with mental retardation and developmental disabilities. The board of the component unit is appointed by the LCBMR/DD. The component unit receives the majority of its funding from the State of Ohio, passed through the LCBMR/DD. The LCBMR/DD has agreed to fund any losses of the component unit which imposes a financial obligation on the County. For report purposes, Community Living Options, Inc. is a governmental component unit. Complete financial statement of the component unit can be obtained from its administrative office at 2001 Collingwood, Toledo, Ohio 43620.

LUCAS COUNTY, OHIO
NOTES TO THE FINANCIAL STATEMENTS (continued)
DECEMBER 31, 2001

Note A—*Description of Lucas County and Basis of Presentation (continued)*

In determining its reporting entity and component units, the County considered all potential component units, including the Lucas County Board of Health, Metropolitan Park District, Lucas County Soil and Water Conservation District, Lucas County Port Authority, Lucas County Improvement Corporation, Toledo Zoological Society, Toledo Area Sanitary District, Toledo Lucas County Public Library, Lucas County Board of Education and Toledo-Lucas County Convention and Visitors Bureau and concluded that such were neither component units nor related organizations of the County and that it would not be misleading to exclude their activities from the County's reporting entity.

Basis of Presentation: The County's basic financial statements consist of government-wide statements, including a statement of net assets and a statement of activities, and fund financial statements which provide a more detailed level of financial information.

Government-wide Financial Statements: The statement of net assets and the statement of activities display information about the County as a whole. These statements include the financial activities of the primary government, except for fiduciary funds. The activity of the internal service funds is eliminated to avoid "doubling up" revenues and expenses. The statements distinguish between those activities of the County that are governmental and those that are considered business-type activities.

The statement of net assets presents the financial condition of the governmental and business-type activities for the County at year-end. The statement of activities presents a comparison between direct expenses and program revenues for each program or function of the County's governmental activities and for the business-type activities of the County. Direct expenses are those that are specifically associated with a service, program or department and therefore clearly identifiable to a particular function. Program revenues include charges paid by the recipient for the goods or services offered by the program, grants and contributions that are restricted to meeting the operational or capital requirements of a particular program and interest earned on grants that is required to be used to support a particular program. Revenues which are not classified as program revenues are presented as general revenues of the County, with certain limited exceptions. The comparison of direct expenses with program revenues identifies the extent to which each business segment or governmental function is self-financing or draws from the general revenues of the County.

As a general rule the effect of interfund activity has been eliminated from the government-wide financial statements. Exceptions to this general rule are payments-in-lieu of taxes and other charges between the County's water and sewer function and various other functions of the County. Elimination of these charges would distort the direct costs and program revenues reported for the various functions concerned.

Fund Financial Statements: During the year, the County segregates transactions related to certain County functions or activities in separate funds in order to aid financial management and to demonstrate legal compliance. Fund financial statements are designed to present financial information of the County at this more detailed level. The focus of governmental and enterprise fund financial statements is on major funds. Each major fund is presented in a separate column. Nonmajor funds are aggregated and presented in a single column. Internal service funds are combined and the totals are presented in a single column on the face of the proprietary fund statements. Fiduciary funds are reported by type.

Fund Accounting: The County uses funds to maintain its financial records during the year. A fund is defined as a fiscal and accounting entity with a self balancing set of accounts. There are three categories of funds: governmental, proprietary and fiduciary.

Governmental Funds: Governmental funds are those through which most governmental functions of the County are financed. Governmental fund reporting focuses on the sources, use and balances of current financial resources. Expendable assets are assigned to the various governmental funds according to the purposes for which they may or must be used. Current liabilities are assigned to the fund from which they will be paid. The difference between governmental funds assets and liabilities is reported as fund balance. The following are the County's major governmental funds.

- General Fund: This fund accounts for the general operating revenues and expenditures of the County not recorded elsewhere. The primary revenue sources are sales and use taxes, property taxes, state and local government fund receipts, investment earnings and charges for services.

LUCAS COUNTY, OHIO
NOTES TO THE FINANCIAL STATEMENTS (continued)
DECEMBER 31, 2001

Note A—*Description of Lucas County and Basis of Presentation (continued)*

- Children Services Board Special Revenue Fund: This fund accounts for County-wide property tax levy, state grants and reimbursements used for County child care programs.
- Board of Mental Retardation Special Revenue Fund: This fund accounts for a County-wide property tax levy, state grants and reimbursements used for care and services for the mentally handicapped and retarded.
- Public Assistance Special Revenue Fund: This fund accounts for various federal and state grants and reimbursements as well as transfers from the General Fund used for human service programs.
- Capital Improvements Capital Projects Fund: This fund accounts for renovation and construction of County owned buildings and facilities, and construction of special assessment projects.
- Debt Service Fund: This fund accounts for revenues received and used to pay principal and interest on debt.

Proprietary Fund: Proprietary fund reporting focuses on the determination of operating income, changes in net assets, financial position and cash flows. These funds are used to account for operations that provide services which are financed primarily by user charges, or activities where periodic measurement of income is appropriate for capital maintenance, public policy, management control or other purposes. The County reports the following major proprietary funds.

- Water Supply System Enterprise Fund: This fund accounts for the distribution of treated water to individuals and commercial users of Lucas County.
- Sewer System Enterprise Fund: This fund accounts for sanitary sewer services provided to individuals and commercial users in Lucas County and portions of Wood County.
- Wastewater Treatment Enterprise Fund: This fund accounts for wastewater treatment services provided to the Sanitary Engineer, cities of Maumee and Sylvania, Village of Waterville, Sylvania Township and other portions of Lucas County and portions of Wood County.

Additionally the County reports which Internal Service Funds account for the goods or services provided by certain County departments to other County funds, departments and other governmental units, on a cost reimbursement basis. The County also reports agency funds that account for and maintain assets held by the County or as an agent for individuals, private organizations, and other governmental units and other funds. These assets include: property and other taxes, as well as other intergovernmental resources that have been collected and which will be distributed to other taxing districts located in Lucas County.

Proprietary funds distinguish operating revenues and expenses from nonoperating items. Operating revenues and expenses generally result from providing services and producing and delivering goods in connection with a proprietary fund's principal ongoing operations. The principal operating revenues of the Water Supply System, Wastewater Treatment Plant, and Sewer System, and of the County's internal service funds are charges to customers for sales and services. The County also recognizes as operating revenue the portion of tap fees intended to recover the cost of connecting new customers to the system. Operating expenses for enterprise funds and internal service funds include the cost of sales and services, administrative expenses, and depreciation on capital assets. All revenues and expenses not meeting this definition are reported as non operating revenues and expenses.

Note B—*Summary of Significant Accounting Policies (in Part)*

The accompanying financial statements of the County are prepared in conformity with GAAP for local government units as prescribed in statements and interpretations issued by the GASB and other recognized authoritative sources. The County has elected not to apply FASB Statements and interpretations issued after November 30, 1989, to its proprietary activities.

Government-wide Financial Statements: The government-wide financial statements are prepared using the economic resources measurements focus. All assets and liabilities associated with the operation of the County are included on the Statement of Net Assets.

Fund Financial Statements: All governmental funds are accounted for using a flow of current financial resources measurement focus. With this measurements focus, only current assets and current liabilities generally are included on the balance sheet. The statement of revenues, expenditures and changes

LUCAS COUNTY, OHIO
NOTES TO THE FINANCIAL STATEMENTS (continued)
DECEMBER 31, 2001

Note B—*Summary of Significant Accounting Policies (in Part)*

in fund balances reports on the sources (i.e., revenues and other financing sources) and uses (i.e., expenditures and other financing uses) of current financial resources. This approach differs from the manner in which the governmental activities of the government-wide financial statements are prepared. Governmental fund financial statements therefore include a reconciliation with brief explanations to better identify the relationship between the government-wide statements and the statements for governmental funds.

Like the governmental-wide statements, all proprietary fund types are accounted for on a flow of economic resources measurement focus. All assets and all liabilities associated with the operation of these funds are included on the statement of net assets. The statement of changes in fund new assets presents increases (i.e., revenues) and decreases (i.e., expenses) in net total assets. The statement of cash flows provides information about how the County finances and meets the cash flow needs of its proprietary activities.

Fiduciary funds are reported using the economic resources measurement focus.

Basis of Accounting: Basis of accounting determines when transactions are recorded in the financial records and reported on the financial statements. Government-wide financial statements are prepared using the accrual basis accounting. Governmental funds use the modified accrual basis of accounting. Proprietary and fiduciary funds also use the accrual basis of accounting. Differences in the accrual and the modified accrual basis of accounting arise in the recognition of revenue, the recording of deferred revenue, and in the presentation of expenses versus expenditures.

Revenues—Exchange and Non-Exchange Transactions: Revenue resulting from exchange transactions, in which each party gives and receives essentially equal value, is recorded on the accrual basis when the exchange takes place. On a modified accrual basis, revenue is recorded in the fiscal year in which the resources are measurable and become available. Available means that the resources will be collected within the current fiscal year or are expected to be collected soon enough thereafter to be used to pay liabilities of the current fiscal year. For the County, available means expected to be received within thirty days of fiscal year-end.

Non-exchange transactions, in which the County receives value without directly giving equal value in return, include property taxes, grants, entitlement and donations. On an accrual basis, revenue from property taxes is recognized in the fiscal year for which the taxes are levied. (See Note K). Revenue from grants, entitlement and donations is recognized in the fiscal year in which all eligibility requirements have been satisfied. Eligibility requirements include timing requirements, which specify the year when the resources are required to be used or the year when use is first permitted, matching requirements, in which the County must provide local resources to be used for a specified purpose, and expenditure requirements, in which the resources are provided to the County on a reimbursement basis. On modified accrual basis, revenue from non-exchange transactions must also be available before it can be recognized.

Under the modified accrual basis, the following revenue sources are considered to be both measurable and available at year-end: delinquent taxes, sales tax, grants, interest, fees and charges for services.

Deferred Revenue: Deferred revenue arises when assets are recognized before revenue recognition criteria have been satisfied.

Property taxes for which there is an enforceable legal claim as of December 31, 2001 but which were levied to finance fiscal year 2002 operations, have been recorded as deferred revenue. Grants and entitlements received before the eligibility requirements are met are also recorded as deferred revenue.

On governmental fund financial statements, receivables that will not be collected within the available period have also been reported as deferred revenue.

Expenses/Expenditures: On the accrual basis of accounting, expenses are recognized at the time they are incurred. The measurement focus of governmental fund accounting is on decreases in net financial resources (expenditures) rather than expenses. Expenditures are generally recognized in the accounting period in which the related fund liability is incurred, if measurable. Allocations of cost, such as depreciation and amortization, are not recognized in the governmental funds.

Budgetary Information: Under Ohio law, the Board of County Commissioners must adopt an appropriations budget by January 1st of a given year, or adopt a temporary appropriation measure with final passage of a permanent budget by April 1st, for all funds except Agency Funds. Budgets are legally

LUCAS COUNTY, OHIO
NOTES TO THE FINANCIAL STATEMENTS (continued)
DECEMBER 31, 2001

Note B—*Summary of Significant Accounting Policies (in Part)*

required for each organizational unit by object (personal services, materials and supplies, charges for services, and capital outlays and equipment).

Each County department prepares a budget that is approved by the Board of County Commissioners. Modifications to the original budget within expenditure objects can be made by the budget manager in the Auditor's Office. The County maintains budgetary control within an organizational unit and fund by not permitting expenditures and encumbrances to exceed appropriations at the object level (the legal level of control). Unencumbered and unexpended appropriations lapse at year-end. Encumbered and unpaid appropriations (reserved for encumbrances) are carried forward to the next year as authority for expenditures.

The County's budgetary process accounts for certain transactions on a basis other than GAAP. The major difference between the budget basis and the GAAP basis are:

(1) Revenues are recorded when received in cash (budget) as opposed to when susceptible to accrual (GAAP).
(2) Expenditures are recorded when encumbered, or paid in cash (budget), as opposed to when susceptible to accrual (GAA).

The actual results of operations, compared to the final appropriation, which include amendments to the original appropriation, for each fund type by expenditure function and revenue source are presented in the *Combined Statement of Revenues, Expenditures and Changes in Fund Balances-Budget and Actual (non-GAAP Budgetary Basis)—All Governmental Fund Types.* The difference between the accrual and cash basis statements was not significant. The reserve for encumbrances is carried forward as part of the budgetary authority for the next year and is included in the revised budget amounts shown in the budget to actual comparisons.

Cash Equivalents: Investments of the cash management pool, and investments with original maturities of three months or less at the time they are purchased by the County are considered to be cash equivalents. Investments with an initial maturity of more than three months are considered to be investments.

Inventory of Materials and Supplies: Inventory is valued at cost using the first-in, first-out method. Inventory is recorded as an expenditure/expense when consumed.

Capital Assets: Capital assets, which include property, plant, equipment, and infrastructure assets (e.g., roads, bridges, sidewalks, and similar items), are reported in the applicable governmental or business-type activities columns in the government-wide financial statements. Capital assets are defined by the government as assets with an initial, individual cost of more than $5,000 (amount not rounded) and an estimated useful life in excess of two years. Such assets are recorded at historical cost or estimated historical cost if purchased or constructed.

Donated capital assets are recorded at estimated fair market value at the date of donation.

The costs of normal maintenance and repairs that do not add to the value of the asset or materially extend assets lives are not capitalized. Major outlays for capital assets and improvements are capitalized, as projects are constructed. Interest incurred during the construction phase of proprietary capital assets is included as part of the capitalized value of the assets constructed.

All reported capital assets are depreciated using the straight line method over the following estimated useful lives:

* Furniture, fixtures and equipment 5–20 years
* Buildings, structures and improvements 20–40 years
* Land improvements (water and sewer lines) 40 years
* Infrastructure 20–40 years

Use of Estimates: The preparation of the basic financial statements in conformity with GAAP requires management to make estimates and assumptions that affect the reported amounts of assets and liabilities and disclosure of contingent assets and liabilities at the date of the financial statements. Estimates also affect the reported amounts of revenues and expenses during the reporting period. Actual results could differ from those estimates.

Required
a. Prepare a vertical common-size analysis of the Statement of Net Assets. Use total assets as the base.
b. Comment on significant items on the vertical common-size analysis.
c. Governmental funds are those through which most governmental functions of the County are financed. List the County's major governmental funds.
d. Proprietary fund reporting focuses on the determination of operating income changes in net assets, financial position, and cash flows. List the County's major proprietary funds.
e. Briefly describe the basis of accounting.
f. The County's budgetary process accounts for certain transactions on a basis other than GAAP. What is the major difference between the budget basis and the GAAP basis?
g. What is the County's definition of capital assets?
h. All reported capital assets are depreciated using the straight-line method over which useful lives?
i. What does the County's report state as to the use of estimates?

Case 13-2   My Mud Hens

Toledo Mud Hens Baseball Club, Inc. is a nonprofit organization that is a separate legal entity and can be sued in its own right.

The Toledo Mud Hens are probably the most famous team in all minor league baseball. They have been named the Toledo Mud Hens since 1896 when the team played at Bay View Park. The surrounding marshland was frequented by these strange birds.

Famous people such as Casey Stengel, Jamie Farr, and Bob Costas, have helped bring the team nationwide fame. Famous players who have contributed to the team's fame include Moses Fleetwood Walker, Addie Joss, Tony Clark, Kirby Puckett, Travis Fryman, and Kirk Gibson.

A famous landmark in Toledo, Ohio, is the Moses Fleetwood Square. Moses Fleetwood Walker, the first African-American major league baseball player, signed with the Toledo Blue Stockings in 1883 where he played catcher barehanded. In 1884 the club was renamed the Toledos and joined the American Association, the major leagues of the era. They were members of the American Association for one season. By 1889 blacks were barred from the high minor leagues and the major leagues. It remained that way until 1947 when Jackie Robinson joined the Brooklyn Dodgers.

Casey Stengel skippered six Toledo teams, including the 1927 squad that won the Junior World Series.

In 2002 the team moved into a new facility. The County issued $20 million in economic development revenue bonds and $6 million in economic development revenue anticipation notes in March 2001. The County retired the notes in March 2002 after receiving revenue for the naming rights (Fifth Third Field) and the lease of the luxury suites.

Lucas County receives rent from the Mud Hens that in the County's opinion is substantially below market rate. The board of the Mud Hens is approved by the Board of County Commissioners.

Source: "Square is Named for Walker," *The Blade* (October 2, 2002), Sec. B, p. 1; Lucas County, Ohio, Comprehensive Annual Financial Report, For Fiscal Year Ended December 31, 2001; and "The Toledo Mud Hens—History in the Making," provided by Toledo Mud Hens Baseball Club, Inc.

Required
a. What form would the Mud Hens statement take?
b. How does Lucas County account for its relationship with the Mud Hens? (Review Case 13-1 Governor Lucas—This is Your County.)

Case 13-3   Jeep

DaimlerChrysler completed its first year of production of the Jeep Liberty in 2001. This production was in a new plant that cost $1.2 billion.

DaimlerChrysler was assisted in financing this new plant by the federal government, state government, the City of Toledo, and Lucas County. The county pledged $2 million by 2002 to help the city of Toledo acquire and improve the site for the new plant.

Required   How would the County account for its $2 million expenditure?

Endnotes

1. *Statement of Position 82-1*, "Accounting and Financial Reporting for Personal Financial Statements," (New York: American Institute of Certified Public Accountants, October 1982).
2. *Statement of Position 82-1*, p. 6.
3. A good article on this subject is "Personal Financial Statements: Valuation Challenges and Solutions," by Michael D. Kinsman and Bruce Samuelson, *Journal of Accountancy* (September 1987), p. 138.
4. *Government Accounting Standards Board Statement No. 1* (July 1984), Appendix B, paragraph 4.
5. *Governmental Accounting, Auditing, and Financial Reporting* (Chicago: Municipal Finance Officers Association of the United States and Canada, 1968), p. 6.
6. Edward M. Klasny and James M. Williams, "Government Reporting Fares an Overhaul," *Journal of Accountancy* (January 2000), pp. 49–51.
7. Walter Robbins and Paul Polinski, "Financial Reporting by Nonprofits," *National Public Accountant* (October 1995), p. 29.
8. *Statement of Financial Accounting Standards No. 93*, "Recognition of Depreciation by Not-for-Profit Organizations" (Stamford, CT: Financial Accounting Standards Board, 1987).
9. *Statement of Financial Accounting Standards No. 116*, "Accounting for Contributions Received and Contributions Made" (Norwalk, CT: Financial Accounting Standards Board, 1993).
10. *Statement of Financial Accounting Standards No. 117*, "Financial Statements of Not-for-Profit Organizations" (Norwalk, CT: Financial Accounting Standards Board, 1993).
11. *Statement of Financial Accounting Standards No. 124*, "Accounting for Certain Investments Held by Not-for-Profit Organizations" (Norwalk, CT: Financial Accounting Standards Board, 1995).
12. *Statement of Position 94-2*, "The Application of the Requirements of Accounting Research Bulletins, Opinions of the Accounting Principles Board and Statements of Interpretations of the Financial Accounting Standards Board to Not-for-Profit Organizations" (New York: American Institute of Certified Public Accountants, September 1994).
13. Charles H. Gibson, "Budgeting by Objectives: Charlotte's Experience," *Management Accounting* (January 1978), p. 39.
14. *Ibid.*, pp. 39, 48.

GLOSSARY

Most of the terms in this glossary are explained in the text. Some terms not explained in the text are included because they represent terms frequently found in annual reports.

A

Accelerated Cost Recovery System (ACRS): Depreciation method introduced for tax purposes in 1981 and subsequently modified. See Modified Accelerated Cost Recovery System (MACRS).

Accelerated depreciation: Any depreciation method in which the charges in earlier periods exceed those in later periods.

Account: A record used to classify and summarize transactions.

Account form of balance sheet: A balance sheet that presents assets on the left-hand side and liabilities and owners' equity on the right-hand side.

Accounting: The systematic process of measuring the economic activity of an entity to provide useful information to those who make business and economic decisions.

Accounting changes: A term used to describe the use of a different accounting principle, estimate, or reporting entity than used in a prior year.

Accounting controls: Procedures concerned with safeguarding the assets or the reliability of the financial statements.

Accounting cycle: A series of steps used for analyzing, recording, classifying, and summarizing transactions.

Accounting equation: Assets = Liabilities + Stockholders' Equity.

Accounting errors: Mistakes resulting from mathematical errors, improper application of accounting principles, or omissions of material facts.

Accounting period: The time to which accounting reports are related.

Accounting policies: The accounting principles and practices adopted by a company to report its financial results.

Accounting Principles Board (APB): A board established by the AICPA that issued opinions establishing accounting standards during the period 1959–1973.

Accounting Research Bulletins (ARBs): Publications of the Committee on Accounting Procedure of the AICPA, that established accounting standards during the years 1939–1959.

Accounting system: The procedures and methods used to collect and report accounting data.

Accounts payable: Amounts owed for inventory, goods, or services acquired in the normal course of business.

Accounts receivable (trade receivables): Monies due on accounts from customers arising from sales or services rendered.

Accrual basis: The accrual basis of accounting dictates: revenue is recognized when realized (realization concept) and expenses are recognized when incurred (matching concept).

Accrued expenses: Expenses incurred but not recognized in the accounts.

Accrued liability: A liability resulting from the recognition of an expense before the payment of cash.

Accrued pension cost: The difference between the amount of pension recorded as an expense and the amount of the funding payment.

Accrued revenues: Revenues for services performed or for goods delivered that have not been recorded.

Accumulated benefit obligation (ABO): The present value of pension benefits earned to date based on employee service and compensations to that date.

Accumulated depreciation: Depreciation allocates the cost of buildings and machinery over the periods of benefits. The depreciation expense taken each period accumulates in the account, Accumulated Depreciation.

Accumulated postretirement benefit obligation (APBO): The present value of postretirement benefits earned to date based on employee service to that date.

Acquisition: A business combination in which one corporation acquires control over the operations of another entity.

Acquisition cost: The amount that includes all of the cost normally necessary to acquire an asset and prepare it for its intended use.

Acquisitions: Companies that have been acquired.

Actuarial assumptions: Assumptions about future events based on historic data such as employee turnover, service lives, and longevity that are used to estimate future costs such as pension benefits.

Additional paid-in capital: The investment by stockholders in excess of the stocks par or stated value as well as invested capital from other sources, such as donations of property or sale of treasury stock.

Adjusting entries: Entries made at the end of each accounting period to update the accounts.

Administrative controls: Procedures concerned with efficient operation of the business and adherence to managerial policies.

Administrative expenses: Result from the general administration of the company's operation.

Adverse opinion: An audit opinion issued whenever financial statements contain departures from GAAP that are too material to warrant only a qualification. This opinion states that the financial statements do not present fairly the financial position, results of operations, or cash flows of the entity in conformity with GAAP.

Aging of accounts receivables: A method of reviewing for uncollectible trade receivables by which an estimate of the bad debts expense is determined. The receivable balances are classified into age categories and then an estimate of noncollection is applied.

Aging schedule: A form used to categorize the various individual accounts receivable according to the length of time each has been outstanding.

Allowance for funds used during construction (AFUDC): The recording of AFUDC is a utility accounting practice prescribed by the state utility commission. It represents the estimated debt and equity costs of financing construction work-in-progress. AFUDC does not represent a current source of cash, but under regulatory rate practices, a return on and recovery of AFUDC is permitted in determining rates charged for utility services. Some utilities report the estimated debt and equity costs of financing construction work-in-progress in separate accounts.

Allowance for uncollectible accounts: A contra accounts receivable account showing an estimate of the accounts receivable that will not be collected.

Allowance method: A method of estimating bad debts on the basis of either the net credit sales of the period or the accounts receivable at the end of the period.

American Accounting Association (AAA): An accounting organization of accounting professors and practicing accountants.

American Institute of Certified Public Accountants (AICPA): A professional organization for CPAs.

Amortization: The periodic allocation of the cost of an intangible asset over its useful life.

Annual report: A formal presentation containing financial statements and other important information prepared by the management of a corporation once a year.

Annuity: A series of equal payments (receipts) over a specified number of equal time periods.

Antidilution of earnings: Assumed conversion of convertible securities or exercise of stock options that results in an increase in earnings per share or a decrease in loss per share.

Antidilutive securities: Securities whose assumed conversion or exercise results in an increase in earnings per share or a decrease in loss per share.

Appropriated retained earnings: A restriction of retained earnings that indicates that a portion of a company's assets are to be used for purposes other than paying dividends.

Arms-length transaction: Transactions that are conducted by independent parties, each acting in their own self-interest.

Assets: Probable future economic benefits obtained or controlled by a particular entity as a result of past transactions or events.

Assignment of receivables: The borrowing of money with receivables pledged as security.

Attestation: Any service performed by a CPA resulting in a written communication that expresses a conclusion about the reliability of a written assertion that is the responsibility of investigating another party.

Audit committee: A committee of the board of directors comprised mainly of outside directors having no management ties to the organization.

Audit report: The mechanism for communicating the results of an audit.

Auditing: A systematic process of objectively obtaining and evaluating evidence regarding assertions and communicating the results to interested users.

Auditor: A person who conducts an audit.

Authorized stock: The maximum number of shares a corporation may issue without changing its charter with the state.

Available-for-sale securities: Stocks and bonds that are not classified as either held-to-maturity or trading securities.

Average cost method (inventory): Averaging methods lump the costs of inventory to determine an average.

B

Balance sheet (Statement of financial position): The financial statement that shows the financial position of an accounting entity as of a specific date. The balance sheet lists assets, the resources of the firm; liabilities, the debts of the firm; and stockholders' equity, the owners' interest in the firm.

Balance sheet (classified): A form that segregates the assets and liabilities between current and noncurrent.

Balance sheet (financial position form): A form that deducts current liabilities from current assets to show working capital. The form adds remaining assets and deducts the remaining liabilities to derive the residual stockholders' equity.

Balance sheet (unclassified): A form that does not segregate the assets and liabilities between current and noncurrent.

Bargain purchase option: Provision granting the lessee the right, but not the obligation, to purchase leased property at a price that, at the inception date, is sufficiently below the expected fair value of the property at exercise date to provide reasonable assurance of exercise.

Bargain renewal option: Provision granting the lessee the right, but not the obligation, to renew the lease at a rental that, at inception, is sufficiently below the expected fair rental at exercise date to provide reasonable assurance of renewal.

Basic earnings per share: The amount of earnings for the period available to each share of common stock outstanding during the reporting period. It does not recognize the potentially dilutive impact on outstanding stock when a corporation has dilutive securities.

Board of directors: A body of individuals who are elected by the stockholders to be their representatives in managing the company.

Bond: A security, usually long-term, representing money borrowed by a corporation. Normally issued with $1,000 face value.

Bond discount: The difference between the face value and the sales price when bonds are sold below their face value.

Bond issue price: The present value of the annuity interest payments plus the present value of the principal.

Bond premium: The difference between the face value and the sales price when bonds are sold above their face value.

Bond sinking fund: A fund established by the segregation of assets over the life of the bond issue to pay the bondholders at maturity.

Bonds (serial): A bond issue that matures in installments.

Book value of an asset: The original cost of an asset less any accumulated depreciation (depletion or amortization) taken to date.

Book value per share: The dollar amount of the net assets of a company on a per share of common stock.

Bottom line: The financial vernacular for net income.

Buildings: A structure used in a business operation.

Business combination: One or more businesses that are merged together as one accounting entity.

Business entity: The viewpoint that the business (or entity) for which the financial statements are prepared is separate and distinct from the owners of the entity.

C

Calendar year: The accounting year ends on December 31.

Callable bonds: Bonds that a corporation has the option of buying back and retiring at a given price before maturity.

Callable obligation: A debt instrument payable on demand of the company that issued the obligation.

Callable preferred stock: Preferred stock that may be redeemed and retired by the corporation at its option.

Capital: Owners' equity in an unincorporated firm.

Capital expenditures: Costs that increase the future economic benefits of an asset above those originally expected.

Capital lease: Long-term lease in which the risk of ownership lies with the lessee and whose terms resemble a purchase or sale; recorded as an asset with a corresponding liability at the present value of the lease payments.

Capital stock: The portion of the contribution by stockholders assignable to the shares of stock as par or stated value.

Capital structure: A firm's strategy for financing its assets with relative amounts of debt and equity.

Capitalization: The process of assigning value to a balance sheet account (asset or liability).

Capitalized interest: Interest added to the cost of a fixed asset instead of being expensed.

Carrying value: The face of a bond plus the amount of unamortized premium or minus the amount of unamortized discount.

Cash: The most liquid asset that includes negotiable checks, unrestricted balances in checking accounts, and cash on hand.

Cash basis accounting: A system of accounting that records revenues when received and expenses when paid.

Cash dividend: The payment (receipt) of a dividend in cash.

Cash equivalents: A company's highly liquid short-term investments considered to be cash equivalents and usually classified with cash on the balance sheet.

Cash flows from financing activities: Cash flows relating to liability and owners' equity accounts.

Cash flows from investing activities: Cash flows relating to lending money and to acquiring and selling investments and productive long-term assets.

Cash flows from operating activities: Generally the cash effects of transactions and other events that determine net income.

Cash surrender value: The investment portion of a life insurance policy, payable to the policyholder if the policyholder cancels the policy.

Certified public accountant (CPA): An accountant who has received a certificate stating that he/she has met the requirements of state law.

Change in an accounting estimate: A change in the estimation of the effects of future events.

Change in an accounting principle: Adoption of a generally accepted accounting principle different from the one used previously for reporting purposes.

Change in reporting entity: An accounting change that reflects financial statements for a different unit of accountability.

Chart of accounts: A listing of all accounts used by a company.

Chief accountant of the SEC: An appointed official of the Securities and Exchange Commission. This individual has a material influence on U.S. accounting standards.

Classified balance sheet: A balance sheet that segregates the assets and liabilities as current and noncurrent.

Closing entries: Temporary account balances are transferred to the permanent stockholders' equity account, retained earnings.

Collateral: Security for loans or other forms of indebtedness.

Commercial paper: Short-term obligations or promissory notes, unsecured, interest bearing with flexible maturities.

Commitment fee: A fee for committing to holding a credit facility available over a period of time to a borrower.

Common-size analysis (horizontal): Common-size analysis expresses comparisons in percentages. Horizontal analysis indicates proportionate change over a period of time.

Common-size analysis (vertical): Common-size analysis expresses comparisons in percentages. Vertical analysis indicates the proportionate expression of each item in a given period to a base figure selected from that same period.

Common stock (capital stock): The stock representing the most basic rights to ownership of a corporation.

Common stock equivalent shares: A security that is not in the form of a common stock, but that contains provisions that enable its holder to acquire common stock.

Comparability: For accounting information, the quality that allows a user to analyze two or more companies and look for similarities and differences.

Comparative statements: Financial statements for two or more periods.

Compensated absences: Payments to employees for vacation, holiday, illness, or other personal activities.

Compensating balance requirements: Provisions in loan agreements requiring the borrower to maintain minimum cash balances with the lending institution.

Compensatory option plans: Stock option plans offered to a select group of employees.

Compilation: A professional service in which the CPA presents information that is the representation of management without undertaking to express any assurance on the statements.

Completed-contract method: A method that recognizes revenues on long-term construction contracts only when the contract is completed.

Composite depreciation: A depreciation method that aggregates dissimilar assets and computes depreciation for the aggregation based on a weighted average life expectancy.

Compound interest: The process of earning interest on interest from previous periods.

Comprehensive income: Net income plus the periods change in accumulated other comprehensive income (accumulated other comprehensive income is a category within stockholders' equity).

Conservatism: The concept that directs that the measurement with the least favorable effect on net income and financial position in the current period be selected.

Conservative analysis: This perspective represents a relatively strict interpretation of the value of assets and what constitutes debt.

Consigned goods: Inventory physically located at a dealer but another company retains title until the consignee sells the inventory.

Consistency: The concept requiring the entity to give the same treatment to comparable transactions from period to period.

Consolidated financial statements: The combined financial statements of a parent company and its subsidiary.

Constant dollar accounting (price-level accounting): The method of reporting financial statement elements in dollars having similar purchasing power. Constant dollar accounting measures general changes in prices of goods and services.

Construction-in-process: Fixed asset account where construction costs are recorded until construction is completed.

Contingencies: Conditions that may result in gains and losses, and that will be resolved by the occurrence of future events.

Contingent asset: An asset that may arise in the future if certain events occur.

Contingent liabilities: Liabilities whose payment is dependent on a particular occurrence such as settlement of litigation or a ruling of tax court.

Contra account: An account used to offset a primary account in order to show a net valuation, e.g., accounts receivable (primary account) less allowance for doubtful accounts (contra account).

Contributed capital: The sum of the capital stock accounts and the capital in excess of par (or stated) value accounts.

Control account: The general ledger accounts that is supported by a subsidiary ledger.

Controller: The chief accounting officer for a company.

Convertible bonds: Bonds that may be exchanged for other securities of the corporation, usually common stock.

Convertible preferred stock: Preferred stock that can be converted into common stock.

Convertible securities: Securities whose terms permit the holder to convert the investment into common stock of the issuing companies.

Copyright: An exclusive right granted by the federal government to publish and sell literary, musical, and other artistic materials.

Corporate officers: Senior executive managers of the company identified by title and name.

Corporation: A separate legal entity having its own rights, privileges, and liabilities distinct from those of its owners.

Cost accounting: Determines product costs and other relevant information used.

Cost/benefit: The process of determining that the benefit of an act or series of acts exceeds the cost of performing the act(s).

Cost of goods manufactured: The total cost of goods completed in the manufacturing process during an accounting period.

Cost of goods sold or cost of sales: The cost of goods sold during an accounting period. Cost of goods available for sale minus ending inventory.

Cost principle: The accounting principle that records historical cost as the appropriate basis of initial accounting recognition of all acquisitions, liabilities, and owners' equity.

Cost recovery: A revenue recognition method that requires recovery of the total cost prior to the recognition of revenue.

Coupon rate: The stated interest rate in a bond contract. Also referred to as the nominal, stated, or face rate.

Covenants: Conditions placed in a loan or credit agreement by the lender to protect its position as a creditor of the borrowing.

Credit: An entry on the right side of an account.

Credit agreement: A contractual arrangement between a lender and a borrower that sets the terms and conditions for borrowing.

Credit ratings: Formal credit risk evaluations by credit rating agencies of a company's ability to repay principal and interest on its debt obligations.

Creditor: A party who lends money to a company.

Cumulative effect of change in accounting principle: The effect that a new accounting principle would have had on net income of prior periods if it had been used instead of the old principle.

Cumulative preferred stock: Preferred stock on which unpaid dividends accumulate over time and must be satisfied in any given year before a dividend may be paid to common stockholders.

Currency swap: An exchange of two currencies as part of an agreement to reverse the exchange on a specific future date.

Current assets: Current assets are assets (1) in the form of cash, (2) that will normally be realized in cash, or (3) that conserve the use of cash during the operating cycle of a firm or for one year, whichever is longer.

Current cost: The current replacement cost of the same asset owned, adjusted for the value of any operating advantages or disadvantages.

Current liabilities: Obligations whose liquidation is reasonably expected to require the use of existing resources properly classifiable as current assets or the creation of other current liabilities.

Current market value: The amount of cash, or its equivalent, that could be obtained by selling an asset in an orderly liquidation.

Current maturity of long-term debt: The portion of a long-term debt payable within the next operating cycle or one year, whichever is longer.

Current replacement cost: The estimated cost of acquiring the best asset available to undertake the function of the asset owned.

Current value: The amount of cash, or its equivalent, that could be received by selling an asset currently.

D

Debenture bonds: Bonds issued on the general credit of a company.

Debit: An entry on the left side of an account.

Debt: Considered to be funds a company has borrowed from a creditor.

Debt securities: Investments in debt instruments such as commercial paper or bonds.

Debt service: A term used by bankers, which refers to a borrower's requirement to make payment of the current maturities on outstanding debt.

Decision usefulness: The overriding quality or characteristic of accounting information.

Declining-balance depreciation: The declining-balance method applies double the straight-line depreciation rate times the declining book value (cost minus accumulated depreciation) to achieve a declining depreciation charge over the estimated life of the asset.

Default risk: The probability that a company will be unable to meet its obligations.

Defeasance: A method of early retirement of debt in which risk-free securities are purchased and then placed in a trust account to be used to retire the outstanding debt at its maturity.

Deferral: The postponement of the recognition of an expense already paid or of a revenue already received.

Deferred charge: A long-term expense prepayment amortized to expense.

Deferred financing costs, net: An asset account usually classified under other assets; costs associated with the issuance of long-term bonds that have not been amortized.

Deferred revenue: A liability resulting from the receipt of cash before the recognition of revenue.

Deferred taxes: A balance sheet account; classified as an asset or liability depending on the nature of the timing differences. The differences are the result of any situation that recognizes revenue or expense in a different time period for tax purposes than for the financial statements.

Deficit: A negative (debit) balance in retained earnings.

Defined benefit pension plan: A pension plan that defines the benefits that employees will receive at retirement.

Defined contribution pension plan: A pension plan that specifies the employer's contributions and bases benefits solely on the amount contributed.

Depletion: Recognition of the wearing away or using up of a natural resource.

Depreciation expense: The process of allocating the cost of buildings, machinery, and equipment over the periods benefitted.

Derivative instruments: Financial instruments or other contracts where rights or obligations meet the definitions of assets or liabilities.

Devaluation: A downward adjustment of the exchange rate between two currencies.

Diluted earnings per share: The amount of earnings for the period available to each share of common stock outstanding during the reporting period and to each share that would have been outstanding assuming the issuance of common shares for all dilutive potential common shares outstanding during the reporting period.

Dilution: Refers to the effect on earnings calculations when the number of shares issued increases disproportionately to the growth in the earnings.

Direct financing type lease: A capital lease in which the lessor receives income only from financing the "purchase" of the leased asset.

Direct method: For preparing the Operating Activities section of the statement of cash flows, the approach in which cash receipts and cash payments are reported.

Direct write-off method: A method of recognizing specific accounts receivable determined to be uncollectible.

Disclaimer of opinion: Inability to render an audit opinion because of lack of sufficient evidence or lack of independence.

Discontinued operations: The disposal of a major segment of a business.

Discount on bonds: A bond is issued below its face amount, indicating that the coupon rate is lower than the market rate for similar bonds.

Discount on notes payable: A contra liability that represents interest deducted from a loan in advance.

Discount rate: The interest rate used to compute the present value.

Discounted note: A noninterest-bearing note where the interest charge has been deducted from the principal in advance.

Discounting: The process of selling a promissory note.

Divestitures: Companies that have been disposed of.

Dividends (cash): Cash payment from current or past income to the owners of a corporation.

Dividends in arrears: The accumulated unpaid dividends from prior years on cumulative preferred stock.

Dividends payable: A current liability on the balance sheet resulting from the declaration of dividends by the board of directors.

Dividends (stock): A percentage of outstanding stock issued as new shares to existing shareholders.

Donated capital: Assets donated to the company by stockholders, creditors, or other parties.

Double-declining-balance deprecation: A method of calculating depreciation by which a percentage equal to twice the straight-line percentage is multiplied by the declining book value to determine the depreciation expense for the period (salvage value is ignored when calculating).

Double-entry accounting: A system of recording transactions in a way that maintains the equality of the equation: Assets = Liabilities + Stockholders' Equity.

Dry holes: Wells drilled that do not find commercial quantities of oil or gas.

E

Early extinguishment of debt: The retirement of debt prior to the maturity date.

Earnings: A term used interchangeably with income and profit.

Earnings per share: A company's bottom line stated on a per-share basis. The computation involves net income, preferred stock dividends, and weighted average number of shares outstanding.

Economic substance: The "real" nature of a transaction, as opposed to its legal form.

Edgar system: The SEC's electronic data gathering analysis and retrieval system.

Effective rate of interest: The yield or true rate of interest.

Efficient market hypothesis: A theory to explain the functioning of capital markets in which share prices reflect all publicly available information.

Emerging Issues Task Force (EITF): A task force of representatives from the accounting profession created by the FASB to deal with emerging issues of financial reporting.

Employee Retirement Income Security Act (ERISA): A legislative act passed by Congress in 1974 that made significant changes in requirements for employer pension plans. This act has been amended several times since 1974.

Employee stock ownership plans (ESOPs): A qualified stock-bonus, or combination stock-bonus and money purchase, pension plan designed to invest in primarily the employer's securities.

Entity assumption: Accounting records are kept for the business entity as distinct from the entity's owners.

Equipment: Assets used in the production of goods or in providing services.

Equity: Equity is the residual interest in the assets of an entity that remains after deducting its liabilities. Synonymous with the expression *shareholders' equity*.

Equity in earnings of nonconsolidated subsidiaries: When a firm has investments in stocks, uses the equity method of accounting, and the investment is not consolidated, then the investor firm reports equity earnings (the proportionate share of the earnings of the investee).

Equity method: A method to value intercorporate equity investments by adjusting the investor's cost basis for the percentage ownership in the investee's earnings (or losses) and for any dividends paid by the investee.

Equity-oriented deferred compensation: The amount of compensation cost deferred and amortized to future periods as the services are provided.

Equity securities: Represent ownership interests in the form of stocks issued by corporations.

ERISA: The acronym for the Employee Retirement Income Security Act of 1974.

Estimated economic life of leased property: The useful life of leased property estimated at inception under conditions of normal maintenance and repairs.

Estimated liability: An obligation of the entity whose exact amount cannot be determined until a later date.

Estimated residual value of leased property: The expected fair or market value of leased property at the end of the lease term.

Estimated useful life: The period of time that a company establishes in order to depreciate a fixed asset.

Ethics: A set of principles referring to ideals of character and conduct.

Event: A happening of consequence to an entity.

Exchange rate: The rate at which one unit of currency may be purchased by another unit of currency.

Executory costs: Insurance, maintenance, and local and property taxes on leased property.

Expectations gap: The disparity between users' and CPAs' perceptions of professional services, especially audit services.

Expenses: Outflows or uses of assets or incurrences of liabilities (or a combination of both) during the process of an entity's revenue-generating operations.

Exposure Draft (ED): A proposed Statement of Financial Accounting Standards.

External expansion: Occurs as firms take over, or merge with, other existing firms.

Extraordinary items: Material events and transactions distinguished by their unusual nature and infrequent occurrence.

F

Face amount, maturity value: The amount that will be paid on a bond (note) at the maturity date.

Face rate of interest: The rate of interest on the bond certificate.

Factor: Selling accounts receivable for cash.

Fair value: The amount at which an asset (liability) could be bought (incurred) or sold (settled) in a current transaction between willing parties.

Feedback value: An ingredient of relevant accounting information.

FIFO method: An inventory costing method that assigns the most recent costs to ending inventory.

Financial accounting: Recording and communication of financial information under GAAP.

Financial Accounting Standards Board (FASB): A body that has responsibility for developing and issuing rules on accounting practice.

Financial analysis: Describes the process of studying a company's financial report.

Financial leverage: The amount of debt financing in relation to equity financing.

Financial statement (report) analysis: The process of reviewing analyzing, and interpreting the basic financial reports.

Financial statements: Generally considered to be the balance sheet, income statement, and statement of cash flows.

Financial summary: A section of the annual report that provides a 5-, 10-, or 11-year summary of selected financial data.

Financing activities: Activities concerned with the raising and repayment of funds in the form of debt and equity.

Finished goods: A manufacturer's inventory that is complete and ready for sale.

First-in, first-out (FIFO) (inventory): The flow pattern assumes that the first unit purchased is the first sold.

Fiscal year: Any 12-month accounting period used by an economic entity, which closes at the end of a month other than December.

Fixed assets: Tangible, long-lived assets, primarily property, plant, and equipment.

Footnotes: Present additional information on items included in the financial statements and additional financial information.

Forecasted transaction: A transaction that is expected to occur for which there is no firm commitment.

Foreign Corrupt Practices Act: Legislation intended to increase the accountability of management for accurate records and reliable financial statements.

Foreign currency: A currency other than the entity's functional currency.

Foreign currency transactions: Transactions that are settled with a nondomestic currency.

Foreign exchange rate: Specifies the number of U.S. dollars (from a U.S. perspective) that are needed to obtain one unit of a specific foreign currency.

Foreign operations: Operational activities that take place in a foreign country.

Form 8-K: A special SEC filing required when a material event or transaction occurs between Form 10-Q filing dates.

Form 10-K: An SEC form required to be filed within 90 days of a company's fiscal year-end. It is like an annual report but with more detail.

Form 20-F: The annual financial report filing with the SEC required of all foreign companies whose debt or equity capital is available for purchase/sale on a U.S. exchange.

Form 10-Q: An SEC form required to be filed within 45 days of the end of a company's 1st, 2nd, and 3rd fiscal year quarters. It contains interim information on a company's operations and financial position.

Form versus substance: Form refers to the legal nature of a transaction or event; substance refers to the economic aspects of the transaction or event.

Forward contract: Agreement to purchase or sell commodities, securities, or currencies on a specified future date at a specified price.

Forward exchange rate: A rate quoted currently for the exchange of currency at some future specified date.

Franchise: A contractual privilege granted by one person to another permitting the sale of a product, use of trade name, or provision of a service within a specified territory and/or in a specified manner.

Fraud: Intent to deceive.

Fraudulent transfer: A transfer of an interest or an obligation incurred by the debtor within one year prior to the date of filing a bankruptcy petition with the intent to defraud creditors.

Full cost accounting: The method of accounting that capitalizes all costs of exploring for and developing oil and gas reserves within a defined area subject only to the limitation that costs attributable to developed reserves should not exceed their estimated present value.

Full disclosure: Accounting reports must disclose all facts that may influence the judgment of an informed reader.

Functional currency: The currency a company uses to conduct its business.

Fund accounting: Accounting procedures in which a self-balancing group of accounts is provided for each accounting entity established by legal, contractual, or voluntary action.

Funding payment: A payment made by the employer to the pension fund on its trustee.

Future contract: Exchange-traded contract for future acceptance or delivery of a standardized quantity of a commodity or financial instrument on a specified future date at a specified price.

Future value of an annuity: Amount accumulated in the future when a series of payments is invested and accrues interest.

G

Gain or loss on redemption: The difference between the carrying value and the redemption price at the time bonds are redeemed.

Gains: Profits realized from activities that are incidental to a firm's primary operating activities.

General journal: A journal used to record transactions not maintained in special journals.

General ledger: A record of all accounts used by a company.

General partnership: An association in which each partner has unlimited liability.

Generally accepted accounting principles (GAAP): Accounting principles that have substantial authoritative support.

Generally accepted auditing standards: Those auditing standards that have been established in a particular jurisdiction by formal recognition by a standard-setting body, or by authoritative support.

Going concern or continuity: Assumes that the entity being accounted for will remain in business for an indefinite period of time.

Goodwill (cost in excess of net assets of companies acquired): Arises from the acquisition of a business for a sum greater than the physical asset value, usually because the business has unusual earning power.

Governmental Accounting Standards Board (GASB): The standards-setting body for governmental accounting and financial reporting.

Governmental funds: General, special revenue, project, debt service, and special assessment funds; each designed for a specific purpose and used by a state or local government to account for its normal operations.

Gross profit margin: Gross profit margin equals the difference between net sales revenue and the cost of goods sold.

Group depreciation: A depreciation method that groups like assets together and computes depreciation for the group rather than for individual assets.

Guarantee of employee stock ownership plan (ESOPs): An employee stock bonus plan used as a financing vehicle for an employer that borrows money to purchase its own stock. The stock is security for the loan, and the ESOP repays the loan from employer contributions.

H

Harmonization of accounting principles: The attempt by various organizations (e.g., the FASB, IASB) to establish a common set of international accounting and reporting standards.

Hedge: A process of buying or selling commodities, forward contracts, or options for the explicit purpose of reducing or eliminating foreign exchange risk.

Hedging contract: A contract to buy or sell foreign currencies in the forward market to protect against the risks of foreign exchange rate fluctuations.

Held-to-maturity securities: Investments in bonds of other companies in which the investor has the positive intent and the ability to hold the securities to maturity.

Historical cost: The cash equivalent price of goods or services at the date of acquisition.

Horizontal analysis: A comparison of financial statement items over a period of time.

Human resource accounting: Attempts to account for the services of employees.

Hybrid securities: A security that is neither clearly debt nor clearly equity.

I

Impairment: A temporary or permanent reduction in asset value.

Imputed interest rate: A rate of interest applied to a note when the effective rate was either not evident or determinable by other factors involved in the exchange.

In-substance defeasance of debt: The debtor irrevocably places cash or other assets in a trust to be used solely for satisfying the payments of both interest and principal on a specific debt obligation.

Income smoothing: An accounting practice that attempts to present a stable measure of income (usually an increasing amount).

Income statement (statement of earnings): A statement that summarizes revenues and expenses.

Income taxes: Taxes levied by federal, state, and local governments on reported accounting profit. Income tax expense includes both tax paid and deferred.

Inconsistency: A change in accounting principle from one period to the next, requiring an explanatory paragraph following the opinion paragraph of the auditor's report.

Incorporation by reference: Direction of the reader's attention to information included in the annual report to shareholders, or proxy, rather than reporting such information in Form 10-K.

Indentures: Provisions and restrictions attached to a bond that make the bond more attractive for investors.

Indirect method: For preparing the Operating Activities section of the statement of cash flows, the approach in which net income is reconciled to net cash flow from operations.

Industry practices: Practices leading to accounting reports that do not conform to the general theory that underlies accounting.

Industry segment: A component of an organization providing a product or related products (or services) to outside parties.

Inflation: An increase in the general price level of goods and services.

Initial public offering (IPO): The first or initial sale of voting stock to the general market by a previously privately held concern.

Insolvent: A condition in which a company is unable to pay its debts.

Installment method: The method in which revenue is recognized at the time cash is collected.

Installment sales: A type of sale that requires periodic payments over an extended length of time.

Institute of Management Accountants (IMA): An organization of management accountants concerned with the internal use of accounting data.

Intangibles: Nonphysical assets, such as legal rights, recorded at historical cost, then reduced by systematic amortization.

Intercompany profit: The profit resulting when one related company sells to another related company.

Intercompany receivables and payables: Receivables and payables among a parent company and its subsidiary(ies).

Interest: The cost for the use of money. It is a cost to the borrower and revenue to the lender.

Interest-bearing note: A debt instrument (note) that pays interest at a stated rate for a stated period.

Interest rate swaps: An agreement to exchange variable rate interest payments based on a specific index for a fixed rate or a variable rate stream of payments based on another index.

Interim reports: Financial reports that cover fiscal periods of less than one year.

Internal control: The process effected by an entity to provide reasonable assurance regarding the achievement of objectives. It consists of three parts—operations controls, financial reporting controls, and compliance controls.

Internal event: An event occurring entirely within an entity.

International Accounting Standards (IAS): The accounting standards adopted by the IASC and later by the IASB.

International Accounting Standards Board (IASB): Established in January 2001 to replace IASC. The new structure has characteristics similar to that of the FASB.

International Accounting Standards Committee (IASC): An organization established in 1973 by the leading professional groups of the major industrial countries. The International Accounting Standards Board (IASB) was established in January 2001 to replace IASC.

International Federation of Accountants (IFAC): An association of professional accounting organizations founded in 1977.

Interperiod tax allocation: The process of allocating the taxes paid by a company over the periods in which the taxes are recognized for accounting purposes.

Introductory paragraph: The first paragraph of the standard audit report, which identifies the financial statements covered by the audit report and clearly differentiates management's responsibility for preparing the financial statements from the auditor's responsibility for expressing an opinion on them.

Inventories: The balance of goods on hand.

Investing activities: A category shown on the cash flow statement. Generally involve long-term assets.

Invoice: Form sent by the seller to the buyer as evidence of a sale.

Inventory-lower-of-cost-or-market (LCM) rule: An inventory pricing method that prices the inventory at an amount below cost if the replacement (market) value is less than cost.

Investments: Usually stocks and bonds of other companies held for the purpose of maintaining a business relationship or exercising control. To be classified as long term, it must be the intent of management to hold these assets as such. Long-term investments are differentiated from marketable securities, where the intent is to hold the assets for short-term profits and to achieve liquidity.

Issued stock: The shares of stock sold or otherwise transferred to stockholders.

J

Joint venture: An association of two or more businesses established for a special purpose; some in the form of partnerships and unincorporated joint ventures; others in the form of corporations jointly owned by two or more other firms.

Journalizing: The act of recording journal entries.

Journals: Initial recordings of a company's transactions.

K

Kiting: A type of misrepresentation fraud used to conceal bank overdrafts or cash misappropriations.

L

Land: Realty used for business purposes. It is shown at acquisition cost and not depreciated. Land containing resources that will be used up, however, such as mineral deposits and timberlands, is subject to depletion.

Land improvements: Expenditures incurred in the process of putting land into a usable condition, e.g., clearing, grading, paving, etc.

Lapping: A form of concealment that involves crediting current customer remittances to the accounts of customers who have remitted previously.

Last-in, first-out (LIFO) (inventory): The flow pattern assumes that those units purchased last are sold first.

Lease: An agreement conveying the right to use property, plant, or equipment (land and/or depreciable assets) for a stated period of time.

Lease improvement: An improvement to leased property that becomes the property of the lessor at the end of the lease.

Leasehold: A payment made to secure the right to a lease.

Ledger: Summarizes the effects of transactions upon individual accounts.

Leverage: The extent to which a company's capital structure includes debt financing.

Lessee: The party to a lease who acquires the right to use the property, plant, and equipment.

Lessor: The party to a lease giving up the right to use the property, plant, and equipment.

Letter to the shareholders: A section of the annual report that presents a message from the company's chairman of the board or president.

Leveraged buy-out (LBO): A purchase of a company where a substantial amount of the purchase price is debt financed.

Liabilities: Future sacrifices of economic benefits arising from present obligations to other entities.

License: Rights to engage in a particular activity.

LIFO liquidation: The reduction of inventory levels below previous levels. This has the effect of increasing income by the amount by which current prices exceed the historical cost of the inventory under LIFO.

LIFO method: An inventory method that assigns the most recent costs to the cost of goods sold.

LIFO reserves (LIFO valuation adjustment): The amount that would need to be added back to the LIFO inventory in order for the inventory account to approximate current cost.

Limited liability: The concept that stockholders in a corporation are not held personally liable.

Line of credit: An agreement that sets the terms and conditions for borrowing up to a set amount of money.

Liquid assets: Current assets that either are in cash or can be readily converted to cash.

Liquidating dividend: A dividend that exceeds the balance in retained earnings.

Liquidation: The process of selling off the assets of a business, paying any outstanding debts, and distributing any remaining cash to the owners.

Liquidity: The nearness to cash of the assets and liabilities.

Listed company: A company whose shares or bonds have been accepted for trading on a securities exchange.

Loan defaults: Violations of loan agreements that could result in loan principal and interest becoming immediately due.

Loan restructuring: Revision of loan terms in a manner mutually acceptable to the lender and borrower.

Long-term liabilities: Long-term liabilities are those due in a period exceeding one year or one operating cycle, whichever is longer.

Lower of cost or market (LCM): A method to value inventories and marketable securities.

Loss on sale of asset: The amount by which selling price is less than book value.

Losses: Losses realized from activities that are incidental to a firm's primary activities.

M

Machinery: An asset listed at historical cost, including delivery and installation, plus any material improvements that extend its life or increase the quantity or quality of service; depreciated over its estimated useful life.

Management accounting: The branch of accounting concerned with providing management with information to facilitate planning and control.

Management discussion and analysis (MD&A): Part of the annual report package required by the Securities and Exchange Commission. Management comments on the results of operations, liquidity, and capital resources for the years under review in the financial statements.

Management report: Management statements to shareholders that acknowledge management's responsibility for the preparation and integrity of financial statements.

Market value (stock): The price investors are willing to pay for a share of stock.

Marketable securities: Ownership and debt instruments of the government and other companies that can be readily converted into cash.

Matching: The concept that determines the revenue and then matches the appropriate cost incurred in generating this revenue.

Materiality: The concept that exempts immaterial items from the concepts and principles that bind the accountant, and allows these items to be handled in the most economical and expedient manner possible.

Maturity date: Date on which the principal of a note becomes due.

Maturity value: The amount of cash the maker is to pay the payee on the maturity of the note.

Merchandise inventory: The account wholesalers and retailers use to report inventory held for sale.

Merger: A combination of one or more companies into a single corporate entity.

Minority interest (balance sheet account): The ownership of minority shareholders in the equity of consolidated subsidiaries that are less than wholly owned.

Minority share of earnings: The portion of income that belongs to the minority owners of a firm that has been consolidated.

Misappropriation: The fraudulent transfer of assets from the firm to one or more employees.

Modified Accelerated Cost Recovery System (MACRS): The accelerated cost recovery system as revised by The Tax Reform Act of 1986.

Monetary assets: Cash and other assets that represent the right to receive a specific amount of cash.

Monetary liabilities: Accounts payable and other liabilities that represent the obligation to pay a specific amount of cash.

Monetary unit: The unit used to measure financial transactions.

Mortgage payable: A liability secured by real property.

Moving average: The name given to an average cost method when it is used with a perpetual inventory system.

Multiple-step income statement: Form of the income statement that arrives at net income in steps.

N

Nasdaq (OTC): The National Association of Securities Dealers Automated Quotations. Represents a computerized communication network that handles the securities transactions of the over-the-counter market.

Natural business year: A 12-month period ending on a date that coincides with the end of an operating cycle.

Natural resources: Assets produced by nature such as petroleum, minerals, and timber.

Net assets: Total assets less total liabilities (equivalent to shareowners' equity).

Net income: Amount by which total revenues exceed total expenses. The bottom line on the income statement.

Net of tax: Indicates that expected tax effects have already been considered as part of a particular calculation or figure. Indicates that taxes have been deducted from a particular financial component.

Net operating loss carryback: When tax-deductible expenses exceed taxable revenues, a company may carry the net operating loss back three years and receive refunds for income taxes paid in those years.

Net operating loss carryforward: When tax-deductible expenses exceed taxable revenues, a company may carry an operating loss forward and offset future taxable income.

Net realizable value: The nondiscounted amount of cash, or its equivalent, into which an asset is expected to be converted less direct costs necessary to make that conversion.

Net sales: Gross sales revenue less any allowances or discounts.

Net worth: Synonymous with shareholders' equity.

Neutrality: A qualitative characteristic of accounting information that involves the faithful reporting of business activity without bias to one or another view.

New York Stock Exchange (NYSE): The New York Stock Exchange is the world's largest securities exchange.

Nominal accounts: The name given to revenue, expense, and dividend accounts because they are temporary and are closed at the end of the period.

Noncash investing and financing activities: A category of investing and financing activities that does not involve cash flows.

Noncurrent or long-term assets: Assets that do not qualify as current assets. In general they take longer than a year to be converted to cash or to conserve cash in the long run.

Nonrecurring: Earnings that do not represent the normal, recurring earnings from operations.

North American Industry Classification System (NAICS): An industry classification system that was adopted in 1997 by the United States. It was created jointly by the United States, Canada, and Mexico.

Note: A written promise to pay signed by the debtor.

Note payable: Payables in the form of a written promissory note.

Note receivable: An asset resulting from the acceptance of a promissory note from another company.

Notes to the financial statements: Information that clarifies and extends the material presented in the financial statements with narrative and detail.

O

Off-balance sheet financing: Refers to a company taking advantage of debt-like resources without these obligations appearing as debt on the face of the balance sheet.

On account: Purchases or sales on credit.

Operating cycle: The period of time elapsing between the acquisition of goods and the final cash realization resulting from sales and subsequent collections.

Operating expenses: Consist of two types: selling and administrative. Selling expenses result from the company's effort to create sales. Administrative expenses relate to the general administration of the company's operation.

Operating lease (lessee): Periodic payment for the right to use an asset, recorded in a manner similar to the recording of rent expense payments.

Option: A financial instrument that conveys to its owner the right, but not the obligation, to buy or sell a security, commodity, or currency at a specific price over a specified time period or at a specific date.

Organizational costs: The legal costs incurred when organizing a business; carried as an asset and usually written off over a period of five years or longer.

Other income and expenses: Income and expenses from secondary activities of the firm not directly related to the operations.

Outstanding shares: The number of authorized shares of capital stock sold to stockholders that are currently in the possession of stockholders (issues shares less treasury shares).

Owners' equity (stockholders' equity, shareholders' equity): The residual ownership interest in the assets of an entity that remains after deducting its liabilities.

P

Paid-in capital in excess of par value (or stated value): The proceeds from the sale of capital stock in excess of the par value (or stated value) of the capital stock.

Par value: An amount set by the firm's board of directors and approved by the state. (The par value does not relate to the market value.)

Parent: Tax term applied to the buyer company in a business combination.

Parent company: A company that owns a controlling interest in another company.

Partnership: An unincorporated business owned by two or more individuals.

Patent: Exclusive legal rights granted to an inventor for a period of 20 years.

Payables (trade): Short-term obligations created by the acquisition of goods and services, such as accounts payable, wages payable, and taxes payable.

Payee: The party that will receive the money from a promissory note at some future date.

Pension Benefit Guaranty Corporation: A United States government agency that insures the pension benefits of workers.

Pension fund: A fund established through contributions from an employer, and sometimes from employees, that pays pension benefits to employees after retirement.

Pension plan: An arrangement whereby an employer provides benefits (payments) to employees after they retire for services they provided while they were working.

Pension plan—contributory: A pension plan where the employees bear part of the cost of the stated benefits or voluntarily make payments to increase their benefits.

Pension plan—funded: A pension plan where the employer sets funds aside for future pension benefits by making payments to a funding agency that is responsible for accumulating the assets of the pension fund and for making payments to the recipients as the benefits become due.

Pension plan—noncontributory: A pension plan in which the employer bears the entire cost.

Pension plan—qualified: A pension plan in accord with federal income tax requirements that permit deductibility of the employer's contributions to the pension fund and tax-free status of earnings from pension fund assets.

Percentage-of-completion method: A revenue recognition method that recognizes profit each period during the life of the contract in proportion to the amount of the contract completed during the period.

Periodic inventory method: A method of accounting for inventory that determines inventory at the end of the period.

Permanent accounts: All balance sheet accounts.

Perpetual inventory method: A method of accounting for inventory that records continuously the sales and purchases of individual items of inventory.

Personal financial statements: Financial statements of individuals, husband and wife, or a larger family group.

Petty cash (fund): Small quantity of funds kept on hand for incidental expenditures requiring quick cash.

Pledging: Using assets as collateral for a bank loan.

Pooling of interest: A method of accounting for a business combination that combines all asset, liability, and stockholders' equity accounts.

Posting: Transcribing the amounts from journal entries into the general ledger.

Postretirement benefits other than pensions: Benefits other than pensions that accrue to employees upon retirement, such as medical insurance and life insurance contracts.

Predictive value: A qualitative characteristic of accounting information based on its relevance and usefulness to a decision maker in forecasting a future event or condition.

Preferred stock: Stock that has some preference over common stock.

Premium: An amount paid in excess of the face value of a security (stock or bond).

Prepaid: An expenditure made in advance of the use of the service or goods.

Present value consideration: The characteristic that money to be received or paid out in the future is not worth as much as money available today. Accountants consider the time value of money when preparing the financial statements for such areas as long-term leases, pensions, and other long-term situations where the future payments or receipts are not indicative of the present value of the asset or the obligation.

Present value factor: Using multiplication, converts a future value to its present value.

Principal: The original or base amount of a loan or investment.

Prior period adjustments: Reported as restatements of retained earnings. They include corrections of errors of prior periods, a change in accounting entity, certain changes in accounting principles, and adjustments that result from the realization of income tax benefits of preacquisition operating loss carryforwards of purchased subsidiaries.

Prior service cost: When a defined pension plan is adopted or amended, credit is often given to employees for years of service provided before the date of adoption or amendment. The cost of taking on this added commitment is called the prior service cost.

Privatization: The sale of all or part of a previously government-controlled entity to the general public.

Pro forma amount: Hypothetical or projected amount. Synonymous with "what if" analyses. Pro forma statements indicate what would have happened under specified circumstances.

Productive-output depreciation: A depreciation method in which the depreciable cost is divided by the total estimated output to determine the depreciation rate per unit of output.

Profitability: The relative success of a company's operations.

Projected benefit obligation (PBO): The present value of pension benefits earned to date based on past service and an estimate of future compensation levels for pay-related plans.

Property dividend: A dividend in a form of asset other than cash.

Property, plant, and equipment: Tangible assets of a long-term nature used in the continuing operation of the business.

Proportionate consolidation: A method of consolidating the financial results of a parent company and its subsidiary in which only the proportion of net assets owned by the parent are consolidated.

Proprietorship: A business owned by one person. The owner and business are not separate legal entities but are separate accounting entities.

Prospectus: A document describing the nature of a business and its recent financial history.

Proxy: A legal document granting another party the right to vote for a shareholder on matters involving a shareholder vote.

Proxy statement: Information provided in a formal written form to shareholders prior to a company's regular annual meeting.

Public company: A company whose voting shares are listed for trading on a recognized securities exchange or are otherwise available for purchase by public investors.

Public Company Accounting Oversight Board (PCAOB): An arm of the Securities and Exchange Commission (SEC). Among the many responsibilities of the PCAOB is to adopt auditing standards.

Purchase accounting: The assets and liabilities of an acquired company accounted for on the books of the acquiring company at their relative fair market values to the acquiring company at the date of acquisition.

Q

Qualified opinion: An audit opinion rendered under circumstances of one or more material scope restrictions or departures from GAAP.

Qualitative characteristics: Standards for judging the information accountants provide to decision makers; the primary criteria are relevance and reliability.

Quarterly statements: Interim financial statements on a quarterly basis.

Quasi-reorganization: An accounting procedure equivalent to an accounting fresh start. A company with a deficit balance in retained earnings "starts over" with a zero balance rather than a deficit. A quasi-reorganization may also include a restatement of the carrying values of assets and liabilities to reflect current values.

R

Ratio analysis: A comparison of relationships among account balances.

Raw materials: Goods purchased for direct use in manufacturing that become part of the product.

Real accounts: The name given to balance sheet accounts because they are permanent and are not closed at the end of the period.

Realization (revenue recognition): A concept that generally recognizes revenue when (1) the earning process is virtually complete and (2) the exchange value can be objectively determined.

Receivables: Claims arising from the selling of merchandise or services on account to customers are referred to as trade receivables. Other claims may be from sources such as loans to employees or a federal tax refund.

Recognition: Recording a transaction on the accounting records.

Redeemable preferred stock: Preferred stock subject to mandatory redemption requirements, or with a redemption feature that is outside the control of the issuer.

Registrar: An independent agent that maintains a record of the number of a company's shares of capital stock that have been issued and to whom.

Relevance: Qualitative characteristic requiring that accounting information bear directly on the economic decision for which it is to be used; one of the primary qualitative characteristics of accounting information.

Reliability: Qualitative characteristic requiring that accounting information be faithful to the original data and that it be neutral and verifiable; one of the primary qualitative characteristics of accounting information.

Replacement cost: The cost to reproduce or replace an asset.

Report form of balance sheet: A balance sheet presentation that presents assets, liabilities, and stockholders' equity in a vertical format.

Reporting currency: The currency used to measure and report.

Representational faithfulness: The agreement of information with what it is supposed to represent.

Research and development (R&D): Funds spent to improve existing products and develop new ones.

Reserves: Accounts classified under liabilities resulting from an expense to the income statement and an equal increase in the reserve account on the balance sheet. These reserve accounts do not represent definite commitments to pay out funds in the future, but they do represent an estimate of funds that will be paid out in the future.

Residual value (salvage value): The estimated net scrap or trade-in value of a tangible asset at the date of disposal.

Restrictive covenants: Limitations imposed by a creditor on a debtor's actions. Covenants are often based on accounting measurements of assets, liabilities, and/or income.

Restructure: The term used to describe corporate downsizing and refocus of operations.

Retail inventory method: An inventory method that converts the retail value of inventory to an estimated cost.

Retained earnings: The undistributed earnings of a corporation consisting of the net income for all past periods minus the dividends that have been declared.

Retained earnings appreciated: The amount of retained earnings that has been restricted for specific purposes.

Retroactively: The method of accounting for accounting principle changes whereby past years' financial statements are restated to reflect the use of the new method.

Revenues: Inflows or other enhancements of assets of an entity or settlements of its liabilities (or a combination of both) from delivering or producing goods, rendering services, or other activities that constitute the entity's ongoing major or central operations.

Risk: The uncertainty surrounding estimates of future cash flows.

Royalties: Payment for a right over some natural resource or payment to an author or composer.

S

Sale and leaseback: Sale of an asset with the purchaser concurrently leasing the asset to the seller.

Sales discounts: Contra-revenue account used to record discounts given customers for early payment of their accounts.

Sales or revenues: Income from the sale of goods or services and lease or royalty payments.

Sales returns and allowances: Contra-revenue account used to record both refunds to customers and reduction of their accounts.

Sales-type lease: A capital lease that generates two income streams. One from the sale of the asset and a second from the financing of the asset.

Salvage value (residual value): The estimated net scrap or trade-in value of a tangible asset at the date of disposal.

Scope paragraph: That paragraph of the audit report that tells what the auditor did. Specifically, it states whether the audit was conducted in accordance with GAAS.

Securities Act of 1933: A federal statute governing the registration of new securities issues traded in interstate commerce.

Securities Act of 1934: A federal statute establishing recurring reporting requirements for public companies once their securities have been registered with the SEC.

Securities and Exchange Commission (SEC): An agency of the federal government that has the legal power to set and enforce accounting practices.

Segment reporting (product segment information): When operations are diversified, the firm may report results on a segmented basis.

Selling expenses: Result from the company's effort to create sales.

Senior debt: Debt obligations that would have a prior claim over junior debt and equity holders on the assets of a company in liquidation.

Serial bonds: A bond issue with several different maturity dates.

Service lives: Working years of employees prior to retirement, as used in accounting for postretirement benefit obligations.

Simple interest: Interest computed on the principal amount only.

Single-step income statement: Form of the income statement that arrives at net income in a single step.

Sinking fund: An accumulation of cash or securities in a special fund dedicated to paying, or redeeming, an issue of bonds or preferred stock.

Social accounting: Attempts to account for the benefits to the social environment within which the firm operates.

Sole proprietorship: A business with a single owner.

Solvency: The ability of a company to remain in business over the long term.

Specific identification (inventory): Identifies the items in inventory as coming from specific purchases.

Standard audit report: The form of audit report recommended by the Auditing Standards Board of the AICPA. This report is rendered at the conclusion of an audit in which the auditor encountered no material scope limitations, and the financial statements conform to GAAP in all material respects.

Standard Industrial Classification (SIC): An industry classification system created in 1987. The manual is the responsibility of the Office of Management and Budget, which is under the executive office of the President.

Stated (contract) rate: The rate of interest used to compute the cash interest payments on bonds or notes.

Stated value: A value assigned by the board of directors to no-par stock.

Statement of cash flows: Provides detailed information on cash flows resulting from operating, investing, and financing activities.

Statement of owners' equity (statement of shareholders' equity): An accounting statement describing transactions affecting the owners' equity.

Statement of retained earnings: A summary of the changes to retained earnings for an accounting period.

Statements of Financial Accounting Concepts (SFACs): Issued by the Financial Accounting Standards Board and provide the Board with a common foundation and basic reasons for considering the merits of various alternative accounting principles.

Statements of Financial Accounting Standards (SFASs): These statements establish generally accepted accounting principles (GAAP) for specific accounting issues.

Statements of Position (SOPs): Issued by the Accounting Standards Division of the AICPA to influence the development of accounting standards.

Stock appreciation rights: Give the holder the right to receive compensation at some future date based on the market price of the stock at the date of exercise over a pre-established price.

Stock certificate: A document issued to a stockholder indicating the number of shares of stock owned.

Stock dividend: A dividend in the form of additional shares of a company's stock.

Stock options: Allow the holder to purchase a company's stock at favorable terms.

Stock split: Increase in the number of shares of a class of capital stock, with no change in the total dollar amount of the class, but with a converse reduction in the par or stated value of the shares.

Stockholder (shareholder): The owner of one or more shares of stock in an incorporated business.

Straight-line amortization of bonds: Writes off an equal amount of bond premium or discount each period.

Straight-line depreciation: A method of depreciation that allocates the cost of a tangible asset in a constant over the life of the asset.

Subordinated debt: A form of long-term debt that is "junior," or in a secondary position vis-à-vis the claim on a company's assets for the payment of its other debt obligations.

Subsequent events: Events that occur after the balance sheet date, but before the statements are issued.

Subsidiary: A company whose stock is more than 50% owned by another company.

Subsidiary ledger: Provides detailed information regarding a particular general ledger account.

Successful efforts accounting: The method of accounting that capitalizes only the costs that result in the discovery of oil and gas reserves.

Sum-of-the-years'-digits depreciation: This method takes a fraction each year times the cost less salvage value. The numerator of the fraction is the remaining number of years of life. The denominator remains constant, and is the sum of the digits of the years of life.

Summary annual report: A simplified annual report in which data required by the SEC is supplied in the proxy statement and the Form 10-K.

Summary of significant accounting policies: A description of all significant accounting policies of the company. An integral part of the financial statements, this information is typically presented as the first footnote.

Supplies: Items used indirectly in the production of goods or services.

T

T-account: A form of ledger page used to record (or illustrate) the entry of debits and credits into ledger accounts.

Take-or-pay contract: An executory contract by which one party agrees to pay for the product regardless of whether the product is physically received.

Tangible assets: The physical facilities used in the operation of the business.

Tax benefit: A reduction in taxes, or a tax credit or refund, due to a particular action or expense incurred by a taxable entity.

Taxable income: Income determined in accordance with income tax regulation.

Taxes payable: Represents unpaid taxes that are owed to a governmental unit.

Temporal method of translation: A method of translating foreign financial statements in which cash, receivables, and payables are translated at the exchange rate in effect at the balance sheet date. Other assets and liabilities are translated at historical rates while revenues and expenses are translated at the weighted-average rate for the period.

Temporary accounts: Accounts closed at the end of an accounting period: includes all income statement accounts and the dividends account.

Temporary differences: Revenue and expense recognized in one period for financial reporting but recognized in an earlier or later period for income tax purposes.

10-K report: Mandatory report filed by a company on an annual basis with the Securities and Exchange Commission.

10-Q report: Mandatory report filed by a company on a quarterly basis with the Securities and Exchange Commission.

Term bonds: The entire bond issue matures at the same time.

Time period: Assumes that the entity can be accounted for with reasonable accuracy for a particular period of time.

Time value of money: The concept that money earns interest over time. This implies that a dollar to be received a year from now is worth less than a dollar received today.

Timeliness: The qualitative characteristic indicating that accounting information should reach the user in time to help in making a decision.

Trademarks: Rights to use distinctive names or symbols granted to the holder. Rights are granted to the holder for 10 years and may be renewed every 10 years, thereafter.

Trading securities: Securities held by firms for brief periods of time that are intended to generate profits from short-term differences in price.

Transaction approach: The recording of events that affect the financial position of the entity and that can be reasonably determined in monetary terms.

Translation adjustments (foreign currency translation adjustment): An account classified under stockholders' equity that represents foreign currency translation gains and losses that have not been charged to the income statement.

Translation gains and losses: Gains and losses due to fluctuations in exchange rates.

Treasury stock: Capital stock of a company, either common or preferred, that has been issued and reacquired by the issuing company but has not been reissued or retired. It reduces stockholders' equity.

Trend analysis: Analysis over more than one accounting period to identify the trend of a company's results.

Trial balance: A listing of all general ledger accounts and their balances for the purpose of verifying that total debits equal total credits.

Troubled debt restructuring: A concession by creditors to allow debtors to eliminate or modify debt obligations.

U

Unappropriated retained earnings: The unrestricted retained earnings.

Unaudited: A term applied to information in the annual or quarterly reports, which is outside the audit conducted by the auditors.

Unconsolidated subsidiaries: Subsidiaries whose financial statements are not combined with the parent company.

Understandability: A user-specific quality directing that accounting information be understandable to users who have a reasonable knowledge of business and economic activities and who are willing to study the information with reasonable diligence.

Unearned income: A liability, either current or long-term, for income received prior to the delivery of goods or the rendering of services (also described as deferred income).

Unexpended industrial revenue bond proceeds: An asset account, classified under other assets, representing funds that have not yet been used for the purpose indicated when the bonds were issued.

Unit-of-production depreciation: Relates depreciation to the output capacity of the asset, estimated for the life of the asset.

Unlimited liability: Each partner is liable for all partnership debts. Limited partners in a limited partnership, which is allowed in some states, do not have unlimited liability.

Unlisted securities: Securities that are not listed on an organized stock exchange.

Unqualified opinion: An audit opinion not qualified for any material scope restrictions or departures from GAAP.

Unrealized decline in market value of noncurrent equity investments: A stockholders' equity account that results from adjusting long-term equity securities to the lower of cost or market value.

Unrealized (gain) loss: A (gain) loss recognized in the financial statements but not associated with an asset sale.

Unusual or infrequent item: Certain income statement items that are unusual or occur infrequently, but not both.

V

Verifiability: The qualitative characteristic indicating that accounting information can be confirmed or duplicated by independent parties using the same measurement technique.

Vertical analysis: A comparison of various financial statement items within a single period with the use of common-size statements.

Vertical integration: The combination of firms with operations in different but successive stages of production and/or distribution.

Vested benefit obligation (VBO): The portion of the pension benefit obligation that does not depend on future employee service.

Vesting: The accrual to an employee of pension rights, arising from employer contributions, not contingent upon the employee's continuing service with the employer.

W

Warrant: A security that gives the holder the right to purchase shares of common stock in accordance with the terms of the instrument, usually upon payment of a specified amount.

Warranty obligations: Estimated obligations arising out of product warranties.

Weighted average cost method: An inventory costing method that assigns the same unit cost to all units available for sale during the period.

Weighted average of outstanding common stock: Gives the proportional shares outstanding in their fraction of the fiscal year.

Work in process: Goods started, but not ready for sale.

Working capital: The excess of current assets over current liabilities.

Write-off: A write-off recognizes that the asset no longer has any value to the firm.

Z

Zero coupon bond: A bond that does not pay periodic interest, but promises to pay a fixed amount at the maturity date.

BIBLIOGRAPHY

CHAPTER 1   INTRODUCTION TO FINANCIAL REPORTING

Ashbough, Holles, Karia M. Johnstone, and Terry D. Warfield. "Corporate Reporting on the Internet," *Accounting Horizons* (September 1999), 241–257.

Beresford, D.R. "The Balancing Act in Setting Accounting Standards," *Accounting Horizons* (March 1988), 1–7.

Beresford, Dennis. "How to Succeed as a Standard Setter by Trying Really Hard," *Accounting Horizons* (September 1997), 79–90.

Bierman, Harold. "Extending the Usefulness of Accrual Accounting," *Accounting Horizons* (September 1988), 10–14.

Chen, Shimin, Zzheng Sun, and Yuetang Wang. "Evidence from China on Whether Harmonized Accounting Standards Harmonize Accounting Practices," *Accounting Horizons* (September 2002), 183–197.

Danaher, Mitchell, and Trevor Harris. "Changing the Rules, the World Gets Serious About Global Accounting Standards," *Financial Executive* (March/April 1999), 28–34.

Geiger, M.A., K. Raghunandan, and D.V. Rama. "Costs Associated with Going-concern Modified Audit Opinions: An Analysis of Auditor Changes, Subsequent Opinions, and Client Failures," *Advances in Accounting* 16 (1998), 117–139.

Geiger, Marshall A., and K. Raghunandan. "Going-Concern Opinions in the New Legal Environment," *Accounting Horizons* (March 2002), 17–26.

Gerboth, Dale L. "The Conceptual Framework: Not Definitions, But Professional Values," *Accounting Horizons* (September 1987), 1–8.

Goldwasser, D.L. "Independence in a Changing Accounting Profession: Is It Possible to Achieve?" *The CPA Journal* (October 1999), 46–51.

Holder-Webb, Lora M., and Michael S. Wilkins. "The Incremental Information Content of SAS No. 559 Going-Concern Opinions," *Journal of Accounting Research* (Spring 2000), 209–219.

Kahn, Jeremy. "Accounting's White Knight," *Fortune* (September 30, 2002), 117, 118, 120, 122.

Koeppen, David R. "Using the FASB's Conceptual Framework: Fitting the Pieces Together," *Accounting Horizons* (June 1988), 18–26.

Levitt, A. "The Importance of High Quality Accounting Standards," *Accounting Horizons* (March 1998), 79–82.

Nogler, G. "The Resolution of Auditor Going-Concern Opinions," *Auditing: A Journal of Practice & Theory* (Fall 1995), 54–73.

Parfet, W.V. "Accounting Subjectivity and Earnings Management: A Prepared Perspective," *Accounting Horizons* (December 2000), 481–488.

Reither, Cheri L. "How the FASB Approaches a Standard-Setting Issue," *Accounting Horizons* (December 1997), 91–104.

Rimerman, Thomas W. "The Changing Significance of Financial Statements," *Journal of Accountancy* (April 1990), 79–83.

Rogero, L.H. "Characteristics of High Quality Accounting Standards," *Accounting Horizons* (June 1998), 177–183.

Shafer, W.E.R.E. Morris, and A.A. Ketchand. "The Effects of Formal Sanctions on Auditor Independence," *Auditing: A Journal of Practice & Theory* (Supplement 1999), 85–101.

Solomons, D. "The FASB's Conceptual Framework: An Evaluation," *Journal of Accountancy* (June 1986), 114–124.

Stamp, Edward. "Why Can Accounting Not Become a Science Like Physics?" *Abacus* (Spring 1981), 13–27.

Sutton, Michael H. "Financial Reporting in U.S. Capital Markets: International Dimensions," *Accounting Horizons* (June 1997), 96–102.

Wyatt, Arthur. "Accounting Standards: Conceptual or Political?" *Accounting Horizons* (September 1990), 83–88.

CHAPTER 2   INTRODUCTION TO FINANCIAL STATEMENTS AND OTHER FINANCIAL REPORTING TOPICS

Adhikari, Ajay, and Shawn Z. Wang. "Accounting for China," *Management Accounting* (April 1995), 27–32.

Ali, Ashiq, and Lee-Seok Hwang. "County-Specific Factors Related to Financial Reporting and the Value Relevance of Accounting Data," *Journal of Accounting Research* (Spring 2000), 1–22.

Benston, Gi, and A. Hartgraves. "Enron: What Happened and What We Can Learn from It," *Journal of Accounting and Public Policy* (August 2002), 105–127.

Beresford, Dennis. "What's the FASB Doing About International Accounting Standards?" *Financial Executive* (May/June 1990), 17–24.

Bernard, Victor L., and Thomas Stober. "The Nature and Amount of Information in Cash Flows and Accruals," *The Accounting Review* (October 1989), 624–652.

Bishop, Ashton, and Rasoul H. Tondkar. "Development of a Professional Code of Ethics," *Journal of Accountancy* (May 1987), 97–100.

Bruns, William J., and Kenneth A. Merchant. "The Dangerous Morality of Managing Earnings," *Management Accounting* (August 1990), 22–25.

Carbridge, Curtis, Walter W. Austin, and David J. Lemak. "Germany's Accrual Accounting Practices," *Management Accounting* (August 1993), 45–47.

Cheney, Glenn A. "Soviet-American Financial Coexistence," *Journal of Accountancy* (January 1990), 68–72.

Choi, Frederick D. "A Cluster Approach to Accounting Harmonization," *Management Accounting* (August 1981), 27–31.

Choi, Frederick D., and Richard M. Levich. "Behavioral Effects of International Accounting Diversity," *Accounting Horizons* (June 1991), 1–13.

Collett, Peter H., Jayne M. Godfrey, and Sue L. Hrasky. "International Harmonization: Cautions from the Australian Experience," *Accounting Horizons* (June 2001), 171–182.

Collins, Stephen. "The Move to Globalization," *Journal of Accountancy* (March 1989), 82–85.

Cook, J. Michael, and Michael H. Sutton. "Summary Annual Reporting: A Cure For Information Overload," *Financial Executive* (January/February 1995), 12–15.

Davidson, Ronald A., Alexander M.G. Gelardi, and Fangyve Li. "Analysis of the Conceptual Framework of China's New Accounting System," *Journal of Accountancy* (March 1996), 58–74.

Dye, Ronald A., and Shyam Sunder. "Why Not Allow FAST and IASB Standards to Compete in the U.S.?" *Accounting Horizons* (September 2001), 257–271.

Epstein, Marc J., and Moses L. Pava. "Profile of an Annual Report," *Financial Executive* (January/February 1994), 41–43.

Erickson, Merle, Brian W. Mayhew, and William L. Felix, Jr. "Why Do Audits Fail? Evidence from Lincoln Savings and Loan," *Journal of Accounting Research* (Spring 2000), 165–194.

Firth, Michael. "Auditor-Provided Consultancy Services and Their Associations with Audit Fees and Audit Opinions," *Journal of Business Finance & Accounting* (June/July 2002), 661–694.

Hartgraves, Al L., and George J. Benston. "The Evolving Accounting Standards for Special Purpose Entities and Consolidations," *Accounting Horizons* (September 2002), 245–258.

Ingberman, M., and G.H. Sorter. "The Role of Financial Statements in an Efficient Market," *Journal of Accounting, Auditing, & Finance* (Fall 1978), 58–62.

Lee, Charles, and Dale Morse. "Summary Annual Reports," *Accounting Horizons* (March 1990), 39–50.

Lowe, Herman J. "Ethics in Our 100-Year History," *Journal of Accountancy* (May 1987), 78–87.

McEnroe, John E., and Stanley C. Martens. "Auditors' and Investors' Perceptions of the Expectation Gap," *Accounting Horizons* (December 2001), 345–358.

Milan, Edgar. "Ethical Compliance at Tenneco Inc.," *Management Accounting* (August 1995), 59.

Millman, Gregory J. "New Scandals, Old Lessons: Financial Ethics after Enron," *Financial Executive* (July/August 2002), 16–19.

Nair, R.D., and Larry E. Rittenberg. "Summary Annual Reports: Background and Implications for Financial Reporting and Auditing," *Accounting Horizons* (March 1990), 25–38.

Perera, M. H. "Towards a Framework to Analyzing the Impact of Culture on Accounting," *International Journal of Accounting* (1989), 42–56.

Rich, Anne J. "Understanding Global Standards," *Management Accounting* (April 1995), 51–54.

Sainty, Barbara J., Gary K. Taylor, and David D. Williams. "Investor Dissatisfaction Toward Auditors," *Journal of Accounting, Auditing, & Finance* (Spring 2002), 111–136.

Schroeder, Nicholas W., and Charles H. Gibson. "Are Summary Annual Reports Successful?" *Accounting Horizons* (June 1992), 28–37.

Schroeder, Nicholas W., and Charles H. Gibson. "Improving Annual Reports by Improving the Readability of Footnotes," *The Woman CPA* (April 1988), 13–16.

Shafer, William E., D. Jordan Lowe, and Timothy J. Fogarty. "The Effects of Corporate Ownership on Public Accountants' Professionalism and Ethics," *Accounting Horizons* (June 2002), 109–124.

Wallace, R.S. Olusegun. "Survival Strategies of a Global Organization: The Case of the International Accounting Standards Committee," *Accounting Horizons* (June 1990), 1–22.

Wallace, Wanda A., and John Walsh. "Apples-to-Apples Profits Abroad," *Financial Executives* (May/June 1995), 28–31.

Wells, Joseph T. "So That's Why It's Called A Pyramid Scheme," *Journal of Accountancy* (October 2000), 91–95.

Wells, Joseph T. "Timing Is of the Essence," *Journal of Accountancy* (May 2001), 78; 81–82; 85–87.

Wyatt, Arthur R., and Joseph F. Yospe. "Wake-Up Call to U.S. Business: International Accounting Standards Are on the Way," *Journal of Accountancy* (July 1993), 80–85.

Zimbelman, M.F. "The Effects of SAS No. 82 on Auditor's Attention to Fraud Risk Factors and Audit Planning Decision," *Journal of Accounting Research* (Supplement 1997), 75–97.

CHAPTER 3   BALANCE SHEET

Barron, Orie E., Donal Byard, Charles Kite, and Edward J. Riedl. "High-Technology Intangibles and Analysts Forecasts," *Journal of Accounting Research* (May 2002), 289–320.

Davis, M.L. "Differential Market Reaction to Pooling and Purchase Methods," *The Accounting Review* (July 1990), 696–709.

Donohue, James, and Cynthia Waller Vallario. "A New Scorecard for Intellectual Property," *Journal of Accountancy* (April 2002), 75–79.

Flamholtz, Eric G., D. Gerald Searfoss, and Russell Coff. "Developing Human Resource Accounting as a Human Resource Decision Support System," *Accounting Horizons* (September 1988), 1–9.

Frischmann, Peter J., Paul D. Kimmel, and Terry D. Warfield. "Innovation in Preferred Stock: Current Developments and Implications for Financial Reporting," *Accounting Horizons* (September 1999), 201–218.

Gibson, Charles H. "Quasi-reorganizations in Practice," *Accounting Horizons* (September 1988), 83–89.

Healy, Paul M., Stewart C. Myers, and Christopher D. Howe. "The R & D Accounting and the Tradeoff Between Relevance and Objectivity," *Journal of Accounting Research* (June 2002), 677–710.

Kim, M., and G. Moore. "Economics vs. Accounting Depreciation," *Journal of Accounting and Economics* (April 1988), 111–125.

Leu, Baruch. "Intangibles at a Crossroads: What's Next?" *Financial Executive* (March/April 2002), 34–36; 38–39.

Moehrle, Stephen R., Jennifer A. Reynolds-Moehrle, and James S. Wallace. "How Informative Are Earnings Numbers That Exclude Goodwill Amortization?" *Accounting Horizons* (September 2001), 243–255.

Samuelson, Richard A. "Accounting for Liabilities to Perform Services," *Accounting Horizons* (September 1993), 32–45.

Sanders, George, Paul Munter, and Tommy Moures. "Software—The Unrecorded Asset," *Management Accounting* (August 1994), 57–61.

Schuetze, Walter P. "What Is an Asset?" *Accounting Horizons* (September 1993), 66–70.

CHAPTER 4   INCOME STATEMENT

Asquith, Paul, Paul Healy, and Krishna Palepu. "Earnings and Stock Splits," *The Accounting Review* (July 1989), 387–403.

Burgstahler, David, James Jiambolvo, and Terry Shevlin. "Do Stock Prices Fully Reflect the Implications of Special Items for Future Earnings?" *Journal of Accounting Research* (June 2002), 585–612.

Elliott, J.A., and D.R. Philbrick. "Accounting Changes and Earnings Predictability," *The Accounting Review* (January 1990), 157–174.

Lilien, Steven, Martin Mellman, and Victor Pastena. "Accounting Changes: Successful Versus Unsuccessful Firms," *The Accounting Review* (October 1988), 642–656.

May, Gordon S., and Douglas K. Schneider. "Reporting Accounting Changes: Are Stricter Guidelines Needed?" *Accounting Horizons* (September 1988), 68–74.

McGough, Eugene. "Anatomy of a Stock Split," *Management Accounting* (September 1993), 58–61.

Pincus, Morton, and Charles Wasley. "The Incidence of Accounting Changes and Characteristics of Firms Making Accounting Changes," *Journal of Accountancy* (June 1994), 1–24.

CHAPTER 5   BASICS OF ANALYSIS

Chang, L.S., K.S. Most, and C.W. Brain. "The Utility of Annual Reports: An International Study," *Journal of International Business Studies* (Spring/Summer 1983), 63–84.

Gibson, C.H., and P.A. Boyer. "Need for Disclosure of Uniform Financial Ratios," *Journal of Accountancy* (May 1980), 78.

Wells, Joseph T. "Irrational Ratios," *Journal of Accountancy* (August 2001), 80–83.

Wittington, G. "Some Basic Properties of Accounting Ratios," *Journal of Business Finance & Accounting* (Summer 1980), 219–232.

CHAPTER 6   LIQUIDITY OF SHORT-TERM ASSETS; RELATED DEBT-PAYING ABILITY

Boer, Germain. "Managing the Cash GAP," *Journal of Accountancy* (October 1999), 27–32.

Davis, H.Z., N. Kahn, and E. Rosen. "LIFO Inventory Liquidations: An Empirical Study," *Journal of Accounting Research* (Autumn 1984), 480–496.

Dopuch, N., and M. Pincus. "Evidence on the Choice of Inventory Accounting Methods: LIFO Versus FIFO," *Journal of Accounting Research* (Spring 1988), 28–59.

Heath, L.C. "Is Working Capital Really Working?" *Journal of Accountancy* (August 1980), 55–62.

Hunt, H.G. III. "Potential Determinants of Corporate Inventory Accounting Decisions," *Journal of Accounting Research* (Autumn 1985), 448–467.

Payne, Stephen. "Working Capital Optimization Can Yield Real Gains," *Financial Executive* (September 2002), 40–42.

CHAPTER 7   LONG-TERM DEBT-PAYING ABILITY

Deakin, Edward B. "Accounting for Contingencies: The Pennzoil-Texaco Case," *Accounting Horizons* (March 1989), 21–28.

Dietrich, J., and R.S. Kaplan. "Empirical Analysis of the Commercial Loan Classification Decision," *Accounting Review* (January 1982), 18–38.

Heian, James B., and James B. Thies. "Consolidation of Finance Subsidiaries: $230 Billion in Off-Balance-Sheet Financing Comes Home to Roost," *Accounting Horizons* (March 1989), 1–9.

Leib, Barclay. "Questioning the Basic Assumptions," *Financial Executive* (September 2002), 35–38.

Thomas, J.K. "Why Do Firms Terminate Their Overfunded Pension Plans?" *Journal of Accounting and Economics* (November 1989), 361–398.

Williams, Georgina, and Thomas J. Phillips. "Cleaning Up Our Act: Accounting For Environmental Liabilities," *Management Accounting* (February 1994), 30–33.

CHAPTER 8   PROFITABILITY

Albrecht, David W., and Niranjan Chipalkalti. "New Segment Reporting," *The CPA Journal* (May 1998), 46–52.

Bradshaw, Mark T., and Richard G. Sloan. "GAAP Versus the Street: An Empirical Assessment of Two Alternative Definitions of Earnings," *Journal of Accounting Research* (March 2002), 41–66.

Lev, B. "On the Usefulness of Earnings and Earnings Research: Lessons and Directions from Two Decades of Empirical Research," *Journal of Accounting Research* (Supplement 1989), 153–192.

Lipe, R.C. "The Information Contained in the Components of Earnings," *Journal of Accounting Research* (Supplement 1986), 37–64.

Liv, Jing, and Jacob Thomas. "Stock Returns and Accounting Earnings," *Journal of Accounting Research* (Spring 2000), 71–102.

MacDonald, Elizabeth. Accounting in the Danger Zone," *Forbes* (September 2, 2002), 138.

Moses, D. "Income Smoothing and Incentives: Empirical Tests Using Accounting Changes," *The Accounting Review* (April 1987), 358–377.

Worthy, F.S. "Manipulating Profits: How It's Done," *Fortune* (June 15, 1984), 50–54.

CHAPTER 9   FOR THE INVESTOR

Ball, Ray. "The Earnings-Price Anomaly," *Journal of Accounting and Economics* (June/September 1992), 319–346.

Beaver, W., and D. Morse. "What Determines Price-Earnings Ratios?" *Financial Analysts Journal* (July–August 1978), 65–76.

Bens, Daniel A., Venky Nagar, and M.H. Franco Wong. "Real Investment Implications of Employee Stock Options Exercises," *Journal of Accounting Research* (May 2002), 359–406.

Block, Frank E. "A Study of the Price to Book Relationship," *Financial Analysts Journal* (January/February 1995), 63–73.

Botosan, Christine A., and Marlene A. Plumlee. "Stock Options Expense: The Sword of Damocles Revealed," *Accounting Horizons* (December 2001), 311–327.

Butler, Kirt C., and Larry H.P. Lang. "The Forecast Accuracy of Individual Analysts: Evidence of Systematic Optimism and Pessimism," *Journal of Accounting Research* (Spring 1991), 150–156.

Chambers, A.E., and S.H. Penman. "Timeliness of Reporting and the Stock Price Reaction to Earnings Announcements," *Journal of Accounting Research* (Spring 1984), 21–47.

Clemente, Holly A. "What Wall Street Sees When It Looks at Your P/E Ratio," *Financial Executive* (May/June 1990), 40–44.

Coggin, T.D., and J.E. Hunter. "Analysts EPS Forecasts Nearer Actual Than Statistical Models," *The Journal of Business Forecasting* (Winter 1982–1983), 20–23.

Cole, Kevin, Jean Helwege, and David Laster. "Stock Market Valuation Indicators: Is This Time Different?" *Financial Analysts Journal* (May/June 1996), 56–64.

Core, John, and Wayne Guay. "Estimating the Value of Employee Stock Option Portfolios Volatility," *Journal of Accounting Research* (June 2002), 613–630.

Holthausen, Robert W., and D.F. Larcker. "The Prediction of Stock Returns Using Financial Statement Information," *Journal of Accounting and Economics* (June/September 1992), 373–411.

Liv, Jing, Doron Nissim, and Jacob Thomas. "Equity Valuation Using Multiples," *Journal of Accounting Research* (March 2002), 135–173.

Molodovsky, Nicholas. "A Theory of Price-Earnings Ratios," *Financial Analysts Journal* (January/February 1995), 29–43.

Ou, Jane A., and James F. Jepen. "Analysts Earnings Forecasts and the Roles of Earnings and Book Value in Equity Valuation," *Journal of Business Finance & Accounting* (April/May 2002), 287–316.

Ou, Jane A., and Stephen H. Penman. "Financial Statement Analysis and the Prediction of Stock Returns," *Journal of Accounting and Economics* (November 1989), 295–329.

Zarowin, P. "What Determines Earnings-Price Ratios Revisited," *Journal of Accounting, Auditing, & Finance* (Summer 1990), 439–454.

CHAPTER 10   STATEMENT OF CASH FLOWS

Casey, C.J., and N.J. Bartczak. "Cash Flow—It's Not the Bottom Line," *Harvard Business Review* (July–August 1984), 61–66.

Largay, J.A. III, and C.P. Stickney. "Cash Flows, Ratio Analysis and the W.T. Grant Company Bankruptcy," *Financial Analysts Journal* (July–August 1980), 51–54.

Livnat, Joshua, and Paul Zarowin. "The Incremental Informational Content of Cash-Flow Components," *Journal of Accounting and Economics* (May 1990), 25–46.

Kronquist, Stacey L., and Nancy Newman-Limata. "Reporting Corporate Cash Flows," *Management Accounting* (July 1990), 31–36.

Nurnberg, Hugo. "Inconsistencies and Ambiguities in Cash Flow Statements Under FASB Statement No. 95," *Accounting Horizons* (June 1993), 60–75.

Rappaport, Alfred. "Show Me the Cash Flow," *Fortune* (September 16, 2002), 192, 194.

Rayburn, J. "The Association of Operating Cash Flow and Accruals with Security Returns," *Journal of Accounting Research* (Supplement 1986), 121–133.

Reichalstein, Stefan. "Providing Managerial Incentives: Cash Flows Versus Accrual Accounting," *Journal of Accounting Research* (Autumn 2000), 243–270.

Sondhi, A.C., G.H. Sorter, and G.I. White. "Cash Flow Redefined: FAS 95 and Security Analysis," *Financial Analysts Journal* (November/December 1988), 19–20.

CHAPTER 11   EXPANDED ANALYSIS

Altman, E.I. "Financial Ratios, Discriminant Analysis and the Prediction of Corporate Bankruptcy," *Journal of Finance* (September 1968), 589–609.

Altman, E.I. *Corporate Financial Distress* (New York: John Wiley & Sons, 1993).

Altman, E.I., and M. Brenner. "Information Effects and Stock Market Response to Signs of Firm Deterioration," *Journal of Financial and Quantitative Analysis* (March 1981), 35–51.

Barwiv, Ran, Anurag Aggarwal, and Robert Leach. "Predicting Bankruptcy Resolution," *Journal of Business Finance & Accounting* (April/May 2002), 497–520.

Beasley, M.S. "An Empirical Analysis of the Relation Between the Board of Director Composition and Finance Statement Fraud," *The Accounting Review* (October 1996), 443–465.

Bell, T.B., and J.V. Carcello. "A Decision Aid for Assessing the Likelihood of Fraudulent Financial Reporting," *Auditing: A Journal of Practice & Theory* (Spring 1999), 169–184.

Beneish, Messod P. "The Detection of Earnings Manipulation," *Financial Analysts Journal* (September–October 1999), 24–36.

Burgess, Deanna Qender. "Graphical Sleight of Hand," *Journal of Accountancy* (February 2002), 45–48, 51.

Casey, C.J., Jr. "Variation in Accounting Information Load: The Effect on Loan Officers' Prediction of Bankruptcy," *Accounting Review* (January 1980), 36–49.

Casey, C.J., and N.J. Bartczak. "Using Operating Cash Flow Data to Predict Financial Distress: Some Extensions," *Journal of Accounting Research* (Spring 1985), 384–401.

Chandra, Uday, Bradley D. Childs, and Bturvg T. Ro. "The Association Between LIFO Reserve and Equity Risk: An Empirical Assessment," *Journal of Accounting, Auditing, & Finance* (Summer 2002), 185–208.

Dambolena, I.G., and S.J. Khorvry. "Ratio Stability and Corporate Failure," *Journal of Finance* (September 1980), 1017–1026.

Dechow, P.A., R.G. Sloan, and A.P. Sweeney. "Causes and Consequences of Earnings Manipulation: An Analysis of Firms Subject to Enforcement Actions by the SEC," *Contemporary Accounting Research* (Spring 1996), 1–36.

Dutta, Sunil, and Frank Gigler. "The Effect of Earnings Forecasts on Earnings Management," *Journal of Accounting Research* (June 2002), 631–656.

Gombola, M.J., and J.E. Ketz. "Financial Ratio Patterns in Retail and Manufacturing Organizations," *Financial Management* (Summer 1983), 45–56.

Grent, C. Terry, Chaunrey M. Depree, Jr., and Gerry H. Grant. "Earnings Management and the Abuse of Materiality," *Journal of Accountancy* (September 2000), 41–44.

Howell, Robert A. "Fixing Financial Reporting: Financial Statement Overhaul," *Financial Executive* (March/April 2002), 40–42.

Jaggi, B. "Which Is Better, D & B or Zeta in Forecasting Credit Risk?" *Journal of Business Forecasting* (Summer 1984), 13–16, 22.

Johnson, W.B., and D.S. Dhaliwal. "LIFO Abandonment," *Journal of Accounting Research* (Autumn 1988), 236–272.

Kasznik, Ron, and Maureen F. McNichols. "Does Meeting Earnings Expectations Matter? Evidence from Analyst Forecast Revisions and Share Prices," *Journal of Accounting Research* (June 2002), 727–760.

Kirschenheiter, Michael, and Nahum D. Melumad. "Can 'Big Bath' and Earnings Smoothing Co-exist as Equilibrium Financial Reporting Strategies?" *Journal of Accounting Research* (June 2002), 761–796.

Largay, James A. "Lessons from Enron," *Accounting Horizons* (June 2002), 153–156.

Lennox, C.S. "The Accuracy and Incremental Information Content of Audit Reports in Predicting Bankruptcy," *Journal of Business Finance & Accounting* (June/July 1999), 757–778.

Lincoln, M. "An Empirical Study of the Usefulness of Accounting Ratios to Describe Levels of Insolvency Risk," *Journal of Banking and Finance* (June 1984), 321–340.

Lynch, David, and Steven Galen, "Got the Picture? CPAs Can Use Some Simple Principles to Create Effective Charts and Graphs for Financial Reports and Presentations," *Journal of Accountancy* (May 2002), 183–187.

Makeever, D.A. "Predicting Business Failures," *The Journal of Commercial Bank Lending* (January 1984), 14–18.

McDonald, B., and M.H. Morris. "The Statistical Validity of the Ratio Method in Financial Analysis: An Empirical Examination," *Journal of Business Finance & Accounting* (Spring 1984), 89–97.

Mendenhall, Richard R. "How Naive Is the Market's Use of Firm-Specific Earnings Information?" *Journal of Accounting Research* (June 2002), 841–864.

Miller, Paul B. "Quality Financial Reporting," *Journal of Accountancy* (April 2002), 70–74.

Parsons, O. "Using Financial Statement Data to Identify Factors Associated with Fraudulent Financial Reporting," *Journal of Applied Business Research* (Summer 1995), 38–46.

Patell, J.M., and M.A. Wolfson. "The Intraday Speed of Adjustment of Stock Prices to Earnings and Dividend Announcements," *Journal of Financial Economics* (June 1984), 223–252.

Patrone, F.L., and D. duBois, "Financial Ratio Analysis in the Small Business," *Journal of Small Business Management* (January 1981), 35–40.

Peterson, M. "Putting Extra Fizz into Profits; Critics Say Coca-Cola Dumps Debt on Spin Off," *New York Times* (August 4, 1998), D1.

Rama, D.V., K. Raghunandan, and M.A. Gerger. "The Association Between Audit Reports and Bankruptcies: Further Evidence," *Advances in Accounting* 15 (1997), 1–15.

Rege, V.P. "Accounting Ratios to Locate Take-Over Targets," *Journal of Business Finance & Accounting* (Autumn 1984), 301–311.

Richardson, F.M., G.D. Kane, and P. Lobingier. "The Impact of Recession on the Prediction of Corporate Failure," *Journal of Business Finance & Accounting* (January/March 1998), 167, 186.

Shelton, Sandra Waller, O. Ray Whittington, and David Landsittel. "Auditing Firms' Fraud Risk Assessment Practices," *Accounting Horizons* (March 2001), 19–33.

Steinbart, Paul John. "The Auditor's Responsibility for the Accuracy of Graphs in Annual Reports: Some Evidence of the Need for Additional Guidance," *Accounting Horizons* (September 1989), 60–70.

Stober, T.L. "The Incremental Information Content of Financial Statement Disclosures: The Case of LIFO Liquidations," *Journal of Accounting Research* (Supplement 1986), 138–160.

Summers, S.L., and J.T. Sweeney. "Fraudulently Misstated Financial Statements and Insider Trading: An Empirical Analysis," *The Accounting Review* (January 1998), 131–146.

Tse, S. "LIFO Liquidations," *Journal of Accounting Research* (Spring 1990), 229–238.

Williamson, R.W. "Evidence on the Selective Reporting of Financial Ratios," *The Accounting Review* (April 1984), 296–299.

Chapter 12   Special Industries: Banks, Utilities, Oil and Gas, Transportation, Insurance, Real Estate Companies

Agnich, J.F. "How Utilities Account to the Regulators," *Management Accounting* (February 1981), 17–22.

Barniv, Ran. "Accounting Procedures, Market Data, Cash-Flow Figures, and Insolvency Classification: The Case of the Insurance Industry," *The Accounting Review* (July 1990), 578–604.

Christensen, Theodore E. "The Effects of Uncertainty on the Informativeness of Earnings: Evidence from the Insurance Industry in the Wake of Catastrophic Events," *Journal of Business Finance & Accounting* (January/March 2002), 223–256.

Gore, R., and D. Stott. "Toward a More Informative Measure of Operating Performance in the REIT Industry: Net Income vs. Funds from Operations," *Accounting Horizons* 12 (1998), 323–339.

Ho, T., and A. Saunders. "A Catastrophe Model of Bank Failure," *The Journal of Finance* (December 1980), 1189–1207.

Lilien, S., and V. Pastena. "Intramethod Comparability: The Case of the Oil and Gas Industry," *Accounting Review* (July 1981), 690–703.

Owhoso, Vincent E., William F. Messer, Jr., and John G. Lynch, Jr. "Error Detection by Industry-Specialized Teams during Sequential Audit Review," *Journal of Accounting Research* (June 2002), 883–900.

Palmon, Dan, and Lee J. Zeidler. "Current Value Reporting of Real Estate Companies and a Possible Example of Market Inefficiency," *The Accounting Review* (July 1978), 776–790.

Rose, P.L., and W.L. Scott. "Return-on-Equity Analysis of Eleven Largest U.S. Bank Failures," *Review of Business and Economic Research* (Winter 1980–81), 1–11.

Shick, R.A., and L.F. Sherman. "Bank Stock Prices as an Early Warning System for Changes in Condition," *Journal of Bank Research* (Autumn 1980), 136–146.

CHAPTER 13 PERSONAL FINANCIAL STATEMENTS AND ACCOUNTING FOR GOVERNMENTS AND NOT-FOR-PROFIT ORGANIZATIONS

Baber, William R., Andrea Alston Roberts, and Gnanakumar Visuana Dran. "Charitable Organizations' Strategies and Program-Spending Ratios," *Accounting Horizons* (December 2001), 329–343.

Barrett, W. "Look Before You Give," *Forbes* (December 27, 1999), 206–214.

Brown, Victor H., and Susan E. Weiss. "Toward Better Not-For-Profit Accounting and Reporting," *Management Accounting* (July 1993), 48–52.

Charnes, A., and W. Cooper. "Auditing and Accounting for Program Efficiency and Management Effectiveness in Not-for-Profit Entities," *Accounting Organizations and Society* 5 (1980), 87–108.

Chase, Bruce. "New Reporting Standards For Not-For-Profits," *Management Accounting* (October 1995), 34–37.

Chase, Bruce W., and Laura B. Triggs. "How to Implement GASB Statement No. 34," *Journal of Accountancy* (November 2001), 71–79.

Downs, G.W., and D.M. Rocke. "Municipal Budget Forecasting with Multivariate ARMA Models," *Journal of Forecasting* (October–December 1983), 377–387.

Gordon, Teresa P., Janet S. Greenlee, and Denise Nitterhouse. "Tax-Exempt Organization Financial Data: Availability and Limitations," *Accounting Horizons* (June 1999), 113–128.

Hay, E., and James F. Antonio. "What Users Want In Government Financial Reports," *Journal of Accountancy* (August 1990), 91–98.

Ives, Martin. "Accountability and Governmental Financial Reporting," *Journal of Accountancy* (October 1987), 130–134.

Kinsman, Michael D., and Bruce Samuelson. "Personal Financial Statements: Valuation Challenges and Solutions," *Journal of Accountancy* (September 1987), 138–148.

Klasny, Edward M., and James M. Williams. "Government Reporting Faces an Overhaul," *Journal of Accountancy* (January 2000), 49–51.

Meeting, David T., Randall W. Luecke, and Edward J. Giniat. "Understanding and Implementing FASB 124," *Journal of Accountancy* (March 1996), 62–66.

Shoulders, Craig D., and Robert J. Freeman. "Which GAAP Should NOPs Apply?" *Journal of Accountancy* (November 1995), 77–78, 80, 82, 84.

Statement of Position of the Accounting Standards Division 82-1, "Accounting and Financial Reporting for Personal Financial Statements" (New York: American Institute of Certified Public Accountants, 1982).

INDEX

PROFITABILITY (CONTINUED)

$$\text{Return on Total Equity} = \frac{\text{Net Income Before Nonrecurring Items} - \text{Dividends on Redeemable Preferred Stock}}{\text{Average Total Equity}}$$

$$\text{Return on Common Equity} = \frac{\text{Net Income Before Nonrecurring Items} - \text{Preferred Dividends}}{\text{Average Common Equity}}$$

$$\text{Gross Profit Margin} = \frac{\text{Gross Profit}}{\text{Net Sales}}$$

INVESTOR ANALYSIS

$$\text{Degree of Financial Leverage} = \frac{\text{Earnings Before Interest and Tax}}{\text{Earnings Before Tax}}$$

$$\text{All-Inclusive Degree of Financial Leverage} = \frac{\text{Earnings Before Interest, Tax, Minority Share of Earnings, Equity Income, and Nonrecurring Items}}{\text{Earnings Before Tax, Minority Share of Earnings, Equity Income, and Nonrecurring Items}}$$

$$\text{Earnings per Common Share} = \frac{\text{Net Income} - \text{Preferred Dividends}}{\text{Diluted Weighted Average Number of Common Shares Outstanding}}$$

$$\text{Operating Cash Flow per Share} = \frac{\text{Operating Cash Flow} - \text{Preferred Dividends}}{\text{Diluted Weighted Average Common Shares Outstanding}}$$

$$\text{Price/Earnings Ratio} = \frac{\text{Market Price per Share}}{\text{Diluted Earnings per Share, before Nonrecurring Items}}$$

$$\text{Percentage of Earnings Retained} = \frac{\text{Net Income before Nonrecurring Items} - \text{All Dividends}}{\text{Net Income before Nonrecurring Items}}$$

$$\text{Dividend Payout} = \frac{\text{Dividends per Common Share}}{\text{Diluted Earnings per Share before Nonrecurring Items}}$$

$$\text{Dividend Yield} = \frac{\text{Dividends per Common Share}}{\text{Market Price per Common Share}}$$

$$\text{Book Value per Share} = \frac{\text{Total Stockholders' Equity} - \text{Preferred Stock Equity}}{\text{Number of Common Shares Outstanding}}$$

$$\text{Operating Cash Flow/Cash Dividends} = \frac{\text{Operating Cash Flow}}{\text{Cash Dividends}}$$

$$\text{Materiality of Options} = \frac{\begin{array}{c}\text{Net Income before} \\ \text{Nonrecurring Items Not} \\ \text{Including Option Expense}\end{array} - \begin{array}{c}\text{Net Income before} \\ \text{Nonrecurring Items} \\ \text{Including Option Expense}\end{array}}{\begin{array}{c}\text{Net Income before Nonrecurring Items} \\ \text{Not Including Option Expense}\end{array}}$$